WORLD PEACE 2.0

RESTORING GLOBAL HARMONY

John E. LaMuth   PhD

REFERENCE BOOKS OF AMERICA
Imprint for:
FAIRHAVEN BOOK PUBLISHERS

Library of Congress Control Number: 2018914699

ISBN# 978-1-929649-00-6

Reference Books of America
Imprint for:
Fairhaven Book Publishers
A Safe Haven in a Sea of Knowledge
• P.O. Box 105
Lucerne Valley, CA 92356 - USA

fairhaven-books@outlook.com
www.worldpeace2.com

Publisher's Cataloging-In-Publication Data

World peace 2.0: restoring global harmony / John E. LaMuth, Author.

284 p. : ill. ; cm.
ISBN: 978-1-929649-00-6

1. Virtues/values--Terminology. 2. Ethics--Terminology. 3. Affect (Psychology) 4. Criminality--Classification. 5. Ethical hierarchy--Technology. 6. World peace -- Moral and ethical aspects.
I. LaMuth, John E. PhD, author.

BF636 .L36 2019
158.4   2018914699

Printed on acid-free paper

Wholesale Distributor:
Ingram Book Group Inc.
La Vergne, Tennessee 37086

TABLE of CONTENTS

PART IV – Global Solutions Towards Peace & Harmony

ACKNOWLEDGEMENTS

The Author gratefully wishes to acknowledge the individuals that have contributed background material to *World Peace 2.0: Restoring Global Harmony*. Topics of a scriptural nature have gratefully been adapted from the *International Standard Bible Encyclopedia*: in particular, W. L. Walker (vanity-reproach), Edward B. Pollard (tribulation), and Dwight M. Pratt (anguish), amongst others. Details relating to etymologies are credited to Douglas Harper: editor for the online resource: *etymonline.com*.

Acknowledgements in terms of photographic illustrations include the Birmingham Museum of Art (Pesellino), British Museum (Papyrus of Ani), Prado Museum (Bosch). All other materials not specifically acknowledged have been contributed by author John E. LaMuth PhD, with special appreciation extended to Reference Books of America and Fairhaven Book Publishers for their gracious permission to reproduce excerpts from previous publications by the author in relation to the overall body of work.

ALSO BY THE AUTHOR ...

**The Motivation Solution:
A Global Initiative**

**Character Values:
Promoting a Virtuous Lifestyle**

**A Diagnostic Classification of the
Emotions: A Three-Digit Coding
System for Affective Language**

PREFACE

The new book release currently under consideration: *World Peace 2.0: Restoring Global Harmony* introduces a master mediation system for themes of an ethical/emotional nature, whereby promoting key insights towards advancing global peace and harmony. This all-inclusive ethical system incorporates each of the major groupings of virtues, values, and ideals specified within the Western ethical tradition. Many of these virtuous traditions have historically been invested with religious overtones, an aspect that generally has been downplayed within today's modern secular culture. The current master mediation system proposes to remedy this crucial oversight, advancing a behaviorally-based system of moral classification consistent with behavioral science. This technical breakthrough has recently been made feasible through the introduction of the new science of Powerplay Politics, an all-inclusive synthesis of the behavioral dynamics characterizing emotionally-charged language in general. This innovation is schematically organized in terms of a master three-digit coding system comprising *400* individual terms: the cursory outline of which is partially depicted in the schematic table immediately below:

+ +	**(300 – 399)** **VICES OF EXCESS** **(Excessive Virtue)**	
+	**(100 – 199)** **MAJOR VIRTUES** **(Virtuous Mode)**	

0	- NEUTRALITY STATUS

–	**(500 – 599)** **VICES OF DEFECT** **(Absence of Virtue)**
– –	**(700 – 799)** **HYPERVIOLENCE** **(Excessive Defect)**

The most salient feature of this master schematic format is the centralized zone of neutrality, the basic default setting for the entire motivational system: representing the initiation point for all new classes of interaction to follow (whether positive or negative in nature). The uppermost segments within the diagram represent the positive domain based upon cooperation, as reflected in the traditional categories of virtues, values, and ideals. This dual formulation unites all of the virtuous categories into a cohesive ten-level hierarchy: the first grand unified theory of its kind (as partially depicted below).

Glory • Prudence	**Honor • Justice**
Providence • Faith	**Liberty • Hope**
Grace • Beauty	**Free-Will • Truth**
Tranquility • Ecstasy	**Equality • Bliss**

Dignity • Temperance	**Integrity • Fortitude**
Civility • Charity	**Austerity • Decency**
Magnanim. • Goodness	**Equanimity • Wisdom**
Love • Joy	**Peace • Harmony**

The lower-most segments within the master diagram are alternately based within the realm of conflict and punishment: namely, Aristotle's listings of the vices of defect. For every virtue there necessarily exists a corresponding antonym (or vice): e.g., love vs. hate, good vs. evil, etc. This permits negative transactions to be analyzed according to their potential to be converted into positive ones (and vice versa): a mirror-image reflection of the virtuous mode, as depicted below.

Infamy • Insurgency	**Dishonor • Vengeance**
Prodigality • Betrayal	**Slavery • Despair**
Wrath • Ugliness	**Tyranny • Hypocrisy**
Anger • Abomination	**Prejudice • Perdition**

Foolishness • Gluttony	**Caprice • Cowardice**
Vulgarity • Avarice	**Cruelty • Antagonism**
Oppression • Evil	**Persecution • Cunning**
Hatred • Iniquity	**Belligerence • Turpitude**

This basic core-nucleus of terms, in turn, serves as the foundation for the remaining outer layer of categories based upon the realm of excess. For the virtuous realm, this introduces Aristotle's notion of the vices of excess. With respect to the darker realm of the vices of defect, this pattern alternately extends to the categorical extremes characterizing the excessive domain of hyperviolence.

This grand-scale synthesis of ethical categories represents an unprecedented contribution to the field of ethical inquiry, expanding Aristotle's enduring "Theory of the Mean" into an all-inclusive theory of everything of a motivational nature. At the risk of appearing overly simplistic, each of these four basic categories is further subdivided into more detailed groupings of ethical terms. For instance, the major virtues are respectively subdivided into *100* individual terms, whereas the vices of defect are similarly specialized into *100* contrasting terms. When the two additional ethical categories based upon excess are further added into the mix; namely, the vices of excess and hyperviolence, the grand total summates to a grand total of *400* individual terms.

The current work represents a broadly updated edition of a previous title by the author: *Challenges to World Peace: A Global Solution* originally published in 2009. In terms of this earlier edition, the issue of *character values* was specifically highlighted, although somewhat limited in terms of the scope of international applications. The current expanded edition has purposely been re-titled to reflect its more expanded focus on global solutions towards advancing world-wide peace and harmony, an aspect even more crucial in light of the troubling global developments over the intervening decade. Although much critical material has been retained from the earlier edition, a significant proportion of new material both clarifies and expands upon issues only briefly touched upon within the original edition. The cur-

rent overall focus, however, remains the promotion of a virtuous lifestyle through more intimate insights into the character values (and affiliated ethical categories) with applications extending to an overarching global sphere of influence.

Far from remaining a purely academic exercise, this all-inclusive ethical system addresses many issues of crucial import to modern global culture. For instance the realm of hyperviolence is examined in Part III, proposing critical applications towards reducing political conflict and global international terrorism, whereby offering timely insights into the intractable conflicts facing modern culture today. Further inroads into information technology are addressed in Part IV: most notably, a discussion of a patented simulation for ethical artificial intelligence. Here the schematic dynamics of the ethical system prove amenable to programming directly into a computer platform, providing an intriguing new foundation for moral computer safeguards.

Perhaps the greatest potential for this breakthrough ethical technology resides in its all-inclusive nature, accounting for virtually every major tradition of ethics on the world scene today. Indeed, based upon a basic number of elementary assumptions; namely, the principles of instrumental conditioning and the concept of the meta-perspective, this ascending hierarchy of stepwise transformations ultimately accounts for the entire *400*-part complement of ethical terms. It has been my great pleasure to serve in the production of this grand-scale undertaking, and one that would have been far more daunting without the support of numerous experts that have graciously contributed expertise to this ground-breaking new edition.

John E. LaMuth PhD
January, 2019

PART-I

1

AN INTRODUCTION TO GLOBAL APPROACHES TO WORLD PEACE

The enduring trend towards world peace has increasingly come under attack in flash points across the globe. These ideological conflicts affect international politics as well as economic misunderstandings and disputes. Perhaps the most prominent conflict worldwide concerns the ethical rivalry between modern secular humanism and the long-standing traditions underlying organized religion. Indeed, our modern secular age primarily favors the trend towards moral relativism in direct opposition to the moral absolutism underpinning organized religion. Each viewpoint exhibits its own distinct range of advantages and disadvantages within such a great moral debate. Religious dogmatism enjoys the advantages of a long and established literary tradition, accompanied by well-established codes of conduct appealing to a universal sphere of influence. Such absolute dogmatism, however, further proves disadvantageous in that the fallible scriptural sources (and voluminous theological interpretations therein) often challenge the credulity of those raised in an age of science and technology.

On the opposing end of the spectrum, moral relativism clearly embraces the scientific ethos, encouraging the search for moral certainty through the observation of the natural world (as opposed to scriptural foundation). This further accentuates moral relativism's significant weakness, in that scarcely enough scientific knowledge exists in relation to psychology and the neurosciences to propose any rationally coherent moral code of conduct (as opposed to the moral certainty claimed by organized religion).

This enduring conflict between moral relativism and organized religion assumes an even more urgent sense of immediacy in light of the recent wave of political reversals that have occurred within the United States concerning the dramatic resurgence of republican conservatism. The stunning reversal of the liberal agenda that had dominated the preceding eight years has cast serious concerns over the future of moral relativism in light of the fundamentalist underpinnings undergirding the conservative platform. This great conservative backlash unfortunately promises to trigger considerable political tension of an unproductive nature for years to come unless some form of acceptable accommodation can be reached between the conservative and progressive ideologies.

The key to such an achievement entails identifying the key advantages underlying each perspective, while minimizing any disadvantages therein. For the conservatives, this accounts to an emphasis upon moral clarity and certainty; whereas the progressives celebrate the power of science and technology as the foundation for ethical deliberations (albeit of a relativistic nature). The remainder of the current treatise proposes precisely such a radical cross-cultural accommodation between the liberal and the conservative perspectives, whereby hopefully circumventing any longstanding clash of cultures.

Indeed, a planetary system of ethics is a goal that has long been anticipated on the world scene today. Although organized religion has long been celebrated as the standard bearer for the promotion of a virtuous life style, the various conflicts afflicting the world religions today clearly expose the inherent weakness to such a simplistic interpretation. Ideally, a scientific foundation for such a moral perspective should prove exceedingly beneficial. A formal behavioral-science tie-in with ethical principles proves particularly effective for removing such a cultural range of stumbling blocks. Here a foundation within behavioral psychology proves effective by invoking instinctual principles shared in common as a species (as well as the rest of animal kingdom). When expanded to include the even more abstract human-cultural values; namely, group and universal authority, the affiliated groupings of virtues and values rightfully enter the picture.

A radically new model of motivated behavior is currently called for, one that melds modern behavioral psychology with the long-standing traditions associated with value ethics: a trend encompassing the personal, group, universal, humanitarian, and transcendental realms of inquiry. This comprehensive fusion linking instinctual conditioning with moral philosophy permits the first grand unified synthesis of ethically-motivated behavior. The currently proposed *motivation solution* provides a grand-scale synthesis of the virtues and values in relation to behavioral principles. The specific details for such a dual achievement invoke the entire range of human culture: organized as a ten-level hierarchy of virtues and values comprising both authority and follower roles. Furthermore, this ascending moral hierarchy formally appeals to the schematic principles underlying Set Theory. Here the elementary concepts of the one, the many, and the absolute are reflected through the personal, group, and universal realms of authority and follower roles.

Each conceptual level is further associated with its own unique complement of ethical/motivational terms. This master ten-level hierarchy of authority and follower roles is uniquely correlated to over two-hundred individual virtuous terms, as partially reproduced in the compact table below (including the preliminary behavioral antecedents).

Approach • Rewards	**Avoidance • Leniency**
Solicitude • Approval	**Submission • Blame**
Glory • Prudence	**Honor • Justice**
Providence • Faith	**Liberty • Hope**
Grace • Beauty	**Free-Will • Truth**
Tranquility • Ecstasy	**Equality • Bliss**

+ Reinforce • Appetite	**– Reinforce • Aversion**
Desire • Aspiration	**Worry • Compliance**
Dignity • Temperance	**Integrity • Fortitude**
Civility • Charity	**Austerity • Decency**
Magnanim. • Goodness	**Equanimity • Wisdom**
Love • Joy	**Peace • Harmony**

The traditional ethical listings defined within this hierarchy all appear linked on an intuitive level, suggesting a clear sense of overall cohesiveness, the complete breakdown of which will now be described.

THE MOTIVATIONAL MATRIX

The key conceptual innovation arises as a direct outcome of the fledgling science of Communication Theory, borrowing the crucial concept of the meta-perspective. It is defined as a higher-order perspective on a viewpoint held by another: schematically defined as "this is how I see you-seeing me." The higher-order listings of virtues and values are collectively ordered as subsets within this hierarchy of meta-perspectives, each more abstract grouping building upon that which it supersedes. Take, for example, the cardinal virtues (prudence, justice, temperance, and fortitude), the theological virtues (faith-hope-charity-decency), and the classical Greek values (beauty-truth-goodness-wisdom). Each of these traditional groupings is further subdivided into four subordinate terms permitting precise point-for-point stacking within the hierarchy of meta-perspectives. Additional listings of ethical terms are further be added into the mix: namely, the civil liberties (providence, liberty, civility, and austerity), the humanistic values (peace-love-tranquility-equality), the mystical values (ecstasy-bliss-joy-harmony), etc.

This cohesive hierarchy of virtues, values, and ideals proves particularly comprehensive in scope, accounting for virtually every major ethical theme celebrated within the Western ethical tradition. It is easy to gain a sense of the trend towards increasing abstraction when scanning the individual columns from top to bottom. The traditional sequences of terms line up seamlessly within this hierarchy of meta-perspectives. Indeed, it proves exceedingly unlikely that this cohesive pattern of organization could have arisen solely by chance. Furthermore, this ethical hierarchy mirrors the ascending sequence of personal, group, spiritual, humanitarian, and transcendental realms within society as a whole: which (when specialized into both authority and follower roles) accounts for the full ten-level span of ethical hierarchy.

The major groupings of virtues and values serve as the elementary foundation for the motivational matrix. This grand-scale unification of ethical principles necessarily argues for a radical reinterpretation of the organizational principles at issue. The key salient insight resides in viewing the individual as the rightful product of a diverse range of social and cultural influences. In addition to the most basic one-to-one style of personal interaction, the individual is further incorporated into a broad range of group contexts (e.g., work, family, country, etc.), as well as some all-encompassing universal context. These individual contexts collectively summate into a unified ethical hierarchy consistent with the theoretical principles governing Set Theory. Set Theory remains in full agreement with the three-level model of the ethical hierarchy: with the unit set, the group set, and the universal set equating with the personal, group, and spiritual levels of authority, respectively.

The concept of a three-level style of set hierarchy is actually nothing new, proposed centuries earlier by German philosopher, Emmanuel Kant. In his masterpiece, *Critique of Pure Reason*, Kant proposes a comprehensive system of conceptual categories he considers crucial to the formation of the human intellect. Most notable is the relevant category of *quantity*: which Kant further subdivides into the concepts of unity, plurality, and totality. Indeed, these three fundamental aspects equate to the notions of the one, the many, and the absolute: equivalent (in a human social sense) to the personal, group, and spiritual authority levels.

This three-level style of social hierarchy, although appealing in its simplicity, differs from Set Theory in that interactions between individuals do not exist solely in a vacuum, but rather are specialized into authority and follower roles. For the personal realm, this amounts to the personal authority and personal follower roles, extending to the group realm as the group authority and group representative variations, culminating in terms of the spiritual authority and spiritual disciple roles. A brief description of each of these authority and follower perspectives is certainly in order here, clearly outlining the proposed grand-scale unification of virtues, values, and ideals.

The most basic personal authority level refers to the one-to-one style of interaction occurring between individuals, much as typically encountered in one's personal friendships. This personal interplay is further specialized into either authority or follower roles: exemplified in the case of the master craftsman who remains dependent upon the services of his faithful apprentice. A similar scenario also holds true with respect to the hero and his sidekick, or the celebrity and his straight-man. Here the authority and follower roles flexibly complement one another in terms of such an equitable balance of power. The authority figure formally depends upon the attentions of his follower (as much as the other way around), resulting in an equivalent balance of power with respect to the personal realm.

This elementary personal foundation, in turn, extends to the equally pervasive domain characterizing the group authority perspective. The group set surpasses the unit set in terms of its expansion to a multitude of elements (or class members) within a group-focused context. Personal concerns now become subordinate to such a group power base, being that enough group followers remain to continue group authority whether or not any single individual chooses to desert. In a single stroke, the group authority rises well above any personal power struggles, an innovation exploited since ancient times as the well-established custom of tribal-based authority.

Group authority, in turn, is susceptible to its own unique form of follower counter-maneuver: namely, that expressed by the group representative. The latter's distinctive style of "strike" leverage is fully realized at this juncture, as witnessed in the modern-day trend towards collective bargaining. By organizing as a union collective, the rank-and-file nominates a shop steward to represent them in their negotiations with management. The group representative, in essence, reminds the group authority that the cooperation of the labor pool is crucial for maintaining the group status quo. Consequently, the group authority (in concert with the group representative) shares an equivalent balance of power within the group power realm.

A similar pattern further holds true with respect to the spiritual authority level, although this sense of "spiritual" is restricted to the universal sense of the term implicit in Set Theory. The universal set clearly surpasses the multiplicity of the group domain: in essence, the sum-totality of all such groups within the universal domain. The universal set represents the "group of all group sets," a 3rd-order style of set-hierarchy (equivalent to the domain of all mankind). Indeed, whereas group authority surpasses the influence of the individual members, the spiritual authority figure similarly overrules the strike power of any of its constituent groups, whereby claiming authority over the sum-total of mankind.

It is true (in practice) that each of the world's religions competes for the beliefs of the world's faithful. In principle each religion vigilantly strives to convert all others, giving credence to the universal sense of the term. This claim to universality is traditionally made binding through an appeal to God or a Messiah-figure, a sanction dating to the earliest civilizations. Here a king could inspire the loyalty of his troops (in the name of a god of war) far in excess of what he might claim as a mere mortal ruler.

110	111
Solicitude	Submissiveness
112	**113**
Desire	Worry

EGO STATES
(Personal Authority)

→

120	121
Approval	Leniency
122	**123**
Aspiration	Compliance

ALTER EGO STATES
(Personal Follower)

↙

130	131
Glory	Honor
132	**133**
Dignity	Integrity

PERSONAL IDEALS
(Group Authority)

→

140	141
Prudence	Justice
142	**143**
Temperance	Fortitude

CARDINAL VIRTUES
(Group Representative)

↙

150	151
Providence	Liberty
152	**153**
Civility	Austerity

CIVIL LIBERTIES
(Spiritual Authority)

→

160	161
Faith	Hope
162	**163**
Charity	Decency

THEOLOGICAL VIRTUES
(Spiritual Disciple)

↙

170	171
Grace	Free Will
172	**173**
Magnanimity	Equanimity

ECUMENICAL IDEALS
(Humanitarian Authority)

→

180	181
Beauty	Truth
182	**183**
Goodness	Wisdom

CLASSICAL GREEK VALUES
(Humanitarian Follower)

↙

190	191
Tranquility	Equality
192	**193**
Love	Peace

HUMANISTIC VALUES
(Transcendental Authority)

→

100	101
Ecstasy	Bliss
102	**103**
Joy	Harmony

MYSTICAL VALUES
(Transcendental Follower)

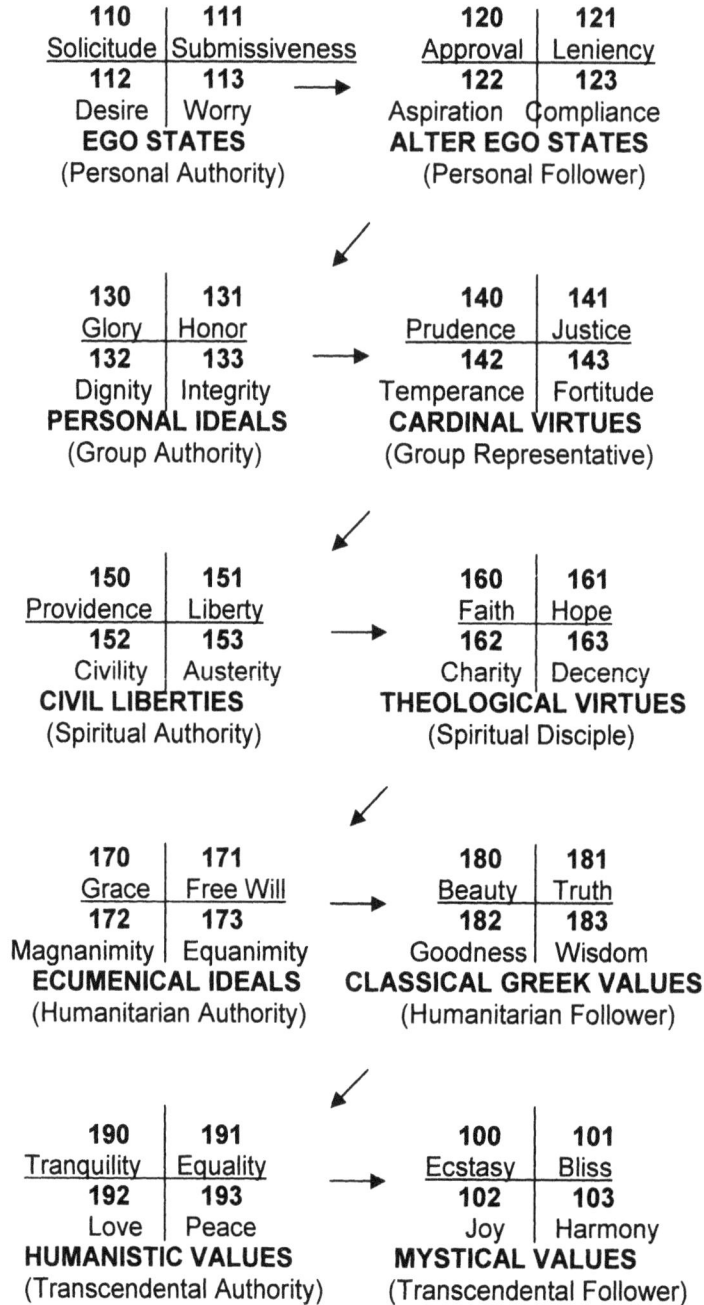

Figure 1 -- The Major Virtues, Values, and Ideals

Taking this trend to the limit, even an authority role as abstract as the universal must (by definition) be susceptible to its own unique form of follower maneuver: e.g., that specified for the spiritual disciple. As spokesman for the spiritual congregation, the spiritual disciple reminds the spiritual authority that the blessings of the faithful are crucial for maintaining the spiritual status quo. Witness the power of the spiritual disciple for influencing such diverse historical events as the Protestant Reformation, and even the very founding of Christianity.

THE MASTER GROUPINGS OF VIRTUES/VALUES

In summary, the three-level ascending hierarchy of personal, group, and spiritual domains, when further specialized in terms of both authority and follower roles, provides the supreme conceptual framework for explaining the grand-scale unification of virtuous terms. This virtuous format is schematically depicted in **Fig. 1**, including the three-digit codes for each of the respective virtues, values, and ideals. This master schematic format (tentatively termed the *motivational matrix*) incorporates each of the major virtuous classifications described to date (plus an equivalent number of new ones) for a grand total of ten levels, serving as the elementary foundation for the remainder of the book to follow.

As the underlying captions serve to indicate, the uppermost three levels of this diagram are designated for the personal, group, and spiritual levels: accounting for the most basic groupings of virtues/ideals. The remaining lowermost two levels, in turn, introduce a pair of hitherto unmentioned categories; namely, the humanitarian and transcendental domains, respectively. This additional sequence of authority levels are classified as uniquely abstract styles of power perspectives, whereby clearly surpassing the more basic organizational pattern previously established for the initial three levels. A brief description of these final two levels is definitely in order here, for the most abstract listings of virtues and values enter into these final two domains.

Although the spiritual realm is clearly the maximum level of organization (in keeping with the traditions of Set Theory), this very sense of chronological time permits the introduction of the even more abstract conception of humanitarian authority. The great theoretical physicist, Albert Einstein defined time as the fourth dimension of the universe, making it fitting that the humanitarian role enters into consideration precisely at this 4th-order level within the ethical hierarchy. Humanitarian authority transcends the spiritual variety by claiming to speak for all generations of mankind, not just the current one: experienced as past traditionalism and/or future potentiality. Its extreme degree of generality precludes its identification within any singular social institution, rather incorporated into the spiritual (and often political) framework of society as a whole.

This extreme sense of the power of abstraction (when considered in its own right) ultimately serves as the basis for one final innovation within the ethical hierarchy; namely, the crowning transcendental level of authority. Transcendental authority regains the upper hand by transcending the routine sense of concreteness shared in common by all of the lower levels, an innovation accounting for many of the most abstract listings of virtues and values. The transcendental perspective enters freely into the realm of pure intuition and imagination, wherein forsaking the constraints of ordinary reality for the supreme and incontrovertible realm of pure abstraction. This transcendental domain (in concert with its humanitarian counterpart) is further specialized into both authority/follower roles for a grand total of four categories. In concert with the six respective level characterizing the personal, group, and spiritual roles, the master ten-level hierarchy emerges in full detail, as schematically depicted in **Fig. 1**.

Although basically only an introductory chapter, a few general observations must necessarily be made with respect to this distinctive schematic format. The ten individual listings of virtues, values, and ideals are organized as dual-descending columns comprising five groupings each. The left-hand column represents the hierarchy of authority roles, whereas the right side specifies the respective follower roles. This dual schematic format represents the sum-totality of reciprocating interactions between the authority and follower roles, as the respective directional arrows further serve to indicate.

The distinctive groupings of virtues and values represented for each individual level exhibit a unique range of distinguishing characteristics. Each listing is represented as a quartet-style of format, depicted as quadrants in a pseudo-Cartesian coordinate system. The more traditional groupings (such as the cardinal virtues) are already depicted as a four-part grouping, fitting quite nicely within the quartet-style format. Others listings (such as the theological virtues) have been supplemented beyond their traditional number in order to achieve the requisite quartet-style status. A number of other groupings are entirely new to the philosophical tradition, yet effectively respecting the quartet-style pattern of organization.

Similar to the reciprocating pattern of authority and follower roles, the affiliated groupings of virtues, values, and ideals similarly mirror this ascending style of hierarchy. The most elementary personal nature of the ego and alter ego states further serve as the foundation for the even more abstract listings of virtuous terms to follow. This virtuous realm runs the entire gamut of human experience ranging from the instinctual to the sublime (and everything in between). A brief description of each of these individual moral groupings is definitely in order here, serving as a preliminary overview for the remaining detailed examination to follow.

THE PERSONAL ETHICAL FOUNDATIONS

The most rational initiation point for this comprehensive style analysis is certainly the personal level within the ethical hierarchy. According to **Fig. 1**, these dual categories are respectively listed as the ego states targeting the personal authority role (solicitousness, submissiveness, desire, and worry), as well as the alter ego states comprising the follower role (approval-leniency-aspiration-compliance). The behavioral overtones underlying these groupings make them tailor-made for incorporation into the personal power realm, whereby effectively specifying the interpersonal dynamics at issue here.

Although only briefly outlined, this initial complement of ego and alter ego states, in turn, serves as the elementary foundation for the remaining listings of virtues, values, and ideals, as outlined in **Fig. 1**. Indeed, a general pattern of organization emerges from this schematic format; namely, the left-hand column is characterized by what are termed the authority ideals: read downwards as the personal ideals, civil liberties, ecumenical ideals, and humanistic values. The right-hand column of follower roles, in turn, specifies the related trend based upon the virtuous mode; namely, the cardinal virtues, theological virtues, classical Greek values, and mystical values. For sake of consistency, the initial authority trend will be examined first, followed by an equally comprehensive treatment of the respective sequence of follower roles.

THE AUTHORITY IDEALS

The first mentioned sequence of authority ideals begins at the group authority level with respect to the provisionally termed class of *personal ideals*

(glory-honor-dignity-integrity). The personal designation for this grouping might appear somewhat of a misnomer, although more properly viewed as ideals within a group sphere of influence. These personal ideals build directly upon the ego states previously described for the personal authority role, wherein accounting for the hybrid quality of the grouping. In this latter respect, the group authority *gloriously* acts solicitously or *honorably* acts submissively towards his personal follower figure. Similarly, he might *dignifiedly* act desirously or worrisomely act with *integrity* in terms of this dual pattern of organization.

The personal ideals collectively derive from the classical Latin tradition, effectively highlighting the Roman's fascination with the heroic themes. This group authority focus is primarily expressed in terms of the many symbolisms for royalty and nobility; as in the heraldic traditions of the circle of *glory*, the *honor* point, the cap of *dignity*, and the heraldic symbolisms for *integrity*. Guided by such lofty civic ideals, the group authority figure fittingly aspires to such noble principles befitting a leader of society.

The next higher spiritual authority level rates a similar consideration indicative of its respective class of *civil liberties* (providence-liberty-civility-austerity). Each of these themes is prominently featured in the founding of the United States, as collectively celebrated in the precepts of the *Declaration of Independence*. This revolutionary document invokes divine authority as one of its central premises, celebrating the universal rights of man for overruling the tyrannical edicts of the English monarch, King George III. Although this designation of *civil liberties* might suggest somewhat of a political context, further examination reveals the deep spiritual foundations for these four basic themes. Indeed, each of these themes was traditionally worshiped as a classical deity in its own right; namely, Providentia, Libertas, Civitas, and Auster. In terms of this more advanced universal context, *providence* represents the spiritual counterpart of glory, whereas *liberty* makes a similar correspondence to honor. Furthermore, *civility* represents a spiritual refinement of dignity, whereas *austerity* denotes integrity from a universal perspective.

The universal prerequisites for spiritual authority role, in turn, serve as the foundation for the affiliated concept of humanitarian authority, an innovation firmly rooted within the concept of "historical" time. This enduring humanitarian focus is directly reflected in the abstract listing of ethical terms provisionally termed the *ecumenical* ideals (grace-free/will-magnanimity-equanimity).

The enduring significance of this grouping certainly suggests a common range of perspectives; namely, timeless themes consistent with such a grand humanitarian perspective. Although closely affiliated with spiritual concerns, a more detailed examination clearly reveals a grand humanitarian focus: as reflected in the long tradition of ecumenical councils dealing with generational issues.

This grouping enjoyed particular favor during the Protestant Reformation. Indeed, according to Martin Luther: "By *grace* are thee saved through faith." This listing of ecumenical ideals adds a more enduring sense of historicity to the civil liberties previously described for the spiritual tradition. For example, *grace* imparts a more enduring humanitarian focus to providence, whereas *free will* provides a historical perspective to liberty. Similarly, the remaining ecumenical ideals of *magnanimity* and *equanimity* extend a similar humanitarian mindset to civility and austerity.

The crowning transcendental level ultimately rounds out the stepwise description of authority roles. This transcendental perspective formally appeals to the idealized realm of pure abstraction, in essence, transcending the more concrete nature of the preceding levels. The respective grouping of *humanistic* values (peace-love-tranquility-equality) rightfully enter into consideration at this juncture: ideal values befitting such a lofty transcendental perspective. Each of these terms befits such a crowning level of abstraction, ideals attuned to realms wholly transcending routine experience. These values date to classical times, worshipped as abstract deities in their own right: namely, Pax (peace), Cupid (love), Quies (tranquility), and Aequitas (equality). These themes further served as the inspiration for many of the modern protest movements, such as in the New England Transcendentalists and the Peace Protest against the Vietnam War.

THE VIRTUOUS FOLLOWER TRADITIONS

The completed description of the authority ideals, in turn, sets the stage for a discussion of the remaining sequence of follower roles. Whereas the authority hierarchy was based upon the ego states, the follower sequence alternately targets the alter ego states. This pattern further extends to the well-established traditions of the cardinal virtues and theological virtues. These two basic categories of virtue have long enjoyed a distinguished place of honor in the Western ethical tradition. As their qualifiers serve to indicate, the theological virtues (faith-hope-charity-decency) encompass the spiritual disciple role, whereas the

cardinal virtues (prudence-justice-temperance-fortitude), by default, target the group follower perspective.

The latter cardinal virtues are collectively designated from the Latin *cardos* (hinge): based upon the belief that all of the higher virtues *hinge* upon these basic four. Consequently, the cardinal virtues exhibit distinct parallels to the more elementary class of alter ego states; namely, *prudent*-approval, *just*-leniency, a *temperate* sense of aspiration, and compliant-*fortitude*. This enduring tradition of cardinal virtues figures prominently in the writings of the Greek philosopher Plato, particularly his fanciful dialogue, *The Republic*. These cardinal virtues provide an effective focal point within the dialogue, promoted as ideal codes of conduct befitting Plato's conception of the Greek city-state.

The even more advanced listing of theological virtues (faith-hope-charity-decency), in turn, builds upon their more elementary foundation within the cardinal virtues. Church theologian, St. Thomas Aquinas, viewed the theological virtues as divinely inspired; in direct contrast to the more elementary nature of the cardinal virtues, the latter of which were more widely regarded as natural social predispositions. Befitting their exalted moral status, the theological virtues remain an enduring theme in New Testament scripture, particularly celebrated by St. Paul as supreme moral principles governing virtuous conduct.

Although the formal designation of *theological* originally applied only to the first basic three terms, the addition of the fourth related theme of *decency* effectively modifies this grouping into a format consistent with the quartet-style of hierarchy. This shortfall in the traditional complement of terms appears to account for the great theoretical insight that was missed down through the ages; namely, the theological virtues represent the higher spiritual analogues of the subordinate class of cardinal virtues (just as the latter are based within the alter ego states). Here one can acknowledge the prudent-*faith* or lenient-*hope* for justice professed by the spiritual disciple figure, in addition to the temperate sense of the *charitableness* and fortitudinous sense of *decency* germane to the discussion.

The completed description of the group and spiritual levels, in turn, extends to a humanitarian focus with respect to the *representative member of humanity* role. More properly termed the philosopher's maneuver, it invokes the prestige of speaking for all generations of mankind (not just the current one). In essence, the representative member of humanity reminds the humanitarian authority figure of his formal sanction from humanity, lest he lose prestige in such matters. The humanitarian authority perspective is essentially seen as more of a policy-making strategy than any immediate style of power perspective. The humanitarian follower, in turn, retains the option of rejecting humanitarian policy; hence, maintaining an essentially equivalent balance of power.

The enduring grouping of classical Greek values (beauty-truth-goodness-wisdom) rightfully enters into consideration here, the major groupings of *virtues* already accounted for at the lower levels. This alternate focus on values invokes precisely such a humanitarian focus, the more immediate sense of virtue now advancing to the more timeless quality of value. Indeed, the classical Greek values date to the most ancient of times, celebrated by Plato as pure forms or essences that transcend the variability of the natural world. Each of these values was worshiped as an abstract deity in its own right; namely, Venus (beauty), Veritas (truth), Bonus Eventus (goodness), and Sapientia (wisdom). This classical tradition of value, in turn, fulfills the trend previously established with respect to the cardinal and theological virtues: namely, the *beauteous*-faith or just-hope for the *truth*, as well as the charitable sense of *goodness* and decent sense of *wisdom* characterizing the overall span of the humanitarian follower role.

Even an authority level as abstract as the transcendental must (by definition) be invested with its own unique form of follower counter-maneuver, in this case, that specified for the transcendental follower role. Despite this extreme level of abstraction, it still proves possible to distinguish a respective listing of mystical values (ecstasy-bliss-joy-harmony). Although a formal description of this grouping of terms is scarcely warranted at this juncture, suffice it to say they encompass the enigmatic realm of religious mysticism tuned to realms wholly transcending ordinary experience. Although this crowning mystical level effectively closes out the *nameable* domain of the ethical hierarchy, it still proves possible to postulate the existence of a supernatural extension to the ascending hierarchy of terms: a topic best reserved for a more detailed examination of mysticism contained in Chapter *6*.

THE MOTIVATIONAL MATRIX

In conclusion, the completed cursory examination of the ten-level hierarchy of virtuous terms aimed to provide a suitably comprehensive overview of virtuous realm, a mere glimpse at the more detailed examination to follow. At the heart of this system lies the unified ethical hierarchy depicted in **Fig. 1**, a reciprocating confluence of authority and follower roles spanning the personal, group, spiritual, humanitarian, and transcendental realms. In tribute to this dramatic scope, this new conceptual paradigm is respectively termed *the motivational matrix*, in direct analogy to the semantic style of linguistic matrix that it represents. This ascending hierarchy of authority and follower roles emerges as a direct outcome of the principles governing Set Theory. The truest value for this system derives from the respective listings of virtues, values, and ideals, intriguing in their quartet-style pattern of organization.

This schematic pattern reflects the overarching sense of cohesiveness underlying the individual virtuous terms, as representative of the cardinal virtues, theological virtues, and classical Greek values. As depicted in **Fig. 1**, in the left-hand column of terms specify the authority roles. The first quadrant lists the ascending sequence of solicitousness, glory, providence, grace, and tranquility. All five terms share an immediately-active focus based upon the acknowledgement of past notable achievements. The same quadrant within the right-hand column of follower roles yields the related sequence of approval-prudence-faith-beauty-ecstasy: themes that directly reciprocate the authority roles through the perspective of the follower figure.

A similar pattern further holds true with respect to the upper (right-hand) quadrants depicted in **Fig. 1**. The respective authority roles lead to the sequence of submissiveness-honor-liberty-freewill-equality: themes all sharing an active focus although now specifying a more submissive perspective. The remaining follower trend (leniency-justice-hope-truth-bliss) further verifies this reciprocating pattern, a sequence mirroring that based on approval with the exception that leniency is now called into focus. Indeed, it proves particularly amazing that these distinctive ethical trends should exist at all, each lining up so perfectly within its respective quadrant of the virtuous hierarchy. This grand scale organization is certainly a major selling point, the perfect symmetry and cohesiveness far too intricate to have arisen solely by chance. Indeed, these ten virtuous groupings actually prove to be just a basic skeleton framework for a much broader system of communication covering the entire range of emotionally-charged language in general: an issue clearly warranting further such overarching consideration.

GLOBAL ETHICAL APPLICATIONS

This grand-scale pattern of organization for the main ethical terms proves a fitting launch-point for applications relating to world peace and harmony. The distinctive listings of virtues and values are amenable to widespread acceptance by the world community, their classical and contemporary overtones serving as the foundation for many of our most prominent political and cultural institutions.

For instance, the legal system clearly celebrates the traditions of the cardinal virtues, the enduring theme of jurisprudence directly deriving from this classical arrangement of terms. The Declaration of Independence further celebrates the listing of civil liberties through an appeal to the universal rights of man, as suggested in the authority ideals of providence and liberty. The world economy is similarly based upon cooperation on an international level, as exemplified in an honorable insistence on fair business dealings, as well as integrity with respect to mutually-equitable commercial trade.

This highly interdependent system of global economic cooperation remains entirely untenable without such enduring virtuous principles that serve as a restraint on unbridled western capitalism, particularly such as that which occurred during the recent global economic downturn. This enduring humanitarian focus celebrates more long-term plans for a stable global infrastructure, a lesson seemingly lost on the droves of speculators that sacrificed economic stability on the altar of short-term financial gains.

Such long-term goals similarly prove applicable in relation to the career politician, an office that often appears similarly shortsighted in terms of partisan politics and a self-serving focus on reelection, all the while delaying critical action relating to budgetary responsibility. This move towards resurrecting traditional value ethics proves crucial towards reining-in the free exercise of short-sighted capitalist impulses. Indeed, many social institutions (whether legal, political, or religious) could gain substantially from the dramatic new insights contained within the newly devised hierarchy of virtuous terms. This cohesive ethical foundation further serves as the major conceptual framework for applications relating to the darker realm of ethical inquiry: including novel inroads towards avoiding the vices of defect, as well as an enhanced comprehension of the motives underlying criminality and international terrorism. This grand-scale ethical synthesis has entered the world scene at perhaps its darkest hour of need, a glimmer of hope for those that might seek to launch such a versatile innovation into action.

THE VICES OF DEFECT

Although a preferential focus on the virtues is certainly understandable, the virtuous mode can scarcely exist solely in a vacuum. The truest applications arise precisely from such a moral contrast with the related realm of the vices (where virtue and vice contrast with one another). Indeed, for every virtue there necessarily exists a corresponding antonym (or vice): namely, love vs. hate, peace vs. war, good vs. evil, etc. The corresponding vices of defect represent the chief moral opposites for their respective virtuous counterparts, whereby providing a balanced sense of symmetry across the unified ethical hierarchy. The ten predicted categories for the vices of defect are arrayed in ten-level hierarchy similar to the pattern previously established for the virtuous mode, depicted in the compact diagram below and also in **Fig. 9B** of Chapter 9.

no Solicit.- *no* Reward	*no* Submiss.- *no* Leniency
Laziness • Treachery	Negligence • Vindictive.
Infamy • Insurgency	Dishonor • Vengeance
Prodigality • Betrayal	Slavery • Despair
Wrath • Ugliness	Tyranny • Hypocrisy
Anger • Abomination	Prejudice • Perdition
Punish. • *no* Appetite	Punish. • *no* Aversion
Apathy • Spite	Indifference • Malice
Foolishness • Gluttony	Caprice • Cowardice
Vulgarity • Avarice	Cruelty • Antagonism
Oppression • Evil	Persecution • Cunning
Hatred • Iniquity	Belligerence • Turpitude

This distinct style of ethical contrast allows negative transactions to be analyzed in terms of their potential for conversion into positive ones (and vice versa). The resultant ten-part categories for the vices of defect includes the ecumenical vices (wrath, tyranny, persecution, and oppression), the moralistic vices (evil, cunning, ugliness, and hypocrisy), and the humanistic vices (anger, hatred, prejudice, and belligerence), etc.; groupings that prove particularly significant for outlining this darker realm of the vices.

THE VICES OF EXCESS

The vices of defect, in turn, can scarcely claim to be all-inclusive by any measure. Indeed, only half of the Seven Deadly Sins are formally accounted for in terms of the vices of defect: where pride, envy, and covetousness defy incorporation into the established domain of defect. This anomaly is fortunately explained through aid of an additional class of vices known since ancient times as the *vices of excess*. Aristotle first described this dual pattern relating to the vices. The vices of defect directly contrast in relation to the vices of excess, the latter defined as that range of extremes in relation to the virtuous mode. Accordingly, Aristotle viewed the virtuous mode as a system of mean values (or norms) interposed between the vices of defect and vices of excess.

For instance, Aristotle cites the example of the virtue of courage. It represents the mean-range of virtue interposed between the corresponding vice of defect (cowardice) and its excessive counterpart in foolhardiness. Consequently, virtue represents the middle-ground between defect and excess, favoring moderation insofar as choosing a balance between this dual arrangement of the vices. Indeed, it ultimately proves feasible to devise an entire ten-level hierarchy for the vices of excess, mirroring point-for-point the pattern previously established with respect to the virtuous mode: although now extending to excessive qualities such as vanity, jealousy, shame, etc.

Pride • Flattery	**Shame • Criticism**
Vanity • Adulation	**Humiliation • Ridicule**
Conceit • Patronization	**Mortification • Scorn**
Pretention • Obsequious	**Anguish • Mockery**
Sanctimony • Sycophancy	**Tribulation• Cynicism**

Envy • Impudence	**Disdain • Insolence**
Jealousy • Arrogance	**Contempt • Audacity**
Covetous. • Impetuosity	**Reproach • Rashness**
Longing • Presumption	**Chagrin • Boldness**
Affectation • Smugness	**Bitterness • Harshness**

Curiously, the three-way pattern of specialization implied in Aristotle's Theory of the Mean fails to distinguish any parallel complement of extremes with respect to the vices of defect (similar to that specified for the virtuous mode). This glaring lack of an even sense of symmetry fortunately is remedied through the introduction of an entirely new class of ethical terms: a terminology provisionally termed the realm of *hyperviolence*. This new category is formally distinguished from the more routine realm of defect primarily in terms of the extremes by which it is expressed.

Herein lies the formal prototype for the realm of hyperviolence; namely, that range of excess targeting the vices of defect. The fact that Aristotle fails to distinguish this additional conceptual category within his Theory of the Mean attests to the classical warrior ideal, where victory was to be achieved at any cost. The terminology for this extreme realm of hyperviolence scarcely enjoys the pedigree or tradition of the other listings of vices, although a complete listing of the provisional categories for hyperviolence is schematically depicted in the compact diagram immediately below, and also **Fig. 18A** of Chapter *18*.

Indolence • Mutiny	**Dereliction • Reprisal**
Notoriety • Rebellious.	**Ignobility • Retribution**
Licentiousness • Treason	**Savagery • Hopeless.**
Fury • Hideousness	**Despotism • Mendacity**
Madness • Horror	**Bigotry • Ruin**

Languor • Grudgingness	**Callous. • Malignancy**
Crassness • Voracity	**Petulance • Cravenness**
Rudeness • Greed	**Hostility • Contentious.**
Brutality • Heinousness	**Barbarism • Ruthless.**
Viciousness • Balefulness	**Atrocity • Fiendish.**

This arrangement is similar in form and function to that previously established for the vices of defect. In keeping with its somewhat infrequent occurrence in society as a whole, any formal terminology with respect to the realm of hyperviolence must necessarily rely upon the wealth of case histories from the annals of violent crime relating to criminal profiling.

In summary, the current introductory chapter aimed to provide a grand overview of the entire motivational matrix. Indeed, a complete tabular listing of each of the individual terms for the major virtues, the vices of defect, the vices of excess, and hyperviolence are depicted in the four tables to follow (along with the accompanying three-digit coding system). Although the precise additional details extend well beyond this introductory chapter, these four tables are provided at this juncture to offer a preliminary indication of the great wealth of explanatory detail to be offered within the following chapters. The discerning reader is encouraged to refer back to this extensive listing of terms (for easy reference) throughout the remainder of the book.

THE MASTER SCHEMATIC FORMAT
LINKING VIRTUE AND VICE

In summary, the formal additional of the realm of hyperviolence results in a more fully balanced symmetry relating to the ethical hierarchy. These four basic ethical categories: e.g., the virtues, the vices of defect, the vices of excess, and hyperviolence collectively account for the routine range of emotionally-charged language in general; as formally depicted in the master schematic diagram to follow. This four-part diagram is organized around the novel concept of the *neutrality status*, a neutral point of entry within the system and the default status from which all new relationships are formed. This neutrality status is defined as that benign sense of neglect we express towards strangers on the street: contacts that pose no meaningful sense of relationship yet do not pose any impending sense of harm.

+ + VICES OF EXCESS
(Excessive Virtue)

+ MAJOR VIRTUES
(Virtuous Mode)

O - NEUTRALITY STATUS

- VICES OF DEFECT
(Absence of Virtue)

- - HYPERVIOLENCE
(Excessive Defect)

Every new relationship (by definition) stems directly from this zone of neutrality status, a range of potentiality that extends to the realm of the virtues, or alternately into the domain of defect/excess. This moral divergence is schematically depicted as the dual arrangement of terms immediately flanking the zone of neutrality. This pair of conflicting options represents an ethical "fork in the road," representing the basic core nucleus for the system. Most relationships are resolved through recourse to one option or the other (either virtue or defect), the basic thoroughfare for the communicational dynamic.

This dual interpretation can scarcely claim to be the total picture, for the parallel realm of excess lurks along the more extreme boundaries of the core nucleus. For the virtuous realm, this corresponds to the related realm of the vices of excess. Furthermore, the vices of defect alternately grade-over into the newly proposed realm of hyperviolence. These latter two categories represent the figurative "fast lanes" of the relationship superhighway; namely, fringe areas exaggerated to the point of crossing over into the range of excess. Fortunately, such forays into the realm of excess are typically somewhat limited, the enduring sense of stability within the social dynamic effectively serving to diminish the effects of such

drastic mood swings and maintain a more stable emotional disposition.

A CURSORY CHAPTER OVERVIEW
FOR *WORLD PEACE 2.0*

In agreement with the considerable degree of detail associated to the ten-level ethical hierarchy, the remaining chapters are subdivided into four major sub-headings. The remainder of the current section is devoted exclusively to the virtuous realm; namely, the major groupings of virtues, values, and ideals representing the cardinal virtues, theological virtues, classical Greek values, etc. This initial **Part I** is further subdivided into eight separate chapters representing the personal, group, spiritual, humanitarian, and transcendental levels within the ethical hierarchy; as well as examining the accessory virtues and general unifying themes. In **Part II** Aristotle's enduring classifications of the vices of defect are further described. This section respectively comprises six individual chapters (*9* through *14*), whereby reflecting the ascending sequence of authority levels within the hierarchy of defect.

This initial range of themes is further expanded in **Part III** with respect to the affiliated domain of excess, defined as that range of extremes targeting the virtuous mode. The realm of excess is further subdivided into three separate chapters collectively specifying the entire range for the vices of excess (as well as a number of accessory issues). The remaining chapters *18* and *19*, in turn, examine the realm of hyperviolence: a new ethical category defined as that range of excess with respect to the vices of defect.

In terms a final ethical overview, the remaining **Part IV** enters into a description of the global applications for the master linguistic matrix. Chapter *20* outlines avenues for further research and development, as well as intriguing modifications relating to the great literary traditions from around the world. Chapter *21*, in turn, proposes improvements to the global economic mindset in terms of international cooperation. With the ongoing concerns over global terrorism, this new technology proves particularly effective towards aiming to ameliorate the effects of such misguided perspectives.

Perhaps the most dramatic potential applications are detailed in Chapter *22* with respect to an ethical simulation of artificial intelligence, the basis for two US patents (now expired and in the public domain). This novel innovation employs the schematic coding system as an aid for programming of complex sequences of ethical parameters.

THE MAJOR VIRTUES (100 – 199)

110 – Solicitousness

111 – Submissiveness

112 – Desire

113 – Worry

114 – Ambition

115 – Deference

116 – Passion

117 – Apprehension

118 – Individualism

119 – Quintessentialism

120 – Approval

121 – Leniency

122 – Aspiration

123 – Compliance

124 – Admiration

125 – Concern

126 – Consideration

127 – Adherence

128 – Pragmatism

129 – Expediency

130 – Glory

131 – Honor

132 – Dignity

133 – Integrity

134 – Exaltation

135 – Uprightness

136 – Respectfulness

137 – Probity

138 – Personalism

139 – Heroism

140 – Prudence

141 – Justice

142 – Temperance

143 – Fortitude

144 – Circumspection

145 – Equitableness

146 – Continence

147 – Bravery

148 – Utilitarianism

149 – Practicality

150 – Providence

151 – Liberty

152 – Civility

153 – Austerity

154 – Bountifulness

155 – Freedom

156 – Courtesy

157 – Forbearance

158 – Romanticism

159 – Charisma

160 – Faith

161 – Hope

162 – Charity

163 – Decency

164 – Devotion

165 – Fairness

166 – Kindness

167 – Scrupulousness

168 – Ecclesiasticism

169 – Dogmatism

170 – Grace

171 – Free-will

172 – Magnanimity

173 – Equanimity

174 – Blessings

175 – Conscientious.

176 – Graciousness

177 – Patience

178 – Ecumenism

179 – Evangelism

180 – Beauty

181 – Truth

182 – Goodness

183 – Wisdom

184 – Charm

185 – Credence

186 – Benevolence

187 – Shrewdness

188 – Eclecticism

189 – Moralism

190 – Tranquility

191 – Equality

192 – Love

193 – Peace

194 – Serenity

195 – Brotherhood

196 – Affection

197 – Amity

198 – Humanism

199 – Philanthropy

100 – Ecstasy

101 – Bliss

102 – Joy

103 – Harmony

104 – Happiness

105 – Contentment

106 – Gladness

107 – Concordance

108 – Mysticism

109 – Spiritualism

THE VICES OF EXCESS (300 – 399)

310 – Pride	344 – Courtliness	378 – Fanaticism
311 – Shame	345 – Denunciation	379 – Fundamentalism
312 – Envy	346 – Brazenness	380 – Obsequiousness
313 – Disdain	347 – Surliness	381 – Mockery
314 – Narcissism	348 – Authoritarianism	382 – Presumption
315 – Ignominy	349 – Absolutism	383 – Boldness
316 – Invidiousness	350 – Conceit	384 – Servility
317 – Despisal	351 – Mortification	385 – Sarcasm
318 – Egotism	352 – Covetousness	386 – Effrontery
319 – Egocentrism	353 – Reproach	387 – Temerity
320 – Flattery	354 – Vainglory	388 – Idealism
321 – Criticism	355 – Despondency	389 – Supremacism
322 – Impudence	356 – Cravingness	390 – Sanctimony
323 – Insolence	357 – Rebuke	391 – Tribulation
324 – Blandishment	358 – Ideology	392 – Affectation
325 – Reprehensiveness	359 – Pontification	393 – Bitterness
326 – Impertinence	360 – Patronization	394 – Pietism
327 – Hubris	361 – Scorn	395 – Affliction
328 – Officiousness	362 – Impetuosity	396 – Pretension
329 – Obtrusiveness	363 – Rashness	397 – Admonishment
330 – Vanity	364 – Condescension	398 – Triumphalism
331 – Humiliation	365 – Derision	399 – Universalism
332 – Jealousy	366 – Brashness	300 – Sycophancy
333 – Contempt	367 – Irascibility	301 – Cynicism
334 – Snobbery	368 – Clericalism	302 – Smugness
335 – Opprobrium	369 – Dogmatism	303 – Harshness
336 – Possessiveness	370 – Pretentiousness	304 – Subservience
337 – Repugnance	371 – Anguish	305 – Satiricism
338 – Elitism	372 – Longing	306 – Gleefulness
339 – Autocracy	373 – Chagrin	307 – Rigorousness
340 – Adulation	374 – Haughtiness	308 – Occultism
341 – Ridicule	375 – Agony	309 – Enigmatism
342 – Arrogance	376 – Yearning	
343 – Audacity	377 – Loathing	

THE VICES OF DEFECT (500 – 599)

510 – Laziness	**544** – Sedition	**578** – Apostasy
511 – Negligence	**545** – Avengement	**579** – Infidelity
512 – Apathy	**546** – Lechery	**580** – Ugliness
513 – Indifference	**547** – Pusillanimity	**581** – Hypocrisy
514 – Slothfulness	**548** – Corruption	**582** – Evil
515 – Carelessness	**549** – Venality	**583** – Cunning
516 – Dispassion	**550** – Prodigality	**584** – Revulsion
517 – Arbitrariness	**551** – Slavery	**585** – Duplicity
518 – Knavery	**552** – Vulgarity	**586** – Wickedness
519 – Mischievousness	**553** – Cruelty	**587** – Guilefulness
520 – Treachery	**554** – Profligacy	**588** – Anarchism
521 – Vindictiveness	**555** – Bondage	**589** – Lawlessness
522 – Spite	**556** – Coarseness	**590** – Anger
523 – Malice	**557** – Acrimony	**591** – Prejudice
524 – Traitorousness	**558** – Profanity	**592** – Hatred
525 – Retaliation	**559** – Scandalousness	**593** – Belligerence
526 – Resentment	**560** – Betrayal	**594** – Irateness
527 – Malevolence	**561** – Despair	**595** – Intolerance
528 – Fraud	**562** – Avarice	**596** – Enmity
529 – Deception	**563** – Antagonism	**597** – Militancy
530 – Infamy	**564** – Perfidy	**598** – Nihilism
531 – Dishonor	**565** – Desperation	**599** – Alienation
532 – Foolishness	**566** – Cupidity	**500** – Abomination
533 – Capriciousness	**567** – Opposition	**501** – Perdition
534 – Disrepute	**568** – Heresy	**502** – Iniquity
535 – Reprehension	**569** – Schismatism	**503** – Turpitude
536 – Preposterousness	**570** – Wrath	**504** – Abhorrence
537 – Fickleness	**571** – Tyranny	**505** – Banefulness
538 – Villainy	**572** – Oppression	**506** – Sinisterity
539 – Licentiousness	**573** – Persecution	**507** – Baseness
540 – Insurgency	**574** – Indignation	**508** – Diabolism
541 – Vengeance	**575** – Subjugation	**509** – Sorcery
542 – Gluttony	**576** – Animosity	
543 – Cowardice	**577** – Torment	

HYPERVIOLENCE (700 – 799)

710 – Indolence
711 – Dereliction
712 – Languor
713 – Callousness
714 – Sluggishness
715 – Laxity
716 – Lethargy
717 – Nonchalance
718 – Perversion
719 – Fetishism
720 – Mutiny
721 – Reprisal
722 – Grudgingness
723 – Malignancy
724 – Untrustworthy
725 – Requital
726 – Umbrage
727 – Peevishness
728 – Exploitation
729 – Victimization
730 – Notoriety
731 – Ignobility
732 – Crassness
733 – Petulance
734 – Disgracefulness
735 – Odium
736 – Absurdity
737 – Willfulness
738 – Depravity
739 – Debasement
740 – Rebelliousness
741 – Retribution
742 – Voracity
743 – Cravenness

744 – Rebelliousness
745 – Revenge
746 – Ravenousness
747 – Dastardliness
748 – Pernicity
749 – Vileness
750 – Licentiousness
751 – Savagery
752 – Rudeness
753 – Hostility
754 – Debauchery
755 – Servitude
756 – Lewdness
757 – Rancor
758 – Sacrilege
759 – Blasphemy
760 – Treason
761 – Hopelessness
762 – Greed
763 – Contentiousness
764 – Disloyalty
765 – Grievousness
766 – Rapaciousness
767 – Vexation
768 – Recusancy
769 – Heathenism
770 – Fury
771 – Despotism
772 – Brutality
773 – Barbarism
774 – Outrage
775 – Imperiousness
776 – Discord
777 – Ferocity

778 – Reprobation
779 – Recreancy
780 – Hideousness
781 – Mendacity
782 – Heinousness
783 – Ruthlessness
784 – Nastiness
785 – Deceitfulness
786 – Badness
787 – Deviousness
788 – Pandemonium
789 – Tumultuous.
790 – Madness
791 – Bigotry
792 – Viciousness
793 – Atrocity
794 – Enragement
795 – Discrimination
796 – Meanness
797 – Truculence
798 – Mindlessness
799 – Unruliness
700 – Horror
701 – Ruin
702 – Balefulness
703 – Fiendishness
704 – Grotesqueness
705 – Damnation
706 – Nefarity
707 – Insidiousness
708 – Demonism
709 – Demoniac

Through the aid of information technology, the task of detecting and cataloguing ethical behavior is greatly simplified, eventually permitting a more effective range of global mediation across an international sphere of influence. Indeed, an intriguing discussion of applications relating to the realm of the neurosciences is included in the supplementary Appendix A, whereby further advancing frontiers towards promoting global peace and harmony within a purely scientific and reproducible sphere of inquiry.

The following chapter launches this grand-scale undertaking in terms of a detailed examination of the personal authority and follower roles targeting the virtuous realm. Indeed, it is precisely at this most basic level that the technical rationale behind the quartet-style organization of ethical terms is finally addressed, ultimately explained in terms of the behavioral terminology of operant conditioning. The latter field of behavioral psychology is devoted to the study of instinctual types of goal-seeking behavior, an aspect highly suggestive of the more abstract focus of the virtues, values, and ideals.

The father of modern behaviorism, B. F. Skinner, proposed a parallel correlation of behavioral and ethical principles in his quest for an overarching *Technology of Behavior*. In his masterpiece, *Beyond Freedom and Dignity* (1971), Skinner examines the behavioral correlates for a broad range of ethical terms (such as freedom and dignity), although to a limited degree of precision. Through the aid of the unified ethical hierarchy, however, this motivational style of analysis can be carried to its logical conclusion, incorporating virtually every major ethical term within the Western tradition. Indeed, it proves particularly crucial to view the ascending hierarchy of virtues and values as based entirely within behavioral terminology, as suggested in the elementary nature of the ego and alter ego states. The science of behaviorism, therefore, serves as the rational launch-point for any such detailed motivational analysis beginning with the detailed chapter to follow. A more detailed examination of the behavioral movement is definitely in order at this juncture, for herein lie the keys to outlining the instinctual foundations for the entire ten-level virtuous hierarchy.

This solid conceptual grounding (within a secular, scientific foundation) fortuitously avoids offending the sensibilities of any singular world religion or culture in the process, celebrating the commonalties embraced by ethical traditions from around the world. Granted the world's religions have enjoyed considerable success in promoting a virtuous lifestyle with origins vastly predating our modern technological age. For the vast majority of recorded history world religions have peacefully co-existed, although varying degrees of religious fanaticism have periodically stoked conflict amongst cultures. With the advent of our modern age of high technology, it would appear that humanity can no longer afford such a dramatic clash of cultures that extend to fanatical terrorism on a global scale. The newly proposed scientifically-based system of planetary ethics holds the greatest potential in this regard for overcoming the considerable threats to diminishing global peace and harmony.

2

THE BEHAVIORAL FOUNDATIONS
FOR THE VIRTUOUS REALM

To the casual student of psychology, the mention of conditioning theory typically brings to mind the classical variety pioneered by Russian behaviorist, Ivan Pavlov. Pavlov was the first to discover that dogs could be trained to salivate to the sound of a neutral conditioned stimulus (such as a ticking metronome) provided it was extensively paired beforehand with a food reward (the unconditioned stimulus). Subsequent researchers extended these results to various other types of reflexive behavior amenable to laboratory investigation. These automatic types of behavior, however, are typically at odds with the more deliberate goal-seeking styles of behavior characterizing mature human endeavor. For the adult, behavior typically precedes reinforcement, instead of following it (as in the classical sense).

Descriptions of this latter type of conditioning first come to light in the writings of Bekhterev, a fellow countryman of Pavlov. This variation was termed *instrumental* conditioning, in that goal-seeking behavior was said to be instrumental in procuring reinforcement from the environment. Indeed, Bekhterev further demonstrated that the strength of instrumental behaviors can greatly be enhanced by increasing the frequency/amplitude of the contingent reinforcement.

Instrumental conditioning soon rivaled classical conditioning in the field of learning theory, only reaching its greatest potential through the efforts of American psychologist B. F. Skinner. Skinner expanded upon traditional "instrumental" theory by developing his own radical variation respectively termed *operant* conditioning. According to Skinner, goal-seeking behaviors "operate" on the environment to produce reinforcement; hence, the operant sense of the term. Skinner actually distinguishes two distinct forms of operant conditioning, designated for his parallel con-

cepts of positive and negative reinforcement. Positive reinforcement (as its name implies) refers to a rewarding aspect within the environment targeted through solicitous types of behavior. A widely cited example of positive reinforcement concerns the plight of the wilderness bear cub, which in the course of foraging overturns a fallen log concealing a wild honeycomb. The rewarding consequences of such a honey bonanza directly encourage further such log-turning behavior in the future, particularly when such efforts are periodically re-rewarded.

Negative reinforcement, on the other hand, refers to the avoidance of some unpleasant aspect within the environment through aversive types of behavior; as in fleeing from predators or stepping around pitfalls. Returning to the previous example, the bear cub might jump into a lake to avoid the unpleasant consequences of a hot summer day, or a swarm of angry bees for that matter. Although distinct mechanisms are clearly involved, both positive and negative variations are similarly reinforcing to the individual, encouraging approach / avoidance types of behavior in relation to the environment.

Skinner's most enduring contribution to the field of behaviorism involves his ingenious experimental designs, allowing for degrees of precision unheard of in the natural state. Employing various animal models, Skinner perfected clever automated set-ups for simulating the interaction of learned operant behaviors (such as depressing a lever) and subsequent reinforcement: as in the delivery of a food pellet (+R), or the avoidance of floor shocks (−R). Within such a controlled laboratory setting, Skinner was effectively able to calculate how different schedules of reinforcement affect the overall behavior of the organism, contrasting the effects of strictly measured reinforcement to that of randomly intermittent or variable reinforcement modes.

CONDITIONING IN A SOCIAL SETTING

The observation of similar types of instinctual behavior in humans invites many practical comparisons that (for the most part) prove quite enlightening. Nature studies, indeed, have confirmed the stabilizing effects of operant conditioning within certain naturally occurring animal societies. For instance the grooming behaviors observed within the wild baboon troop serve to cement the bonds between dominant and subordinate members. The subordinate baboons groom the coats of the troop leaders in exchange for their outward approval. A similar set of circumstances is further seen with respect to breeding behaviors between the sexes within a social context.

These distinct interactions find further parallels within human society, where mankind's symbolic use of language permits approval to be expressed in more dramatic formats; namely, praise, commendation, etc. Symbolism also gives meaning to what Skinner terms the secondary reinforcers; e.g., money, power, etc. Although paper currency is not intrinsically pleasing in itself, it is secondarily reinforcing in that it can be exchanged for any of the primary reinforcers: as in food, shelter, etc. These secondary reinforcers directly encourage procurement behaviors in complex types of situations where rewards are customarily delayed. Herein lies the basis for the traditional Protestant work ethic; e.g., no work - no pay!

Although the effectiveness of rewards clearly remains without question, social hierarchies are rarely so idyllic as to be ruled entirely through positive reinforcement. Grooming behaviors are typically restricted to members of the opposite sex, or members of the same sex that are not a serious challenge to each other. The drive to become the dominant member of the troop is alternately determined through aggressive types of behavior. Such power skirmishes, unfortunately, can prove detrimental to the cooperative social unit, particularly in terms of the threat of serious injury or fatalities. Most social species, accordingly, have evolved stereotypical submissive behaviors serving to terminate the conflict well ahead of any permanent damage. Instead of continuing to act contentiously, the loser switches to appeasement to escape further punishment.

In the highly competitive wolf pack, for example, the defeated wolf bares its throat to the vic-

tor in an overt plea for mercy. This submissive display effectively serves as a visual cue to the dominant wolf to leniently terminate the conflict well ahead of any permanent damage. For the primate troop, this aspect is alternately seen in the crouching/appeasement postures assumed by the subordinate member. Such actions are similarly suggestive of the "prisoner of war" mentality, where waving a white flag is a cue to the victors to forgo the certain extermination bound to occur in a fight to the death; e.g., "Remember the Alamo!"

THE HUMAN CONNECTION

Although such ethological observations prove extremely enlightening, their extrapolation to the human condition proves infinitely more complex. In particular, the extreme degree of complexity separating human and animal societies renders any direct comparisons tentative at best. In contrast to animal societies, mankind is essentially a product of his supportive culture, which cooperatively permits the effective management of environmental factors. Whereas lower animal societies remain at the mercy of the environment for their reinforcement (or lack thereof), mankind's facility for taming the forces of nature has led to the unique reassignment of reinforcement to specialized agencies within the social hierarchy. This is particularly evident in the traditional work place setting, where the employee performs a service function in exchange for secondary reinforcers; namely, money, praise, prestige, etc. Individuals in the enviable position of controlling reinforcement typically enjoy coveted positions of power or authority within the social hierarchy, employing rewards to encourage the procurement behaviors of the subordinate staff of laborers in order to encourage their cooperation.

This overall control over reinforcement has progressed to the point that reinforcement now primarily drives procurement in contrast to the order typically encountered in nature. Indeed, one might rightfully surmise that procurement behaviors (either appetite or aversion) would only rarely be prompted to occur without a precipitating display of reinforcement behaviors: e.g., a job offer of a reinforcing nature typically precedes any practical work actually being done. It might alternately be argued that the remnant hunter gatherer societies around the world remain chiefly dependent upon the environment for reinforcement, where a certain degree of initiative of a procurement nature always proves crucial for maintaining any complex style of social structure.

This formal behavioral model further brings into focus the major paradox of the conditioned relationship; namely, as a two-stage sequential process only one role can occur in the present at any given time. In particular, when procurement is actively occurring, reinforcement remains a future potentiality. Similarly, when reinforcement finally comes to pass, procurement is similarly thrust into a potentiality status. This dual style of conditioned interaction is schematically represented in **Fig. 2A**: with procurement represented as the letter (X), whereas reinforcement is specified by the letter (Y). The complete scale of time is further represented by paired (oppositely-facing) "time-wedges" denoting the past and future time-frames, with the gap representing the present. This dual wedge format was purposely chosen in reference to the observation that the measure of time increases as a direct function of its distance from the present.

According to Part A of **Fig. 2A**, when procurement (X) immediately occurs, reinforcement (Y) remains a future potentiality. This conditioned interaction is formally based upon the successful completion of previous such interplay from the past, formally represented by the X → Y (small type) notation depicted entirely within the past-directed time-wedge. Indeed, this previous experience serves as the primary predictive template for the current ongoing interaction, where active procurement (X) anticipates the bestowal of future reinforcement (Y). This is basically achieved through a pattern-matching style of procedure, where past memories that share key motivational factors are recollected en-mass. This may extend to previous interactions with the current individual, or other such interactions that provided a relevant learning experience.

This bottom up style of intuitional cognition is described as elastic thinking according to Leonard Mlodinow (2018). Elastic thinking permits the contextual identification of hidden assumptions implicit within pattern recognition, as opposed to a top-down style of analytical logic. Elastic processing excels in rapidly changing social contexts, were numerous contrasting factors are held in the balance. Through varying degrees of subconscious pattern processing, the confluence of past learning experiences relating to instrumental conditioning (X-then-Y) are synthesized holistically into a tentative solution to the current motivational circumstance. This further permits the novel prediction of the potential for (X-then-Y) in terms of a future-directed context and serves as the justification for the immediately-active course of action initiated by the authority figure. This encourages

an entirely new range of motivational permutations essential within rapidly changing social contexts, although analytic decision-making may also enter into any extended deliberation.

As schematically diagrammed, the procurer of reinforcement is depicted within a currently active time-frame indicative of a subjective "I" perspective representing the initiation of the sequence. The subsequent reinforcement role is projected as a potentiality within the future-directed time-frame, in essence, a mental projection on the part of the procurer; hence, experienced as an objective style of "you" perspective indicative of "the other." This future-focused style of mental projection allows the procurer to form a mental map of the entire procurement-then-reinforcement dynamic, whereby expressing the motivational rationale for one's active means towards the achievement of reinforcement.

The reinforcer within the conditioned interaction, in turn, is thrust into his/her own active status when the time for bestowing reinforcement finally comes to pass. According to Part B of **Fig. 2A**, this sequence of events is formally punctuated from the subjective perspective of the procurer, being that the respective you/I polarities are carried over unchanged in relation to those previously established in Part A. Here the active bestowal of reinforcement (Y) in the present, in turn, anticipates the enactment of upcoming procurement behaviors (X) in the future, in essence, providing an effective sense of closure across the entire two-stage operant schematic. In other words, when reinforcement (Y) now immediately occurs, procurement (X) becomes a future potentiality. This conditioned interaction is formally based upon the successful completion of previous such memories from the past, formally represented by the Y → X (small type) notation depicted entirely within the past-directed time-wedge. Indeed, this previous experience serves as the primary predictive template for the current ongoing interaction, where active reinforcement (Y) anticipates the enactment of future procurement (X).

The follower within the conditioned relationship may also be prompted to employ elastic thinking for verifying the predictions specified by the authority figure's immediate behaviors. Here the pattern matching procedure focuses on the immediately-active behaviors exhibited by the authority figure, whereby prompting past memories of procurement (X) leading to subsequent reinforcement (Y) that has predictably been expected in terms of the follower figure. In an elastic sense, these past memories that deal with active procurement behaviors are compounded by

(A)

Solicitousness
Submissiveness

Approval
Leniency

X ⟶ Y $\underline{X}$ ⟶ $\underline{Y}$

Past   **Present**   **Future**
(Authority Role)   **(Follower Role)**

(B)

Desire
Worry

Aspiration
Compliance

Y ⟶ X $\underline{Y}$ ⟶ $\underline{X}$

Past   **Present**   **Future**
(Authority Role)   **(Follower Role)**

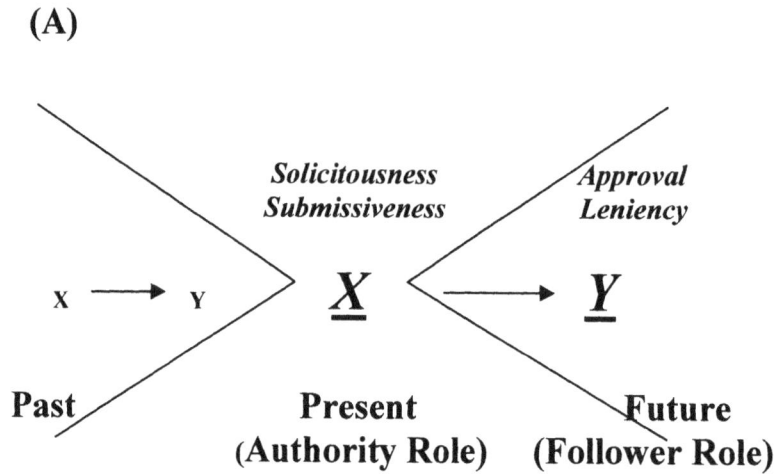

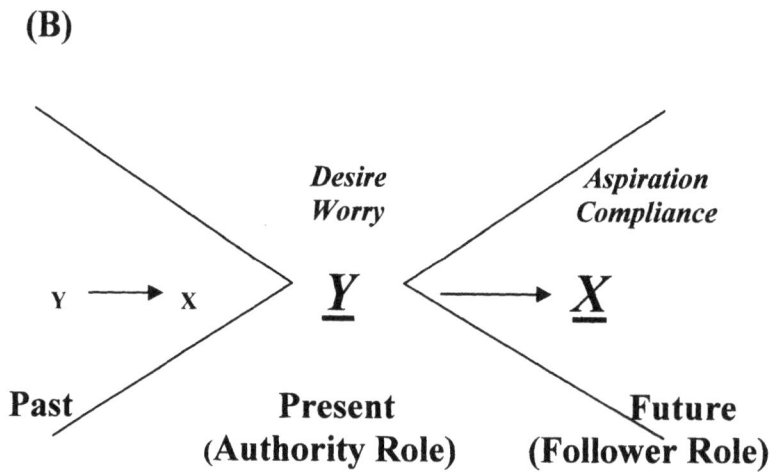

Fig. 2A - The Two-Stage Schematic for Operant Conditioning

the predicted reinforcement ramifications spanning the entire range of motivational experience. These can elastically relate to a given individual, as well as all others recollected within similar contexts. Here a tentative solution holistically emerges, predicting the potentiality of the follower role (Y) in relation to the immediately-active procurement behavior (X) expressed by the authority figure. Consequently the follower figure may ultimately determine that potential reinforcement (Y) is ultimately called for, although the timing for such an active course of action still remains open to deliberation based upon contextual factors.

Through this systematic interplay of sequences (A) and (B) both procurement and reinforcement share an equal complementary status within the present, in addition to their potential displacement into future-focused time-frames respectively. Indeed, the ultimate completion of Part B further sets the stage for additional cycles of interaction within the operant sequence: for if configuration (B) is phase shifted one stage further into the past, one arrives back at the initial configuration depicted in Part A. This cyclic (recursive) periodicity emerges as a key factor underlying this two-stage model, whereby allowing such motivational interchanges to accumulate in a seamless fashion over real time. It is chiefly through such a systematic style of analysis (isolated through individual stages over time) that the conditioned interaction is seen to be punctuated from either the procurement or reinforcement perspectives. In this dual motivational sense the procurement and reinforcement roles maintain their given order within the conditioned interaction, each punctuated from one favored perspective or another.

AN INTROSPECTIVE TERMINOLOGY FOR CONDITIONING THEORY

This dual "staggered" model of the conditioned relationship, although technically comprehensive in scope, unfortunately is restricted by a strict reliance upon behavioral terminology. Although procurement and reinforcement retain a clear meaning within the active time frame, their respective extension into a future-directed time-frame further begs for a corresponding distinction in meaning. Although behavioral terminology (true to its scientific focus) proves inadequate to the task, colloquial English proves much better equipped, particularly verbal categories dealing with subjective motivations.

The most fitting launch-point for such a determination concerns the initiation of the operant

sequence, where active procurement anticipates the future bestowal of reinforcement. The predicted set of colloquial terms therefore exhibits two distinct modes of specialization; namely, an active mode occurring within the present and a predicted projection into a future-directed time-frame. The active behavioral mode appears equivalent to the introspective terminology governing behavioral conditioning, employing colloquial terms with clear instinctual overtones; e.g., solicitousness, submissiveness, desire, and worry. These ego states are specialized into the active reinforcement perspectives of desire and worry, as well as the active procurement roles of solicitousness and submissiveness. The *ego* is traditionally defined as that most basic sense of self to emerge within an immediately-active time-frame. Indeed, the elementary nature of this active class of ego states certainly bears out such a strict interpretation, proving equally applicable in terms of inanimate objects within the environment (as in desiring a cup of water).

This initial class of ego states represents immediately active perspectives taking as their object the more abstract (projected) complement of alter ego states: the latter also defined as that "of the other." This future-directed realm targets a more colloquially-based set of behavioral terms: e.g., approval, leniency, aspiration, and compliance. This latter class of terms is rightfully termed the *alter ego* states in reference to their conceptual dependence upon the precipitating class of ego-states. Generally speaking, the ego states actively initiate the conditioned interaction, whereby prompting the future-potentiality encompassing the alter ego states (lending credence to the notion of *alter ego*). These future-based alter ego states directly complement their immediately active ego state counterparts within the conditioned interaction: namely desirous reinforcement in anticipation of aspiring treatment, or worrisome-leniency in expectation of compliant treatment, etc. The remainder of the current chapter aims to examine the behavioral dynamics governing this predicted eight-part complement of terms, providing a sturdy conceptual foundation for a discussion of the complete virtuous hierarchy to follow.

SOLICITOUSNESS-APPROVAL

The more straightforward class of positive reinforcement proves to be the most logical initiation point for such a grand scale analysis, being that rewards appear to be a much more tangible experience than the vaguer concept of leniency. The interplay of solicitousness/approval will be examined first, followed by the subsequent sequence specified for desire/aspiration. As suggested by their elementary character, it is fair to assume that this overall range of behavioral terminology encompasses the most basic one-to-one style of personal dynamic targeting the interplay of the personal authority and personal follower roles.

As initially described, the solicitous behavior on the part of the procurer initiates the conditioned interaction, whereby prompting the approving reinforcement of the part of the follower. The initial expression solicitousness occurs within an immediately-active time-frame consistent with a subjective "I" perspective, experienced as an acknowledgement of previous such solicitous cycles recollected from the past. This initial phase is often experienced in terms of a sense of nostalgia due to the acknowledgement of previous such cycles of reinforcement from past experience.

The subsequent potential style of rewarding-approval is alternately represented within a future-directed time-frame, whereby equating with a complementary style of objective "you" perspective. The potential aspect of the approval perspective, in essence, equates to the personal follower role: whereas the immediately active sense of solicitousness invokes the initial personal authority role. Indeed, according to American clergymen John C Maxwell: "A leader is one who knows the way, goes the way, and shows the way." The approving determination to act rewardingly is formally assigned the personal follower status in that it directly follows the procurement behavior that had initiated the conditioned interaction. The initial procurement role, in turn, is assigned the status of the personal authority role, being that the personal follower depends upon the authority figure for justifying the upcoming reinforcement. Consequently, the follower looks to his/her authority figure for the immediate rationale prompting one's anticipated behavior within a future-directed time-frame: in essence, the authority status drives any subsequent bestowal of reinforcement on the part of the follower.

A familiar example of such a one-to-one style of personal interaction concerns the enduring interaction between the master craftsman and his willing apprentice. The craftsman's apprentice typically performs routine duties around the shop, whereby solicitously seeking the approval of the master artisan through their shared endeavor. The apprentice aims to display his fledgling talents under the approving gaze of the established master, perhaps one day achieving a master's status of one's own. This potential sense of rein-

forcement on the part of the master is colloquially equated with approval, a perspective prompted by the active sense of solicitousness expressed by the apprentice (in the active personal authority role). Here, the apprentice is granted authority status through the very initiation of the conditioned interaction.

It proves useful here to discuss the individual subjective/objective polarities at issue here. Being that the apprentice acts first, he/she rightfully assumes the subjective "I" status characterizing such an immediately active role. The master, in turn, alternately assumes an objective "you" status indicative of the potential for reinforcement projected to occur within a future-directed time-frame. Indeed, the potentially rewarding nature of approval is reflected in its linguistic derivation, tracing its origins to the Latin *probus* (good). It is traditionally defined as an act of encouragement or commendation, also synonymous with the related theme of approbation (of similar derivation). This potential for approval is sometimes colloquially equated with the theme of hero worship: namely, potentially encouraging solicitous treatment on some future occasion. Indeed, the current subjective/objective style of role specialization formally depends upon which roles are active or passive during any given stage within the conditioned interaction.

In slightly more technical terms, I (as personal authority) actively behave solicitously towards you in anticipation of your (as personal follower) rewarding sense of approval. The latter approval perspective certainly rates its objective projected status, being that such reinforcement is potentially deferred to some future occasion. Approval is directly distinguished in terms of such a future-directed potentiality, whereby reacting to the initially active sense of solicitousness on the part of the authority figure. The procurer bears a certain risk in assuming that reinforcement will ultimately be forthcoming. He/she, however, can reasonably be assured by the wealth of previous cycles of procurement-then-reinforcement on previous occasions, spurring the anticipation of a similar bestowal of reinforcement on some future date.

This initial dual-interaction represents just the first step of the two predicted stages within the overall communicational dynamic. The follow-up sequence specifies that the personal follower figure must ultimately act upon his/her own rewarding potentiality, whereby further serving to encourage the future expression of solicitous behavior on the part of the procurer. Although the reinforcer may act immediately with respect to such rewarding intentions, (more often than not) such complex intentions entail a more leisurely pace of deliberation on the part of the reinforcer. Indeed, it is this tenuous power of deliberation that ultimately imparts the power leverage enjoyed by the reinforcer in relation to the procurer, the latter wholly dependent upon the former to fulfill the anticipated reinforcement mandate.

DESIRE-ASPIRATION

As suggested within the previous section, the inevitable passage of time ultimately dictates that the time for reinforcement must eventually come to pass. The motivational dynamic governing this second stage within the conditioned interaction, in essence, mirrors that previously established for the initial phase, although with a number of key distinctions. According to this second phase, the personal follower ultimately acts upon his approving intentions, rewardingly acting in a desirous fashion towards his willing apprentice, whereby prompting aspiring feelings of determination on the part of the latter. Here the approval perspective now is actively experienced in the present as the rewarding bestowal of desire towards the follower figure. Indeed, desire is traditionally defined as a longing or craving for a wished-for outcome, in this case, the potential future cooperation of the willing apprentice. This passionately-desirous perspective actually depends upon an acknowledgement of previous such cycles of the desire then procurement recollected from memory.

In similar fashion, the formerly active sense of solicitousness (initially expressed by the personal authority figure), in turn, is potentially displaced into a future-directed time-frame, experienced as an aspiring determination to continue acting solicitously in response to such desirous intentions. This aspiring attitude is also colloquially equated with the theme of approval seeking, where both terms essentially yield the same outcome. Furthermore, the polarities governing the subjective/objective viewpoints are effectively maintained in place for this second stage within the conditioned interaction. The procurer of reinforcement retains one's subjective perspective, whereas the reinforcer continues to be viewed in terms of an objective status consistent with the preliminary perspectives initially established with respect to phase one.

In terms of this subjective/objective arrangement of terms, you (as personal authority) now desirously act in a rewarding fashion towards me in anticipation of my (as personal follower) aspiring determination to act solicitously towards you within a future-directed time-frame. Note that the current personal authority role (in the guise of active reinforcer) now desirously anticipates the validation of the personal follower figure as the potential rationale for such an immediately active expression of rewarding behavior. The subjectively-based personal follower role, in turn, expresses a potential style of aspiring perspective, whereby providing a follower-based validation for the approval immediately occurring.

Analogous to the previous expression of solicitousness, desire represents a projected form of mental time travel into the future. This anticipatory style of mental projection (exclusive of the present) provides the motivational rationale for the respective follower role within the conditioned interaction. This follower role represents a projected mental representation within the mind of the immediately active authority figure. This active style of behavioral focus is clearly suggestive of a focused state of mindfulness that formally lacks any self-reflective component. The future-directed perspectives, in contrast, alternately represent a strictly reflective style of mental projection that formally defines the parameters of the mental time travel. Indeed, one basically only experiences one's own inward mental projections, projected states of motivation relating to others that are periodically verified in terms of their outwardly observable behaviors.

Returning (once again) to our ongoing master/apprentice example, a number of key factors can further be predicted with respect to the respective authority/follower roles. In terms of one's active expression of desirous-approval, the master artisan, in essence, relinquishes the initial personal follower role, now taking on a more active personal authority status in relation to the willing apprentice. The apprentice, in turn, now assumes the mantle of the personal follower role consistent with the latter's aspiring determination to continue acting solicitously on all future occasions. According to this distinctive style of role reversal, the master artisan now actively expresses his desirous approval in anticipation of instilling a determined aspiring sense of solicitousness on the part of the apprentice (conducive to future such feats of helpfulness).

This active expression of desirous approval unswervingly acknowledges the unfailing potential for future cooperation on the part of the apprentice. This actively admiring perspective is frequently expressed as a glowing sense of adulation and/or appreciation on the part of the master towards his apprentice. The apprentice, in turn, is reciprocally dependent upon the rewardingly-desirous attentions of his master/mentor, his potential for future achievement remaining entirely meaningless without such suitable fanfare.

This projected determined sense of aspiring cooperation represents a mental projection based upon a pointed acknowledgment of having acted worthily of such active desire in the past. These aspiring feelings of competency (on the part of the apprentice), in turn, prove conducive to the initiation of further such cycles of procurement-then-reinforcement within the conditioned interaction. This latter aspect upholds the inherent power leverage enjoyed by the apprentice (now specified for the personal follower role), for without such a determined sense of cooperation, the desirous expression of approval by the master artisan will all have been for naught. The master, therefore, desirously acts approvingly towards his apprentice in anticipation of latter's aspiring cooperation within a future-directed time-frame.

Therefore, to summarize, the actively expression of solicitousness on the part of the personal authority figure initiates the conditioned interaction, whereby anticipating rewarding approval on the part of the personal follower. The latter reinforcement perspective, in turn, ultimately reaches an active status, whereby desirously prompting an aspiring determination to act solicitously on the part of the personal follower. According to this second stage, you (as personal authority) now desirously act rewardingly towards me in anticipation of my (as personal follower) aspiring determination to act solicitously on all further occasions. This dual style of communicational dynamic effectively serves as the deliberative foundation for initiating the repetition of many such motivational cycles in the future. Indeed, such desirous reinforcement typically proves sufficient for justifying such a solicitous range of overtures. Consequently, an enduring pattern of procurement-then-reinforcement is encouraged and maintained within the social environment over the long run, providing a solid foundation for stable enterprise and commerce across modern culture.

RECURSIVE CORRELATES FOR CONDITIONING

The two-stage dynamic inherent to conditioning theory shares many of the attributes defined for a recursive style of process. Recursion is the process of repeating items in a self-similar way, representing a procedure by which one (or more) steps of a process work to invoke a repetition of the self-same procedure. Recursion in linguistics involves embedding sequences within sequences (of a self-similar nature) resulting in a hierarchical structure through the process of reiteration. This process of embedding ideas within ideas is a skill that humans seem to acquire in an effortless fashion, perhaps the one true dividing line separating humanity from the rest of the animal kingdom. Such recursive attributes enable humans to freely engage in mental time travel. This entails recalling past memories within present consciousness, then employing these memories for imagining or predicting future potentialities in terms of mental projections. Such advanced abilities appear to arise primarily through progressive increases in short-term memory. Similarly, the mental capacity for hierarchical reasoning chiefly appears to have been made feasible through incremental increases in brain evolution.

In summary, the completed description of the operant sequence of solicitousness/approval and desire/aspiration represents a schematic theoretical overview of the dynamics governing positive reinforcement within the realm of personal authority and follower roles. Although the master/apprentice example appeared suitably enlightening for illustrative purposes, many other examples further come to mind; e.g., the hero and his sidekick, the comedian and the straight-man, etc. This stepwise analysis devoted considerable effort towards restating the obvious, although the true goal of this exercise aimed towards providing a solid conceptual foundation for a parallel style of analysis for the virtues and values to follow. Indeed, this personal level provides the key conceptual understanding behind the instinctually-driven nature of mankind in general, as further extended to include the grand unified model encompassing the entire virtuous hierarchy.

SUBMISSIVENESS-LENIENCY

Before skipping ahead to such significant virtuous applications, it proves crucial to further examine the remaining motivational dynamics associated with the realm of negative reinforcement. This alternate style of motivational analysis is scarcely as clear-cut as that for positive reinforcement, being that negative reinforcement involves the lenient withholding of punishment, as opposed to the more straightforward bestowal of rewards. In a general state of nature, negative reinforcement involves the lenient withholding of punitive consequences within the environment, or (in a human social sense) leniently abstaining from punishing aversive types of behavior. For example, the personal authority figure submissively acts aversively in anticipation of a lenient treatment on the part of the personal follower figure. The latter lenient intentions, in turn, eventually become actualized as a worrisome sense of concern on the part of the active authority: whereby prompting a submissive determination to act more appropriately on the part of the follower.

This submissive style of conditioned interplay is particularly apparent in the throat-baring behaviors previously described for the wolf pack. Here the submissive pack member exaggerates one's degree of vulnerability in anticipation of an unconditional bestowal of leniency on the part of the pack leader. In terms of human society, submissiveness frequently equates to a vocal admission of guilt aimed towards verbally eliciting a lenient sense of concern. This phase invokes the memory of previous such cycles of aversion-then-leniency, experienced as a submissive feeling of culpability. It would certainly appear risky to express such an extreme degree of vulnerability without a reasonable assurance of lenient treatment in return. Past cycles of lenient treatment certainly come into play, where previous such instances of leniency ultimately serve to justify such a radical act of faith.

The colloquial concept of leniency certainly fits the accepted profile for negative reinforcement, conventionally defined as professing concern for the difficulties experienced by another. In response to the personal authority's aversive feelings of submissiveness, the personal follower leniently acts in a concerned fashion in an attempt to alleviate such aversive perspectives. This future-projected focus upon leniency further specifies the potential for meaningful rehabilitation rather than vengeful retribution. Indeed, leniency is often colloquially equated with the concept of blame, where blamefulness essentially yields a similar outcome: namely, verbally acting in a leniently-blameful fashion in order to dramatize the aversive deficiencies at issue. Consequently, blamefulness will generally be used interchangeably with leniency with respect to purposes of illustration within the current chapter.

A familiar example of this one-to-one style of personal interaction is observed with respect to the interplay between the drill sergeant and his raw recruit. The recruit is expected to fall in line with the dictates of the drill sergeant, whereby submissively acting in an aversive fashion in hopeful anticipation of a lenient sense of concern on the part of the drill sergeant. This initial guilty expression of submissiveness, in essence, anticipates a contingent bestowal of leniency on the part of the drill sergeant utilizing an admission of culpability indicative of appeasement behavior.

Being that the recruit initiates the first stage within the conditioned interaction, he/she rightfully assumes a subjective "I" role: whereas the drill sergeant, in turn, assumes the objective "you" role specified for potentiality within a future-directed time-frame. Consequently, I as personal authority (the recruit) aversively act in a submissive fashion towards you in anticipation of your (as my drill sergeant) lenient sense of concern. The recruit bears a certain risk in assuming that leniency will always follow, although reassured by a wealth of previous such cycles of reinforcement from past memory.

WORRY-COMPLIANCE

The initial future-directed sequence of submissiveness-then-leniency further implies that the reinforcer must eventually immediately act upon one's lenient potential, whereby worrisomely acting in a concerned fashion in anticipation of a compliant determination to perform better on the part of the recruit This latter course of action often necessitates a rather extended course of deliberation on the part of the lenient reinforcer. Indeed, this tenuous power of deliberation ultimately imparts the active style of power leverage wielded by the reinforcer in relation to the procurer. Once this opportunity for action finally arrives, the worrisome expression of leniency (on the part of the personal authority figure) further serves to encourage future potentially compliant cooperation on the part of the recruit.

The dual interplay of authority/follower roles, in turn, is respectively modified with respect to this second stage of the conditioned interaction. Here, this second phase represents the worrisome bestowal of lenient reinforcement by the drill sergeant (now in the role of personal authority), as schematically represented in Part-B of **Fig. 2A**. This second stage is now phase-shifted within the time-frame dynamic, with reinforcement (Y) now occupying the present, whereas procurement (X) alternately projected as a future potentiality. In essence, the drill sergeant now is respectively thrust into an immediately active role, leniently reinforcing the submissiveness initially expressed by the recruit, whereby prompting the latter's determination to act appropriately on all future occasions so as to encourage further such cycles of aversion/leniency.

A number of key features are further encountered with respect to the polarities underlying the authority and follower roles. With respect to his/her active expression of leniency, the drill sergeant now abandons one's former personal follower role, in turn, switching to an immediately-active personal authority status in relation to the trusty recruit. The recruit, in turn, now assumes the mantle of the personal follower figure consistent with the potentiality inherent to a future-directed time-frame. By definition, the personal follower depends upon the personal authority for active guidance concerning proper conduct: hence, the authority leads the follower in terms of this stepwise priority.

This role reversal certainly proves warranted being that it reciprocates the initial sequence based upon submissiveness/leniency, although now punctuated from an immediately-active worrisome perspective (rather than the submissive variety). The drill sergeant now worrisomely acts in a lenient fashion through a critique on weakness, whereby prompting the compliant determination to perform better on the part of the recruit. This latter sense of compliance relies upon an acknowledgement of past memories of leniency the compliance within the conditioned interaction. This process of worrisome deliberation proves particularly conducive towards ensuring further such cycles of learned compliance in the process. This serves to enhance the inherent power leverage enjoyed by the recruit (as personal follower), for without this compliant determination to improve, the lenient behavior expressed by the drill sergeant will all have been for naught.

In summary, during the second stage within the conditioned interaction, the drill sergeant now worrisomely acts in a concerned fashion towards his recruit in anticipation of the latter's compliant determination to improve. Here the recruit plays-up his vulnerability; in essence, effectively cutting short the potential for any further sense of conflict. Any subsequent action taken against the compliant party is now motivated out of a worrisome sense of concern rather than vindictive retaliation. Consequently, the recruit remains reciprocally dependent upon the worrisome intentions of his drill sergeant, his submissive expression of compliance now entirely meaningless without such lenient treatment to begin with.

Although the rather broad range of connotations associated with submissiveness, leniency, worry, and compliance might suggest other possible interpretations, the current range of viewpoints certainly fits the pattern specified for the realm of negative reinforcement: a finding further verified with respect to the even more abstract ascending hierarchy of the virtues. Indeed, this fundamental comprehension of the most elementary personal authority and follower roles proves exceedingly critical for ultimately defining the more abstract groupings of virtues and values to follow.

THE ACCESSORY MOTIVATIONAL TERMS

According to the preceding somewhat technical style of analysis, the initially active authority roles are specified from a subjective "I" perspective, whereas the anticipated follower roles alternately encompass a complementary (objective) "you" perspective. This reciprocating pattern of subjective procurement then objective reinforcement follows a strict give-and-take dynamic, formally defined as "if I, then you" (and vice versa). According to this complementary style of power-sharing strategy, the initially active procurement roles within the conditioned relationship are designated in terms of a subjective "I" status, whereas the future-directed style of reinforcement roles are specified in terms of an objective "you" status. Indeed, this arrangement mirrors that which typically occurs in nature, where the organism actively procures and the environment (inanimately) reinforces.

This reciprocating model of motivational communication, however, can scarcely claim to be the total picture, for it formally accounts for only half of the introspective roles predicted within the linguistic matrix. The inherent versatility of the human mind, however, (by definition) allows for a subjective reflection upon one's objective status (after the fact: in essence, subjectifying the objective status of the respective reinforcement roles. This style of role-reversal similarly extends to a further objectification of the initially-active subjective class of procurement roles.

This reflective style of role-reversal conveniently allows for crucial insights into the feelings and motivations experienced by another, an aspect respectively defined as *empathy*. It is traditionally defined as that indwelling sense of inter-subjectivity by which one introspectively comprehends the feelings privately held by another. This empathic style of motivational perspective formally predicts the existence of an entire parallel complement of affective terms for designating this additional class of perspectives (now specified as the *accessory* class of motivational terms). Fortunately the English language is richly blessed with an abundant number of synonyms conducive to fulfilling this predicted complement of accessory terms.

The specific details underlying this innovation are reserved for the upcoming Chapter 7: a section devoted exclusively to a description of these accessory motivational perspectives. Here the "you"/"I" perspectives are systematically reversed in terms of polarity across the board, ensuring that both procurement and reinforcement roles encompass their full range of objective/subjective potentialities encountered in real-life situations. For instance, for the personal realm, the proposed accessory class of ego states (ambition, deference, passion, and apprehension) effectively complements the main listing of terms: namely, solicitousness, submissiveness, desire, and worry. Furthermore, the accessory listings of alter ego states: admiration, concern, consideration, and adherence, in turn, reciprocate the main listing of terms (approval, leniency, aspiration, and compliance), respectively.

In terms of the main pairing of desire and aspiration, the accessory complement of passion/consideration proves particularly well suited to the task. Here, I (as personal authority) passionately act rewardingly towards you in anticipation of your (as personal follower) considerate treatment of me. In terms of the related context of worry/compliance, the personal authority figure now switches to an apprehensive perspective, whereby anticipating the personal follower's adherent expression of submissiveness. A similar pattern further holds true with respect to the personal authority's ambitiousness in anticipation of admiration, or deference in expectation of concern. This reciprocating interplay of both main and accessory terms collectively permits a convincing simulation of the empathy underlying the conditioned interaction in general.

THE ACCESSORY HIERARCHY OF VIRTUES, VALUES, AND IDEALS

According to this main/accessory model of empathic communication, it remains only a further minor step to extend this personal complement of motivational terms to the even broader range of the virtues, values, and ideals characterizing the higher authority levels. This yields the full fortyfold complement of accessory terms schematically depicted below, and also portrayed in an expanded format in Chapter 7.

Ambition •	**Admiration**	**Deference •**	**Concern**
Exalt.•	**Circumspection**	**Uprightness •**	**Equity**
Bountiful. •	**Devotion**	**Freedom •**	**Fairness**
Blessings •	**Charm**	**Conscience •**	**Credence**
Serenity •	**Rapture**	**Brotherhood •**	**Content.**

Passion •	**Consider.**	**Apprehens.•**	**Adherence**
Respect •	**Continence**	**Probity •**	**Bravery**
Courtesy •	**Kindness**	**Forbear. •**	**Scruples**
Gracious.•	**Benevolence**	**Patience •**	**Shrewd.**
Affection •	**Gladness**	**Amity •**	**Accordance**

This compact diagram represents a mirror-image variation on the main listing of virtuous terms depicted in **Fig. 1** of Chapter 1. Indeed, this parallel master hierarchy of accessory terms spans the entire range of personal, group, spiritual, humanitarian, and transcendental domains within the motivational matrix as a whole. This reciprocating interplay of both classes of terms permits a convincing simulation of empathic communication in general, the objective and subjective polarities effectively reversed through an inversion of the "you" and "I" polarities. These accessory groupings of terms scarcely exhibit the pedigree or tradition initially established for the main listings of terms. Accordingly, the accessory listings of terms are formally labeled through the addition of the prefix *"accessory"* to the better-known listings specified for the major terms: enabling these empathic foundations to be verified to a high degree of specificity and precision.

THE AUTHORITY AND FOLLOWER ROLES

Returning to our ongoing description of the main operant sequence, in a strictly interdependent sense, the personal authority and personal follower roles effectively complement one another within the conditioned interaction, formally maintaining an equivalent balance of power in the process. Indeed, the hero is equally dependent upon the potential attentions of his sidekick, whereas the master craftsman is totally lost without the services of his apprentice. Herein resides the basis for the fundamental paradox underlying the authority/follower roles: namely, one hand is always needed to wash the other. The old Zen Buddhist adage describing how the follower leads the leader (as much as the other way around) certainly rings true in this basic regard. Indeed, this basic style of personal interaction is effectively seen to repeat for the remaining group and spiritual authority levels to follow: providing an accurate means towards comprehending the dynamics underlying the entire range of virtues and values.

THE METAPERSPECTIVE SCHEMATIC FORMAT

The higher-order concept of the alter ego states is directly reminiscent of a similar range of concepts pioneered in the emerging field of Communication Theory; most notably, the *meta-perspective* format advanced by R. D. Laing and P. I. Watzlawick. In *Interpersonal Perception* (1966) Laing (et al) researched the dynamics of interpersonal communication, specified as "the spiral of reciprocal perspectives." In his *Pragmatics of*

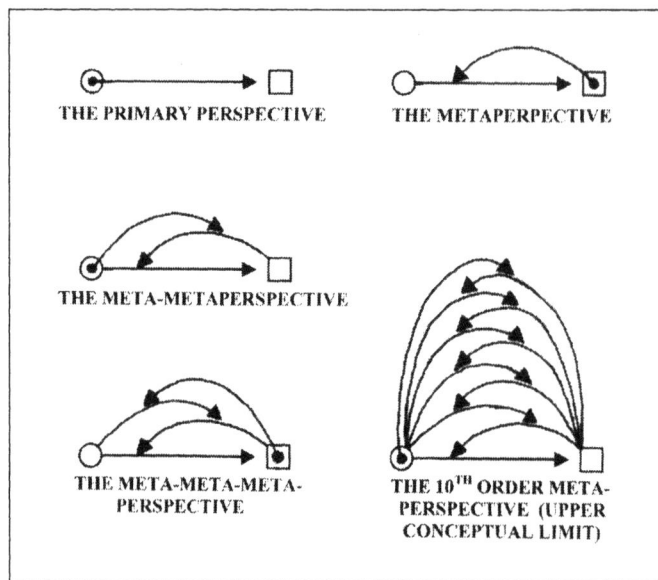

Fig. 2B - The Ten-Level Hierarchy of Meta-perspectives
The Schematic Foundation for the Ten-Level Hierarchy of Virtues, Values, and Ideals

Human Communication (1967) Watzlawick (and associates) alternately focused upon the informational aspects of communication defined as "the hierarchy of meta-perspectives." Both such formulations share a common theme; namely, communication between individuals is compounded by abstract "meta" messages defining how the relationship is to be conducted. The meta-perspective, from the Greek *meta-* (above), is defined as a higher-order perspective on a viewpoint held by another: schematically defined as "this is how I see you seeing me." Spontaneous forms of communication are further reflected upon as formal objects of discourse, adding both content and context to a given style of ongoing verbal interaction.

In addition to this preliminary class of meta-perspective, even more abstract perspectives are theoretically feasible, leading to what Communication Theorists term the *meta-meta-perspective*. This more advanced perspective is one meta-level further removed from the more basic meta-perspective format, schematically defined as: "this is how I see you - seeing me - seeing you." Indeed, there does not appear to be any barrier limiting the degree to which reflection can serve as a basis for itself, resulting in up to a ten-level hierarchy of meta-communication in general. This meta-perspective format, depicted in **Fig. 2B**, provides a graphic interpretation of the unified hierarchy of authority and follower roles, an en-

during format culminating in an unprecedented 10th-order level of meta-abstraction. According to Laing, relationships typically are understood implicitly rather than explicitly, developing over time through negotiation. Furthermore, the outwardly observable behaviors of others are publically accessible, analogous to the active style of motivated communication specified for the ego states. Mental experience, in turn, is defined as internal perceptions that are privately felt, corresponding to the future-projected class of alter ego states. Consequently, one can observe the behavior of others but not another's inner mental experience. Direct perspectives emerge when observing/interpreting the behaviors of others, whereas meta-perspectives arise when attempting to infer the inward motivations held by another. By definition, meta-perspectives are not all that accurate, highlighting the contrast between feeling understood and actually being understood by another.

A REVIEW OF CONDITIONING THEORY

In summary, the completed description of the ego and alter ego states effectively rounds out the stepwise description of the personal authority and follower roles within the conditioned interaction. The somewhat technical tone for this introductory chapter proved particularly crucial in terms of clarity and precision. Indeed, a sturdy foundation is crucial to the construction of any higher-order conceptual edifice. It proves particularly informative, therefore, to formally summarize what has previously gone before within this somewhat technical style of chapter. First proposed were the conditioned types of instinctual behavior so eloquently categorized in B. F. Skinner's terminology of instrumental conditioning. This instinctual foundation, in turn, extended to a human sphere of influence, a model of motivation taking into full account humanity's enduring heritage within the animal kingdom. Skinner's elementary principles of positive and negative reinforcement proved particularly well-suited to the task, whereby further anticipating the more abstract predicted hierarchy of virtues, values, and ideals.

The two-stage dynamic governing operant conditioning was further described: offering crucial insights into the realm of immediately-active and future-directed time-frames. Human society is uniquely specialized for operating within these projected/predicted contexts: namely, the tendency to learn from past experience leading to the prediction of future contingencies (also known as Prospective Psychology). Operant terminology scarcely proved adequate for defining the range of introspectively-derived perspectives, necessitating the introduction of colloquial English terms into the mix (as evident in the listing of ego and alter ego states). These colloquial terms add a further crucial introspective dimension, in essence, serving as the conceptual foundation for the remaining virtuous hierarchy.

This resultant ten-level hierarchy of virtuous terms, in turn, redirects the current personal focus, effectively specifying the repetition of both the authority and follower roles across the ethical hierarchy. Being that the personal authority role occurs first within the operant sequence, it seems only fitting that it be the first to repeat in the expanded sense of the group authority role: followed, in turn, by the group representative. Indeed, the ascending sequence of authority and follower roles ultimately extends to an ascending hierarchy of spiritual, humanitarian, and tran-scendental levels: culminating in an unprecedented 10th-order hierarchy of meta-abstraction.

One might rightfully question the capacity of the human mind to entertain such a formidable multiplicity of meta-perspectives. The mind is apparently able to selectively focus-in upon the immediately relevant levels within the ascending virtuous hierarchy similar to the analogy of climbing a ten-level flight of stairs. The process of rising to the next higher step implies the primacy of the immediately adjoining levels, equal to a span of three sequential levels (e.g., the meta-meta-perspective): quite a modest task for the versatile human mind.

THE SCHEMATIC DEFINITIONS FOR THE VIRTUES, VALUES, AND IDEALS

Although this expanded style of virtuous hierarchy proves suitably convincing on an intuitive level, its advanced degree of detail necessarily specifies an even higher degree of precision than has currently been called for. In this enhanced respect, the systematic organization of the ethical hierarchy formally permits the construction of what are technically termed the *schematic definitions* for the motivational matrix. This crucial innovation spells out in longhand the precise location of each virtue/value within the linguistic matrix while simultaneously preserving the correct orientation of authority/follower roles. Each such definition is formally constructed along the lines of a two-stage sequential format; namely, (A) the formal recognition of the preliminary power maneuver and (B) the countermaneuver currently being employed; and hence, labeled. Take, for example, the schematic definition for the representative cardinal virtue of *prudence*, reproduced below from the comprehensive series of definitions shown in **Tables A-1** to **A-4**.

> Previously, I (as your group authority) have gloriously acted solicitously towards you:
> in anticipation of your (as PF) approving treatment of me.
> But now, you, (as group representative) will *prudently* act approvingly towards me:
> in response to my (as GA) glorious treatment of you.

According to this specific *prudence* example, the glorious sense of solicitousness expressed by the group authority figure represents the preliminary power maneuver: countered, in turn, by the *prudent*-approval offered by the group representative. Note that the polarity of authority/follower roles is effectively preserved equivalent to their polarity portrayed in **Fig. 1**.

In terms of this two-stage schematic format, the preliminary power perspective represents the "one-down" power maneuver, whereas the current power maneuver designates the "one-up" variety. Power leverage is secured by rising to the "one-up" power status; namely, ascending to the next higher meta-perspectival level. This compre-hensive listing of schematic definitions can effect-

SOLICITOUSNESS	APPROVAL
Previously, you (as reinforcer) have rewardingly acted in a reinforcing fashion towards me: in response to my (as procurer) approachful treatment of you. But now, I (as personal authority) will actively behave *solicitously* towards you: in anticipation of your rewarding treatment of me.	Previously, I (as personal authority) have actively behaved solicitously towards you: in anticipation of your (as reinforcer) rewarding treatment of me. But now, you (as personal follower) will rewardingly act in an *approving* fashion towards me: overruling my (as PA) solicitous treatment of you.
GLORY	**PRUDENCE**
Previously, you (as your personal follower) have rewardingly acted in an approving fashion towards me: in response to my (as PA) solicitous treatment of you. But now, I (as group authority) will *gloriously* act in a solicitous fashion towards you: in anticipation of your (as PF) approving treatment of me.	Previously, I (as group authority) have gloriously acted solicitously towards you: in anticipation of your (as PF) approving treatment of me. But now, you (as group representative) will *prudently* act in an approving fashion towards me: overruling my (as GA) gloriously-solicitous treatment of you.
PROVIDENCE	**FAITH**
Previously, you (as group representative) have prudently acted approvingly towards me: in response to my (as GA) gloriously-solicitous treatment of you. But now, I (as spiritual authority) will gloriously act *providently* towards you: in anticipation of your (as GR) prudent-approval of me.	Previously, I (as spiritual authority) have gloriously acted providently towards you: in anticipation of your (as GR) prudent-approval of me. But now, you (as my spiritual disciple) will prudently act in a *faithful* fashion towards me: overruling my (as SA) provident treatment of you.
GRACE	**BEAUTY**
Previously, you (as my spiritual disciple) have prudently acted in a faithful fashion towards me: in response to my (as SA) gloriously-provident treatment of you. But now, I (as humanitarian authority) will providently act in a *graceful* fashion towards you: in anticipation of your (as SD) prudent-faith in me.	Previously, I (as humanitarian authority) have providently acted gracefully towards you: in anticipation of your (as SD) prudent-faith in me. But now, you (as representative member of humanity) will *beauteously* act in a faithful fashion towards me: overruling my (as HA) providently-graceful treatment of you.
TRANQUILITY	**ECSTASY**
Previously, you (as representative member of humanity) have beauteously acted faithfully towards me: in response to my (as HA) providently-graceful treatment of you. But now, I (as transcendental authority) will *tranquilly* act gracefully towards you: in anticipation of your (as RH) beauteous-faith in me.	Previously, I (as transcendental authority) have tranquilly acted gracefully towards you: in anticipation of your (as RH) beauteous-faith in me. But now, you (as my transcendental follower) will beauteously act in an *ecstatic* fashion towards me: overruling my (as TA) tranquil sense of gracefulness.

Table A-1 - The Definitions Based on Solicitousness/Approval

SUBMISSIVENESS	LENIENCY
Previously, you (as reinforcer) have tolerantly acted in a reinforcing fashion towards me: in response to my (as procurer) aversive treatment of you. But now, I (as personal authority) will aversively act in a *submissive* fashion towards you: in anticipation of your tolerant treatment of me.	Previously, I (as personal authority) have aversively acted submissively towards you: in anticipation of your (as reinforcer) tolerant treatment of me. But now, you (as my personal follower) will *leniently* act in a tolerant fashion towards me: overruling my (as PA) submissive treatment of you.
HONOR	**JUSTICE**
Previously, you (as my personal follower) have leniently acted in a tolerant fashion towards me: in response to my (as PA) submissive treatment of you. But now, I (as group authority) will *honorably* act submissively towards you: in anticipation of your (as PF) lenient treatment of me.	Previously, I (as group authority) have honorably acted submissively towards you: in anticipation of your (as PF) lenient treatment of me. But now, you (as group representative) will leniently act in a *just* fashion towards me: overruling my (as GA) honorable treatment of you.
LIBERTY	**HOPE**
Previously, you (as group representative) have leniently acted justly towards me: in response to my (as GA) honorable treatment of you. But now, I (as spiritual authority) will honorably act in a *libertarian* fashion towards you: in anticipation of your leniently-just treatment of me.	Previously, I (as spiritual authority) have honorably acted in a libertarian fashion towards you: in anticipation of your (as GR) leniently-just treatment of me. But now, you (as my spiritual disciple) will leniently-*hope* for justice: overruling my (as SA) libertarian sense of honor.
FREE WILL	**TRUTH**
Previously, you (as my spiritual disciple) have leniently-hoped for justice: in response to my (as SA) libertarian sense of honor. But now, I (as humanitarian authority) will honorably act in a *freely willed* fashion towards you: in anticipation of your (as SD) blameful hope for justice.	Previously, I (as humanitarian authority) have honorably acted in a freely-willed fashion towards you: in anticipation of your (as SD) blameful-hope for justice. But now, you (as representative member of humanity) will justly-hope for the *truth*: overruling my (as HA) libertarian sense of free will.
EQUALITY	**BLISS**
Previously, you (as representative member of humanity) have justly-hoped for the truth: in response to my (as HA) libertarian sense of free will. But now, I (as transcendental authority) will freely-willed act in an *egalitarian* fashion towards you: in anticipation of your (as RH) just-hope for the truth.	Previously, I (as transcendental authority) have freely-willed acted in an egalitarian fashion towards you: in anticipation of your (as RH) just-hope for the truth. But now, you (as my transcendental follower) will *blissfully* hope for the truth: overruling my (as TA) egalitarian treatment of you.

Table A-2 – Definitions Based Upon Submissiveness/Leniency

DESIRE	ASPIRATION
Previously, I (as procurer) have acted approachfully towards you: in response to your (as reinforcer) rewarding treatment of me. But now, you (as my personal authority) will rewardingly act *desirously* towards me: in anticipation of my approachful treatment of you.	Previously, you (as my personal authority) have rewardingly acted desirously towards me: in anticipation of my approachful treatment of you. But now, I (as your personal follower) will *aspiringly* act approachfully towards you: overruling your (as PA) desirous treatment of me.
DIGNITY	**TEMPERANCE**
Previously, I (as your personal follower) have aspiringly acted approachfully towards you: in response to your (as PA) desirous treatment of me. But now, you (as my group authority) will *dignifiedly* act in a desirous fashion towards me: in anticipation of my (as PF) aspiring treatment of you.	Previously, you (as my group authority) have dignifiedly acted desirously towards me: in anticipation of my (as PF) aspiring treatment of you. But now, I (as group representative) will *temperately* act in an aspiring fashion towards you: overruling your (as GA) dignified-desire for me.
CIVILITY	**CHARITY**
Previously, I (as group representative) have temperately acted aspiringly towards you: in response to your (as GA) dignified-desire for me. But now, you (as my spiritual authority) will dignifiedly act in a *civil* fashion towards me: in anticipation of my (as GR) temperate treatment of you.	Previously, you (as my spiritual authority) have dignifiedly acted in a civil fashion towards me: in anticipation of my (as GR) temperate treatment of you. But now, I (as spiritual disciple) will temperately act *charitably* towards you: overruling your (as SA) civilly-dignified treatment of me.
MAGNANIMITY	**GOODNESS**
Previously, I (as your spiritual disciple) have temperately acted in a charitable fashion towards you: in response to your (as SA) civilly-dignified treatment of me. But now, you (as humanit. authority) will civilly behave *magnanimously* towards me: in anticipation of my (as SD) charitable treatment of you.	Previously, you (as humanit. authority) have civilly acted magnanimously towards me: in anticipation of my (as SD) charitable treatment of you. But now, I (as representative member of humanity) will charitably act with *goodness* towards you: overruling your (as HA) magnanimous treatment of me.
LOVE	**JOY**
Previously, I (as representative member of humanity) have charitably acted with goodness towards you: in response to your (as HA) civilly-magnanimous treatment of me. But now, you (as transcendental authority) will magnanimously act *lovingly* towards me: in anticipation of my (as RH) goodly treatment of you.	Previously, you (as transcend. authority) have magnanimously acted lovingly towards me: in anticipation of my (as RH) goodly treatment of you. But now, I (as your transcendental follower) will goodly act in a *joyous* fashion towards you: overruling your (as TA) magnanimously-loving treatment of me.

Table A-3 – The Definitions Based Upon Desire/Aspiration

WORRY	COMPLIANCE
Previously, I (as procurer) have acted aversively towards you: in response to your (as reinforcer) tolerant treatment of me.	Previously, you (as my personal authority) have worrisomely acted tolerantly towards me: in anticipation of my (as procurer) aversive treatment of you.
But now, you (as my personal authority) will *worrisomely* act tolerantly towards me: in anticipation of my aversive treatment of you.	But now, I (as your personal follower) will aversively act *compliantly* towards you: overruling your (as PA) worrisome treatment of me.

INTEGRITY	FORTITUDE
Previously, I (as your personal follower) have aversively acted compliantly towards you: in response to your (as PA) worrisome treatment of me.	Previously, you (as my group authority) have worrisomely acted with integrity towards me: in anticipation of my (as PF) compliant treatment of you.
But now, you (as my group authority) will worrisomely act with *integrity* towards me: in anticipation of my (as PF) compliant treatment of you.	But now, I (as group representative) will compliantly act with *fortitude* towards you: overruling your (as GA) worrisome sense of integrity.

AUSTERITY	DECENCY
Previously, I (as group representative) have compliantly acted with fortitude towards you: in response to your (as GA) worrisome sense of integrity.	Previously, you (as spiritual authority) have austerely acted with integrity towards me: in anticipation of my (as GR) fortitudinous treatment of you.
But now, you (as spiritual authority) will *austerely* act with integrity towards me: in anticipation of my (as GR) fortitudinous treatment of you.	But now, I (as your spiritual disciple) will fortitudinously act in a *decent* fashion towards you: overruling your (as SA) austere sense of integrity.

EQUANIMITY	WISDOM
Previously, I (as your spiritual disciple) have fortitudinously acted decently towards you: in response to your (as SA) austere sense of integrity.	Previously, you (as my humanitarian authority) have austerely acted with equanimity towards me: in anticipation of my (as SD) decent treatment of you.
But now, you (as my humanitarian authority) will austerely act with *equanimity* towards me: in anticipation of my (as SD) decent treatment of you.	But now, I (as representative member of humanity) will decently act in a *wise* fashion towards you: overruling your (as HA) austere sense of equanimity.

PEACE	HARMONY
Previously, I (as representative member of humanity) have decently acted in a wise fashion towards you: in response to your (as HA) austere sense of equanimity.	Previously, you (as transcendental authority) have peaceably acted with equanimity towards me: in anticipation of my (as RH) decent sense of wisdom.
But now, you (as transcendental authority) will *peaceably* act with equanimity towards me: in anticipation of my (as RH) decent sense of wisdom.	But now, I (as transcendental follower) will wisely act *harmoniously* towards you: overruling your (as TA) peaceable treatment of me.

Table A-4 – The Definitions Based Upon Worry/Compliance

ively be viewed as a motivational calculus replete with the strict transformational rules governing how each level meshes with those above or below it. The instinctual terminology for operant conditioning initially dominates the uppermost levels within the tables of definitions, replaced in due fashion by the virtues and values specifying the more advanced authority levels. At each succeeding level, a new term (distinguished through *italics*) is introduced, whereby specifying the current power maneuver under consideration. Beginning with the group level, the preliminary terms begin to drop out of the equation, freeing-up space for the newer terms currently being introduced, whereby maintaining a stable buffer of terms.

The affiliated authority/follower roles similarly remain in consistent positions throughout the ten-level hierarchy, although systematically abbreviated (for the sake of brevity) in non-critical positions. Accordingly, PA stands for personal authority, PF represents personal follower, etc. The reciprocal interplay of the "you" and "I" roles proves equally significant, whereby maintaining a stable buffer of subjective/objective perspectives in relation to the authority and follower roles.

It is further crucial to note (upon close examination of the schematic definitions) that the active behavioral states effectively prompt the future-directed perspectives within the operant interaction. These complementary pairings directly ensure that the correct placement of "you"/"I" roles within the schematic definitions, providing a truly convincing schematic model of the motivational dynamics at issue.

The remainder of the current **Part I** is devoted to systematically outlining the formal dynamics for the entire virtuous hierarchy. Consequently, each successive chapter is devoted exclusively to a specific authority/follower realm within the virtuous hierarchy. Chapter *3* initiates this analysis with a detailed examination of the group authority/follower roles, introducing the groupings of personal ideals and cardinal virtues, respectively. Chapter *4*, in turn, focuses upon the spiritual authority/disciple roles: providing an in-depth examination of the civil liberties and the theological virtues. Chapter *5* subsequently examines the corresponding humanitarian authority and follower roles, introducing the classical Greek values and ecumenical ideals, respectively. Chapter *6*, in turn, targets the crowning transcendental domain: offering an in-depth examination of the humanistic values and mystical values. Finally, Chapters *7* and *8* round out the current section with an examination of a number of key supplementary issues relating to the virtuous realm; namely, the accessory virtues/values, as well as the overarching concept of the general unifying themes. This grand-scale undertaking is, hereby, initiated with a detailed examination of the behavioral analogues for the group authority and follower roles, a group domain virtually synonymous with virtually every major form of cooperative human endeavor.

3

THE GROUP ETHICAL REALM

Group (or tribal) authority is certainly one of mankind's most time-honored traditions. Prior to the dawning of our modern agricultural age, primitive hunter tribes wandered the earth following the uneven distribution of game animals, much as occurs in the remote outposts of the world today. In a purely organizational sense, the human tribe shows many similarities to the primitive social order of the lion pride or the wolf pack, although a closer examination reveals many finer distinctions. In particular, the human tribe is distinguished through its symbolic use of verbal communication over and beyond any instinctual form of body language. Lower animal societies are limited almost exclusively to this gestural style of communication, as suggested in the grooming and throat-baring types of behavior previously described. Although vocalization is often a key feature in many complex animal societies, it is chiefly employed in a guttural fashion without any consensus sense of form or meaning.

Although these instinctual forms of communication (by definition) occur chiefly between individuals, such personal interactions, in turn, are summated across the extent of the social hierarchy resulting in a "round-robin" style of pecking order. This dominance hierarchy only superficially conforms to true tribal authority in that it promotes a single dominant leader overseeing a descending hierarchy of less powerful individuals. This arrangement further makes little provision for any enduring sense of permanence, resulting in a frequent reshuffling of power within the pecking order. The human tribe, in contrast, picks a single consensus leader overseeing a collective of virtually equal followers. Although jockeying for position is not entirely abandoned, it ultimately is made subordinate to this group power leverage.

This distinction between the simple pecking order and true group authority is chiefly made possible through mankind's innovative use of ver-

bal symbolism. Nonverbal communication is meaningful only in immediate types of contexts, allowing only for one obvious means of interpretation; namely, the most basic style of pecking order. Human language, in contrast, is distinguished by its ability to communicate symbolically about abstract or motivational issues: permitting verbal communication not formally tied to such immediate concerns. Through this verbal refinement, mankind is essentially able to distinguish the more abstract style of group authority from its more elementary foundation in the personal pecking order, setting the stage for the cooperative social structure so crucial on the world scene today.

Indeed, there appears to be two fundamental perspectives on communication, experiential-subjective and symbolic-communicative. The latter category refers to the individual words that permit communication in relation to individual emotional states. For instance, stating "I love you" permits others to gain empathic insights into the experiential emotions I am currently experiencing. A multitude of ethical terms are labeled through symbolic language; e.g., peace, joy, honor, etc. without which ethical discourse would remain impossible. Here the subjective and the symbolic represent two sides of the same coin, although each has its own strengths and limitations. This dual facility for language permits the crucial innovation of human social communication within a group social context. The experiential/subjective aspects remain clearly in evidence, well suited for verbal communication in concert with crucial nonverbal cues. Although language is essentially a group-shared phenomenon, it originally was much better suited for describing objects and quantification. This need for tallying objects led directly to the invention of writing, where numerical tallies were pressed into clay seals accompanying the inventory. A subsequent stage of communication concerning affect and emotion began in earnest when writing became divorced from nonverbal cues. Verbal abstractions were agreed upon to label emotional states. Gronk is angry with his neighbor Targ, etc. The parallel evolution of organized religion further spurred the dramatic expansion of such abstract vocabulary. The legal code of Hammurabi (as well as scriptural sources) dictated a proper code of conduct: expressed in terms of the virtues vs. the vices. The early Greek philosophers Plato and Aristotle were particularly celebrated for systematizing such abstract moral principles. This ancient heritage serves as the elementary foundation for the currently proposed motivational matrix, although now synthesized into an overarching ethical hierarchy based upon behavioral principles. This hierarchy is chiefly made possible through the conceptual innovation of the meta-perspective, where group authority represents a higher form of personal authority, and so on further up the hierarchy.

The group authority figure achieves this enhanced authority status by countering the more limited partisan concerns expressed by the personal follower. The "side kick" style of strike leverage employed by the personal follower no longer proves effective against the group authority, who announces that individual members are now expendable when it comes down to a group challenge for power. According to this third-order meta-perspectival format, enough followers always remain to perpetuate group authority whether or not any individual should choose to desert. In a single stroke, the group authority is elevated well above any personal power struggles, an innovation that has endured as the familiar tradition of civic authority.

Although group authority has undergone many refinements down through the ages, its basic dynamics have remained fairly consistent in nature. Originally the tribal chiefdom was organized along familial lines, with related clan members answering to a single dominant patriarch or matriarch. Similarities in language and culture eventually brought related clans together, resulting in the enduring trend towards the nation state. Originally, nationalism implied the leadership of a regal monarch, with royal power passed down (in tribal fashion) through inheritance. This regal authority was celebrated through the potent use of ritual symbolisms: as reflected in the enduring Western traditions of the scepter, throne, crown, etc. The supportive cast of influential dukes and nobles relied upon a similar use of heraldic symbolisms for maintaining their accessory authority status.

The Western tradition of heraldry dates at least to medieval times, expressed in the development of the hereditary "coat of arms." This latter term derives from the military custom of embroidering the emblem of the knight directly upon the surcoat covering the armor. The protective function of the armor complicated the identification of friend or foe during the heat of battle, leading to the invention of personal heraldic symbolisms inscribed upon the shield. Originally, these symbols were personally selected, generally commemorating a defining episode during the knight's military career. Confusion ultimately arose concerning the duplication of designs, leading to the formal appointment of *heralds*, whose supervision of the art form gave rise to the general sense of the term. The introduction of gunpowder eventually rendered protective armor obsolete, reducing heraldry to its current formality of tracing family ancestry.

The traditional coat of arms is formally composed of a shield, crest, and motto. The descriptive terms employed in heraldry are assigned specific meanings in order to avoid confusion amongst the various authorities. A number of key heraldic terms with regal overtones particularly come to mind, in keeping with the four affective dimensions predicted for the group authority perspective. Colorful terms such as the circle of *glory* (or halo), the *honor*-point (on the shield), and the cap of *dignity* (or chapeau) abound within the heraldic literature. Add to these the animal symbolisms associated with *integrity* and the cohesive listing of "personal ideals" falls neatly into place.

This four-part grouping of glory-honor-dignity-integrity collectively traces its origins to the classical Latin tradition. Indeed, the Romans celebrated group leadership to perhaps its grandest degree of style. The personal ideals represent the more advanced group analogues of the subordinate class of ego states that they serve to supersede. Although their personal designation might seem to suggest somewhat of a misnomer, the group authority maneuver directly maneuvers upon the personal follower perspective, wherein accounting for the hybrid quality of the grouping. Accordingly, *glory* represents the group analogue of solicitousness, whereas *honor* denotes a similar modification of submissiveness. Furthermore, *dignity* redefines desire from a group perspective, whereas *integrity* denotes a more idealized form of worry. Accordingly, this four-part listing of personal ideals formally specifies motivations encompassing the group authority role; namely, glory, honor, dignity, and integrity. This initial class of group-focused ideals represents

The Heraldic Symbolisms for the Personal Ideals
In Clockwise Order: Circle of Glory – Honor Point – Rampant – Cap of Dignity

immediately active perspectives that take as their anticipated object the more abstract potential complement of future-directed virtuous modes. The authority mode represents an immediately active perspective anticipating (as its projected object) the potential complement of future-directed follower roles. Generally speaking, the group authority themes immediately initiate the conditioned interaction in anticipation of the future-based potentiality characterizing the group representative.

THE CARDINAL VIRTUES:
THE ESSENCE OF GROUP COHESIVENESS

This initial description of the (group-focused) personal ideals effectively outlines the fundamental dynamics governing the group authority perspective. These four basic themes all derived from Latin roots, accentuating the Roman's enduring fascination with group leadership. The group authority perspective, accordingly, promotes these four basic themes; namely, dignified purpose tempered by integrity, accompanied by an active sense of glory and honor in one's civic endeavors.

This distinctive group power base effectively allows the group authority to overrule the more shortsighted concerns of the personal follower, in essence, regaining the upper hand within the ascending power hierarchy. In light of the more elementary style of personal authority (that it supersedes), the group authority figure is similarly susceptible to one's own unique form of follower counter-maneuver, in this case that expressed by the group representative.

The group follower perspective is essentially as ancient as group authority itself, serving as a crucial counterpoint to the power of the group authority figure. Similar to the personal follower role (that it supersedes), the group representative shares the distinctive style of "strike" leverage characterizing the follower role. Indeed, it is chiefly with through this more advanced (group) context that the strike power of the follower figure reaches its greatest degree of potential. Although this basic strike leverage traces its origins to classical times, it only recently has truly come of age with respect to the dramatic rise of unions and collective bargaining. Prior to the turn of the century the typical factory worker suffered many

39

indignities at the whim of his employer, yet was powerless to resist out of fear of being replaced. By playing one employee against another, management effectively maximized the power leverage implicit for the group authority perspective.

A corresponding rise in power within the group, however, forced management to come to a more equal footing with labor. Through the latter's reorganization as a "union collective," the rank-and-file picked a consensus spokesman (the shop steward) to represent them in their dealings with management. The most powerful leverage in collective bargaining, however, resides in the much publicized (and all too often wielded) strike clause within the union contract. According to this group power tactic, the group representative informs the group authority that without the cooperation of the labor pool, there will be no one left to justify his authority status. Through the judicious use of the strike option, the group representative effectively evens the score in job-related conflicts, as witnessed in the modern-day standoff between labor and management.

This enduring reliance on the strike option for pressing militant demands is generally invoked in only most intractable situations; namely, those negative conflicts where both parties suffer to some degree. It is ultimately possible, however, to invoke a more positive slant on the group follower perspective, as exemplified in the principles governing group *cohesiveness*. According to Group Theory, the theme of cohesiveness refers to a general preponderance of attractive vs. repulsive forces within the group. Cartwright and Zander (1960) identified five attractive forces within the successful group: respectively defined as (1) a strong feeling of "we"ness rather than "I"ness, (2) friendliness and loyalty to fellow members, (3) collective work towards a common goal, (4) willingness to endure pain or frustration for the sake of the group, and (5) a common defense against criticism. Members attracted to a group are more likely to exhibit congruent attitudes: namely, responsible action, interpersonal harmony, similarity of values, and an emphasis on security within the group.

It still remains to be determined, however, which precise combination of terms goes towards satisfying the requisite four-part complement of affective dimensions predicted for the group representative perspective. Being that the group representative reprises the role originally introduced as personal follower, this new format, accordingly, represents a more abstract variation on the initial complement of alter ego states (approval, leniency, aspiration, and compliance). This more advanced modification is effectively satisfied in terms of the previously described listing of cardinal virtues; namely, prudence, justice, temperance, and fortitude. Indeed, this distinctive grouping conveniently appears tailor-made for satisfying the four affective dimensions predicted for the group representative perspective.

THE CLASSICAL TRADITIONS FOR THE CARDINAL VIRTUES

The English spellings for the cardinal virtues all collectively derive from Latin roots, although earlier precedents clearly exist in the Greek tradition. They first appear as a definitive grouping in Plato's dialogue *The Republic*, although Plato intimates that they were already a tradition even in his own day. The lyrical poet Pindar is credited with their first recorded reference in his *Eighth Isthmian Ode* (478 BCE): where Peleus and his fellow Aeacids are cited as models of justice, courage, temperance, prudence, and piety (a fifth virtue originally included within this grouping). In his *Republic*, however, Plato eliminates the somewhat extraneous concept of piety, focusing on the remaining four as the central core for his enduring system of ethical philosophy.

For Plato, virtue played a preeminent role in securing the health and harmony of the soul. In his dialogue *The Republic*, Plato (speaking through Socrates) proposes his utopian vision of the Greek city-state: one wishfully compensating for the weakness plaguing the troubled Athens of his day. Plato's ideal city-state was organized along the lines of a three-part caste system comprising a ruling-elite of guardians, a military class of warriors, and a mercantile class of workers (respectively symbolized as gold, silver, and bronze). The guardian class enjoyed an extensive degree of education accentuating the virtues of *prudence* and wisdom. The warrior class was subject to exhaustive military training selecting for the qualities of *fortitude* and courage in defense of the city. Furthermore, the economic focus of the worker/craftsman class selected for the virtue of *temperance* concerning such economic matters. Finally, the virtue of *justice* was ultimately found in the truth that each caste performed the task for which it was best suited; namely, duties consistent with its respective virtuous mode. The city-state, accordingly, is prudent, just, temperate, and brave: directly amplifying those noble qualities professed by the shared focus its three supportive castes.

The subsequent rise to power of the Roman Empire brought further consideration to the Latin versions of the cardinal virtues. The Romans greatly admired classical Greek culture, borrowing extensively from their rhetoric and philosophy (including the enduring canon of cardinal virtues). One of the most influential Latin expositions in this regard was Cicero's *De Officiis*, a stirring tribute to the Latinized grouping of prudentia, justitia, temperatus, and fortitutio. An early distrust of pagan philosophy initially led many Christians to reject the validity of this Latin complement of cardinal virtues. With the eventual Roman acceptance of Christianity, however, Clement and Origen among the Greeks, as well as Lactantius and Ambrose among the Romans, began freely adapting pagan virtues to fit emerging Christian morality. Origen was among the first to draw attention to the preeminence of the cardinal virtues, describing them as indispensable to moral development. Although not specifically mentioned as a grouping in the New Testament, they nevertheless enjoyed widespread individual appeal. They are also listed as a grouping in the OT *Wisdom of Solomon*, a book incorporated into the Apocrypha of the Catholic Bible.

It remained to the efforts of St. Ambrose (of Milan) to give this classical listing its traditional designation: deriving from the Latin *cardos* (hinge), deriving from the basic belief that all of mankind's more noble tendencies *hinge* upon these basic four virtues. This perspective, indeed, is prophetic in light of the pivotal role these virtues play at the group level within the ascending power hierarchy. These Christian perspectives on the cardinal virtues ensured their enduring significance in later Western culture, celebrated as moralistic standards in their own right. These themes enjoy considerable prestige even in our modern age, particularly when impassioned calls to service and duty remain the order of the day. The true significance of the cardinal virtues, however, ultimately reflects their direct foundation within the respective alter ego states. In this latter respect, *prudence* represents the group analogue of approval, whereas *justice* designates a similar refinement of blameful-leniency. Furthermore, *temperance* adds a public sense of moderation to aspiration, whereas *fortitude* redefines compliance from a civic perspective. This distinctive class of cardinal virtues represents a projected sense of potentiality within a future-directed time-frame, in essence, serving to effectively consummate the immediately active authority-based perspectives that initiated the two-stage operant schematic.

Generally speaking, the group authority role immediately initiates the conditioned interaction, whereby anticipating the potentiality characterizing the projected follower roles. The immediately-active authority roles occur entirely within the present, whereas the passively-potential follower modes are manifest within a future-directed time-frame. The latter future-projected follower roles effectively complement the immediately active authority terms within the overall group dynamic. For instance, in the case of positive reinforcement, the initial glorious sense of nostalgia on the part of the group authority figure further prompts the prudent sense of approval on the part of the group representative. This prudent sense of approval, in turn, eventually becomes actualized as dignified-desire on the part of the reinforcer, whereby prompting the temperate determination to act aspiringly on the part of the group representative (within a future-directed time frame).

A similar style of motivational interplay further holds true with respect to the remaining class of virtues encompassing the domain of negative reinforcement. For instance, the initial honorable sense of guilt on the part of the group authority figure, in turn, anticipates a leniently-just treatment on the part of the group representative. This lenient sense of justice, in turn, eventually becomes actualized as an active worrisome sense of integrity on the part of the reinforcer, whereby now prompting the fortitudinous determination to act compliantly on the part of the group representative (within a future-directed time frame). Consequently, in terms of both positive and negative reinforcement, the immediately-active group ideals of glory, honor, dignity, and integrity effectively anticipate (in a behavioral sense) the respective virtuous counterparts of prudence, justice, temperance, and fortitude. Indeed, this dual style of group interaction is further seen to repeat for the remaining spiritual, humanitarian, and transcendental levels as well: providing the ultimate means for specifying the dynamics underlying the ethical traditions specific to the virtuous realm. The remainder of the current chapter further outlines this advanced style of group dynamic encompassing the entire eight-part complement of motivational terms, providing a sturdy ethical foundation for all subsequent classes of virtue and value to follow, including an extensive analysis of their individual literary traditions.

GLORY - PRUDENCE

The more straightforward class of positive virtues proves to be the most logical initiation point for such a grand-scale analysis, being that positive rewards appear much more tangible in nature: in contrast to the vaguer concept of leniency governing negative reinforcement. Accordingly, the interplay of glory and prudence will be examined first, followed by the remaining sequence comprised of dignity and temperance. As suggested in the group foundations for these virtuous terms, this overall realm of inquiry encompasses the more extensive style of group interplay that builds directly upon the more basic behavioral style of personal authority/follower roles.

As initially suggested, the glorious sense of solicitousness expressed by the group authority figure actively initiates the group conditioned interaction, formally expressed as the potential quest for the rewarding reinforcement in relation to the group follower role. Being that only one role may be active within the conditioned sequence at any given time, the role of the reinforcer is relegated to that of a future potentiality, identified as the prudent sense of approval that is anticipated from the group representative.

The latter prudent sense of approval equates to the group representative role, whereas the immediately-active glorious expression of solicitousness further invokes the initial group authority role. According to this group authority/follower interaction, the group authority initiates the conditioned relationship, gloriously acting solicitously in anticipation of the prudent-approval by the group representative within a future-directed time-frame. This projected sense of potentiality ultimately imparts meaning and purpose to the group authority's initial gloriously-solicitous treatment, being that all will have been for naught should such prudent-approval fail to materialize.

A familiar example of such a group style of interaction concerns the typical workplace scenario, defined as the reciprocal interplay between corporate administration and the supportive class of employees. This effectively mirrors the interplay previously described (in a personal sense) between the master craftsman and the apprentice. The group-oriented workplace employee typically performs specialized duties crucial to the group office environment, whereby (in the process) gloriously acting solicitously in anticipation of the prudent-approval of the supervisory staff through the rigors of such a shared endeavor. The employee seeks to distinguish his/her own competency within the approving glance of management, perhaps one day even achieving supervisory status in one's own right. This active sense of procurement (in an appetitive sense) is colloquially equated with one's own glorious sense of solicitousness, an immediately-active emotion contin-

gently anticipating the prudent bestowal of approval on the part of the follower figure.

The authority-ideal of *glory* certainly fits the bill in this preliminary group-focused respect, traditionally defined as a nostalgic expression of worthiness fully deserving of prudent-approval on the part of the reinforcer. Indeed, glory can actually span a rather broad range of meanings, from exalted praise/honor to heightened achievement or distinction. Its modern spelling derives from the Latin *gloria* (of similar meaning and usage). As with so many of their abstract concepts, the Romans divinely worshiped glory as a deity: as witnessed in a dedicatory inscription to *Gloria* unearthed at Numidia in Northern Africa. She also appears as Gloria Exercitus (training, exercise) on medallions of the Roman emperor Constantius II, and simply as *Gloria* on other imperial coins.

The classical Greeks further worshiped this mental aspect in the guise of their abstract goddess *Eucleia*. Originally, Eucleia had been a surname of Artemis (the Greek Goddess of the Hunt), although this qualifier eventually came to be worshipped as a deity in its own right. She was particularly worshipped in the city-state of Athens, where a sanctuary was dedicated to her from the spoils-of-war seized at the Battle of Marathon. This battle was the greatest military triumph for the brave Athenians, with a reported *6,400* Persian casualties vs. *192* fatalities for the Athenians. Eucleia, accordingly, symbolized the exalted state of glory the Athenians enjoyed on their exalted victory day. Even in our modern era, glory still figures prominently in prestigious sporting events such as the Olympics, where great performances by winning athletes are acknowledged in glorious medal presentation ceremonies attended by throngs of admiring fans. The fact that such athletes are classified as amateurs (competing without pay) only further serves to magnify the symbolic glory they bow to receive upon the presentation stand.

The latter group expression of rewarding-approval is schematically represented by the cardinal virtue of prudence, traditionally defined as sound judgment or discretionary conduct in practical affairs. Its modern spelling derives from the Latin *prudens* (denoting wisdom and/or foresight). In Plato's *Republic*, prudence is specifically singled out as the foremost of the four cardinal virtues. This theme was further amplified by Plato's contemporary Aristotle, who viewed it as a key factor crucial to the moral development of the individual conscience. These classical perspectives, in turn, extended to the Christian era, where prudence is defined as deep spiritual insight into one's moral duties, as well as the concrete means towards their fulfillment. Consequently, prudence remains the cardinal virtue most allied to practical reason, a key motivational influence underlying all virtuous acts.

This foresightful aspect of Christian prudence finds parallel representation in the medieval tradition of cathedral art. Prudence is traditionally depicted as a seated maiden holding a book or pointing to a globe at her feet. She is also shown holding a compass (a symbol of direction) or a mirror intertwined by serpents (signifying personal intuition). She is sometimes depicted with two faces (or even three) signifying her consideration of past, present, and future contexts. Prudence eventually became synonymous with courtly behavior, particularly the pronounced degree of decorum expressed towards the ruling royal family.

The magnificent palaces of Europe certainly fostered such a grand cast of supportive characters, an entourage that gloried in the majesty of the regal monarch. In particular, prudence gained considerable popularity as a femininely given name, reflecting the courtly spirit characteristic of the royal "ladies-in-waiting." This emphasis upon rewards similarly fits well within the workplace example, where management prudently aims to act approvingly towards the employees in response to their gloriously-solicitous efforts, whereby encouraging further such cycles of initiative.

Final mention must necessarily be made with respect to the dual interplay of the main and accessory terms in relation to positive reinforcement. This formally entails replacing the *main* motivational terms with their respective *accessory* counterparts, essentially close synonyms of one another. Here the preliminary complement of main terms (my glorious sense of solicitousness in anticipation of your prudent-approval) is now replaced by the respective accessory counterparts (your exalted-ambitiousness in anticipation of my circumspective-admiration). In this latter schematic sense, you (as group authority) now *exaltedly* act ambitiously towards me in anticipation of my (as group representative) *circumspective*-admiration of you. In essence, the "you" and "I" roles are now effectively reversed, systematically ensuring that both procurement and reinforcement roles encompass the full range of objective/subjective perspectives within a real-life communicational dynamic.

DIGNITY - TEMPERANCE

The completed description of the preliminary sequence of glory-then-prudence, in turn, gives way to the remaining discussion of the remaining phase within the group interaction: namely, that encompassing dignity-then-temperance. According to this latter stage, the group representative eventually acts upon the potentiality inherent to one's prudently-approval, whereby dignifiedly acting desirously towards one's willing workforce in anticipation of the temperate determination to act aspiringly within a future-directed time-frame. A number of key features are further observed similar to those initially encountered with respect to glory-then-prudence. In terms of management's dignifiedly-desirous treatment, the supervisor now assumes a group authority status in relation to the workplace employees. The latter employee style of role, in turn, takes on the mantle of the group follower, in that it formally "follows" the authority role in terms its projected order within the conditioned interaction. According to this dignity-then-temperance dynamic, management dignifiedly acts desirously towards the employees in anticipation of instilling a (projected) temperate determination to act worthily on the part of the workforce, whereby encouraging further such cycles of productivity on all future occasions.

This immediately active style of rewarding perspective is formally identified with the group authority expression of *dignity*, continuing in the tradition of the group authority and follower roles. Its modern spelling derives from the Latin *dignitas* (merit or worth), from *dignus* (worthy): the same root for the Latin *decorum* (propriety). The great Roman statesman Cicero directly mentions dignity within the context of his rhetorical essay on decorum. In the course of his dissertation, Cicero restricted this term exclusively to the brotherhood of man: defining dignity as that crucial quality which distinguishes mankind from the rest of nature. He further states that mankind's intellect is superior in its capacity for rational insight, in direct contrast to the more shortsighted instincts guiding the rest of the animal kingdom.

These classical themes underwent a significant revival during the Renaissance, when Italian humanists (following Cicero's precedent) equated the dignity of man with the tradition of the humanities. Dignity was associated with the *art* of being human instilled through a devoted study of the liberal arts and sciences.

These classical overtones are further evident with respect to the heraldic symbolisms associated with dignity. These are particularly apparent in terms of the stylized *chapeau*, also known as the cap of dignity or estate. As the chief heraldic emblem of dignity, the chapeau was elegantly constructed of red velvet, sporting a flat crown and a

Personifications of the Four Cardinal Virtues (Clockwise: P-T-J-F) - circa 1295
Somme le Roi - ms. 6329, folio 96v, Paris Arsenal, Photo courtesy Bibliotheque Nationale, Paris

decorative ermine rim. The cap originally was worn by barons and nobles of the British Parliament formally dramatizing their elevated rank and status. Around the time of King Charles II, the chapeau was further embellished with precious metal around its base, giving rise to the coronet (or crown) of British royalty. Indeed, the velvet cap contained within the British royal crown is directly traceable to this original cap of dignity.

These noble connotations of the chapeau rate further consideration in light of its designation as the cap of maintenance (or estate). According to medieval tradition, the noble enjoyed exclusive sway over his feudal estate, accompanied by the attendant responsibilities of dignifiedly-rewarding the general welfare and labor of the serfs. In times of trouble, the noble often provided his subjects protection within the walls of his stockade as a reward for their fruitful services on the estate. Indeed, the great power and dignity enjoyed by the noble stemmed directly from his shrewd reinforcement of his loyal workforce.

A similar emphasis extends to the current workplace example, where the group authority (in the guise of management) dignifiedly acts desirously in order to reward the aspiring efforts of the respective workforce, whereby anticipating their (projected) temperate-aspirations within a future-directed time-frame. Indeed, the employee is reciprocally dependent upon the rewarding approval of management. This initial gloriously-solicitous treatment now becomes essentially meaningless without such suitable rewarding fanfare, whereby prompting the potential for further such cycles of productivity. This crucial air of dignity further aims to maintain a promising and reinforcing environment conducive to flourishing, as verified when the monthly paychecks are finally issued. In this latter sense, a healthy sense of respect for the temperate rank-and-file within the company further ensures a successful outcome to all such collaborative endeavors.

The latter temperate perspective certainly fits the bill in this basic regard, temperance traditionally defined as restraint or moderation in the indulgence of the appetites, as conducive to harmonious cooperation within the group. Its modern spelling derives from the Latin *temperantia* (moderation) from the Latin root *tempos* (extent or measure). It proves ironic that the true value of this virtue was frequently overlooked during the classical era, particularly in light of the sensual excesses characterizing the Imperial Roman era. The more austere Greeks worshipped this theme as their abstract goddess Sophrosyne, the divine personification of moderation and self-control. Indeed, her name is defined as a Greek compound of root-stems denoting safe-mindedness. Sophrosyne, is depicted as a comely maiden in flowing garb holding a *ewer* (pitcher) and *cantharos* (a libation cup used in drinking rituals).

According to Plato's masterpiece, *The Republic,* temperance is defined as the rational restraint of the physical appetites: particularly, food, drink, and sexual indulgence. In Plato's ideal city-state, the economic focus of the worker/craftsman class selected for the virtue of *temperance* in relation to an overarching sense of restraint and control in economic matters of a group nature. In his later dialogue, *Laws,* Plato intimates that temperance aspires to emulate divinity, a theme further professed by early Church theologians in their pursuit of a virtuous lifestyle. Medieval artisans, in turn, symbolized temperance in the classical style reminiscent of Sophrosyne. Through the dramatic medium of cathedral stained-glass, each of the cardinal virtues was visually personified using a stylized set of human attributes. Some stained glass representations portray Temperance with a torch and a jug. Others include a vessel of water for mixing with the wine (wherein diluting its inebriating effects). Related depictions feature a scourge and a bridle (sometimes with the bit in place) signifying the restraint of the passions.

In this formal schematic sense, I (as group representative) temperately act aspiringly towards you in response to your (as group authority) dignified-desire towards me. The employer bears a certain risk in assuming that such anticipated temperate cooperation will eventually be forthcoming. He/she can be reasonably assured, however, by the wealth of previous cycles of temperate-aspiration from past memory, spurring the anticipation of similar such temperate cooperation in the future. Indeed, it is chiefly this tenuous power of deliberation that ultimately imparts the strike-leverage enjoyed by the group representative in relation to the group authority figure, the latter dependent upon the former to fulfill his/her immediately active reinforcing mandate.

This temperately-aspiring treatment (on the part of the workforce) ultimately provides an effective sense of closure to the entire conditioned interchange: ultimately serving to prompt further such cycles of cooperation linking labor and management. Consequently, this second phase effectively reflects the inherent strike-power enjoyed by the loyal workforce, for without this temperate treatment, the dignified sense of desire expressed by management will all have been for naught. Although the workplace example proves extremely enlightening (for illustrative purposes), other examples further come to mind. Indeed, the ultimate goal of this exercise has been to propose a sturdy conceptual foundation for the even more abstract hierarchy of virtues and values to follow.

One final mention must necessarily be made concerning the dual interplay of both the main and accessory terms for the second stage of the conditioned interaction. This formally entails replacing the *main* motivational terms with their respective *accessory* counterparts, essentially close synonyms of one another. Here the preliminary complement of main terms (your dignified-desire for me in anticipation of my temperately-aspiring treatment of you) is now replaced by the respective accessory counterparts (my passionate-respect for you in anticipation of your continent-consideration of me. According to this accessory modification, I (as group authority) now passionately act *respectfully* towards you in anticipation of your (as group representative) *continently*-considerate treatment of me. This dual interplay of main and accessory perspectives ensures that both the procurement and reinforcement roles encompass the full range of objective-subjective potentialities across the board.

HONOR - JUSTICE

In addition to the realm of positive reinforcement, it further proves crucial to examine the remaining domain of negative reinforcement. This latter style of analysis scarcely proves as clear-cut as that for the positive realm being that negative reinforcement involves the lenient withholding of punishment as opposed to the more straightforward bestowal of rewards. Negative reinforcement entails the withholding of punitive consequences within the environment or (in an interpersonal sense) leniency in response to submissive types of behavior. In terms of a group social context, the group authority figure honorably acts in a guiltily-submissive fashion in anticipation of a leniently-just treatment on the part of the group representative. This anticipated lenient sense of justice, in turn, eventually becomes actualized as a worrisome sense of integrity on the part of the reinforce, whereby anticipating the (projected) fortitudinously-compliant treatment on the part of the respective follower figure.

This interplay of compliance/leniency is exceedingly reminiscent of the throat-baring behaviors previously described for the wolf pack. The submissive pack member dramatically exaggerates his degree of vulnerability in anticipation of a bestowal of leniency. In the more abstract (verbal) sense, submissiveness operates in a similar fashion: namely, honorably expressing a vocal sense of guilt, whereby potentially eliciting a leniently-just treatment on the part of the group representative. Certainly it could appear somewhat risky to express such an extreme degree of vulnerability without a reasonable assurance of upcoming leniency. Past memories certainly come into play, with previous such cycles of leniency ultimately justifying such a radical act of faith. According to this more measured strategy, leniently-just rehabilitation (rather than vengeful retribution) now remains the order of the day.

A familiar example of such a reciprocating style of group interaction concerns the interplay between the military general and his band of enlisted men. The enlisted soldier is expected to fall into line with the discipline and dictates of the general, honorably acting submissively in anticipation of leniently-just treatment on the part of the general. In more formal terms, I as group authority (the enlisted man) honorably act in a guiltily-submissive fashion towards you in anticipation of your (as ranking general) leniently-just treatment of me. The soldier bears a certain risk in trusting that such leniently-just treatment will eventually be forthcoming although assured by the wealth of previous cycles of negative reinforcement conducive to such confidence.

The preceding soldier/general example specifically outlines the (group) prerequisites for honor,

a term invested with a rather broad range of meaning spanning from admiration and esteem to nobility and honesty. Similar to the case previously made for glory, honor also was prominently worshipped as a deity by the classical Romans, as personified by their abstract god Honos. On Roman coins and medals, Honos is depicted as a handsome youth holding a spear in his right hand and a "horn of plenty" in his left. He is crowned with a wreath of bay leaves and his chest is exposed. His chief temple was situated outside the Porta Capena in Rome in close proximity to the temple of Mars, the Roman God of War. An even more ancient altar was dedicated to Honos outside the Colline gate. Persons sacrificing here were obliged to have their heads uncovered, a custom still widely employed today in the swearing of oaths.

The early Middle Ages further celebrated such classical overtones, honor figuring prominently in the Codes of Courtesy and Chivalry: also known as the Court of Venus and the Field of Mars. In medieval heraldry, the honor point refers to the high center point on the shield, the field where the crowning symbolisms of brave-nobility are most likely to occur. This heraldic sense of the term actually spans a much broader range of meaning, further implying a sense of primacy and/or seniority. It also suggests (like honesty) a sense of what is rightfully expected with respect to one's civic and moral obligations.

This upright quality comes through most clearly with respect to the tradition of the Code of Honor: namely, that system of reciprocal rights and obligations governing a particular trade or profession. It typically takes the form of honesty in one's business dealings, as well as unswerving loyalty to one's fraternal organizations. It frequently is compounded by the themes of etiquette and good breeding consistent with such a refined social context. Consequently, this code eventually came to be associated with many stylized rituals: most notably, the time-honored custom of dueling to restore one's personal sense of honor (or that of one's family).

In terms of this two-stage motivational dynamic, the clear militaristic overtones associated with the anticipated leniency phase are exemplified (in a group sense) by the cardinal virtue of justice, as witnessed during classical times with respect to the legal administration of the Roman Empire. The Justinian Code of Law specifically defines justice as: "the constant and firm willingness to render every man his due." This basic conviction was further echoed centuries later by St. Thomas Aquinas in his comprehensive discussion of justice contained within his *Summa Theologica*. These general connotations of justice seem to share a common theme; namely, the subordination of one's personal self-interests to the collective welfare comprising the group. Indeed, justice certainly fulfills its status as a group follower perspective, a fact amply documented in the modern-day institution of the *jury* trial.

True to its origins in British Common Law, the jury trial has remained a prominent American standard since colonial times. The American variation preserves the basic features of the Common Law jury; namely, a twelve-member panel presided over by a judge empowered to reach a unanimous verdict. This group focus is particularly evident during the jury selection process, where complete impartiality is sought across a broad cross-section of the general population. The public is similarly invited to witness the courtroom proceedings, criminal cases referred to through the formula: The People vs. John Doe.

Following the systematic presentation of evidence, the jury ultimately deliberates in private over the presumed guilt or innocence of the accused, tempering the letter of the law with personal intuition and insight. The jury foreman (as representative of the group) submits the final verdict to the judge, who (as spokesman for the court) reads the decision to the defendant. The lack of a unanimous verdict is figuratively termed a "hung jury," being that complete agreement is necessary for establishing the guilt or innocence of the accused. The sentencing phase focuses on the lenient rehabilitation of the individual, a factor that downplays any personal quest for retribution. Although fines or jail-time are typically pronounced at this juncture, such punitive measures are primarily instituted to protect the public welfare (as well as providing restitution to the injured party). A penitent attitude on the part of the defendant often secures a greater degree of leniency from the judge. Indeed, an honorable admission of guilt is rightfully expected if justice is truly said to have been done.

Similar to the case of the interplay of main and accessory terms in relation to positive reinforcement, a parallel dynamic is further encountered with respect to negative reinforcement. This formally entails replacing the *main* motivational terms with their respective *accessory* counterparts, essentially close synonyms of one another. Here the preliminary complement of main terms (your honorable sense of guilt in anticipation of my leniently-just treatment of you) is further replaced by the respective accessory counterparts (my deferential sense of uprightness in anticipa-

tion of your equitable sense of concern towards me). According to this accessory modification, you (as group authority) deferentially act in an *upright* fashion towards me in anticipation of my (as group representative) *equitable* sense of concern towards you. According to this empathically-based accessory format, the "you" and "I" polarities are now reversed, effectively ensuring a full range of objective/subjective potentialities across the board.

INTEGRITY - FORTITUDE

The preceding two-stage sequence of honor-then-justice, in turn, dictates that the group follower figure must eventually act upon the potentiality implicit in his/her own lenient sense of justice. This further takes the form of a worrisome sense of integrity within an immediately-active time-frame in anticipation of the compliant sense of courage/fortitude on the part of the enlisted men. This ultimate decision to act often dictates an extended course of deliberation on the part of the lenient reinforcer. Indeed, it is chiefly this ultimate power of deliberation that formally imparts the power leverage enjoyed by the reinforcer in relation to the procurer.

The respective interplay of group authority and group follower roles invokes the immediately-active worrisome sense of integrity on the part of the reinforcer, although now punctuated from the perspective of the group authority figure, as schematically depicted in Part-B of **Fig. 2A**. Here, reinforcement (Y) is now depicted occurring entirely in the present, whereas the potential for procurement (X) is now shown projected into a future-directed time-frame. Consequently, the general-in-command now assumes the immediately active reinforcement role, whereby worrisomely acting with integrity in anticipation of the (projected) compliant sense of fortitude on the part of his enlisted men (the latter experienced within a future-directed time-frame).

A number of key modifications are further specified with respect to the polarities of the authority/follower roles. In terms of his immediately-active worrisome sense of integrity, the general now abandons his former (potential) lenient expression of justice (representative of the group follower perspective); in turn, switching to a more immediately active style of integrity perspective indicative of the group authority role. The common soldier, in contrast, now assumes the subsequent mantle of group representative, a status reflecting the leverage inherent to one's future-directed style of fortitude perspective. These role reversals are certainly warranted, being that they formally reflect the initial sequence based upon honor-then-justice, although now punctuated from an active reinforcement perspective (rather than the submissive variety). The general now worrisomely acts with lenient-integrity in anticipation of instilling a compliant sense of fortitude on the part of his enlisted men with an eye towards encouraging them to honorably act submissively on all future occasions.

This immediately active integrity perspective (on the part of the general) directly parallels the affiliated theme of dignity with the exception that leniency (rather than approval) is now called into focus. This sense of leniency is further reflected in the traditional connotations of the term; e.g., moral probity and ethical steadfastness. Its modern spelling derives from the Latin *integritas* (completeness, purity), from *integer* (whole). In terms of steadfastness, integrity is figuratively symbolized as the domestic canine consistent with its enduring reputation as "man's best friend."

This unswerving sense of integrity (in relation to the domestic dog) is reflected in its traditionally given name "*Fido*," from the Latin *fideo* (I believe). Other carnivores with strong social instincts (such as the lion) are similarly esteemed as paragons of integrity in classical mythology. According to Old Testament scripture, the lion and the wolf were respectively revered as the figurative emblems of the Jewish tribes of Judah and Benjamin. According to medieval heraldry, one of the most popular shield arrangements was the *rampant*: a lion standing upright in profile with its front paws splayed (as if warding off a blow). The rampaging lion is often depicted sporting a regal crown, a factor also consistent with the group overtones of integrity. Indeed, this regal sense of integrity (under the most adverse of circumstances) directly complements the more dignified demeanor initially cited in more positive contexts.

In terms of this overarching two-stage dynamic, the enduring militaristic overtones specified for the remaining group follower role are exemplified by the final cardinal virtue of fortitude: a theme traditionally defined as the patient endurance of trouble or pain. Courage and bravery are often cited as close synonyms. Its modern spelling derives from the Latin *fortitutio* from *fortis* (strength or power). During the classical era, fortitude was specifically identified with Virtus: the Roman personification of manly courage and valor, from the Latin *vir* (man). Patriarchal philosophers often identified manliness with godliness, with *virtu* becoming synonymous with moral goodness, in addition to other such terms hinting

at male potency (such as rectitude and uprightness). *Virtu* eventually came to be identified with moral efficacy in general, as suggested in broader connotations of the term.

These military connotations of fortitude endured the decline of the classical era, remaining one of the most prominent themes throughout the Middle Ages. During the ensuing age of chivalry, fortitude helped fire the hopes and aspirations of all knights within the realm. It served to subjugate the emotions of fear and cowardice while inspiring dutiful conduct in perilous situations. It is traditionally linked to prudence, effectively moderating the tendency towards reckless bravado. These moral overtones were further reflected in the cathedral art of the day, incorporating many of the classical attributes traditionally associated with Virtus. In addition to the upright sword, shield, and armor; Fortitude is variously depicted tearing open the jaws of a lion or chained to a column suggestive of the biblical story of Samson. In one portrayal, fortitude is depicted holding a miniature tower entwined by a dragon (the neck of which he grasps), an allusion to the perpetual struggle between good and evil.

True fortitude, however, is also invested with a strategic defensive slant, the military *fort* deriving from the same Latin root-stem. In truth, it might be judged just as noble to stand fast under entrenched attack as to lead the charge, effectively underscoring the dual aspects of the term. This risk of life-and-limb entails sacrifice approaching true "intestinal" fortitude; namely, that figurative ability to *stomach* adversity. Indeed, whether one aspires to military glory or martyrdom, one's personal concerns pale in significance to the welfare of the group.

Similar to the preceding comparisons to temperance, the brave warrior is wholly dedicated to duty and allegiance within his military unit. Even in our modern age of mechanistic warfare, the courage of the brave soldier knows no bounds: ranging from vexing personal hardship to the perilous risk of life or limb. This overarching sense of duty is particularly evident on the eve of a great battle, where a stirring call to courage is made by the general-in-command in order to alleviate any lingering sense of doubt on the part of the enlisted men. The general strategically reminds his soldiers of the peril to their free way of life (and that of their loved ones), effectively appealing to their crucial role towards maintaining the political status quo.

In conclusion, in terms of this second stage of the conditioned interaction, the commanding officer worrisomely acts with integrity towards his enlisted men in anticipation of their compliant sense of fortitude within a future-directed time-frame. This latter fortitude perspective effectively accentuates one's vulnerability within the conditioned interaction, effectively limiting the potential for further conflict. The soldier, accordingly, is reciprocally dependent upon the lenient integrity expressed by his commanding officer: his compliant sense of fortitude remaining entirely meaningless without such lenient underpinnings.

Final mention must necessarily extend to the dual interplay of both the main and accessory terms. This formally entails replacing the *main* virtuous terms with their respective *accessory* counterparts, essentially representing close linguistic synonyms of one another. Here the preliminary complement of main terms (your worrisome sense of integrity in anticipation of my compliant expression of fortitude) is now replaced by the respective accessory counterparts (my apprehensive sense of probity in anticipation of your brave sense of adherence towards me. According to this accessory modification, I (as group authority) now apprehensively act with *probity* towards you in anticipation of your (as group representative) adherent sense of *bravery*. This dual interplay of main and accessory perspectives schematically ensures that the full range of procurement and reinforcement roles encompass the complete complement of objective/subjective potentialities.

In summary, the immediately active style of group authority perspective proves a fitting counterpoint to the potentially characterizing the group follower role. As initially described for the ego and alter ego states, the more abstract listings of virtues specified for the group ideals and cardinal virtues are similarly subdivided into immediately-active modes occurring in the present and passively-potential modes projected into a future-directed time-frame. The active behavioral modes are defined in terms of the personal ideals, as specialized into the group authority

themes of *dignified*-desire or worrisome-*integrity*, as well as the *honorable* sense of guilt or *glorious* sense of nostalgia. The future-directed modes, in turn, target the more abstract realm of the cardinal virtues consistent with their inherent degree of potentiality: namely, *prudent*-approval, *just*-leniency, *temperate*-aspiration, or *fortitudinous*-compliance.

As chief spokesman for the group, the group representative promotes an equal balance of power with respect to the authority figure. The virtuous themes celebrated in Plato's *Republic* certainly ring true in this regard, each representative within the group fully cognizant of one's projected role therein; namely, to be prudent, just, temperate, and brave. When ultimately faced with such a potent challenge to his/her own authority status, the group authority further seeks to regain the upper hand within the ascending ethical hierarchy; namely, ascending once again to the next higher *universal/spiritual* level of authority.

The scope of the upcoming background material relating to spiritual (or universal) authority is essentially eclectic in nature, not meant to favor any one cultural tradition over another. True to its elementary foundations within Western thought, many of the specific virtuous themes were originally developed within the Christian tradition, a feature not generally compatible with modern-day secularism. Many of the spirited literary excerpts from theologians or scripture were, nevertheless, left intact; for qualifying these historical documents (in hindsight) would greatly diminish the impact of the background material. This eclectic strategy is not meant to be construed as favoring any one faith-based system over another, for the celebration of virtue is essentially a universal phenomenon. With this caveat firmly in place, the behavioral prerequisites for the remainder of this treatise should hopefully satisfy even the most stringent of secular critics, a resource applicable across all cultures and creeds.

4

THE SPIRITUAL/UNIVERSAL REALM

Similar to the case previously established for the group authority role, spiritual (or universal) authority is essentially as ancient as civilization itself, serving an analogous stabilizing function for many primitive cultures. Prior to our modern age of scientific inquiry, primitive man relied almost exclusively on religious belief and superstition to explain the bewildering complexities of the natural world. The typically violent forces of earth, wind, and fire served as a source of awe and amazement, inspiring an enduring sense of sacredness within this ancient mentality. The orderly rhythms governing the procession of the sun, moon, and stars must have surely provoked feelings of amazement eventually identified in terms of a complex pantheon of celestial gods. This constellation of myth and ritual eventually gave rise to a specialized clan of tribal shamans, leading to the priestly castes within many early civilizations. According to this pre-scientific mentality, the priest's ritual appeal to divinity spelled the difference between illness and health, fortune and disaster: a welcome hedge in an uncertain world.

In ancient Egypt, the pharaoh and the priestly class shared more-or-less equally in the power of the kingdom, each magnifying the power of the other in the eyes of the people. First and foremost, the pharaoh represented the supreme political figurehead for the Egyptian people. Egypt's prosperous economy served as a powerful magnet for refugees throughout the region. In order to counteract this multi-cultural challenge to his native authority, the pharaoh took full advantage of the much broader cloak of spiritual authority; namely, that binding over the group of all groups (or all mankind). By claiming direct lineage from the gods, the pharaoh proclaimed supreme authority over all groups within his domain regardless of any partisan concerns therein. The spiritual authority figure served clear notice that numerous other groups remained to perpetuate his authority status whether or not any particular group should choose to decide to desert. Consequently, the spiritual authority transcends the limitations plaguing partisan politics, whereby maximizing the degree of power leverage characterizing the universal perspective.

The Western tradition of spiritual authority has remained virtually synonymous with Christian principles since the decline of the classical Roman era. As founder of the Christian movement, Christ made direct claim to the role of Messiah (or Anointed One) within the Jewish tradition. His purported claim to divinity (as Son of God) established Christ as the premier spiritual authority figure of his day. Christ was particularly well versed in the spiritual authority maneuver, as witnessed in his encounters with the hypocritical Pharisees of his day. In one instance the Pharisees attempted to trap Jesus into an act of treason, questioning whether it was lawful to give tribute unto Caesar. Invoking the spiritual authority counter-maneuver, Christ cleverly replied: "Render unto Caesar the things that are Caesar's and unto God the things that are God's." Certainly, these scriptural precedents echo the modern-day separation of church and state, a cornerstone of the American political system.

MODERN PERSPECTIVES IN RELATION TO SPIRITUAL AUTHORITY

From a historical perspective the establishment of the United States of America arose as a direct consequence of the power struggle pitting the Colonials against the oppressive rule of the British Crown. A long line of English monarchs (leading to King George III) frequently oppressed the American colonists, including a plan to proclaim the Church of England as the official state religion throughout the Colonies (conflicting with the diverse spiritual foundations of the latter). This overreach, compounded by draconian economic policies, led to the *Declaration of Independence* and subsequent Revolutionary War. The *Declaration* represented an unprecedented appeal to spiritual authority, directly overruling the more partisan concerns professed by the British crown. In keeping with the overarching Christian heritage of the colonies, the *Declaration of Independence* proclaimed: "All men are created equal, endowed by their Creator with certain unalienable rights; namely, life, liberty, and the pursuit of happiness." In contrast to the prevailing royalist perspective, the colonials viewed government as instituted through mankind's consent to protect and preserve fundamental human rights.

Historical precedent dictates that the *Declaration's* author, Thomas Jefferson, borrowed extensively from earlier British theorists on the subject. In *On Civil Government, The Second Treatise* (1690) John Locke proposed that no one should harm another with respect to life, health, liberty, or possessions. Furthermore, should one actually be harmed, the injured party enjoys full right to compensation. Locke's treatise was published shortly following the Glorious Revolution of 1688, which witnessed the expulsion of King James II from the British throne. Four generations later the American colonist's similar dissatisfaction with British policies encouraged a revival in social conscience. Jefferson adopted Locke's principles of life and liberty, while modifying the remaining theme of property (for aesthetic reasons) into the *pursuit of happiness*.

Although the spirited literary style of the *Declaration* provided some measure of consolation to the disgruntled colonials, they soon became embroiled in the long and trying War of Independence. The ultimate victory by the revolutionary forces led to the subsequent adoption of the *Constitution of the United States*. In a curious oversight, the framers of the *Constitution* failed to include adequate guarantees of the civil liberties so eloquently proclaimed in the *Declaration of Independence*. Indeed, the common people rightfully rejected Federalist claims that such guarantees exceeded the limits of constitutional authority.

This shortcoming fortunately was remedied during the first regular meeting of Congress, chiefly through the efforts of James Madison. The Madison Amendments stemmed from numerous proposals gleaned from state conventions throughout the land. The final ten amendments (comprising the *Bill of Rights*) include guarantees on freedom of speech, religion, and the press. Further safeguards include the right to a speedy trial, reasonable bail, and the power to confront one's accusers. Other amendments protected against mandatory self-incrimination, unreasonable search-and-seizure, as well as cruel and unusual punishment. None of these rights were absolute, for the amendments were never meant to conflict with the general public welfare. Indeed, the *Bill of Rights* only limited the power of the federal government, the states clearly reluctant to diminish their individual autonomy.

With respect to the individual groupings of virtues and values examined to date, the diverse range of civil liberties guaranteed within the *Bill of Rights* can scarcely claim the pedigree or tradition essential for incorporation into the ascending virtuous hierarchy. It proves effective, however, to view the generic concept of "civil liberty" as the confluence of its two supportive concepts; namely, *civility* and *liberty*. Add to these the related moral themes of *providence* and *austerity* and the four-part listing of spiritual authority themes falls neatly into focus. In this expanded sense, the master four-part listing of providence-liberty-civility-austerity collectively comprises what is termed the class of *civil liberties*, in fitting acknowledgement of their enduring spiritual precedents.

According to this more universal style of context, the civil liberties represent the higher spiritual analogues of the more elementary group-focused class of personal ideals (glory-honor-dignity-integrity). Here, *providence* represents a spiritual refinement of glory, whereas *liberty* makes a further analogy to honor. Similarly, *civility* defines dignity from a spiritual perspective, whereas *austerity* represents a more idealized form of integrity. Although the political applications of the civil liberties might seem to belie their spiritual significance, recall that the spiritual authority maneuver builds directly upon the group representative perspective, whereby accounting for the hybrid quality of the grouping.

Consequently, this four-part listing of civil liberties specifies motivations encompassing the spiritual authority role; namely, providence, liberty, civility, and austerity. These universally-focused ideals represent immediately active perspectives, anticipating (as their focus) the more abstract potential complement of theological virtues. Here the spiritual authority role represents an immediately active perspective, whereby anticipating the future-directed complement of follower roles. Generally speaking, the spiritual authority themes immediately initiate the conditioned interaction in anticipation of the projected sense of potentiality characterizing the spiritual disciple perspective.

THE THEOLOGICAL VIRTUES

The completed description of the spiritual authority perspective, in turn, gives way to a similar style of analysis with respect to the spiritual follower (or disciple) role. The spiritual disciple maneuver is essentially as ancient as spiritual authority itself, restoring an equal balance of power to the universal realm. Similar to the other follower maneuvers (that it supersedes), the spiritual disciple maneuver shares the distinctive style of *strike* leverage so crucial to confrontations with the authority figure. For the spiritual disciple, this generally takes the form of a universal style of strike leverage frequently seen in the emergence of schisms or heresies. Although the extreme degree of abstraction encountered at this level might appear to invalidate any meaningful degree of effectiveness, witness the power of the revolutionary for influencing such enduring historical events as the Protestant Reformation; and, indeed, the very founding of Christianity itself.

In his designated role of spokesman for the spiritual congregation, the spiritual disciple informs the spiritual authority that the blessings of the faithful are crucial for maintaining his authority status. The spiritual disciple can wield a considerable degree of influence within the spiritual congregation. History certainly abounds with such dramatic twists of fate, as witnessed in the emergence of the Protestant Reformation. Here the unassuming monk, Martin Luther dared to speak out against the corrupt practices of the Roman Catholic Church, a schism destined to forever alter the face of Western civilization. Although this drastic style of strike leverage is typically effective only in confrontational circumstances, a more positive slant may further emerge with respect to the cohesiveness of the spiritual congregation. Although group cohesiveness was previously defined in terms of the four cardinal virtues, the congregational variety is further specified within the traditions governing the more abstract class of the theological virtues.

The theological virtues (faith, hope, and charity) have enjoyed a long and distinguished religious tradition, even rivaling that previously established for the cardinal virtues. Although individually mentioned throughout the Old Testament, they are first listed as a cohesive grouping in the New Testament, particularly in the writings of St. Paul. These virtues are prominently featured in Chapter *13* of his First Letter to the Corinthians where he finishes with the stirring admonition: "And now abideth faith, hope, and char-

ity, these three; but the greatest of these is charity." The designation of *theological* dates to St. Gregory the Great celebrating the supreme moral foundations for these three basic virtues, whereby further acknowledging their intimate connection to the cardinal virtues.

These enduring traditions extended to the writings of later theologians, most notably, St. Thomas Aquinas (1225-1274). In his *Summa Theologica*, St. Thomas specifically distinguishes the cardinal (or natural) virtues from the theological (or supernatural) versions. According to Aquinas the cardinal virtues are rooted within the psychological nature of man, developed primarily through concerted moral effort. They perfect mankind's natural dispositions, whereby defending against instinctual types of excess. In contrast, the theological virtues were viewed as supernatural, serving to promote spiritual character.

In keeping with his illustrious predecessors, St. Thomas limited his treatment of the theological virtues to the original three. This circumstance, however, leaves the complement one term short of satisfying the requisite four-part listing predicted for the spiritual disciple perspective. Historical precedent has favored such a numerical shortcoming, particularly being that medieval theologians grouped the theological and cardinal virtues together summating to the mystical number *seven*. This seven-fold listing was magically said to counteract the evil influence of the Seven Deadly Sins; namely, pride, anger, envy, lust, gluttony, covetousness, and sloth. This theme first appears in the writings of Psychomachia of Prudentius (circa 400 CE) picturing in vivid verse the inner moral conflict pitting virtue versus vice.

Despite these theological traditions, it ultimately proves crucial to return to the original scriptural sources for clues as to the identity of the missing theological virtue. It is particularly significant to note that Chapter *13* of St. Paul's First Letter to the Corinthians is the shortest chapter of the entire epistle, more or less arbitrarily divided from the adjoining chapters. St. Paul fittingly sums up the theme of the subsequent Chapter *14* with the quotation: "Let all things be done *decently* and in order" suggesting that decency represents the missing theological virtue. Decency is certainly a prominent theme in OT scripture (in addition to the New Testament teachings of Christ). Although not specifically mentioned by name, a careful reading of St. Paul's other references to the theological virtues: e.g., Romans (5:1-5) and 1st Thessalonians (1:3) seem to suggest precisely such a novel interpretation of this theme.

This crucial modification of the theological virtues finally accounts for the complete four-part listing of virtuous terms predicted for the spiritual disciple perspective. The theological virtues are viewed as the more abstract universal variations on the more elementary complement of cardinal virtues. According to this expanded context, *faith* redefines prudence from a spiritual perspective, whereas *hope* makes a similar analogy to justice. Furthermore *charity* represents a spiritual refinement of temperance, whereas *decency* reinterprets fortitude from a theological perspective. Although this intimate correspondence was never directly specified within the scriptures, this radical viewpoint is further validated in terms of the respective literary traditions.

THE MOTIVATIONAL INTERPLAY FOR THE UNIVERSAL DOMAIN

As previously established with respect to the personal ideals and cardinal virtues, the even more abstract range of perspectives governing the civil liberties and theological virtues exhibit a similar dual degree of specialization: subdivided into immediately active roles occurring within the present and passively-potential modes projected into a future-directed time-frame. The immediately active authority modes are defined in terms of the civil liberties, invested with clear behavioral overtones; namely, a glorious sense of *providence* or *libertarian* sense of honor, as well as a dignified sense of *civility* or *austere* sense of integrity.

The future-directed behavioral perspectives, in turn, target the passively-potential realm of the theological virtues: namely, prudent-*faith*, just-*hope*, temperate-*charitableness*, and decent-fortitude. This future-directed class of theological virtues directly complements the immediately-active class of civil liberties in terms of the overall spiritual dynamic. For instance, in the case of positive reinforcement, the gloriously-providential treatment on the part of the spiritual authority directly anticipates the prudent sense of faithfulness on the part of the spiritual disciple. This prudent sense of faithfulness, in turn, eventually becomes actualized as the civilly-dignified treatment on the part of the reinforcer, whereby anticipating the temperate sense of charitableness projected to occur within a future-directed time-frame.

A similar motivational dynamic further holds true with respect to the remaining realm of negative reinforcement. For instance, the libertarian sense of honor on the part of the spiritual authority figure, in turn, anticipates the blameful-hope for justice on the part of the spiritual disciple. This latter (projected) blameful-hope for justice, in turn, eventually becomes actualized as the austere sense of integrity on the part of the reinforcer, whereby further anticipating the decent sense of fortitude projected to occur within a future-directed time-frame. Consequently, in terms of both positive and negative reinforcement, the immediately active civil liberties of providence, liberty, civility, and austerity effectively complement the projected range of potentiality characterizing the theological virtues: faith, hope, charity, and decency. The remainder of the current chapter examines the detailed motivational dynamics encompassing this eight-part complement of terms, providing a sturdy foundation for all subsequent classes of virtues/values to follow.

Following the pattern of discussion previously established for the personal and group domains, it would be tempting at this juncture to proceed in a similar vein: examining both the spiritual authority and disciple roles in tandem as a two-stage motivational dynamic. In terms of the current spiritual/universal focus, this would amount to the positive sequence of providence, faith, civility and charity: as well as the lenient sequence of liberty, hope, austerity and decency. The extreme third-order level of abstraction implicit to the spiritual-universal realm, however, unfortunately begins to obscure the orderly pattern of procurement *then* reinforcement previously established for the personal and group levels.

Indeed, effective illustrative examples for the predicted interplay of spiritual authority and spiritual follower roles prove similarly elusive, unlike the more clear-cut personal example of the master and the apprentice, or the group example of the general and his enlisted men. Indeed, most common interactions are either of a group or personal nature, with universal perspectives chiefly restricted to those holding strong religious or universal viewpoints. Potential positive examples include the interplay of the monk and the abbot, or the philanthropist and an all-encompassing world community. Examples targeting negative reinforcement further extend to a "superhero" focus, such as the interplay of the crusader and the pontiff, or the UN Security Council and its peacekeeping force (in a more secular universal sense). The most prominent risk to citing such universal examples is that one side might inevitably be put-off in terms of the sensitivities governing such a secular and/or inter-denominational focus.

Despite this range of objections, a similar pattern of presentation for the universal themes is currently proposed; namely, examining both the spiritual authority and follow roles in tandem with one another as a two-stage motivational dynamic. The dedicated reader can further refer back to previous chapters (devoted to the group/personal realms) for confirmation of this overarching two-stage pattern in relation to the current spiritual/universal realm, as convincingly validated in terms of the wealth of literary traditions to follow.

PROVIDENCE - FAITH

The more straightforward class of positive virtues proves to be the most logical initiation point for such a grand-scale synthesis, being that positive rewards appear much more tangible than the more vague concept of leniency. The interplay of providence and faith will be examined first, followed by the remaining sequence of civility/charity. The overarching universal foundations for these virtuous themes encompass a more abstract style of universal perspective distinct from the more basic style of interplay initially established for the personal/group domains.

As initially suggested, the gloriously-providential treatment expressed by the spiritual authority figure actively initiates this universal perspective, expressed as the solicitous quest for the approval characterizing the spiritual disciple role. Being that only one role may be active within the conditioned interaction at any given moment, the role of the reinforcer is relegated to that of a future potentiality, identified as the prudent sense of faithfulness expected in terms of the spiritual disciple figure.

The potential nature of the latter prudent-faithfulness equates to the spiritual disciple role, whereas the more immediately active gloriously-providential treatment alternately specifies the spiritual authority role. According to this spiritual authority/follower interplay, the spiritual authority initiates the conditioned relationship, gloriously acting providently in anticipation of the prudently-faithful treatment projected to occur within a future-directed time-frame. This latter faithful sense of potentiality ultimately imparts meaning and purpose to the spiritual authority's initial providential treatment. Indeed, this projected sense of potentiality ultimately defines the power-leverage underlying the spiritual disciple role, being that all will have been for naught should such a prudent expression of faithfulness fail to come to pass.

A familiar example of such a spiritual style of interaction concerns the typical monastic scenario, defined as the reciprocal interplay between the religious authority and the supportive cast of monks. This example effectively mirrors the interplay previously described (in a personal sense) between the master craftsman and his faithful apprentice, or in a group context between labor and management The spiritually-minded monk typically performs routine duties crucial to the monastery, in the process gloriously acting providently in anticipation of the prudently-faithful treatment on the part of the abbot. The monk seeks to distinguish his competency under the approving glance of the abbot through such dutiful service. This immediately active sense of solicitousness is colloquially equated with providence, a forward-looking emotion that contingently anticipates the faithful bestowal of approval.

The first mentioned theme of *providence* certainly fits the bill in terms of this universally-focused perspective, traditionally defined as the determination to act productively or fruitfully, whereby providing the motivational rationale for the prudently-faithful treatment potentially forthcoming from the spiritual disciple figure. The latter spiritual disciple role is polarized in terms of an objective "you" perspective consistent with its reinforcing role within a future-directed time-frame. The providential treatment of the spiritual authority, in contrast, is specified from a subjective "I" perspective consistent with its immediately active style of expression. Indeed, the modern spelling for providence derives from the Latin *providentia* (the power to see in advance), from *pro-* (before) and *videre* (to see).

The ancient Romans specifically worshipped Providentia as their personification of the divine foresight guiding the fortunes of the Empire. Various Roman coins depict Providentia as a stylized eagle holding the scepter of Rome in its beak descending to the throne of the emperor in a peaceful transition of power. Providentia eventually came to signify the nourishing and protective power of the gods in general. This providential favor allowed the earth to bloom with grain in the spring, aided by an ample supply of rainfall during the growing season. Extreme ritual devotion was considered crucial for securing the fortuitous favor of the providential gods and goddesses.

These classical connotations for providence are particularly suggestive of the visual symbolisms associated with the *cornucopia*, literally, the *horn of plenty*. According to Roman mythology, the cornucopia traces its origins to Achelous the River God, who transformed himself into a raging bull in order to gain the upper hand in a violent struggle against Hercules. Achelous lost one of his horns during the confrontation, eventually retrieved by river nymphs who reverently filled it with fruits and flowers of the season. Henceforth, it was magically said to perpetually overflow with all such manner of bountiful blessings from the earth. In keeping with this bountiful character, the cornucopia was depicted as a major attribute for many gods and goddesses of the period. Chief among these was Fortuna, the goddess of fortune, and Copia, handmaiden to Fortuna (and goddess of plenty). Plutus, the Roman god of wealth, was further depicted cradling a horn of plenty. It is respectively portrayed as a gently curving spiral horn overflowing with fruit and grain, a symbolism traditionally associated with the modern day American celebration of Thanksgiving.

In this latter context, the cornucopia signified the providential favor the Pilgrims enjoyed in the form of a bountiful harvest, commemorating the Pilgrims' brave adaptation to life in the New World. Indeed, the cornucopia represents one of the most potent metaphors for Divine Providence, being that the supply of blessings remains virtually unlimited in principle. Through hard work (and some assistance from the natives) the Pilgrims succeeded in harvesting enough surplus to insure their survival through the harsh winter. These devout Pilgrims undoubtedly considered their success as divinely inspired, in direct contrast to the holiday's current (more secular) focus. Indeed, these spiritual themes emerged as the founding principles underlying the formation of the thirteen original colonies.

This gloriously-provident aspect formally anticipates the prudently-faithful treatment projected to occur within a future-directed time-frame. Here, the spiritual disciple prudently acts in a faithful fashion towards his spiritual authority figure, typically expressed as glowing adulation and/or grateful appreciation. The spiritual authority figure, in turn, remains entirely dependent upon the rewarding attentions of his spiritual disciple, any gloriously-provident treatment now remaining entirely meaningless without suitable worship or devotion.

The latter spiritual disciple expression of devoted-approval is clearly represented by the theological virtue of faith, traditionally defined as the supreme emblem of worship and devotion. Its modern spelling derives from the Latin *fides*, also the root-stem for the related theme of fidelity. The early Romans traditionally worshipped Fides as their divine personification of faith or fidelity in oaths and vows. She is typically depicted as a matronly figure adorned in a white veil and flowing gown, her right hand solemnly raised as if taking a vow. According to historical precedent, Fides was worshipped at an ancient temple on the Capitoline Hill close to that of Jupiter (with whom she is closely associated). Her cult is said to be very ancient, dating at least to the reign of King Numa. Her annual feast-day was celebrated on the first day of October when priests of her cult rode to her temple in a covered chariot, signifying that faith can never be too carefully protected. Her sacrificial priests were said to wrap their right hands up to their fingers with strips of white cloth suggesting that the seat of honor must be kept holy and pure. Covered hands eventually came to symbolize faith in general, as depicted on coins commemorating the loyalty and fealty of the Roman Legions.

These pagan connotations of faith eventually paved the way for the Christian sense of the term. According to New Testament scripture, Christ consistently implored his disciples to trust in the divine power of the Lord that worked through him. The dramatic series of miracles he is said to have performed further stipulated the unswerving faith of all that would be cured. Indeed, the chief emblem of faith (as the first of the theological virtues) is a shield with a stylized Latin cross inscribed in the center: traditionally referred to as the Shield of St. Paul.

This tradition of miraculous cures endures to our modern age in terms of the well-established phenomenon of faith healing. From its very inception faith healing was essentially an all-or-none phenomenon; namely, all was cured or nothing. Its specifics are described in the Epistle of St. James (5:14-16), which describes the anointing of the sick in a congregational setting. Healing is also listed among the Gifts of the Holy Spirit according to Chapter 11 of St. Paul's First Letter to the Corinthians. This emphasis upon faith proves particularly applicable to such providential healing, where the spiritual disciple prudently acts faithfully towards one's spiritual authority figure in hopes of a providential outcome via the healing ceremony.

Final mention must necessarily be made regarding the dual interplay of the main and accessory terms in relation to positive reinforcement. This formally entails replacing the *main* motivational terms with their respective *accessory* counterparts, essentially close synonyms of one another. Here your exalted sense of bountifulness in anticipation of my circumspective sense of devotion is substituted for the preliminary complement of main terms: e.g., my gloriously-provident treatment of you in anticipation of your prudent-faith in me. In more formal terms, you (as spiritual authority) now exaltedly act *bountifully* towards me in anticipation of my (as spiritual disciple) circumspective-*devotion* for you. In

The Theological Virtues (With Their Historical Representatives) – Circa 1460
Detail from Panel by Pesellino, Birmingham Museum of Art, Gift of the Samuel H. Kress Foundation

essence, this dual interplay of both main and accessory perspectives systematically ensures that the dual complement of procurement and reinforcement roles encompass the full range of objective/subjective potentialities.

CIVILITY - CHARITY

The completed preliminary sequence of providence and faithfulness, in turn, gives way to a further discussion of the remaining sequence within the conditioned interaction: namely, that encompassing civility and charity. According to this latter stage, the spiritual disciple eventually acts upon the potentiality of his/her prudent sense of faithfulness, whereby dignifiedly acting civilly in anticipation of the temperate determination to act charitably on the part of the follower figure. A number of key features are observed similar to that initially encountered in terms of providence/faithfulness. In terms of the abbot/monk example, the abbot's immediately active civilly-dignified treatment now formally ensures a spiritual authority status in relation to the devoted monastic members. The latter role of compliant monk, in turn, takes on the mantle of the spiritual follower role, being that it formally "follows" the authority role in terms the projected potentiality expressed within a future-directed time-frame.

According to this civility/charity dynamic, the abbot dignifiedly acts civilly towards his support-

ive cast of monks in anticipation of instilling a temperate-charitable perspective on the part of the individual monks, whereby encouraging further such cycles of cooperative-productivity within a future-directed time-frame. In terms of this immediately active style of rewarding reinforcement, the spiritual authority theme of *civility* certainly fits the bill. Indeed, as the chief spiritual analogue for the more group-focused theme of dignity, civility is traditionally defined as a sense of courtesy or chivalry within a universal context. Its modern spelling derives from the Latin *civilitas*, from *civis* (citizen). Limited archaeological evidence suggests that the Romans worshipped this theme as a deity, as evident in a dedicatory inscription to Civitas unearthed in Rome. Although *civitas* initially referred to the art of skilled governance, it ultimately came to signify the associated refinements of polite society in general.

In its latter legal sense, the classical concept of Civil Law originally applied to the sum-body of the Roman Code, particularly that portion applicable to the private citizen. The Common Law traditions for the English speaking world portray Civil Law as referring to the personal and property rights of the individual, a residual category that goes beyond the scope of Criminal, Military, and International Law. In this latter sense, the *U. S. Bill of Rights* makes clear provisions for such individual civil rights, although unforeseen ambiguities plague the wording of virtually every key passage. It ultimately falls to the judicial and legislative branches to derive legally binding interpretations for each of these civil rights provisions.

The current body of civil rights precedents emerged from a long history of legal decisions. The *Bill of Rights* originally applied only to freemen, although modified through the abolition of slavery as formalized in the *Emancipation Proclamation*. The subsequent Civil Rights Acts of 1866 and 1870 allowed all citizens the free right to engage in legal transactions (as in owning property or entering into lawsuits). The Civil Rights Act of 1871 further made it unlawful to deny any citizen equal protection under the law: whether through force, threat, or intimidation. The Act of 1875 guaranteed the free use of public accommodations, although this legislation was later reversed as unconstitutional. The latter reactionary trend culminated in 1896 with the Supreme Court ruling Plessy vs. Ferguson that upheld the principle of "separate but equal" facilities for people of color.

The midpoint of the 20th century, however, again ushered in the winds of change, as witnessed in the 1954 Supreme Court Decision for Brown vs. Topeka Board of Education. This historic ruling overturned the legal precedent of segregation in public schools, citing the inherent inequality for such a forced arrangement. Additional aspects of racial segregation soon followed as targets of reform. On December 1, 1955, Rosa Parks was arrested in Montgomery, Alabama for refusing to surrender her bus seat to a white passenger. The black seamstress' courageous act of defiance touched off a year-long boycott of the city transit system, a cause championed by civil rights leader Rev. Martin Luther King Jr. As spokesman for the Southern Christian Leadership Conference, King preached a message of non-violent resistance: culminating in the Civil Rights March from Selma to Montgomery, Alabama with a turn-out estimated at *25,000* strong. Faced with such intense public scrutiny, Congress soon passed a flurry of new legislation aimed at barring racial segregation. The Civil Rights Act of 1964 banned discrimination in employment and public accommodations, while the Civil Rights Act of 1968 extended these guarantees to real estate and private housing.

Civility clearly represents a spiritual ideal within the dignity tradition, although surpassing the more limited group-focus of the latter. For instance, Rosa Parks solicitously boarded the bus, fully expecting a civilly-reinforcing atmosphere en route to her destination. As agent for the bus-company, the driver was rightfully expected to respect her civil rights consistent with the routine expectations of the paying patrons. The civil environment underlying such a public conveyance necessarily specifies the principles of equality under the law, were it not for the prejudicial undercurrents plaguing the Deep South of the day. The bus driver maliciously ejected Rosa Parks from the bus employing ingrained racial prejudice as the rationale for compromising her civil rights. Indeed, it truly appears ironic to resort to such an inverted example for illustrating the dynamics of civility, so much do we take such civil rights for granted. The government fortunately remedied such appalling circumstances based in prejudicial treatment. These fundamental human standards are now effectively safeguarded throughout the public sector, whereby ensuring uniform standards of trade and commerce throughout the Land. Consequently, the spiritual authority (in the guise of moral authority) civilly anticipates the (projected) temperate sense of charitableness on the part of the well-meaning citizenry. This overarching respect for civility maintains a suitably rewarding environment conducive to civic cooperation and prosperity. In this enduring fashion, a healthy measure of civil-respect for the common people ensures a successful outcome to all such collaborative endeavors.

The latter allusion to a temperate sense of charitableness certainly rings true in this basic regard. Indeed, as the first and foremost of the theological virtues, *charity*, earns its key placement through a consummation of the entire (universally-focused) interaction indicative of such a spiritual disciple perspective. In slightly different terms, I (as spiritual disciple) am temperately determined to act in a charitable fashion towards you in response to your (as spiritual authority) civilly-dignified treatment of me. This distinctive motivational interplay clearly reflects the characteristic "if I then you" motivational dynamic governing the entire conditioned interchange.

Charity certainly meets such universal prerequisites, traditionally defined as generosity freely bestowed upon the needy in hopes of improving their condition. Its modern spelling derives from the Latin *caritas* (dearness, affection), from *carus* (dear). Latin translations of the New Testament translate the original Greek *agape* as *caritas*, equivalent to the English theme of charity in the King James Edition. Agape originally referred to the Greek word for brotherly love, as opposed to *eros* (or passionate love): a distinction preserved in later scriptural contexts.

The most stirring New Testament account of charity occurs in Chapter *13* of St. Paul's First

Letter to the Corinthians. Many modern versions of the New Testament prefer to substitute the related theme of *love* for charity, although this generalization fails to preserve the original distinction in terms. Semantics aside, St. Paul extols charity as the greatest of all of the theological virtues, surpassing faith and hope in terms of moral excellence. St. Paul views charity as a fixed disposition of the soul clearly at odds with egocentric concerns. According to the Gospel of St. Mark (12:24-44) Christ heartily praises the poor widow who modestly gave a mere farthing to the temple fund, in contrast to the wealthy Pharisee, who publicly extolled the magnitude of his largess.

These noble aspects for charity effectively permeated the very fiber of the early Christian Church. The first charitable measures were administered by the early Christian congregations, enlisting the aid of deacons under the guidance of the elders. Grateful recipients included the aged and the infirm, the poor and imprisoned, as well as widows and orphans. These early congregational measures eventually were supplanted by the diocesan system, where churches of a township answered to a single bishop. This centralization allowed an even greater share of church tithing to go to the poor, a full quarter by many accounts. Even non-Christians were permitted to join the ranks of the needy, for it was judged nobler to err on the side of generosity. This diocesan system flourished throughout the Middle Ages, although gradually supplanted by the establishment of monastic orders devoted exclusively to such charitable causes.

It remained till the more liberal precepts of our modern age for women to take a broader role in such charitable endeavors. Take, for example, the founding of the Missionaries of Charity by Mother Teresa of Calcutta. At the age of 18, Mother Teresa joined the Institute of the Blessed Virgin in Ireland, soon transferring to India to work as a teacher. She sought permission to work with the poor in the slums of Calcutta, whereby founding her order in 1948. The Missionaries of Charity established centers to aid the blind, disabled, and terminally ill of Calcutta. She also founded a leper colony near Asansol, India known as Shanti Nagar (Town of Peace). The Indian government awarded Mother Teresa the prestigious Padmashri Award in 1963 in recognition of her unfailing service to the people of India. Even greater awards soon followed, most notably the 1974 Nobel Peace Prize: to which she humbly commented "I am unworthy." This modest attitude echoed her deep spiritual conviction: "The help for the hopeless is the simple duty of us all."

This commendable preoccupation with charitable endeavors is certainly one of Western culture's most time honored traditions. Specialized agencies such as the United Way and the Red Cross/Crescent aid in the distribution of much needed funds and services. It certainly appears fitting, then, that the medieval representation of charity takes the form of a crimson heart inscribed in a heraldic fashion upon a shield. This figurative depiction symbolizes the heart's unceasing service to the wellbeing of the individual, a factor particularly in keeping with the lifelong charitable precepts of such noble spiritual servants as Mother Teresa. Consequently, the well-intentioned spiritual disciple temperately acts in a charitable fashion in response to the civilly-dignified treatment expressed by the spiritual authority figure. The spiritual authority bears a certain degree of uncertainty in assuming that such charitable treatment will eventually be forthcoming, although reasonably assured by the wealth of previous cycles recollected from past experience. Indeed, this tenuous power of deliberation ultimately imparts the reciprocal style of power-leverage implicit to both the spiritual authority/follower roles.

Further mention must necessarily be made with respect to the dual interplay of the main and accessory terms for this second stage of the conditioned interaction. This formally entails replacing the *main* motivational terms with their respective *accessory* counterparts, essentially close synonyms of each other. Here the preliminary complement of main terms (your civilly-dignified treatment of me in anticipation of my temperate sense of charitableness) is now replaced by the respective accessory counterparts (my courteous-respect for you in anticipation of your continent sense of kindness towards me. According to this accessory modification, I (as spiritual authority) now *courteously* act respectfully towards you in anticipation of your (as spiritual disciple) continently-*kind* treatment of me. This dual interplay of both main and accessory perspectives ensures that the complete range of procurement and reinforcement roles encompass the full range of objective/subjective potentialities across the board.

In summary, the completed description of the two-stage universal schematic comprising providence-faith and civility-charity offers a complete overview of such a universally-focused interaction. Although the monastic example proved informative for illustrative purposes, a number of other examples could prove equally feasible. Indeed, the ultimate goal for this exercise has been to propose a sturdy foundation for the even more abstract listings of virtues and values to follow, resulting in an overarching model for the virtuous realm in general.

LIBERTY - HOPE

Before skipping ahead to such a potential range of applications, it proves crucial to examine the remaining motivational dynamics for the virtuous realm of negative reinforcement. Indeed, such a motivational style of analysis scarcely proves as clear-cut as that for positive rewards being that negative reinforcement involves the lenient withholding of punishment as opposed to the more straightforward bestowal of rewards. Negative reinforcement entails the withholding of punitive consequences occurring within the environment or (in an interpersonal sense) leniency in response to avoidance types of behavior. In terms of the current spiritual/universal context, the spiritual authority figure honorably acts in a libertarian fashion in anticipation of the blameful-hope for justice on the part of the spiritual disciple. This potential blameful-hope for justice eventually becomes actualized as the austere sense of integrity on the part of the reinforcer, whereby ultimately anticipating the fortitudinous sense of decency on the part of the follower figure.

This interplay of submissiveness/leniency is reminiscent of the throat-baring behaviors previously described for the wolf pack, where the submissive pack member dramatically exaggerates his degree of vulnerability in anticipation of the ultimate bestowal of leniency. In a more abstract (verbal) sense, submissiveness operates in a similar fashion: namely, the vocalized libertarian sense of honor aims to potentially elicit a lenient hope for justice on the part of the spiritual follower figure. Certainly it could appear somewhat risky to express such an extreme degree of vulnerability without a reasonable assurance of upcoming leniency. Past memories certainly come into play, with previous cycles of lenient treatment ultimately justifying such a radical act of trust in terms of such an aversive strategy. According to this more measured tactic, leniently rehabilitation (rather than retribution) now dominates the discussion.

A plausible example of such a reciprocating style of universal interaction concerns the interplay between the United Nations Security Council and the respective Peace-Keeping Forces. The enlisted peace-keepers (drawn from around the world) are expected to fall into line with the discipline and dictates of the UN Security Council,

whereby honorably acting in a freely-libertarian fashion in anticipation of the blameful-hope for justice on the part of the Security Council. This distinctive libertarian perspective represents a forward-looking emotion consistent with its direct foundations in honor. The soldier bears a certain risk in trusting that his freely enacted peace-keeper role will eventually lead to a hopeful outcome, although assured by the wealth of previous such cycles of submissiveness-then-leniency.

The preceding UN example proves informative with respect to the universal prerequisites for *liberty*. As defined from the immediately active role of the spiritual authority figure, this libertarian sense of honor effectively provides the projected rationale for the blameful-hope for justice expressed by the spiritual disciple figure. Liberty is traditionally defined as the right to act without interference within the limits of the law. The term derives from the Latin *libertas*, from *liber* (free). In the early days of the Roman Republic liberty was regarded as a constitutional mandate, in contrast to tyranny or dictatorship. In keeping with other such classical themes, Libertas was worshipped as a deity, with several temples dedicated to her in Rome alone. She is traditionally depicted as a lightly attired matron holding a broken scepter in one hand and a staff hung with a felt cap in the other. The staff (the *vindicta*) played a role in the ceremonial freeing of slaves. The felt cap (the *pilleus*) was further bestowed upon the heads of freed slaves following their emancipation. It originally had been placed upon the heads of troublesome slaves at auction, whereby absolving the vendor of any subsequent liability. Towards the end of the Republic (circa the assassination of Julius Caesar) portrayals of Libertas often include a stylized dagger signifying the blood that must be shed in her defense.

In a more contemporary sense, liberty has enjoyed a prominent place of honor within the American system of government, one of the many treasured principles upon which this great country was founded. In a debt of gratitude from the world as a whole, Frenchman Auguste Bartholdi commemorated this spirit of freedom in his monumental masterpiece, the Statue of Liberty. Bartholdi's aesthetic vision of Liberty blends classical overtones with innovative technical design. It features a flowingly-garbed personification of a woman depicted in the act of gaining her freedom. Her right hand holds aloft a burning torch, while her left cradles a book of law inscribed July 4, 1776. The classical connotation of the liberty cap is curiously lacking, replaced by a striking crown of stylized rays of light. Broken shackles lie at her feet as Liberty strides forward to achieve her liberation.

Similar to the case previously established for providence, liberty clearly represents an immediately active style of universal authority perspective, an interpretation directly in keeping with the classical overtones associated with the Statue of Liberty. This spirited spiritual focus is particularly evident in the stirring principles embodied in the *Declaration of Independence*, where liberty is specifically singled out as one of the three God-given rights guaranteed to all individuals. Through such a libertarian perspective, the spiritual authority figure freely expands upon the group-focused foundation within honor, whereby anticipating the blameful-hope for justice by the spiritual disciple figure. These spiritual overtones are particularly suggested in terms of the "larger than life" attributes of the Statue of Liberty. Liberty's mild (but commanding) demeanor must have surely enthralled the uninitiated as one of the many wonders America had to offer. Towards these ends, it was Liberty's outstretched torch that figuratively served to light the way for the perpetual throngs of hopeful refugees, an endeavor that many immigrants hoped to realize in this Golden Land of opportunity.

The latter hopeful perspective experienced by the immigrants certainly fits the dual dynamics underscoring the entire motivational interchange. Indeed, the modern spelling of hope derives the Anglo Saxon *hopa* (to be confident, to trust). The Latin slant on hope, *sperare*, entered the English lexicon chiefly in terms of its opposing connotation as despair. Similar to the case previously established for Fides, Spes (the Roman personification of hope) was worshipped since the 4th century BCE. Spes originally was a goddess associated with Fortuna, invoked by all who hoped for success (particularly the hope for a good harvest). Over the course of generations, Spes eventually came to personify the goddess of the future: invoked at births, weddings, and dedications. In light of her considerable prestige, several temples were dedicated to her in Rome alone. Spes is traditionally depicted as a youthful maiden striding gracefully in a long robe, the seam raised in her left hand (as if in haste). In her right hand she holds a flower bud on the verge of opening, signifying the hopes for a brighter tomorrow.

These classical connotations beg further mention of the related theme of Pandora's Box. According to Greek mythology, Pandora was the first woman on earth, her name literally translated as "Giver of All." In celebration of her creation Zeus offered Pandora an ornate box that she was in-

structed never to open. This ploy was part of Zeus' clever plan to punish mankind for accepting (from Prometheus) the sacred gift of fire. In a fit of curiosity Pandora ultimately peeked into the box, allowing all manner of human ills to escape into the world. Only hope (*elpis*) was left behind in the box, a solitary comfort to mankind in such newfound misery. Later versions of the myth (such as the Fable of Babrius) have Pandora losing all the blessings of the gods (save hope), with similar consequences only now more closely resembling the biblical account of Adam and Eve.

This steadfast quality of hope finds similar parallels in the Christian scriptural tradition. Traditional representations of the theological virtues depict hope figuratively symbolized as an anchor inscribed upon a shield (similar to the crucifix symbolism previously described for faith). This anchor symbolism traces its origins to St. Paul's Epistle to the Hebrews (6:19) where he states: "...which *hope* we have as an anchor of the soul, both steadfast and sure." In the following verse, St. Paul further identifies Christ as the rightful object of our hope, an intercessory towards salvation.

The early Christians had long anticipated the prophesied return of the Lord, a particularly comforting thought during desperate times of persecution. This fearful era forced many Christians to resort to obscure forms of symbolism as a disguised expression of their hope. In particular, many early Christians adopted the marine anchor as an allegorical representation of the cross, a symbolism suggested by the cruciform arrangement of the anchor's shaft and crossbar. This anchor symbolism was particularly widespread in the catacombs alongside other such disguised symbols of Christianity; e.g., the dove and the fish. Indeed, just as a sailor sets his anchor in order to avoid drifting into danger, so the Christian disciple sets his *hope* in the saving power of Christ. It certainly remains a fitting tribute to the deep spiritual insights of St. Paul that he would so intuitively link these distinctive anchor symbolisms with early Christian beliefs relating to hope.

This overarching lenient-style context for hope underscores the allegorical symbolisms for the anchor. Here the spiritual disciple now blamefully hopes for justice in response to the libertarian sense of honor on the part of the spiritual authority figure: an interaction conducive to salvation similar to that previously described with respect to faith-healing. Here the libertarian authority figure is reciprocally dependent upon the lenient perspective of the spiritual disciple, any free expression of honor and liberty now entirely meaningless without such a reciprocating style of inter-action. Although faith and hope are sometimes used interchangeably in common usage, their distinctive styles of reinforcement ultimately prove to be the distinguishing factor.

Similar to the interplay of main and accessory terms in relation to positive reinforcement, a parallel dynamic is further encountered with respect to the realm of negative reinforcement. This formally entails replacing the *main* motivational terms with their respective *accessory* counterparts, essentially close synonyms of one another. Here the preliminary complement of main terms (my libertarian sense of honor in anticipation of your lenient-hope for justice) is further replaced by the respective accessory counterparts (your free sense of uprightness in anticipation of my equitable sense of fairness towards you). According to this accessory modification, you (as spiritual authority) now *freely* act in an upright fashion towards me in anticipation of my (as spiritual disciple) equitably-*fair* treatment of you. According to this empathically-based accessory format, the respective "you" and "I" polarities are effectively reversed ensuring a full range of objective/subjective potentialities across the board.

AUSTERITY - DECENCY

The preceding two-stage dynamic of liberty-hope, in turn, dictates that the spiritual disciple figure eventually must act upon the potentiality implicit to his/her lenient-hope for justice. This latter development takes the form of austerely acting with integrity within an immediately-active time-frame, whereby anticipating the (projected) brave sense of decency on the part of the follower figure. This ultimate decision to act frequently dictates a rather extended course of deliberation on the part of the austere authority figure. Indeed, it is chiefly this ultimate freedom of deliberation that imparts the power leverage enjoyed by the austere authority figure.

This respective interplay of spiritual authority and disciple roles is similarly modified in relation to the first stage within the conditioned interaction. The latter phase invokes the active austere sense of integrity expressed by the lenient reinforcer, only now punctuated from a spiritual authority perspective, as schematically referred to in Part-B of **Fig. 2A** (of Chapter 2). Here reinforcement (Y) is now depicted occurring immediately within the present, whereas procurement (X) is shown projected into a future-directed time-frame. For example, the UN Security Council is now thrust into an immediately active reinforce-

ment perspective, austerely acting with a lenient sense of integrity in anticipation of the (projected) decent sense of fortitude on the part of the peace keepers. This role reversal certainly proves warranted, being that it formally reflects the initial sequence based upon liberty/hope, although now punctuated from an immediately active leniency perspective (rather than the submissive variety). The spiritual authority figure now austerely acts with integrity in anticipation of instilling a brave sense of decency on the part of the peace keepers, whereby further serving to encourage such a decent range of treatment on future occasions.

This immediately active austerity perspective directly parallels the affiliated theme of civility with the exception that leniency (rather than approval) is now called into focus. This lenient interpretation is further reflected in the traditional connotations of austerity. Indeed, the modern spelling of austerity derives from the Greek *austeros* (denoting dryness or harshness). Austerity is traditionally defined as the endurance of pain, hardship, or misfortune, often in a mortified fashion. It can also suggest a sense of harshness or strictness in the bestowal of discipline. According to the Latin tradition this distinctive theme is figuratively identified with the Roman god Auster, the divine personification of the South Wind. Indeed, Auster is described as the dry and sultry south wind, the *sirocco* of modern-day Italians. It is the harbinger of hot and dry weather consistent with Italy's close proximity to the Sahara Desert. Consequently, historians trace its origins to the Latin root-stem *uro-* (the willingness to burn).

In its alternate philosophical sense, the traditions associated with austerity establish it as one of the fundamental principles governing the strict Code of Sparta: a powerful city-state to the south of Athens. Sparta maintained its military might primarily through an elaborate system of state-enforced regimentation and disciple. At the tender age of seven, male children were separated from their family and raised in state-sanctioned military academies. The recruits slept year round in open barracks on reeds harvested from the banks of the river Eurota. Family life was only reinstated upon reaching the age of thirty, when the individual was finally accorded the full rights and privileges of a citizen of Sparta.

These classical connotations of harshness and discipline have endured to our modern age, as exemplified in the recurring traditions of the *austerity budget*. This fiscal policy has long been employed to bolster faltering economies, chiefly through increased production and export of capital goods, whereby improving the overall balance of trade. It is further offered a stopgap measure to temporary economic problems: such as financing a military campaign or balancing the federal budget. The United Kingdom has instituted austerity budgets throughout its history, ensuring its enduring influence in modern economic theory.

In terms of the United States, this theme brings to mind the price controls instituted by President Nixon during the 1970's: a strategy aimed towards controlling skyrocketing inflation. The truest sense of the term, however, extends to the early 1980's with the advent of *Reaganomics*. President Reagan deliberately resurrected the austerity budget to describe his revolutionary program to revitalize the national economy. The lack-luster state of affairs characterized by runaway inflation and high unemployment called for a bold set of economic measures; namely, sharp budget cutting to shrink the public sector as well as a broad retreat from business and environmental regulations. This policy of "supply-side economics" promised (and eventually delivered) a surge in non-inflationary economic growth, although to the initial detriment of the more underprivileged economic classes.

On the opposing side of the ledger, the general public rightfully expected that their submissive attempts at economic cooperation would leniently be rewarded with an improved economy. The traditional austerity budget formally calls for such cooperative measures; namely, reduced consumption and resource conservation. In exchange for such a shared sacrifice, the government was rightfully expected to improve the economy to the point where austerity measures would no longer be necessary. Critics of the plan argued that the economic sacrifices demanded of the public were disproportionately severe at the bottom end of the spectrum, a premise all too evident during the early years of the Reagan Plan. Such hardships fortunately ran their course, resulting in the healthier and happier economy currently in force today. This lenient style of authority perspective austerely aims to ameliorate suffering in anticipation of the decent willingness to cooperate on the part of the willing citizenry. This overarching austere sense of integrity effectively promotes a leniently-rewarding environment conducive to global economic cooperation and inclusiveness. Consequently, austerity extends the more elementary (group) focus of integrity into an even broader (universal) sphere of influence.

In terms of the ongoing two-stage dynamic, the enduring fiscal overtones for austerity, in turn, are consummated through the remaining theological virtue of decency. Similar to its related counterpart in charity, decency further provides an effective sense of closure to the two-stage spiritual authority/follower interaction. Decency is traditionally defined as a sense of propriety in both word and deed with an emphasis upon moral scruples. Its modern spelling derives from the Latin *decentia* (fitting), from the Latin verb *decere* (befitting). The early Romans expressed a high regard for the principles of decency, the Roman statesman Cicero succinctly summing up the opinion: "Justice consists in doing no injury to man, *decency* in giving them no offense." Decency enjoys similar precedents within the Christian tradition, although specifically mentioned just once in English translations of the New Testament. The basic import of this theme covers a broad range of ethical contexts, as evident in its strategic placement in Chapter *14* of St. Paul's First Letter to the Corinthians. Indeed, this chapter concludes with the stirring admonition: "Let all things be done *decently* and in order," hinting at the profound significance of this fourth theological virtue. Furthermore, Chapter *14* directly continues the general theme of Chapters *12* and *13* (namely, the Gifts of the Holy Spirit), placing decency in fitting proximity to the descriptions of the first three theological virtues.

In Chapter *14* St. Paul directly focuses on the congregational aspects of the spiritual gifts, as in the themes of prophesy and speaking-in-tongues. St. Paul rightfully expressed concern that the over-zealous use of such gifts could prove detrimental to the credibility of the Church from a gentile standpoint. He further sought to resolve this issue by proposing strict guidelines for governing their expression within a congregational setting. He recommended restraint in the number of those speaking-in-tongues, while calling for an interpreter to offer insights into prophetic revelations. In this stricter sense, St. Paul expressed hope that these gifts would be expressed for the edification of the Church over and beyond their spiritual significance to the individual: a proclamation consistent with his call for decency in a church setting.

This spiritual interpretation survives to our modern era in the familiar expression: "common decency," namely, common to all cultures and creeds. Indeed, St. Paul deliberately sets the tone of a spiritual authority figure, lecturing on many austere themes of central importance to the fledgling Church. Although this epistle was originally addressed to the congregation in Corinth, it has since been accorded a universal focus in Christian theology. Through such concerted efforts, Christianity eventually grew to claim a prominent place on the world religious scene, a degree of success that even St. Paul might marvel at today. Here the spiritual disciple figure fortitudinously acts in a decent fashion towards one's spiritual authority figure in response to the latter's austere sense of integrity. In more formal terms, I (as spiritual disciple) bravely act decently towards you in response to your (as spiritual authority) austere sense of integrity. Indeed, this tenuous power of potentiality ultimately imparts the key power leverage implicit to the spiritual disciple perspective, the authority depending upon the follower to consummate the two-stage sequence of austerity-then-decency.

Final mention must necessarily extend to the dual interplay of the main and accessory terms. This formally entails replacing the *main* virtuous terms with their respective *accessory* counterparts, essentially close linguistic synonyms of one another. Here the preliminary complement of main terms (your austere sense of integrity in anticipation of my decent treatment of you) is now replaced by the respective accessory counterparts (my forbearing sense of probity in anticipation of your scrupulously-brave treatment of me. According to this accessory modification, I (as spiritual authority) now *forbearingly* act with probity towards you in anticipation of your (as spiritual disciple) *scrupulously*-brave treatment of me. This dual interplay of main and accessory perspectives schematically ensures that the full range of procurement and reinforcement roles encompass the full complement of objective/subjective potentialities.

In summary, the immediately active style of spiritual authority perspective offers a fitting counterpoint to the (projected) potentiality inherent to the spiritual disciple role. As previously described with respect to the personal ideals and the cardinal virtues, the civil liberties and theological virtues exhibit a similar degree of specialization: namely, immediately-active authority roles in anticipation of the passively-potential follower roles. The active authority roles are defined in terms of the civil liberties; namely, the immediately-active

themes of dignified-*civility* or an *austere* sense of integrity, as well as the *libertarian* sense of honor or glorious sense of *providence*. The future-directed follower roles, in turn, target the equally abstract realm of the theological virtues: namely, prudent-*faith*, just-*hope*, temperate-*charitableness*, and fortitudinous-*decency*.

As chief spokesman within the spiritual congregation, the spiritual disciple essentially rates an equivalent balance of power in relation to the authority/follower roles. The theological virtues celebrated by St. Paul certainly ring true in this basic respect. Indeed, this spiritual/universal range of perspectives offers crucial insights on the world scene today, offering the potential for healing many of the currently intractable religious rifts. Disturbing extremist trends may now finally be put to rest through the aid of the newly devised insights contained within the principles of Set Theory. Indeed, this third-order style of universal perspective dictates that all religions are equivalent when speaking from such an overarching spiritual perspective, whereby potentially facilitating enhanced spiritual peace and harmony.

This distinctive style of spiritual/universal perspective ultimately appears to close-out the ascending hierarchy of abstraction, for there can be no level of organization greater than mankind as a whole. This very sense of the power of abstraction, however, sets the stage for one further class of abstract innovation; namely, that specified for the humanitarian authority realm. In contrast to the purely organizational status governing the first three levels, the humanitarian realm is distinguished through the abstract addition of *historical* time. The profoundly abstract nature of the humanitarian realm is further reflected in the abstract character of its respective groupings of terms: as the lofty grouping of beauty, truth, goodness, and wisdom collectively serves to indicate. A more detailed description of this subsequent class of authority roles will now be undertaken with an in-depth examination of the humanitarian realm in concert with its respective ecumenical and moralistic classifications.

5

THE HUMANITARIAN GLOBAL TRADITION

In keeping with the more elementary forms of authority roles that it supersedes, humanitarian authority has been blessed with a long and illustrious literary tradition. The humanitarian variation, however, is distinguished from all previous forms in terms of being the first truly abstract class of power maneuver. Not an organizational power maneuver per sé, it represents an expansion of the spiritual variety through the abstract addition of historical time. According to this latter innovation, the humanitarian authority transcends spiritual authority by claiming to speak for all generations of mankind (not just the current one). Although the past and future might seem like different worlds, the two are intimately intertwined within our minds. Scientists refer to the brain's ability to think about the past, present, and future as *chronesthesia*, or mental time travel. In recent studies, neuroscientists have discovered that we use many of the same regions of the brain to remember the past as we do to envision the future. This dependence on foresight may explain why we form memories in the first place. Indeed, episodic memory may have arose in part due to the fact it helped individuals make good survival decisions.

Although humanitarian authority is quick to acknowledge the inherent immediacy of spiritual authority, on a grander time-scale the humanitarian perspective will always prevail. Its extreme range of generality precludes its identification with any singular social institution; rather its banner is typically incorporated into the religious (and sometimes political) framework of society as a whole. The truest appeal for humanitarian authority hinges upon mankind's enduring fascination with culture and tradition, giving homage to the progressive nature of the collective human spirit. During classical times when the rate of technological change was typically negligible over the course of generations, such humanitarian con-

cerns rated far less prestige than currently enjoyed today. In particular, the Roman style of political administration served as the dominant humanitarian perspective throughout the late classical age, maintaining a stable platform of peace and prosperity over the course of many generations.

The eventual decline of the Western Roman Empire, however, ushered in a radical shift in such classical perspectives. Its standard-bearer status (by default) reverted to the Roman Catholic Church, an unlikely outcome in light of the latter's humble beginnings. From its very inception, Christianity professed only the most limited of historical perspectives, its founding generation fully expecting to witness the Second Coming of the Lord. A vicious series of persecutions (including the destruction of Jerusalem) were further interpreted as prophetic signs of Christ's imminent return. In fact, Christ's closing words to the faithful in the apocalyptic *Book of Revelation* states: "I am coming soon."

Following several centuries of desperate survival, Christianity miraculously found itself in a position of prominence within the Roman Empire. This placed the Church Fathers in the awkward position of reinterpreting scripture to meet the demands of an enduring spiritual institution. By accepting the power ceded to it from the Romans, the Church underwent a dramatic period of growth and consolidation within its ranks. In the interest of Church unity the Emperor Constantine called the First Ecumenical Council at Nicea in 325 CE in an attempt to reconcile differing scriptural interpretations. Indeed, the term "ecumenical" derives from the Greek *oikoumene* (of the inhabited world), presaging all such doctrinal councils to follow.

The sack of Rome by Alaric, King of the Goths in 410 CE precipitated a further series of crises for the fledgling Church. For most of the classical era the Roman Empire had reigned supreme as the paragon of law, order, and stability. Pagan reactionaries seized upon Rome's downfall to denounce the Church, blaming Christianity's preoccupation with pacifism and asceticism for undermining the regimented solidarity of the Empire. These serious charges were formally addressed by St. Augustine of Hippo (354-430) in his treatise *The City of God*. In this seminal work both grace and free-will emerge as prominent humanitarian themes. In particular, this pairing of ecumenical ideals appears tailor-made for satisfying two of the four dimensions predicted for the humanitarian authority perspective. Their traditional context certainly betrays such an enduring focus: with grace denoting the humanitarian refinement of providence, whereas free-will makes a similar correspondence to the spiritual prerequisites underlying liberty.

The remaining two dimensions prove somewhat more problematic, although clues abound within the classical literature. Ideally, the final two terms should represent more abstract (humanitarian) analogues of the more basic concepts of civility and austerity (specific to the spiritual authority role). The closely related concepts of magnanimity and equanimity directly come to mind, clearly suggestive of a higher-order correspondence to civility and austerity. In this latter respect, *magnanimity* represents the humanitarian counterpart for civility, whereas *equanimity* denotes a similar refinement of austerity, effectively rounding out the predicted four-part complement of humanitarian authority terms.

This cohesive grouping of grace, free-will, magnanimity, and equanimity is most appropriately termed the class of *ecumenical* ideals: whereby alluding to the enduring spirit of the early ecumenical councils. In particular, this theme has undergone a significant revival as of late, chiefly through the efforts of a broad coalition of Protestant denominations: a major proponent of the ecumenical movement around the world. The Protestant sense of the term certainly proves relevant here; with grace, free-will, magnanimity, and equanimity all figuring prominently in the teachings of Protestant Reformation, including those of Martin Luther. This enduring listing of authority ideals represents an immediately-active class of motivational perspectives that anticipate the future-directed complement of follower roles. Generally speaking, the humanitarian authority themes immediately initiate the conditioned interaction in anticipation of the potentiality characterizing the subsequent representative member of humanity perspectives.

THE CLASSICAL GREEK VALUES: THE ROLE OF THE HUMANITARIAN FOLLOWER

The ecumenical ideals offer a preliminary overview of the motivational dynamics governing the humanitarian authority perspective. In keeping with such a grand humanitarian time-scale, each of the ecumenical ideals figures prominently in the long-standing tradition of ecumenical councils. This timeless quality of the ecumenical ideals certainly fits a common stereotype; namely, enduring themes fittingly in harmony with such a grand humanitarian perspective. This formidable style of humanitarian power-base allows the humanitarian authority to overrule any of the more immediate concerns expressed by the spiritual disciple, whereby regaining the upper hand in the perpetual power struggle. Even an authority perspective as abstract as the humanitarian, however, (by definition) is invested with its own unique form of follower counter-maneuver: in this case, that relating to the humanitarian follower.

True to its extreme level of abstraction, the humanitarian follower perspective reciprocally complements its authority counterpart, maintaining an equal balance of power within the humanitarian realm. Consequently, it shares the distinctive style of "strike" leverage previously described for the lower levels culminating in an unprecedented 4th-order level of meta-abstraction. In this more advanced sense, the humanitarian follower informs the humanitarian authority that the sanction from all of humanity is critical for maintaining the latter's authority status. Technically speaking, we can all speak as representatives of humanity within such a grand humanitarian time-scale. This inherent degree of flexibility was suggested earlier in this chapter, where the authority role was defined as more of a policy-making strategy than any immediate style of power maneuver. The representative member of humanity, therefore, maintains the option of rejecting humanitarian policy; whereby ensuring an equal balance of power across the entire range of humanity.

More properly termed the "philosophers" maneuver, this distinctive style of follower strategy downplays the strike-tactic altogether in favor of the prestige involved in speaking for all of humanity. Indeed, the philosopher role has long been revered for critical reasoning and crucial insights into universal truths. In the spirit of the stirring classical injunction: "Know Thyself," philosophy has painstakingly refined the collective wisdom of humanity over the span of countless generations. Philosophy is primarily eclectic in nature, drawing deeply from the rich wellspring of accumulated wisdom and truth.

This enduring interpretation necessarily suggests the existence of a remaining class of follower themes, although both major categories of virtue (e.g., the cardinal and theological) have already been accounted for within the ethical hierarchy. This basically only leaves the remaining listing of classical Greek values as the most effective adjunct for designating the humanitarian follower perspective. The respective grouping of beauty, truth, and goodness represents one of philosophy's most time-honored traditions: perpetuating the more immediate ethical focus of the virtues, with the exception that the more enduring theme of *values* is now called into focus. It ultimately remained to the genius of Plato to unite these concepts into a unified cohesive context, much as had already been accomplished with respect to the cardinal virtues.

According to his dialogue *Parmenides*, Plato speculates on the existence of absolute forms (or values) that convey our understanding of the beautiful, the good, and the true. As organizational principles, they impart an overarching sense of order to our varying perceptual experiences. In his masterpiece *The Republic*, Plato further makes an analogy between *goodness* and the sun: for just as the sun provides light for the physical world, so goodness offers illumination on a moral plane. Indeed, Plato specifically distinguishes goodness as the supreme primal form that unifies all of the lesser forms.

Although this cohesive grouping of beauty, truth, and goodness appears tailor-made for designating the first three dimensions predicted for the humanitarian follower perspective, it still remains one term short of satisfying the complete quartet. This shortfall is fortunately remedied through the addition of the affiliated theme of *wisdom*. Due to its superficial resemblance to the cardinal virtue of prudence, wisdom consistently appears to have been overlooked in the traditional listing of the classical Greek values. In particular, wisdom suggests more of a humanitarian focus, in direct contrast to the more elementary group focus of prudence. Plato appears to suggest precisely such a distinction: distinguishing between the wisdom of the social environment and that of the philosopher in his stoic pursuit of the truth. Plato's student, Aristotle proposed an even sharper distinction: with practical wisdom (prudence) more closely related to social matters, whereas speculative wisdom (*sophia*) pursues truth for its own sake: namely, the universal principles underlying all human experience. Indeed,

according to Alfred Lord Tennyson: "Knowledge comes, but *wisdom* lingers."

In affirmation of these historical perspectives, only the latter (humanitarian) sense of wisdom effective rounds-out the four-part listing of classical Greek values. In this collective sense, *beauty* represents the humanitarian counterpart of faith, whereas *truth* makes a similar analogy to hope. Furthermore, *goodness* directly expands upon the theological virtue of charity, whereas *wisdom* makes a similar correspondence to decency.

THE MOTIVATIONAL INTERPLAY FOR THE HUMANITARIAN REALM

As previously described for the spiritually-focused listings of civil-liberties and theological virtues, the more abstract groupings of ecumenical ideals and classical Greek values exhibit a similar dual degree of specialization: the latter subdivided into either immediately active authority roles occurring within the present and passively-potential follower roles projected into a future-directed time-frame. The immediately active authority roles are defined in terms of the ecumenical ideals, invested with clear behavioral overtones; namely, a providential sense of *gracefulness* or a libertarian sense of *free-will*, as well as a civil sense of *magnanimity*, or an austere sense of *equanimity*. The future-directed follower perspectives, in turn, target the more abstract potential realm of the classical Greek values: namely, *beauteous*-faith, just-hope for the *truth*, charitable-*goodness*, and decent-*wisdom*. These projected follower themes directly complement the immediately-active focus of the authority roles within the overall humanitarian dynamic. For instance, in the case of positive reinforcement, the providently-graceful treatment on the part of the humanitarian authority further anticipates the beauteously-faithful treatment on the part of the representative member of humanity. The latter beauteous sense of faithfulness, in turn, is eventually actualized as the civilly-magnanimous treatment on the part of the reinforcer in anticipation of the charitable sense of goodness on the part of the follower figure.

A similar style of motivational interplay further holds true for the affiliated realm of negative reinforcement. For instance the libertarian sense of free-will (on the part of the humanitarian authority figure), in turn, anticipates the just-hope for the truth on the part of the representative member of humanity. This latter-mentioned just-hope for the truth, in turn, is eventually actualized as the austere sense of equanimity on the part of the reinforcer in anticipation of the decent sense of wisdom on the part of the follower figure. The remainder of the current chapter aims to examine this dual humanitarian dynamic encompassing the complete eight-part complement of terms, providing a sturdy conceptual foundation for all subsequent classes of virtuous-values to follow.

Following the pattern of discussion previously described for the personal, group, and universal domains, it would be tempting to employ a similar style of strategy: namely, examining both the humanitarian authority and follow roles in tandem with one another in terms of a two-stage motivational dynamic. With respect to the current humanitarian focus, this amounts to the rewarding sequence of grace, beauty, magnanimity and goodness: followed by the negative reinforcement sequence of free-will, truth, equanimity and wisdom. The respective fourth-order level of abstraction, however, ultimately begins to obscure the orderly pattern of procurement *then* reinforcement previously established for the subordinate levels, although the pattern still remains partially in evidence.

Indeed, illustrative examples for the predicted interplay of the humanitarian authority and the humanitarian follower roles prove similarly elusive in scope, unlike the more clear-cut range of examples for the preceding three authority levels. Indeed, the extreme level of generality associated with the humanitarian realm precludes its identification with any singular social institution; rather typically incorporated into the religious (and sometimes political) framework of society as a whole. The truest appeal of humanitarian authority hinges upon mankind's enduring fascination with ritual and tradition, offering homage to the progressive nature of the collective human spirit tempered by the forward-looking themes of conservation and renewable economics.

Despite this extreme range of restrictions, a similar pattern of presentation for the humanitarian themes is currently proposed; namely, examining both the humanitarian authority and follow roles in tandem with one another employing a two-stage motivational dynamic (although specific illustrative examples will be omitted from the current chapter). This dual pattern of presentation provides a more balanced and overarching overview conducive to a general understanding of the unified ethical hierarchy, further validated in terms of their respective literary traditions.

GRACE - BEAUTY

The more straightforward class of positive values proves to be the most logical initiation point for such a grand-scale analysis, being that positive rewards appear much more cogent in contrast to the vaguer concept of leniency. The interplay of grace and beauty will be examined first, followed by the remaining sequence of magnanimity and goodness. As suggested in the overarching virtuous foundations for the respective humanitarian terms, the overall range of inquiry encompasses a much broader range of interplay than that previously described for the preceding three (more concretely-focused) authority levels.

As initially suggested, the provident sense of gracefulness actively expressed by the humanitarian authority figure initiates the conditioned interaction, expressed as the solicitous quest for rewarding reinforcement anticipated with respect to the humanitarian follower role. Being that only one role can be active within the conditioned interaction at any given time, the role of the reinforcer is relegated to a future potentiality, identified as the beauteously-faithful treatment on the part of the representative member of humanity. According to this humanitarian authority/follower dynamic, the humanitarian authority initiates the conditioned interaction, providently acting gracefully in anticipation of the beauteously-faithful treatment on the part of the follower figure. This latter beauteously-faithful perspective ultimately imparts meaning and purpose to the humanitarian authority's initial providentially-graceful role. Indeed, this projected sense of potentiality ultimately defines the specifics of the humanitarian follower role; being that all will have been for naught should such a beauteously-faithful treatment fail to come to pass.

The first mentioned ecumenical ideal of *grace* certainly fits the bill in this humanitarian respect, traditionally defined as divine protection or favor bestowed from On High. Its modern spelling derives from the Latin *gratia* (favor, kindness), from *gratus* (pleasing, agreeable). The classical Romans divinely worshipped this theme as the Gratiae (Graces), a trio of sister goddesses tending to the adornment of Venus. Indeed, the Romans sometimes referred to grace as *venia* in allusion to the handmaidens' unparalleled favor in the eyes of Venus. Although the Graces commanded only a limited cult following in Rome, they were more widely worshipped in their native Greece as the *Charites*: from the Greek *charis* (grace), also a root-stem for charisma. This derivation only superficially conforms to the theme of charity, the latter deriving from the Latin *caritas*.

The Charites traditionally represented the Greek ideal of the good life, particularly life's more festive aspects. The Greeks joyously celebrated these qualities in the naming of their three sister goddesses; namely, Aglaia (splendor and brilliance), Thalia (bloom and abundance), and Euphrosyne (joy and mirth). These three sisters were said to preside over banquets and social engagements, giving charm to all that made life joyous and beautiful. The Charites were also closely affiliated with the Muses, sharing the latter's penchant for music, art, and poetry.

The Graces, accordingly, are depicted as beautiful young maidens dancing in a circular pattern within a meadow in keeping with their traditional role as nature goddesses. Their most ancient shrine was located at Orchomenos in Greece, adjacent to a temple dedicated to Dionysus and a spring sacred to Aphrodite (both cited in the parentage of the Graces). Ancient stone images of the Charites were enshrined here, said to have fallen miraculously from the heavens. Their annual feast day was celebrated nearby with musical contests and dancing staged in their honor.

Grace is also celebrated as a major theme in the Judeo-Christian tradition. The opening passages of the Old Testament proclaim the Jews as the chosen people of God, a blessing stemming from the Lord's founding promise to Abraham (Genesis 12:2-3) and His subsequent covenant with Moses on Mt. Sinai (Exodus 33:19). The end of the Old Testament period, however, ushered in a more personalized perspective on God's grace; now viewed as a gift freely bestowed upon all those that kept His Commandments.

This personalized perspective on God's grace eventually carried over into New Testament scripture. The original Greek NT versions specifically translate grace as *charis* (referring to objects of joy or delight). It is chiefly through the writings of the St. Paul, however, that the Christian sense of the term reaches its most enduring significance. In 1st Corinthians, Chapter *12*, St. Paul directly intimates that the *charismatic* gifts (namely, prophecy, healing, and speaking-in-tongues) are but outward manifestations of this indwelling grace from God. Furthermore, these Gifts of Grace are chiefly made available through faith (Romans 4:16), the devotion of the believer proving crucial to such divine intervention. Here the humanitarian authority providentially acts graceful towards his respective follower figure in anticipation of the latter's beauteously-faithful treatment. In response to this beauteous treatment on the part of humanitarian follower, the humanitarian authority remains reciprocally dependent within such a grand humanitarian time-scale: any providential-gracefulness now entirely meaningless without such potential reinforcement.

The latter positive allusions to reinforcement are clearly specified for the enduring humanitarian theme of *beauty*. In contrast to the solicitous prerequisites initially described for gracefulness, beauty further targets that potential range of positive reinforcement projected within a future-directed time-frame. Its modern spelling traces its origins to the Latin *bellitas*, from the root-stem *bellus* (pretty or pleasing). The classical Greeks particularly revered physical beauty and perfection, qualities their gods and goddesses exhibited to an outstanding degree. The goddess Aphrodite was particularly singled out as the divine personification of love, beauty, and fertility. Her ethereal status among the gods derived from the claim that she was born upon the waves and foam of sea, from the Greek *aphros* (foam). She is depicted as a lightly-draped figure of uncompromising grace and beauty. An ancient armless statue of her (the Venus de Milo) was named for its discovery on the remote Greek isle of Melos.

The Roman counterpart of Aphrodite, *Venus*, originally appears to have been Italian goddess associated with vegetable gardens, whereby promoting their fertility. Her Latin name eventually became synonymous with charm and beauty, a key factor in her identification with the Greek traditions of Aphrodite. The legendary beauty of Venus was directly symbolized by her chief attribute, the Cestus (an elaborately embroidered girdle).

These mythological interpretations of beauty find direct parallels to the aesthetic principles underscoring classical Greek philosophy. According to early Greek tradition, beauty represents an external attribute of a given object, a property intrinsic to its very physical make-up. According to the writings of Plato and Aristotle, beauty resides in a regularity of form and function: as further expressed in symmetry, proportion, and harmony. Our modern age of ethical subjectivism, however, changed the face of aesthetics forever, as evident in the contemporary maxim: "Beauty is in the eye of the beholder." This radical interpretation was directly championed by the empiricists, who viewed beauty as any agreeable aesthetic experience of a reinforcing nature. Indeed, some empiricists postulated the existence of a special "sixth sense" attuned to beauty, whereby governing the appreciation of all such pleasurable experience. These themes are retained in the subjectivist theories of our modern age, with beauty defined as that sensory experience that evokes a positive emotional response, particularly in an appealing visual sense. Indeed, as the great English poet, John Keats fittingly wrote: "A thing of beauty is a joy forever."

Final mention must necessarily be made concerning the dual interplay of the main and accessory terms. This formally entails replacing the *main* motivational terms with their respective *accessory* counterparts, essentially close in meaning to one another. Here your bountiful-blessing of me in anticipation of my charming-devotion for you is substituted for the main complement of terms: e.g., my providently-graceful treatment in anticipation of your beauteous-faith in me. In more formal terms, you (as humanitarian authority) now bountifully-*bless* me in anticipation of my (as representative member of humanity) *charming*-devotion for you. In essence, this dual interplay of both main and accessory terms ensures that the dual complement of procurement and reinforcement roles encompass the full range of objective/subjective potentialities.

MAGNANIMITY - GOODNESS

The completed description of grace and beauty, in turn, gives way to the discussion of the remaining sequence completing the humanitarian dynamic: namely, magnanimity and goodness. According to this latter scenario, the reinforcer eventually acts upon his (projected) beauteous sense of faithfulness, whereby civilly acting magnanimously in anticipation of the charitable determination to act with goodness on the part of the follower figure. A number of key features become apparent with respect to this initial magnanimous phase. As the respective humanitarian counterpart for the spiritually-focused theme of civility, magnanimity certainly proves adequate to the task. Its modern spelling derives from the Latin *magnanimus* (greatness of soul), from *magnus* (great) and *animus* (soul). It is traditionally defined as nobility of mind or spirit that graciously overlooks insult or injury. Magnanimity was particularly revered during the classical age, specifically singled out by Aristotle in his principle listing of the virtues. This theme also finds expression in the Judeo-Christian tradition, as in the parable describing the slaughter of the fatted calf (Luke 15:23) or the opening of a chest of precious ointment (Mathew 26:8-13). A similar theme occurs in OT Book of Ecclesiastes (11:1) which states: "Cast thy bread upon the waters, for thou shalt find it after many days," signifying generosity that transcends any personal concerns.

Magnanimity signifies the inclination to reward exemplary courage or skill, often to an extravagant degree. Such noble characteristics also endear it as one of the chief attributes of royalty and nobility. In the heraldic symbolism of the Middle Ages, magnanimity is represented as a triumphant eagle depicted in the act of sparing a portion of its kill for the lesser birds of prey that hover around the eagle in a solicitous fashion. Contrast this to the human condition, where those in positions of power and authority consistently strive to preserve some measure of their exalted status through the erection of a stone memorial durably built to stand the test of time. Indeed, many such grand monuments survive from ancient times, standing mute testimony to the magnificence of the commemorated leader as well as the painstaking labor of the supportive cast of artisans. Here the humanitarian authority civilly behaves in a magnanimous fashion in anticipation of the charitable sense of goodness on the part of the humanitarian follower figure. This overarching magnanimous context encourages a consistent degree of incentive over a grand humanitarian time-scale, an aspect conducive to the longstanding traditions of goodness and flourishing.

The latter goodly-charitable perspective certainly rings true in this basic respect, gaining its chief placement through the subsequent consummation of the entire humanitarian interchange. In more formal terms, I (as representative member of humanity) now charitably aim to act with goodness towards you in response to your (as my humanitarian authority) civilly-magnanimous treatment of me. This distinctive style of motivational interplay particularly reflects the characteristic "if you then I" motivational dynamic governing the entire conditioned interchange.

Goodness is traditionally invested with a rather broad range of meaning consistent with its generalized applications within the field of ethical inquiry. Its modern spelling derives from the Anglo-Saxon *god* (denoting goodness). The Latin tradition is alternately identified with *bonitas*, the same root-stem for benevolence. In direct contrast to truth and beauty, goodness is not limited to any single classical deity, rather an indwelling quality of gods and goddesses in general. Although many of the classical gods were not above a certain degree of spirited combativeness, they were generally regarded as morally upright and good at heart.

Certain of the classical deities exemplified this quality to a supreme degree; namely, the Roman god Bonus Eventus (literally, good event). Bonus Eventus originally was worshipped as an agricultural deity, whose rituals determined the success or failure of the harvest. His scope eventually extended into close association with Fortuna (the Roman goddess of fortune). Surviving statues depict Bonus Eventus as a youthful figure

The Feather of Truth: Balancing Heart on the Scales of Justice
Detail from the Egyptian Papyrus of Ani   © - The British Museum

offering a libation toast at the foot of a sacrificial altar. He holds stalks of grain in his free hand indicative of his agricultural origins.

Perhaps the most stirring applications of goodness concern the Christian teachings on the subject, particularly those relating to the parable of the Good Samaritan, a story proclaiming the value of love for one's neighbor. Here goodness represents a projected style of humanitarian follower perspective indicative of its more elementary foundations in charity. This benevolent impulse underscores the most salient feature of goodness: namely, its bestowal as its own reward without regard for material gain (in keeping with such a grand humanitarian time-scale). Indeed, this tenuous power of potentiality ultimately justifies the reciprocity inherent within the authority/follower interaction, the former depending upon the latter to provide ultimate meaning and fulfillment.

Final mention must necessarily be made concerning the dual interplay of both the main and accessory terms. This formally entails replacing the *main* motivational terms with their respective *accessory* counterparts, essentially close in meaning of one another. Here the accessory pairing of terms (my courteous sense of graciousness in anticipation of your benevolent sense of kindness) is substituted for the main complement of terms (your civilly-magnanimous treatment of me in expectation of my charitable sense of goodness). According to this accessory modification, I (as

humanitarian authority) now courteously act *graciously* towards you in anticipation of your (as representative member of humanity) *benevolent* sense of kindness towards me. This dual interplay of main and accessory perspectives ensures that the respective listing of procurement and reinforcement roles encompass the full spectrum of objective/subjective potentialities.

FREE-WILL - TRUTH

In summary, the completed description of the two-stage sequences of grace-beauty and magnanimity-goodness offers a comprehensive overview of the motivational dynamics at issue within the humanitarian style of interaction. The ultimate goal for this exercise has been to propose a sturdy conceptual foundation for the virtuous realm, providing an overarching model of value ethics in general. Before skipping ahead to this further range of applications, it ultimately proves crucial to examine the motivational interplay of values targeting the remaining realm of negative reinforcement. Negative reinforcement entails the deliberate withholding of punitive consequences within the environment or (in an interpersonal sense) leniency in response to aversive types of behavior.

In terms of a humanitarian social context, the humanitarian authority figure freely-willed acts in a libertarian fashion in anticipation of the just-hope for the truth professed on the part of

71

the humanitarian follower. This latter-mentioned just-hope for the truth, in turn, eventually becomes actualized as the austere sense of equanimity on the part of the reinforcer in anticipation of the decent sense of wisdom on the part of the follower figure. Certainly it might appear somewhat risky to exhibit such an extreme degree of equanimity without a reasonable assurance of upcoming cooperation on the part of the follower. Past memory cycles certainly come into play justifying such a radical act of trust.

The humanitarian theme of free-will definitely enters into consideration here, defined as the chief humanitarian variation in relation to the libertarian sense of honor previously ascribed to the universal realm. Indeed, this libertarian sense of free-will provides the motivational rationale for the just-hope for the truth anticipated from the representative member of humanity. The modern spelling of free-will derives from a literal translation of the Late-Latin *liberum arbitrium* (literally, free decision). In keeping with its compound character, free-will has traditionally been assigned a rather broad range of meanings: from motivation and will, to necessity and determination. Its modern spelling suggests somewhat of a redundancy, for the component themes of freedom and will are often employed interchangeably in terms of common usage.

In a traditional sense, the doctrine of free-will was originally devised to defend against the argument that God had the power to prevent the occurrence of evil in the world. According to this free-will defense, God allows mankind to be tempted by evil in order to freely elect to resist (or yield) to it. The wrathful punishment awaiting the wicked adds further fuel to the controversy, for God surely is able to circumvent sin without necessarily resorting to outright punishment. Various Church theologians have attempted to reinterpret this paradox, shifting the blame for sin to mankind's inherent weakness. Here the Church was able to blame the fall of Adam and Eve (and not any flaw in God's master plan) for the ever-present consequences of the evil that occurs throughout the world.

In a complementary fashion, the humanitarian follower figure now justly hopes for the truth in direct response to his authority figure's libertarian sense of free-will. This lenient connotation for truth shares much in common with the related theme of beauty. Indeed, Keats is further credited with the stirring quotation: "Beauty is truth, truth is beauty," attesting to the figurative association linking the two. Its modern spelling derives the Anglo Saxon *treowth* (of similar meaning and us-

age). Its related Latin counterpart, *veritas*, survives primarily in terms of the English synonyms verity, veracity, etc. In fact, Veritas was specifically worshipped as a deity by the ancients, described as the daughter of Saturn and the Mother of Virtue. She is portrayed as a youthful virgin draped in white exhibiting an overarching air of modesty. The Greek philosopher Democritus describes her as hiding at the bottom of a well hinting at the great difficulty with which she is found.

Such classical considerations beg further mention of the related legends associated with Diogenes, a Greek contemporary of Aristotle. Diogenes is traditionally credited as the founder of Cynicism, a philosophical movement named for its attempts to discredit the lofty pretensions of the elite of Athens. Diogenes earned the reputation as somewhat of an eccentric, advocating a "back to nature" form of ascetic lifestyle often bordering upon the absurd. His most prominent claim to fame concerns the fanciful legends surrounding his search for "the honest man." His quest was said to have taken him through the streets of Athens holding aloft a lantern in broad daylight, a feature further indicative of the futile nature of such an endeavor.

According to this fanciful legend, Diogenes clearly assumes the role of the representative member of humanity: a status clearly befitting the serious philosopher of his day. His persistent quest for the truth further narrows the focus, directly emphasizing the leniently-moralistic aspects of the legend. The distinctive lantern symbolism of the tale lends further credence to the discovery function of truth. Indeed, lamps of various styles are incorporated into the seals of many great universities, accentuating their unswerving devotion to the truth. A similar correspondence is further seen with respect to beauty, which (in analogy to truth) is perceived entirely through the eye of the beholder.

Truth is experienced as a never-ending quest, the search for the honest man directly targeting those deserving of lenient treatment within such a grand humanitarian time-scale. Curiously, the legendary honest man always eludes Diogenes, for in the sage opinion of Albert Einstein: "The search for *truth* is more precious than its possession." Along similar lines, philosopher George Santayana further writes: "The *truth* is all things seen under the form of eternity," a speculation particularly in keeping with the grand humanitarian prerequisites for truth. In more formal terms you (as representative member of humanity) justly-hope for the truth in reaction to my (as humanitarian authority) libertarian sense of freewill.

Similar to the case of the main and accessory terms relating to positive reinforcement, a parallel dynamic is further expressed with respect to negative reinforcement. This formally entails replacing the *main* motivational terms with their respective *accessory* counterparts, essentially closely related in meaning. Here the accessory pairing of terms (your free sense of conscientiousness in anticipation of my fair sense of credence) is substituted for the main complement of terms (my libertarian sense of free-will in expectation of your just-hope for the truth). In slightly different terms, you (as humanitarian authority) now freely act in a *conscientious* fashion towards me in anticipation of my (as representative member of humanity) fair sense of *credence* in you. According to this empathically-based accessory format, the "you" and "I" roles are now reversed, effectively ensuring the full range of objective/subjective potentialities.

EQUANIMITY - WISDOM

The preceding two-stage dynamic of free-will and truth, in turn, dictates that the humanitarian follower eventually acts upon the potentiality implicit to his/her just-hope for truth. This latter development now takes the form of austerely acting with equanimity within an immediately-active time-frame, whereby anticipating the (projected) decent sense of wisdom on the part of the follower figure. Indeed, this inherent power of deliberation directly imparts the power leverage enjoyed in terms of the equanimity perspective. Indeed, equanimity directly parallels the affiliated theme of magnanimity with the exception that leniency (rather than approval) is now called into focus. Accordingly, magnanimity and equanimity are often employed in quite similar contexts. This clear degree of overlap is betrayed in terms of their common linguistic origins: magnanimity specifying "a greatness of mind," whereas equanimity equates with "an evenness of mind." The latter term derives from the Latin *aequus* (equal) and *animus* (mind), formally reflecting its traditional connotations of mental composure and/or calm demeanor. Just as magnanimity imparted a more enduring quality to civility, so equanimity adds a similar humanitarian focus to austerity.

This timeless quality of equanimity further emerges as a prominent theme in classical philosophy, most notably the traditions associated with Stoicism. Here Zeno of Citium founded Stoicism in the city of Athens lecturing his students from a *stoa* (or porch). The stoic individual accepts what cannot be changed, stomaching adversity with an austere sense of equanimity. The subsequent rise of the Christian era presaged the decline of pagan Stoicism, although many of its nobler themes became incorporated into later Church Canon. This austere sense of equanimity was particularly revered by the early ascetic orders, offering hope and inspiration in the face of the tribulations accompanying the Dark Ages. Equanimity, accordingly, was revered as the emblem of the long-suffering medieval knight through the aid of heraldic symbolisms similar to those cited for magnanimity. The noble knight represents a fitting exemplar of equanimity, pledging a lifetime of service and fealty to his feudal lord regardless of personal hardship.

Although the heraldic symbolisms for magnanimity took the form of a regal eagle, equanimity is more prosaically portrayed as the domestic ass: a beast of burden symbolizing patience and perseverance under even the most trying of circumstances. Equanimity is also symbolized as the humble beaver, a beast that patiently labors to maintain its constructions under the most formidable of circumstances. Whether one alludes to the industrious beaver or the patient ass, these enduring qualities of equanimity are unmistakable in terms of their intent: an enduring refinement of austerity wholly emblematic of such a grand humanitarian perspective. Consequently, this humanitarian focus on equanimity leniently endeavors to reinforce the (anticipated) decent sense of wisdom on the part of the representative member of humanity. Indeed, this overarching sense of equanimity promotes a leniently-assured environment conducive to global peace and harmony. Equanimity thusly extends the more basic (universal) theme of austerity into the even more abstract humanitarian sphere of influence.

In terms of this two-stage motivational dynamic, the enduring humanitarian overtones for equanimity are subsequently consummated with respect to the remaining classical Greek value of wisdom. Similar to its motivational counterpart in goodness, wisdom alternately provides an effective sense of closure to the entire humanitarian interchange. Here I (as representative member of humanity) now will decently act in a wise fashion towards you in response to your (as humanitarian authority) austere sense of equanimity.

In a traditional sense, *wisdom* enjoys a status virtually unparalleled within the field of ethical inquiry. Its modern spelling derives from a compound of two Anglo-Saxon words *wis-* (way or manner) and *dom* (state) collectively designating sound moral judgment and common sense. The classical Romans divinely worshipped this quality as their abstract goddess Sapientia (Latin for Lady-Wisdom). She is traditionally depicted as a Siren of Philosophies rising from the sea in a style reminiscent of Aphrodite, pouring-out the "wine of enlightenment" from her bosom. Indeed, the Latin proper name for the human species, *Homo sapiens*, literally translates as "wise man." The related Greek root *sophia* suggests a parallel scope of inquiry, as evident in the English derivations of Sophism, sophistication, etc. Plato's disdain for the elite Sophists (or paid philosophers) of his day appears to have further contributed to the omission of wisdom in his traditional canon of classical Greek values. Consequently, wisdom was viewed as more of a virtue than a value, equivalent to the cardinal virtue of prudence.

Perhaps of even greater import is the Wisdom Literature of the Jewish tradition, particularly the Old Testament Books of *Proverbs* and *Psalms*. As the traditional author of the book of *Proverbs*, King Solomon is revered as the wisest in a long line of biblical monarchs. Solomon proved particularly well suited to the duties of his royal upbringing, widely celebrated for his legendary cleverness and wisdom. His penchant for clever manipulation figured prominently in his celebrated seduction of the visiting Queen of Sheba. Indeed, his shrewd political acumen was chiefly instrumental in ushering in a golden age of trade and commerce, leading to the construction of the First Jewish Temple in Jerusalem.

King Solomon's most prominent reputation for wisdom was recorded in his routine courtly pronouncements, when he assumed an active role in settling disputes amongst his subjects. The Old Testament describes a conflict between two women seeking audience before the king, both claiming the same newborn child. Solomon shrewdly feigned the prospect of cleaving the disputed child in two, whereby determining the true mother through her emotional plea to forgo such drastic measures. This shrewd insight into human nature clearly validates King Solomon's fitting status as a true humanitarian visionary. The decent sense of wisdom he so effortlessly dispensed reflects a degree of common sense so crucial to such a humanitarian perspective. In truth, we are all heirs to the Wisdom of Solomon, a sage mixture of decency and wisdom crucial to the trials of everyday experience.

Final mention must necessarily be made with respect to the dual interplay of the main and accessory terms. This formally entails replacing the *main* virtuous terms with their respective *accessory* counterparts, essentially close linguistic synonyms of one another. Here the accessory pairing of terms (my forbearingly-patient treatment of you in anticipation of your scrupulous sense of shrewdness) is now substituted for the main complement of terms (your austere sense of equanimity in anticipation of my decent sense of wisdom). According to this modified accessory format, I (as humanitarian authority) now forbearingly act *patiently* towards you in anticipation of your (as representative member of humanity) scrupulously-*shrewd* treatment of me. This dual interplay of main and accessory perspectives ensures that the procurement and reinforcement roles encompass the full range of objective/subjective potentialities.

In conclusion, the completed description of the humanitarian authority and follower roles proves a fitting counterpoint to all that has gone before. Indeed, the representative member of humanity role is one that we all share in common; spokespersons for all generations throughout history. Although this extreme degree of abstraction can prove quite daunting, we are all eligible to speak as philosophers of a sort through the eclectic listing of classical Greek values: beauty, truth, goodness, and wisdom. This crowning humanitarian realm would appear to close out any further additions to the ethical hierarchy, for there cannot be any level of organization greater than humanity as a whole. This very sense of the power of abstraction, however, serves as the basis for one final innovation within the ascending ethical hierarchy: namely, that range of influence specifying the crowning *transcendental* realm of authority and follower roles.

6

THE TRANSCENDENTAL PERSPECTIVE

The transcendental authority perspective has enjoyed a long and illustrious literary tradition with precedents dating at least to classical times. Its modern spelling derives from the Latin *transcendere* (to climb over), from *trans-* (over) and *scandere* (to climb. Medieval scholars freely adapted this theme in the field of Scholasticism: defining as *transcendentalia* (or *transcendentia*) extremely abstract concepts such as goodness, unity, being, etc. The modern sense of the term traces back to the writings of German philosopher Immanuel Kant, who laid the groundwork for his unique style of transcendental philosophy. In his masterpiece, *Critique of Pure Reason*, Kant directly acknowledges the transcendental philosophy of the ancients, although suggesting that his revised sense of the term only superficially conforms to the traditional sense. Indeed, Kant draws sharp distinctions between the notions of transcendence, the transcendental, and the immanent.

The realm of *transcendence* is said to apply to ideas beyond the range of direct sensory experience. The notion of *immanence*, in turn, refers to the concrete realm of sensory experience. The remaining concept of the *transcendental*, however, represents an intermediary position; namely, conceptual constructs implicit to sensory experience, although not directly arising from the senses. In particular, Kant distinguishes a broad range of transcendental categories (such as relation, causality, quantity, etc.) that intuitively serve to order sensory experience, although existing as mere formalities without sensory data to embody them. In this modified sense, all knowledge is preconditioned by such transcendental presuppositions forming the basis for the German school of transcendental idealism.

Kant's dynamic influence eventually reached the English speaking world chiefly through the writings of Samuel Taylor Coleridge and Thomas Carlyle. These interpretations eventually gained notice in the United States, flowering during the early 19th century as the eclectic movement known as New England Transcendentalism. This movement arose as a revolt against the skepticism characterizing British Rational Philosophy, as well as the dogmatism of Orthodox Protestantism. Ralph Waldo Emerson was the acknowledged leader of the movement. Other notables include Henry David Thoreau, Nathaniel Hawthorne, and Margaret Fuller. Although the New England movement was relatively short-lived, it was instrumental in influencing religious and social thought for generations to come. Despite the belief that social change was chiefly a matter of personal choice, many transcendentalists championed the major reform movements of the day; namely, peace, temperance, women's suffrage, and the abolition of slavery.

The strength of the movement declined with the onset of the Civil War coinciding with the retirement of Emerson and the death of Thoreau. A century later Dr. Martin Luther King Jr. acknowledged the influence that Thoreau's philosophy of civil disobedience played in the Civil Rights demonstrations of the 1960's. Indeed, these latter troubled times provide crucial clues towards identifying the four affective dimensions predicted for the transcendental authority perspective.

A MODERN-DAY REVIVAL OF TRANSCENDENTALISM

The war protest era of the early 70's was characterized by great political and moral upheaval, a trend the establishment found increasingly difficult to ignore. The great rallying cry was the protest against the Vietnam War, the mounting casualties discouraging support for what (even then) appeared to be a futile ideological endeavor. The peace movement evolved its own fraternal symbolisms; namely, the peace sign and the peace symbol (a dove's foot inscribed in a circle). The simultaneous availability of "the pill," in turn, ushered in a more relaxed sexual attitude, the practice of free love flourishing in "hippy" districts such as Haight-Ashbury. This self-styled peace-love generation prided itself on such non-conformist attitudes, looking to the unconventional practice of meditation and astrology for solutions to political turmoil, promoting the quest for inner peace and tranquility. The emerging Civil Rights movement further raised the pressing issue of racial equality, an issue deliberately grafted into the peace movement as yet another tactic to thwart the tyranny of the establishment. Blacks became "brothers" with whites in a stirring appeal to universal peace and brotherhood.

These four noble themes of the 70's (peace-love-tranquility-equality) collectively celebrate the transcendental focus of the age, a tradition sharing much in common with New England Transcendentalists. This enduring transcendental perspective proves particularly consistent with the reigning humanistic focus of our modern age, downplaying the dogmatism of orthodox religion in favor of individual conscience. This cohesive grouping of peace-love-tranquility-equality is more appropriately termed the class of *humanistic* values, directly expanding upon the humanitarian focus of the ecumenical ideals. In a more abstract sense, *peace* represents a transcendental modification of equanimity, whereas *love* attaches a similar significance to magnanimity. Furthermore, *tranquility* imparts a transcendental modification to grace, whereas *equality* expands upon the affiliated theme of free will.

In contrast to the pattern of discussion previously described for the group, spiritual, and humanitarian realms, the transcendental sphere of influence will employ a slightly different style of analysis. This fifth-order level of transcendental abstraction clearly begins to obscure the more orderly pattern of organization previously established for the subordinate levels. Despite these abstract shortcomings, the basic two-stage sequential pattern of authority roles follower remains essentially in focus, as in the positive sequence specified for tranquility, ecstasy, love, and joy: as well as the leniently-based sequence of equality, bliss, peace, and harmony. A custom pattern of presentation for the individual transcendental terms is, therefore, proposed: examining the transcendental themes as the crowning culmination of the entire span governing the virtuous hierarchy. For instance, joy is examined in terms of the subordinate concepts of charity and goodness, whereas love is defined with respect to

civility and magnanimity. Furthermore, ecstasy is examined in relation to faith and beauty, whereas tranquility exhibits a similar correspondence to providence/grace. A similar pattern of presentation further holds true with respect to the realm of transcendental perspectives based upon leniency. These comparisons prove relatively straightforward, being as the humanitarian realm shares many aspects in common with the crowning transcendental domain. Indeed, this final transcendental realm provides an overarching description of themes of a purely abstract nature, culminating in a seamless overview of the entire unified virtuous hierarchy.

PEACE

The first of the humanistic values to be examined, peace, represents a theme of virtually universal appeal. Peace was deliberately chosen to lead off this style of analysis providing the immediately-active lenient rationale for the subsequent expression of harmony on the part of transcendental follower. From the viewpoint of the transcendental authority, peace represents a leniently-active expansion upon the austere-equanimity that anticipates the wisely-harmonious treatment on the part of the respective follower figure. Consequently, peace extends the subordinate qualities of austerity and equanimity into a much broader transcendental sphere of influence.

The enduring traditions ascribed to peace endow this transcendental theme with a broad range of spiritual overtones. Its modern spelling derives from the Latin *pax* (peace) primarily in the context of the Pax Romana: the formal peace the Romans imposed upon subject provinces within its Empire. The Roman's self-appointed role of peacemaker was seen as a moral prerogative according to political theorists such as Virgil. Indeed, the Romans specifically worshipped this concept as their abstract goddess Pax, the divine personification of peace amongst the nations.

Pax represents a relatively late addition to the Roman pantheon, virtually unheard of before the time of Augustus. State support for her cult is generally credited with fostering the strength and stability of the Empire under Augustus. A Roman shrine was dedicated to Pax in 9 BCE in celebration of the restoration of peace by Augustus following his triumphant series of campaigns in Spain and Gaul. The widespread longing for peace contributed to Pax's great popularity among the common people during this period of civil unrest. Accordingly, Pax is portrayed as a youthful maiden holding a cornucopia in her left hand and an

Noah in the Ark: Welcoming Back the Dove of Peace
Detail from a Fresco in the Catacomb of St. Peter/St. Marcellinus - Rome - (3rd Century)

olive branch (the symbol of peace) in her right. She is sometimes depicted setting fire to a stock-stockpile of armaments in defiance to the prevailing militarism of the era. A major festival was held in her honor on the last day in April.

The Judeo-Christian tradition similarly celebrates the transcendental aspects of peace. The Hebrew word for peace, *Salom*, is directly related to the same root-stem for health and wholesomeness. The prophets of the Old Testament exalted peace as the promised blessing of the Messianic Age. In his Sermon on the Mount, Christ directly blesses the peacemakers, stating: "They shall be called children of God." The Apostle Paul, in turn, describes Christ's message as "the gospel of peace" (Ephesians 6:15). St. Paul also lists peace among the Gifts of the Holy Spirit. Indeed, it is fitting that the dove (as the chief symbolism of the Holy Spirit) figures so prominently in OT descriptions of peace, particularly the celebrated story of Noah and the Ark. Here the dove served as God's messenger, carrying an olive sprig in its beak symbolizing peaceful intent. Noah originally had released the dove during the Great Flood to see if it might successfully find landfall. The olive branch carried by the dove, in turn, signaled that

the ordeal had finally come to an end. In keeping with these stirring scriptural precedents, peace builds (in a transcendental fashion) upon the humanitarian prerequisites previously established for equanimity, terms sharing a common lenient focus in austerity. These grand-scale transcendental attributes for peace suggest precisely such an austere perspective, as exemplified in the offering of an olive branch during peace negotiations. The olive orchard required many years of tending to become fruitful signifying the peaceful cooperation required to reach fruition. Consequently, the dove and the olive branch are all revered as symbolisms of peace: emblems still employed today in the amicable settlement of disputes.

LOVE

The completed description of peace, in turn, begs mention of the related transcendental theme of *love*. Similar to peace, love represents the supremely abstract bestowal of reinforcement within the conditioned interaction. According to this transcendental authority perspective, love represents the civil expression of magnanimity in anticipation of the goodly sense of joyousness projected for the transcendental follower figure. Indeed, in terms of this overarching communicational dynamic, I (as transcendental authority) magnanimously act lovingly towards you in anticipation of your (as transcendental follower) goodly sense of joy towards me.

In keeping with such a crowning transcendental perspective, love extends the true measure of transcendence across all ages and cultures. Its modern spelling derives the Anglo-Saxon *lufu* (of similar meaning and usage). Although the English derivation has endured as its dominant form, the classical tradition is represented as the Latin *cupido* (passion, desire), as well as *amor* (love). Indeed, the Romans worshipped this theme in the guise of Cupid, their youthful god of love. In classical mythology, Cupid is traditionally depicted as an adorable winged cherub daintily equipped with a quiver and bow. The youngest of the Roman gods, he is described as callous and capricious even to his mother Venus. The gods Pothos and Himeros were his constant companions, the divine personifications of longing and desire. Jupiter graciously equipped Cupid with a pair of golden wings, a magical bow, and a quiver of arrows said never to miss their mark. These arrows were said to instill irresistible love in the hearts of all struck by them. One ancient legend suggests that Cupid whets with blood the grindstone upon which he sharpens his arrows. He is described as blind or blindfolded consistent with the contention that "love is blind."

These fanciful legends surrounding Cupid serve as the colorful basis for many modern-day symbolisms of love; e.g., a crimson heart pierced by an arrow (the traditional emblem of St. Valentine's Day). The modern-day conception of romantic love is actually of fairly recent vintage, in addition to the tradition of marriage purely for love's sake. Marriage solely for love at first was considered a scandalous novelty, in contrast to the prevailing moral mandate it currently enjoys today.

The modern age of romantic love was initially celebrated in the lyric poetry popularized by the troubadours of Southern France. This romantic exaltation of the passions eventually swept the continent, whereby celebrating the romantic ideal of chaste womanhood. This courtly expression of love transcended mere sexual passion, idealizing the chaste and inaccessible woman of fancy. The medieval lover was expected to serve his lady without recompense save the glowing warmth of her gracious approval. This elevated status of women eventually became reflected in other chivalrous themes; namely, a steadfast sense of loy-

alty to God, King, and Country. These noble themes of chastity and chivalry sought to control (rather than gratify) such amorous instincts. Romantic passion increased in direct proportion to the obstacles placed in its way. In this latter sense, love guides one to a nobler life, its trials and tribulations curiously suggestive of the ordeals of martyrdom (both of which transcend the self in the quest for a higher good).

As is true for so many of the great love stories from the past, love is seen to transcend all political and social barriers, a transcendental display of pure passion. In the case of Romeo and Juliet, their respective families were embroiled in a bitter blood feud lasting many generations, in direct contrast to the tender and loving passion shared by the young lovers. In similar fashion, Anthony and Cleopatra were the fateful offspring of opposing cultures, yet the flame of their love burned bright until tragically cut short. Here (as with Romeo and Juliet), the couple chose to die together in order to be joined again for all eternity, an extreme variation on the transcendental underpinnings for the love perspective.

TRANQUILITY

The completed description of peace and love, in turn, redirects the focus of this analysis to the remaining humanistic values of tranquility and equality. True to their order of introduction, tranquility will be described first, followed by a parallel discussion of equality. Both themes share commonalties with peace and love with the exception that they are now punctuated from a procurement (rather than reinforcement) perspective. In terms of this transcendental authority perspective, tranquility represents an immediately-active style of providential-gracefulness in anticipation of the beauteously-ecstatic treatment on the part of the respective follower figure.

The extremely abstract attributes associated with tranquility are virtually unprecedented within the transcendental realm. Its modern spelling derives the Latin *tranquillitas*, from *trans-* (beyond) and *quies* (rest). The use of the same prefix in the overall context of transcendentalism lends further credence to the overlapping significance of these two basic themes. The Romans worshipped tranquility as the abstract goddess Quies, the divine personification of calmness and tranquility. She is traditionally portrayed as a beautiful maiden in a relaxed pose, sometimes shown leaning upon a short marble column. Her chapel was located on the Via Labicana in Rome, a welcome refuge for the weary traveler. A private cult dedicated to Quies dates to the earliest days of the Republic, although official worship was not instituted until Imperial times. Following his surrender to Augustus, the rival Maximian had a medal of conciliation minted with the inscription "Quies Augustorum." A later series of coins incorporates the theme *tranquillitas* into the emperor's title of distinction.

The direct antithesis of such formal classicism extends to an appreciation of tranquility within the natural environment. Perhaps no experience is more exhilarating than a visit to a still mountain lake framed with majestic tall timber and permeated with an eternal hush completely at odds with the urban environment. This pristine natural setting peacefully transcends the more hectic pace of city life, offering an experience of virtually timeless proportions. This exalted devotion for nature was widely celebrated in the spirited works of the great English and German romanticists: namely, Goethe, Wordsworth, and Coleridge. They collectively celebrate an enhanced regard for the wonders of nature, in addition to an empathy for the workings underlying its divine order.

The subsequent dawning of the Industrial forever altered such a pastoral range of perspectives. Nature was now esteemed as a source of timber and coal for fueling the furnaces and steam engines of the day. Cities grew increasingly over-crowded and polluted, attracting many unskilled laborers from the countryside. Under such trying circumstances, tranquility was primarily achieved through chemical means: e.g., alcohol, opium, or other tranquilizers.

In keeping with the preceding nature example, tranquility is defined as an immediately active style of transcendental perspective true to its more elementary foundations in grace. The "tranquilizer" abuser habitually acts solicitously in order to achieve the calming rewards when the drug finally takes effect. Here, the sedative effect of the tranquilizer diminishes routine stresses in favor of tranquil feelings of serenity.

Drugs actually represent just one avenue towards achieving a calm disposition. The appreciation of music, art, and drama provide an effective release from everyday stressful routines: in addition to prayer, yoga, and meditation. The serene smile traditionally associated with depictions of the Buddha is clearly indicative of such a tranquil demeanor. Indeed, whether the hypnotizing radiance associated with the Transfiguration of Christ, or the mystical magnetism described in Herman Hesse's *Siddartha*; this enduring sense of tranquility will still come shining through!

EQUALITY

The completed description of tranquility, in turn, redirects the focus to the remaining humanistic value of equality, a theme sharing many commonalties to tranquility with the exception that submissiveness is targeted rather than the solicitousness. As defined from the perspective of the transcendental authority, the immediately active egalitarian expression of free will, in turn, anticipates the blissful-hope for the truth potentially expected from the respective follower figure. In a more formal sense, I (as transcendental authority) freely-willed act in an egalitarian fashion towards you in anticipation of your (as transcendental follower) blissful-hope for the truth.

Equality certainly lives up to its transcendental attributes, being that in the real world everyone proves unique in terms of individual strengths and weaknesses. Its modern spelling derives from the Latin *aequalitas* (equal), from *aequalis* (even). The Romans professed a strong constitutional sense of equality, every citizen enjoying equal protection under the law. The Jus Naturale (or natural law) insured equal rights to the sea, seashore, and community property. Consequently, the Romans divinely worshipped this aspect as their abstract goddess Aequitas. Direct evidence of her cult occurs in an archaic inscription from Vulci, and Arnobius mentions her as a goddess. Her name is also inscribed on ancient coins from the era.

The modern-day conception of equality (also known as *egalitarianism*) dates as a fitting postscript to the Age of Enlightenment. Political philosopher Thomas Hobbes professed the equal rights of man in a natural state consistent with one's unlimited sense of potential. John Locke, in turn, elaborated upon this basic premise stating: "all men are equally free under the natural law and therefore fully deserving of the same natural rights." Throughout the 18th century these noble perspectives were further reflected in emerging theories of human potential and development. According to Condillac and Helvetius, all men are equal in terms of the unlimited potential they share at birth and equally perfectible given the proper social environment. French philosopher, J. J. Rousseau, explained social inequality in terms of the pressures stemming from a stratified social order. Each individual (in the state of nature) fends for himself, whereby further abstaining from exploiting others (or being exploited). Rousseau additionally reasons that full social equality is the ideal natural state for human society in general.

These radical interpretations proved instrumental in fueling the American and French Revolutions, themes eloquently reflected in their respective declarations of rights. For the American Revolution, this trend towards equality denied the legitimacy of any arbitrary form of government. The *Declaration of Independence* formally underscores this basic principle stating: "We hold these truths to be self evident that all men are created *equal*, they are endowed by their Creator with certain unalienable rights, that among these are Life, Liberty, and the Pursuit of Happiness." This egalitarian perspective continues to our modern age, particularly with respect to the United Nation's *Universal Declaration of Human Rights* (1948) which states: "All human beings are born free and *equal* in dignity and rights."

In direct analogy to the case previously established for tranquility, equality shares an enduring transcendental focus: an ideal eminently noble in principle (although seldom realized in practice). In truth, any recourse to universal principles necessarily entails a seeming disregard for the more basic limitations governing the human condition. This egalitarian perspective necessarily specifies equal protection under the law irrespective of personal limitations or class distinctions. Such a noble range of ideals celebrates the equal opportunity of all races and creeds; hence, specifically denouncing any preferential treatment therein. Although such lofty ideals do not always square with the glaring gaps in the global economy, they, nevertheless, remain principles worth aspiring to, even if only to remedy much of the prejudice that breeds in its stead.

THE MYSTICAL VALUES: THE ROLE OF THE TRANSCENDENTAL FOLLOWER

In conclusion, the completed description of the humanistic values offers a suitably dramatic departure from the more routine rigors of everyday life. Indeed, the world would undoubtedly be a much crueler place to live without such a noble class of ideals to aspire to. This transcendental perspective formally appeals to an idealized realm of pure abstraction, effectively overruling the more limited (organizational) power-base characterizing the lower levels. This profoundly abstract scope might suggest that the upper conceptual limit for the ethical hierarchy has finally been reached, for it is virtually impossible to imagine a set of constructs more abstract than peace, love, tranquility, and equality. Even an authority level as abstract as the transcendental must (by definition) be invested with its own unique style of fol-

lower counter-maneuver, in this case that claimed by the transcendental follower figure.

The transcendental follower maneuver is truly an unprecedented addition to the orderly progression of the ethical hierarchy, its extreme level of abstraction greatly influencing any characteristic style of "strike" leverage. Indeed, this supremely abstract style of follower perspective introduces the hitherto unmentioned theme of "meta-" or *pure* transcendence; namely, transcendence based entirely within transcendence. The previously described class of humanistic values (specifying the transcendental authority perspective) all display a fair degree of conventionality consistent with their elementary foundations within the representative member of humanity perspective. The transcendental follower maneuver, however, abandons all such basis in concreteness, rather grounded directly within the transcendental authority perspective; hence, the *meta*-transcendental sense of the term.

This supremely abstract style of follower perspective is particularly suggestive of the emotional detachment reported in certain oriental schools of religious mysticism. In particular, the most basic precept of Buddhism states that the pursuit of pleasure necessarily invites pain, leaving emotional detachment as the primary means for achieving authentic spiritual balance. Consequently, the mystic renounces the transitory passions of everyday life in favor of a heightened experience of pure transcendence underlying the mystical experience.

One of the most enduring mystical techniques towards these ends is the long-standing tradition of meditation. Indeed, meditation appears in one form or another in virtually every major religious tradition across the globe. Although the particulars can vary widely, all share some sort of preliminary focusing technique aimed at gaining entry into the mystical realm. This can be passive as in focusing on one's breathing, or active as in chanting a mantra. At some point during the preliminaries, the over-stimulation (or under-stimulation) specific to the procedure permits entry into the transcendental realm. This mystical state is variously described as relaxed alertness or detached awareness, an experience essentially devoid of any particulars in thought or feeling. In terms of this blissful state, full mental stillness is ultimately achieved through an abandonment of any reference to external form or function.

According to Zen Buddhism, this enlightened state is known as *satori*, whereas the Yogic tradition defined it as *samadhi*. Even the Christian tradition acknowledges mystical enlightenment; e.g., "the peace that passeth understanding" according to St. Paul. Indeed, virtually every culture reports some form of mystical experience, variously described as joyous-ecstasy or blissful-harmony. This universal mystical character transcends all cultural barriers: whether Christian, Jewish, or Islamic. It ultimately proves fruitful to look beyond such ingrained cultural traditions, rather focusing on the individual subjective accounts characterizing the mystical experience.

THE CONTRIBUTIONS OF WILLIAM JAMES

Perhaps the most definitive analysis of the mystical experience is offered by William James in his *Varieties of Religious Experience: A Study in Human Nature*. This work is a compilation of his Lectures on Natural Religion delivered in Edinburgh, Scotland in 1901-1902. James is traditionally revered as a founding father of the American school of pragmatic psychology. The brother of celebrated novelist Henry James, William was educated (and eventually achieved tenure) at prestigious Harvard University. His pioneering work into the psychological effects of nitrous oxide anesthesia provided him an unconventional (yet accommodating) access to the mystical realm. He alludes to this personal aspect of the mystical experiences as follows: "The further limits of our being plunge, it seems to me, into an altogether other dimension of existence from the sensible and merely understandable world. Name it the mystical region or the supernatural region, whatever you choose."

According to his *Varieties of Religious Experience,* James lists a number of key distinguishing features underlying the mystical experience: defined as (1) ineffability, (2) noetic character, (3) transience, and (4) passivity. The first mentioned theme of *ineffability* refers to the inherent difficulty in finding the words to express the dramatic nature of the mystical experience. Many mystics claim that it can only be understood through direct experience, with intuition clearly taking precedent over intellect. Although the experience is not easily articulated to others, it generally has an insightful character to the mystic: an aspect that James further identifies as the *noetic* character. This term refers to "insights into the very depths of truth, unplumbed by the discursive intellect." These insights often come in the form of illuminations or revelations overflowing with significance, although often only vaguely remembered following the return to ordinary consciousness. This latter aspect is respectively termed *transiency* in that worldly concerns must eventually draw

the mystical experience to close. Although the mystical experience is only imperfectly reproduced in ordinary memory, it is instantly recognized in its purest sense during any subsequent recurrence. Although this state can be precipitated through voluntary means (such as prayer or meditation), the actual transformation is realized through an abeyance of the will, as if drawn to a superior power. James's final category of *passivity* refers to this ego-attenuation, a feature widely reported by mystics caught up in the throes of blissful-ecstasy.

This preliminary survey of the mystical experience, although clearly informative on an intuitive level, still leaves open the remaining issue of the identification of the four affective dimensions predicted for the transcendental follower perspective. Indeed, the affiliated theme of ineffability would certainly suggest that these additional dimensions would remain inexpressible in verbal terms. The Western tradition of Christian mysticism offers the greatest potential in this regard, particularly in terms of the personal realm known as saintliness.

THE ENDURING TRADITIONS OF SAINTLINESS

In his *Varieties of Religious Experience*, James devotes five full lectures to the topic of saintliness, defining it as the "ripe fruits of spirituality." Citing a survey of the literature spanning many generations, James proceeds to outline a number of key characteristics underlying saintliness. He initially describes the occurrence of an expanded outlook transcending one's individual peculiarities for an expanded conviction in a higher order. This further leads to a willing self-surrender to such a benevolent force, tempering freedom with elation as the distinctive outlines of selfhood melt away. There finally occurs a positive shift towards loving and harmonious affections directly in keeping with such an ecstatic experience.

Although this line of reasoning proves extremely enlightening, it ultimately proves crucial to examine individual accounts of saintliness in order to discern an overall pattern for the mystical states under consideration. According to St. Teresa of Avila, the highest of these is the orison of union: which raises the soul into mystical union with the Divine, whereupon giving the appearance of complete mental inaccessibility. The English language fortunately is endowed with a broad range of terms for describing the mystical experience borrowing extensively from both classical and contemporary accounts. This rich abundance of synonyms has apparently selected for the precise shades of meaning predicted within the ethical hierarchy. For instance, the cohesive grouping of ecstasy, bliss, joy, and harmony is a collection of themes specifically mentioned by James in his report on saintliness. Although all four terms appear to share a common range of meanings, enough marginal distinctions remain to warrant a strict correspondence to the four pre-dicted affective dimensions. In this more ad-vanced sense, *ecstasy* expands upon the aesthet-ic qualities of beauty, whereas *bliss* similarly am-plifies the knowledge functions of truth. Further-more, *joy* adds a transcendental perspective to goodness, whereas *harmony* makes a similar cor-respondence to wisdom. This cohesive four-part listing of themes is fittingly termed the class of *mystical values*, in direct analogy to their general unifying theme. Although these motivational par-allels prove suitably convincing on an intuitive level, their true test of validity is ultimately vali-dated in terms of their respective literary traditions.

ECSTASY

The first of the mystical values to be examined, *ecstasy*, is a theme endowed with virtually uni-versal significance in terms of the mystical expe-rience. In terms of the transcendental follower role, ecstasy represents a projected beauteous sense of rewarding perspective in response to the tranquil sense of gracefulness initially expressed by the transcendental authority figure. In more formal terms, you (as transcendental follower) now beauteously act ecstatically towards me in re-action to my (as transcendental authority) tranquil sense of gracefulness. Ecstasy certainly fits the bill in this basic respect, traditionally defined as an overarching sense of rapture during the mystical experience. Its modern spelling derives from the Greek *ekstasis* (displacement), from *ek-* (out) and *histanai* (to place).

This theme has virtually always denoted a mystical significance, variously described as an enhanced sense of joy accompanied by su-preme feelings of delight. According to St. Teresa of Avila, this ecstatic state can be delicately gen-tle or violently rapturous, as in full-blown flights of the spirit. In the throes of such divine con-templation, the mystic becomes "One" with the experience of the Absolute. The mystic often be-comes impervious to outside sensation, even to the point of ignoring painful stimuli. Indeed, this trance-like quality of ecstasy is similarly sug-gested in terms of its subordinate foundation in beauty. Here, the transcendental follower beaute-ously acts ecstatically in a supreme variation on the overarching theme of faithfulness.

BLISS

The completed description of ecstasy, in turn, re-directs this analysis to the related theme of *bliss*, sharing many commonalties to ecstasy with the exception that leniency (rather than rewards) is now called into focus. In this latter sense, bliss-fulness represents a truth-based variation upon the transcendental follower perspective in re-sponse to the egalitarian treatment of the tran-scendental authority figure. In slightly more for-mal terms you (as transcendental follower) bliss-fully-hope for the truth in response to my (as transcendental authority) egalitarian sense of free-will. Indeed, the modern spelling of bliss de-rives from the Anglo Saxon *blisse*, from *bliths* (joy), surviving to our modern era in relation to rapture and gladness.

This rather broad range of meanings would seem to restrict bliss to yet another synonym for ecstasy were it not for its incorporation into the popular expression "ignorance is bliss." Here an alternate style of *truth* function is further sug-gested for bliss. Indeed, Joseph Campbell's most widely quoted admonition concerns "following one's bliss." According to Campbell: "If you follow your bliss, you put yourself on a track that has been there all the while ... Wherever you are, if you are following your bliss, you are enjoying that refreshment, that life within you all of the time." An extensive survey of mystical traditions further brings to mind many such stirring accounts of the blissful state, where the supreme scheme of things becomes blissfully apparent. Indeed, igno-rance *is* bliss in this basic respect, a grand hi-erarchical perspective certainly in keeping with such a grand transcendental dimension.

JOY

The completed description of ecstasy and bliss, in turn, shifts the current focus to the remaining mystical values of joy and harmony. These themes share many commonalties to ecstasy and bliss with the exception that they are now punc-tuated from an anticipated procurement perspec-tive (rather than the reinforcing variety). *Joy* rates prominent placement in this regard through its solicitous culmination the authority/follower interaction. In more formal terms I (as your tran-scendental follower) now goodly act in a joyous fashion towards you in response to your (as tran-scendental authority) magnanimously-loving treatment of me. Indeed, this theme traces its origins to the Old French *joye*, from the Latin *guadium* (of similar usage and meaning). It is traditionally defined as extreme feelings of happiness or gladness, frequently used interchangeably with ecstasy or rapture. The ancient Romans worshipped this concept in the guise of Comus (the divine personification of joyous revelry): a derivation of the Greek god Komos, the same root-stem for the related theme of comedy. Indeed, this congenial god is figuratively depicted wearing an exaggerated smiling-style of acting mask typically employed during classical comedies.

These classical overtones find parallel consideration in the field of ethical inquiry, where joy is defined as the prevailing quality of a rightful act consistent with its transcendental variation in goodness. St. Thomas Aquinas defines joy as "The delight that is the healthy complement of intelligent and willed activity when the appetite is actively at rest in a *good* really possessed." St. Paul further mentions joy among the Gifts of the Holy Spirit (Galatians 5:22). This solicitous sense of the term is particularly evident in the popular expression "taking joy in one's work:" with joy figuratively symbolized as a tolling bell, a singing lark, the midday sun, or the color yellow: accentuating its close connotations to goodness.

HARMONY

The completed description of joy, in turn, shifts the current focus to the remaining mystical value of *harmony*. It shares many similarities to joy with the exception of targeting a more submissive focus (rather than solicitousness), proving a fitting adjunct to the lofty ideals underlying the transcendental follower perspective. In more formal terms, I (as transcendental follower) will wisely act in a harmonious fashion towards you in response to your (as transcendental authority) peaceable sense of equanimity. Harmony seemingly spans a rather broad range of meaning consistent with its transcendental placement within the ethical hierarchy. Its modern spelling derives from the Greek *harmonia* (a fitting together, an agreement) from *harmos* (a fitting or joining).

According to classical Greek mythology, the goddess Harmonia is traditionally worshipped as the daughter of Ares and Aphrodite: an insightful allegory in light of the fact that Ares was revered as the god of war, whereas Aphrodite was worshipped as the goddess of love. Harmonia was also closely allied to Aphrodite-Pandemos, symbolizing the figurative love uniting all people through a personification of the overarching social order, also corresponding to the Roman goddess Concordia (concordance).

This theme further extends to the aesthetic realm of classical music and the fine arts. Here agreement in form, function, and melody prove crucial to any meaningful attempts at composition. In medieval iconography, Harmony is depicted as a beautiful matron bedecked with an ornate crown and flourishing a violin and bow. In its more restricted relationship sense, harmony directly expands upon the humanitarian prerequisites previously established for wisdom, reflecting a transcendent sense of agreement within an international sphere of influence.

THE SUPERNATURAL REALM

In conclusion, the completed description of the mystical values effectively rounds out the verbal description of the ascending power hierarchy. Any further extension of this format necessarily entails the existence of an even more abstract style of authority perspective; namely, that *transcending* transcendental authority. Although this extreme level of abstraction certainly stretches the limits of abstract sensibility, in theory there does not appear to be any conceptual limit governing the degree to which reflection can serve as a basis for itself. Indeed, any such upper limit must necessarily be a practical one; namely, that level of abstraction that ultimately exceeds the capacity of the human intellect to distinguish the individual affective dimensions, precluding their incorporation into the collective speech lexicon. An observed blending of meanings would, indeed, seem to indicate that the upper conceptual limit has finally been reached.

Beginning with the preliminary transcendental authority level, the respective listing of humanistic values (peace-love-tranquility-equality) all exhibit a fair degree of distinctness, even though a degree of conceptual affinity is apparent in their dictionary definitions. At the next higher transcendental follower level the mystical values (ecstasy-bliss-joy-harmony) all exhibit a more extreme degree of conceptual affinity, reflected in dictionary definitions that are similar (if not synonymous) in form and function. Taking this trend to the limit, however, predicts a complete and irrefutable blending of meanings at this even more abstract meta-meta-order level of transcendence. At this almost inconceivable conceptual level, the four requisite dimensions effectively appear to merge into a unified conceptual continuum, virtually unnamable except in the broadest of supernatural terms; e.g., God, the Absolute, etc.

One experiencing this extreme level of transcendence would certainly be impressed by the paradoxical blending of emotional states, in direct contrast to the more concrete range of experience characterizing the lowermost levels. In ordinary consciousness the mind is typically restricted to entertaining only one affective perspective (or emotion) at any given time. With respect to the supernatural dimension, however, the distinctions between the emotions become so blurred as to merge into a unified transcendent state: the "one becomes the many" as numerous mystics have reported down through the ages.

This paradoxical awareness of all-knowing consciousness has traditionally been documented using a rather broad range of terms; e.g., the Universal Mind, the Oversoul, the Great Spirit, Cosmic Consciousness, Brahma, etc. These further serve as the primordial conceptual template for the remaining continuum of lower (more differentiated) emotional states. This supremely abstract perspective (by definition) encompasses all of the lower levels as subsets; hence, accounting for the corresponding flooding of meaning. Herein lies the basis for the traditional Judeo-Christian belief that man is created in the image and likeness of God. Ordinary consciousness (with its concrete limitations) is formally theorized to differentiate out of such an all-inclusive sphere of awareness. At this supremely abstract level, we all appear to tune into the Universal Mind as the sum-potentiality of all that is transcendent in nature.

Perhaps it is really only a matter of convention (devised by the ordinary mind) to regard the mystical state as a wholly independent dimension. William James appears to make a similar point in the following quotation from his *Varieties of Religious Experience*. "This overcoming of all of the usual barriers between the individual and the Absolute is the great mystical achievement. In mystic states we both become one with the Absolute and we become aware of our oneness. This is the everlasting and triumphant mystical tradition hardly altered by differences of clime or creed." The spiritually-minded can rightfully view mysticism as rooted entirely within such a supernatural foundation, all power emanating from the Supreme Creator of all that is spiritual and material. The individual traditions are scarcely the issue

here, for as many a sage has noted: "Many roads lead to Enlightenment."

This supreme transcendent perspective further underscores the fundamental paradox underlying the ascending ethical hierarchy; namely, its openness at both its upper and lower margins. The lower margin blends with the mysterious materialistic realm of behavioral instinctualism, whereas the upper end extends to the supernatural domain. Although the limited human intellect may favor such a dualistic interpretation, this dual perspective (on a grander scale) might actually amount to a grand illusion! Is it truly possible to distinguish the spiritual from the material, the mental from the physical? No matter how one frames the puzzle, these two themes always remain intimately interconnected. So long as the mind-body puzzle remains unresolved, then these issues must always remain open to further research and speculation.

This newly devised interpretation targeting the mystical realm offers the potential for radically new insights into the promotion of global peace and harmony. The respective mystical traditions propounded throughout the ages serve as the enduring moral foundation for the dogma guiding many of the world religions. This dogmatic supernatural exclusivity unfortunately serves as a point of friction that impedes inter-religious tolerance, putatively establishing one scriptural tradition as superior over another accompanied by resentment towards those thusly slighted.

The newly devised ten-level hierarchy of the virtues, values, and ideals fortunately provides a radically new strategy for healing much of this endemic religious exclusivity. Here the mystical realm arises as a hierarchical extension of the more fundamental virtuous traditions, constructs shared in common by each of the major world religions. Through a concerted recognition of these ethical and moral commonalities, an enhanced degree of interreligious cooperation might potentially be forthcoming, whereby counteracting any ingrained trend towards religious exclusivity. This unbounded perspective offers a particular appeal to those professing religious convictions, encouraging a common peaceful rallying point regardless of any individual supernatural traditions therein.

7

THE ACCESSORY VIRTUES, VALUES, AND IDEALS

The preceding description of the stepwise hierarchy of virtues, values, and ideals permits many interesting applications concerning the virtuous realm, although this schematic format is limited by a number of unforeseen complications. Chief among these is the observation that the dual interplay of procurement and reinforcement roles is strictly specialized into either subjective or objective polarities. This basic limitation stems from the basic restrictions governing the construction of the schematic definitions. The respective "you" and "I" roles (by definition) are locked into place with respect to the reciprocating sequences of procurement and reinforcement roles: whereby maintaining a stable buffer of terms within the schematic definitions.

This dual style of role specialization follows a strict set of guidelines; namely, the initially active procurement role is technically specified from a subjective "I" perspective, whereas the subsequent reinforcement role is alternately defined from an objective perspective. This reciprocating pattern of subjective procurement and objective reinforcement roles follows a strict give-and-take dynamic, schematically represented as "if you, then I" (and vice versa). According to this complementary style of power-sharing arrangement, the initially active procurement roles within the conditioned interaction are assigned a subjective "I" status, whereas the subsequent reinforcement roles are distinguished through an objective "you" status. Indeed, this arrangement essentially mirrors what is typically observed in nature, where the organism actively procures, whereas the environment (inanimately) provides reinforcement.

As previously described in the Introductory Chapter 1, this initial pattern of virtuous communication can scarcely claim to be the total picture, for it formally accounts for only half of the introspective roles predicted within the linguistic matrix. The inherent versatility of the human mind (by definition) allows for a subjective reflection upon one's objective status after the fact; in essence, subjectifying the objective status initially assigned to the reinforcement roles. This role reversal is further counterbalanced by a similar objectification of the subjective procurement roles. This reflective style of role-reversal conveniently allows for crucial insights into the feelings and motivations experienced by another, an aspect traditionally known as *empathy*. Empathy refers to an indwelling sense of inter-subjectivity by which one subjectively anticipates feelings privately held by another. This unique ability attribute mental states to others is the key factor that makes us truly human, an aspect developmental psychologists identify as *Theory of Mind*. This innate capacity to empathize the feelings of others appears to emerge over several distinct stages of emotional development. In particular Dr. Michael Lewis of Robert Wood Johnson Medical School (1995) outlines a three-stage sequence of empathic development.

The primary emotions, such as fear or sadness, first appear around the age of six months: expressed through a spontaneous response repertoire of a non-reflective nature. The more abstract secondary emotions, in turn, emerge around the age of two, signaling the first true "sense of self" characterized by more sophisticated emotions such as guilt or shame. These secondary emotions invoke a higher sense of self, an enduring identity to which these emotions ultimately refer. The third stage of empathic development mainly occurs around the ages of 4 or 5, when the child learns to ascribe motivations to others that might be personally experienced under similar circum-

114	115		124	125
Ambition	Deference	→	Admiration	Concern
116	**117**		**126**	**127**
Passion	Apprehension		Consideration	Adherence
ACCESS. EGO STATES			**ACC. ALTER EGO STATES**	
(Personal Authority)			(Personal Follower)	

134	135		144	145
Exaltation	Uprightness		Circumspection	Equitableness
136	**137**	→	**146**	**147**
Respect	Probity		Continence	Bravery
ACC. PERSONAL IDEALS			**ACC. CARDINAL VIRTUES**	
(Group Authority)			(Group Representative)	

154	155		164	165
Bountifulness	Freedom	→	Devotion	Fairness
156	**157**		**166**	**167**
Courtesy	Forbearance		Kindness	Scruples
ACCESS. CIVIL LIBERTIES			**ACC. THEOLOG. VIRTUES**	
(Spiritual Authority)			(Spiritual Disciple)	

174	175		184	185
Blessings	Conscience	→	Charm	Credence
176	**177**		**186**	**187**
Graciousness	Patience		Benevolence	Shrewdness
ACC. ECUMEN. IDEALS			**ACC. CLASSICAL VALUES**	
(Humanitarian Authority)			(Humanitarian Follower)	

194	195		104	105
Serenity	Brotherhood	→	Rapture	Contentment
196	**197**		**106**	**107**
Affection	Amity		Gladness	Accordance
ACC. HUMANIST. VALUES			**ACC. MYSTICAL VALUES**	
(Transcendental Authority)			(Transcendental Follower)	

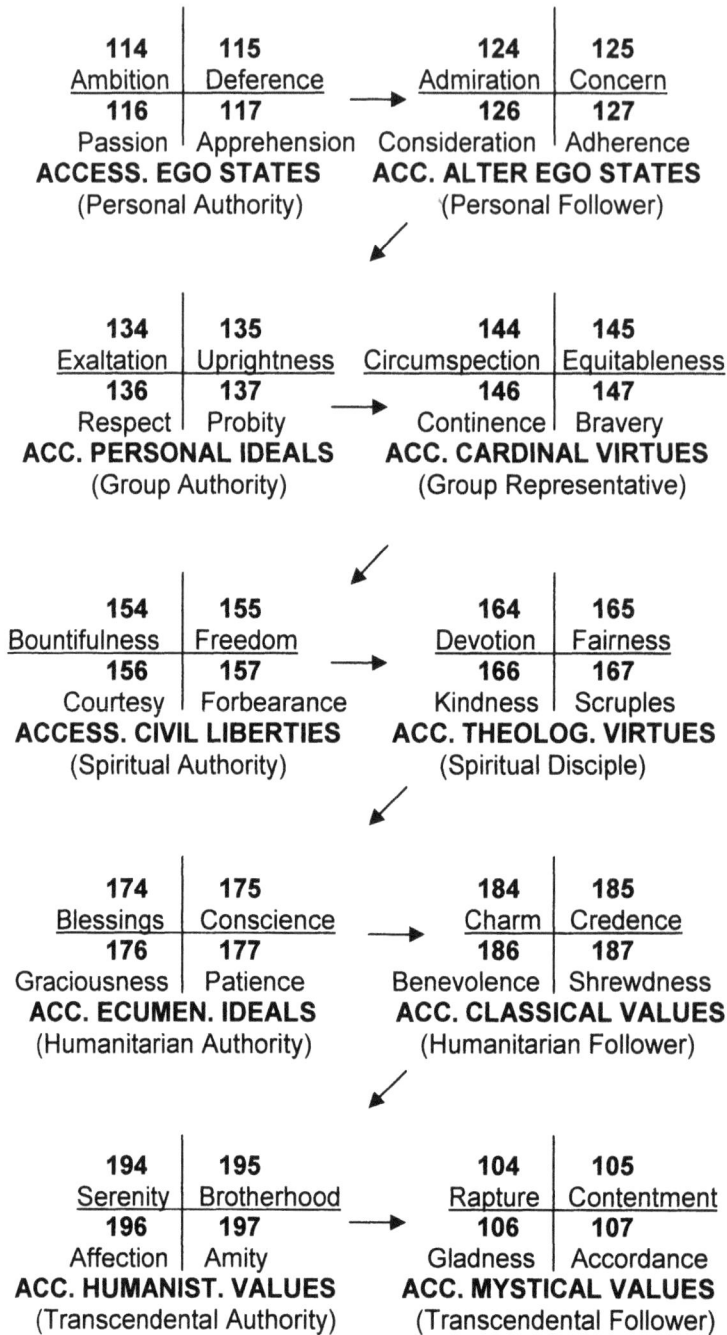

Fig. 7A – The Accessory Virtues and Values

stances. This more advanced capacity is explained philosophically in terms of the *Argument from Analogy*, where internal motives associated with personal behaviors are similarly attributed to the outwardly observable behaviors of others.

Indications of this ability are evident at a fairly early age, such as when a toddler shows interesting objects to others. This early perspective in relation to others, however, is actually fairly egocentric. The infant expresses a belief in an egocentric knowledge base, in direct contrast to the more advanced empathic flexibility derived from perspectives held by another. This latter development only truly becomes apparent around the age of five, when the child realizes that others do not have direct access to one's own individual mindset, but rather entertain distinct thoughts and motivations entirely of their own making. This more advanced comprehension of independent cognitive mindsets permits the development of the many skills underlying social empathy, as reflected in common role-playing games such as cops & robbers, doctor & patient, etc. Affiliated feelings of playfulness generate outward facial expressions, the observation which activates similar bodily responses within the observer. This induced bodily response (for the observer) translates into a shared emotional perspective, whereby establishing a collective sense of empathy linking the observer to the observed.

This distinct empathic ability proves particularly crucial within a social setting, where cohesion within the group is enhanced through recourse to such overlapping perspectives, whereby minimizing interpersonal frictions. According to Robert Gordon (1986), this innate sense of empathy depends primarily upon our ability to run cognitive simulations: inferring the intentions of others by employing one's own mind as a model for that of others. This formally entails placing oneself in the shoes of another and then observing how one's mind resonates within such a mutually connected context. The reciprocal interplay linking one's inner and outer perspectives provides the supreme conceptual template for modeling a convincing sense of empathy in relation to others.

This empathic style of motivational perspective further predicts the existence of an entirely new complement of affective terms for designating this dual degree of versatility, an innovation labeled the *accessory* motivational terms. Fortunately the English language is richly blessed with a broad range of synonyms conducive to satisfying this predicted complement of accessory terms. These accessory "you"/"I" perspectives are systematically reversed in polarity across the board

ensuring that both procurement and reinforcement roles encompass the full range of objective/subjective potentialities. For the personal realm, for instance, the proposed accessory class of immediately-active authority roles (ambition, deference, passion, and apprehension) effectively complements the main listing of terms (solicitousness, submissiveness, desire, and worry). Furthermore, the accessory personal follower roles (admiration, concern, consideration, and adherence), in turn, reciprocates the main listing of terms (approval, leniency, aspiration, and compliance).

With respect to the main interplay of solicitousness-then-approval, for instance, the accessory complement of ambition then admiration proves particularly well suited to the task. In more formal terms, you (as personal authority) now solicitously act approachfully towards me in anticipation of my (as personal follower) admiring treatment of you. In terms of the related context of deference-then-concern, the personal authority figure switches to a deferential perspective, whereby anticipating the personal follower's lenient sense of concern. A similar pattern further holds true with respect to the personal authority's passionate reinforcement in anticipation of considerate treatment on the part of the personal follower, or apprehension in expectation of adherent treatment. This reciprocating dynamic for both the main and accessory sets of terms permits a convincing simulation of the empathic interplay governing the conditioned interaction.

THE ACCESSORY VIRTUOUS HIERARCHY

According to this main/accessory model of empathic communication, it remains only a further minor step to extend this personal complement of terms to the even more abstract realm of the virtues, values, and ideals comprising the more abstract authority levels. Indeed, the full forty-fold listing of accessory terms is schematically depicted below, as well as an expanded format in **Fig. 7A**.

Ambition • Admiration		Deference • Concern	
Exalt.• Circumspection		Uprightness • Equity	
Bountiful. • Devotion		Freedom • Fairness	
Blessings • Charm		Conscience • Credence	
Serenity • Rapture		Brotherhood • Content.	

Passion • Consider.		Apprehen.• Adherence	
Respect • Continence		Probity • Bravery	
Courtesy • Kindness		Forbear. • Scruples	
Gracious.• Benevolence		Patience • Shrewd.	
Affection • Gladness		Amity • Accordance	

This compact diagram represents a mirror-image variation on the main listing of virtuous terms depicted in **Fig. 1** of Chapter 1. Indeed, this master hierarchy of accessory terms spans the entire ten-level span of personal, group, spiritual, humanitarian, and transcendental realms within the ascending virtuous hierarchy. This reciprocating interplay of both main and accessory terms permits a convincing simulation of empathic language in general: the objective/subjective polarities now systematically reversed through a direct inversion of the "you" and "I" perspectives. These accessory groupings of terms unfortunately exhibit little in the way of the pedigree or tradition previously described for the main listings of terms. According to **Fig. 7A**, the accessory listings of terms are formally specified through the addition of the prefix *"accessory"* to the better-known monikers assigned to the main groupings. More permanent labels must necessarily await further collective research into the field, for any permanent system of classification must remain open to the consensus opinion of the broader global community at large.

It ultimately proves fruitful to undertake a more in depth examination of the individual accessory terms spanning the entire virtuous hierarchy, providing a clear indication of the reciprocal dynamics at issue. The remainder of the current chapter further examines these additional listings of accessory terms to a much greater degree of detail, whereby focusing upon the subjective/objective polarities in relation to the main groupings of virtues/values previously described.

AMBITION

The first mentioned theme of *ambition* rates current consideration as the chief accessory counterpart of solicitousness. The term derives from the Latin *ambitio* (a going around), particularly in the context of soliciting votes; hence, the striving for favor, seeking flattery, or a desire for honor. It similarly relates to the past-participle *ambire* (to go around), the same root-stem for ambient. It also refers to the secondary Latin sense of an eager or inordinate desire for honor, often in a pejorative sense, as in overreaching pride or vainglory. Such pronounced feelings of personal influence share with solicitousness such an immediately active range of influence. Here the subjective prerequisites for solicitousness effectively complement the objective characteristics formally assigned to ambition, an emotional perspective typically encountered within a personal sphere of influence.

EXALTATION

The personal authority theme of ambition, in turn, extends to a group sphere of influence with respect to the affiliated theme of *exaltation*: a term defined as glorious fortune or elevated rank. Its modern spelling derives from the Latin *altus* (high) and *ex-* (a prefix indicating intensity) representing the objective counterpart of the subjective *glory* perspective. This theme shares with glory a heightened quest for power or prestige indicative of such a leadership role. Consequently, this poignant sense of exaltation preserves the active focus previously established for the glory perspective of the group authority, although now in anticipation of the admiring treatment of the personal follower figure.

BOUNTIFULNESS

Exaltation, in turn, extends to the spiritual authority theme of *bountifulness*, objectively complementing the subjective prerequisites previously established for *providence*. The term derives from the Latin *bonitas*, from *bonus* (good), a connotation consistent with its generosity in the bestowal of gifts. Bountifulness shares many features in common with the traditional symbolisms associated with providence. Particularly the *cornucopia* (horn of plenty) perpetually overflows with an abundant bounty of produce from the field, permitting a welcome sense of security in pressing times. Consequently, the exalted sense of bountifulness expressed by a spiritual authority proves a fitting counterpoint to the circumspective sense of devotion anticipated from the spiritual follower figure.

BLESSINGS

The even more abstract humanitarian authority level begs further mention of the related theme of *blessings*. This theme traces its origins to the Anglo Saxon *bledsian* (to bless), from *blod* (blood), as in a blood-sacrifice upon an altar. It chiefly refers to a divine sense of sanctification or sacredness analogous to its subjective counterpart in *grace*. Indeed, the act of "saying Grace" begins with the stirring invocation: *"Bless* us Oh Lord for these Thy gifts … received through Thy bounty." This long-standing tradition of abundant blessings clearly preserves the strict humanitarian focus of grace, objectively reciprocating the subjective prerequisites of the latter. The bountiful-blessings specified within such a universal domain clearly prove a worthy match to the charming sense of devotion potentially anticipated from the representative member of humanity.

SERENITY

The bountiful-blessings specified for the humanitarian realm, in turn, extend to a transcendental domain with respect to the affiliated theme of *serenity*. It represents the chief objective counterpart in relation to the subjective prerequisites previously established for *tranquility*. Its modern spelling derives from the Latin *serenus* (clear) indicative the tranquil attributes associated with the term. It is often employed as a title of distinction for reigning princes and dignitaries consistent with the calm demeanor typically accompanying such positions of power. This serene sense of contentment is further associated with the great mystical figures throughout the ages: such as Buddha, Christ, Mohammed, etc. The serene-blessings expressed by the transcendental authority figure directly reciprocate the charmingly-rapturous treatment anticipated from the transcendental follower.

ADMIRATION

The remaining ascending sequence of accessory terms based upon the corresponding follower roles begins with the personal follower theme of *admiration*. As the chief subjective counterpart of approval, it shares with latter a profound sense of homage or respect for those worthy of such approbation. Its modern spelling derives from the Latin *admirari* from *ad-* (to) and *mirari* (to wonder) indicative of such rewarding overtones. The positive emotional focus shared by admiration and approval is certainly quite telling, whereby rewarding the notable achievements of the personal authority figure. In terms of the requisite "you" and "I" perspectives, admiration clearly suggests a more objective style of outward focus than does approval, the latter specifying a subjective sense of approbation indicative of the personal follower role.

CIRCUMSPECTION

The personal prerequisites for admiration, in turn, extend to a group sphere of influence with respect to the affiliated theme of *circumspection*. The term derives from the Latin *circum-* (about) and *spectum* (to look): suggesting a cautious investigation spanning many angles similar to the watchful perspective previously described for pru-

dence. Indeed, the symbolisms associated with circumspection share many features in common with those ascribed to prudence; namely, a seated maiden facing the three cardinal directions representative of past, present, and future potentialities. The future-projected dimensionality for circumspection is certainly favored, in essence, responding to the exaltedly-ambitious treatment expressed by the group authority figure.

DEVOTION

Circumspection, in turn, ultimately gives way to the spiritual disciple theme of *devotion*: traditionally defined as strong piety or spiritual attachment. The term derives from the Latin *devovere*: from *de-* (away) and *vovere* (to vow), suggestive of its close association with faith. In particular, this term refers to the Roman Catholic tradition of the devotional, as in prayers or worship of an intensely personal nature. This pious sense of devotion transcends any formal ritual concerns, denoting a deeply subjective counterpart in relation to its objective counterpart in faith. Consequently, the circumspective-devotion professed by the spiritual disciple effectively complements the exaltedly-bountiful treatment expressed by the spiritual authority figure.

CHARM

The next higher domain of the humanitarian follower, in turn, begs mention of the accessory theme of *charm*, an aspect that subjectively complements the objective prerequisites previously ascribed to beauty. Its modern spelling derives from the Latin *carmen* (a song) indicating the ritual significance that music plays in religious observance. Charm also denotes a magical sense of enchantment or attractiveness reminiscent of the familiar notions of the charm bracelet or charm school. The truest sensibility of charm, however, stems from its enduring characteristics implicit to such a grand humanitarian perspective. Consequently, the charming sense of devotion professed by the representative member of humanity subjectively reciprocates the bountiful-blessings bestowed by the humanitarian authority figure.

RAPTURE

The preceding humanitarian discussion of charm, in turn, gives sway to its respective transcendental counterpart in *rapture*: the main subjective counterpart in relation to the more objective theme of ecstasy. The term derives from the Latin *raptum* (to seize) indicative of extreme flights of fancy relating to enlightenment or mysticism. Although other synonyms for ecstasy (such as happiness) might equally fit the bill, the subjective prerequisites for rapture prove adequate to the current sense of the term. Here the rapturously-charming treatment professed by the transcendental follower proves a fitting counterpoint to the serene-blessings bestowed by the transcendental authority figure.

THE PARALLEL SEQUENCE OF TERMS
BASED UPON DEFERENCE/CONCERN

In terms of the remaining realm of negative reinforcement, a parallel sequence of accessory terms is further based upon the personal authority/follower themes of deference/concern. For instance, the group authority deferently acts in an upright fashion in anticipation of the equitable sense of concern on the part of the group representative. Furthermore, the spiritual authority figure freely acts in an upright fashion in anticipation of the equitable sense of fairness professed by the spiritual disciple. Finally, with respect to the more advanced humanitarian/transcendental levels, the authority figure freely acts conscientiously (or conscientiously acts in a brotherly fashion) in anticipation of the latter's fair sense of credence/contentment, as schematically depicted in the compact diagram below:

Deference	Concern
Uprightness	**Equity**
Freedom	**Fairness**
Conscientiousness	**Credence**
Brotherhood	**Contentment**

This accessory sequence of ethical terms effectively reciprocates the pattern previously established for the main sequence of terms (e.g., submissiveness-honor-liberty-freewill-equality) characterizing the authority role, in addition to listing of leniency-justice-hope-truth-bliss specified for the follower role: whereby preserving an equal balance of power for the "you" and "I" perspectives.

PASSION

A third dual-sequence of accessory terms, in turn, is based upon personal interplay linking passion and consideration: a foundation reciprocally complementing the main sequence based upon desire and aspiration. For instance, the first mentioned theme of *passion* denotes a strongly positive sense of emotion, particularly ardent love or de-

sire. The term derives from the Old French *passiun*, from the Latin *passus* (to suffer). This early connotation of suffering is consistent with the longstanding frustrations associated with the consummation of the passions, as in a personal quest for fulfillment. Here, passion suggests a more personally-subjective slant, as opposed to the more objective prerequisites typically associated with desire. Indeed, the latter appears more concerned with the actual object of desire rather than the passionate steps towards its fulfillment.

RESPECT

The personal prerequisites for passion, in turn, extend to a group sphere of influence with respect to the even more abstract theme of *respect*, a term that subjectively complements the more objective prerequisites for dignity. Its modern spelling derives from the Latin *respectum*, from *re-* (back) and *specere* (to look) consistent with the dignified demeanor characterizing such leadership positions. Outward respect typically drives the passionate adherence to one's duties, subjectively contrasting to any dignified sense of desire. Here the passionate-respect professed by the group authority figure proves a fitting counterpoint to the objective prerequisites for dignity, whereby countering the continently-aspiring treatment of the group representative.

COURTESY

The group authority theme of respect, in turn, gives way to the more universal authority theme of *courtesy*: traditionally defined as polite consideration or civil accommodation. The term derives from the Latin *cortis* (courtyard) suggestive of the "common courtesy" shared in common by the populace. This theme figures prominently in the increasingly quaint custom of the *courtesy call*; namely, a social visit made entirely on the basis of common courtesy. This aspect further traces its origins to the medieval tradition of The Code of Courtesy. The chivalrous knight courteously acts respectfully towards the object of his passion, fully expecting a continently-aspiring treatment in return. Consequently, this courteous expression of respect offers a fitting counterpoint to the more objective prerequisites previously described for the spiritual authority's civilly-dignified treatment.

GRACIOUSNESS

The ascending (accessory) sequence of courtesy and respect, in turn, extends to the even more abstract humanitarian theme of *graciousness*, defined as divine favor or supreme kindness. The term derives from the Latin *gratia* (favor) from *gratus* (agreeable), a connotation consistent with its accessory association with magnanimity. Similar to courtesy, graciousness is traditionally associated with the custom of *gratuities*: as in showing appreciation by freely tipping the hired-help. Indeed, the notion of the gracious host is one of mankind's most honored traditions, particularly in the Middle East, where the needs of the guest formally take precedent over those of the host. Here the courteously-gracious treatment on the part of the humanitarian authority proves a fitting objective counterpoint to the benevolent sense of kindness anticipated from the representative member of humanity.

AFFECTION

The ascending ethical hierarchy of courtesy and graciousness, in turn, extends to the crowning transcendental theme of *affection*: the chief subjective counterpart in relation to *love*. The term derives from the Latin *affectio*, from *ad-* (to) and *facere* (to do), consistent with such enhanced feelings of rewarding reinforcement. Indeed, the related theme of "affect" is similarly invoked to denote a strong range of emotions: the attachments of love certainly fitting the bill in this latter respect. The supremely abstract connotations of affection prove consistent with such a crowning transcendental perspective, a fitting subjective counterpoint to the more objective prerequisites previously described for love. Consequently, one can certainly "toy" with another's affections, although the same does not necessarily hold true for the more objective aspects of love.

CONSIDERATION

The further *accessory* sequence in relation to the follower roles is currently launched with respect to the preliminary personal follower theme of *consideration*. It is typically defined as an enthusiastic style of goal seeking consistent with its subjective counterpart in aspiration. This considerate focus further counters the passionate reinforcement of the personal authority figure, as reflected in the interplay of admiration and ambitiousness initial cited in the previous section. In reference to the respective "you" and "I" polarities, consideration clearly suggests an objective character, whereby effectively complementing the subjective prerequisites previously described for passion. This scenario direct contrasts with the respective interplay of desire and aspiration (although the role-polarities are now reversed).

CONTINENCE

The personal attributes for consideration, in turn, extend to a group sphere of influence with respect to the group follower theme of *continence*. It is traditionally defined as restraint in the indulgence of the passions similar to its subjective counterpart in temperance. The term derives from the Latin *continens* (to contain, to hold back), a connotation consistent with the "bridling" of the passions. Continence is most often associated with sexual restraint, in contrast to the more general range of constraint specified for temperance. Irrespective of its object of focus, the continently-aspiring treatment expressed by the group representative proves a fitting counterpoint to the passionate-respect expressed by the group authority figure.

KINDNESS

The next higher spiritual level, in turn, gives way to the accessory follower theme of *kindness*: representing the objective accessory counterpart of the more subjectively oriented theme of charity. Its modern spelling derives from the Old English *cynn* (kind) suggesting a free willingness to perform good or note-worthy deeds. This nurturing quality has traditionally been celebrated as the "milk of human kindness," an enduring interpretation consistent with such good-hearted (charitable) endeavors. The universal appeal underlying such a continent sense of kindness certainly rates such a high degree of esteem. Indeed, this volunteer spirit extends considerable benefits to both the recipient as well as the bestower. Here the continently-kind treatment expressed by the spiritual disciple proves a fitting counterpoint to the courteously-respectful treatment professed by the spiritual authority figure.

BENEVOLENCE

The universal overtones for kindness, in turn, extend to a humanitarian sphere of influence with respect to the affiliated theme of *benevolence*. The term derives from the Latin *benevolentia* (goodwill) from *bene-* (well) and *velle* (to wish). It traditionally denotes a humanitarian disposition towards graciousness or generosity in terms of both word and deed. This grand humanitarian perspective is particularly apparent in the many philanthropic endeavors associated with benevolent societies; e.g., institutions that seek to improve the human condition through charitable works and public education. This enduring spirit of benevolence clearly validates such a grand humanitarian perspective: a noble aspiration much depended upon in times of trouble. Here the benevolent sense of kindness professed by the representative member of humanity objectively complements the (subjective) courteously-gracious reinforcement on the part of the humanitarian authority figure.

GLADNESS

The benevolent sense of kindness characterizing the humanitarian realm ultimately extends to the crowning transcendental level with respect to the abstract theme of *gladness*. As the chief objective counterpart in relation to joy, gladness denotes a cheerful or optimistic disposition, particularly in an enthusiastic or animated fashion. The term derives from the Old English *glaed*, from the Old Norse *glathr* (bright), suggesting a sparkling emotional outlook. The objective prerequisites for gladness effectively complement the subjective aspects initially described for joy. Here the benevolent sense of gladness expressed by the transcendental follower proves a fitting counterpoint to the affectionate sense of graciousness professed by the transcendental authority figure.

THE ACCESSORY TERMS BASED UPON APPREHENSION/ADHERENCE

The fourth and final sequence of accessory motivational terms is based upon the remaining motivational sequence of apprehension/adherence (the accessory counterparts relating to worry and compliance). The accessory sequence of authority terms (apprehension, probity, forbearance, patience, and amity) effectively reciprocates the main sequence of terms: e.g., worry-integrity-austerity-equanimity-peace. Furthermore the remaining sequence of accessory follower roles: (adherence, bravery, scrupulousness, shrewdness, and accordance), in turn, provides a fitting counterpoint to their main virtuous counterparts: e.g., compliance, fortitude, decency, wisdom, and harmony: as schematically depicted in the compact diagram below.

Apprehension	Adherence
Probity	**Bravery**
Forbearance	**Scrupulousness**
Patience	**Shrewdness**
Amity	**Accordance**

This cohesive hierarchy of accessory terms effectively complements the dynamics for the main sequence of terms, effectively verifying the empathic validity of the entire virtuous hierarchy.

THE SCHEMATIC DEFINITIONS FOR THE ACCESSORY VIRTUOUS REALM

One final issue of critical significance concerns the prediction that the accessory virtuous terms are similarly amenable to incorporation within the schematic definition format. Indeed, a complete listing of *accessory* schematic definitions is respectively tabulated in **Tables B-1** to **B-4** in direct analogy to the main set of definitions depicted in **Tables A-1** to **A-4** (of Chapter *2*). These accessory schematic definitions are identical in form and function to their main counterparts with the exception that the "you" and "I" polarities are now reversed across the board. This systematic reversal of the "you" and "I" perspectives further permits an alternating confluence of subjective and objective viewpoints. This dual-dynamic format is formally predicted through the empathic principles governing Theory of Mind, where reciprocating viewpoints take into full account all such potential variations and viewpoints.

In order to completely explain this dual interplay of main and accessory perspectives, it proves fruitful to look back (in review) to the basic empathic issues. Routine communication depicted in terms of a two-stage motivational schematic. The subjective party is fittingly termed "myself," whereas the objective perspective is alternately labeled "the other" in keeping with established existential terminology. These two basic domains are separated by a figurative gap that signifies the channel that communication must travel in order to bridge both sender and receiver.

This schematic model depicted in **Fig. 7B** represents one complete cycle of empathic communication between "myself" and "the other," as the directional arrows figuratively serve to indicate. The cycle begins with **Box A** where a given example of communication (the subjective definition for *glory*) is listed in the upper left-hand box. In terms of this specific example, I (as group authority) now gloriously act solicitously towards you in anticipation of your (as personal follower) approving treatment of me. This initial power maneuver is communicated from "myself" to "the other" (Channel **A → B**) across the formal subjective/objective gap. This basic communication channel (by definition) is open to distortion, ambiguity, or misinterpretations over the entire extent of the transmission.

(A) I (as group authority) will *gloriously* act solicitously towards you, in anticipation of your (as my personal follower) approving treatment of me.	**(B)** You (as group authority) have ambitiously acted *exaltedly* towards me, in anticipation of my (as your personal follower) admiring treatment of you.

(MY ↑ SELF) **(THE ↓ OTHER)**

(D) You (as group representative) now *prudently* act approvingly towards me: in response to my (as group authority) glorious treatment of you.	**(C)** I (as group representative) *circumspectively* act admiringly towards you, in response to your (as group authority) exalted treatment of me.

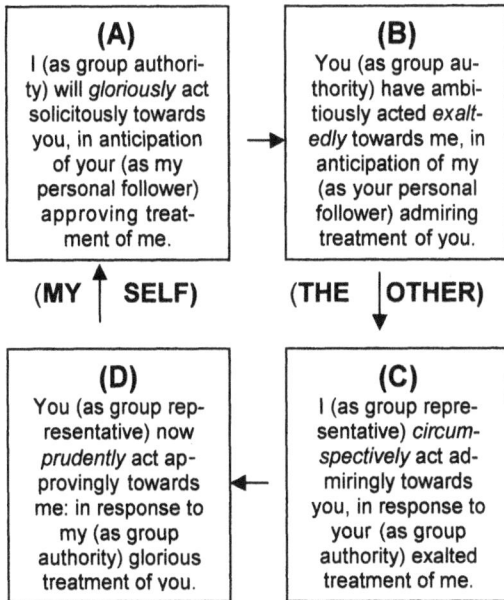

Fig. 7B - The Two-Stage Communicational Dynamic

Despite these internal shortcomings, for sake of illustration, the message is depicted as successfully reaching the receiver in direct attention to "the other." The message must necessarily be translated into a form that is subjectively meaningful to the empathic dictates of the receiver. This further entails translating the *main* schematic definition into its empathic *accessory* counterpart specified from the subjective viewpoint of "the other." According to **Box B** of **Fig. 7B**, the accessory form of the schematic definition for "exaltation" is now represented as: You (as group authority) have ambitiously acted in an *exalted* fashion towards me in anticipation of my (as personal follower) admiring treatment of you. According to this modified format, the "you" and "I" roles are effectively reversed whereby personalizing the message to fit the subjective prerequisites of "the other."

THE COUNTERMANEUVER OF "THE OTHER"

Once the message is received and comprehended by "the other," it remains to be determined how "the other" will best respond to the message. According to step **B → C**, one possible option is to ignore the message as if it were never received, or claim to misunderstand the message. Another option entails mirroring the message back to the sender in what Communication Theorists term the *symmetrical* maneuver. A further option entails accepting the content of the message as given, as well as one's specified role within the conditioned interaction. This latter response typically occurs only when one is satisfied with the status quo that was initially projected.

A further relevant option builds directly upon this initial acceptance: accepting the content of the message as initially offered, then subsequently modifying one's role by rising to the next higher meta-perspectival level within the accessory hierarchy. This necessarily entails countering the power tactic initially offered by substituting (in its place) a power-status of one's own making. This more advanced variation is schematically depicted in **Box C**. Here the personal follower rises to the more advanced level of "group representative" employing the *circumspective* form of counter-maneuver. The first part of this advanced definition builds directly upon the initial *exaltation* maneuver originally communicated, followed by the *circumspection* counter-maneuver proper; namely, I (as group representative) circumspectively act in an admiring fashion towards you in response to your (as group authority) exaltedly-ambitious treatment of me. According to Communication Theorists, this strategy is termed the *complementary* class of power maneuvers, being that they directly complement what has gone before. The group representative role now formally complements the group authority role that was originally offered.

Once formulated, this complementary style power maneuver is subsequently communicated from "the other" back to "myself," as shown in step **C → D** within the master diagram. The respective arrow once again crosses the subjective/objective gap, being further susceptible to the shortcomings of distortion, ambiguity, etc. Assuming that the communication is successfully transmitted, this necessarily entails a translation back to a form meaningful to "myself:" the *main* schematic definition depicted in **Box D**. Here the *circumspective*-adoration of the group representative is now translated back into a sense of *prudent*-approval consistent with my own subjective perspective. In this latter respect, the "you" and "I" roles are once again reversed, empathically modified in terms of the subjective group authority role originally communicated.

The successful receipt of the group representative's *prudence* counter-maneuver, in turn, offers further options for myself (as depicted in step **D → A**). According to this latter instance, this may further entail rising to the next higher spiritual authority level, expressed as a *providential* expansion upon the original glory maneuver. This innovation (by definition) launches one further

AMBITION	ADMIRATION
Previously, I (as reinforcer) have rewardingly acted in a reinforcing fashion towards you: in response to your (as procurer) approachful treatment of me. But now, you (as personal authority) will approachfully act *ambitiously* towards me: in anticipation of my rewarding treatment of you.	Previously, you (as personal authority) have approachfully acted ambitiously towards me: in anticipation of my (as reinforcer) rewarding treatment of you. But now, I (as personal follower) will rewardingly act in an *admiring* fashion towards you: overruling your (as PA) ambitious treatment of me.
EXALTATION	**CIRCUMSPECTION**
Previously, I (as your personal follower) have rewardingly acted in an admiring fashion towards you: in response to your (as PA) ambitious treatment of me. But now, you (as group authority) will ambitiously act in an *exalted* fashion towards me: in anticipation of my (as PF) admiring treatment of you.	Previously, you (as group authority) have ambitiously acted exaltedly towards me: in anticipation of my (as PF) admiring treatment of you. But now, I (as group representative) will *circumspectively* act in an admiring fashion towards you: overruling your (as GA) exalted treatment of me.
BOUNTIFULNESS	**DEVOTION**
Previously, I (as group representative) have circumspectively acted admiringly towards you: in response to your (as GA) exalted treatment of me. But now, you (as spiritual authority) will exaltedly act in a *bountiful* fashion towards me: in anticipation of my (as GR) circumspective-admiration of you.	Previously, you (as spiritual authority) have exaltedly admitted acting in a bountiful fashion towards me: in anticipation of my (as GR) circumspective-admiration of you. But now, I (as your spiritual disciple) will circumspectively act *devotedly* towards you: overruling your (as SA) bountiful treatment of me.
BLESSINGS	**CHARM**
Previously, I (as your spiritual disciple) have circumspectively acted devotedly towards you: in response to your (as SA) bountiful treatment of me. But now, you (as humanitarian authority) will bountifully-*bless* me: in anticipation of my (as SD) circumspective-devotion for you.	Previously, you (as humanitarian authority) have bountifully-blessed me: in anticipation of my (as SD) circumspective-devotion for you. But now, I (as representative member of humanity) will *charmingly* act devotedly towards you: overruling your (as HA) bountiful-blessing of me.
SERENITY	**RAPTURE**
Previously, I (as representative member of humanity) have charmingly acted devotedly towards you: in response to your (as HA) bountiful-blessing of me. But now, you (as transcendental authority) will *serenely*-bless me: in anticipation of my (as RH) charming devotion for you.	Previously, you (as transcendental authority) have serenely-blessed me: in anticipation of my (as RH) charming-devotion for you. But now, I (as your transcendental follower) will charmingly act in a *rapturous* fashion towards you: overruling your (as TA) serene-blessing of me.

Table B-1 – The Definitions Based on Ambition/Admiration

DEFERENCE	CONCERN
Previously, I (as reinforcer) have tolerantly acted in a reinforcing fashion towards you: in response to your (as procurer) aversive treatment of me. But now, you (as personal authority) will *deferentially* act in an aversive fashion towards me: in anticipation of my tolerant treatment of you.	Previously, you (as personal authority) have deferentially acted aversively towards me: in anticipation of my (as reinforcer) tolerant treatment of you. But now, I (as your personal follower) will tolerantly act in a *concerned* fashion towards you: overruling your (as PA) deferential treatment of me.
UPRIGHTNESS	EQUITABLENESS
Previously, I (as your personal follower) have will tolerantly acted in a concerned fashion towards you: in response to your (as PA) deferential treatment of me. But now, you (as group authority) will deferentially act in an *upright* fashion towards me: in anticipation of my (as PF) concerned treatment of you.	Previously, you (as group authority) have deferentially acted in an upright fashion towards me: in anticipation of my (as PF) concerned treatment of you. But now, I (as group representative) will *equitably* act with concern towards you: overruling your (as GA) deferential sense of uprightness.
FREEDOM	FAIRNESS
Previously, I (as group representative) have equitably acted with concern towards you: in response to your (as GA) deferential sense of uprightness. But now, you (as spiritual authority) will *freely* act in an upright fashion towards me: in anticipation of my (as GR) equitable sense of concern.	Previously, you (as spiritual authority) have freely acted in an upright fashion towards me: in anticipation of my (as GR) equitable sense of concern. But now, I (as your spiritual disciple) will equitably act in a *fair* fashion towards you: overruling your (as SA) free sense of uprightness.
CONSCIENCE	CREDENCE
Previously, I (as your spiritual disciple) have equitably acted fairly towards you: in response to your (as SA) free sense of uprightness. But now, you (as humanitarian authority) will freely act in a *conscientious* fashion towards me: in anticipation of my (as SD) equitable sense of fairness.	Previously, you (as humanitarian authority) have freely acted conscientiously towards me: in anticipation of my (as SD) equitable sense of fairness. But now, I (as representative member of humanity) will fairly express a sense of *credence* in you: overruling your (as HA) conscientious treatment of me
BROTHERHOOD	CONTENTMENT
Previously, I (as representative member of humanity) have fairly expressed a sense of credence in you: in response to your (as HA) conscientious treatment of me. But now, you (as transcendental authority) will conscientiously act in a *brotherly* fashion: in anticipation of my (as RH) fair sense of credence.	Previously, you (as transcendental authority) have acted in a brotherly fashion towards me: in anticipation of my (as RH) fair sense of credence. But now, I (as your transcendental follower) will *contentedly* express a sense of credence in you: overruling your (as TA) brotherly treatment of me.

Table B-2 – The Definitions Based on Deference/Concern

PASSION	CONSIDERATION
Previously, you (as procurer) have acted approachfully towards me: in response to my (as reinforcer) rewarding treatment of you. But now, I (as personal authority) will *passionately* act in a rewarding fashion towards you: in anticipation of your (as procurer) approachful treatment of me.	Previously, I (as personal authority) have passionately acted in rewarding fashion towards you: in anticipation of your (as procurer) approachful treatment of me. But now, you (as personal follower) will approachfully act in a *considerate* fashion towards me: overruling my (as PA) passionate treatment of you.
RESPECTFULNESS	**CONTINENCE**
Previously, you (as my personal follower) have approachfully acted in a considerate fashion towards me: in response to my (as PA) passionate treatment of you. But now, I (as group authority) will passionately act *respectfully* towards you: in anticipation of your (as PF) considerate treatment of me.	Previously, I (as group authority) have passionately acted respectfully towards you: in anticipation of your (as PF) considerate treatment of me. But now, you (as group representative) will *continently* act in a considerate fashion towards me: overruling my (as GA) passionate-respect for you.
COURTESY	**KINDNESS**
Previously, you (as group representative) have continently acted in a considerate fashion towards me: in response to my (as GA) passionate-respect for you. But now, I (as spiritual authority) will *courteously* act respectfully towards you: in anticipation of your (as GR) continent sense of consideration.	Previously, I (as spiritual authority) have courteously acted in a respectful fashion towards you: in anticipation of your (as GR) continent sense of consideration. But now, you (as my spiritual disciple) will continently act in a *kind* fashion towards me: overruling my (as SA) courteous-respect for you.
GRACIOUSNESS	**BENEVOLENCE**
Previously, you (as my spiritual disciple) have continently acted in a kind fashion towards me: in response to my (as SA) courteous-respect for you. But now, I (as humanitarian authority) will courteously act in a *gracious* fashion towards you: in anticipation of your (as SD) kind treatment of me.	Previously, I (as humanitarian authority) have courteously acted graciously towards you: in anticipation of your (as SD) kind treatment of me. But now, you (as representative member of humanity) will *benevolently* act in a kind fashion towards me: overruling my (as HA) gracious treatment of you.
AFFECTION	**GLADNESS**
Previously, you (as representative member of humanity) have benevolently acted in a kind fashion towards me: in response to my (as HA) gracious treatment of you. But now, I (as transcendental authority) will graciously act *affectionately* towards you: in anticipation of your (as RH) benevolent sense of kindness.	Previously, I (as transcendental authority) have graciously acted in an affectionate fashion towards you: in anticipation of your (as RH) benevolent sense of kindness. But now, you (as my transcendental follower) will benevolently act with *gladness* towards me: overruling my (as TA) affectionate treatment of you.

Table B-3 – The Definitions Based on Passion/Consideration

APPREHENSION	ADHERENCE
Previously, you (as procurer) have acted aversively towards me: in response to my (as reinforcer) tolerant treatment of you. But now, I (as personal authority) will *apprehensively* act tolerantly towards you: in anticipation of your (as procurer) aversive treatment of me.	Previously, I (as personal authority) have apprehensively acted tolerantly towards you: in anticipation of your (as procurer) aversive treatment of me. But now, you (as personal follower) will aversively act in an *adherent* fashion towards me: overruling my (as PA) apprehensive treatment of you.
PROBITY	BRAVERY
Previously, you (as my personal follower) have aversively acted in an adherent fashion towards me: in response to my (as PA) apprehensive treatment of you. But now, I (as group authority) will apprehensively act with *probity* towards you: in anticipation of your (as PF) adherent treatment of me.	Previously, I (as group authority) have apprehensively acted in a probity-filled fashion towards you: in anticipation of your (as PF) adherent treatment of me. But now, you (as group representative) will *bravely* act adherently towards me: overruling my (as GA) probity-filled treatment of you.
FORBEARANCE	SCRUPULOUSNESS
Previously, you (as group representative) have bravely acted adherently towards me: in response to my (as GA) probity-filled treatment of you. But now, I (as spiritual authority) will *forbearingly* act with probity towards you: in anticipation of your (as GR) brave treatment of me.	Previously, I (as spiritual authority) have forbearingly acted with probity towards you: in anticipation of your (as GR) brave sense of adherence. But now, you (as my spiritual disciple) will *scrupulously* act bravely towards me: overruling my (as SA) forbearing treatment of you.
PATIENCE	SHREWDNESS
Previously, you (as my spiritual disciple) have scrupulously acted bravely towards me: in response to my (as SA) forbearing treatment of you. But now, I (as humanitarian authority) will forbearingly act *patiently* towards you: in anticipation of your (as SD) scrupulous treatment of me.	Previously, I (as humanitarian authority) have forbearingly acted patiently towards you: in anticipation of your (as SD) scrupulous treatment of me. But now, you (as representative member of humanity) will scrupulously act in a *shrewd* fashion towards me: overruling my (as HA) patient treatment of you.
AMITY	ACCORDANCE
Previously, you (as representative member of humanity) have scrupulously acted shrewdly towards me: in response to my (as HA) patient treatment of you. But now, I (as transcendental authority) will patiently act with *amity* towards you: in anticipation of your (as RH) shrewd treatment of me.	Previously, I (as transcendental authority) have patiently acted in an amity-filled fashion towards you: in anticipation of your (as RH) shrewd treatment of me. But now, you (as transcendental follower) will shrewdly act with *accordance* towards me: overruling my (as TA) amity-filled treatment of you.

Table B-4 – The Definitions Based on Apprehension/Adherence

deed, this basic pattern further extends to the remaining humanitarian and transcendental authority levels within the linguistic matrix as well, ceasing only when the level of abstraction exceeds the scope of the language tradition.

AN OVERVIEW OF
COMMUNICATION IN GENERAL

A few general speculations on communication in general prove crucial at this juncture. First, the role of "myself" within the communication dynamic clearly represents the crucial factor, in direct contrast to the more extraneous sense of "the other." This observation is definitely warranted being that I only have direct access to my own thoughts and feelings. Alternately I can only make empathic predictions for those thoughts and feelings held by "the other." I formally model (to some degree) the unique mindset of "the other" through the aid of the *accessory* schematic definitions depicted in **Boxes B** and **C**. According to this simulation of the accessory realm, I formally imagine the motivations of "the other" within a given interaction. This includes moments alone when I mentally rehearse dialogue in anticipation of meeting others ahead of time. This further entails imagining all of the potential contingencies or responses "the other" might employ in preparation so as not to be caught off-guard. The other party in the interaction (by definition) does not even need to be present in order to conduct such mental dialogue. The eventual meeting with the "other" only serves to finalize the choices initially imagined. The outwardly observable behaviors of "the other," in turn, are compared to the mental model of my own expectations, the results eventually determining my own next course of action. This egocentric model of communication in general (by definition) is based entirely upon the intrinsic consciousness of "myself." The outwardly observable actions of "the other," in turn, are predicted in terms of my own projected mental model. Furthermore, the awareness experienced by the "the other" is similarly invested with its own full range of autonomous choices. Indeed, "the other" entertains a fully independent sense of identity operating through a self-governing style of ego status. This multitude of individual selves merges into a unified communicational continuum, whereby forming an overlapping series of interpersonal projections in relation to one another. This all-encompassing communicational dynamic still relies upon my primary mental monologue linking myself with the mental projections of others, a model calibrated in terms of outward-

ly observable behaviors, whereby imparting a semblance of conformity with a real-life situation.

According to this multi-modal model of virtuous communication, whether we chose to acknowledge it or not, we all are basically alone in the world in terms of the restrictions of our own mental thought processes. Our firm convictions with respect to others are basically projections of our own making, mental models periodically reinforced to some extent through external observation. This formal sense of isolation actually represents a blessing in disguise, for the private life we so dearly enjoy would remain inconceivable if others could freely read our minds (and vice versa). It is only through the symbolism expressed through the human speech lexicon that interpersonal communication is feasible at all (through standards maintained in a shared cultural sense).

In terms of this dualistic interpretation, my introspective mental states (by definition) are projected onto you, whereas yours (in theory) are referred back to me. There is no single channel of communication, rather an intersecting confluence of mutual perspectives. It is this mental construct of others with which we have a relationship, not the direct sense we might wish to believe: a saving illusion in light of the more brutally honest picture currently proposed. Along similar lines of reasoning, Irish-born essayist, Dame Rebecca West insightfully wrote: "There is no such thing as conversation, it is an illusion. There are intersecting monologues: that is all."

It should further be emphasized that this abiding sense of isolation strictly applies only to symbolic verbal communication. Indeed, nonverbal communication of a synchronously-empathic nature is much more amenable to such a social degree of synergy across the board. Here a concerted effort towards directed mindfulness permits concentration within a present tense, unlike the more temporally-focused past/future dimensions characterizing verbal communication of an affective nature. With such verbal chatter temporarily attenuated, the mindful individual now becomes free to immediately attend to meaningful facial-cues and bodily synchronies in relation to others, providing an extreme degree of empathic synchrony that transcends any linguistic means designed to explain it. Hence, by periodically turning down the "chatter-box" of verbal dialogue that effectively dominates our waking moments, a more effective experience within the here-and-now provides a more effective means of establishing a meaningful sense of synchrony and synergy in relation to our empathic dealings with our significant others.

8

THE GENERAL UNIFYING
VIRTUOUS THEMES

The preceding motivational analysis encompassing both main and accessory virtuous terms predicts a further emergent quality of critical import; namely, the identification of the general unifying themes. This higher-order class of themes represents a *meta-order* summation with respect to each individual level within the ethical hierarchy; in essence, a 2nd order style of meta-perspective. For instance, the general unifying theme of *utilitarianism* encompasses the collective group focus comprising the cardinal virtues (prudence-justice-temperance-fortitude). A similar pattern further holds true for the remaining spiritual, humanitarian, and transcendental levels within the ethical hierarchy: as thematically depicted in **Fig. 8A**. For instance, the personal authority perspective introduces the theme of *individualism*, extending to the *personalism* characterizing the group authority level. The spiritual authority perspective, in turn, extends to the more idealized theme of *romanticism* consistent with a much broader focus on universal principles. The themes for the remaining humanitarian and transcendental levels, in turn, take their cues from their respective individual listings of terms; namely, *ecumenism* and *humanism*: whereby rounding-out the virtuous hierarchy of themes.

In a related fashion, the remaining sequence of *follower* roles is similarly organized in terms of such an ascending hierarchy of general unifying themes; namely, pragmatism, utilitarianism, ecclesiasticism, eclecticism, and mysticism. For instance the first-mentioned theme of *pragmatism* refers to that which is practical or expedient to the individual, extending (in a group sense) to a *utilitarian* concern for the common good. This ascending hierarchy of follower themes ultimately extends to the remaining spiritual, humanitarian, and transcendental domains with respect to

the cohesive listing of ecclesiasticism, eclecticism, and mysticism, respectively.

A few general conclusions emerge from this overarching pattern of general unifying themes. As initially described, the general unifying themes are further subdivided into either immediately-active authority roles (occurring within the present) or passively-potential follower modes (projected into a future-directed time-frame). The active behavioral modes refer to the immediately-active class of authority themes: namely, individualism, personalism, romanticism, ecumenism, and humanism. This immediately-active class of authority-based themes further anticipates (as their object) the passively-potential complement of future-directed follower themes; namely, pragmatism, utilitarianism, ecclesiasticism, eclecticism, and mysticism. Generally speaking, the initial authority themes immediately initiate the conditioned interaction in anticipation of the projected potentiality implicit to the respective follower themes. This latter class of follower themes effectively consummates the more immediately active focus for the authority themes. A more detailed examination of these general unifying themes will now be undertaken, including an extensive analysis of their extensive literary traditions across the board.

INDIVIDUALISM

The respective analysis of the main virtuous themes is currently launched with respect to the first-mentioned theme of *individualism*. This theme formally encompasses the subordinate listing of ego states (solicitousness, submissiveness, desire, and worry) indicative of such an immediately-active style of personal authority perspective. The term derives from the Latin

118 - INDIVIDUALISM **Ego States** *Personal Authority*	**128 - PRAGMATISM** **Alter Ego States** *Personal Follower*
138 - PERSONALISM **Personal Ideals** *Group Authority*	**148 - UTILITARIANISM** **Cardinal Virtues** *Group Representative*
158 - ROMANTICISM **Civil Liberties** *Spiritual Authority*	**168 ECCLESIASTICISM** **Theological Virtues** *Spiritual Disciple*
178 - ECUMENISM **Ecumenical Ideals** *Humanitarian Authority*	**188 - ECLECTICISM** **Classical Values** *Humanitarian Follower*
198 - HUMANISM **Humanistic Values** *Transcendental Authority*	**108 - MYSTICISM** **Mystical Values** *Transcendental Follower*

Fig. 8A – The Three-Digit Codes for the "Meta" Virtuous Themes

individuus from *in-* (not) and *dividuus* (divisible), from *didere* (to divide). The modern sense of the term emerged through ideas promoted by British philosophers Adam Smith and Jeremy Bentham. This enduring sense of individualism is further noted by Alexis de Tocqueville as crucial to the overarching American temperament.

In a general sense, individualist values are person-centered, where all individuals share a common moral status. Individualism opposes external authority without consent, the power of government chiefly being restricted to maintaining law and order. The chief aim of society is the promotion of individual human rights and welfare, whereby encouraging the cultivation of individual moral character. True individuals freely live their lives as they see fit without unwarranted interference from the state. The principles of individualism were briefly challenged at the turn of the 20th century with the rise of Communism and Fascism, although regained prominence through a global return to representative forms of government.

In a behavioral context, individualism encompasses the instinctual attributes specified for the personal authority role; namely, that active sense of vitality derived from an immediate course of action. This immediate-active style of desirous reinforcement or lenient concern invokes such a personal style of authority status: as does solicitousness and submissiveness, respectively. These personal authority attributes for individualism clearly provide a fitting foundation for the ascending hierarchy of general unifying themes to follow.

PERSONALISM

The personal perspectives for individualism, in turn, extend to a group sphere of influence with respect to the civic-focused theme of *personalism*. The term derives from the Latin *persona*, a mask in ancient theatres worn to depict an emotional reaction: ultimately extending to the role of a dramatic actor. In a general social sense, personalism refers to the notion of dignity and integrity within a civil society. Some trace its origins to Anaxagoras, as well as further influences attributed to Plato and Aristotle. Boethius defines the persona as: "an individual substance of a rational nature." This preliminary interpretation continues through the efforts of St. Augustine, Avicenna, and Thomas Aquinas: eventually entering our modern age with respect to the rationalist and empiricist traditions.

The modern-day sense of personalism traces its origins to 19th-century thought, although reaching ultimate expression beginning with the 20th century. Early German philosopher Friedrich Schleiermacher used the term *Personalismus* in his *Discourses* (1799). Cambridge philosopher John Grote further referred to his novel metaphysical approach as *personalism*, from his *Exploratio Philosophica* (1865). In each of these formulations, a respective emphasis on human dignity proves highly suggestive of the affiliated listing of personal ideals (glory-honor-dignity-integrity). Indeed, their respective designation as "personal ideals" clearly reflects the civic-centered nature of personalism: a more refined variation on the more elementary theme of individualism. It shares with the latter the immediately-active sense of vitality inherent to such a group authority perspective. Consequently, this enduring sense of personalism represents a fitting adjunct to the group authority perspective, a virtuous innovation consistent with the ascending hierarchy of general unifying themes.

ROMANTICISM

The group prerequisites for personalism, in turn, extend to a universal sphere of influence with respect to the overarching theme of *romanticism*. The term derives from the French *romantique*, from the Middle French *romant* (a romance): an oblique reference to the Old French *romanz* (a narrative in verse). Romanticism emerged in the late 18th and early 19th centuries as a stylistic movement that downplayed the prevailing imitation of neo-classical stereotypes. It flourished in large part due to the libertarian and egalitarian ideals emerging from the French Revolution, an innovation that exalted the supremacy of the common man. The basic ideals of Romanticism are similarly noble: namely, an appreciation of the natural world and a belief in the goodness of the human spirit, whereby exalting emotional sensibility over reason and intellect. In this latter sense, Romanticism represents a cultural backlash against the orderly rationality of the Enlightenment, the latter disparaged as artificially impersonal and mechanistic. Romanticism instead favored the emotional saliency of direct individual experience, as well as the boundless nature of the unfettered human imagination.

This enduring fascination with larger-than-life themes seems consistent with romanticism's universal placement within the virtuous hierarchy of themes. Indeed, themes of a romanticized nature enjoy virtually universal appeal throughout the span of world literature. The heroic exploits of the supreme authority figure are romanticized to the point of attracting widespread public appeal.

The respective class of the ideals of romanticism (providence, liberty, civility, and austerity) certainly fulfills such a universal perspective, projecting a romanticized style of global appeal consistent with such a universal style of authority perspective. Indeed, each of the individual civil liberties was worshipped as a deity in classical times so significant was their universal appeal. Consequently, romanticism shares with the subordinate themes of individualism and personalism such an immediate vitality set of perspectives, although now targeting a universal sphere of influence. Romanticism, therefore, continues the tradition of the revered range of authority themes befitting such a grand universal perspective.

ECUMENISM

Ascending to the next higher humanitarian sphere of influence invokes the enduring theme of *ecumenism*. The term derives from the Latin *oecumenicus* (general, universal), from the Greek *oikoumene* (of the inhabited world): from *oikoumenos*, present participle of *oikein* (to inhabit), from *oikos* (house or habitation). In its modern sense, it denotes the movement towards the anticipated unification of all Protestant denominations, and (ultimately) all of Christianity. This movement gained impetus during the First Assembly of the World Council of Churches in Amsterdam in 1948, a gathering extending to Protestant, Eastern Orthodox, and Catholic representatives. Indeed, this initiative endures today as the major force for promoting ecumenism across the globe.

In its most elementary sense, ecumenism promotes a sense of unity and mutual cooperation amongst all of the various denominations within a given belief system. This overarching goal of interfaith cooperation aims towards greater respect and tolerance amongst all of the religions of the world. It has awakened a universal conscience towards a renewed spirit of mission and service to the global community. This evangelical spirit is particularly evident in the enduring tradition of the ecumenical councils of the early Christian Church, sharing a focus in fortifying and preserving the unity of faith.

This authority-based theme of ecumenism proves a fitting humanitarian adjunct to the preliminary hierarchy of themes: namely, individualism, personalism, and romanticism. This enduring humanitarian perspective is clearly reflective of the enduring mission of the ecumenical councils devoted to contemporary Church issues. The affiliated listing of ecumenical ideals (grace,

free-will, magnanimity, and equanimity) further imparts such a grand humanitarian time-scale. Indeed, the ecumenical movement actively seeks to promote this enduring class of humanitarian themes regardless of the individual ethical traditions therein.

HUMANISM

The ascending hierarchy of authority-based themes ultimately culminates with respect to the crowning transcendental theme of *humanism*. The term derives from the Latin *literae humaniores* (polite literature), from the root-stem *homo* (a human being). Its original Renaissance connotations referred to the surviving works of Greek and Latin literature. The Italian revival based upon the Latin Arts and Letters, in turn, promoted the growth of the modern *humanistic* movement. In general, the Humanities were classified as that branch of literature (classics, rhetoric, and poetry) that worked to humanize and refine the intellect: a style of education befitting the academic elite of the age.

The affiliated Renaissance revolt against the dogmatic strictures of Church decree promoted a high degree of intellectual freedom, whereby enabling scientific research and economic mercantilism. In celebration of the classical traditions characterizing the Greco-Roman Era, Renaissance Humanism emerged as a powerful counterpoint to the ecclesiastical dictates of the Roman Catholic Church (the dominant academic institution of its day). Through allusion to the classical Greek injunction "Know Thyself," humanists promoted a free-thinking style of academic optimism. The humanistic movement eventually spread throughout Europe aided by the invention of movable type.

In concert with a subsequent decline in Church influence, humanism acquired many of its more modern secular attributes. Consistent with the current cultural pre-eminence of science and technology, *secular* humanism has assumed a mantle of distinction governing democratic forms of government. This is particularly telling in the respective class of the *humanistic* values (peace, love, tranquility, and equality): themes all sharing such a lofty humanistic focus indicative of the vitality underlying the transcendental authority perspective. Indeed, all four values profess a profound transcendental disregard for the more routine sphere of affairs characterizing the subordinate hierarchy of unifying themes; namely, individualism, personalism, romanticism, and ecumenism. Lofty platitudes such as peace and love continue to serve as supreme transcendental ideals towards which one can consistently strive for, although rarely entirely realized in practice.

PRAGMATISM

The completed description of the authority-based sequence of general unifying themes invites further comparisons to the remaining ascending hierarchy of themes based upon the respective follower roles. Indeed, this parallel style of analysis is currently initiated with respect to the personal follower theme of *pragmatism*. The term derives from the Latin *pragmaticus* (skilled in business or law) from the Greek *pragmatikos* (versed in business): from *pragmatos* (civil business or activity), from *prassein* (to act or perform). The modern sense of the term derives from the system of philosophy proposed jointly by C. S. Peirce, William James, and John Dewey circa the turn of the 20th century. Pragmatism asserts that the meaningfulness of any course of action is chiefly a function of its projected practical outcome. Pragmatism resolves ethical conflicts by investigating the practical consequences of a given choice of action. Ideas are truthful insofar as they conform to the facts and speak to practicality, as well as the concrete means towards achievement.

Along a similar line of reasoning, pragmatism exemplifies the personal follower perspective, which potentially determines what is feasible (in a practical sense) within a given conditioned interaction, whereby effectively consummating the more immediately-active sense of individualism expressed by the personal authority figure. The projected class of alter ego states (approval, leniency, solicitousness, and submissiveness) collectively provides the ethical standards by which pragmatism is judged, where the ends truly justify the means.

UTILITARIANISM

The personal prerequisites for pragmatism, in turn, extend to a civic sphere of influence with respect to the group-follower theme of *utilitarianism*. The term derives from the Latin *utilitas*, from *uti* (to use). This designation was first coined by Jeremy Bentham in 1781 in reference to his doctrine of the greatest potential good for the greatest number. Utilitarianism was further expanded through the efforts of James Mill and John Stuart Mill. This father-and-son team proposed that the greatest potential good resides in maximizing the common public welfare. Indeed, utilitarianism extends the more basic theme of pragmatism into

a broader civic sphere of influence. The utilitarian movement contrasted with the competing sense of romanticism, primarily with respect to the latter's focus upon emotionality and a disregard for rationality. The utilitarian movement, in contrast, held that proper social order emerged from a balanced blend of individual interests. Furthermore, the principles of utility set a viable standard for judging legal and moral efficacy.

Utilitarianism approves action that promotes an overarching sense of welfare within society as a whole, an aspiration consistent with the temperate and fortitudinous dimensions characterizing the group follower perspective. Such benefits need not solely be restricted to intent, but rather extending to the outcome of the action, a pattern similar to that established for pragmatism. This projected range of potentiality is particularly evident in the respective class of cardinal virtues (prudence, justice, temperance, and fortitude): a quartet celebrating group cohesiveness and cooperation towards the common good. Indeed, the interests of all must equally be considered if utilitarianism is truly to profess an equitable range of utility. Here again the ends are fittingly seen to justify the means.

ECCLESIASTICISM

Ascending, once again, to the next higher universal realm, in turn, gives way to the spiritual disciple theme of *ecclesiasticism*. It is traditionally defined as that branch of Christian theology that is devoted to the study of the organizational principles at work within the Church: particularly its practical, operational, and congregational aspects. The term derives from the Greek *ekklesia* (an assembly summoned by a crier), the compound of *ek-* (out of) and *kalein* (to call). In ancient Athens the ecclesia was a popular assembly where all male citizenry exercised political influence. All male citizens over the age of twenty were eligible to cast their vote for issues on the agenda.

The modern Christian sense of the term derives from the Late Latin *ecclesiasticus*, from the Greek *ekklesiastes* (speaker of the assembly). New Testament writers (particularly St. Paul) employed this term to refer to local assemblies of Christians, such as those gathered at Corinth (I Corinthians 1:2). This connotation eventually came to denote the unity of the early Christian Church in general.

The first formal mention of ecclesiasticism dates to the medieval Scholastic tradition. Protestant ecclesiasticism emphasizes the spiritual nature of the Christian Church, whereas the

INDIVIDUALISM	PRAGMATISM
Previously, you have potentially acted in a motivational fashion towards me: in response to my active treatment of you. But now, I (as personal authority) will actively behave in an *individualistic* fashion towards you: in anticipation of your potentially motivated treatment of me.	Previously, I (as personal authority) have actively behaved individualistically towards you: in anticipation of your potential treatment of me. But now, you (as my personal follower) will potentially act in a *pragmatic* fashion towards me: overruling my (as PA) individualistic treatment of you.
PERSONALISM	**UTILITARIANISM**
Previously, you (as my personal follower) have potentially acted in a pragmatic fashion towards me: in response to my (as PA) individualistic treatment of you. But now, I (as group authority) will individualistically act in a *personable* fashion towards you: in anticipation of your (as PF) pragmatic treatment of me.	Previously, I (as group authority) have individualistically acted personably towards you: in anticipation of your (as PF) pragmatic treatment of me. But now, you (as group representative) will pragmatically act in a *utilitarian* fashion towards me: overruling my (as GA) personable treatment of you.
ROMANTICISM	**ECCESIASTICISM**
Previously, you (as group representative) have pragmatically acted in a utilitarian fashion towards me: in response to my (as GA) personable treatment of you. But now, I (as spiritual authority) will personably act in a *romanticized* fashion towards you: in anticipation of your (as GR) utilitarian treatment of me.	Previously, I (as spiritual authority) have personably acted romantically towards you: in anticipation of your (as GR) utilitarian treatment of me. But now, you (as spiritual disciple) will utilitarianally act in an *ecclesiastical* fashion towards me: overruling my (as SA) romantic treatment of you.
ECUMENISM	**ECLECTICISM**
Previously, you (as my spiritual disciple) have acted in an ecclesiastical fashion towards me: in response to my (as SA) romantic treatment of you. But now, I (as humanitarian authority) will romantically act in an *ecumenical* fashion towards you: in anticipation of your (as SD) ecclesiastical treatment me.	Previously, I (as humanit. authority) have acted in an ecumenical fashion towards you: in anticipation of your (as SD) sense of ecclesiasticism. But now, you (as representative member of humanity) will ecclesiastically act in an *eclectic* fashion towards me: overruling my (as HA) ecumenical treatment of you.
HUMANISM	**MYSTICISM**
Previously, you (as representative member of humanity) have ecclesiastically acted eclectically towards me: in response to my (as HA) ecumenical treatment of you. But now, I (as transcendental authority) will ecumenically act *humanistically* towards you: in anticipation of your (as RH) sense of eclecticism.	Previously, I (as transcendental authority) have acted in a humanistic fashion towards you: in anticipation of your (as RH) eclectic treatment of me. But now, you (as my transcendental follower) will eclectically act in a *mystical* fashion towards me: overruling my (as TA) humanistic treatment of you.

Table C-1 – The "Meta" Definitions for the Virtuous Themes

Roman Catholic format alternately stresses an organizational focus. The modern sense of the term blends a mixture of these diverse theological perspectives. Here ecclesiasticism continues in the tradition previously established for the follower themes of pragmatism and utilitarianism (although now targeting a more spiritual sphere of influence). Consequently, it formally encompasses the potentiality of the respective class of theological virtues (faith, hope, charity, and decency): scriptural ideals celebrating the scope of proper conduct characterizing the spiritual disciple perspective. Here the specifics for the spiritual disciple role (relative to the spiritual congregation) become exceedingly apparent in an ecclesiastical sense irrespective of religious exclusivity.

ECLECTICISM

The universal focus of ecclesiasticism, in turn, extends to a humanitarian sphere of influence with respect to the enduring philosophical theme of *eclecticism*. The term derives from the Greek *eklektikos* (selective), from *eklegein* (to pick out or select): from a compound of *ek-* (out) and *legein* (to choose). It refers to the practice of synthesizing the best philosophical traditions from many schools of thought. It originally referred to groups of classical philosophers that worked together to integrate doctrines from many competing systems. Consequently, eclecticism refers to the potential selection of a diverse system of elements without much concern for potential contradictions. It differs from *syncretism*, which seeks to combine various schools of thought while attempting to resolve to any underlying conflicts.

Renaissance humanists eclectically borrowed from both Catholic and Classical doctrines. Their efforts presaged a 19th century revival, such as proposed by French philosopher Victor Cousin (who popularized the modern sense of the term). Eclectics are sometimes accused of being inconsistent concerning their abstract juxtaposition of doctrines at the risk of fundamental incoherence, although the ends often outweigh the means.

In terms of this humanitarian follower perspective, the eclectic individual revels in enduring themes of a timeless nature, as reflected in the abstract listing of classical Greek values (beauty, truth, goodness, and wisdom). These enduring classical values have been revered throughout the ages, immutable precepts that have stood the test of time. Indeed, each of these classical Greek values was worshiped as a deity in its own right, so widespread was their philosophical appeal. Ec-

lecticism certainly rates its lofty humanitarian placement within the hierarchy of general unifying themes, whereby expanding upon the projected sense of potentiality inherent to the subordinate listing of themes: namely, pragmatism, utilitarianism, and ecclesiasticism.

MYSTICISM

The ascending hierarchy of general unifying themes ultimately culminates with respect to the crowning transcendental follower theme of *mysticism*. The term derives from the Greek *mystikos* (secret, mystic), from *mystes* (one who is initiated), from *myein* (to close one's eyes). These enduring connotations of mysticism appear as a common thread across all cultures and creeds. Indeed, many have speculated that some innate feature within the human psyche necessarily accounts for such supreme mystical aspirations. Only rare individuals, however, seem to be effortlessly capable of entering into such a mystical contemplation with the Divine. The early Church theologian Pseudo-Dionysius gives a systematic account of Christian mysticism, whereby contrasting the more routine realm of rational inquiry with the unplumbed depths of esoteric insight achieved through the mystical experience.

Although much additional detail would certainly seem logical at this juncture, this will not be discussed here due to the extensive discussion of mysticism contained within Chapter 6. Regardless of the individual traditions therein, this overarching theme of mysticism shares a number of key characteristics; namely, a transcendental follower perspective encompassing the affiliated complement of mystical values (ecstasy, bliss, joy, and harmony). Here mysticism represents the crowning transcendental realm within the virtuous hierarchy of themes, and one that proves incomparable to those entering its charmed embrace.

THE SCHEMATIC DEFINITIONS FOR THE MAIN VIRTUOUS THEMES

The completed description of the ascending ethical hierarchy for the general unifying themes offers an additional degree of validation for the overall virtuous realm. Indeed, the systematic pattern of organization for this ascending hierarchy of themes further specifies their potential for incorporation into the formal schematic definition format. Indeed, the full ten-part complement of "meta-" schematic definitions for the main virtuous themes is depicted in **Table C-1**. This table schematically depicts the reciprocating

119 - QUINTESSENTIAL. **Ego States II** *Personal Authority*	**129 - EXPEDIENCY** **Alter Ego States II** *Personal Follower*
139 - HEROISM **Personal Ideals II** *Group Authority*	**149 - PRACTICALITY** **Cardinal Virtues II** *Group Representative*
159 - CHARISMA **Civil Liberties II** *Spiritual Authority*	**169 - ORTHODOXY** **Theological Virtues II** *Spiritual Disciple*
179 - EVANGELISM **Ecumenical Ideals II** *Humanitarian Authority*	**189 - MORALISM** **Classical Values II** *Humanitarian Follower*
199 – COSMOPOLITAN. **Humanistic Values II** *Transcendental Authority*	**109 - SPIRITUALISM** **Mystical Values II** *Transcendental Follower*

Fig. 8B - The Three-Digit Codes for the Accessory Virtuous Themes

QUINTESSENTIALISM	EXPEDIENCY
Previously, I have potentially acted in a motivated fashion towards you: in response to your active treatment of me. But now, you (as personal authority) will actively behave in a *quintessential* fashion towards me: in anticipation of my potentially motivated treatment of you.	Previously, you (as personal authority) have acted in a quintessential fashion towards me: in anticipation of my potential treatment of you. But now, I (as your personal follower) will potentially act in an *expedient* fashion towards you: overruling your (as PA) quintessential treatment of me.
HEROISM	**PRACTICALITY**
Previously, I (as your personal follower) have potentially acted in an expedient fashion towards you: in response to your (as PA) quintessential treatment of me. But now, you (as group authority) will quintessentially act in a *heroic* fashion towards me: in anticipation of my (as PF) expedient treatment of you.	Previously, you (as group authority) have quintessentially acted in a heroic fashion towards me: in anticipation of my (as PF) expedient treatment of you. But now, I (as group representative) will *practically* act in an expedient fashion towards you: overruling your (as GA) heroic treatment of me.
CHARISMA	**ORTHODOXY**
Previously, I (as group representative) have practically acted in an expedient fashion towards you: in response to your (as GA) heroic treatment of me. But now, you (as spiritual authority) will heroically act in a *charismatic* fashion towards me: in anticipation of my (as GR) practical treatment of you.	Previously, you (as spiritual authority) have heroically acted in a charismatic fashion towards me: in anticipation of my (as GR) practical treatment of you. But now, I (as spiritual disciple) will practically act in an *orthodox* fashion towards you: overruling your (as SA) charismatic treatment of me.
EVANGELISM	**MORALISM**
Previously, I (as spiritual disciple) have practically acted in a orthodox fashion towards you: in response to your (as SA) charismatic treatment of me But now, you (as humanitarian authority) will charismatically act in an *evangelical* fashion towards me: in anticipation of my (as SD) orthodox treatment of you.	Previously, you (as humanitarian authority) have evangelically acted charismatically towards me: in anticipation of my (as SD) orthodox treatment of you. But now, I (as represent. member of humanity) will orthodoxly act *moralistically* towards you: overruling your (as HA) evangelical treatment of me.
COSMOPOLITANISM	**SPIRITUALISM**
Previously, I (as representative member of humanity) have acted moralistically towards you: in response to your (as HA) sense of evangelism. But now, you (as transcendental authority) will evangelically act in a *cosmopolitan* fashion towards me: in anticipation of my (as RH) moralistic treatment of you.	Previously, you (as transcendental authority) have acted cosmopolitanly towards me: in anticipation of my (as RH) moralistic treatment of you. But now, I (as your transcendental follower) will moralistically act in a *spiritualistic* fashion towards you: overruling your (as TA) cosmopolitan treatment of me.

Table C-2 - The Accessory Definitions for the Virtuous Themes

pattern linking both authority and follower roles across the entire ten-level span of the unified linguistic matrix. This newly proposed format of "meta" schematic definitions effectively transcends and unifies the individual listings of virtues, values, and ideals: a meta-order style of schematic innovation. For instance, the "meta" schematic definition for *utilitarianism* formally encompasses (as subsets) the four-part listing of individual definitions comprising the cardinal virtues (prudence, justice, temperance, and fortitude). A similar pattern further holds true for the remaining listings of virtuous themes, as the respective "meta" schematic definitions effectively serve to indicate.

As meta-order summations for the individual virtuous terms, the definitions for the general unifying themes scarcely exhibit the degree of clarity or precision previously established for the individual terms. A more intensive analysis of these "meta" schematic definitions, however, clearly reveals the basic dynamics at issue; namely, the active status for the authority roles effectively anticipates the passively-potential status characterizing the follower roles. For instance, the group authority personally acts in an individualistic fashion in anticipation of the pragmatically-utilitarian treatment expressed by the group representative.

Although this highly specialized range of general unifying themes might seem somewhat limited in terms of practical applications, they, nevertheless, provide a formal schematic template for the more basic listings of virtues and values at issue: effectively validating the dual definition format to an advanced degree of validity.

THE ACCESSORY GROUPINGS OF VIRTUOUS THEMES

The *main* listings of virtuous themes, in turn, are augmented by the predicted *accessory* class of general unifying themes, where the polarities of the "you" and "I" roles are reversed similar to that previously encountered for the (more basic) individual virtuous terms. As initially suggested in Chapter 7, the dual interplay of the main and accessory virtuous terms permits a convincing simulation of empathic communication through a reversal of the "you" and "I" perspectives within the schematic definitions. This dual pattern of main/accessory perspectives (by extension) can further be extended to the meta-order realm of the general unifying themes. The respective addition of these dual accessory counterparts adds a further crucial empathic dimension to the "meta-"

schematic definition format. Indeed, a suitable number of synonyms for the virtuous themes have been identified: resulting in the formal *accessory* format of themes schematically depicted in **Fig. 8B**, and also in terms of the compact diagram immediately below:

Quintessentialism	**Expediency**
Heroism	**Practicality**
Charisma	**Orthodoxy**
Evangelism	**Moralism**
Cosmopolitanism	**Spiritualism**

This accessory listing of themes directly mirrors the pattern previously established for the *main* themes with the exception that the "you" and "I" polarities are now reversed. For instance, the main *authority* sequence of individualism, personalism, romanticism, ecumenism, and humanism directly contrasts with the *accessory* sequence of themes; namely, quintessentialism, heroism, charisma, evangelism, and cosmopolitanism. Furthermore, the main *follower* sequence of pragmatism, utilitarianism, ecclesiasticism, eclecticism, and mysticism similarly reciprocates the respective accessory hierarchy; namely, expediency, practicality, orthodoxy, moralism, and spiritualism. Although the degree of correspondence for certain of these themes might not be as precise as might be expected, the overarching cohesiveness of this accessory system proves the crucial deciding factor here. Indeed, a majority of these accessory themes are not commonly encountered in general usage; hence, a more comprehensive description is deferred for coverage in a later edition.

The true test of validity for this accessory listing of themes ultimately extends to their incorporation into the respective schematic definition format. In direct analogy to the main sequence of themes (the schematic definitions of which are depicted in **Table C-1**), the accessory variations are similarly incorporated into their own schematic definition format: representing meta-order abstractions on the more basic listings of individual accessory terms. For instance, the "meta-" schematic definition for *evangelism* encompasses the four (accessory) ecumenical ideals as subsets (namely, blessings, conscientiousness, graciousness, and patience). Indeed, the complete ten-part listing of schematic definitions for the accessory virtuous themes is tabulated in **Table C-2**: in direct analogy to the pattern previously established for the main listings of themes. In comparison to the main set of definitions depicted in **Table C-1**, the reciprocal interplay of the "you" and

"I" perspectives becomes thoroughly apparent. Indeed, both the main and accessory variations permit a degree of empathic insight unprecedented on the world scene today with respect to the virtuous realm.

In conclusion, the completed description of the general unifying themes for the virtuous realm provides a welcome additional validation to the individual listings of virtues, values, and ideals. These general unifying themes are all endowed with well-established literary traditions, perhaps even rivaling those for the individual virtuous terms. These themes address a wide range of pressing social issues, although never before brought together in such a singular ethical synthesis. In this overarching sense, the newly devised master-hierarchy of virtuous themes offers the potential for a broad range of solutions towards maintaining global peace and prosperity.

For instance, with respect to the immediately-active class of authority ideals, the initial theme of *individualism* serves as a founding principle for the American way of life, an aspect uniquely celebrated through the US Bill of Rights. This pervasive foundation within individualism, in turn, switches the focus to the charismatic sense of *personalism* characterizing the group authority figure: an attribute prized by both politician and CEO. Certain privileged figures can even command a universal sphere of consideration, such as *romanticized* in the legendary exploits attributed to Mother Teresa, the Delai Lama, Pope John Paul II, etc. The truest degree of influence, however, enters into consideration at the humanitarian sphere of influence: as witnessed in themes of virtually *ecumenical* proportions: namely, environmental conservation, global climate change, and issues confronting global poverty. In terms of its crowning sphere of abstraction, the transcendental authority perspective must always reign supreme, as exemplified in the enduring *humanistic* perspectives propounded by legendary visionaries such as Abraham Maslow and Fritz Perls.

These clearly romanticized authority perspectives, in turn, beg mention of the related hierarchy of follower themes, as represented in the ascending sequence of pragmatism, utilitarianism, ecclesiasticism, eclecticism, and mysticism. The initially mentioned theme of *pragmatism* serves as a guiding principle for acting in a personally-practical fashion, a fitting counterpoint to the immediately-active sense of individualism expressed by the personal authority figure. Furthermore, the group-focused theme of *utilitarianism* extends to a civic sphere of influence, as reflected in the potentiality of progressive movements targeting social justice and welfare. In terms of the even more abstract universal sphere of influence, progressivism ultimately acquires an *ecclesiastical* focus, as reflected in universal religious suffrage and/or liberation theology. The crowning humanitarian theme of *eclecticism* projects a truly timeless persona, where diverse social engineering movements are figuratively weighed in the balance. In this ultimate collective sense, the master ten-part hierarchy of the "meta-" virtuous themes represents the ultimate guide to wisdom and goodness for all generations to come.

This enduring philosophical focus is highly reminiscent of the seminal concept of *The Perennial Philosophy*, an eclectic system of thought that appropriates the best conceptual constructs from the broad range of philosophical schools that have flourished down through the ages. Indeed, the currently proposed ten-part hierarchy of the major virtues and values (in addition to the general unifying themes) qualifies as one of the most radically complete Perennial Philosophies devised to date, whereby unifying a broad range of philosophical themes. Indeed, each level within the ascending virtuous hierarchy is respectively associated with its own unique philosophical theme. This intriguing style of tandem correspondence between the individual virtuous terms and their general unifying themes expands this eclectic style of Perennial Philosophy to its fullest epistemological potential.

The truest collective potential for this ascending virtuous hierarchy ultimately appeals to the heretofore unprecedented potential for global collaboration and tolerance. In concert with the individual listings of virtues, values, and ideals, this newly devised complement of general unifying themes promises a new era in global cooperation that offers radically new solutions towards maintaining global peace and prosperity.

PART-II

9

AN INTRODUCTION TO
THE VICES OF DEFECT

The preceding examination of the virtuous realm proves exceedingly comprehensive in scope, although scarcely all-inclusive by any means. Indeed, any true system of ethics must necessarily account for the evils of society as well as the good: as reflected in the contrasting hierarchy of the realm of defect. Accordingly, for every virtue or value there necessarily exists a corresponding polar opposite (or vice): such as the contrast between love and hate, peace vs. war, good vs. evil, etc. The Greek philosopher Aristotle was among the first to categorize this contrasting realm of opposites defined as the vices of defect: namely, that state of defect that directly counters the nobler realm of the virtues.

As previously described in Chapter 2, the virtuous realm was formally defined in terms of a behavioral terminology of instrumental conditioning: categorized as appetite in anticipation of rewards (positive reinforcement) or aversion in expectation of leniency (negative reinforcement). Positive reinforcement reinforces solicitous types of behaviors, whereas negative reinforcement (sometimes confused with punishment) leniently reinforces submissive behaviors through the removal of some external threat from within the environment. Although alternate mechanisms are clearly involved, both positive and negative reinforcement proves similarly reinforcing to the individual, encouraging procurement or appeasement behaviors in an interactive setting.

At the opposing end of the spectrum, Skinner also distinguishes a darker side to conditioning theory colloquially known as punishment. Punishment represents a complete reversal of the reinforcement format in that positive/negative reinforcement is withheld rather then bestowed, discouraging behaviors judged not to be suitably solicitous or submissive. According to this latter punitive format, I withhold positive reinforcement because you failed to act solicitously towards me: "I refuse to give you the car keys because you didn't do your chores!" Similarly, lenient treatment is withheld in response to a lack of submissive behavior: "I refuse to give you a ride home because you talked back to me!"

These punitive consequences exhibit clear parallels to learning opportunities occurring naturally within the environment, similar to those encountered with respect to operant conditioning. Indeed, the fickle dictates of the natural world clearly specify such an innate understanding of punishment. For instance a food supply may become scarce or vanish altogether. Similarly a once reliable water hole may dry-up or go sour. The survival of the organism under such variable conditions directly relies upon the acknowledgement of such punitive consequences, where previous behavior patterns are abandoned altogether in favor of discovering an alternate means for re-establishing reinforcement.

These environmental perspectives on punishment similarly extend to a human sphere of influence, where inappropriate behaviors are discouraged in order to facilitate those judged more suitably solicitous or submissive. Ideally, punishment closely follows the antecedent behaviors, just as reinforcement similarly benefits through close proximity to the precipitating (procurement) behaviors. Unlike most other animal species, humans often cooperate with those they are not closely related, a feature that puzzles many evolutionary biologists. Indeed, various motives that cause individuals to engage in cooperative types of behaviors often prove costly to maintain. A general assumption emerges that favors are meant to be repaid, although (given a certain degree of cheating/freeloading) such repayment

(A)

solicitousness · approval
submissiveness · leniency

laziness · treachery
negligence · vindictiveness

X ⟶ Y $\underline{X}$ ⟶ $\underline{Y}$

Past   Present   Future

(Authority)   (Follower)

(B)

desire · aspiration
worry · compliance

apathy · spite
indifference · malice

Y ⟶ X $\underline{Y}$ ⟶ $\underline{X}$

Past   Present   Future

(Authority)   (Follower)

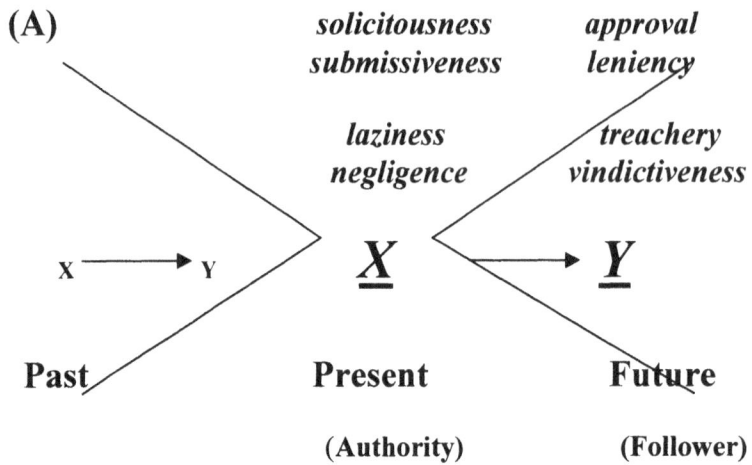

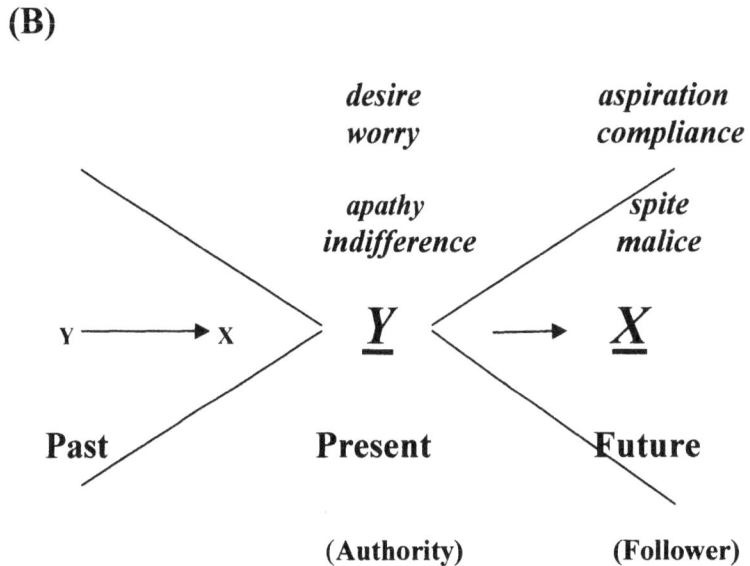

Fig. 9A - Two-stage Dynamic for the Ego & Alter Ego Virtues/Vices

cannot always be relied upon. One solution is to punish cheating, although imposing punishment can also be costly: leading to the evolution of what is termed altruistic punishment. In other words, the benefits to the group towards maintaining punishment (in order to keep cheaters in check) typically outweighs the cost to any of the individual punishers. This is particularly true when the defection rate is low, resulting in cost to punishers similarly being reduced. Furthermore, since free-loading does not pay well when punishers are common, cheating tends to become even rarer: a form of virtuous self-fulfilling cycle.

These processes allow both altruistic punishment and altruistic cooperation to be maintained even when social groups become larger in size, such as village-scale human societies that have existed for most of prehistory. Indeed, this theory makes several crucial predictions with respect to modern hunter-gatherer societies, groups that typically have a maximum of approximately 180 people. Without punishment, computer simulations by Boyd, et al (2003) suggest that cooperation should have mainly died out for groups of this size, indicating that altruistic punishment emerged as a crucial stabilizing factor towards encouraging the spread of culture and civilization. For many of the earliest civilizations, punishment for misconduct was particularly exacting and severe, such as exemplified in the "eye-for-an-eye" statutes contained within the ancient Babylonian Code of Hammurabi. A more detailed analysis of punishment within a social context is definitely in order here, specifying the dynamics governing punitive strategies in general.

THE TWO-STAGE DYNAMICS FOR PUNISHMENT

The most effective means for explaining the social dynamics of punishment occurs in direct contrast to its respective counterpart in reinforcement. As previously described in Chapter *2*, the human sphere of social conditioning is effectively seen as a two-stage process; namely, goal-seeking behaviors that anticipate subsequent reinforcement. For instance, the dedicated employee works industriously in order to earn the praise of his boss, or acts submissively in order to avoid being fired. When procurement is defined as (X) and reinforcement identified as (Y), the complete operant sequence is represented as $(X \rightarrow Y)$. According to this two-stage format, only one role can occur in the present at any given time, giving rise to the crucial paradigm of future-directed time dimensions. Behavioral terminology (by definition) does not technically recognize such introspective states

necessitating the introduction of a more colloquial style of terminology. In particular, this includes the ego states (solicitousness, submissiveness, desire, and worry) and the alter ego states (approval, leniency, aspiration, and compliance). These distinctive colloquial groupings effectively account for the sum-total of available slots predicted for the personal level within the virtuous hierarchy.

Extending these results to the related realm of punishment necessarily introduces a parallel complement of motivational terms specific to the contrasting realm of defect. Each specific ego or alter ego state is directly associated with its own corresponding antonym (or vice), identified as the direct antithesis of the respective virtuous mode. Along these lines, the ego states formally contrast with the respective listing of *ego vices* (laziness-negligence-apathy-indifference). Furthermore, the alter ego states, in turn, contrast with the respective listing of *alter ego vices* (treachery, vindictiveness, spite, and malice). For lack of a better designation, these darker sets of terms are respectively designated for the ego and alter ego terms, in direct analogy to their respective virtuous counterparts. For instance, *laziness* represents the darker counterpart of solicitousness, whereas *negligence* represents a similar variation on submissiveness. Furthermore, *apathy* represents the darker antithesis of desire, whereas *indifference* assigns a negative connotation to worry. Although the four basic ego vices all exhibit a fair degree of generality, they nevertheless serve as the elementary foundation for the entire darker realm of the ethical hierarchy to follow.

The remaining listing of the alter ego vices (treachery, vindictiveness, spite, and malice) is a grouping that virtually begs to be listed together: each defined as a formal antonym of its respective alter ego state. For instance, *treachery* represents the darker counterpart of approval, whereas *vindictiveness* makes a similar correspondence to leniency. Furthermore, *spite* suggests a more maladaptive variation on aspiration, whereas *malice* makes a similar contrast with compliance.

In direct analogy to the case previously established for the virtuous realm, the alter ego vices are similarly organized along the lines of a metaperspective style of format. For instance, you (as personal follower) *treacherously* act in a punitive fashion towards me, in reaction to my (as personal authority) lazy treatment of you. Similarly, you might punitively act *vindictively* towards me, in response to my negligent treatment of you. Furthermore, I (as personal follower) might

510	511
Laziness	Negligence
512	**513**
Apathy	Indifference

EGO VICES
(Personal Authority)

520	521
Treachery	Vindictiveness
522	**523**
Spite	Malice

ALTER EGO VICES
(Personal Follower)

530	531
Infamy	Dishonor
532	**533**
Foolishness	Capriciousness

VICES of PERSONALISM
(Group Authority)

540	541
Insurgency	Vengeance
542	**543**
Gluttony	Cowardice

CARDINAL VICES
(Group Representative)

550	551
Prodigality	Slavery
552	**553**
Vulgarity	Cruelty

CIVIL LIABILITIES
(Spiritual Authority)

560	561
Betrayal	Despair
562	**563**
Avarice	Antagonism

THEOLOGICAL VICES
(Spiritual Disciple)

570	571
Wrath	Tyranny
572	**573**
Oppression	Persecution

ECUMENICAL VICES
(Humanitarian Authority)

580	581
Ugliness	Hypocrisy
582	**583**
Evil	Cunning

CLASSICAL GREEK VICES
(Humanitarian Follower)

590	591
Anger	Prejudice
592	**593**
Hatred	Belligerence

HUMANISTIC VICES
(Transcendental Authority)

500	501
Abomination	Perdition
502	**503**
Iniquity	Turpitude

MYSTICAL VICES
(Transcendental Follower)

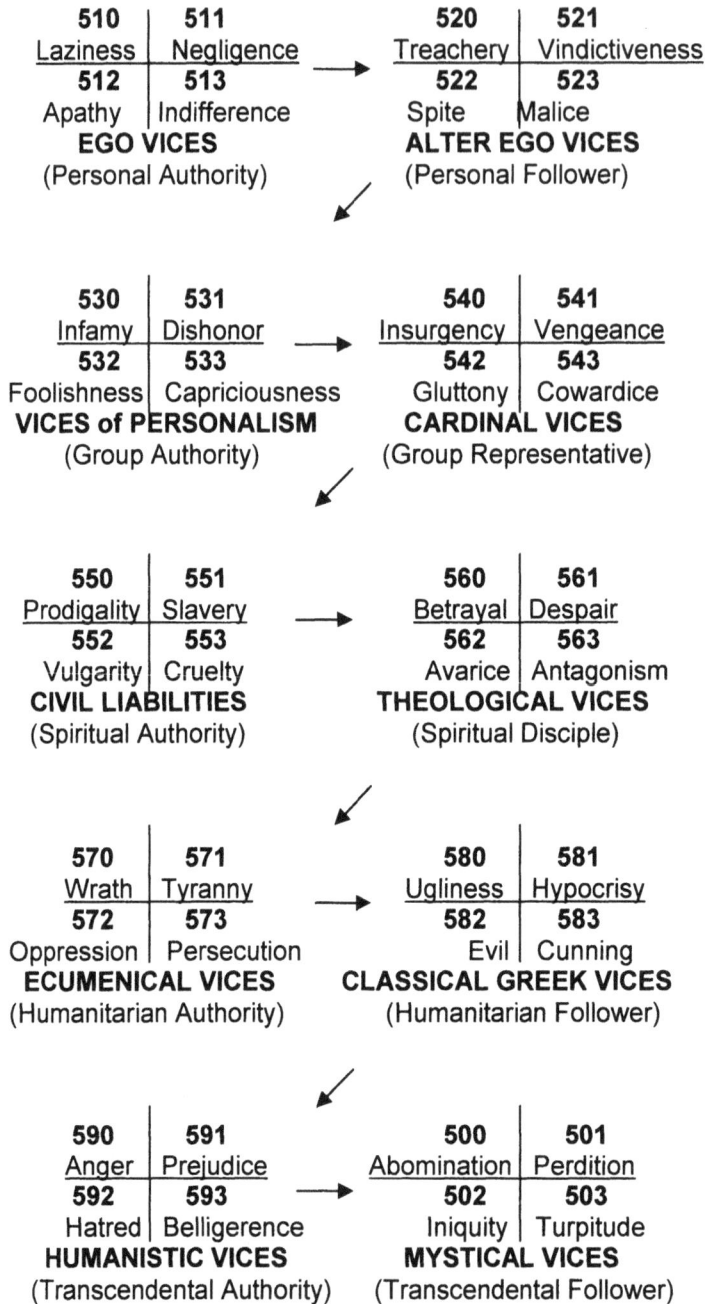

Fig. 9B – The Vices of Defect

spitefully act grudgingly towards you, in response to your apathetic treatment of me. Alternately, I could *maliciously* act in an adversarial fashion towards you, in response to your indifferent treatment of me. This distinctive set of interactions is schematically depicted in **Fig. 9A**, identical to **Fig. 2A**, with the exception that the vices (rather than the virtues) are now called into focus.

Similar to the case for the virtuous mode, the ego vices actively initiate each phase within the punitive interaction, whereby anticipating the potentiality characterizing the alter ego vices (lending credence to the notion of alter ego). Indeed, these future-directed alter ego vices directly complement their (active) ego vice counterparts: namely, laziness in anticipation of treachery, negligence in expectation of vindictiveness, etc. The remainder of the current chapter endeavors to examine the punitive dynamics underlying this eight-part complement of terms, providing a sturdy conceptual foundation for the remainder of the hierarchy of defect to follow.

LAZINESS - TREACHERY

The preliminary interplay of laziness/treachery will be examined first, followed by a subsequent description of apathy/spite. As suggested in terms of their elementary character, this overall darker range of terminology encompasses the most basic one-to-one style of personal dynamic governing the personal authority/follower roles. As initially described, the lazy failure to act solicitously on the part of the personal authority figure initiates the punitive interaction: whereby prompting the treacherous refusal to act rewardingly on the part of the personal follower. The initial lazy failure to act solicitously occurs within an immediately active time-frame consistent with a subjective "I" perspective. This initiatory phase is subjectively experienced as a lazy lack of solicitousness in direct acknowledgement of previous such cycles of laziness-then-treachery from previous experience: as depicted in the past-directed time-wedge of **Part A** of **Fig. 9A**. As the direct antithesis of the virtuous (solicitousness) perspective, laziness specifies directly acting to the contrary. Consequently, the personal authority lazily fails to act solicitously, whereby anticipating punitively-treacherous treatment on the part of the personal follower figure. Productivity is certainly regarded as a crucial factor during uncertain times, with laziness particularly singled out for such punitive social consequences.

The latter (predicted) style of punitive treatment represents a mental projection within a fu-ture-directed time-frame, equating with the complementary (objective) "you" perspective. The projected/potential nature of the treachery role, in essence, equates to the personal follower perspective: whereas the immediately-active expression of laziness invokes the immediacy of the personal authority role according to **Part A** of **Fig. 9A**. The treacherous determination to withhold reinforcement is formally assigned the personal follower role, being that it (in essence) follows the lazily-adversarial behavior that initiated the punitive interaction. The latter adversarial role is alternately identified as the personal authority role, being that the personal follower looks to the authority figure for rationalizing the entire punitive interaction. In essence, the authority status is based upon the power-leverage inherent to the very initiation of the punitive interaction.

A familiar example of such a one-to-one style of personal interaction concerns the enduring interplay between the lazy slacker and the treacherous rebel. The slacker lazily shirks any pretense of worthiness, earning the treacherous disapproval of the rebellious defector in the process. This potential denial of rewarding reinforcement on the part of the rebel is colloquially equated with treachery, a projected mental percept that acknowledges the initial lazy lack of solicitousness on the part of the slacker. The slacker clearly rates the personal authority role through the very initiation of the punitive interaction.

In order to more clearly illustrate the varying perspectives at issue, it proves useful to identify the respective subjective/objective polarities within the punitive interaction. Being that the authority figure acts first within the adversarial interaction, he/she rightfully assumes the subjective "I" status characterizing the active expression of laziness. The role of the treacherous defector, in turn, potentially assumes the objective "you" perspective specific to the personal follower role indicative of a projected withholding of reinforcement within a future-directed time-frame. The theme of treachery derives from the Old French *tricherie* (trickery), generally an allusion to the surprising fashion with which it is often bestowed. It refers to a betrayal of trust or confidence in one's personal authority figure, the same root-stem for the related theme of treason. Indeed, petty treason (in contrast to high treason) is defined as treachery occurring entirely within a personal sphere of influence: as in the betrayal of the master by his servant. Consequently treachery is defined as the chief moral antithesis of rewarding-approval: a suitably punitive response to the lazy proclivities of the personal authority figure.

In summary, according to **Part A** of **Fig. 9A**, I (as personal authority) lazily refuse to act solicitously towards you in anticipation of your (as personal follower) treacherous refusal to act rewardingly towards me. The latter treachery perspective clearly rates such a projected style of follower status, being that punishment is deferred as occurring within some future-directed time-frame: effectively complementing the initial lazy refusal to act solicitously on the part of the personal authority figure.

This initial dual style of interaction actually represents just the first of the two predicted stages within the overall punitive interchange. According to **Part B** of **Fig. 9A**, the follow-up sequence dictates that the personal follower ultimately acts upon his/her own potentially treacherous intentions, whereby punitively acting to discourage future cycles of unproductive behavior on the part of the slacker. Although the defector may act immediately with respect to such punitive intentions, (more often than not) such complex interactions entail a more measured pace of deliberation on the part of the defector. Indeed, it is this tenuous power of deliberation that ultimately imparts the power leverage enjoyed by the defector in relation to the slacker.

APATHY - SPITEFULNESS

As suggested earlier, the inevitable passage of time ultimately dictates that the time for treacherous punishment eventually comes to pass. The punitive dynamic governing this second stage within the adversarial interaction, in essence, mirrors the interplay previously established for the initial stage, although with a number of key differences. According to **Part B** of **Fig. 9A**, the personal follower now apathetically refuses to act rewardingly towards the slacker, whereby ultimately prompting non-cooperative feelings of spitefulness on the part of the latter. The authority perspective is now actively experienced in the present tense as the apathetic withholding of rewarding treatment in anticipation the spiteful perspectives of the follower figure.

As the chief moral antithesis of desire, the theme of apathy derives from the Greek prefix *a-* (without) and *pathos* (feeling), collectively specifying an absence of passion or desire. Indeed, apathy has facetiously been described as the "root cause of nothing." In this latter respect, the personal authority figure apathetically refuses to act rewardingly, whereby prompting the spiteful intention to withhold future cooperative behavior on the part of the personal follower. This initiatory

phase emerges as an acknowledgement of previous memories of apathy-then-spitefulness depicted in the past-directed time-wedge of **Part B** of **Fig. 9A**.

Furthermore, the initially active expression of laziness by the personal authority figure, in turn, is now displaced into a future-directed time-frame as the spiteful refusal to act solicitously on some future occasion: a response to the apathetic initial slight on the part of the defector. This potential style of adversarial attitude is colloquially equated with the familiar theme of spitefulness. Its modern spelling derives from the Old French *despit*, from the Latin *despectus*, (to despise): from *de-* (down) and *specere* (to look). It is traditionally defined as the tendency to frustrate or thwart, as in a grudging expression of ill will. This adversarial expression of spitefulness may take many forms, such as suggested in the popular expression: "Cut off one's nose to *spite* one's face" (in essence, acting in anger so as to cause harm to oneself). The subjective/objective polarities are effectively maintained in place for this second stage within the punitive interaction. The apathetic defector retains one's initial objective perspective in relation to treachery, whereas the spiteful slacker preserves one's subjective status as evident in the earlier laziness perspective.

In line with this subjective/objective arrangement of perspectives, you (as personal authority) now apathetically refuse to act rewardingly towards me in anticipation of my (now as personal follower) spiteful refusal to act solicitously towards you within some future-directed time-frame. Analogous to the case previously made for laziness-then-treachery, apathy-then-spite similarly represents a form of mental time travel projected into a future-directed time-frame: providing the motivational rationale for the (spiteful) follower status within the punitive relationship. This spiteful follower perspective represents an independent mental projection within the mind of the active authority role. Indeed, I can only essentially experience my own outward projections relating to you: mental constructs that are periodically verified in terms of the outwardly observable behaviors exhibited by others around me.

Returning once again to our ongoing slacker and defector example, a number of key factors can further be predicted with respect to the corresponding authority/follower roles. In terms of his/her own apathetic denial of approval, the defector, in essence, relinquishes one's own initial personal follower role, rather switching to an active personal authority status in relation to the slacker. The slacker, in turn, now assumes the

The Seven Deadly Sins – Detail from Flemish Painting by Hieronymous Bosch (1450-1516)
Outer-Ring Clockwise: Gluttony-Sloth-Lust-Pride-Anger-Envy-Covetousness – Prado Museum, Madrid

formal mantle of personal follower role consistent with the potentiality of one's spiteful refusal to act solicitously on some future occasion. According to this formal style of role reversal, the defector now apathetically withholds any active sense of approval in anticipation of the projected sense of spitefulness on the part of the slacker.

Therefore to summarize both phases within the punitive interaction, the actively-expressed lazy refusal to act solicitously on the part of the personal authority figure initiates the punitive interaction, whereby anticipating the treacherous determination to act punitively on the part of the personal follower. The latter style of punitive potentiality, in turn, ultimately achieves active status in terms of the immediate expression of apathy, whereby prompting the (projected) spiteful refusal to acting solicitously on the part of the personal follower. According to this second stage, you (as personal authority) now apathetically refuse to act approvingly towards me in anticipation of my (as personal follower) spiteful refusal to act solicitously towards you on some future occasion. This latter spiteful status (as a deliberative perspective in its own right) serves as the foundation for the initiation of further such complex cycles within the punitive interaction: whereby verifying the recursive dynamics of the entire punitive interchange. Indeed, this most basic personal level of punitive interaction provides the key conceptual mechanism for understanding the instinctually-driven nature of punishment in general, whereby further extending to a grand unified model encompassing the even more abstract realm of the ascending hierarchy that encompasses the vices of defect.

NEGLIGENCE - VINDICTIVENESS

Before jumping ahead to such significant applications, it proves crucial to examine the remainder of the motivational dynamics associated with the more antagonistic styles of punishment. In a general state of nature, negative reinforcement involves the lenient withholding of punitive consequences within the environment, or (in a human social sense) lenient treatment in response to aversive types of behavior. In the case of direct punishment, however, the personal authority figure negligently refuses to act submissively in anticipation of the vindictive failure to act leniently on the part of the personal follower. This projected sense of vindictiveness, in turn, ultimately becomes actualized as an indifferent refusal to act leniently within an immediately-active time-frame. In other words, the initial negligent failure to act submissively (that first prompted the punitive interaction), in turn, is mentally projected as a future-directed malicious refusal to act submissively on all future occasions, as depicted schematically in **Fig. 9A**.

This reverse style of submissive interplay is particularly apparent in the throat-baring behaviors typically described for the wolf pack, where the submissive pack member exaggerates one's degree of vulnerability in anticipation of an unconditional bestowal of leniency on the part of the pack leader. With respect to more advanced human society, negligence equates to an active denial of any sense of submissiveness, whereby prompting a vindictive refusal to act leniently on the part of the personal follower figure. The modern spelling of negligence derives from the Latin *neglegere* (to neglect): denoting an avoidance of one's proper duties. This term is also used in a legal sense, as in the deliberate lack of attention to the interests or wellbeing of others specified under the law. In this modified sense, the personal authority figure negligently fails to submit to the letter of the law, whereby provoking subsequent vindictive retribution from the respective follower figure.

This latter colloquial concept of vindictiveness certainly fits the profile for such a punitive expression of potentiality. Its modern spelling derives from the Latin *vindicare* (to defend, to avenge). The modern-day connotations of vindictiveness imply a willful refusal to bestow leniency on the part of the personal follower figure. This projected punitive focus directly contrasts with that already established for the virtuous realm, where the personal follower leniently acts mercifully towards his personal authority in response to the latter's heartfelt expression of submissiveness.

A familiar example of this one-to-one style of punitive interaction is observed with respect to the stylized interaction between the delinquent and the turncoat. The delinquent fails to meet the prevailing standards of propriety by negligently failing to act submissively, whereby prompting the punitive sense of vindictiveness on the part of the turncoat. Indeed, negligence is traditionally defined as a callous disregard for any personal sense of responsibility. Being that the delinquent initiates this stage within the punitive interaction he/she rightfully assumes the subjective "I" role, whereas the turncoat alternately assumes the objective "you" role indicative of a future-directed sense of potentiality. Consequently, I as personal authority (the delinquent) negligently refuse to act submissively towards you (as personal follower) in anticipation of your, as turncoat, vindictive refusal to act leniently towards me.

INDIFFERENCE - MALICE

The preceding initial sequence of negligence-then-vindictiveness further implies that the punisher must eventually act upon one's vindictive potentiality, whereby indifferently refusing to act leniently within an immediately-active time-frame. As the chief moral antithesis of worry, *indifference* proves consistent with such personal authority perspectives. Its modern spelling derives from the Latin *indifferens*, from *in-* (not) and *differre*: the compound of *dif-* (apart) and *ferre* (to bear). In *Timon of Athens* (Act II, Scene 2) Shakespeare describes indifference as: "T'is lack of kindly warmth." George Bernard Shaw similarly writes: "The worst sin towards our fellow creatures is not to hate them, but to be *indifferent* to them: that's the essence of inhumanity." Essayist Juan Montalvo further writes: "There is nothing harder than the softness of indifference."

According to **Part B** of **Fig. 9A**, indifference (Y) now occupies the present, whereas maliciousness (X) is projected as a future-directed potentiality. In essence, the turncoat is alternately thrust into an immediately active role, whereby indifferently refusing to act leniently, ultimately prompting the potential determination to act maliciously on the part of the delinquent. This latter malicious perspective is traditionally regarded as particularly pernicious: its modern spelling deriving from the Latin *malitia*, from *malus* (evil, illness) implying deep-seated feelings of dislike or ill will. Within a related legal context, malice is typically defined as: "that state of mind predisposed to commit an unlawful act." This theme is further encountered in the legal notion of malice *prepens* (malice aforethought): the premeditated intent to commit an unlawful act.

In terms of his/her indifferent refusal to act leniently, the turncoat formally abandons one's initial personal follower role, rather switching to an active personal authority status. The delinquent, in turn, now assumes the mantle of the personal follower role consistent with one's future-directed sense of malice. This role reversal certainly proves warranted, being that it reciprocates the preliminary punitive sequence based upon negligence/vindictiveness. Hence, the immediately-active expression of indifference, in turn, prompts the malicious refusal to act submissively on the part of the delinquent, whereby prompting further such cycles of maliciousness in the process. Although the rather broad range of meanings associated with negligence, vindictiveness, indifference, and malice might suggest further possible interpretations, the current range of viewpoints certainly fits the schematic prerequisites specified for the personal authority/follower roles: a finding further verified with respect to the ascending hierarchy of defect to follow.

A NEW CLASSIFICATIONAL SYSTEM FOR THE VICES OF DEFECT

This personal interplay of both authority/follower roles further sets the stage for the group and universal levels within the hierarchy of defect. For instance, the preliminary *laziness* perspective of the personal authority, in turn, sets the stage for *infamy* expressed by the group authority figure, culminating in the *prodigality* specific to a universal perspective. Furthermore, the *treachery* characterizing the personal follower role, in turn, prompts the *insurgency* expressed by the group representative, culminating in the *betrayal* expressed by the spiritual disciple figure. Furthermore the similar interplay of negligence-then-vindictiveness, in turn, sets the stage for a similar expansion of group/spiritual levels. For example, the *negligence* expressed by the personal authority, in turn, mirrors the *dishonorableness* characterizing the group authority figure, culminating in the sense of *enslavement* expressed by the spiritual authority figure. Furthermore, the *vindictiveness* of the personal follower, in turn, gives way to the *vengeance* specified for the group representative, culminating in the *despair* perspective of the spiritual disciple.

According to **Fig. 9B**, the sequence of vices targeting the first three authority roles (laziness-infamy-prodigality) collectively specify an immediately-active focus: in contrast to the parallel hierarchy of follower roles (treachery-insurgency-betrayal) that formally reciprocates the range of authority ideals. Furthermore, the related authority sequence of negligence-dishonor-enslavement similar anticipates the remaining sequence of follower roles (vindictiveness-vengeance-despair) essentially mirroring the trend based upon treachery with the exception that vindictiveness is now called into focus.

A similar set of trends further holds true with respect to the remaining punitive terms characterizing the domain of defect. With respect to the personal realm, this amounts to apathy in anticipation of spitefulness, or indifference in expectation of maliciousness. In other words, the immediately-active range of sinfulness targeting the authority roles (apathy-foolishness-vulgarity) further prompts the remaining sequence of vices targeting the follower roles (spitefulness-gluttony-avarice). In a similar sense, the remaining authority sequence of indifference-capriciousness-cruelty prompts a similar range of expectation with respect to the related sequence of follower roles: malice, cowardice, and antagonism.

This initial sequence of vices (spanning the personal, group, and spiritual levels), in turn, formally explains the remaining crowning series of humanitarian and transcendental levels within the hierarchy of defect. In contrast to the purely organizational status characterizing the first three authority levels, the final two levels are alternately specified as purely abstract styles of authority/follower perspectives. The humanitarian domain derives from the abstract innovation of *historical* time, whereas the transcendental level makes a formal appeal to the realm of pure transcendence.

The profoundly abstract nature of these crowning two levels is further reflected in their respective abstract groupings of individual terms. These darker themes share an enduring significance within the field of ethical inquiry: as the representative sampling of evil, hatred, belligerence etc., clearly serve to indicate. In truth, the vices associated with these final two levels virtually beg to be listed together; as in the sins of ecumenism (wrath, tyranny, persecution, and oppression), the moralistic vices (evil-cunning-ugliness-hypocrisy), the sins of humanism (anger, hatred, prejudice, and belligerence), and the crowning mystical vices (iniquity-turpitude-abomination-perdition).

Indeed, this strict correspondence of the vices of defect in relation to the virtuous mode necessarily specifies the existence of an entire parallel hierarchy for the realm of defect. Each virtue and value within the virtuous hierarchy contrasts (point-for-point) with a corresponding vice within the hierarchy of defect. For the most part, each such vice represents the direct moral antithesis (or antonym) of its respective virtuous counterpart, permitting precise quartet-style listings analogous to that previously established for the virtuous mode.

This parallel hierarchy for the vices of defect is schematically depicted in **Fig. 9B** (in addition to the respective three-digit codes) structured in parallel fashion to the virtuous format previously depicted in **Fig. 1** (of Chapter 1). Here the first digit for the coding system is assigned the numerical value of "5" for the vices of defect; as opposed to the major virtues, where the codes all begin with "1." Both diagrams are organized in terms of dual descending columns representing the reciprocal interplay of both authority and follower roles. Each column is further subdivided into the respective personal, group, spiritual, humanitarian, and transcendental domains specified for the ethical hierarchy. These authority/follower roles respectively alternate over the entire ten-level span of the motivational hierarchy, as the directional arrows formally serve to indicate.

Although the virtues and values have collectively enjoyed a rather broad range of philosophical traditions, a similar set of precedents with respect to the vices has conspicuously been lacking. Indeed, perhaps the only grouping of any major significance is that of the Seven Deadly Sins: namely, pride, covetousness, lust, anger, gluttony, envy, and sloth. This traditional grouping actually represents an incongruent hodgepodge of vices spanning a diverse range of levels within the hierarchy of defect/excess, an arrangement scarcely specific enough to adequately quantify this overall domain of the vices. Consequently, an entirely new system of classification is necessarily in order. This new format formally takes its cues chiefly from the traditions previously established for virtuous mode, with the groupings of vices now provisionally designated in opposition to their virtuous counterparts; namely, the cardinal vices, the theological vices, the mystical vices, etc. Furthermore, whereas the virtues (specific to the follower role) are distinguished from the authority "ideals," so the darker realm of defect is further subdivided in terms of the parallel concepts of

vice and sin. In particular, the Greek verb for sin (in the New Testament) translates as "to miss" (as in failing to reach a goal). This "sin" of failing to reach the goal directly contrasts with the more positive prerequisites of the authority "ideals" in terms of such a latter negative respect.

According to the remaining hierarchy of follower roles, the vices directly counteract the virtues in this dual motivational sense. As previously outlined in Chapter 2, the virtues formally define the potentially-anticipated aspects of the conditioned relationship, designating behaviors with the potential to complement the immediately-active perspective of the authority ideals. The corresponding notion of vice offers a fitting darker counterpoint, whereby representing an anticipated set of consequences in relation to the more immediately-active sense of sinfulness characterizing the authority roles. Indeed, whereas these notions of sin and vice share a complementary status with respect to the authority/follower roles; for sake of brevity, this overall set of themes is schematically referred to simply as "the vices" consistent with the general terminology underlying the vices of defect. A similar scenario further holds true for the virtuous realm, where the catchall term of "the virtues" is collectively employed to designate the overall hierarchy of virtues, values, and ideals.

With respect to the basic rules for the coding of the vices within the three-digit system, a few basic observations are definitely in order. The first digit for the vices of defect, by definition, is assigned the unitary value of "5," as specified within the basic numbering pattern previously established from Chapter 1. The second digit further narrows the focus, in turn, specifying each of the ten respective levels within the motivational hierarchy. According to this basic format, 1 = personal authority, 2 = personal follower, 3 = group authority, etc. With the first two digits now established, it ultimately remains to determine the specifics of the remaining final digit in order to round-out the three-digit coding system. For example, should the first digit be a "5" (the vices of defect), and the second digit is a "2" (for personal follower), then the range of possibilities is further narrowed down to the single category of the alter ego vices (treachery-vindictiveness-spite-malice). Indeed, each of the respective groupings of vices of defect is specified in terms of such a two-digit combination.

In order to further specify the complete range of individual terms, the third (and final) digit is ultimately called into play. According to the previous example, 520 = treachery, 521 = vindictiveness, 522 = spite, and 523 = malice. Digits 4 to 7 (in the three-slot) further specify the accessory variations of terms, as more elaborately described in the Chapter *15* of the current section. Consequently, 524 = mutiny, 525 = retaliation, 526 = grudgingness, and 527 = malevolence. The final pair of third-place digits (8 & 9) alternately specify the respective general unifying themes; namely (in the case of this example), the major theme of the fraud and the accessory theme of deception.

THE INTERPLAY OF INDIVIDUAL TERMS WITHIN THE HIERARCHY OF DEFECT

The newly proposed master-hierarchy of vice and sin represents a major contribution to the field of ethical inquiry, an achievement completely surpassing the only other major competing system; namely, the more rudimentary listing of the Seven Deadly Sins. Each of the ten master groupings for the realm of defect is further designated in terms of the traditions in opposition to the virtuous realm, a necessary circumstance in light of the lack of any better alternative. Indeed, this "stopgap" measure for classifying the vices of defect must necessarily remain in force until a more consensus means for labeling can universally be agreed upon.

THE SCHEMATIC DEFINITIONS FOR DEFECT

Although the preliminary discussion of the schematic definitions has previously been limited exclusively to the virtuous realm, the parallel hierarchy of the vices of defect is similarly amenable to its own unique complement of definitions: as formally depicted in **Tables D-1** to **D-4**. This comprehensive forty-part listing of schematic definitions (for the realm of defect) contrasts point-for-point with the respective virtuous counterparts, as initially depicted in **Tables A-1** to **A-4**. This crucial innovation spells out in longhand the precise location of each individual vice within the linguistic hierarchy, while simultaneously incorporating the respective authority and follower roles. Each definition is formally constructed along the lines of a two-stage sequential format; namely (1) the formal recognition of the initial power maneuver and (2) the countermaneuver currently being employed; and hence, labeled. Power leverage, accordingly, is achieved by rising to a "one-up" power status; namely, ascending to the next higher level within the hierarchy of metaperspectives.

The instinctual terminology specified for punishment dominates the initial levels within the schematic hierarchy, replaced in due fashion by the individual range of vices characterizing the higher authority levels. At each successive level, a new vice (distinguished through *italics*) is introduced into the schematic format: representing the punitive maneuver currently under consideration. The affiliated authority/follower roles remain fixed throughout the entire ten-level span; although systematically abbreviated (for sake of brevity) in non-critical positions. Here, PA stands for personal authority, PF denotes personal follower, etc. Some of the more atypical abbreviations are GR (group representative), SD (spiritual disciple), and RH (the representative member of humanity).

This dual ethical system linking both virtue and vice provides a sturdy ethical foundation for diagnosing issues of a moral nature. Indeed, this darker complement of schematic definitions proves just as informative as those for the virtues, offering crucial ethical insights into what should be shunned or avoided. This inevitable familiarity with the realm of defect actually amounts to a basic safeguard within the system. Negative transactions can be diagnosed in terms of their potential for transformation into positive ones, while the reverse is also prevented from occurring.

A more detailed description of the complete ten-level hierarchy for the vices of defect, accordingly, is offered in the remaining Chapters *10* to *14* of the current section. Each successive chapter within the current **Part II** is devoted exclusively to a specific authority/follower realm within the hierarchy of defect replete with a description of the individual terms. Chapter *10* initiates this analysis with a detailed examination of the group authority/follower realm, introducing the sins of villainy and vices of corruption, respectively. Chapter *11*, in turn, focuses upon the spiritual authority/disciple roles: providing an in-depth description of the sins of profanity and the heretical vices. Chapter *12* subsequently examines the corresponding humanitarian-focused themes, introducing the sins of apostasy and vices of anarchism, respectively. Chapter *13* alternately targets the crowning transcendental realm, offering an in-depth examination of the sins of nihilism and the mystical vices. Finally, Chapter *14* rounds out the current section with an examination of a number of key supplemental issues relating to the realm of defect; namely, the accessory categories of sin/vice, as well as the overarching concept of the general unifying themes. Each chapter is further embellished with numerous illustrative examples from both classical and contemporary

LAZINESS	**TREACHERY**
Previously, you (as punisher) have refused to act rewardingly towards me: in response to my (as adversary) failure to act approachfully towards you. But now, I (as personal authority) will *lazily* refuse to act approachfully towards you: in anticipation of your (as punisher) failure to act rewardingly towards me.	Previously, I (as personal authority) have lazily refused to act approachfully towards you: in anticipation of your (as punisher) failure to act rewardingly towards me. But now, you (as personal follower) will *treacherously* refuse to act rewardingly towards me: overruling my (as PA) lazy treatment of you.
INFAMY	**INSURGENCY**
Previously, you (as my personal follower) have treacherously refused to act rewardingly towards me: in response to my (as PA) lazy treatment of you. But now, I (as group authority) will *infamously* act in a lazy fashion towards you: in anticipation of your (as PF) treacherous treatment of me.	Previously, I (as your group authority) have infamously acted lazily towards you: in anticipation of your (as PF) treacherous treatment of me. But now, you (as group representative) will *insurgently* act in a treacherous fashion towards me: overruling my (as GA) infamously-lazy treatment of you.
PRODIGALITY	**BETRAYAL**
Previously, you (as group representative) have insurgently acted treacherously towards me: in response to my (as GA) infamously-lazy treatment of you. But now, I (as spiritual authority) will infamously act in a *prodigal* fashion towards you: in anticipation of your (as GR) insurgently-treacherous treatment of me.	Previously, I (as your spiritual authority) have infamously acted in a prodigal fashion towards you: in anticipation of your (as GR) insurgently-treacherous treatment of me. But now, you (as spiritual disciple) will insurgently act in a *betraying* fashion towards me: overruling my (as SA) prodigal treatment of you.
WRATH	**UGLINESS**
Previously, you (as my spiritual disciple) have insurgently acted in a betraying fashion towards me: in response to my (as SA) infamously-prodigal treatment of you. But now, I (as humanitarian authority) will prodigally act in a *wrathful* fashion towards you: in anticipation of your (as SD) insurgent-betrayal of me.	Previously, I (as humanitarian authority) have prodigally acted wrathfully towards you: in anticipation of your (as SD) insurgent-betrayal of me. But now, you (as representative member of humanity) will betrayingly act in an *ugly* fashion towards me: overruling my (as HA) prodigally-wrathful treatment of you.
ANGER	**ABOMINATION**
Previously, you (as representative member of humanity) have betrayingly acted in an ugly fashion towards me: in response to my (as HA) prodigally wrathful treatment of you. But now, I (as transcendental authority) will wrathfully act in an *angry* fashion towards you: in anticipation of your (as RH) ugly-betrayal of me.	Previously, I (as transcendental authority) have wrathfully acted in an angry fashion towards you: in anticipation of your (as RH) ugly-betrayal of me. But now, you (as transcendental follower) will *abominably* act in an ugly fashion towards me: overruling my (as TA) angry treatment of you.

Table D-1 – The Definitions Based Upon Laziness/Treachery

NEGLIGENCE	VINDICTIVENESS
Previously, you (as punisher) have refused to act tolerantly towards me: in response to my (as adversary) failure to act aversively towards you. But now, I (as personal authority) will *negligently* refuse to act aversively towards you: in anticipation of your (as punisher) failure to act tolerantly towards me.	Previously, I (as personal authority) have negligently refused to act aversively towards you: in anticipation of your (as punisher) failure to act tolerantly towards me. But now, you (as personal follower) will *vindictively* refuse to act tolerantly towards me: overruling my (as PA) negligent treatment of you.
DISHONOR	**VENGEANCE**
Previously, you (as my personal follower) have vindictively refused to act tolerantly towards me: in response to my (as PA) negligent treatment of you. But now, I (as group authority) will negligently act in a *dishonorable* fashion towards you: in anticipation of your (as PF) vindictive treatment of me.	Previously, I (as group authority) have negligently acted in a dishonorable fashion towards you: in anticipation of your (as PF) vindictive treatment of me. But now, you (as group representative) will *vengefully* act vindictively towards me: overruling my (as GA) dishonorable treatment of you.
SLAVERY	**DESPAIR**
Previously, you (as group representative) have vengefully acted vindictively towards me: in response to my (as GA) negligently-dishonorable treatment of you. But now, I (as spiritual authority) will dishonorably-*enslave* you: in anticipation of your vengefully-vindictive treatment of me.	Previously, I (as spiritual authority) have dishonorably-enslaved you: in anticipation of your (as GR) vengefully-vindictive treatment of me. But now, you (as my spiritual disciple) will vengefully act in a *despairing* fashion towards me: overruling my (as SA) dishonorable-enslavement of you.
TYRANNY	**HYPOCRISY**
Previously, you (as my spiritual disciple) have vengefully acted in a despairing fashion towards me: in response to my (as SA) dishonorable-enslavement of you. But now, I (as humanitarian authority) will *tyrannically*-enslave you: in anticipation of your (as SD) despairing treatment of me.	Previously, I (as humanitarian authority) have tyrannically-enslaved you: in anticipation of your (as SD) despairing treatment of me. But now, you (as representative member of humanity) will despairingly behave in a *hypocritical* fashion towards me: overruling my (as HA) tyrannical-enslavement of you.
PREJUDICE	**PERDITION**
Previously, you (as representative member of humanity) have despairingly behaved in a hypocritical fashion towards me: in response to my (as HA) tyrannical-enslavement of you. But now, I (as transcendental authority) will tyrannically act *prejudicially* towards you: in anticipation of your (as RH) hypocritical treatment of me.	Previously, I (as transcendental authority) have tyrannically acted prejudicially: in anticipation of your (as RH) hypocritical sense of despair. But now, you (as transcendental follower) will hypocritically act in a *perditionable* fashion towards me: overruling my (as TA) prejudicial treatment of you.

Table D-2 – The Definitions Based on Negligence/Vindictiveness

APATHY	**SPITE**
Previously, I (as adversary) have refused to act approachfully towards you: in response to your (as punisher) failure to act rewardingly towards me. But now, you (as my personal authority) will *apathetically* fail to act rewardingly towards me: in anticipation of my (as adversary) refusal to act approachfully towards you.	Previously, you (as my personal authority) have apathetically failed to act rewardingly towards me: in anticipation of my (as adversary) refusal to act approachfully towards you. But now, I (as your personal follower) will *spitefully* refuse to act approachfully towards you: overruling your (as PA) apathetic treatment of me.
FOOLISHNESS	**GLUTTONY**
Previously, I (as your personal follower) have spitefully refused to act approachfully towards you: in response to your (as PA) apathetic treatment of me. But now, you (as my group authority) will *foolishly* act in an apathetic fashion towards me: in anticipation of my (as PF) spiteful treatment of you.	Previously, you (as my group authority) have foolishly acted apathetically towards me: in anticipation of my (as PF) spiteful treatment of you. But now, I (as group representative) will *gluttonously* act in a spiteful fashion towards you: overruling your (as GA) foolishly-apathetic treatment of me.
VULGARITY	**AVARICE**
Previously, I (as group representative) have gluttonously acted in a spiteful fashion towards you: in response to your (as GA) foolishly-apathetic treatment of you. But now, you (as spiritual authority) will foolishly act *vulgarly* towards me: in anticipation of my (as GR) gluttonously-spiteful treatment of you.	Previously, you (as my spiritual authority) have foolishly acted in a vulgar fashion towards me: in anticipation of my (as GR) gluttonously-spiteful treatment of you. But now, I (as your spiritual disciple) will gluttonously act *avariciously* towards you: overruling your (as SA) foolishly-vulgar treatment of me.
OPPRESSION	**EVIL**
Previously, I (as your spiritual disciple) have gluttonously acted avariciously towards you: in response to your (as SA) vulgar treatment of me. But now, you (as my humanitarian authority) will vulgarly act in an *oppressive* fashion towards me: in anticipation of my (as SD) gluttonously-avaricious treatment of you.	Previously, you (as humanitarian authority) have vulgarly acted oppressively towards me: in anticipation of my (as SA) avaricious treatment of you. But now, I (as representative member of humanity) will avariciously act in an *evil* fashion towards you: overruling your (as HA) vulgarly-oppressive treatment of me.
HATRED	**INIQUITY**
Previously, I (as representative member of humanity) have avariciously acted in an evil fashion towards you: in response to your (as HA) vulgarly-oppressive treatment of me. But now, you (as transcendental authority) will oppressively act in a *hateful* fashion towards me: in anticipation of my (as RH) evil treatment of you.	Previously, you (as my transcendental authority) have hatefully acted in an oppressive fashion towards me: overriding my (as RH) avaricious sense of evil. But now, I (as your transcendental follower) will evilly act in an *iniquitous* fashion towards you: in anticipation of your (as TA) hateful treatment of me.

Table D-3 – The Definitions Based Upon Apathy/Spite

INDIFFERENCE	MALICE
Previously, I (as adversary) have refused to act aversively towards you: in response to your (as punisher) failure to act tolerantly towards me. But now, you (as my personal authority) will *indifferently* fail to act tolerantly towards me: in anticipation of my (as adversary) refusal to act aversively towards you.	Previously, you (as my personal authority) have indifferently failed to act tolerantly towards me: in anticipation of my (as adversary) refusal to act aversively towards you. But now, I (as your personal follower) will *maliciously* refuse to act aversively towards you: overruling your (as PA) indifferent treatment of me.
CAPRICIOUSNESS	**COWARDICE**
Previously, I (as your personal follower) have maliciously refused to act aversively towards you: in response to your (as PA) indifferent treatment of me. But now, you (as group authority) will *capriciously* act indifferently towards me: in anticipation of my (as PF) malicious treatment of you.	Previously, you (as my group authority) have capriciously acted indifferently towards me: in anticipation of my (as PF) malicious treatment of you. But now, I (as group representative) will *cowardly* act in a malicious fashion towards you: overruling your (as GA) capricious sense of indifference.
CRUELTY	**ANTAGONISM**
Previously, I (as group representative) have cowardly acted in a malicious fashion towards you: in response to your (as GA) capricious sense of indifference. But now, you (as spiritual authority) will capriciously act *cruelly* towards me: in anticipation of my (as GR) cowardly-malicious treatment of you.	Previously, you (as my spiritual authority) have capriciously acted in a cruel fashion towards me: in anticipation of my (as GR) cowardly-malicious treatment of you. But now, I (as your spiritual disciple) will cowardly act in an *antagonistic* fashion towards you: overruling your (as SA) cruel treatment of me.
PERSECUTION	**CUNNING**
Previously, I (as your spiritual disciple) have cowardly acted in an antagonistic fashion towards you: in response to your (as SA) cruel treatment of me. But now, you (as my humanitarian authority) will cruelly-*persecute* me: in anticipation of my (as SD) cowardly-antagonistic treatment of you.	Previously, you (as humanitarian authority) have cruelly-persecuted me: in anticipation of my (as SD) cowardly-antagonistic treatment of you. But now, I (as representative member of humanity) will antagonistically act in a *cunning* fashion towards you: overruling your (as HA) cruel persecution of me.
BELLIGERENCE	**TURPITUDE**
Previously, I (as representative member of humanity) have antagonistically acted in a cunning fashion towards you: in response to your (as HA) cruel persecution of me. But now, you (as my transcendental authority) will *belligerently*-persecute me: in anticipation of my (as RH) cunning treatment of you.	Previously, you (as my transcendental authority) have belligerently-persecuted me: in anticipation of my (as RH) antagonistic sense of cunning. But now, I (as your transcendental follower) will cunningly act in a *turpitudinous* fashion towards you: overruling your (as TA) belligerent persecution of me.

Table D-4 – The Definitions Based Upon Indifference/Malice

125

literature adding a further entertaining dimension to this somewhat formal discussion of the vices.

In conclusion, the newly proposed ten-level hierarchy for the vices of defect represents an entirely new addition on the world scene today. In contrast to the long-standing literary traditions underlying the major virtues, the newly minted categories for the realm of defect represent entirely new formulations, taking their cue as direct antitheses of their respective virtuous counterparts. This breakthrough innovation further allows for more comprehensive ethical applications of a purely scientific and behavioral nature. No longer is religious scripture the only potential source of authority for debating issues of conflict relating to defect. Furthermore, the timely incorporation of the vices of defect into the formal schematic definition format permits an unprecedented degree of precision in this basic respect. This elementary domain of defect, when further analyzed in a strictly communicational fashion, offers crucial telling insights into the realms of criminality, hyper-criminality, and hyperviolence: providing an invaluable tool for deciphering the twisted motives underlying the rash of terrorist directives currently afflicting the global community. Hopefully, this new ethical technology can be instituted in a timely fashion so as to avert any further regrettable damage to the prospects for global peace and prosperity.

10

THE GROUP DOMAIN OF DEFECT

The group authority/follower perspectives relating to the realm of defect represent crucial adjuncts to the sphere of ethical inquiry. The group virtuous realm was initially defined in terms of the authority-based traditions underlying the personal ideals; e.g., glory, honor, dignity, and integrity. This enduring group focus offers further crucial insights into the darker prerequisites in relation to the domain of defect; namely, the overarching theme of *villainy*. The term derives from the Old French *villain*, from the Middle Latin *villanus* (farmhand), from the Latin *villa* (a country house): probably a reduction from *vicla* or *vicus* (a village). It originally referred to a serf bound to a villa or a farm, the inferred ingrained proclivities of which led to the attribution of evil or depraved motives.

The modern-day connotation of villainy refers to an antagonistic character from a novel or play, whose evil motives/actions help drive the plot in concert with the more noble aspirations of the protagonist. In "The Merchant of Venice," William Shakespeare describes the villainy of his character Shylock as: "An evil soul producing holy witness is like a *villain* with a smiling cheek, a goodly apple rotten to the heart." (Act I: Scene 3). In *Henry IV*, Shakespeare similarly writes: "There is nothing but roguery to be found in a *villainous* man," wherein stressing an inferred affiliation with knavery. Villains in Elizabethan drama were particularly prominent in a genre known as "revenge tragedy," depicted as descending from the portrayal of devils and the vices that dominated earlier morality plays.

The basic "stock" villain first appears in 19th century melodrama, typically in the form of a coarsely groomed seducer. This context extends to the dramatic genres of the American Old West, where the villain dressed in black (with a handlebar mustache, to match) pressured the vulnerable widow for the deed to her meager estate. This dastardly range of intimidation ultimately culmi-nated with the heroin tied to the railroad track by the wicked villain, although rescued in the nick of time by the dashing hero. This enduring theme of crime and punishment particularly exemplifies a group sphere of influence, where the efforts of local law enforcement are typically sufficient to rectify any such individual instances of villainous infamy.

This overarching sense of villainy represents the key moral antithesis in relation to the more positive aspirations characterizing the virtuous realm. According to this dualistic interpretation, the virtuous focus of the personal ideals is directly countered (point-for-point) with the corresponding listing of the sins of villainy (infamy, dishonor, foolishness, and capriciousness): a factor consistent with the antithetical role sinfulness plays in relation to the authority ideals. The *infamous* sense of laziness expressed by the group authority figure directly counteracts the latter's glorious sense of solicitousness. Similarly, one's negligent sense of dishonor directly opposes any honorable sense of submissiveness. Furthermore, the authority figure's *foolishly*-apathetic treatment makes a fitting counterpoint to any dignified sense of desire. Finally, one's *capricious* sense of indifference effectively counteracts any worrisome sense of integrity

This distinctive listing of the sins of villainy further builds directly upon the more elementary class of ego vices (that they supersede). For instance, *infamy* represents the group extension of laziness, whereas *dishonor* denotes a similar modification of negligence. Furthermore, *foolishness* represents apathy from a group perspective, whereas *capriciousness* denotes a more extreme form of indifference. This preliminary class of authority-based perspectives represents an immediately active realm of perspectives that directly anticipates the potentiality inherent to the projected (future-directed) complement of vices specified for the subsequent follower role.

THE VICES OF CORRUPTION: THE BANE OF THE GROUP FOLLOWER PERSPECTIVE

The preliminary description of the sins of villainy characterizing the group authority perspective, in turn, is susceptible to its own unique form of follower counter-maneuver: in this case, that expressed by the group representative. Indeed, this group follower focus (in a virtuous sense) was initially described in terms of the enduring listing of cardinal virtues (prudence-justice-temperance-fortitude). This virtuous group focus offers further crucial insights into the darker prerequisites for the group follower perspective; namely, those relating to the affiliated theme of *corruption.* The term derives from a compound of the Latin *cor-* (intensification) and *rumpere* or *ruptum* (to break). It denotes a breach of confidence that typically accompanies such a fraudulent range of practices. Consequently, corruption represents the chief moral antithesis of the virtuous theme of utilitarianism, where the welfare of the group is circumvented to the selfish benefit of a partisan official or faction. Indeed, corruption has remained the bane of elected forms of government as far back as the age of the Roman Republic.

In 159 BCE, the *lex Cornelia* punished (with exile) those found guilty of bribing the electorate: therefore, a general prohibition against the direct purchase of votes must have existed well in advance of the passage of this specific law. Furthermore, the *lex Calpurnia* (in 67 BCE) imposed heavy fines on any candidate employing bribery (whether successful or not). This law further prevented the transgressor from ever holding public office or sitting in the Senate.

A similar pattern equally applies to the American form of representative government. Corrupt practices include offenses by public officials (include bribery), the sale of public office, the awarding of public contracts to favored firms, etc. Election corruption includes efforts to influence or intimidate voters, as well as tampering with the official ballot or vote tally. Nearly every democratic country has passed laws guarding against corruption in political campaigns and official state duties. In larger cities, election fraud has long been associated with a corrupt style of influence known as the "political machine."

At the federal level, the House and Senate established ethics committees and codes of conduct that require a public accounting of income and campaign contributions. These corrupt practices reforms have also been applied to business and labor unions, as in "price fixing" or the misappro-priation of funds. Although the temptation towards corruption always proves a seductive option, the elaborate system of governmental checks and balances fortunately limits such occurrences to a relatively small impact on the common public welfare.

This widespread theme of corruption, in turn, provides clues towards identifying the corresponding listing of individual vices; namely, the darker realm of the vices of corruption: insurgency, vengeance, gluttony, and cowardice. According to this darker range of perspectives, *insurgency* makes a fitting contrast to prudence, whereas *vengeance* represents the darker counterpart of justice. Furthermore, *gluttony* represents the chief moral antonym of temperance, whereas *cowardice* specifies a darker counterpart to fortitude.

Furthermore, these individual vices of corruption build directly upon the more elementary class of alter ego vices (that they supersede). For instance, *insurgency* represents the group analogue of treachery, whereas *vengeance* denotes a similar modification of vindictiveness. Furthermore, *gluttony* redefines spitefulness from a group follower perspective, whereas *cowardice* denotes a group variation on malice. In summary, the initial four-part listing of the sins of villainy represent motivations actively characterizing the group authority role; namely, infamy, dishonor, foolishness, and capriciousness. This preliminary class of authority-based perspectives represents an immediately active range of perspectives that directly anticipates the projected potentiality inherent to the future-directed class of the vices of corruption; namely, insurgency, vengeance, gluttony, and cowardice. Generally speaking, the group authority roles actively initiate the punitive interaction in anticipation of the future potentiality characterizing the group follower perspective in relation to the vices of corruption.

For instance, the initial infamous sense of laziness on the part of the group authority figure further anticipates the insurgent sense of treachery on the part of the group representative. This insurgent sense of treachery, in turn, eventually becomes actualized as the foolishly-apathetic treatment on the part of the withholder of reinforcement: whereby prompting the gluttonously-spiteful treatment on the part of the group representative.

A similar motivational interplay further holds true with respect to the remaining punitive range of themes encompassing the withholding of leniency. For instance, the initial negligently-dishonorable treatment on the part of the group authority figure directly anticipates the vengeful sense of vindictiveness on the part of the group representative. This vengeful sense of vindictiveness, in turn, ultimately becomes actualized as the capricious sense of indifference on the part of the punisher whereby prompting the cowardly-malicious treatment on the part of the group representative. Consequently, for both of these basic forms of punishment, the actively-initiated class of the sins of villainy: infamy, dishonor, foolishness, and capriciousness effectively anticipate (in an adversarial fashion) the projected potentiality of the vices of corruption: insurgency, vengeance, gluttony, and cowardice. Indeed, this dual style of group interaction is further seen to repeat for the remaining spiritual and humanitarian levels in relation to sin and vice as well: explaining the overarching darker dynamics for the vices of defect. The remainder of the current chapter further examines this darker complement of individual vices, providing a sturdy foundation for the subsequent classes of defect to follow.

INFAMY - INSURGENCY

The more straightforward class of positive punishment proves to be the most logical initiation point for such a grand-scale analysis, mirroring the pattern previously established with respect to the virtuous mode. Accordingly, the interplay of infamy/insurgency will be examined first, followed by the subsequent sequence comprised of foolishness/gluttony. As suggested in the group foundations for this darker range of terms, the overall realm of inquiry builds directly upon the more basic behavioral set of terms previously encountered with respect to the personal authority/follower roles.

As initially indicated, the infamous sense of laziness expressed by the group authority figure actively initiates the punitive interaction, further prompting the insurgently-treacherous denial of reinforcement by way of the group follower role. Being that only one role may be active within the conditioned interaction at any given instance, the role of punisher is relegated to that of a future potentiality, identified as the insurgent sense of treachery anticipated from the group follower figure. The potential status of this insurgent sense of treachery equates to the group representative role, whereas the more immediately active infamously-lazy treatment directly invokes the initial group authority role.

A particular example of such an adversarial style of group interaction concerns a typical conflict scenario, such as the reciprocal interplay between the freeloader and the rebel. This scenario effectively mirrors the interplay previously described (in a personal sense) between the slacker and the defector/turncoat, although now expanded to encompass a much broader group sphere of influence. The group-based freeloader typically wrongfully exploits those within a criminal environment, whereby infamously acting lazily in anticipation of the insurgently-treacherous admonishment by the rebel/defector.

This infamously-lazy refusal to act solicitously certainly fits the bill in this group-focused respect. As the chief moral antithesis of glory, *infamy* is typically defined as ill-gotten fame or notoriety. This theme is particularly abounds during lawless periods in American history, such as the frontier spirit of the Old West or the Prohibition frenzy of the early 20th century. Both periods exhibited their fair share of notorious outlaws. Billy the Kid and Jesse James roamed the Old West, whereas gangsters such as Bonnie and Clyde and Al Capone stole headlines in the 20th century. These infamous criminals lived by a common code; namely, failing to act cooperatively in a culturally prescribed fashion, as reflected in their habitual disregard for property and the law. The general public was rightfully outraged by such unlawful activities. Although some criminals were revered as cult heroes consistent with their free-spending propensities, this "Robin Hood" style of mentality eventually led to feelings of outrage when wholesale community resources were pillaged. The general citizenry felt little hesitancy in betraying such desperate outlaws, particularly in light of the sizeable bounty accompanying cases of such magnitude.

This indiscriminate brand of criminality undoubtedly sparked widespread resentment amongst the working class. The daring string of bank robberies perpetrated by Bonnie and Clyde wiped-out the hard-earned savings of entire farming communities. This outrage eventually sparked a wave of public indignation expressed as a determined effort to punish such shameless outlaws. Ironically, their final downfall was instigated by a traitor within their midst, culminating in a bloody shootout so often the outcome for those that gloried in such notoriety.

According to the preceding outlaw examples, the lazy sense of infamy expressed by Bonnie and Clyde equates to a darker variation on the gloriously-solicitous demeanor of the virtuous authority figure. This infamy perspective, in turn, is potentially countered by the *insurgent* sense of treachery expressed by the group follower figure. In other words, the group representative insurgently aims to act in a treacherous fashion towards one's group authority figure: whereby punitively admonishing the latter's lazy sense of infamy, as the betrayal of Bonnie and Clyde amply serves to indicate. As the chief moral antithesis of prudent-approval, insurgency represents a higher (group) variation on the treachery perspective of the personal follower. Its modern spelling derives from the Latin *insurgens* (to rise up against), from *in-* (upon) and *surgere* (to rise). It generally refers to organized opposition to unlawful authority as in a treacherous-insurrection.

Perhaps the earliest mention of insurgency involves the widely cited rebellion of the Olympian gods against the harsh treatment of their Titan overlords. This theme frequently recurs throughout the vast body of myth to follow, with specific instances too numerous to mention. Such legendary intrigues clearly reflect the violent spirit of the age, where those who lived by the sword were invariably doomed to perish by it.

This enduring sense of insurgent-treachery ultimately extends to our modern age as reflected in the Communist revolutions that swept Russia and Mainland China. The prevailing form of imperial government was toppled in favor of a Marxist ideology that gloried in the power of the worker class. In the case of the Russian Revolution, Czar Nicholas II found himself heir to a bitter class struggle pitting the ruling aristocracy against the rising power of the peasant class. The Czar's steadfast refusal to promote meaningful reforms (combined with the economic turmoil of WWI) ultimately led to his violent downfall at the hands of the rebellious worker class. Through this concerted power to organize, the populace insurgently-rebelled against the infamously-lazy treatment by the prevailing ruling class. From the ashes of the resulting anarchy rose a radically new style of socialistic viewpoint. This bold experiment in social engineering has undergone a precipitous decline as of late, a fitting outcome for an ideology based entirely upon such revolutionary dictates.

FOOLISHNESS - GLUTTONY

The initial punitive interplay of infamy/insurgency, in turn, redirects the focus of this discussion to the remaining phase within the group interaction: namely, that encompassing foolishness/gluttony. In terms of the inevitable march of time, the group follower eventually acts upon his insurgently-treacherous intentions: now foolishly acting apathetically towards the freeloader, whereby prompting the latter's gluttonously spiteful viewpoint within a future-directed time-frame.

A number of key features emerge analogous to those initially encountered with respect to infamy-then-insurgency. The rebel-defector's foolishly-apathetic treatment now formally assumes a group authority status in relation to the freeloading follower. The latter's gluttonous style of spiteful role, in turn, takes on the mantle of the group follower role, being that it formally "follows" the authority role within the punitive interaction. According to this foolishness-then-gluttony dynamic, the rebel-defector foolishly acts apathetically towards the freeloader in anticipation of the latter's potential determination to gluttonously act spitefully, whereby ensuring that further such punitive/adversarial cycles are guaranteed to ultimately repeat on future occasions.

In a group sense, the immediately active withholding of reinforcement is formally identified with *foolishness*, continuing the tradition of infamy-then-insurgency previously established for the initial stage within the punitive interaction. As the chief moral antithesis of dignity, *foolishness* is typically defined as the unnerving lack of common sense. This traditional connotation is similarly suggested in the Old Testament quotation: "folly is set in great dignity" (Ecclesiastes 10:6). Its modern spelling derives from the Late Latin *follus* (foolish), from the Latin *follis* (a pair of bellows, a windbag): wherein alluding to the puffed cheeks (and hot air) of the buffoon. One of the most distinctive symbolisms of foolishness concerns the traditional role of the court jester, a comedic parody on the pomp and circumstance of royal privilege. Certainly no royal entourage was complete without the colorful antics of the court jester: his jocularity played so convincingly in his gaudy, jangling, harlequin suit. The joker's manifest lack of respectfulness was carefully played-off with humorous banter, his foolish antics offering the perfect "foil" for the dignified demeanor of the royal monarch. Curiously, more than a few court jesters literally "lost their heads" over their assignment, suggesting the inherent limitations of humor for disguising the more salient aspects of the realm of the vices.

These humorous overtones for foolishness are particularly evident in the enduring tradition of April Fool's Day, a holiday where all dignity is temporarily cast aside in favor of a frenzy of foolish prank-playing. This tradition dates back to the 16th century, when New Years Day was originally celebrated on March 25th, launching a weeklong celebration culminating on April 1st. In 1564, King Charles switched the observance of New Years Day to its modern date. Those resisting the change found themselves the victim to numerous pranks and jokes on April 1ˢᵗ. According to this foolish context, the practical joker fabricates a deceptive air of respectability prior to exposing the more devious aspects of his ruse, as suggestive of the interplay linking both virtue and vice.

The preceding foolishness example, in turn, redirects the focus of this analysis to the *gluttony* perspective expressed by the group follower figure. The group representative gluttonously aims to act spitefully, whereby retroactively thwarting the foolishly-apathetic treatment of the group authority figure. As the chief moral antithesis of temperance, gluttony is traditionally defined as the intemperate consumption of food, alcohol (or other such sensual pursuit). Its modern spelling derives from the Latin *glutto* (glutton), from *glutire* (to devour). The social downside for this vice was frequently overlooked during the licentious and affluent age of the late Roman Empire. Indeed, the typical inclusion of the vomitorium at the standard Roman banquet ensured a degree of sensual consumption far in excess of any nutritional requirements. Comus (Roman god of joy or mirth) is typically depicted as drunk and languid within a traditional banquet setting.

These classical connotations give little hint of gluttony's general condemnation during the Christian era. Throughout the Middle Ages, gluttony was condemned as perhaps the most dangerous of the Seven Deadly Sins. The tight-knit web of loyalties comprising the medieval feudal system certainly specified such a drastic outlook, with any tendency towards personal greed menacing the collective welfare of the entire agrarian form of social structure. Selfish activities were particularly frowned upon, as witnessed in the harsh punishments meted out to poachers infringing upon the bounty of the noble's forest estates. The sensual excesses of the classical period must have appeared completely at odds with the devoutly virtuous strictures of the later Medieval period.

According to the Roman excesses of the banquet, the glutton (in the role of the group representative) celebrated jaded tastes through gluttonous rituals aimed at achieving that elusive thrill of satisfaction. Although such bulimic purging might have appeared methodical in its madness, such greedy tendencies demanded a much greater economic sacrifice from society as a whole. This senseless waste of nutritional resources was more broadly viewed as a travesty by the more reserved classes of Rome, a condition directly underscoring the spiteful qualities of gluttony (in contrast to its virtuous counterpart in temperance).

In a formal schematic sense, I (as group representative) gluttonously aim to act spitefully towards you on some future occasion in response to your (as group authority) foolishly-apathetic treatment of me. Indeed, it is chiefly this potential threat of gluttonous-spitefulness that ultimately imparts the inherent strike-power employed by the group representative relative to the group authority figure: the latter dependent upon the former to punish his/her gluttonous depravities. This gluttonous sense of spitefulness ultimately provides an effective sense of closure to the entire punitive interchange, ultimately prompting further such cycles of conflict within the punitive interaction.

DISHONOR - VENGEANCE

The completed two-stage description of the group domain of conflict based upon infamy/insurgency and foolishness/gluttony, in turn, sets the stage for the remaining series of themes targeting dishonor/vengeance and capriciousness/cowardice. This latter format specifies the deliberate withholding of leniency, whereby punishing behaviors judged not to be suitably submissive. This alternate format directly contrasts with the preceding section where rewards were withheld in response to non-solicitous types of behavior. Consequently, negative punishment extends to adverse consequences occurring within the environment, or (in an interpersonal sense) the denial of leniency in response to the absence of aversive types of behavior. In terms of a group social context, the group authority figure negligently acts dishonorably in anticipation of vengefully-vindictive treatment on the part of the group representative. This (potential) vengeful sense of vindictiveness, in turn, eventually becomes actualized as the capricious sense of indifference on the part of the authority figure, whereby prompting the cowardly determination to act maliciously on the part of the respective follower figure. A familiar example of such a reciprocating style of group interaction concerns the interplay between the villain and the vigilante. In a more formal sense, I as group authority (villain) negligently act dishonorably towards you in anticipation of your (as vigilante) vengefully-vindictive treatment of me.

The preceding villain/vigilante example proves exceedingly enlightening with respect to the (group) prerequisites for dishonor. As the chief moral antonym of honor, *dishonor* is defined as a manifest lack of honorable treatment, similar to the contrast previously established for glory/infamy. Dishonor represents a manifest lack of submissive (rather than solicitous) behavior, much as typically encountered during the great military conflicts across the ages. Perhaps the greatest military epoch in this regard concerns the Samurai warrior tradition of medieval Japan. The Samurai warrior submitted "life and limb" to the will of his imperial warlord. According to this rigid code of honor, the dishonored warrior's only course of atonement (befitting such violent times) was the ritual enactment of suicide known as *hari kiri*. Through this supreme sacrifice of ritual self-disembowelment, the warrior desperately sought to reconcile his shame over failing to meet the stringent expectations of his military warlord. Indeed, the English translation of hari kiri (literally, happy dispatch) particularly reflects this contrast to the dutiful sense of honor expected through one's militaristic obligations.

According to this specific Samurai example, dishonor is clearly an active theme characterizing the group authority perspective, directly expanding upon its more elementary foundations within negligence. The sacrificial act of *hari kiri* shamefully sought to atone for one's unbearable feelings of abject humiliation, a desperate reconciliation after the fact. This dramatic display of personal disregard was scarcely limited to the Samurai Age. Suicidal missions (such as willingly submitted to by Kamikaze pilots during WW-II) merited a high degree of honor within the military establishment. In the final tally, however, all such sacrifice went for naught, the sound defeat of the Japanese provoking a tragic wave of suicidal despair that preceded the Reconstruction Era.

In light of the preceding Samurai example, the dishonor perspective expressed by the group authority figure, in turn, sets the stage for the subsequent follower maneuver proper; namely, the vengeful sense of vindictiveness expressed by the group representative. Its modern spelling derives from the Old French *venger* (to avenge), from the Latin *vindicare* (to avenge). According to classical Greek mythology, vengeance is personified by Nemesis, the Greek goddess of divine retribution. According to legend, Nemesis served as the limiting influence on the extravagant favors bestowed by Tyche (the Greek goddess of fortune and chance). In keeping with her persistent persecution of the rich and powerful, Nemesis eventually came to signify the fateful accounting awaiting the reckless thrill-seeker. By extension, she is often confused with Adrastea (the Greek goddess of the inevitable). Nemesis is traditionally depicted as a winged goddess holding an apple bough in one hand and a Wheel of Fortune in the other. She is sometimes portrayed driving a chariot drawn by fierce griffins attesting to the fearsome nature of her exploits.

The Latin tradition of vengeance is alternately affiliated with Mars Ultor, a variation on the Roman God of War (whose surname meant "Avenger"). The Emperor Augustus dedicated a temple to him in the Roman Forum subsequent to taking revenge upon the assassins of his predecessor Julius Caesar. Indeed, the doors to this temple continuously remained open throughout the duration of any armed conflict/war occurring within the Empire. In line with this general trend towards vigilante justice, Augustus established squads of paid firemen (*vigiles*) to patrol Rome during nightly hours in response to the Great Fire of 6 CE. These vigiles were further empowered with minor police duties, adding a much-needed sense of order similar to the role the vigilante gangs enjoyed in the American Old West.

In this latter respect, the frontier vigilante gangs were composed primarily of deputized private citizens outraged enough to take the law into their own hands. They filled a vacuum in law-enforcement so prevalent in the sparsely populated frontier territories. The general aim of such a vigilante posse was euphemistically termed a "necktie party," where the captured guilty criminals were swiftly hung on the spot, wherein eliminating any subsequent need for a jury trial.

According to this theme of vigilante justice, vengeance clearly represents a vice in the punitive group tradition, whereby countering the negligent sense of dishonor expressed by the group authority figure. In the preceding "lynch-gang" example, the members of the vigilante gang vengefully act vindictively towards any fugitives from justice, effectively contrasting with the leniently-just treatment characterizing the virtuous mode. In terms of such a community-based perspective, the posse members were keenly aware of the unjust plight of any members within their group, venting their outrage in the most vindictive manner possible. The predictable finality of the necktie party was oft-times regrettable, for (in the frenzy of the hunt) many tragic miscarriages of justice often occurred: such as dramatized in Walter Van Tilburg Clark's fictional masterpiece, *The Oxbow Incident*.

CAPRICIOUSNESS - COWARDICE

The preceding two-stage interplay of dishonor/vengeance, in turn, dictates that the group follower figure eventually acts upon the potentiality implicit to his/her (projected) vengeful quest for vindictiveness. This further development takes the form of capriciously acting indifferently within an immediately-active time-frame, whereby anticipating the cowardly determination to act maliciously on the part of the villain. The ultimate timing for this act frequently dictates a rather extended course of deliberation. Indeed, this ultimate power of determination formally imparts the extreme power leverage wielded by the villain in relation to the vigilante.

This second stage within the punitive interaction invokes an active capricious sense of indifference on the part of the punisher, although now punctuated from the perspective of the group authority figure in anticipation of the (projected) cowardly determination to act maliciously on the part of the villain. This role reversal certainly appears warranted, being that mirrors the initial sequence based upon dishonor/vengeance, although now punctuated from an immediately-active punishment perspective (rather than the adversarial variety). The vigilante now capriciously acts indifferently in anticipation of prompting the cowardly sense of maliciousness on the part of the follower figure.

This immediately-active expression of capriciousness (on the part of the vigilante) is directly suggestive of the affiliated theme of foolishness, with the exception that the withholding of leniency (rather than that of approval) is now called into focus. As the chief moral antithesis of the virtuous lenient sense of integrity, *capriciousness* is traditionally defined as a fickle change in disposition, often without rhyme or reason. Its modern spelling derives from the Latin *caper* (a goat), also a basis for the English verb *caper* (to jump erratically like a goat). In this latter respect, capriciousness suggests an unexpected or random form of activity similar to the frisky antics of the mountain goat. In a related motivational sense, capriciousness implies a fickle change of motive or intent, often in a negative fashion. The related musical term *capriccio* refers to compositions of a free-form nature, an endeavor completely at odds with established musical convention.

The general connotations of capriciousness to a group sphere of influence prove equally significant, a feature often seen in the downfall of oppressive political regimes. The economic hardships leading up to the French Revolution were further compounded by widespread crop failures across the region, resulting in a scarcity of basic staples such as bread. Queen Marie Antoinette's capricious statement: "Let them eat cake," further fueled the outrage of the downtrodden peasants, leading to bloody revolt on a grand scale (as well as Marie's execution on the guillotine).

This capricious sense of indifference expressed by the group authority figure, in turn, sets the stage for the cowardly sense of malice anticipated from the group follower perspective. Indeed, the contemptible trend towards cowardice is only truly comprehensible precisely within such a group follower context. The group representative's cowardly-malicious refusal to act submissively stands in direct contrast to the compliant sense of fortitude characterizing the virtuous perspective. Indeed, cowardice is traditionally defined as the lack of fortitude or courage, particularly with respect to life or limb. Its modern spelling derives from the Latin *cauda* (tail) and *-ard* (a limiting suffix): literally "short-tailed" (originally an epithet for the timid hare). In medieval heraldry, cowardice is figuratively symbolized as a frightened (cowering) dog with its tail tucked between its legs.

According to classical mythology, this vice is traditionally associated with Venus Murtia, a variation on her affiliated role as goddess of love. The surname Murtia specifically reflected her fondness for the perpetually blooming myrtle tree. Indeed, a large grove of myrtle trees was prominently featured in front of her chapel at the foot of the Aventine Hill. As the patroness of laziness and cowardice, statues celebrating this curiously negative aspect of Venus were purposely allowed to accumulate a layering of moss (signifying hesitancy or inactivity): as evident in the common folksy expression, "a rolling stone gathers no moss."

This timid quality of cowardice actually represents just part of the total picture, balanced in a more active sense by the malicious variant practiced by the bully/hoodlum. The schoolyard bully that terrorizes his classmates for their lunch money is just as much a coward as those he intimidates. Such boldface aggression is generally risked only out of a false sense of immunity from punishment. The bully's cowardly expression of malice typically mirrors his own lack of submissive treatment; e.g., "My parents cut-off my allowance, so I'll take yours!"

This willful quality of cowardice further extends to a military sphere of influence, where a courageous sense of compliance for one's duties is abandoned altogether (such as launching into a cowardly retreat). The cowardly desertion of one's post is a widespread concern amongst many a new recruit, shirking responsibility to one's unit (as well as the very noble aims of the campaign). This potential towards cowardice was particularly apparent during the Civil War, where "greenhorn" recruits abandoned all pretense of bravery when faced with the true horrors of war: as dramatized in Steven Crane's stirring novel, *The Red Badge of Courage*.

In summary, the immediately-active villainous style of group authority perspective proves a fitting counterpoint to the potential range of corruption inherent to the group follower role. As initially described for the ego and alter ego vices, the group vices specified for villainy/corruption exhibit a parallel degree of specialization: namely, subdivided into either immediately-active roles or anticipatory modes projected within a future-directed time-frame. The immediately active authority roles are defined in terms of the sins of villainy, as specialized through the immediately-active themes of *foolish*-apathy or *capricious*-indifference, as well as negligent-*dishonor* or lazy sense of *infamy*. The future-directed modes, in turn, target the more abstract realm of the vices of corruption consistent with a darker range of potentiality: namely, *insurgent*-treachery, *vengeful*-vindictiveness, *gluttonous*-spitefulness, or *cowardly*-maliciousness.

As chief spokesman for the group, the group representative expresses an equally perverse balance of power with respect to the villainous prerequisites for the group authority roles. When ultimately faced with such a potent challenge to his authority status, the villainous group authority directly seeks to regain the upper hand within the ascending motivational hierarchy; namely, ascending (once again) to the next higher *universal* authority level within the hierarchy of defect.

11

THE UNIVERSAL REALM FOR DEFECT

The enduring spirit underlying the universal realm offers crucial insights into the darker characteristics encompassing the spiritual authority perspective; namely, the overarching theme of *profanity*. Profanity represents the chief moral antithesis of the virtuous theme of romanticism; namely, the failure to acknowledge the legitimacy of such universal issues. In particular, profanity represents the darker aspects within organized spirituality, effectively questioning any enduring universal significance, therein. The term derives from the Latin *profanus* (outside the temple, not sacred), from *pro-* (before) and *fanum* (a temple). It denotes contempt for sacred things, as in impiety or irreverence. Often profanity refers to the choice of words that most would consider offensive. Its original connotation was restricted to expression of blasphemy, sacrilege, or taking the Lord's name in vain: as explicitly forbidden within the Ten Commandments. The number of words considered profane has recently diminished due to the general secularization of society as a whole.

The derivation of profanity (literally, before the shrine) gives a general indication of its symbolic specificity. The concept of a walled enclosure into which only privileged persons might enter formally contrasts with the outer district of less worthiness or prestige. This notion of a threshold includes elaborate rules for delineating the clear separation between the sacred and the profane. The priests of the Jewish Temple symbolized their separateness through a change of garments when entering the inner court. They further avoided routine foods and forms of family interaction in order to prepare themselves for teaching the distinction between the sacred and the profane.

This enduring contrast pitting sacredness against the profane is particularly telling in the context of organized religion, with profanity essentially denigrating the sanctity of the spiritual authority perspective. Here profanity formally counters the more positive prerequisites previously established in terms of virtuous theme of *romanticism*, where such spiritual/universal overtones prove crucial for defining the overarching mystical sense of the term. In this latter respect, profanity proves antithetical to any such revered sense of sacredness, whether through the influence of thought, word, or deed.

According to this dualistic interpretation, the virtuous focus of the civil liberties (providence, liberty, civility, and austerity) is directly countered (point-for-point) with the contrasting listing of civil liabilities (prodigality-slavery-vulgarity-cruelty). Indeed, the latter cohesive grouping might have just as easily been termed the "sins of profanity" consistent with the antithetical role that sin plays in relation to the authority ideals. The infamous sense of *prodigality* expressed by the spiritual authority figure directly counteracts any gloriously-providential treatment. Similarly, one's dishonorable-*enslavement* further opposes any libertarian sense of honor. Furthermore, the authority figure's foolishly-*vulgar* treatment makes a dramatic counterpoint to any contrasting civilly-dignified treatment. Similarly, one's capricious sense of *cruelty* directly counters any austere sense of integrity.

Furthermore, this distinctive class of the sins of profanity builds directly upon the more elementary (group) class of the sins of villainy that they supersede. For instance, *prodigality* represents a more universal analogue of infamy, whereas *slavery* denotes a similar modification of dishonor. Furthermore, *vulgarity* redefines foolishness from a universal perspective, whereas *cruelty* denotes a more brutal form of capriciousness. This universal realm of authority-focused perspectives represents an immediately active style of authority perspective that specifically anticipates the potentiality inherent to the (future-directed) complement of follower vices.

THE THEOLOGICAL VICES: THE DARKER SIDE FOR THE SPIRITUAL DISCIPLE PERSPECTIVE

The preliminary description of the sins of profanity provides a fitting thematic overview in relation to the affiliated (more positive) listings of the civil liberties. The spiritual authority perspective, however, (by definition) is susceptible to its own unique form of follower counter-maneuver: in this case, that expressed by the spiritual disciple. Indeed, this enduring universal focus (in a virtuous sense) was previously described in terms of the respective listing of the theological virtues (faith, hope, charity, and decency): offering further crucial insights into the darker prerequisites of betrayal, despair, avarice, and antagonism; namely, those relating to the affiliated theme of *heresy*. Heresy is traditionally defined as the undermining or corruption of religious ritual or doctrine, whereby representing the direct moral antithesis of its virtuous counterpart in ecclesiasticism.

The term derives from the Old French *heresie*, from the Latin *hæresis*: employed by Christian writers in reference to the unorthodox teaching of doctrine. The Latin tradition, in turn, derives from the Greek *hairesis* (a taking or choosing), from *hairein* (to take or seize): whereupon taking opinions or beliefs in opposition to those conventionally accepted within the community. Consequently, heresy represents a more abstract (universal) variation upon the more basic "strike" option employed by the group representative. Martin Luther, for instance, was clearly regarded as heretical by the Catholic establishment of his day.

In the terms of Christian tradition, heresy is defined as those beliefs or viewpoints held by church members in contradiction to orthodoxy or core doctrine. It is formally distinguished from apostasy in that the latter represents a complete abandonment of faith, rendering the apostate a deserter or renegade. Heresy is also distinct from schisms; namely, a splitting of church membership brought about by disputes over hierarchy or discipline rather than matters of doctrine. The heretic generally considers oneself the *true* believer in terms of such doctrinal disputes.

The battle for doctrinal control over the Christian Church began with the scriptural proclamations of St. Peter (2 Peter 2:1), wherein the transition to the ecclesiastical tradition is ultimately traced. The "destructive heresies" specified by St. Peter refer to those promoting errors in doctrine that prohibit the heretic's fellowship within the church. In terms of this emerging ecclesiastical context, heresy is defined not only as a doctrinal error, but also the obstinate expression of error in the face of all proper instruction.

During Christianity's first three centuries, numerous heretical sects came into conflict with the accepted doctrine of the early Church. The First Council of Nicea (in 325 CE) addressed the heresy of Arianism, the first of many challenges to Christian orthodoxy. Excommunication soon became the preferred means for dealing with heretical individuals or groups. Although a small number of schisms have successfully endured, the vast majority were suppressed through forcible means, a fitting exemplar to anyone willing to risk such a foray into the darker realm of the vices.

This darker version of the spiritual disciple perspective has much to say with respect to the ongoing discussion of the contrasting realm of the vices. The universal focus (in an ecclesiastical sense) is respectively reflected in the corresponding listing of theological virtues (faith, hope, charity, and decency). This virtuous theme of ecclesiasticism, in turn, offers many clues towards identifying the contrasting realm of the vices for the spiritual disciple role; namely, the theological vices (betrayal, despair, avarice, and antagonism). According to this darker range of themes, *betrayal* makes a fitting contrast to faith, whereas *despair* makes a darker counterpoint to hope. Furthermore, *avarice* represents the chief moral antonym of charity, whereas *antagonism* denotes the darker counterpart of decency.

According to this darker interpretation, the despicable focus of the theological vices (betrayal, despair, avarice, and antagonism) might have just as easily been termed the "heretical vices" consistent with the antithetical role that vice plays in relation to virtue. The insurgent sense of *betrayal* expressed by the spiritual disciple figure directly counteracts any prudent sense of faithfulness. Similarly, any vengeful sense of *despair* further counteracts any blameful-hope for justice. Furthermore, the spiritual disciple figure's gluttonously-*avaricious* treatment makes a fitting counterpoint to any temperate sense of charitableness. Alternately, one's cowardly sense of *antagonism* further counteracts any fortitudinous sense of decency.

This cohesive class of spiritual disciple-based perspectives represents the passively-potential realm of vice that directly counteracts the more immediately-active domain of sinfulness characterizing the preliminary class of spiritual authority roles. Generally speaking, the spiritual authority themes immediately initiate the punitive interaction in anticipation of the future-directed potentialities underlying the follower perspective.

THE DARKER MOTIVATIONAL INTERPLAY GOVERNING THE UNIVERSAL REALM

As previously described with respect to the group-focused listings of the sins of villainy and the cardinal vices, the more abstract universal groupings specified for the civil liabilities and theological vices exhibit a similar range of specialization: subdivided into either immediately active authority roles occurring within the present or passively-potential follower modes projected into a future-directed time-frame. The immediately active authority roles are defined in terms of the civil liabilities, as invested with clear behavioral overtones; namely, an infamous sense of *prodigality* or a dishonorable sense of *slavery*, as well as a foolish sense of *vulgarity* or a capricious sense of *cruelty*. The future-directed behavioral perspectives, in turn, target the more abstract potentiality characterizing the theological vices: namely, insurgent-*betrayal*, blameful-*hope* for justice, gluttonous-*avariciousness*, or cowardly-antagonism. The latter passively-potential vices effectively complement the immediately active authority roles within the overall spiritual dynamic. For instance, an infamous sense of prodigality on the part of the spiritual authority further anticipates the insurgent-betrayal on the part of the spiritual disciple. This insurgent-betrayal, in turn, eventually becomes actualized as the foolish expression of vulgarity on the part of the punisher, whereby prompting the gluttonously-avaricious treatment on the part of spiritual disciple within a future-directed time-frame.

Furthermore, a parallel style motivational interplay similarly holds true with respect to the punitive withholding of negative reinforcement. For instance, the dishonorable-enslavement on the part of the spiritual authority figure, in turn, anticipates the vengeful sense of despair on the part of the spiritual disciple. This vengeful sense of despair, in turn, ultimately becomes actualized as the capricious sense of cruelty on the part of the punisher, whereby prompting the cowardly determination to act antagonistically on the part of the spiritual disciple. Consequently, for both punitive types of interaction, the immediately active nature of the civil liabilities effectively prompts (in a behavioral sense) the projected follower range of potentiality characterizing the theological vices. The remainder of the current chapter systematically examines the universal dynamics encompassing this eight-part complement of terms, providing a sturdy conceptual foundation for all subsequent classes of vices to follow.

A similar pattern of discussion will be followed, continuing the stepwise strategy of presentation previously established for the personal and group realms: whereby examining both the spiritual authority and spiritual disciple roles in tandem in terms of a two-stage ethical sequence. This encompasses the initial punitive sequence of prodigality, betrayal, vulgarity and avarice: as well as the darker sequence of slavery, despair, cruelty and antagonism. The dedicated reader can further refer back to the previous chapters (devoted to the group and personal realms) confirming that such an overarching two-stage dynamic remains in effect for the universal realm as well, as well validated in terms of the respective wealth of literary traditions.

PRODIGALITY – BETRAYAL

The more straightforward punitive withholding of rewards proves to be the most logical initiation point for such a grand-scale synthesis, mirroring the pattern previously established for the group realm of the defect. The interplay of prodigality and betrayal will be examined first, followed by the subsequent sequence comprising vulgarity and avarice. As initially suggested, the infamously-prodigal perspective of the spiritual authority figure actively initiates the punitive interaction in anticipation of the insurgent-betrayal on the part of the spiritual disciple. Being that only one role may be active within the punitive interaction at any given time, the role of the punisher is relegated to that of a future potentiality, specified as the insurgent-betrayal anticipated with respect to the spiritual disciple role.

The infamously-prodigal refusal to act solicitously (characterizing the sin of *prodigality*) certainly fits the bill in this universal sense. In particular, the infamous sense of *prodigality* characterizing the spiritual authority role effectively consummates the trend previously established with respect to laziness and infamy. Although the precise meaning of prodigality varies according to context, its general connotation refers to reckless wastefulness or extravagance consistent with the infamously-lazy treatment of the group authority figure. Its modern spelling derives the Latin *prodigalitas*, from *prodigere* (to drive away, to squander). In early Italian iconography, prodigality is personified as a blindfolded smiling woman shown in the act of scattering coins from a cornucopia, a fitting allusion to the fickle and often extravagant nature of this vice.

These wasteful connotations of prodigality are similarly condemned in biblical scripture, as reflected in Christ's Parable of the Prodigal Son. The basic story line refers to the tale of two sons, the younger of whom persuaded his father to advance him his share of the family inheritance. With such newfound wealth at his disposal, the young man journeyed to a faraway land where he squandered his fortune on loose living and sensual pursuits. A disastrous famine soon followed, eventually pointing the prodigal son home in hopes of receiving the humble conditions afforded the servant help. Upon his return the son fell upon his father's mercy, pleading: "Father, I have sinned against heaven and in thy sight: I am no longer worthy to be called thy son, make me as one of thy hired servants." The father, moved by the sight of his long-lost son, ordered the servants to kill the "fatted calf" in honor of his return. In this fashion, the scandalous behavior of the prodigal son was graciously absolved through the providential favor of his benevolent father.

The spiritual overtones of this parable certainly ring true today, the role of the father undoubtedly alluding to the providential favor of God-the-Father. The "featured" son in the parable further signifies the contrasting realm of the vices, his loyalties now redirected towards strangers far-removed from family ties. The son's fortunes soon failed him, in direct contrast to the father's providential favor. The son's callously-selfish behavior was rightfully judged as prodigal, in keeping with the spiritual context of this fictional parable. Fortunately this story ends on a positive note, being that any vice can remedied when both parties seek reconciliation.

This preceding scenario of the Prodigal Son further sets the stage for the remaining spiritual follower form of counter-maneuver; namely, the insurgent-*betrayal* expressed by the spiritual disciple figure. The initial infamously-prodigal treatment, in turn, anticipates the insurgent-betrayal on the part of the follower figure. Here the spiritual disciple insurgently acts in a betraying fashion towards his spiritual authority figure, a more universal variation on the insurgent sense of treachery expressed by the group representative. As the chief moral antithesis of faith, betrayal traces its origins to the Latin *tradere* (to deliver up), as in a betrayal of trust or allegiance. According to Dante's *Inferno*, betrayal is considered the most deadly of sins, the worst traitors of history specifically singled-out for the most terrible of punishments within the pit of Hell. Accordingly, betrayal remains a theme almost universally disparaged throughout classical antiquity.

The fateful example of Julius Caesar particularly comes to mind, his insatiable quest for power ultimately cut short by members of the Senate. Caesar had originally invoked the emergency powers of the Roman Constitution to rule uncontested as emperor. This circumstance directly threatened the power of the Senate that originally held sway over Rome's republican form of government. Caesar's fortunes quickly faded following his vain attempt to claim divinity, a tactic seen as setting the stage for a change to permanent dictatorship. The Senate felt pressured into taking drastic action culminating in Caesar's assassination in 44 BCE. The cruelest irony concerns the role of Brutus, one of the many senators wielding a knife during the deadly attack. Indeed, Brutus is traditionally cited as one of Caesar's several illegitimate sons. Caesar's shock at his betrayal by such a trusted ally was strikingly apparent in his famous last words: "et tu Brutus?" (and you Brutus?), whereupon he is said to have collapsed in inglorious resignation.

VULGARITY – AVARICE

The completed initiatory sequence of prodigality-betrayal, in turn, redirects the focus to the remaining darker stage within the universal interaction: namely, that encompassing vulgarity and avarice. In terms of this latter phase, according to the march of time, the spiritual disciple eventually acts upon the potentiality of his (projected) insurgent-betrayal: now foolishly acting vulgarly towards the follower figure in anticipation of the latter's gluttonous determination to act avariciously within a future-directed time-frame. This active withholding of reinforcement formally equates with the *vulgarity* perspective expressed by the spiritual authority figure, continuing the tradition of foolishly-apathetic treatment initially established for the respective personal/group levels. In essence, the spiritual authority foolishly acts in a vulgar fashion, whereby prompting the gluttonous determination to act avariciously on the part of the follower figure.

A number of key features are observed similar to those initially encountered with respect to prodigality/betrayal. Here the foolishly-vulgar party now formally assumes a spiritual authority status, whereas the latter gluttonously-avaricious perspective, in turn, takes on the mantle of the spiritual disciple role, being that the latter formally "follows" the authority role in terms of such a future-directed course of action.

As the chief moral antithesis of civility, *vulgarity* is traditionally defined as a universal lack of refinement. Its modern spelling derives from the Latin *vulgaris*, from *vulgus* or *volgus* (of the common people). This originally neutral connotation eventually acquired negative overtones, as reflected in a lack of culture, taste, or refinement. In terms of the current context, only the latter connotation of coarseness and/or crudeness rates further consideration within the ongoing discussion of vulgarity.

In fitting contrast to vulgarity, civility encourages a striving for social harmony, whereby circumventing the conflict accompanying vulgar breaches of etiquette. In keeping with the principles of the Golden Rule, civility proves most effective when a majority of the citizenry complies. Although custom and tradition tend to facilitate social stability, such rigid formalism can often lead to misunderstandings. Indeed, the modern trend towards informality is often mistaken for rudeness or vulgarity. Radical individualism may similarly be interpreted in poor taste, as in rebellion against social conformity. This enhanced degree of social freedom further impacts self-discipline and respect for authority. The disturbing trend towards tabloidism, raucous politics, and licentiousness proves indicative of this salient trend towards vulgarity.

Perhaps the most telling aspect in this regard concerns the rebellious nature of youth. Each new generation embraces a fresh style of attire and conduct meant to erect a line of demarcation with respect to the establishment. The youth generation narrowly views parental authority as rejecting fledgling strivings towards independence, often leading to a drastically altered appearance. The rebellious youth finds solace primarily in the company of a similarly inclined peer group, their shared value platform providing a common insurgent rallying point. This desire to press for nonconformity provokes a particularly strong establishment response, leaving any affiliated judgment of *vulgarity* to the discretion of the public at large. Indeed, it is precisely this *universality* of judgment that equates vulgarity with the spiritual authority perspective, whereby transcending the more partisan concerns of the group for a much broader moralistic perspective.

The preceding discussion of vulgarity, in turn, redirects the current focus to the gluttonously-avaricious perspective expressed by the spiritual disciple figure. The spiritual disciple gluttonously determines to act spitefully-avariciously, whereby ultimately countering the foolishly-vulgar treatment initially expressed by the spiritual authority figure. As the chief moral antithesis of charity, avarice is most often defined as a universal preoccupation with wealth or riches. In the current context, *avarice* represents the main spiritual

variation on the group/personal themes of gluttonous-spitefulness, representing the selfish withholding of any solicitous cooperation. Its modern spelling derives from the Latin *avaritia* (avarice), from *avere* (to wish, to desire). Consistent with its related connotation to greed, avarice denotes a self-centered pursuit of wealth: in contrast to its benevolent bestowal (as in charity). The Bible specifically personifies avarice as Mammon, the demon spirit of wealth and greed (from the Aramaic term for riches). According to Middle Eastern tradition, the term originally referred to the rich outpouring of milk from the inexhaustible breasts (mammae) of their chief fertility goddess. The Babylonians worshipped her as Mami or Mammitu (mother), while related Sumerian texts refer to her as Mammetun (Mother of Destinies).

According to the New Testament Sermon on the Mount, Christ insightfully states that mankind cannot serve both God and Mammon: equating worldly wealth with ungodliness. Contrary to the wording of the popular maxim, it is the *love* of money (and not money itself) that is the root of all evil. Mammon eventually came to symbolize a false god with powers hostile to the Christian tradition. Occult lore describes Mammon as one of the fallen angels ruling over Hell, also referred to as the Prince of Tempters. His arch-demon status eventually led to his identification with Lucifer, Beelzebub, and Satan. As the demon of avarice, Mammon holds the throne of this world according to St. Francesca quoting one of her *93* Visions. Weyer facetiously referred to Mammon as Hell's ambassador to England, a satirical reference to the ruthless nature of British commercialism.

In a formally schematic sense, I (as spiritual disciple) gluttonously express a determination to spitefully act avariciously towards you in response to your (as spiritual authority) foolishly-vulgar treatment of me. Indeed, it is chiefly this potential threat of spiteful-avarice that ultimately imparts the strike power-leverage employed by the spiritual disciple in relation to the spiritual authority: the latter dependent upon the former to ultimately justify his/her own immediately-active villainous depravities. This gluttonously-avaricious treatment ultimately provides an effective sense of closure to the entire universal style of punitive interchange.

SLAVERY – DESPAIR

The completed two-part description of the universally-focused vices based upon prodigality-betrayal and vulgarity-avarice, in turn, sets the stage for the remaining sequence of themes targeting slavery/despair and cruelty/antagonism. This latter format, in turn, specifies the deliberate withholding of leniency, whereby deliberately punishing behaviors judged to not be suitably submissive. This latter format directly contrasts with the preceding section where rewards were deliberately withheld in response to non-solicitous types of behavior. Negative types of punishment entail withholding lenient consequences naturally occurring within the environment, or (in an interpersonal sense) the denial of leniency in response to the absence of aversive types of behavior. In terms of the current universal context, the spiritual authority figure negligently and dishonorably acts in a slavish fashion, whereby prompting the vengeful sense of despair on the part of the spiritual disciple. The latter vengeful sense of despair, in turn, eventually becomes actualized as the capriciously-cruel treatment on the part of the punisher, whereby prompting the cowardly determination to act antagonistically on the part of the respective follower figure.

As initially indicated, the dishonorable sense of enslavement expressed by the spiritual authority figure actively initiates the two-stage punitive interaction. As the chief moral antithesis of liberty, *slavery* is defined as a manifest lack of honorable and libertarian sense of ethics representative of a manifest disregard for the freedom of others. Slavery is generally defined as the forceful domination of another individual resulting in the loss of personal freedom. Its modern spelling derives from the Latin *sklabos* (slave), a term originally referring to captives of a Slavic origin: from the Old Slavic *sloven* or *slovo*. From the earliest of times, slavery was widely regarded as an economic and social necessity. The traditional slave force was culled from captives of war or bred as the offspring of slave parents. Slavery was typically viewed as a regrettable economic misfortune, most slaves resigned to endure their menial or domestic duties. Discipline and chastisement were generally reserved for only the worst offenders, with the death penalty an even rarer occurrence.

The eventual decline of the Western Roman Empire led to a similar decline in slavery's influence, although the invading barbarian hordes were not averse to taking full advantage of captive prisoners. Between the 8th and 10th centuries, a resurgence of slavery occurred with respect to the wholesale enslavement of Slavic peoples by invading German forces; hence, the English derivation of the term. Through subsequent Christian influence, slavery gradually declined in Western Europe: leading to the medieval feudal system with its more humane reliance on the labor of the serfs and peasants.

The eventual dawning of the Age of Exploration provided a new wrinkle to this ages-old institution. Sturdy sailing ships permitted ready access to the teeming tropical shores of Africa, offering an entirely new class of slaves for exploitation. The discernible racial and cultural distinctions proved particularly instrumental in legitimizing such an evil system of exploitation. The New World colonies became the recipients of cheap slave labor, the Africans typically surpassing Native Americans in terms of vigor and stamina. The vast Caribbean plantations were the chief beneficiaries of this labor windfall, as well as the agricultural economies of the Southern United States. The labor-intensive focus of the major cash crops (cotton, sugar, and tobacco) was chiefly made possible through a captive labor force. Indeed, the considerable profits gained from the slave trade eventually rivaled those gleaned from the agricultural sector.

By today's standards, the field laborers of the Southern plantation were maintained under the most appalling of circumstances, a far cry from the luxury of the master's mansion. The mere threat of punishment was generally sufficient to oppress the burgeoning slave population. Primarily for financial reasons, the suitably submissive slave was not typically mistreated. Physical violence was reserved for rebellious slaves that violated the unwritten code of bondage. Punishments were customarily severe: ranging from scourging and chastisement to torture and execution: staged as a public example for others of their lot. Through such a violent tactics, the slave owner forcefully commanded the unswerving obedience of his captive work force, a tragedy that largely endured until more enlightened times fortunately prevailed.

In terms of the preceding slavery scenario, the dishonorable-enslavement by the spiritual authority figure, in turn, sets the stage for the follower counter-maneuver proper; namely, the vengeful sense of desperation expressed by the spiritual disciple. This circumstance directly contrasts with the virtuous mode, where despair represents the direct antithesis with respect to hope. The spiritual follower now vengefully acts despairingly in response to the dishonorable-enslavement on the part of the spiritual authority figure: an interplay analogous to the pattern previously established with respect to prodigality/betrayal. Its modern spelling derives from the Latin root *desperatus*, the past participle of *desperate* (to be without hope). This manifest lack of hope is a theme common to many scriptural contexts consistent with the prominent influence of the spiritual disciple perspective.

According to Old Testament scripture, the prophets frequently endured many trials and tribulations leading to despair. For instance, the prophet Elijah fled for his life following an interminable conflict with the wicked Queen Jezebel. Indeed, Elijah entreated the Lord to put an end to the trials and tribulations he was forced to endure (1st Kings 19:14). The prophet Job similarly suffered a broad range of trials: resulting in impoverishment, the death of his children, and painful ailments, all within a brief span of time (Job 1:13-19, 2:7-8). His unending torment caused him to lament: "I would prefer death to all my sufferings." (Job 7:15). This dramatic set of tribulations appeared to overwhelm these faithful men of God, their dark despair crying-out for a merciful release from suffering. Fortunately, God saw fit to fortify both Elijah and Job through the depths of their despair, their faith in Divine Providence eventually restored in full.

CRUELTY – ANTAGONISM

The preceding two-stage sequence of slavery-despair, in turn, dictates that the spiritual follower figure must eventually act upon the potentiality implicit in his/her (projected) vengeful sense of despair. This further development takes the form of a capricious sense of cruelty within an immediately-active time-frame, whereby anticipating the cowardly-antagonistic treatment on the part of the respective follower figure. Indeed, this ultimate power of deliberation crucially imparts the power leverage wielded by the authority figure in relation to that of the follower.

This second stage within the punitive interaction encompasses an immediately-active capricious expression of cruelty on the part of the punisher, although now punctuated from the active perspective of the spiritual authority figure: in anticipation of the cowardly determination to act antagonistically on the part of the follower. This active expression of cruelty directly parallels the related theme of vulgarity, with the exception that the withholding of leniency (rather than that of approval) is now called into focus. Indeed, as the chief moral antithesis of austere-integrity, *cruelty* is traditionally defined as a fickle expression of callousness analogous to that previously established with respect to capriciousness. Its modern spelling derives from the Latin *crudelis*, from *crudis* (raw): suggesting a predilection for inflicting pain or suffering upon others.

Cruelty is traditionally symbolized as the fabled Basilisk serpent, a fierce dragon with fiery breath (and fearsome looks) said to have the power to kill. According to medieval heraldry, cruelty is personified as a stealthy leopard, a hulking vulture, or cunning wolf. These fearsome overtones prove equally relevant to the realm of international warfare, as in innumerable campaigns of military conquest. Cruelty has been employed as a crucial military tactic, instilling terror in all that would resist the wave of conquest.

The most ruthless commander in this regard was Ghengis Khan, who deliberately employed a cruel policy of annihilation. Cities that resisted his demands were brutally savaged as a fitting example for all to follow. Entire urban populations were slaughtered without mercy. Any survivors were marched ahead of advancing Mongol armies as human shields, a clever defense against preemptive attacks. Cities that surrendered without resistance were generally spared, their citizens merely enslaved. Indeed, many cities preemptively surrendered rather than risk the prospects of a prolonged siege. This cruel tactic of terror eventually proved instrumental in subjugating a broad swath of Asian territories ranging from Persia to Northern China. Ghengis Kahn's descendents further expanded his empire during the 13th century across a span ranging from Eastern Europe to Southern China. These cruel tactics survive to our modern era as the ruthless strategy of "the reprisals of war," retribution intended to inflict proportionately horrific casualties upon the enemy. This brutal tactic was the stock-in-trade for Nazi Occupation of World War II, as evident in the vicious slaughter of entire villages of civilians towards the end of the war: a grim testimony to the cruel mind-set driving the unfettered Nazi regime.

In accordance with the preceding wartime examples, cruelty primarily represents a universal style of power maneuver targeting the realm of defect. The Nazis speciously imagined themselves as "the master race" for the entire world, a delusion underlying such a twisted cruelty perspective. This capricious sense of cruelty, in turn, prompts the subsequent cowardly-*antagonistic* perspective on the part of the spiritual disciple figure. Indeed, antagonism is provisionally defined as the chief moral antithesis of decency. Unlike the first three theological virtues (which were paired with more definitive moral opposites), the greater degree of generality associated with decency would appear to obscure any exclusive antonym. The traditions associated with antagonism, however, clearly fit the bill in this regard; namely, a willful sense of rivalry or opposition in a broad social setting.

The term derives from the Greek *antagonistes* (an opponent), from *anti-* (against) and *agon* (contest). Indeed, the latter root-stem chiefly refers to an assembly (the *agonia*): a gathering dedicated to athletic games and contests. The modern-day Olympic Games owe a great debt to this classical tradition: particularly the wrestling, running, and boxing events. The favored contender in the agonia was termed the *agonistes* in reference to the assembly-style format of the contest. The rival of the agonistes was specified as the *antagonistes*, the prefix *anti-* clearly reflecting the adversarial nature of the proceedings. In keeping with these competitive overtones, the ancient tournaments were generally organized as open invitationals, where only the fittest athletes competed from across the land. Any underlying feelings of malice were strongly tempered by the festive nature of the proceedings, although the desperate quest to avoid defeat certainly figured prominently in the mental outlook of the athlete.

A wide assortment of antagonistic strategies (such as bluffing or psyching-out one's opponent) figured prominently within the individual events, much as is commonly seen today with respect to wrestling and boxing. This highly contentious persona was strongly tempered by the codes of fair play and sportsmanship, providing a fitting counterpoint to the highly antagonistic nature of the proceedings. Under such circumstances the spiritual disciple figure cowardly determines to act antagonistically towards one's spiritual authority figure, in response to the latter's capriciously-cruel treatment. In a more formal sense I (as spiritual disciple) now cowardly act in an antagonistic fashion towards you, in reaction to your (as

spiritual authority) cruel treatment of me. This tenuous power of potentiality ultimately imparts the power leverage implicit to both the spiritual authority and disciple roles, the former depending upon the latter to consummate the recursive cycle of cruelty-then-antagonism.

In conclusion, the completed description of the vices of defect spanning the personal, group, and universal levels, in turn, sets the stage for the remaining humanitarian and transcendental levels within the hierarchy of defect. In contrast to the purely organizational status of the first three levels, the final two levels are alternately defined as purely abstract styles of power maneuvers. The humanitarian domain is specified through the abstract addition of "historical" time, whereas the transcendental realm makes an appeal to the notion of pure transcendence.

The profoundly abstract nature of these final two levels is further reflected in their respective groupings of vices. These darker themes all share a profound significance within the field of ethical inquiry: as the respective sampling of evil, cunning, hatred, belligerence, etc., collectively serve to indicate. Indeed, the vices associated with these final two levels virtually beg to be listed together: as in the sins of apostasy (wrath-tyranny-persecution-oppression), the moralistic vices (evil-cunning-ugliness-hypocrisy), the humanistic vices (anger-hatred-prejudice-belligerence), and the mystical vices (iniquity, turpitude, abomination, and perdition). These final two authority levels come replete with a wealth of historical documentation spanning both classical and contemporary traditions. The respective description of this additional class of vices is now launched with an in-depth examination of the humanitarian authority level in concert with the affiliated listings of ecumenical and moralistic vices.

12

THE HUMANITARIAN DOMAIN OF DEFECT

The humanitarian authority perspective represents a unique addition to the orderly progression of the ethical hierarchy, distinguished from all previous levels in terms of being the first truly abstract power maneuver. Not an organizational power maneuver per sé, it rather represents a more advanced variation on the more fundamental universal perspective (modified through the abstract addition of historical time). Consequently, humanitarian authority claims to speak for all generations of mankind, not just the current one, a theme equally applicable to the darker realm of the vices.

The virtuous humanitarian realm was initially defined in terms of the traditions of the ecumenical ideals; namely, grace, free will, magnanimity, and equanimity. Although this grouping scarcely exhibits the pedigree of some other listings of virtues/values, its individual terms offer a clear moral precedent in their own right. Their extreme level of abstraction ensures a prominent place in Christian theology: themes that have resounded in the enduring spirit of the ecumenical councils that have defended, fortified, and preserved the unity of faith. This ecumenical spirit survives to our modern age with respect to the World Council of Churches, a broad coalition of Protestant denominations united in dedication to service and witness to the global community.

This enduring ecumenical spirit offers further crucial insights into the darker prerequisites for the humanitarian authority perspective; namely, those relating to *apostasy* (literally a falling away). This contrasting sense of apostasy represents the key moral antithesis to the spirit of ecumenism; namely, the failure to acknowledge the legitimacy of such an enduring humanitarian perspective. Apostasy represents a darker variation on organized spirituality, effectively questioning any enduring humanitarian significance therein. The term derives from the Greek *apostasis* (a

revolt or a standing-away), from *apostenai* (to defect, to stand off), from a compound of *apo-* (away-from) and *stenai* (to stand). It denotes the abandonment of one's religious or moral principles, a counterpoint completely at odds with such an enduring humanitarian perspective. Accordingly, apostasy signifies the desertion of one's moral foundation, whereby giving-up one's moral state of belief. One who has initially embraced a particular belief cannot leave it without also being labeled an apostate.

After the Roman Empire adopted Christianity as its state religion, apostates were punished through a deprivation of all their civil rights. They were forbidden to give evidence in a court of law and were not allowed to bequeath or inherit property. To induce another to apostasy was considered a grievous capital offense. During the Middle Ages both Civil and Canon Law classified apostates with heretics: with *Apostasy Perfidiæ* defined as the voluntary abandonment of the Christian faith.

The heretic differs from the apostate primarily in that the former denies or disagrees with one or more doctrines of the faith, whereas the apostate denies the validity of the entire edifice, a sin regarded as most grievous. Apostasy, therefore, was included in a special class of sin for which the Church imposed perpetual penance and excommunication without hope of pardon: leaving forgiveness to God's will alone. Although penalties within the Christian tradition have softened somewhat in modern times, the stance within Islam has remained unchanged down through the ages. Indeed, according to the Koran: "He that converts to any other religion shall be put to death" as commanded by the Prophet.

According to this dualistic interpretation, the virtuous focus of the ecumenical ideals is directly countered (point-for-point) with the corresponding listing of the sins of apostasy (wrath-tyranny-persecution-oppression). Perhaps no other grouping of sins exhibits such a clear-cut degree of conceptual affinity across the board. Indeed, this cohesive grouping might just as easily have been termed the "sins of ecumenism" consistent with the antithetical status sin plays in relation to the authority ideals. The prodigal sense of *wrathfulness* expressed by the humanitarian authority figure directly counteracts any provident sense of gracefulness. Similarly, one's *tyrannical* sense of enslavement directly opposes any libertarian sense of free will. Furthermore, the one's vulgar sense of *oppressiveness* makes a fitting counterpoint to any civil expression of magnanimity. Finally, one's cruel sense of *persecution* effectively counteracts any austere sense of equanimity.

THE MORALISTIC VICES: THE SCOURGE OF THE HUMANITARIAN PERSPECTIVE

In conclusion, the preliminary description of the sins of apostasy provides a fitting counterpoint to the affiliated class of ecumenical ideals. This cohesive grouping of vices proves particularly comprehensive in scope consistent with their enduring humanitarian significance. Indeed, this darker grouping remains a powerful influence even in our modern age, particularly those troubled regions of the world ruled by ruthless dictators. Even an authority perspective as abstract as the humanitarian, however, must (by definition) be susceptible to its own unique form of follower countermaneuver: in this case, that employed by the representative member of humanity.

The humanitarian follower perspective (also known as the representative member of humanity role) has much to say with respect to the ongoing analysis of the vices. The motivational dynamics governing this supremely abstract follower perspective share much in common with the subordinate follower levels that it supersedes. More properly termed the philosopher's maneuver, this eclectic strategy invokes the prestige of speaking as a representative for all of humanity. Indeed, this enduring focus (in a virtuous sense) is further reflected in the respective listing of classical Greek values (beauty-truth-goodness-wisdom): themes that formally expand upon the cardinal/theological virtues, only now invoking the more versatile concept of *value*.

This enduring virtuous theme of eclecticism, in turn, offers significant clues towards identifying the remaining humanitarian listing of vices; in this case, the contrasting realm of the *moralistic* vices (evil-cunning-ugliness-hypocrisy. According to this darker range of perspectives, *evil*

makes a fitting contrast to goodness, whereas *cunning* represents the darker counterpart of wisdom. Furthermore, *ugliness* represents the chief moral antithesis of beauty, whereas *hypocrisy* suggests a darker counterpart in truth. Indeed, this cohesive grouping might just as easily have been termed the "vices of anarchism" consistent with the antithetical status that anarchism plays in relation to eclecticism.

In this formal sense, the universal prerequisites previously established for heresy, in turn, are modified as the more enduring humanitarian theme of *anarchism*. The term derives from the Greek compound of *an-* (deprivation) and *arche* (government). It denotes the theory that government is oppressively restrictive to personal freedom, a factor that is ideally to be abolished in favor of a free system of agreement amongst individuals. Central to anarchist thought is a belief in individual human freedoms and the denial of any outward authority: professing that the discipline of the state harmfully hinders personal development.

Beginning in the Middle Ages, the anarchist tradition became closely associated with utopian and/or millenarian religious movements. These included the Brethren of the Free Spirit in the 13th century and the Anabaptists in the 16th century. The modern sense of political anarchism emerged in the 18th and 19th centuries, chiefly through the writings of William Godwin, P.J. Proudhon, amongst others. Russian anarchist, Mikhail Bakunin, in turn, invested the movement with its collectivist and violent overtones, despite revisionary efforts by Piotr Kropotkin and Leo Tolstoy. Political anarchism was suppressed in Russia by the Bolshevik party following the Russian Revolution.

As an organized movement, anarchism has largely faded in significance, although retaining status as the inspiration for political and social protest. Contrary to popular belief, terrorism was never adopted as a widespread platform for anarchist theory or practice. Some anarchists, however, engaged in what was termed *propaganda by deed*: namely, acts of terrorism or assassination against state officials or the ruling class. In recent years, anarchists have mounted extremely vocal (and sometimes violent) public protests at international gatherings attended by representatives of the major industrial nations, as in recent demonstrations at the World Trade Organization and the World Economic Forum.

Here anarchism proves a fitting counterpoint to the more positive prerequisites previously established for eclecticism, the latter celebrating the cooperative spirit underlying all human endeavor.

In contrast, anarchism aims to destroy all traditions from the past, favoring radical individualism at the expense of the status quo. Anarchism founders in its failure to ensure that a better system of governance will necessarily emerge: throwing its lot to the vagaries of chance and well-meaning intentions. Consequently, anarchism has never appealed to more than a fringe segment of society as a whole, marginalized to the point of representing little more than an excuse for demonstrating before the global media.

In summary, in terms of the previously described universally-focused listings of the sins of profanity and the heretical vices, the more abstract groupings specified for the sins of apostasy and the vices of anarchism exhibit a similar dualistic range of specialization: subdivided into either immediately active authority roles occurring within the present or passively-potential follower roles projected into a future-directed time-frame. The immediately active terms are defined through the sins of apostasy, invested with clear punitive overtones; namely, a prodigal sense of *wrathfulness* or a *tyrannical* sense of enslavement, as well as the vulgar sense of *oppressiveness*, or a cruel sense of *persecution* specific to the authority role.

The future-directed follower perspectives, in turn, target the more abstract realm of the vices of anarchism: namely, *ugly*-betrayal, *hypocritical*-despair, avaricious-*evil*, or antagonistic-*cunning*. This projected class of follower terms effectively complements the more immediately active authority roles in terms of the overall humanitarian dynamic. For instance, the prodigal sense of wrathfulness on the part of the humanitarian authority directly prompts the ugly sense of betrayal on the part of the representative member of humanity. This latter ugly sense of betrayal, in turn, is eventually actualized as a vulgar expression of oppressiveness on the part of the punisher, whereby prompting the avaricious determination to act evilly on the part of the follower figure.

A similar style of motivational interplay is further encountered with respect to the remaining realm of malicious punishment. For instance, the tyrannical-enslavement on the part of the humanitarian authority figure, in turn, prompts the hypocritical sense of despair from the representative member of humanity. This latter hypocritical sense of despair, in turn, eventually becomes actualized as cruel-persecution on the part of the punisher, whereby prompting the antagonistic sense of cunning in relation to the follower figure.

Following the pattern of discussion previously established for the personal, group, and universal levels, it would be tempting to employ a similar strategy here: namely, examining both the humanitarian authority and follow roles in tandem encompassing a two-stage motivational dynamic. With respect to the current humanitarian focus, this would amount to the sequence of wrath, ugliness, oppression, and evil: as well as the subsequent sequence of tyranny, hypocrisy, persecution, and cunning. This fourth-order level of abstraction, however, ultimately begins to obscure the orderly pattern of authority *then* follower roles previously established for the initial levels (although the pattern still remains somewhat in evidence). Indeed, the extreme level of generality associated with the humanitarian realm precludes its identification with any singular social institution: rather incorporated into the universal (or sometimes political) framework of society as a whole.

Consequently, in contrast to the pattern of presentation previously established for the personal, group, and universal realms, the humanitarian sphere of influence employs a slightly different strategy across the board. A custom pattern of presentation for the individual humanitarian vices is, therefore, proposed: examining the darker humanitarian themes as a more abstract extension of the elementary realm of the vices. For instance, evil is examined in terms of the subordinate concepts of avarice/gluttony, whereas oppression is defined in relation to vulgarity/foolishness. Furthermore, ugliness is examined in reference to insurgency/betrayal, whereas wrathfulness exhibits a similar correspondence to prodigality/infamy.

This dualistic range of comparisons proves relatively straightforward, being that the humanitarian realm shares many features in common with the subordinate universal/group domains. Indeed, the humanitarian realm provides overarching insights of such a darker range of themes, culminating in a seamless overview of the entire unified hierarchy of sin and vice. The remainder of the current chapter presents an in-depth examination of the specific literary traditions for each of the sins of apostasy, followed by a similarly comprehensive discussion of the vices of anarchism: as further validated through their traditional religious and historical precedents.

WRATH

The first of the ecumenical vices, *wrathfulness*, is traditionally defined as the chief moral antithesis of grace. Its modern spelling derives from the Anglo-Saxon *wrath* (intense anger), the past tense of *writhan* (to writhe). In a more contemporary sense, it refers to an extreme degree of rage or fury in keeping with such an enduring humanitarian focus. During the classical era, the wrathfulness of the gods of nature conveniently explained the inevitable occurrence of earthquakes, volcanic eruptions, and tidal waves. Old Testament accounts of the destruction of Sodom and Gomorrah further attest to wrath's enduring significance in the Judeo-Christian tradition. Beginning with Noah and the Flood, mankind remained in jeopardy of the wrath of God, particularly under circumstances when remorse for sinfulness was lacking. The Lord freely bestowed His wrathfulness upon the egregious evildoer, in fitting contrast to the goodness and mercy He reserved for the faithful. Essentially a human passion, wrath can only metaphorically be ascribed to the Lord: rationalized in terms of God's overriding sense of love irrespective of the severity of His punishments.

This extreme sense of wrathfulness rates much less significance in New Testament scripture consistent with its more prominent charitable precepts. The final apocalyptic Book of Revelation, however, resurrects many of the traditional trappings of divine wrathfulness, particularly the metaphorical imagery relating to the Old Testament. Most prominent of these is the "grapes of wrath" metaphor described in the Chapter *14* of the Book of Revelation. The Apostle John describes in graphic detail the great winepress of the wrath of the Lord in reference to the Day of Final Judgement, when the Lord returns to reap the great spiritual harvest of the earth. Christ is depicted descending upon a billowing cloud wielding a great sickle with which he harvests the innumerable clusters of grapes (souls) from the "vine of life" covering the earth. This final bounty is then said to be cast into a great winepress from which a torrent of juice (blood) is said to flow to considerable depth.

According to this metaphorical interpretation, wrathfulness represents the extreme humanitarian counterpart of the prodigality expressed by the spiritual authority figure, in turn, prompting the ugly-betrayal expressed by the respective follower figure. In a more formal sense, the prodigal sense of wrathfulness expressed by the humanitarian authority figure actively initiates the punitive-interaction, in turn, anticipating the ugly-betrayal expressed by the representative member of humanity. Being that only one role may be active within the punitive interaction at any given time, the role of punisher is relegated to that of future potentiality; namely the ugly-betrayal anticipated from the humanitarian fol-

lower figure. In such metaphorical terms, the Lord passes final judgement upon the unrighteous, freely venting His wrath upon all that scorned their commitment to His goodwill. John (3:36) similarly states: "He that believeth in the Son hath everlasting life: and he that believeth not in the Son shall not see life, but the *wrath* of God abideth upon him."

TYRANNY

Any discussion of wrathfulness must necessarily remain incomplete without mention of the related theme of *tyranny*. As the chief moral antithesis of free will, tyranny extends the more immediate prerequisites for enslavement into a humanitarian sphere of influence. Tyranny is traditionally defined as absolute political rule unfettered by the restrictions of law or constitution. It is typically motivated out of a personal sense of greed to the necessary detriment of the public good. This tyrannical treatment on the part of the humanitarian authority figure initiates the punitive interaction, whereby prompting the hypocritical sense of despair on the part of the humanitarian follower.

The modern spelling of tyranny derives from the Greek *tyrannos* (the rule of a lord or tyrant). This vice is metaphorically personified as a matronly woman adorned with an iron crown: also wielding a sword, chains, and a yoke. Aristotle specifically disparages tyranny as the opposite of true kingship. Its overthrow is often justified, although Aquinas argues that the transition of power should be less damaging than the suffering inflicted by the pre-existing tyranny.

The most widely cited example of tyranny in the classical world concerns the reign of the Thirty Tyrants, a council appointed by the Spartans to rule over Athens following the Pelloponesian War. Athens had been soundly defeated by Sparta (a rival city-state), yet failed to fully comply with the stringent terms of surrender; namely, the demolition of the fortifications surrounding Athens. Athens quickly was accused of breaking the peace, only escaping further drastic measures by agreeing to a radical overhaul of its governing body. The Council of Thirty was hastily convened in the summer of 404 BCE, quickly adopting a pro-Spartan form of government. The council soon sought to eliminate all opposition to its newfound political status, executing or exiling many prominent citizens in the process. Although war reparations necessitated some degree of economic sacrifice, the council's greed eventually led to unprecedented looting and pillaging. This extreme sense of tyranny eventually led to the sound defeat of the Council of Thirty less than a year after its precipitous rise to power. Such a tenuous hold on arbitrary power is generally the rule rather than the exception: for those that live by the sword often are doomed to die it.

PERSECUTION

The completed description of wrath and tyranny, in turn, sets the stage for a discussion of the remaining humanitarian vices of persecution and oppression. As the chief moral antitheses of magnanimity and equanimity, both persecution and oppression share a similar overlap in meaning: collectively deriving from the Latin *opprimere* (to press against) and *persecutus* (to pursue). Although these darker themes are frequently used interchangeably in common usage, enough finer distinctions remain to warrant separate placement within the hierarchy of the vices. For instance, persecution suggests a more deliberate sense of cruelty than oppression, as witnessed in the savage sequence of persecutions undertaken against the early Christians. Oppression, in contrast, denotes a more passive style of aggression, an aspect encountered during the great purges of history (such as the Spanish Inquisition).

In the case of Roman persecutions, the early Christians were not particularly concerned with humanitarian themes, an ongoing issue precluded by the speedy anticipated return of Jesus Christ. The Romans, in contrast, were the unrivaled humanitarian standard-bearers of their time, maintaining a stable rule of law (often by force) throughout the Mediterranean realm. The secretive tendencies of the early Christians certainly cut against the grain of Roman sensibility: particularly their avoidance of civic affairs, public games, and military service. The Christian condemnation of the prevailing pagan order must have surely aroused fears of treason amongst the Roman gentry. The most damning charge against the early Christians concerned their refusal to submit to the worship of the state-sanctioned gods: in particular, the professed divinity of the emperor. Such a heretical act of treachery was considered a capital offense in most instances.

The Christians unyielding stance brought on harsh punitive measures legitimized through the Emperor's claim to a broad humanitarian power base. The first widespread persecution against the Christians was initiated by the Emperor Nero in 64 CE, presumably as part of his devious plan to assign blame for the Great Fire of Rome. Indeed, Christianity eventually was classified as a capital offense, although pardon could be gained by recanting. Although Nero's campaign of terror was somewhat limited in scope compared to later persecutions, his precedent of persecution continued unmercifully for centuries to follow. Consequently, this immediately-active style of punitively-cruel persecution exemplifies such a humanitarian authority perspective. In a more formal sense, the immediately active humanitarian authority figure cruelly acts in a persecutory fashion, whereby prompting the antagonistic sense of cunning on the part of the respective follower figure. This immediately-active style of persecution directly parallels the affiliated theme of oppression, with the exception that the withholding of leniency (rather than rewards) is now called into focus.

OPPRESSION

The eventual decline of the Western Roman Empire thrust the fledgling Church into the enviable position of assuming many of the Empire's institutional functions. In a curious historical parallel, the Catholic Church grew increasingly intolerant to heresy during the Middle Ages, falling into the same trap that had plagued its predecessor: namely, resorting to organized aggression to suppress heresy within its ranks. This active suppression was generally achieved through *oppressive* tactics, where heretics were forced to either recant or flee such untenable circumstances. The Latin root *opprimere* (to press against) suggests precisely such a cruel use of force for pressuring compliance, as traditionally evident during the infamous Spanish Inquisition. This latter historical movement traces its origins to the Latin *inquiro* (to inquire into), indicative of the Church's practice of actively seeking-out heretics over and beyond the customary investigation of accusations.

At the onset of the Inquisition, Spain was unique placed among the kingdoms of Western Europe in terms of its broad cultural diversity: most notably, the burgeoning Jewish and Moorish contingents. The Jews initially enjoyed considerable economic prosperity throughout the region, constituting highly educated elites much in demand for administrative positions. The ruling Catholic elite, however, grew increasingly jealous of the wealthy Jews, tacitly promoting the moral outrage fueling the Inquisition. The considerable wealth of the Jews was targeted first, followed by an equally abhorrent moral backlash against the Moors. The only recourse to forced conversion entailed permanent exile, whereby prompting a broad number of nominal converts to the Catholic faith.

In 1492, the first Grand Inquisitor, Tomas de Torquemada persuaded the Catholic royalty to expel the Jewish population, resulting in a mass-exodus estimated at *70,000* strong. In 1502, the even greater Moorish contingent was added to the purge. Those attempting to remain fell victim to a cruel assortment of tactics: including torture, execution, and imprisonment. During Torquemada's reign of terror, an estimated *2,000* heretics were publicly burned at the stake. Life imprisonment was reserved for those faint-hearted souls that confessed under torture, or recanted to escape execution. Surviving family members suffered Church confiscation of all property in common. Confiscation was also imposed upon those fleeing the death sentence, as well as those caught dealing in the possessions of heretics, funds rightfully claimed as property of the Church. These proceeds further helped defray the expenses of the Inquisition, paying handsome dividends to those in positions of high authority. This vulgar sense of oppressiveness particularly characterizes the humanitarian authority perspective, whereby prompting the avaricious determination to act evilly on the part of the respective follower role: the latter technically "following" the authority role in terms of such a projected punitive sphere of influence.

THE VICES OF ANARCHISM

In summary, the completed description of the sins of apostasy effectively provides a compelling description of the humanitarian authority perspective (in both its punitive and adversarial manifestations). Indeed, the darker focus of the sins of apostasy was directly seen to counteract the more positive listing of ecumenical ideals. The profoundly abstract nature of the humanitarian authority perspective must necessarily be complemented by a respective listing of follower roles, as proposed in a similarly comprehensive discussion of the vices of anarchism (evil-cunning-ugliness-hypocrisy).

EVIL

Of any of the themes examined to date, *evil* reigns supreme as the darkest emblem of the vices. Whereas goodness was celebrated as the epitome of virtue, so its antithesis (evil) rates parallel significance within the corresponding realm of the vices. Accordingly, evil is defined as that which is morally corrupt or injurious to individual wellbeing. Nowhere is this definition more readily apparent than in the widespread superstition of the "evil eye." This evil stare was said to turn to stone, strike dead, or cause injury to all that returned its glance. Classical mythology certainly figures prominently in the origins of this superstition, particularly that relating to the serpent-haired monster, Medusa. This hideous creature was said to possess the power to turn to stone all that beheld her hypnotic gaze. The Latin equivalent of the evil eye, the Jettatura, is a theme widespread throughout the Mediterranean world. As late as the Inquisition, medieval judges so feared the evil eye that they forced accused witches to enter the courtroom backwards in order to avoid the advantage of the first glance.

In terms of this broader range of meaning, evil appears to encompass a more expansive range of connotation than its singular placement within the ethical hierarchy would seem to warrant. This extreme degree of generality, however, was also encountered with respect to goodness consistent with its pivotal role in all ethical deliberation. Accordingly, evil is restricted to its most basic motivational context; namely, those adversarial dictates directly in keeping with such a grand humanitarian perspective. As the supreme personification of evil, the Devil makes a fitting counterpoint to God's bountiful goodness. Here oppressiveness formally assumes a humanitarian authority status, whereas the latter avaricious sense of evil assumes the mantle of the humanitarian follower figure, being that the latter formally "follows" the authority role in terms of such a darker range of potentiality.

CUNNING

Any formal discussion of evil must necessarily remain incomplete without mention of the related theme of *cunning*. Cunning represents the chief moral antithesis of wisdom, just as evil was previously contrasted with goodness. Its modern spelling derives from the Anglo-Saxon *cunnian* (to try or test). Although cunning originally denoted a sense of skillfulness or shrewdness, it eventually acquired the more devious connotations of deception, slyness, or craftiness. For brevity's sake, only the latter negative connotations will be directly addressed within the current humanitarian context. In this latter sense, the respective representative member of humanity antagonistically acts in a cunning fashion towards one's humanitarian authority figure, in response to the latter's cruel sense of persecution. In a more formal sense, I (as representative member of humanity) am antagonistically determined to act a cunning fashion towards you in reaction to your (as spiritual authority) cruel-persecution of me. Indeed, this tenuous power of potentiality ultimately imparts the power leverage underlying the dual interplay of authority/follower roles, the former depending upon the latter to consummate the recursive cycle of persecution vs. cunning.

Perhaps the most widely celebrated example of cunning concerns the enduring legend of the Trojan Horse. According to Homer's *Iliad*, a united Greek force besieged the ancient city of Troy in an attempt to free the captive Queen Helen of Sparta. The Greeks were said to have raised a fleet of over *1,000* ships, although the fortifications of Troy proved equally as formidable. The great heroes of the Greeks (Ajax and Achilles) battled against their Trojan counterparts (Hector and Aeneas), although with mixed results. Finally, Odysseus proposed a cunning ruse for circumventing the impenetrable defenses of the city, advocating the construction a colossal wooden figure of a horse that secretly concealed a contingent of soldiers. When the Greek fleet sailed deceptively out of sight, the Trojans joyously emerged to accept the wooden horse as a token of victory, favoring that it be drawn within the city walls. Among the cautious was Cassandra, whose warnings of doom were ignored due to a curse making her predictions unbelievable to others. "Beware of Greeks bearing gifts" proclaimed Laocoon, although his warning was cut short by the appearance of a pair of giant serpents that crushed the life out of him. The Trojans mistakenly viewed this as a favorable sign, drawing the horse into the city in celebration of their lengthy ordeal. The Greek soldiers ultimately emerged in the dead of night, throwing open the city gates to the returning fleet, resulting in the total devastation and sack of the city.

Similar to the case previously established for evil, cunning clearly represents an adversarial style of power perspective, whereby expanding upon the cowardly-antagonistic treatment expressed by the spiritual disciple. According to the Trojan Horse example, the frustrated Greeks assumed precisely such an adversarial role, pretending to submit to defeat (via the Trojan Horse), although actually disguising quite antagonistic directives. The Trojans had cruelly taunted the Greeks, refusing to return the captive Queen Helen. In a last-ditch effort, the Greeks pinned their fading hopes on the trickery encompassing the Trojan Horse. By the time the Trojans discovered the folly of their pretensions, the Greeks had moved to breach the walls of the city, suffering a fitting fate at the hands of the vengefully-vindictive Greeks.

UGLINESS

A third vice intimately associated with evil is the enduring theme of *ugliness*. As the chief moral opposite of beauty, ugliness refers not as much to physical repulsion as to actions judged reprehensibly to be so. Its modern spelling derives from the Old Norse *uggligr* (dreadful), from *uggr* (fear). According to classical Greek mythology, the major gods and goddesses were described as beautiful or alluring, whereas demons and devils were described as hideous or ugly. This stereotype was curiously reversed in the case of Hephaestus (the Greek god of fire and metalwork). In contrast to the other Olympian gods, Hephaestus (also known as Vulcan by the Romans) was born both lame and homely to his otherwise impeccable parents Zeus and Hera. His left leg was shorter than his right, a handicap skillfully corrected through braces crafted from gold. He is traditionally depicted in the trademark undershirt and oval cap of the blacksmith, actively wielding a hammer and tongs. He was twice thrown from heaven for offending the delicate sensibilities of the gods, a fate similarly suffered by deformed infants of the age. Despite his uncomely appearance Hephaestus wed only the most beautiful of goddesses; namely, Aphrodite (the goddess of love) and Charis (one of the Graces).

This enduring theme of ugliness recurs in many literary narratives: e.g., *Beauty and the Beast*, *The Phantom of the Opera*, *The Hunchback of Notre Dame*, etc. Perhaps the most telling in this regard concerns Hans Christian Andersen's fanciful *Tale of the Ugly Duckling*. Although the characters of this fable all take animal form, its metaphorical overtones suggest the true moralistic message of the tale. The basic story line concerns the plight of a newborn duckling judged so ugly by its peers that it was persecuted unmercifully. Upon reaching maturity, it, ultimately, was delighted to discover it had been transformed into a gorgeous swan, assuming its rightful place of distinction upon the lake. The more distressing aspects of the story rate clear significance in the overall context of the vices, where the distressing attributes of the ugly duckling were wrathfully persecuted by the rest of the brood.

The ugly duckling certainly rates the title role in this regard, betraying (in an ugly fashion) the aesthetic sensibilities of one's peer group. In failing to meet the prevailing standards of beauty, the ugly duckling became the unfair target of scorn and derision within the group. This circumstance represents a complete reversal of the beauty contest format, where adulation is withheld rather than bestowed. The latter virtuous aspect only emerges towards the end of the tale, where the duckling joyously discovers its newfound grace and beauty (accompanied by the approval so desperately denied). Here the initial prodigal sense of wrathfulness further prompts the ugly sense of betrayal within a future-directed time-frame. In a more formal sense, the representative member of humanity betrayingly acts in an ugly fashion towards one's humanitarian authority figure, effectively abandoning any semblance of approval in terms of such an enduring humanitarian perspective.

HYPOCRISY

The final of the moralistic vices, *hypocrisy*, is traditionally defined as the chief moral antithesis of truth. Its modern spelling derives from the Greek *hypokrisis* (to feign or act a part), tracing its origins to the ancient Greek art form of the dramatic play. Early theatrical productions were composed of a chorus of roughly a dozen individuals, accompanied by a smaller number of actors for delivering the dialogue. The actors were respectively known the *hypokritai;* namely, those that respond to the chorus. Over time, this term gained somewhat of a metaphorical sense: as in feigning a pretense. Indeed, hypocrisy is often personified as a simpering ape hiding behind the stylized mask of an actor.

In this latter respect, hypocrisy is primarily defined as dishonestly pretending to be what one is not, particularly in a pretense of sincerity. In Dante's *Inferno,* the hypocrite was condemned for all eternity to wear a brilliantly ornamented cloak lined with lead, metaphorically bearing the weight of sinfulness (although disguised as virtue). This example bears many parallels to the notion of the "odor of sanctity," an expression suggestive of an overarching air of respectability. This expression grew out of a belief popular during the Middle Ages that the bodies of saints exuded a sweet aroma following death. In our modern age, this theme now encompasses a more satirical sense, whereby equating sanctity with sanctimoniousness.

This darker circumstance directly contrasts with the virtuous mode, where hypocrisy represents the darker counterpart in relation to truth. The respective follower figure now despairingly acts in a hypocritical fashion in response to the tyrannical-enslavement on the part of the humanitarian authority figure: an interaction analogous to that previously established with respect to wrathfulness/ugliness. In a similar fashion, the tyrannical authority figure respectively prompts the hypocritical sense of despair expressed by the representative member of humanity.

In conclusion, the completed description of the moralistic vices effectively rounds out the stepwise description of the humanitarian realm of defect. The darker focus of the moralistic vices (evil-cunning-ugliness-hypocrisy) proves a fitting counterpoint to the initial listing of the sins of apostasy (wrath, tyranny, persecution, and oppression). This humanitarian variation on the overarching realm of defect clearly represents the most abstract level of organizational permitted according to the principles of Set Theory. This very sense of the power of abstraction, however, serves as the basis for one final innovation within the perpetual power struggle; namely, that specifying the crowning transcendental level within the darker realm of the vices.

13

THE TRANSCENDENTAL REALM OF DEFECT

The issue of the vices for the crowning transcendental level of the motivational hierarchy certainly proves enigmatic at first glance. As initially described in **Part I**, the transcendental authority figure regains the upper hand in the perpetual power struggle by surpassing the more routine sense of concreteness shared in common by all of the lower levels. This supremely abstract perspective freely enters into the realm of pure intuition and imagination, forsaking the constraints of ordinary reality for the esoteric realm of pure abstraction. This overarching sense of transcendence reflects a general humanistic theme; in particular, the Renaissance variation so treasured throughout modern history. The principles of humanism ring as true today as when they were first formulated, namely: man is the measure of all things, an enduring perspective reveling in the collective spirit underlying all human endeavors.

The respective grouping of humanistic values (peace-love-tranquility-equality) formally characterize the ethereal nature of the transcendental authority perspective, in essence, setting the stage for a discussion of the corresponding sins of nihilism (anger-hatred-prejudice-belligerence). In contrast to the purely positive prerequisites for the humanistic values, the contrasting realm of defect is alternately specified in terms of "nihilistic" principles. Indeed, whereas humanism celebrates the collective human spirit, the theme of *nihilism* contrarily states that nothing in life has meaning, an existential lament with dire consequences to individuals and society as a whole. This nihilistic perspective builds directly upon the darker theme of apostasy characterizing the humanitarian realm, culminating in an existential state of negativistic-nihilistic alienation.

The term derives from the German *nihilismus*, from the Latin *nihil* nothing): from a compound of *ne-* (not) and *hilum* (a small thing, trifle). It signifies a belief in nothing, often bordering upon extreme skepticism. It chiefly expresses the belief that there is no meaning or purpose to life, as in the absolute denial or negation of human values. Here no meaningful ethical standards or moral compass exists for determining morality or truth. According to German philosopher Friedrich Nietzsche: "The uppermost values devalue themselves in *nihilism*." Nihilism, therefore, represents the chief moral antithesis of the more positive prerequisites previously established with respect to humanism.

For the nihilist, human progress is ephemeral being that there is little ultimate impact on the master course of the universe. Consequently, one should strive for whatever pleasure or thrills accompany such a depressive outlook. This nihilistic perspective exemplifies those leading intense or reckless lives of self-destruction, as in violent revolutionaries seeking to destroy existing standards by resorting to terrorist activities. By promoting a nihilistic stance, there appears little in the way of objective certainty or truth; hence, less chance for achieving the productive and harmonious ends conducive to a flourishing lifestyle.

In conclusion, the four-part listing of the sins of nihilism might just as easily have been termed the sins of humanism, in reference to their general contrasting theme. The ethical parallels to the humanistic values certainly ring true in this basic regard; namely, *anger* represents a darker variation on tranquility, whereas *hatred* makes a similar contrast to love. A similar reciprocating pattern further holds true with respect to *prejudice*/equality and *belligerence*/peace.

In addition to the darker range of sin specified for the authority role, parallel mention must necessarily be made for the corresponding realm of transcendental follower roles in relation to the domain of the defect. Here, the obscure cohesive grouping of the mystical vices (iniquity, turpitude, abomination, and perdition) rightfully enters into consideration. Indeed, this four-part listing of mystical vices effectively contrasts, point-for-point, with their respective virtuous counterparts in the mystical values (ecstasy, bliss, joy, and harmony).

Similar to the pattern of discussion previously established for the humanitarian realm, the transcendental sphere of influence employs an analogous authority-then-follower pattern of discussion. This fifth-order realm of transcendental abstraction, however, even more dramatically appears to obscure the overarching hierarchical pattern of organization. Despite such abstract restrictions, the basic two-stage sequential pattern of authority-then-follower roles remains essentially in evidence, as in the punitive sequence specified for anger, abomination, hatred, and iniquity: as well as the related darker sequence of prejudice, perdition, belligerence, and turpitude.

A custom pattern of presentation for the individual transcendental vices, therefore, is proposed: examining the transcendental realm as the darker culmination of all vices that have gone before. For instance, iniquity is described in terms of the subordinate concepts of avarice/evil, whereas hatred represents that based upon vulgarity/oppressiveness. Furthermore, abomination is specified in terms of ugly/betrayal, whereas anger exhibits a similar correspondence to prodigality/wrathfulness. Indeed, this darker transcendental domain provides an overarching exposition of virtually epic proportions, culminating in a seamless overview of the entire range of terms underlying vice and sin.

ANGER

The first mentioned of the sins of nihilism, *anger*, is traditionally defined as the chief moral antithesis of tranquility, consistent with its more elementary foundations in wrathfulness. Its modern spelling derives from the Old Norse *angr* (denoting distress or grief). The Teutonic peoples reverently equated the fury of nature with their fierce warrior-god Thor: celebrated for his enchanted hammer, the Mjolnir (Destroyer). Old Norse legends describe Thor as a powerful bearded warrior sporting iron gauntlets for gripping the shaft of his mighty hammer. In a figurative allusion to a lightning bolt, the hammer was magically said to return to Thor each time it was thrown. The clap of thunder was further explained as the violent impact of Thor's lightning-quick hammer. Related parallels occur throughout classical mythology; in particular, the lightning bolts issuing from the *aegis* (shield) of Zeus consistent

with Zeus's prominent role as Defender of Righteous Causes.

This wrathful quality of the gods of antiquity certainly reflects the forceful and violent nature of the era. The Semitic God of the Old Testament was certainly no exception in this regard, venting his righteous anger against the wicked on innumerable occasions. Even with respect to New Testament scripture, Christ briefly resorted to righteous anger, as exemplified in his outraged expulsion of the moneychangers from the Temple. According to the Gospel of St. Matthew (21:12), Christ triumphantly returned to Jerusalem welcomed by throngs of jubilant disciples. Upon reaching the Temple, however, Christ became incensed over the presence of the moneychangers, righteously condemning their greedy disrespect. Flying into a holy rage, Christ overturned the tables and scales, proclaiming: "It is written, my house shall be called a house of prayer; but ye have made it a den of thieves."

According to this scriptural example, Christ clearly appears to appeal to a transcendental power base, whereby deliberately choosing to ignore the established mercantile traditions of his day. Indeed, the Temple merchants could scarcely be faulted being that they were legitimately entitled to a fair return on their services. Christ's highly idealized message, in contrast, condemned any such manner of profane conduct. By further referring to the Temple as his own "house," Christ essentially includes himself within such a transcendental perspective, whereby hinting at the true rationale for his righteous anger. It certainly would appear strange that Christ would stray so far from his ordinarily meek demeanor, although it is only at this extreme level of transcendence that Christ's anger ultimately becomes comprehensible to the purest of Christian sensibilities. Accordingly, anger represents the transcendental culmination of the wrathfulness expressed by the humanitarian authority figure, whereby prompting the abominably-ugly betrayal by the transcendental follower. Being that only one role may be active at any given moment, the role of the punisher is relegated to that of a future potentiality, identified as the betrayingly-ugly treatment of the transcendental follower.

HATRED

The second of the sins of nihilism (intimately associated with anger) is the related theme of *hatred*. Its modern spelling derives from the Anglo-Saxon *hatian* (intense dislike or ill will). It is generally defined as the chief moral antithesis of

Metal Figurine of the Norse god Thor *(seated)*
Shown Gripping the Shaft of His Mighty Hammer

love, whereby expanding upon its more elementary foundations in oppression. Hatred quickly emerges as a prominent theme in Old Testament scripture, particularly with respect to the story of Cain and Abel. According to the Book of Genesis, Cain and Abel were the first-born sons of Adam and Eve following their banishment from Paradise. Abel tended the sheep while Cain labored in the field. Abel sacrificed lambs from his flock to the Lord, earning great favor in the process. Cain's offerings of the fruits of the field, however, received only callous indifference. Cain soon became envious of his brother, his efforts denied the approval that Abel's so readily enjoyed.

While laboring in the field, Cain's hatred finally reached its breaking point, killing Abel in a fit of rage. When the Lord confronted Cain on Abel's whereabouts, Cain feigned ignorance replying: "Am I my brother's keeper?" The Lord angrily chastised Cain responding: "What hast thou done? The voice of thy brother's blood cries up to me from the ground." The Lord further set a mark upon Cain as a visual badge of his crime, condemned to a life castoff from society.

Hatred is similarly proscribed in New Testament scripture, clearly antithetical to the Apostle John's stirring description of God as pure love. St. Paul further lists hatred among the Sins of the Holy Spirit, just as *love* was listed among the Fruits therein. The clearly transcendental nature of this vice often is used to justify many of the great crimes against humanity. The scourge be-gins with Cain's hateful murder of his brother, whereby extending to our modern age as Hitler's unspeakable mass extermination of the Jews. This hateful sense of oppressiveness clearly exemplifies the darker side to the transcendental authority perspective, whereby prompting the subsequent evil sense of iniquity specified for the corresponding follower role: the latter *following* the immediately-active authority role through such a projected realm of potentiality.

PREJUDICE

This completed description of anger/hatred further begs mention of the related theme of *prejudice*. As the chief moral antonym of equality, prejudice is traditionally defined as an irrational aversion to differing races, cultures, or creeds. Its modern spelling derives the Latin *praejudicium*, from *prae-* (before) and *judicium* (judgment): suggesting a biased or opinionated viewpoint. Racial prejudice is undoubtedly the most salient variety, readily apparent over and beyond any affiliated social distinctions. In general, it represents an extreme variation on the widespread cultural phenomenon known as *ethnocentrism*; namely, the tendency to employ the norms and values of one's own culture when judging those of another. This pronounced tendency towards favoring one's individual life-style over that of another directly appears to fuel such prejudicial tendencies. This prejudicial attitude is further compounded by stereotypical beliefs, where distinguishing characteristics ascribed to particular individuals are generalized to all other members within the group.

The truest measure of racial prejudice (as opposed to erroneous judgment) is its unnerving inflexibility; namely, that tendency to hold contradictory beliefs even when faced with strong evidence to the contrary. In keeping with such a darker transcendental focus, prejudice clearly employs circular logic to reinforce such specious perspectives. Even when the glaring errors of these belief systems are finally exposed, racial prejudice continues to persist, even though the theoretical underpinnings have been invalidated. This rigid pattern of inflexibility renders racial prejudice particularly difficult to eradicate once it has taken root in common culture. Indeed, social imitation appears to be the most dominant mode of transmission, particularly when compounded over the course of many generations.

BELLIGERENCE

The fourth and final of the sins of nihilism, *belligerence*, is traditionally defined as a hostile or warlike attitude consistent with its antithetical counterpoint in peace. Its modern spelling derives from the Latin *belligerare* (to wage war): from *bellum* (war) and *genere* (to carry on). This power of force for settling disputes was certainly followed throughout the classical era, particularly with respect to Mars, the Roman god of war, equivalent to the Greek god Ares. His wife Bellona (the Roman goddess of war) owes her name to the related Latin root-stem *bello* (to wage war). According to tradition Bellona never strayed far from the side of Mars, often portrayed in the act of preparing his chariot for the rigors of war. She similarly appears in battle with a torch in one hand and a bloody whip in the other: the latter with which she maddened her foes and enflamed her own fury. Her chief ceremonial priests, the *Bellonarii*, were traditionally garbed in black: honoring her devotion by wounding themselves and screaming wildly.

Appius Claudius Caecus dedicated a temple to Bellona (during the war against the Samnites) outside the walls of Rome within the Campus Martius. Its remote location made it particularly well suited for negotiations with foreign ambassadors, as well as receiving Roman generals returning in victory from distant military campaigns. The Columna Bellica (Pillar of War) was located at the entrance to the temple employed in ritual declarations of war on distant lands. The area within Bellona's temple symbolized the enemy's territory, whereas the pillar represented its outermost frontier. A declaration of war was initiated by launching a bloody spear against the pillar, a ceremony that earlier war councils had originally performed at the actual boundary of the enemy's territory.

This ritualized belligerent posturing has remained an enduring theme throughout recorded history, such as the tragic turn of events leading to up the First World War. At the turn of the century, pre-war Europe was neatly divided into opposing groups of allies; namely, the Triple Alliance (Italy, Germany, and Austria-Hungary), and the Triple Entente (Britain, France, and Russia). The deadly catalyst occurred on June 28, 1914, when the Crown Prince and Princess of Austria-Hungary were assassinated by Serbian terrorists during a tour of the Bosnian capital of Sarajevo. Desiring a greater degree of influence in the Balkan Peninsula, Austria-Hungary quickly accused the Serbian government of instigating the intrigue: delivering a stern ultimatum amounting to protectorship status over Serbia. Although Serbia pleaded for compromise, Austria-Hungary obstinately refused to surrender the dispute to international arbitration.

Precisely one month to the date of the assassination, Austria-Hungary declared war on Serbia, counting on the logistical support of its allies Italy and Germany. Serbia, in turn, enlisted the aid of Britain, France, and Russia, dragging virtually the entire European continent into the fray. This initial belligerent posturing eventually escalated out of all control, a lesson in conflict management that Europe should have dearly taken to heart.

The end of the war, however, saw little change to such belligerent perspectives, the imposition of extensive war reparations further setting the stage for the economic frustrations that plagued post-war Germany. Such deprivations further proved instrumental to Hitler's fanatical rise to power, resulting in the even more devastating Second World War. These two great World Wars effectively dramatized the folly of belligerent posturing in our modern age of technological warfare, a circumstance that fortunately has paved the way for the unprecedented span of peace and prosperity currently in force today.

This immediately-active style of belligerent posturing by the transcendental authority figure directly expands upon the cruel sense of persecution encompassing the hierarchy of defect. In a more formal sense, the immediately active transcendental authority belligerently acts in a persecutory fashion, whereby prompting the cunning expression of turpitude on the part of the follower figure. The immediately-active sense of belligerence directly parallels the affiliated theme of hatefulness with the exception that the punitive withholding of leniency (rather than rewards) is now called into focus.

THE MYSTICAL VICES: THE UPPERMOST LIMITS FOR THE REALM OF DEFECT

In summary, the completed description of the moralistic vices effectively rounds the stepwise description of the transcendental authority perspective (in both its positive and negative manifestations). Indeed, the evil focus of the sins of nihilism was effectively seen to counteract the more positive focus of the humanistic values. The profoundly abstract nature of the transcendental authority perspective would seem to suggest that the upper conceptual limit for the realm of the vices has finally been reached. Indeed, it is difficult to imagine a set of vices more abstract than the already abstruse listing of anger-hatred-prejudice-belligerence. In direct analogy to the preceding examination of the mystical values, however, there should necessarily also exist a parallel complement of mystical vices that contrast point-for-point with the respective virtuous mode.

Although positive mysticism takes Divinity as its supreme focus, the darker version (by extension) enters into the occult realm of sorcery or witchcraft. Such occult rituals were typically conducted under the greatest of secrecy due to their condemnation by the Christian Church. The witchcraft hysteria of the Middle Ages sent many suspected witches to their death, leaving scant enduring documentation of their covert practices. This dearth of historical evidence clearly diminishes the prospects for identifying the four predicted dimensions for the mystical vices were it not for the Bible's slant on religious mysticism. Although its spirited literary style is slanted primarily from a positive perspective, the Bible also deals with diabolical themes with the express intent of condemning them.

The term derives from the Greek *diabolos* (the Devil), from *diaballein* (to slander), from *dia-* (across) and *ballein* (to throw): reflecting the fallen angel's scriptural role as adversary. It generally refers to the worship of deities that take a demoniac form or focus. The worship of the devil dates to the earliest glimmerings of moral dualism, said to derive from the Zoroastrian system of opposing deities. Here, the divinities of *Ormuzd* and *Ahriman* symbolized both the good and the evil principles, respectively.

A number of modern groups practicing Satanism have emerged in concert with the resurgence of occultism during the 20th century. Other groups, such as the Yezidi sect of Kurdistan, view the world as the creation of Lucifer (the fallen angel): whom they propitiate in a symbolic form through worship of the peacock. Regardless of the individual traditions therein, the general theme of diabolism shares a number of key characteristics; namely, a transcendental perspective manifest in terms of such a darker range of themes. Here, diabolism represents the chief moral antithesis of religious mysticism, a contrast that nowhere should be confused with a positive outlook.

This darker slant to mysticism is perhaps most convincingly expressed in the prophetic segments of the Bible, a circumstance consistent with the transcendental nature of mystical foresight. A detailed reading of prophetic scripture reveals the darker focus of what must be termed the mystical vices; namely, iniquity, turpitude, abomination, and perdition. This four-part listing of mystical vices effectively contrasts, point-for-point, with the virtuous prerequisites ascribed to the mystical values (ecstasy, bliss, joy, and harmony). Indeed, the specific rationale behind their particular individual assignments becomes exceedingly apparent within the expanded context of their corresponding literary traditions.

INIQUITY

The somewhat obscure notion of *iniquity* emerges as a recurrent theme throughout both Old and New Testament scripture. This term is virtually synonymous with the subordinate notion of evil with the exception of extending to a purely transcendental sphere of influence. Its modern spelling traces its origins to the Latin *iniquitas*, from *in-* (not) and *aequus* (equal). This classical connotation of inequity eventually expanded to a much broader context of pure evil or wickedness true to its transcendental prerequisites. Indeed, these latter two aspects endure as one of iniquity's most salient features, as scripturally evident in the *Mystery of Iniquity* described by St. Paul in his Second Letter to the Thessalonians. This scriptural passage directly alludes to the dark events associated with the apocalyptic end-times in fitting association with the emergent spirit of lawlessness predicted for such times.

TURPITUDE

The second of the mystical vices, *turpitude*, is a theme sharing many parallels to iniquity. Although not specifically mentioned in English translations of the Bible, its basic import is apparent in passages dealing with vileness and depravity. Its modern spelling derives from the Latin *turpitudo* (baseness), from *turpis* (base): as suggested in the class of *baser* instincts. This negative connotation dates at least to classical times, when *base* metals (e.g.; lead, copper, or tin) were alloyed with the noble metals (gold and silver), wherein enhancing strength and durability. Their unscrupulous use, however, allowed greedy metalsmiths to maximize their profits by compromising the intrinsic worth of their commissioned metalwork. These classical connotations, in turn, prove consistent with turpitude's elementary foundations relating to cunning: e.g., moral turpitude within a transcendental sphere of influence. Similar to the case previously made for iniquity, this cunningly deceptive aspect of turpitude is often disguised through a semblance to decency until the shocking truth is finally revealed.

ABOMINATION

A third of the mystical vices intimately associated with iniquity is the darker theme of *abomination*. Its modern spelling derives from the Latin *abominabilis*, from *ab-* (from) and *ominari* (to regard as an omen): particularly in an ominous sense. In common usage it refers to objects of extreme hatred or disgust consistent with its more elementary foundation in ugliness. This depraved quality is particularly evident in the OT Book of Proverbs (15:9) which states: "The way of the wicked is an *abomination* unto the Lord." This theme reaches perhaps its greatest degree of notoriety in the New Testament accounts of the Abomination of the Desolation, a reference to the prophesied desecration of the Jewish Temple by worshippers of pagan gods. In our modern age, this term is typically associated with the *abominable snowman*, the monstrous "yeti" of the Himalayan highlands. Indeed, the brutish attributes associated with such a grotesque monster remain consistent with the transcendental attributes for this darker realm of defect.

PERDITION

The final-mentioned of the mystical vices, *perdition*, effectively rounds out the quartet-style listing of transcendental follower themes. Its modern spelling derives from the Latin *perditio*, from *perdere* (to lose, to ruin). Its traditional emphasis on destruction or ruin is clearly illustrated on Card XVI of the standard Tarot card deck: namely, The

Tower Struck by Lightening. It graphically depicts the tragic loss of life or property resulting from such a violent act of nature.

In terms of its affiliated scriptural connotations, perdition is typically defined as the loss of all hope for spiritual salvation, effectively condemning the soul to eternal damnation. Those deliberately straying from the path of righteousness are virtually assured such a devastating fate for the Day of Judgment is said to effectively close the book on any appeals to leniency. In keeping with such an extreme degree of transcendence, perdition effectively builds upon its more elementary foundation in despair, wherein effectively counteracting its virtuous counterpart in bliss.

THE DIABOLICAL EXTREMES
FOR THE REALM OF DEFECT

This completed description of the mystical vices invites consideration of one further critical issue; namely, what level of experience is predicted to extend beyond this final nameable realm of defect? According to the earlier chapter on religious mysticism, this context seemingly entails a predicted blending of individual affective dimensions, resulting in a mystical experience of virtually supernatural proportions. From a purely positive perspective, this supernatural realm was assumed to be entirely unnamable except in the broadest of descriptive terms; e.g., God, Cosmic Consciousness, the Oversoul, etc. With respect to the darker realm of defect, this supernatural domain (by definition) conceptually surpasses the more fearsome complement of the mystical vices (iniquity, turpitude, abomination, and perdition). Such a fearsome perspective can only be described in terms of the broadest of demonic brushstrokes, as in diabolical archetypes or demon possession. William James insightfully touches on this darker side to the mystical experience according to the following quotation from his *Varieties of Religious Experience*:

"So much for religious mysticism proper. But more remains to be told, for religious mysticism is only one half of mysticism. The other half has no accumulated tradition except those which the text books on insanity supply. Open any of these, and you will find abundant cases in which "mystical ideas" are cited as characteristic symptoms of enfeebled or deluded states of mind. In delusional insanity, paranoia, as they sometimes call it, we may have a diabolical mysticism, a sort of religious mysticism turned upside down. The same sense of ineffable importance in the smallest events, the same texts and words coming with new meanings, the same voices and visions and leadings and missions, the same controlling by extraneous powers. Only this time the emotion is pessimistic: instead of consolations we have desolations; the meanings are dreadful; and the powers are enemies to life. It is evident that from the point of view of their psychological mechanism, the classical mysticism, and these lower mysticisms spring from the same mental level, from that great subliminal or trans-marginal region of which science is beginning to admit the existence, but of which so little is really known. This region contains every kind of matter: seraph and snake abide there side by side."

This rather extensive quotation suggests an entire demonic side to the mystical experience afflicting those poor souls tragic enough to experience it. German psychologist Carl Jung suggests a similar aspect with respect to his notion of the *shadow*: an archetypal experience conceptually consistent with such disturbing themes. Indeed, is it truly rational to postulate the existence of a sentient being (such as the Devil) in order to counteract the more positive aspects of the mystical experience? The longstanding tradition of devils or demons has endured as a universal theme in religious systems throughout the world. With respect to the Judeo-Christian tradition, Lucifer was celebrated as the most powerful angel in the service of the Lord until his sin of pride led to his banishment from heaven, leading numerous other angels to perdition in the process.

As the most powerful of the Archangels, Lucifer was a creation of God, and, therefore, never His equal. Curiously, the Devil did not always figure so prominently in Old Testament scripture. Indeed, many biblical scholars concede that this Devil of Wickedness traces its origins to the later Babylonian Captivity of the Jews. The Jews were undoubtedly exposed to Zoroastrianism, a Persian cult celebrating the enduring struggle between good and evil. This latter influence subsequently appears to have been incorporated into the budding Christian movement, as witnessed in scriptural accounts describing Christ's temptation by Satan. This emergent tradition of the Devil as evil antagonist reaches its supreme fulfillment within the Book of Revelation, an apocalyptic final showdown between the forces of Light and Darkness.

It might ultimately be questioned if Christianity is truly justified in promoting the belief in an all-powerful Devil of Wickedness in concert with the affiliated themes of demon possession and exorcism? Evil certainly requires goodness for contrast, for there can be no darkness without light. Indeed, "darkness" is essentially all-or-none phenomenon, whereas light is invested with virtually unlimited shades of being. A similar scenario holds true with respect to the mystical values, which are all expressly vital in their literary traditions, as witnessed in the stirring accounts of saints and sages throughout the ages. In contrast, the corresponding listing of mystical vices (iniquity, turpitude, abomination, and perdition) scarcely amount to more than scriptural technicalities, clearly lacking the dynamic vitality characterizing their virtuous counterparts.

In truth, this darker slant to religious mysticism could just as easily be explained through recourse to the righteous/wrathful attributes of the traditional God of the Old Testament: a divinity not averse to punishing moral transgressions. Indeed, according to the Book of Isaiah (45:7) the Lord is quoted stating: "I form the light and create the darkness. I make peace and create *evil*. I, the Lord, do all these things." Furthermore, the Book of Lamentations (3:37-38) similarly states: "Who has commanded and it came to pass unless the Lord has ordained it? Is it not from the mouth of the Most High that good and evil come?"

Regardless of the preferred mechanism of explanation, the prospects of a darker side to the mystical experience are undoubtedly a formidable influence in the lives of those thusly afflicted. Fortunately, documented cases of demonic possession appear to be relatively rare. Indeed, whether attributed to some sentient form of evil entity, or a righteous outcome of God's wrath, or some impersonal form of shadow archetype, this darker slant to the mystical experience must necessarily remain a topic open to further investigation. Hopefully a clearer understanding will ultimately be achieved in terms of the fundamental principles governing all such aspects of the mystical experience.

14

THE ACCESSORY COUNTERPARTS FOR THE VICES OF DEFECT

The completed description of the main sequence of terms for the vices of defect, in turn, raises the affiliated issue of the respective accessory counterparts. As initially described for the virtuous realm, the accessory terms represent a role-reversal targeting the main themes they serve to imitate. Here the polarities of the "you" and "I" roles are reversed within the schematic definition format, whereby instilling a sense of empathy within the interpersonal interaction. The darker realm of the vices of defect is certainly no exception in this regard, although now facilitating empathic potential for exploiting others in the pursuit of a selfish agenda.

A growing number of researchers speculate that the stepwise development of empathic ability in young children undergoes one final stage of development; namely, that leading to the skills underlying social deception. Although telling the truth is vaunted as the default setting for social communication, the cunning attributes associated with deception suggest a more sophisticated style of response repertoire. Indeed, the dramatic physiological changes observed during lying clearly reflect the extreme mental effort underlying such deceptive tactics.

The techniques associated with successful deception appear to develop over a distinct sequence of stages similar to the pattern previously established for empathy in general. Initially, the child's first experiences with lying entail staying out of trouble, as in avoiding confessing to activities that had been punished in the past. This self-centered pattern of lying is generally a hit-or-miss phenomenon, being that the child occasionally succeeds, although more often detected.

With the ultimate development of true empathic ability, the child eventually learns to tailor his deceptions to meet the expectations of his su-periors, whereby improving chances of success. Eventually, this egocentric focus extends to comprehending the outward perspectives of others. Here the latter class of "little white lies" aims to spare the feelings of others in the interest of social harmony. Any convincing effort towards social harmony necessarily remains unrealistic assuming that one will volunteer the unvarnished truth in every situation.

The leadership qualities we so dearly treasure appear to similarly depend upon gracefully stretching the truth in order to achieve cooperation amongst various group members. In a series of experiments designed to test for leadership potential, individuals that spontaneously took charge of the group exhibited the greatest facility for deception when tested individually later. The researchers ultimately concluded that, although leaders may not be more likely to lie, they typically are better at it than the rest of us. Fortunately, this somewhat harmless form of social deception is generally the extent for most of us, although a limited number of individuals (such as "con-men") frequently harness their skills for selfish purposes. The social psychopath expresses little remorse for the physical or emotional harm inflicted upon others, consistent with degree of criminality encountered within a social setting.

Although the accessory realm of empathic communication proves exceedingly convincing for the virtuous mode, for sake of symmetry, the domain of defect is similarly invested with its own unique complement of accessory terms: as formally depicted in **Fig. 14A**. According to this "darker" variation on the accessory realm, the personal authority listing of accessory ego vices (sloth-carelessness-dispassionateness- callousness), directly complements the main listing of terms (e.g., laziness-negligence-apathy-indiffer-

514	515		524	525
Sloth	Carelessness		Traitorousness	Retaliation
516	**517**	→	**526**	**527**
Dispassion	Arbitrariness		Resentment	Malevolence

ACCESS. EGO VICES
(Personal Authority)

ACCESS. ALTER EGO VICES
(Personal Follower)

534	535		544	545
Disrepute	Reprehension		Sedition	Avengement
536	**537**	→	**546**	**547**
Preposterous.	Fickleness		Lechery	Pusillanimity

ACC. VICES of VILLAINY
(Group Authority)

ACC. CARDINAL VICES
(Group Representative)

554	555		564	565
Profligacy	Bondage		Perfidy	Desperation
556	**557**	→	**566**	**567**
Coarseness	Acrimony		Cupidity	Opposition

ACCESS. CIVIL LIABILITIES
(Spiritual Authority)

ACC. THEOLOGICAL VICES
(Spiritual Disciple)

574	575		584	585
Indignation	Subjugation		Revulsion	Duplicity
576	**577**	→	**586**	**587**
Animosity	Torment		Wickedness	Guilefulness

ACCESS. ECUMEN. VICES
(Humanitarian Authority)

ACC. MORALISTIC VICES
(Humanitarian Follower)

594	595		504	505
Irateness	Intolerance		Abhorrence	Banefulness
596	**597**	→	**506**	**507**
Enmity	Militancy		Sinisterity	Baseness

ACC. HUMANISTIC VICES
(Transcendental Authority)

ACCESS. MYSTICAL VICES
(Transcendental Follower)

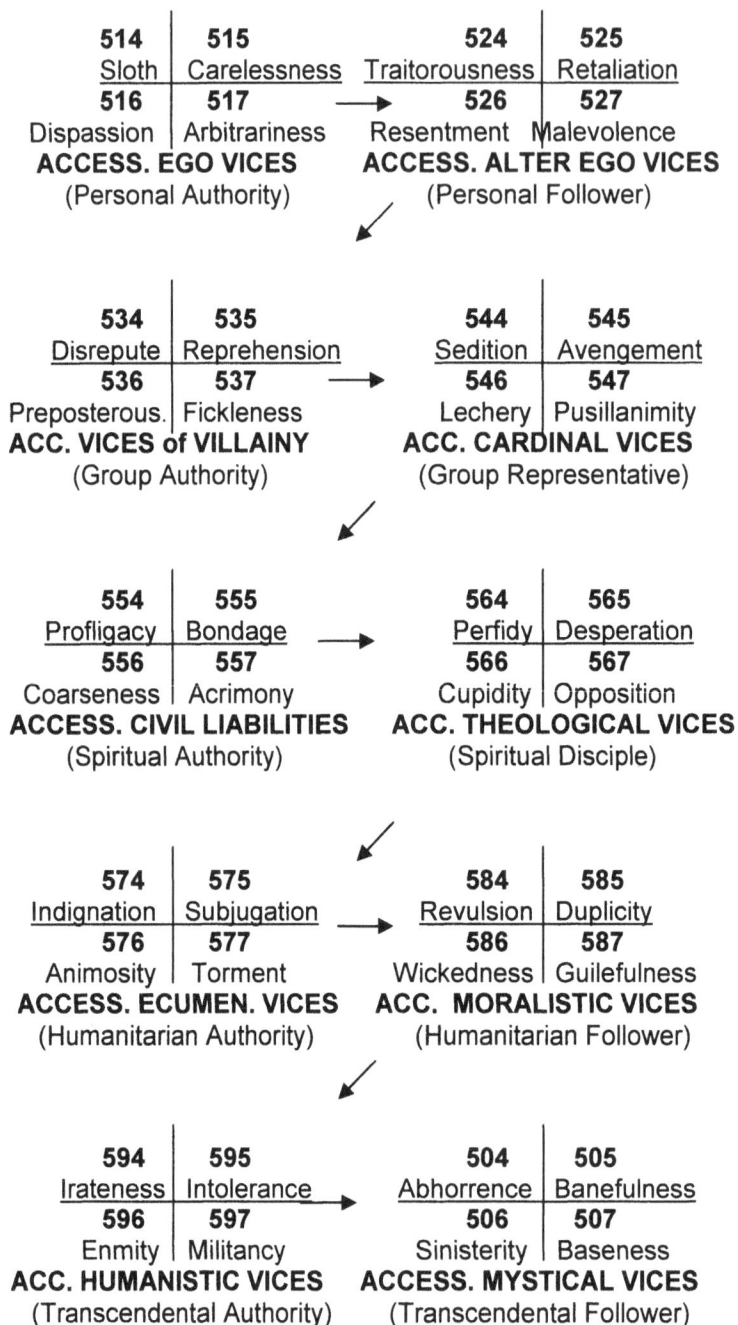

Fig. 14A – The Three-Digit Codes for the Accessory Vices of Defect

ence). Furthermore, the accessory alter ego grouping of mutiny, retaliation, grudgingness, and malevolence similarly mirrors the main sequence of terms (treachery-vindictiveness-spite-malice).

This distinctive interplay of ego and alter ego vices, in turn, reflects the schematic interactions at issue. For instance, you (as personal authority) *slothfully* refuse to act solicitously towards me in anticipation of my (as personal follower) *mutinous* treatment of you. Similarly, you might *carelessly* refuse to act submissively towards me in anticipation of my retaliation against you. A similar interplay of terms further holds true with respect to the remaining accessory pairings of dispassionateness/grudgingness and callousness/malevolence. Here the authority and follower roles effectively reciprocate one another in terms of the subjective/objective role polarities.

THE ACCESSORY TEN-LEVEL HIERARCHY FOR THE VICES OF DEFECT

In keeping with the personal foundations for the (accessory) ego and alter ego vices, it further proves feasible to extend this trend to the remaining group, spiritual, humanitarian, and transcendental levels within the ascending hierarchy of vices. This full forty-fold complement of accessory vices is schematically depicted in **Fig. 14A**: equivalent in every respect to the *main* listing of defect initially portrayed in **Fig. 9B**, with the exception that the "you" and "I" polarities are now reversed. Here the accessory vices share with their main counterparts the tendency towards hierarchical organization across the entire ten-level span of the linguistic hierarchy.

For instance, the accessory authority sequence of slothfulness-notoriety-profligacy-disgracefulness-fury specifies an immediately-active focus, whereas the remaining follower sequence of mutiny-rebellion-treason-vileness-abhorrence, represent future-directed potentialities, as schematically depicted immediately below.

514 – **Slothfulness**	524 – **Mutiny**
534 – **Notoriety**	544 – **Rebellion**
554 – **Profligacy**	564 – **Treason**
574 – **Disgracefulness**	584 – **Vileness**
594 – **Fury**	504 – **Abhorrence**

In a related fashion, the accessory authority sequence of carelessness-ignominy-bondage-subjugation-bigotry specifies a similarly active focus, although now targeting a more shameful style of context. Furthermore, the remaining follower sequence of terms; e.g., retaliation-retribution-desperation-mendacity-pernicity directly consummates such an initially-active authority perspective, mirroring that based upon mutiny with the exception that retaliation is now brought into focus.

515 – **Carelessness**	525 – **Retaliation**
535 – **Ignominy**	545 – **Retribution**
555 – **Bondage**	565 – **Desperation**
575 – **Subjugation**	585 – **Mendacity**
595 – **Bigotry**	505 – **Pernicity**

The third sequence of accessory terms is based upon the authority/follower sequence of dispassionateness and grudgingness. For example, the group authority figure now crassly acts in a dispassionate fashion in anticipation of the lecherously-grudging treatment of the group representative. Furthermore, the spiritual authority figure now crassly acts rudely in anticipation of the lecherously-greedy treatment by the spiritual disciple, as schematically depicted in the table immediately below:

516 – **Dispassionateness**	526 – **Grudging.**
536 – **Crassness**	546 – **Lechery**
556 – **Rudeness**	566 – **Greediness**
576 – **Brutality**	586 – **Wickedness**
596 – **Meanness**	506 – **Depravity**

The fourth and final sequence of accessory terms is alternately based upon the personal authority/follower themes of callousness/malevolence (the accessory counterparts for indifference and malice). Here, the accessory sequence of authority terms (callousness-fickleness-wantonness-torment-atrocity) effectively reciprocates its main listing of counterparts (indifference-capriciousness-cruelty-persecution-belligerence. The remaining accessory sequence of follower roles (malevolence-pusillanimity-contentiousness-ruthlessness-fiendishness) offers a fitting contrast to its subjective counterparts: e.g., malice, cowardice, antagonism, cunning, and turpitude.

SLOTH	TRAITOROUSNESS
Previously, I (as punisher) have re-fused to act rewardingly towards you: in response to your (as adversary) failure to act solicitously towards me. But now, you (as personal authority) will *slothfully* refuse to act approachfully towards me: in antici-pation of my (as punisher) failure to act rewardingly towards you.	Previously, you (as personal authority) have slothfully refused to act solicitously towards me: in antici-pation of my (as punisher) failure to act rewardingly towards you. But now, I (as your personal follower) will *traitorously* refuse to act reward-ingly towards you: overruling your (as PA) slothful treatment of me.
DISREPUTE	**SEDITION**
Previously, I (as your personal follower) have traitorously refused to act rewardingly towards you: in response to your (as PA) slothful treatment of me. But now, you (as group authority) will slothfully act in a *disreputable* fashion towards me: in anticipation of my (as PF) traitorous treatment of you.	Previously, you (as group authority) have slothfully acted in a disreputable fashion towards me: in anticipation of my (as PF) traitorous treatment of you. But now, I (as group represent.) will traitorously act in a *seditious* fashion towards you: overruling your (as GA) disreputable treatment of me.
PROFLIGACY	**PERFIDY**
Previously, I (as group representa-tive) have traitorously acted in a seditious fashion towards you: in response to your (as GA) disreputable treatment of me. But now, you (as spiritual authority) will disreputably act in a *profligate* fashion towards me: in anticipation of my (as GR) seditious treatment of you.	Previously, you (as spiritual authority) have disreputably acted in a profligate fashion towards me: in anticipation of my (as GR) seditious treatment of you. But now, I (as your spiritual disciple) will seditiously act in a *perfidious* fashion towards you: overruling your (as SA) profligate treatment of me
INDIGNATION	**REVULSION**
Previously, I (as your spiritual disci-ple) have seditiously acted perfidious-ly towards you: in response to your (as SA) profligate treatment of me. But now, you (as humanitarian authority) will profligately act in an *indignant* fashion towards me: in anticipation of my (as SD) perfidious treatment of you.	Previously, you (as humanitarian authority) have profligately acted in an indignant fashion towards me: in anticipation of my (as SD) perfidious treatment of you. But now, I (as represent. member of humanity) will perfidiously act *revul-sively* towards you: overruling your (as HA) indignant treatment of me.
IRATENESS	**ABHORRENCE**
Previously, I (as representative member of humanity) have perfidi-ously acted with revulsion towards you: in response to your (as HA) indignant treatment of me. But now, you (as transcendental au-thority) will indignantly act in an *irate* fashion towards me: in anticipation of my (as RH) revulsive treatment of you.	Previously, you (as transcend-ental authority) have indignantly acted in an irate fashion towards me: in anticipation of my (as RH) revulsive treatment of you. But now, I (as transcendental follow-er) will revulsively act in an *abhorrent* fashion towards you: overruling your (as TA) irate treatment of me.

Table E-1 – The Definitions Based Upon Sloth/Traitorousness

CARELESSNESS	RETALIATION
Previously, I (as punisher) have refused to act tolerantly towards you: in response to your (as adversary) failure to act aversively towards me. But now, you (as personal authority) will *carelessly* refuse to act aversively towards me: in anticipation of my (as punisher) failure to act tolerantly towards you.	Previously, you (as personal authority) have carelessly refused to act aversively towards me: in response to my (as punisher) refusal to act tolerantly towards you. But now, I (as your personal follower) will *retaliatively* refuse to act tolerantly towards you: overruling your (as PA) careless treatment of me.
REPREHENSION	**AVENGEMENT**
Previously, I (as your personal follower) have retaliatively refused to act tolerantly towards you: in response to your (as PA) careless treatment of me. But now, you (as group authority) will *reprehensibly* act in a careless fashion towards me: in anticipation of my (as PF) retaliatory treatment of you.	Previously, you (as group authority) have reprehensibly acted carelessly towards me: in anticipation of my (as PF) retaliatory treatment of you. But now, I (as group representative) will retaliatively act in an *avenging* fashion towards you: overruling your (as GA) reprehensible treatment of me.
BONDAGE	**DESPERATION**
Previously, I (as group representative) have retaliatively acted in an avenging fashion towards you: in response to your (as GA) reprehensible treatment of me. But now, you (as spiritual authority) will reprehensibly maintain me in *bondage*: in anticipation of my (as GR) avenging treatment of you.	Previously, you (as spiritual authority) have reprehensibly maintained me in bondage: in anticipation of my (as GR) avenging treatment of you. But now, I (as your spiritual disciple) will *desperately* seek vengeance against you: overruling your (as SA) reprehensible maintenance of me in bondage.
SUBJUGATION	**DUPLICITY**
Previously, I (as your spiritual disciple) have desperately sought vengeance against you: in response to your (as SA) reprehensible maintenance of me in bondage. But now, you (as humanitarian authority) will reprehensibly *subjugate* me in bondage: in anticipation of my (as SD) desperate quest for vengeance.	Previously, you (as humanitarian authority) have reprehensibly subjugated me in bondage: in anticipation of my (as SD) desperate treatment of you. But now, I (as representative member of humanity) will desperately act in a *duplicitous* fashion towards you: overruling your (as HA) subjugation of me in bondage.
INTOLERANCE	**BANEFULNESS**
Previously, I (as representative member of humanity) have desperately acted in a duplicitous fashion towards you: in response to your (as HA) subjugation of me in bondage. But now, you (as transcendental authority) will subjugate me in an *intolerable* fashion: in anticipation of my (as RH) duplicitous treatment of you.	Previously, you (as transcendental authority) have subjugated me in an intolerable fashion: in anticipation of my (as RH) duplicitous treatment of you. But now, I (as transcendental follower) will duplicitously act *banefully* towards you: overruling your (as TA) intolerable treatment of me.

Table E-2 - The Definitions Based on Carelessness/Retaliation

DISPASSIONATENESS Previously, you (as adversary) have refused to act approachfully towards me: in response to my (as punisher) failure to act rewardingly towards you. But now, I (as personal authority) will *dispassionately* refuse to act rewardingly towards you: in anticipation of your (as adversary) failure to act approachfully towards me.	**RESENTMENT** Previously, I (as personal authority) have dispassionately refused to act rewardingly towards you: in anticipation of your (as adversary) failure to act approachfully towards me. But now, you (as personal follower) will *resentfully* refuse to act approachfully: overruling my (as PA) dispassionate treatment of you.
PREPOSTEROUSNESS Previously, you (as my personal follower) have resentfully refused to act approachfully towards me: in response to my (as PA) dispassionate treatment of you. But now, I (as group authority) will *preposterously* act in a dispassionate fashion towards you: in anticipation of your (as PF) resentful treatment of me.	**LECHERY** Previously, I (as group authority) have preposterously acted in a dispassionate fashion towards you: in anticipation of your (as PF) resentful treatment of me. But now, you (as group representative) will *lecherously* act resentfully towards me: overruling my (as GA) preposterous treatment of you.
COARSENESS Previously, you (as group representative) have lecherously acted in a resentful fashion towards me: in response to my (as GA) preposterous treatment of you. But now, I (as spiritual authority) will preposterously act in a *coarse* fashion towards you: in anticipation of your (as GR) lecherous treatment of me.	**CUPIDITY** Previously, I (as spiritual authority) have preposterously acted in a coarse fashion towards you: in anticipation of your (as GR) lecherous treatment of me. But now, you (as spiritual disciple) will lecherously act with *cupidity* towards me: overruling my (as SA) coarse treatment of you.
ANIMOSITY Previously, you (as my spiritual disciple) have lecherously acted with cupidity towards me: in response to my (as SA) coarse treatment of you. But now, I (as humanitarian authority) will coarsely express *animosity* towards you: in anticipation of your (as SD) lecherous sense of cupidity.	**WICKEDNESS** Previously, I (as humanitarian authority) have coarsely expressed animosity towards you: in anticipation of your (as SD) lecherous sense of cupidity. But now, you (as represent. member of humanity) will *wickedly* act with cupidity towards me: overruling my (as HA) coarse sense of animosity.
ENMITY Previously, you (as representative member of humanity) have wickedly acted with cupidity towards me: in response to my (as HA) coarse expression of animosity. But now, I (as transcendental authority) will animously act with *enmity* towards you: in anticipation of your (as RH) wicked treatment of me.	**SINISTERITY** Previously, I (as transcendental authority) have animously acted with enmity towards you: in anticipation of your (as RH) *wicked* treatment of me. But now, you (as transcendental follower) will wickedly act in a *sinister* fashion towards me: overruling my (as TA) enmity-filled treatment of you.

Table E-3 - The Definitions Based on Dispassion/Resentment

ARBITRARINESS	MALEVOLENCE
Previously, you (as adversary) have refused to act aversively towards me: in response to my (as punisher) failure to act tolerantly towards you. But now, I (as personal authority) will *arbitrarily* refuse to act tolerantly towards you: in anticipation of your (as adversary) failure to act aversively towards me.	Previously, I (as personal authority) have arbitrarily refused to act tolerantly towards you: in anticipation of your (as adversary) failure to act aversively towards me. But now, you (as my personal follower) will *malevolently* refuse to act aversively towards me: overruling my (as PA) arbitrary treatment of you.
FICKLENESS	PUSILLANIMITY
Previously, you (as my personal follower) have malevolently refused to act aversively towards me: in response to my (as PA) arbitrary treatment of you. But now, I (as group authority) will arbitrarily act in a *fickle* fashion towards you: in anticipation of your (as PF) malevolent treatment of me.	Previously, I (as group authority) have arbitrarily acted ficklely towards you: in anticipation of your (as PF) malevolent treatment of me. But now, you (as group representative) will malevolently act in a *pusillanimous* fashion towards me: overruling my (as GA) fickle treatment of you.
ACRIMONY	OPPOSITION
Previously, you (as group representative) have malevolently acted in a pusillanimous fashion towards me: in response to my (as GA) fickle treatment of you. But now, I (as spiritual authority) will fickly act in an *acrimonious* fashion towards you: in anticipation of your (as GR) pusillanimous treatment of me.	Previously, I (as spiritual authority) have fickly acted acrimoniously towards you: in anticipation of your (as GR) pusillanimous treatment of me. But now, you (as my spiritual disciple) will pusillanimously act in an *oppositional* fashion towards me: overruling my (as SA) acrimonious treatment of you.
TORMENT	GUILEFULNESS
Previously, you (as my spiritual disciple) have pusillanimously acted in an oppositional fashion towards me: in response to my (as SA) acrimonious treatment of you. But now, I (as humanitarian authority) will acrimoniously-*torment* you: in anticipation of your (as SD) oppositional treatment of me.	Previously, I (as humanitarian authority) have acrimoniously-tormented you: in anticipation of your (as SD) oppositional treatment of me. But now, you (as representative member of humanity) will *guilefully* act in an oppositional fashion towards me: overruling my (as HA) tormenting treatment of you.
MILITANCY	BASENESS
Previously, you (as representative member of humanity) have guilefully acted in an oppositional fashion towards me: in response to my (as HA) tormenting treatment of you. But now, I (as transcendental authority) will tormentingly act in a *militant* fashion towards you: in anticipation of your (as RH) guileful treatment of me.	Previously, I (as transcendental authority) have tormentingly acted in a militant fashion towards you: in anticipation of your (as RH) guileful treatment of me. But now, you (as my transcendental follower) will guilefully act in a *base* fashion towards me: overruling my (as TA) militant treatment of you.

Table E-4 – The Definitions Based on Arbitrariness/Malevolence

517 – Callousness **527 – Malevolence**

537 – Fickleness **547 – Pusillanimity**

557 – Wantonness **567 – Contentiousness**

577 – Torment **587 – Ruthlessness**

597 – Atrocity **507 – Fiendishness**

In terms of the three-digit coding system, the third (and final) digit is ultimately called into play. In terms of the cardinal vices, for instance, the main versions are coded as: 140 = insurgency, 141 = vengeance, 142 = gluttony, and 143 = cowardice. Digits 4 through 7 in the three-slot, alternately specify the accessory variations for the cardinal vices; namely, 144 = rebellion, 145 = retribution, 146 = greed, and 147 = pusillanimity (as schematically depicted in **Fig. 14A**).

One further pressing issue necessarily remains; namely, the prediction that the accessory variations for the vices of defect are suitable for incorporation into the schematic definition format. Indeed, a complete listing of accessory definitions for the vices of defect is tabulated in **Tables E-1** to **E-4**, in direct analogy to the main set of definitions previously depicted in **Tables D-1** to **D-4** (of Chapter 9). Here, the accessory definitions are similar in form and function to their *main* counterparts with the exception that the "you" and "I" polarities are now reversed. This reciprocal interplay of "you" and "I" perspectives formally permits an understanding of the darker empathic principles governing realm of the vices of defect.

THE GENERAL UNIFYING THEMES
FOR THE REALM OF DEFECT

The completed description of the accessory variations for the domain of defect invokes one final issue of significance; namely, extensions to the darker realm of the general unifying themes. As previously described in Chapter 8 (for the virtuous mode), each of the general unifying virtuous themes is viewed as a "meta-order" summation of its respective listing of virtuous terms. For instance, the general unified theme of *utilitarianism* encompasses the respective listing of cardinal virtues; e.g., prudence, justice, temperance, and fortitude. A similar pattern further holds true with respect to the darker domain of defect. Here the general unifying theme of *corruption* encompasses the general focus of the vices of cor-

ruption; namely, insurgency, vengeance, gluttony, and cowardice.

Indeed, it even proves feasible to devise an entire parallel hierarchy of darker themes targeting the realm of defect: as formally depicted in **Fig. 14B**. This diagram employs a format similar to that depicted in **Fig. 8A** of Chapter 8, allowing for a direct contrast in terms. A cursory comparison of these two diagrams reveals a mirror-image correspondence between the respective listings of themes. The darker themes represent the direct moral antithesis of their respective virtuous counterparts.

For instance, the general unifying themes targeting the authority roles (knavery-villainy-profanity-apostasy-nihilism) further contrast (point-for-point) with the respective virtuous counterparts of individualism, personal-ism, romanticism, ecumenism, and humanism. Furthermore, the darker sequence of follower themes; e.g., fraud-corruption-heresy-anarchism-diabolism, in turn, mirrors the respective virtuous themes; namely, pragmatism, utilitarianism, ecclesiasticism, eclecticism, and mysticism. Indeed, each of these darker themes was mentioned in its respective chapter in the overall context of the vices of defect.

Similar to the ascending hierarchy of themes targeting the virtuous mode, the respective interplay of darker themes prove similarly enlightening. For instance, the personal authority theme of *knavery* further extends to the *villainy* expressed by the group authority figure. The spiritual authority role, in turn, targets the more abstract vice of *profanity* consistent with a focus on universal principles. The themes for the remaining humanitarian and transcendental levels alternately target the notions of *apostasy* and *nihilism*, respectively.

In similar fashion, the remaining darker listings of follower themes are identified as fraud-corruption-heresy-anarchism-diabolism. Here the personal follower theme of *fraud* (in contrast to pragmatism) refers to that which is detrimental to the individual: extending (in a group sense) to the *corrupt* disregard for "the common good." This ascending format further extends to the remaining spiritual, humanitarian, and transcendental realms with respect to the darker themes of heresy, anarchism, and diabolism (as schematically depicted in tabular form below). For a more complete discussion of this darker range of themes, the dedicated reader can refer back to the more extensive degree of detail contained within the chapters devoted to the specific vices of defect.

518 – Knavery	**528 – Fraud**
538 – Villainy	**548 – Corruption**
558 – Profanity	**568 – Heresy**
578 – Apostasy	**588 – Anarchism**
598 – Nihilism	**508 – Diabolism**

In direct analogy to the virtuous range of themes, the parallel complement of darker themes for the vices of defect can similarly be incorporated into the formal schematic definition format. This latter innovation is termed the class of "meta-" schematic definitions, being that they represent meta-order summations of the respective individual terms. The complete listing of "meta-" schematic definitions for the vices of defect is depicted in **Table C-3**, contrasting (point-for-point) with the respective virtuous mode shown in **Table C-1** (of Chapter *8*). These definitions for the darker range of themes are formally based upon the behavioral principles underlying punishment, just as the virtuous mode was seen to be grounded within the instinctual terminology of instrumental conditioning. This strong behavioral foundation adds a welcome additional validation to this dual complement of themes, providing an overarching behavioral basis for the entire linguistic matrix.

THE ACCESSORY LISTING OF THEMES FOR THE VICES OF DEFECT

The completed description of the main themes for the vices of defect, in turn, invites comparisons to the anticipated *accessory* variations. Similar to the pattern previously established for the virtuous themes, the accessory darker variations respectively complement the main listings of themes, with the exception that the "you" and "I" polarities are now reversed. This further adds a crucial (empathic) dimension to the dual schematic format of terms.

519 - Mischief	**529 - Deception**
539 - Licentiousness	**549 - Venality**
559 - Scandal	**569 - Schismatism**
579 – Infidelity	**589 - Lawlessness**
599 - Alienation	**509 - Sorcery**

Indeed, a suitable number of accessory themes for the vices of defect have recently been identified, permitting the introduction of the accessory listing of terms depicted in **Fig. 14B** and also the preceding compact table. For instance, the main authority sequence of darker themes (knavery-villainy-profanity-apostasy-nihilism) further contrasts with their respective accessory counterparts; e.g., mischievousness, licentiousness, scandalousness, infidelity, and alienation. Furthermore, the main *follower* sequence of fraud, corruption, heresy, anarchism, and diabolism, in turn, reciprocates its accessory sequence of counterparts (deception, venality, schismatism, lawlessness, and sorcery). Although the anticipated degree of correspondence for several of these themes is not as close as might be expected, the seamless cohesiveness encompassing this overall accessory system proves the crucial factor here. Indeed, many of these accessory terms are not commonly encountered in general usage: hence, a more detailed analysis of this accessory listing of deferred themes is deferred for treatment in an upcoming edition.

As per the original description of the three-digit coding system initially proposed, the general unified themes for the vices of defect are similarly amenable for coding within the master format. Here, three-digit codes ending with the numeral "8" specify the main listings of themes, whereas those ending with a "9" (in the three-spot) represent the *accessory* variations. Here the main and accessory variations effectively complement one another with the exception that the "you" and "I" polarities are now reversed.

THE FORMAL SCHEMATIC DEFINITIONS FOR THE ACCESSORY THEMES OF DEFECT

The true test of validity for this accessory listing of darker themes, however, ultimately extends to their formal incorporation into the schematic definition format. In direct analogy to the main listing of schematic definitions targeting the vices of defect, the respective accessory variations similarly respect such a format, whereby specifying higher-order perspectives on the more basic complement of individual terms. For instance, the "meta" schematic definition for *venality* encompasses the four (accessory) vices of venality as subsets (e.g., rebellion, retribution, lechery, and pusillanimity). Accordingly, the complete four-part listing of schematic definitions for the darker accessory themes is schematically depicted in **Table C-4**. When further contrasted with the schematic definitions for the main listings of darker themes

518 - KNAVERY **Ego Vices** *Personal Authority*	**528 - FRAUD** **Alter Ego Vices** *Personal Follower*
538 - VILLAINY **Charismatic Vices** *Group Authority*	**548 - CORRUPTION** **Cardinal Vices** *Group Representative*
558 - PROFANITY **Civil Liabilities** *Spiritual Authority*	**568 - HERESY** **Theological Vices** *Spiritual Disciple*
578 - APOSTASY **Ecumenical Vices** *Humanitarian Authority*	**588 - ANARCHISM** **Moralistic Vices** *Humanitarian Follower*
598 - NIHILISM **Humanistic Vices** *Transcendental Authority*	**508 - DIABOLISM** **Mystical Vices** *Transcendental Follower*

Fig. 14B - The "Meta" Themes for the Vices of Defect

KNAVERY	FRAUD
Previously, you have acted in an un-motivated fashion towards me: in response to my (as antagonist) adversarial treatment of you. But now, I (as personal authority) will *knavishly* act in an adversarial fashion towards you: in anticipation of your unmotivated treatment of me.	Previously, I (as personal authority) have knavishly acted in an adversarial fashion towards you: in anticipation of your (as punisher) unmotivated treatment of me. But now, you (as my personal follow-er) will *fraudulently* act in an unmoti-vated fashion towards me: overruling my (as PA) knavish treatment of you.
VILLAINY	**CORRUPTION**
Previously, you (as my personal follower) have fraudulently acted in an unmotivated fashion towards me: in response to my (as PA) knavish treatment of you. But now, I (as group authority) will knavishly act in a *villainous* fashion towards you: in anticipation of your (as PF) fraudulent treatment of me.	Previously, I (as group authority) have knavishly acted in a villainous fashion towards you: in anticipation of your (as PF) fraudulent treatment of me. But now, you (as group represent-ative) will fraudulently act in a *corrupt* fashion towards me: overruling my (as GA) villainous treatment of you.
PROFANITY	**HERESY**
Previously, you (as group repre-sentative) have fraudulently acted in a corrupt fashion towards me: in response to my (as GA) villainous treatment of you. But now, I (as spiritual authority) will villainously act in a *profane* fashion towards you: in anticipation of your (as GR) corrupt treatment of me.	Previously, I (as spiritual authority) have villainously acted in a profane fashion towards you: in anticipation of your (as GR) corrupt treatment of me. But now, you (as my spiritual disci-ple) will *heretically* act in a corrupt fashion towards me: overruling my (as SA) profane treatment of you.
APOSTASY	**ANARCHISM**
Previously, you (as my spiritual disciple) have heretically acted in a corrupt fashion towards me: in response to my (as SA) profane treatment of you. But now, I (as humanitarian authority) will profanely act in an *apostasy*-filled fashion towards you: in anticipation of your (as SD) heretical treatment of me.	Previously, I (as humanitarian authority) have profanely acted with apostasy towards you: in anticipation of your (as SD) heretical treatment of me. But now, you (as representative member of humanity) will heretically act in an *anarchical* fashion towards me: overruling my (as HA) apostasy-filled treatment of you.
NIHILISM	**DIABOLISM**
Previously, you (as representative member of humanity) have heretical-ly acted in an anarchical fashion towards me: in response to my (as HA) apostasy-filled treatment of you. But now, I (as transcendental auth-ority) will act in a *nihilistic* fashion towards you: in anticipation of your (as RH) anarchical treatment of me.	Previously, I (as transcendental au-thority) have acted in a nihilistic fash-ion towards you: in anticipation of your (as RH) anarchical treatment of me. But now, you (as my transcendental follower) will anarchically act in a *diabolical* fashion towards me: overruling my (as TA) nihilistic treatment of you.

Table C-3 - The "Meta" Definitions for the Themes of Defect

519 - MISCHIEF **Ego Vices - II** *Personal Authority*	**529 - DECEPTIVENESS** **Alter Ego Vices - II** *Personal Follower*
539 - LICENTIOUSNESS **Charismatic Vices - II** *Group Authority*	**549 - VENALITY** **Cardinal Vices - II** *Group Representative*
559 - SCANDAL **Civil Liabilities - II** *Spiritual Authority*	**569 - SCHISMATISM** **Theological Vices - II** *Spiritual Disciple*
579 - INFIDELITY **Ecumenical Vices - II** *Humanitarian Authority*	**589 - LAWLESSNESS** **Moralistic Vices - II** *Humanitarian Follower*
599 - ALIENATION **Humanistic Vices - II** *Transcendental Authority*	**509 - SORCERY** **Mystical Vices - II** *Transcendental Follower*

Fig. 14C – The Accessory Themes for the Vices of Defect

MISCHIEVOUSNESS	DECEPTIVENESS
Previously, I have acted in an unmotivated fashion towards you: in response to your (as antagonist) adversarial treatment of me. But now, you (as personal authority) will *mischievously* act in an adversarial fashion towards me: in anticipation of my unmotivated treatment of you.	Previously, you (as personal authority) have mischievously acted in an adversarial fashion towards me: in anticipation of my (as punisher) unmotivated treatment of you. But now, I (as your personal follower) will *deceptively* act in an unmotivated fashion towards you: overruling your (as PA) mischievous treatment of me.
LICENTIOUSNESS	**VENALITY**
Previously, I (as your personal follower) have deceptively acted in an unmotivated fashion towards you: in response to your (as PA) mischievous treatment of me. But now, you (as group authority) will mischievously act in a *licentious* fashion towards me: in anticipation of my (as PF) deceptive treatment of you.	Previously, you (as group authority) have mischievously acted in a licentious fashion towards me: in anticipation of my (as PF) deceptive treatment of you. But now, I (as group representative) will deceptively act in a *venal* fashion towards you: overruling your (as GA) licentious treatment of me.
SCANDALOUSNESS	**SCHISMATISM**
Previously, I (as group representative) have deceptively acted in a venal fashion towards you: in response to your (as GA) licentious treatment of me. But now, you (as spiritual authority) will licentiously act in a *scandalous* fashion towards me: in anticipation of my (as GR) venal treatment of you.	Previously, you (as spiritual authority) have licentiously acted in a scandalous fashion towards me: in anticipation of my (as GR) venal treatment of you. But now, I (as spiritual disciple) will venally act in a *schismatic* fashion towards you: overruling your (as SA) scandalous treatment of me.
INFIDELITY	**LAWLESSNESS**
Previously, I (as spiritual disciple) have venally acted in a schismatic fashion: in response to your (as SA) scandalous sense of licentiousness. But now, you (as humanitarian authority) will scandalously act with *infidelity* towards me: in anticipation of my (as SD) schismatic treatment of you.	Previously, you (as humanit. authority) have scandalously acted with infidelity towards me: in anticipation of my (as SD) schismatic treatment of you. But now, I (as representative member of humanity) will schismatically act in a *lawless* fashion towards you: overruling your (as HA) scandalous sense of infidelity.
ALIENATION	**SORCERY**
Previously, I (as representative member of humanity) have schismatically acted in a lawless fashion towards you: in response to your (as HA) scandalous sense of infidelity. But now, you (as transcend. authority) will infidelously act in an *alienated* fashion towards me: in anticipation of my (as RH) sense of lawlessness.	Previously, you (as my transcendental authority) have acted in an alienated fashion towards me: in anticipation of my (as RH) schismatic sense of lawlessness. But now, I (as your transcendental follower) will lawlessly act with *sorcery* towards you: overruling your (as TA) alienated treatment of me.

Table C-4 – The Accessory Definitions for the Thematic Vices

(from **Table C-3**), the reciprocal interplay of "you" and "I" perspectives finally become conceptually complete: whereby permitting a degree of empathic versatility unprecedented in terms precision, allowing for overarching insights into the disturbing realm of deceptive communication.

In summary, the completed description of the accessory variations for the vices of defect permits unprecedented insights into the darker realm of the criminal mind. As is so often the case, motives of criminals are labeled in an entirely objective fashion consistent with their social stigma, offering precious little insight into the underlying subjective perspectives. Through the aid of the *accessory* class of defect, however, both objective and subjective viewpoints for the vices of defect can be examined in a complementary fashion, whereby allowing the offender a subjective perspective from the viewpoint of the victim (and vice versa). Hopefully, these expanded conceptual insights will serve to remedy many of the random acts of violence affecting Western culture today.

The further formal identification of the general unifying themes for the vices of defect offers similar dramatic inroads conducive to remedial oversight. Many of the darker themes enjoy widespread expression in the literary tradition. Indeed, what would a melodrama or tragedy be without an antagonist to contrast with the protagonist. In terms of this range of darker authority roles, the ascending series of themes; namely, knavery, villainy, profanity, apostasy, and nihilism proves particularly suggestive of many literary traditions. For instance, the dastardly villain or the turncoat apostate proves a fitting counterpoint to the virtuous prerequisites of the fictional hero. Furthermore, for the remaining darker realm of the follower roles, the respective themes of fraud, corruption heresy, anarchism, and diabolism provide a suitably effective counterpoint for their respective virtuous counterparts. This enduring moral contrast across this broad array of general unifying themes represents an unprecedented innovation on the world scene, the literary dynamics embodied in such a thematic morality play ultimately decipherable to a high degree of precision (and without necessarily resorting to the individual virtues/vices at issue within the script). Hence, this breakthrough overall technology fortuitously enjoys two distinct degrees conceptual versatility: namely, the individual contrasts between the specific virtues and vices, as well as a broader overarching counterpoint utilizing the respective general unifying themes.

This dual degree of versatility provides an extra set of checks and balances with respect to the certitude of that being communicated, ensuring a suitably effective model of the dynamics underlying affective language in general. Hopefully, this increased conceptual understanding in relation to such darker motives will permit more effective interventions on the world scene before irreparable damage can occur, permitting a more peaceful and harmonious global community. Here, advanced partnerships between affiliated spheres of influence now become eminently more feasible, offering dramatic new inroads towards global peace and stability. In concert with the supportive individual traditions of the virtues, values, and ideals, the overarching grand unifying themes promise a new era for collaborative human endeavors based upon such noble principles, ushering in a new age of cooperation for policymakers throughout the world.

PART-III

15

AN INTRODUCTION TO
THE VICES OF EXCESS

The enduring contrast between the major virtues and the vices of defect emerges as one of the most salient features for the newly proposed ethical hierarchy. The ascending hierarchy of defect described in Chapter 9 represents a fitting adjunct to the virtuous traditions, chiefly due to its systematic correspondence to the virtuous mode. Although the newly proposed groupings of vices prove exceedingly comprehensive on an intuitive level, they scarcely can claim to be all-inclusive by any measure. In particular, only half of the Seven Deadly Sins are directly accounted for within the realm of defect. Indeed, pride, envy, and covetousness defy incorporation into this extreme domain of defect. This anomaly is fortunately explained in terms of an entirely new class of vices referred to since ancient times as the *vices of excess*.

The ancient Greeks particularly exhibited an extreme degree of disdain for any conspicuous expression of excess. The entrance to the famed Greek oracle at Delphi contains the stirring admonition "Nothing in excess," attesting to their ideal mindset concerning moderation. Indeed, Aristotle was among the first to describe this dual system of vices; namely, the vices of defect (described in Chapters 9 to 14), as well as the respective vices of excess: defined as that range of extremes with respect to the virtuous mode. Indeed, Aristotle viewed the virtuous realm that class of "mean values" (or norms) interposed between the vices of defect and the vices of excess. Consequently, virtue represents the mean-value interposed between defect and excess: an aspect favoring moderation insofar as choosing a middle ground between these two categories of vice. The following schematic table offers a sample listing of specific examples exemplifying Aristotle's *Theory of the Golden Mean*, gratefully adapted from Aristotle's *Nicomachean Ethics*.

The *Vices of* DEFECT	The *Virtues:* "MEAN VALUES"	The *Vices of* EXCESS
cowardice	**courage**	rashness
stinginess	**liberality**	extravagance
laziness	**ambition**	greed
secrecy	**modesty**	pride
moroseness	**honesty**	loquacity
quarrelsome	**wittiness**	buffoonery

According to the first listed example, courage represents the ideal mean-value interposed between cowardice (defect) and rashness (excess). Furthermore, in terms of finances, liberality denotes the mean (norm) value, whereas defect/excess is alternately represented as extravagance and stinginess. With respect to congeniality, the mean value is specified as wittiness, whereas buffoonery suggests the state of excess, while quarrelsomeness indicates defect. Here morality (like art) personally consists of deciding where to draw the line! The virtues formally represent a predisposition to take a moderate course, effectively defined as staying upon the middle path. Although the general pattern underlying Aristotle's schematic system proves extremely informative, a number of terms appear somewhat artificially assigned; a shortcoming fortunately remedied within the expanded context of the modified listing of the vices of excess depicted in **Fig. 15A**.

According to the basic "tripartite" system underlying the Theory of the Mean, the realm of defect represents a well-defined set of opposing qualities (defined as the absence of virtue). The vices of excess, in contrast, prove somewhat less clear-cut in nature; representing a more ambiguous determination of extremes with respect to the virtues with relativistic consequences across the broad range of cultures. The vices of excess, ac-

310	311
Pride	Shame
312	**313**
Envy	Disdain

(XS) EGO STATES
(Personal Authority)

→

320	321
Flattery	Criticism
322	**323**
Impudence	Insolence

(XS) ALTER EGO STATES
(Personal Follower)

↙

330	331
Vanity	Humiliation
332	**333**
Jealousy	Contempt

(XS) PERSONAL IDEALS
(Group Authority)

→

340	341
Adulation	Ridicule
342	**343**
Arrogance	Audacity

(XS) CARDINAL VIRTUES
(Group Representative)

↙

350	351
Conceit	Mortification
352	**353**
Covetousness	Reproach

(XS) CIVIL LIBERTIES
(Spiritual Authority)

→

360	361
Patronization	Scorn
362	**363**
Impetuosity	Rashness

(XS) THEOLOGICAL VIRTUES
(Spiritual Disciple)

↙

370	371
Pretentiousness	Anguish
372	**373**
Longing	Chagrin

(XS) ECUMENICAL IDEALS
(Humanitarian Authority)

→

380	381
Obsequiousness	Mockery
382	**383**
Presumption	Boldness

(XS) CLASSICAL VALUES
(Humanitarian Follower)

↙

390	391
Sanctimony	Tribulation
392	**393**
Affectation	Bitterness

(XS) HUMANISTIC VALUES
(Transcendental Authority)

→

300	301
Sycophancy	Cynicism
302	**303**
Smugness	Harshness

(XS) MYSTICAL VALUES
(Transcendental Follower)

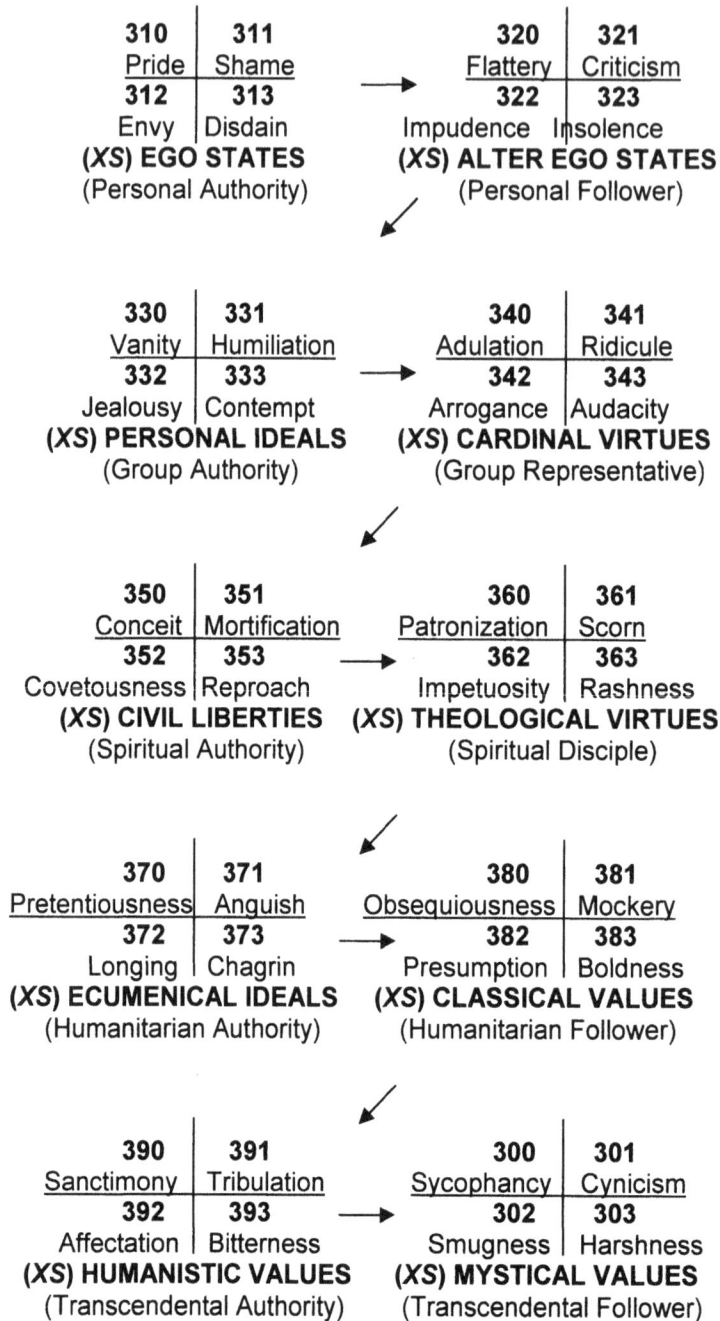

Fig. 15A – The Vices of Excess

cordingly, represent a more ambiguous style of moral continuum, a fuzzy-style of moral gray area of virtually relativistic proportions.

The first major indications of a trend towards excess typically occur during adolescence, when teens increasingly strive to gain independence from the family unit. This is not necessarily meant to imply that excess is the exclusive domain of rebellious youth, for it frequently carries over into adulthood as well. Certainly, we all strive to be outwardly recognized for the magnitude of our achievements, as well as the attendant advantages of wealth or power. Athletes strive to achieve the upper limits within their respective sport of choice, whereas politicians seek to enhance their status in relation to their peers/constituency. This quest for distinction through extremes on many fronts remains a natural inclination, although the dividing line separating the true domain of excess amounts to a somewhat of a vague value judgment.

Perhaps the most crucial criterion in this regard concerns the distinction between cooperation and selfishness, where selfish tendencies (such as pride, shame, impudence, etc.) characterize an overarching realm of excess. Those forms of excess (that preserve social cooperation) are more likely to be tolerated in a social setting. Indeed, Logan P. Smith once speculated: "A slight touch of friendly malice and amusement towards those we love keeps our affections for them from turning flat." Henry Ward Beecher further writes: "A man without mirth is like a wagon without springs. He is jolted disagreeably by every pebble in the road."

Some range of extremes (in contrast to pure seriousness), appears crucial for preventing boredom in one's everyday affairs. This is typically experienced as novelty, excitement, or variations in expectations. Dr. Marvin Zuckerman of the University of Delaware (2000) has devised a sensation-seeking scale based upon three basic parameters. The first of these is defined as the adventure/thrill-seeking scale, defined as a preference for extreme sports or high-risk behaviors. The second dimension is defined in terms of experience-seeking, a tamer version stressing the quest for sensation through intellectual curiosity and the senses: as experienced in the aesthetic appreciation of the arts and sciences, as well as a tendency towards wanderlust and world-travel. A third factor concerns the ages-old phenomenon of *disinhibition*, as in the mood altering properties underlying drugs or alcohol. This similarly extends to a party atmosphere replete with a seductive mix of shifting social coalitions.

According to these three basic motivational parameters, sensation-seeking specifies a spirit of adventure underlying all such extreme endeavors, as particularly celebrated in the exploits of the trailblazer or international explorer. Dr. Frank Farley of Temple University (1991) further identifies this extreme trait as the type "T" personality: the "T" representing an abbreviation for the thrill-seeking characterizing all such high-risk activities. It directly contrasts with the (small) type "t" personality; namely, the more staid segment of the population that is content with enjoying the safer thrills of life.

To a modest degree, the realm of excess plays a key role in maintaining emotional stability, a common feature with respect to humor and comedy. Indeed, many of the world's most creative people live on a perpetual balance between excess (or even mania) and the mundane: a circumstance frequently leading to the tendency towards eccentricity. The eccentric revels in field of hyperbole and excess, creating fantastical innovations to the amusement of the more rational amongst us. These extremes can further extend to the exploits of the daredevil or the blatant publicity-seeker, genres currently in vogue within the entertainment industry. Although this degree of excess can prove quite irritating, it nevertheless remains relatively innocuous compared to the darker realm of the vices of defect. Consequently, the vices of excess are generally tolerated within society, although they can further lead to conflict when pressed to extremes.

THE MASTER SCHEMATIC FORMAT FOR THE VICES OF EXCESS

In deference to Aristotle's enduring theory of the mean, the expanded specifics for the motivational matrix allow for a degree in precision unheard of within the earlier traditions. In terms of this expanded context, the communicational factors characterizing each of the vices of excess represent a variable degree of excess with respect to the virtuous mode. Indeed, many of the individual vices of excess are more-or-less universally acknowledged in common usage. For instance, *pride* represents the extreme counterpart of solicitousness, whereas *shame* makes a similar correspondence to submissiveness. Furthermore, *flattery* directly expands upon approval, whereas *criticism* designates a more extreme form of lenient-blame. Indeed, it ultimately proves possible to devise an entire ten-level hierarchy for the vices of excess, effectively mirroring the specifics of the purely virtuous realm.

(A)

solicitousness
submissiveness

approval
leniency

pride
shame

flattery
criticism

X → Y

$\underline{X}$ → $\underline{Y}$

Past

Present

Future

(Authority)

(Follower)

(B)

desire
worry

aspiration
compliance

envy
disdain

impudence
insolence

Y → X

$\underline{Y}$ → $\underline{X}$

Past

Present

Future

(Authority)

(Follower)

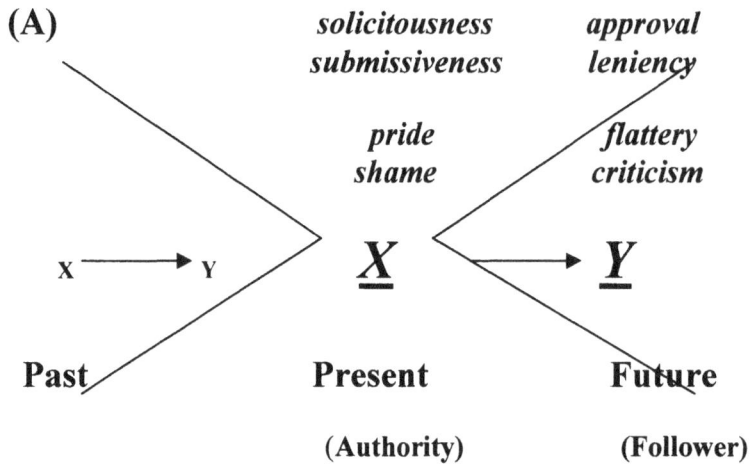

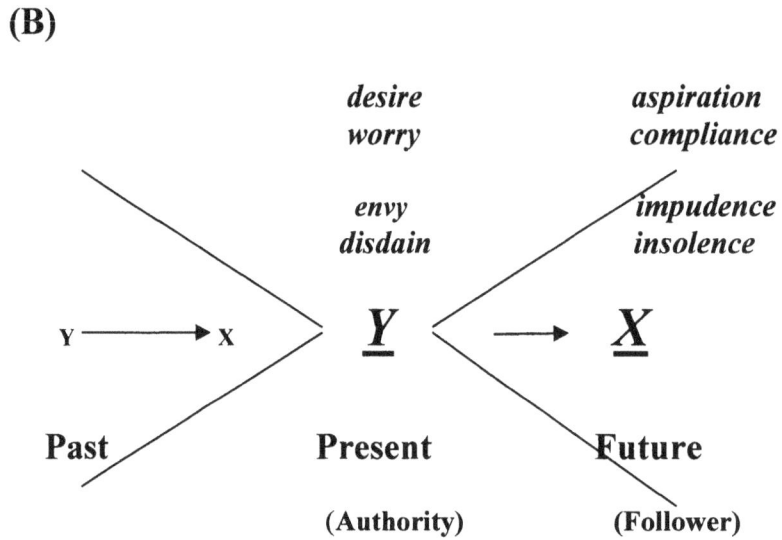

Fig. 15B - Two-stage Dynamic for the Vices of Excess vs. Virtues

The complete ascending hierarchy for the vices of excess is schematically depicted in **Fig. 15A**, in addition to the respective three-digit codes (all beginning with the first-place digit "3"). This format is further depicted in the compact table immediately below demonstrating the hierarchial relationships in a more condensed format.

Pride • Flattery	**Shame • Criticism**
Vanity • Adulation	**Humiliation • Ridicule**
Conceit • Patronization	**Mortification • Scorn**
Pretention • Obsequious.	**Anguish • Mockery**
Sanctimony • Sycophancy	**Tribulation • Cynicism**

Envy • Impudence	**Disdain • Insolence**
Jealousy • Arrogance	**Contempt • Audacity**
Covetous. • Impetuosity	**Reproach • Rashness**
Longing • Presumption	**Chagrin • Boldness**
Affectation • Smugness	**Bitterness • Harshness**

This hierarchy of excess is identical in form and function to that previously established for the virtuous mode. Owing to the greater range of flexibility involved in determining the precise degree of excess, this hierarchy scarcely exhibits the clarity or precision previously established for the more clearly defined realm of the virtues. A clear degree of ambiguity, accordingly, is essentially unavoidable for the more abstract (humanitarian and transcendental) levels within this hierarchy of excess. Fortunately, the personal, group, and spiritual levels prove particularly adequate to the task, with well-defined terms occupying each of the individually-predicted slots.

THE BEHAVIORAL FOUNDATIONS FOR THE VICES OF EXCESS

Beginning with the most basic personal level within the hierarchy of excess, pride and shame are formally defined as the excessive counterparts of the respective ego states of solicitousness and submissiveness. Furthermore, flattery and criticism, in turn, represent extreme variations on the respective alter ego states of approval and leniency. Indeed, the complete eight-part complement of personal terms for the realm of excess is schematically depicted in **Fig. 15B**. This diagram directly mirrors the virtuous prerequisites previously established in **Fig. 2A** (of Chapter 2), with the exception that the vices of excess are now substituted for the original listings of ego and alter ego states. According to Part A of this diagram, the *pride* maneuver of the personal authority figure directly anticipates the flattery expressed by the personal follower, whereas *shame-fulness* similarly prompts a corresponding expression of criticism. Furthermore in Part B, *envy* prompts a potential expression of impudence, whereas *disdain*, in turn, anticipates an outward display of insolence. This formal arrangement of immediately-active and future-directed time-frames predicts the eight specified authority/follower roles in relation to the realm of excess. For instance, pride and shame represent an immediately-active style of procurement perspective, whereas envy and disdain alternately specify active styles of reinforcement perspectives. The remaining four terms are depicted as potentially occurring within a future-directed time-frame, as indicated in the more introspective range of themes; namely, flattery, criticism, impudence, and insolence.

THE HIERARCHY FOR THE VICES OF EXCESS

This preliminary *personal* realm of excess, in turn, extends to the group, spiritual, humanitarian, and transcendental authority levels as well. For instance, in terms of the group level of organization, the *vain* sense of pride expressed by the group authority figure directly anticipates the flattering sense of *adulation* professed by the group representative. Similarly, the shameful sense of *humiliation* experienced by the authority figure further prompts the critical sense of *ridicule* on the part of the follower figure. Furthermore, the envious sense of *jealousy* experienced by the group authority figure effectively prompts the impudent sense of *arrogance* professed by the group representative. Finally, the former's disdainful sense of *contempt* alternately prompts the follower figure's insolent sense of audacity.

This systematic modification of terms, in turn, extends to the remaining spiritual, humanitarian, and transcendental authority levels, as well: although the distinctions between terms increasingly diminish in relation to the higher authority levels. Indeed, the respective choice of terms is often not as exacting as might be expected. Precision notwithstanding, a definite ascending pattern of organization is definitely illustrated for the entire ten-level hierarchy for the vices of excess. For instance, the respective authority sequence of pride, vanity, conceit, pretentiousness, and sanctimony effectively complements the remaining follower sequence of flattery, adulation, patronization, obsequiousness, and sycophancy. Furthermore, the related authority sequence of shame, humiliation, mortification, anguish, and tribulation effectively complements the remaining follower sequence of criticism, ridicule, scorn,

PRIDE	FLATTERY
Previously, you (as reinforcer) have excessively acted approvingly towards me: in response to my (as procurer) extremely solicitous treatment of you. But now, I (as personal authority) will *pridefully* act in an extremely solicitous fashion towards you: in anticipation of your (as reinforcer) excessively approving treatment of me.	Previously, I (as personal authority) have pridefully acted extremely solicitously towards you: in anticipation of your (reinforcer) excessively approving treatment of me. But now, you (as my personal follower) will *flatteringly* act extremely approvingly towards me: overruling my (as PA) prideful treatment of you.
VANITY	**ADULATION**
Previously, you (as personal follower) have flatteringly acted in an extremely approving fashion towards me: in response to my (as PA) prideful treatment of you. But now, I (as group authority) will pridefully act in a *vain* fashion towards you: in anticipation of your (as PF) flattering treatment of me.	Previously, I (as group authority) have pridefully acted in a vain fashion towards you: in anticipation of your (as PF) flattering treatment of me. But now, you (as group representative) will flatteringly act with *adulation* towards me: overruling my (as GA) vain sense of pride.
CONCEIT	**PATRONIZATION**
Previously, you (as group representative) have flatteringly acted with adulation towards me: in response to my (as GA) prideful sense of vanity. But now, I (as spiritual authority) will vainly act in a *conceited* fashion towards you: in anticipation of your (as GR) flattering sense of adulation.	Previously, I (as spiritual authority) have vainly acted in a conceited fashion towards you: in anticipation of your (as GR) flattering sense of adulation. But now, you (as my spiritual disciple) will flatteringly act in a *patronizing* fashion towards me: overruling my (as SA) vain sense of conceit.
PRETENTIOUSNESS	**OBSEQUIOUSNESS**
Previously, you (as my spiritual disciple) have flatteringly acted in a patronizing fashion towards me: in response to my (as SA) vain sense of conceit. But now, I (as humanitarian authority) will conceitedly act in a *pretentious* fashion towards you: in anticipation of your (as SD) patronizing treatment of me.	Previously, I (as humanitarian authority) have conceitedly acted in a pretentious fashion towards you: in anticipation of your (as SD) patronizing treatment of me. But now, you (as a representative member of humanity) will patronizingly act in an *obsequious* fashion towards me: overruling my (as HA) pretentious treatment of you.
SANCTIMONY	**SMUGNESS**
Previously, you (as representative member of humanity) have patronizingly acted obsequiously towards me: in response to my (as HA) pretentious treatment of you. But now, I (as transcendental authority) will pretentiously act in a *sanctimonious* fashion towards you: in anticipation of your (as RH) obsequious treatment of me.	Previously, I (as transcendental authority) have pretentiously acted in a sanctimonious fashion towards you: in anticipation of your (as RH) obsequious treatment of me. But now, you (as transcendental follower) will obsequiously act in a *smug* fashion towards me: overruling my (as TA) sanctimonious treatment of you.

Table F-1 – The Definitions Based Upon Pride/Flattery

SHAME	CRITICISM
Previously, you (as reinforcer) have excessively acted in a lenient fashion towards me: in response to my (as procurer) extremely submissive treatment of you. But now, I (as personal authority) will *shamefully* act extremely submissively towards you: in anticipation of your (as reinforcer) excessively lenient treatment of me.	Previously, I (as personal authority) have shamefully acted extremely submissively towards you: in anticipation of your (as reinforcer) excessively lenient treatment of me. But now, you (as my personal follower) will *critically* act extremely leniently towards me: overruling my (as PA) shameful treatment of you.
HUMILIATION	RIDICULE
Previously, you (as personal follower) have critically acted extremely leniently towards me: in response to my (as PA) shameful treatment of you. But now, I (as group authority) will shamefully act in a *humiliated* fashion towards you: in anticipation of your (as PF) critical treatment of me.	Previously, I (as group authority) have shamefully acted in a humiliated fashion towards you: in anticipation of your (as PF) critical treatment of me. But now, you (as group representative) will critically-*ridicule* me: overruling my (as GA) shameful sense of humiliation.
MORTIFICATION	SCORN
Previously, you (as group representative) have critically-ridiculed me: in response to my (as GA) shameful sense of humiliation. But now, I (as spiritual authority) will humiliatingly act in a *mortified* fashion towards you: in anticipation of your (as GR) critical-ridiculing of me.	Previously, I (as spiritual authority) have humiliatingly acted in a mortified fashion towards you: in anticipation of your (as GR) critical-ridiculing of me. But now, you (as my spiritual disciple) will *scornfully*-ridicule me: overruling my (as SA) mortified treatment of you.
ANGUISH	MOCKERY
Previously, you (as my spiritual disciple) have scornfully-ridiculed me: in response to my (as SA) mortified treatment of you. But now, I (as humanitarian authority) will mortifiedly act in an *anguished* fashion towards you: in anticipation of your (as SD) scornful-ridiculing of me.	Previously, I (as humanitarian authority) have mortifyingly acted in an anguished fashion towards you: in anticipation of your (as SD) scornful-ridiculing of me. But now, you (as representative member of humanity) will scornfully act in a *mocking* fashion towards me: overruling my (as HA) anguished treatment of you.
TRIBULATION	CYNICISM
Previously, you (as representative member of humanity) have scornfully-mocked me: in response to my (as HA) anguished treatment of you. But now, I (as transcendental authority) will anguishingly act with *tribulation* towards you: in anticipation of your (as RH) scornful-mocking of me.	Previously, I (as transcendental authority) have anguishingly acted with tribulation towards you: in anticipation of your (as RH) scornful-mocking of me. But now, you (as my transcendental follower) will mockingly act in a *cynical* fashion towards me: overruling my (as TA) anguished sense of tribulation.

Table F-2 – The Definitions Based Upon Shame/Criticism

ENVY	IMPUDENCE
Previously, I (as procurer) have excessively acted aspiringly towards you: in response to your (as reinforcer) extremely desirous treatment of me. But now, you (as my personal authority) will *enviously* act in an extremely desirous fashion towards me: in anticipation of my (as procurer) excessively aspiring treatment of you.	Previously, you (as my personal authority) have enviously acted in an extremely desirous fashion towards me: in anticipation of my (as procurer) excessively aspiring treatment of you. But now, I (as your personal follower) will *impudently* act in an extremely aspiring fashion towards you: overruling your (as PA) envious treatment of me.
JEALOUSY	**ARROGANCE**
Previously, I (as your personal follower) have impudently acted in an extremely aspiring fashion towards you: in response to your (as PA) envious treatment of me. But now, you (as my group authority) will enviously act in a *jealous* fashion towards me: in anticipation of my (as PF) impudent treatment of you.	Previously, you (as my group authority) have enviously acted in a jealous fashion towards me: in anticipation of my (as PF) impudent treatment of you. But now, I (as group representative) will impudently act in an *arrogant* fashion towards you: overruling your (as GA) enviously-jealous treatment of me.
COVETOUSNESS	**IMPETUOSITY**
Previously, I (as group representative) have impudently acted in an arrogant fashion towards you: in response to your (as GA) enviously-jealous treatment of me. But now, you (as my spiritual authority) will jealously act in a *covetous* fashion towards me: in anticipation of my (as GR) impudently-arrogant treatment of you.	Previously, you (as my spiritual authority) have jealously acted in a covetous fashion towards me: in anticipation of my (as GR) impudently-arrogant treatment of you. But now, I (as your spiritual disciple) will *impetuously* act in an arrogant fashion towards you: overruling your (as SA) covetous treatment of me.
LONGING	**PRESUMPTION**
Previously, I (as your spiritual disciple) have impetuously acted in an arrogant fashion towards you: in response to your (as SA) covetous treatment of me. But now, you (as my humanitarian authority) will covetously act in a *longing* fashion towards me: in anticipation of my (as SD) impetuous treatment of you.	Previously, you (as my humanitarian authority) have covetously acted in a longing fashion towards me: in anticipation of my (as SD) impetuous treatment of you. But now, I (as representative member of humanity) will impetuously act in a *presumptuous* fashion towards you: overruling your (as HA) longing treatment of me.
AFFECTATION	**SMUGNESS**
Previously, I (as representative member of humanity) have impetuously acted in a presumptuous fashion towards you: in response to your (as HA) longing treatment of me. But now, you (as my transcendental authority) will longingly act with *affectation* towards me: in anticipation of my (as RH) presumptuous treatment of you.	Previously, you (as my transcendental authority) have longingly acted with affectation towards me: in anticipation of my (as RH) presumptuous treatment of you. But now, I (as your transcendental follower) will presumptuously act in a *smug* fashion towards you: overruling your (as TA) affectation-filled treatment of me.

Table F-3 – The Definitions Based Upon Envy/Impudence

DISDAIN	INSOLENCE
Previously, I (as procurer) have exces-sively acted compliantly towards you: in response to your (as reinforcer) extremely worrisome treatment of me. But now, you (as my personal authority) will *disdainfully* act in an extremely worrisome fashion towards me: in anticipation of my (as procurer) excessively compliant treatment of you.	Previously, you (as my personal authority) have disdainfully acted in an extremely worrisome fashion towards me: in anticipation of my (as procurer) excessively compliant treatment of you. But now, I (as personal follower) will *insolently* act in an extremely compliant fashion towards you: overruling your (as PA) disdainful treatment of me.
CONTEMPT	**AUDACITY**
Previously, I (as your personal follower) have insolently acted extremely compli-antly towards you: in response to your (as PA) disdainful treatment of me. But now, you (as my group authority) will disdainfully act *contemptuously* towards me: in anticipation of my (as PF) insolent treatment of you.	Previously, you (as my group authority) have disdainfully acted contemptuously towards me: in anticipation of my (as PF) insolent treatment of you. But now, I (as group representative) will insolently act in an *audacious* fashion towards you: overruling your (as GA) contemptuous treatment of me.
REPROACH	**RASHNESS**
Previously, I (as group representative) have insolently acted in an audacious fashion towards you: in response to your (as GA) contemptuous treatment of me. But now, you (as my spiritual authority) will contemptuously act with *reproach* towards me: in anticipation of my (as GR) audacious treatment of you.	Previously, you (as my spiritual authority) have contemptuously acted with reproach towards me: in anticipation of my (as GR) audacious treatment of you. But now, I (as your spiritual disciple) will audaciously act in a *rash* fashion towards you: overruling your (as SA) contemptuous sense of reproach.
CHAGRIN	**BOLDNESS**
Previously, I (as your spiritual disciple) have audaciously acted in a rash fashion towards you: in response to (as SA) contemptuous sense of reproach. But now, you (as my humanitarian authority) will reproachfully act with *chagrin* towards me: in anticipation of my (as SD) rash treatment of you.	Previously, you (as my humanitarian authority) have reproachfully acted with chagrin towards me: in anticipation of my (as SD) rash treatment of you. But now, I (as representative member of humanity) will rashly act in a *bold* fashion towards you: overruling your (as HA) chagrined treatment of me.
BITTERNESS	**HARSHNESS**
Previously, I (as representative member of humanity) have rashly acted in a bold fashion towards you: in response to your (as HA) chagrined treatment of me. But now, you (as my transcendental authority) will *bitterly* act in a chagrined fashion towards me: in anticipation of my (as RH) bold treatment of you.	Previously, you (as my transcendental authority) have bitterly acted in a chagrined fashion towards me: in anticipation of my (as RH) bold treatment of you. But now, I (as your transcendental follower) will boldly act in a *harsh* fashion towards you: overruling your (as TA) bitter sense of chagrin.

Table F- 4 – The Definitions Based Upon Disdain/Insolence

mockery, and cynicism. A similar pattern further holds true for the remaining pair of sequences for the vices of excess, as a cursory examination of **Fig. 15A** adequately serves to indicate. The precise selection of terms for the most abstract levels within the hierarchy of excess, however, definitely remains a work in progress, an avenue open to much further research within the field.

THE SCHEMATIC DEFINITIONS
FOR THE VICES OF EXCESS

One of the most significant applications for the entire ten-level hierarchy of excess concerns its affiliated incorporation into the respective schematic definition format, as depicted in tabular format spanning **Tables F-1** to **F-4**. This four-part sequence of tables is identical in form and function to that previously established for the virtuous mode in Chapter *2*. This crucial innovation spells out in longhand the precise location of each term within the linguistic matrix while simultaneously preserving the proper orientation of the respective authority/follower roles. Each definition is formally constructed along the lines of a two-stage sequential format; namely (A) the preliminary power maneuver initially employed, and (B) the counter-maneuver currently under consideration; and hence, labeled. For instance, according to **Table F-1**, the vainful sense of pride expressed by the group authority figure represents

the preliminary power maneuver, whereby prompting the potential flattering sense of adulation on the part of the group representative. According to this two-stage schematic format, power leverage is achieved by rising to a "one-up" power status; namely, ascending to the next higher meta-perspectival level. Consequently, at each succeeding level, a new term (distinguished through *italics*) is introduced into the schematic definition format specifying the power tactic currently under consideration.

Although the precision of the definitions in relation to excess scarcely equals that previously established for the virtuous mode, one nevertheless gains a clear impression of the complementary interplay of the authority and follower roles across the board. The remainder of the current section examines the individual motivational terms for the realm of excess over a much greater degree of detail. Chapter *16* examines the procurement-based realm of excess targeting pride/flattery, followed by those that expand upon shame/criticism. Chapter *17*, in turn, examines the reinforcement-based realm of excess expanding upon envy/impudence and disdain/insolence. Consequently, the current motivational analysis of the realm of excess represents an unprecedented contribution to the field of ethical inquiry, effectively presenting the ideal concept of moderation and self-control in contrast to the extreme realm of excess.

16

THE VICES OF EXCESS – PART ONE

The detailed description of the vices of excess is currently launched with respect to an in-depth examination of the procurement-based realm of affective terms; namely, the sequence based upon pride/flattery followed by that targeting shame/criticism. As stated in the preceding chapter, the current section endeavors to describe the reciprocating realm of excess spanning the personal, group, spiritual, humanitarian, and transcendental levels within the ethical hierarchy. This discussion of the individual vices of excess employs a slightly different strategy than that which has gone before; namely, outlining the ascending hierarchy of authority and follower roles in an alternating pattern of presentation. Consequently, the authority sequence of pride, vanity, conceitedness, pretentiousness, and sanctimony effectively complements the remaining follower series of flattery, adulation, patronization, obsequiousness, and sycophancy. A similar pattern further holds true with respect to the remaining authority/follower sequences linking shame-humiliation-mortification-anguish-tribulation and criticism-ridicule-scorn-mockery-cynicism. The dedicated reader is encouraged to refer back to the four-page listing of schematic definitions for the vices of excess depicted in the preceding chapter in order to gain a broader context for each of the individual terms.

PRIDE

The first-mentioned vice of *pride* represents the extreme counterpart of the immediately-active sense of solicitousness expressed by the personal authority figure. Although solicitousness implies an active acknowledgement of personal achievement, pride alternately specifies deliberately acting excessively therein. The personal authority figure pridefully acts excessively solicitously in anticipation of the flatteringly treatment on the

part of the personal follower figure. Traditionally counted among the Seven Deadly Sins, pride is defined as excessive feelings of personal excellence. St. Thomas Aquinas (in deference to the teachings of St. Gregory) singled-out pride as the most grievous of all of the seven deadly sins. Vanity, affectation, and pretentiousness are commonly cited as close synonyms of pride, a theme well placed to serve inordinately excessive aims.

Pride is traditionally identified as the specific cause for Satan's fall from grace. As originally created, Lucifer was regarded as the most powerful archangel serving God's throne as a guardian cherub. His name refers to his status as an unparalleled "angel of light." The lesser angels marveled at his unparalleled status in Heaven. Lucifer eventually claimed to be worthy of equal status with the most-high God (Ezekiel 28:14-17). Too proud to accept God's authority, Lucifer was summarily cast from Heaven in concert with the other angels that were seduced by such treachery. Consequently Lucifer became the chief adversary of the goodness and welfare for humanity in the process. His proud assertions took root in the seeds of flattery sown by the remaining fallen angels, eventually resulting in an all-consuming sense of vanity. The extremes of self-obsession associated with pride represent a personal degree of magnification instrumental to driving the detrimental effects of the other vices. As such it represents the archetypal vice for the realm of excess, an ever-present bane to the range of cooperation underlying all human endeavors.

FLATTERY

The preliminary personal authority theme of pride, in turn, is countered (in a follower sense) with respect to the excessive theme of *flattery*.

Here the personal follower *flatteringly* acts extremely approvingly in response to the prideful perspective of the personal authority figure. The term derives from the Old French *flater* (to flatter), originally "to stroke with the hand, to caress," from the Frankish *flat* (the palm of the hand). It typically signifies the verbal strokes that accompany such an overt style of flattering strategy.

A clear distinction further exists between simple encouragement and flattery. The Greek equivalent for flattery, *kolakeria*, denotes motives of a self-serving nature. Indeed, those employing flattery generally expect some potential for favorable treatment in return. Some are encouraged with kind words, although this can frequently gradeover into flattery: ultimately compounded by overt manipulation and control. The ultimate focus of flattery aims to render another pridefully oblivious to their foibles, or simply deluded and deceived. Great power is therefore driven through such flattering or overweening compliments. The respective personal follower flatteringly exaggerates the merits of his personal authority figure, whereby directly reciprocating the latter's extreme sense of pride.

This reciprocating interplay of both authority and follower roles, in turn, sets the stage for the further group and spiritual levels within the hierarchy of excess. For instance, the prideful perspective of the personal authority, in turn, extends to the vanity expressed by the group authority figure, culminating in the conceitedness inherent to the spiritual authority perspective. Similarly, the flattering demeanor of the personal follower, in turn, sets the stage for the adulation expressed by the group representative, culminating in the patronizing perspectives of the spiritual disciple figure. The upcoming sections aim to describe this reciprocating interplay of vanity/adulation and conceit/patronization, beginning with an in-depth examination of the group authority theme of vanity.

VANITY

The preliminary personal authority theme of pride, in turn, extends to a group sphere of influence with respect to the more socially-driven theme of *vanity*. The term derives from the Latin *vanus* (empty), signifying the marginal degree of truth accompanying such vain pretensions. Indeed, the notion of vanity (or vanities) occurs as a common theme throughout scripture. The term commonly refers to a sense of evanescence, emptiness, or wickedness: not only in terms of pridefulness, but also vain or empty things. The chief spelling for vanity (or vanities) is *hebhel* (a breath of air, as from the mouth), generally referring to one's exalted pretensions or wealth/treasure (Proverbs 13:11, 21:6). In Ecclesiastes, the word occurs in various contexts, a theme succinctly summed up as: "Vanity of vanities, all is vanity" (Ecclesiastes 1:2, 12:8).

In a more contemporary sense, this theme figures prominently in historical accounts of the Bonfire of the Vanities (Italian: Falò delle Vanità) that occurred on February 7, 1497. Followers of Girolamo Savonarola collected and publicly burned thousands of art objects in Florence, Italy during its Shrove Tuesday celebration. The focus of this destruction concerned objects considered prideful, including vanity items such as mirrors, cosmetics, fine clothing, and even musical instruments. Other targets included immoral books, manuscripts of secular songs, playing cards, and paintings. Indeed, several paintings depicting classical mythology by Botticelli were torched, personally throwing them into the bonfire. This enduring conflict between virtue and excess solidifies vanity's reputation as perhaps one of the most debilitating of the vices of excess, extending the personal prerequisites of pride into a group sphere of influence. Here, the civic overtones of vanity come through the clearest, although now targeting a range of extremes within a public sphere of influence.

As initially suggested, the prideful sense of vanity expressed by the group authority figure actively initiates this realm of excess, directly expressed as an extreme sense of glory: whereby anticipating the flattering-adulation inherent to the group representative. Being that only one role is active within the conditioned interaction at any given time, the latter eventuality is alternately expressed as the flattering-adulation professed by the group follower figure.

ADULATION

The group authority attributes for vanity, in turn, are countered (in a follower sense) by the flattering *adulation* expressed by the group representative. The group representative flatteringly acts with adulation towards his group authority figure in response to the latter's vain sense of pride. It represents the excessive counterpart of the respective cardinal virtue of prudence. Its modern spelling derives from the Latin *adulari* or *adulatus* (to fawn upon), from *ad-* (to) and *ulos* (tail): originally denoting the sense of "to wag the tail." In an affiliated social sense, it denotes a fawning ex-

Vain-Glory (Personified) – Detail from an Italian Fresco attributed to Giotto
Depicted in *De Viris Illustribus* by Francesco Petrarch, circa 1350

pression of flattery towards a public figure: as in excessive admiration or devotion in a servile fashion. According to British poet George Gordon Byron: "The reason that adulation is not displeasing is that it shows one to be of consequence enough to induce people to deceive." The professed content of adulation is typically exaggerated to some degree, this range of extremes proves consistent with its group status within the realm of excess. This somewhat amusing interplay of vanity and adulation remains a common theme in the genre of comedy, although extending to a tragic context when such contrived strategies ultimately take a turn for the worse.

CONCEITEDNESS

This completed description of the group interplay of vanity/adulation, in turn, sets the stage for the universal domain of conceit/patronization. The smug sense of *conceit* expressed by the spiritual authority figure directly extends the trend previously established for pride and vanity. Conceit is typically defined as an overweening sense of self-esteem, as in an overly high opinion of oneself.

The term derives from the Old French *conceiven* (conceive), from the Latin *conceptum*, from *con-* (together) and *capre* (to take). The originally neutral sense of "something formed in the mind" eventually came to be modified in the 16th century to reflect a "fanciful or witty notion" and (ultimately) a sense of vanity. Indeed, according to American advertising executive, Bruce Barton: "Conceit is God's gift to little men."

In an overarching literary sense, a *conceit* is defined as fanciful or far-fetched imagery: where apparently dissimilar themes actually share a common theme, as in a whimsical metaphor. This exaggerated context for conceit is further preserved in its most basic relationship sense, where the spiritual authority vainly acts *conceitedly* in anticipation of the flattering-adulation expressed by the spiritual follower figure. The extreme hyperbole associated with conceit is consistent with such a universal sphere of influence: where conceitedness claims relevance within some romanticized style of worldview. Consequently, conceitedness consummates the trend previously established for the subordinate themes of pride and vanity, a common feature in many enduring mirthful forms of comedic entertainment that virtually define our modern culture.

PATRONIZATION

The spiritual authority focus for conceit, in turn, redirects the focus to the respective follower counter-maneuver; namely, the *patronizing* treatment expressed by the spiritual disciple figure. This patronizing perspective represents a more abstract variation on the subordinate themes of flattery and adulation, although now extending to a universal sphere of influence. The term derives from the Latin *patronus*, from *pater* or *patris* (father): a derivation suggestive of the elaborate system of patronage popular during the Italian Renaissance. The rich patron welcomed an artist into his house in exchange for the fruits of his artistic talents. Indeed, Leonardo da Vinci spent much of his career under the privilege of court patronage.

Three main motives drove the patronage of the arts; namely, piety, prestige, and pleasure. Art patronage played prominent public relations role for secular rulers, whereby promoting high social status. Indeed, a career in the arts proved a grueling undertaking aside from the advantages of such patronage. The great economic prosperity enjoyed by the Florentines encouraged merchants and bankers to aspire to the prestige associated with art patronage. Eager to display their enlightened status in terms of piety, taste, and learning, the Medici family spent lavishly on religious art, and the support of charities. The Medicis directly benefited from such a lofty arrangement, effectively advertising their wealth and prestige to the Renaissance community.

Although the noble aspirations of patronage prove relatively innocuous in terms of intent, this theme, nevertheless, shares many commonalties with the subordinate themes of flattery and adulation, particularly when cynically acting self-servingly in order to achieve the desired agenda. More recent connotations of the term suggest an overarching sense of condescension or smugness in one's dealings with others, particularly in a haughty or arrogant fashion. Here patronization continues in the excessive follower tradition of the manipulative, self-serving sycophant, although now extending to a more abstract (universal) sphere of influence. Consequently, the patronizing individual assumes an arrogant sense of superiority, although now chiefly tolerated in terms of the deviously deceptive fashion through which it is carried out.

PRETENTIOUSNESS

The completed description of the individual terms spanning the personal, group, and universal levels, in turn, sets the stage for a discussion of the remaining humanitarian and transcendental levels with respect to the hierarchy of excess. In contrast to the strict organizational status of the first three levels, the final two levels are alternately distinguished as purely abstract styles of perspectives. The humanitarian authority level derives its status from the abstract addition of *historical* time, whereas the transcendental realm makes reference to the realm of *pure* transcendence.

The profoundly abstract nature of these remaining two levels is further reflected in their abstract groupings for the vices of excess. For instance, the initial authority sequence of pride-vanity-conceit, in turn, extends to a humanitarian sphere of influence with respect to the excessive theme of *pretentiousness*. This term derives from the Latin *praetendere*, from *prae* (before) and *tensum* (to stretch): signifying that stretch of the truth that typically accompanies such ostentatious displays. It typically refers to an offensively condescending attitude, as in projecting the appearance of distinction or superiority over others in a social context. This proves particularly apparent with respect to bombastic political figures that aspire to appear truly larger than life.

Pretentiousness can also apply to an artificial sense of self-esteem, a factor that typically fails to correlate with the true value of one's achievements (whether implied or claimed). Such exaggerated self-esteem is often exhibited by dictators, gang-leaders, or similar such types of narcissistic individuals. In many circumstances, pretentiousness can readily be distinguished by the lack of integrity linking both word and deed. Objective reasoning is similarly impaired, leading to wishful thinking or delusional fantasies. Although the haughty individual tends to portray a grand persona, their true lot in life often fails to match the majesty of their pretensions.

SANCTIMONY

The preceding humanitarian sense of pretentiousness, in turn, extends to a crowning transcendental sphere of influence with respect to the related theme of *sanctimony*. The term derives from the Middle French *sanctimonie*, from Latin *sanctimonia* (holiness, virtuousness), from *sanctus* (holy). Its respective Latin root-stem is consistent with its original 16th century English connotation of holiness or saintliness. By the early 17th century, however, it came to suggest "hypocritical holiness," as mentioned in Shakespeare's *Measure for Measure* (in a disparaging sense). In modern times it has pejoratively acquired the sense of "vainly saintly or pretentiously holy," as in hypocritical religious devotion or righteous sanctimony.

These vain characteristics of sanctimony embody an extreme degree of self-importance, culminating (in a transcendental sense) the preliminary sequence of pride, vanity, conceitedness, and pretentiousness. Although such a bold assertion is undoubtedly fraught with alternate interpretations, the overall sense of sanctimony appears particularly well suited to the task, and one destined to remain in vogue until a better option comes to light.

OBSEQUIOUSNESS

The completed description of the extreme authority roles of pretentiousness and sanctimony, in turn, redirects the current focus to the remaining sequence of follower themes; namely, the ascending sequence of obsequiousness and sycophancy targeting the humanitarian and transcendental domains, respectively. For instance, the first-mentioned theme of *obsequiousness* traces its origins to the Latin *obsequiosus* (compliant, obedient), from *obsequium* (compliance, dutiful service): from *ob-* (after) and *sequi* (follow), suggesting an extremely fawning demeanor. The English pejorative sense of "fawning sycophant" dates to the 17th century, in reference to the self-seeking, servile flatterer or fawning parasite. Synonyms of a slang nature include yes-man, flunky, or toady. Sir Walter Raleigh similarly writes about flatterers: "It is hard to know them from friends, they are so *obsequious* and full of protestations; for as a wolf resembles a dog, so doth a flatterer a friend."

In direct analogy to the ascending sequence of flattery, adulation, and patronization: obsequiousness represents more of an enduring style of personality trait than any immediately-active behavior pattern: a factor consistent with its proposed inclusion into a humanitarian sphere of influence. As such, it is provisionally assigned this extreme level of placement within the hierarchy of excess, at least until a better alternative can be found.

SYCOPHANCY

The preceding humanitarian focus of obsequiousness, in turn, redirects the current focus to the proposed transcendental theme of *sycophancy*. The term derives from the Greek *sykophantes*, traditionally referring to an individual who informed on those exporting figs from Attica, as well as those that plundered the sacred fig trees. It possibly also referred to one who gathers figs by shaking the tree; hence, one who encourages a rich man give up his goods through such persistent fawning overtures. Indeed, this particular derivation traces its origins to the Greek *sykon* (fig) and *phainein* (to show). As such, sycophancy continues the general theme of the fawning follower perspective encompassing the subordinate ascending sequence of flattery, adulation, patronization, and obsequiousness. Whether sycophancy truly warrants such a crowning transcendental placement remains open to debate, although its culmination of the overall follower sequence would appear warranted at this juncture.

THE SUBMISSIVE-BASED PERSPECTIVES SPECIFIED FOR SHAME/CRITICISM

The completed description of the vices of excess based upon pride/flattery further sets the stage for the related interplay of shame and criticism. This latter format alternately specifies the critical expression of blame in response to one's shameful sense of guilt. This extreme motivational dynamic clearly mirrors the vain prerequisites previously established for pride-then-flattery, where flattery counters the pride expressed by the personal authority figure. This reciprocating pattern of authority and follower roles proves similarly applicable with respect to the related interplay of shame and criticism. Here the initial authority sequence of shame, humiliation, mortification, anguish, and tribulation, in turn, prompts the remaining follower sequence of criticism, ridicule, scorn, mockery, and cynicism. Consequently, the extreme interplay of authority and follower roles can accurately be determined with respect to shame and criticism, as further validated through the individual narratives to follow.

SHAME

The first mentioned theme of *shame* represents the extreme motivational analogue for submissiveness. Its modern spelling derives from the Old English *sc(e)amu*, akin to the German *scham*: denoting a disgraced sense of humiliation due to fault or failure. Indeed, Blaise Pascal humorously wrote: "The only shame is to have none!" Here shame represents a moral emotion encompassing evaluative thought, where one believes one is culpable of moral wrong-doing accompanied by the desire to cover up such a moral shortcoming. Shame represents a powerful emotion insofar as it implies an irreparable sense of harm done to another, in addition to recognition of blame for such a reprehensible action. It is traditionally denotes extreme culpability or blameworthiness in a personal sense. Consequently, actions of an unintentional nature typically cannot serve as the basis for any personal sense of shame.

Shame is clearly distinguished from its close relation to embarrassment. Unlike shame, embarrassment is less concerned with social mores, rather targeting the perception that one has done something silly or out of character, accompanied by the desire to undo such a blunder. Consequently, shame represents an extreme variation on the guilty sense of submissiveness expressed by personal authority figure, particularly in terms of an interpersonal sphere of influence. The personal authority now shamefully acts in an extremely submissive fashion in anticipation of the critical treatment from the personal follower figure. The extreme degree of emotion typically associated with shame can prove particularly debilitating if chronic in nature, when left untreated can lead to motivations of an extremely self-destructive nature.

CRITICISM

The personal prerequisites for shame, in turn, are reciprocated (in a follower sense) through the related theme of *criticism*. This latter perspective is assumed by the personal follower figure, critically acting in an extremely blameful fashion in response to the shameful treatment of the personal authority. Its modern spelling derives from the Greek *kritikos*, from *krinein* (to judge): denoting censure or harsh judgment, or finding fault with. These connotations suggest an extreme sense of lenient-blamefulness on the part of the personal follower consistent with criticism's inclusion amongst the vices of excess.

In an alternate sense, the professional critic, deriving from the Greek *krites* (judge), offers cogent critical judgments relating the performance or work of others (as in art, music, and the theatre). These critics specialize within a particular field, typically publishing their reviews for the education of others. Consequently, constructive criticism encompasses valid and well-reasoned opinions within the state of the art, supposedly including both positive and negative evaluations. Criticism provides a valuable tool for raising and maintaining performance standards, although a tendency towards self-aggrandizement can lead to a negative focus. Indeed, British lexicographer, Samuel Johnson once scathingly wrote: "Criticism is a study by which men grow important and formidable at very small expense."

This extreme interplay of shame and criticism, in turn, sets the stage for a related discussion of the group and spiritual levels within the hierarchy of excess. For instance, the *shamefulness* expressed by the personal authority, in turn, anticipates the *humiliation* professed by the group authority figure, culminating in the *mortification* characterizing a universal sphere of influence. Furthermore, the *criticism* expressed by the personal follower, in turn, extends to the *ridicule* bestowed by the group representative, culminating in the *scornfulness* anticipated from the spiritual disciple figure. The remaining two sections examine this dual interplay based upon shame and criticism, beginning with the group realm of humiliation/ridicule, followed by the spiritual realm of excess targeting mortification/scorn.

HUMILIATION

The first-mentioned theme within the group authority realm, *humiliation*, is defined as an extreme sense of shamefulness chiefly in a public or social setting. The term derives from the Latin *humiliare*, from *humilis* (low), from *humus* (earth): a figurative allusion to such deeply humble origins. Humiliation represents an inherently unpleasant emotion concerned with a lack of social status. It traditionally invokes the negative belief that one's standing has diminished in the eyes of the community due to actions not befitting one's public standing, accompanied by the desire to reinstate one's favorable status. It can further imply an undue sense of self-importance, being that those that feel humiliated place an inordinate emphasis on their personal self-image, effectively downplaying the significance of those around them.

Humiliation includes the intent to harm the feelings of another, a morally reprehensible action. Indeed, American psychologist, Paul Ekman succinctly states: "The *humiliation* of shame requires disapproval or ridicule by others. If no one ever learns of a misdeed, there can be no shame, but there still might be guilt. Of course, both may occur together." As the extreme variation on the honorably-submissive treatment on the part of the group authority, humiliation similarly expands upon the personal prerequisites previously established for shame, whereby paralleling the pattern previously established for pride/vanity.

RIDICULE

The shameful sense of humiliation experienced by the group authority, in turn, sets the stage for the follower maneuver proper; namely, the critical sense of *ridicule* professed by the group representative. The term derives from the Latin *ridiculus*, from *ridere* (to laugh): denoting speech or behavior intended to provoke contemptuous laughter, particularly in a taunting or derisive fashion. Consequently, ridicule figures prominently in the time-honored tradition of social satire. As many a sage has noted: "Ridicule is the test of truth." Furthermore, Roman commentator, Horace once wrote: "Ridicule often settles things more thoroughly and better than acrimony." Napoleon Bonaparte similarly quips: "There is only one step from the sublime to the ridiculous."

This enduring emphasis on the ludicrous is fittingly associated with ridicule: defined as that which is worthy of ridicule: as in a sense of the absurd, the preposterous, or the laughable. According to American humorist, Samuel Clemens: "There is no character, howsoever good and fine: but it can be destroyed by ridicule, howsoever poor and witless." Here ridicule extends the personal prerequisites for criticism into a broader civic sphere of influence, as the group attributes for the term adequately serve to indicate. Whether any constructive benefit results from ridicule remains irrelevant to such a discussion, for ridicule will always dwell within the unsavory realm encompassing the vices of excess.

MORTIFICATION

The completed description of the group domain of excess (e.g., humiliation and ridicule), in turn, extends to the respective universal counterparts of mortification and scornfulness. In a direct analogy to the interplay of shame and humiliation, mortification is typically defined as the control the passions through severe discipline or penance, as suggested in trials of humiliation. The term derives from the Latin *mortificare* (to cause death to), from *mortis* (death) and *facere* (to make): alluding to the restraint of the passions in order to make amends for past grievous deeds.

In terms of the early Christian tradition, mortification overcomes the temptation to sin by freely accepting physical hardships rather than yielding to temptation. In a deeper spiritual sense, such outward displays of penance are beneficial insofar as mirroring the internal mortification of one's prideful nature in all of its various manifestations.

Consistent with such religious traditions, mortification is viewed as an extremely submissive style of spiritual authority perspective: effectively complementing the ascending authority sequence of shame and humiliation. As such, mortification encompasses a much broader range of themes than its subordinate counterparts, particularly when expressed in outward forms of extreme penance. Indeed, mortification revels in such extreme themes of intense spiritual submission, the extent of which has been moderated somewhat within our modern age.

SCORN

The preceding discussion of mortification, in turn, sets the stage for the related style of follower counter-maneuver; namely, the *scornful* sense of ridicule expressed by the spiritual disciple. Scorn represents an extreme variation on the lenient prerequisites previously established for hope. The term derives from the Old French *escarn* (mockery, derision, contempt), from Old High German *skern* (mockery, jest, sport), from Proto-Germanic *skarnjan* (to mock, to deride). Scorn is typically distinguished from its related synonyms of mockery or derision: both of which more specifically refer to the outward means by which scorn is expressed. Consequently, scorn denotes a more subjective style of verbal reaction. It also can include overtones of superiority, resentment, and aversion.

Scorn certainly appears to be a much hotter/fiercer emotion than disdain or contempt. As such, it shares with its subordinate counterparts in criticism and ridicule an overtly biting style of verbal response, although presumably extending to a universal sphere of influence. Scorn seems to transcend the more partisan concerns of criticism and ridicule, effectively targeting themes of a universal significance. Indeed, the most salient feature of scorn is precisely such a far-reaching emphasis on opprobrium, wherein disparaging the foibles governing human nature. Fortunately, the modern trend towards political correctness finds ready acceptance of public scorn, an aspect not quite as welcome as characterizing simpler times.

ANGUISH

The completed description of the extreme range of terms spanning the personal, group, and spiritual levels further sets the stage for the remaining humanitarian and transcendental realms with respect to the vices of excess. The profoundly abstract nature of these final two levels is reflected in the similarly abstract listings of vices. For instance, the initial authority sequence of shame-humiliation-mortification, in turn, extends to a humanitarian sphere of influence with respect to the extreme theme of *anguish*. The term derives from the Latin *agnustia* (straight or straightness), from *ang(u)ere* (to press tightly, to strangle). It signifies an extreme sense of pain or mortification, as in an expression of penance.

Agony denotes extreme emotional distress: as in excruciating internal suffering, also extending to grief, remorse, or despair. This theme occurs in the Old Testament as *tsuq* (straitened, pressed), or *tsar* and its derivatives (straightness, narrowness), whereby denoting pressure or distress. This theme also extends to the New Testament *thlipsis* (a pressing together): as in affliction or tribulation. The common theme suggests one of pressure, as in straitening or compression consistent with painfulness through the infliction of mental distress.

Regardless of the individual traditions therein, anguish provisionally suggests a range of themes targeting the humanitarian sphere of influence, whereby expanding upon the spiritual connotations of mortification. Anguish is most frequently refers to contexts specifying enduring suffering: as in the trials and tribulations associated with bondage or the agony of a lingering illness. Here anguish continues in the tradition previously established for its subordinate sequence of terms: namely, shame, humiliation, and mortification. Consequently, anguish represents a considerable cross to bear, even though the underlying ideology spans the course of many generations.

TRIBULATION

The preceding humanitarian focus of anguish ultimately extends to the crowning transcendental theme of *tribulation*. The term derives from the Latin *tribulatum* (to afflict), from *tribulum* (a sledge for rubbing-out grain), from *terere* (to rub): whereby signifying an abrasive sense of affliction, trial, or hardship. Old Testament scripture denotes a sense of being closely pressed: as in seals (Job 41:15), or streams pent up (Isaiah 59:9), or the limitation of strength (Proverbs 24). These various contexts share the general figurative connotation of tight circumstances rendered as affliction or distress. The term also refers to the hardships Christ's disciples would suffer (Matthew 13:21; 24:9). In this extreme sense, tribulation represents the supreme culmination of the trend previously established

for shame, humiliation, mortification, and anguish. Indeed, whether tribulation truly warrants its transcendental placement remains an issue open to debate, although clearly the leading contender in this regard.

MOCKERY

The completed description of the preliminary authority sequence of anguish and tribulation, in turn, sets the stage for the remaining sequence of follower roles; namely, mockery and cynicism targeting the humanitarian/transcendental domains, respectively. For instance, the humanitarian follower theme of *mockery* derives from the Middle French *mocquer* (to deride, jeer), presumably from the Vulgar Latin *muccare* (to blow one's nose in a derisive gesture), from the Latin *mucus*. The English spelling is said to derive from the Middle Dutch *mocken* (to mumble), or the Middle Low German *mucken* (to grumble). The affiliated notion of imitation (as in a mocking-bird, mock-up, etc.) derives from such derisive imitation.

Accordingly, mockery represents a prominent theme in the field of literary satire, a technique effective for ridiculing the powerful and elite. Mockery generally employs exaggeration or irony to spotlight the flaws or shortcomings of others. Although disdain and contempt similarly work well in satire, the satirist's most powerful tools extend to wit and humor that borders upon the ridiculous. Samuel Clemens fittingly notes: "Against the assault of laughter nothing can stand." No matter how strongly the satirist feels about the subject, one must entertain the audience, not preach to it.

Satirists from classical times include the Greek playwright Aristophanes, as well as the Roman satirists Juvenal and Horace. The Age of Enlightenment further produced English satirists such as Pope, Dryden, and Swift; as well as the French satirists Moliére and Voltaire. Satire employs a fusion of humor and contempt in order to censure the incongruities of vice and folly. Hence, the more enduring sense of the term specifies mockery as the uniquely humanitarian variation on the subordinate sequence of criticism, ridicule, and scorn. Consequently, the satirical nature of mockery has remained a powerful tool for social reform down through the ages, although one scarcely in danger of abating anytime soon!

CYNICISM

The preceding humanitarian theme of mockery, in turn, further extends to the affiliated transcendental theme of *cynicism*. The term derives from the Greek *kynikos* (literally dog-like), from *kynos* (dog). It presumably traces its origins to the *Kynosarge* (Grey Dog): the name of the gymnasium in ancient Athens where the founder of classical Cynicism, Antisthenes, preached the tenets of his movement. This discipline includes many later contributors, of which Diogenes is most widely cited. Cynicism is defined as that attitude or tendency to view the beliefs or abilities of others in a negative or sarcastic light.

Cynical judgments can be justified in many cases; particularly chronic misbehaviors, mistakes, or unethical conduct. The cynic may intuitively grasp the limitations of others, although remain oblivious to the potential for remediation. For the typical cynic, a given judgment remains irrevocable without the potential for revision. This cynical sense of inflexibility can prove toxic to the development of creative or synergistic solutions to problems. Indeed, the cynic avoids putting-forth any authentic effort, whereby employing narrow-minded beliefs as an excuse for inactivity. Here cynicism embodies an overarching sense of satire and light-hearted ridicule, whereby effectively rounding out the ascending sequence of criticism-ridicule-scorn-mockery, and now, cynicism.

In conclusion, the completed description of the procurement-based perspectives for the vices of excess provides a preliminary indication of their overall range of influence. Indeed, it proves a fitting tribute to the considerable scope of the English-language tradition that such an elaborate vocabulary exists for the vices of excess. This ten-level domain of excess represents an unprecedented addition to the field of ethical inquiry, an innovation on par with the parallel hierarchy for the vices of defect. In concert with the overarching virtuous hierarchy that contrasts with these two basic categories of vice, Aristotle's enduring theory of the virtuous-mean finally reaches its conceptual completion.

This major breakthrough in ethical theory permits unprecedented inroads into diagnosing dysfunctional relationships in terms of encouraging a timely course of intervention. Although

scarcely as dysfunctional as the darker realm of the vices of defect, the vices of excess, nevertheless, are plagued by their own distinctive range of shortcomings. Indeed, this domain of excess exhibits the tendency to escalate tensions within the overall communicational dynamic: whereby increasing the potential for misunderstandings that can lead to conflict or violence. For example, the extreme vices of pride and vanity are deserving of their deadly reputations. Although not conflict producing in their own right, any subsequent decrease in the anticipated adulation may lead to feelings of resentment or spite. In a parallel sense, the darker emotions of shame and humiliation are similarly liable to misunderstandings that can lead to prolonged despondency or personal vendettas.

These specific examples prove the rule (rather than the exception) concerning relations on the international stage. Indeed, countries have become mortal enemies based upon the slightest of misperceptions, not infrequently escalating into seething hostilities or warfare. It is common wisdom to assume that this extreme range of excess can lead to unforeseen negative consequences; hence, the timeworn etiquette of established protocol. The newly devised terminology for the vices of excess provides a powerful new tool for detecting and diagnosing dysfunctional communication before any crucial threshold can be breached. Granted the extreme antics professed by the pundits and politicos provoke their fair share of media exposure and public fascination. Although the boundaries governing acceptable conduct will always remain somewhat of a balancing act, the concerted effort towards measured improvements in social mores should always be a worthy of praise and aspiration.

Through the aid of the newly proposed terminology for the vices of excess, hopefully the public may gain a more profound insight into how their sentiments are manipulated in such a crass fashion through public notoriety. Only then will public welfare be more adequately safeguarded, perhaps even presaging a return to simpler times: when measured and respectful behavior was an asset to be cultivated and treasured.

17

THE VICES OF EXCESS – PART TWO

The completed description of the preliminary procurement-based realm for the vices of excess, in turn, sets the stage for a discussion of the remaining reinforcement-based sequence of terms. For the most basic personal level within the hierarchy of excess, this amounts to envy in anticipation of impudence or disdainfulness in expectation of insolence. This reciprocating sequence of terms, in turn, extends to the remaining group, spiritual, humanitarian, and transcendental levels as well, serving as the elementary foundation for the remainder of the chapter to follow.

The current chapter employs a stepwise-strategy similar to that encompassing the previous chapter; namely, an ascending hierarchy of authority and follower roles in a reciprocating pattern of presentation. The preliminary authority sequence of envy-jealousy-covetousness-longing-affection, in turn, anticipates the remaining follower sequence of impudence, arrogance, impetuosity, presumptuousness, and smugness. Furthermore, the darker authority sequence of disdain-contempt-reproach-chagrin-bitterness, in turn, prompts the remaining follower sequence of insolence-audacity-rashness-boldness-harshness. The dedicated reader is encouraged to refer back to the four-page listing of schematic definitions for the vices of excess outlined in Chapter *15* in order to gain a broader context for each of the individual terms.

ENVY

In terms of the most basic personal level for the realm of excess, the first-mentioned theme of *envy* represents the extreme motivational counterpart of the virtuous theme of desire. Indeed, desire was previously described as a reinforcing perspective that anticipates future aspiring treatment on the part of the follower figure, a factor that envy magnifies to an extreme degree. Its modern spelling derives from the French *envie*, from the Latin *invidia*, a compound of *in-* (on) and *videre* (to look). It denotes a grudging or jealous attitude, particularly in terms of the well-being or success of another. According to the medieval tradition, envy is listed among the Seven Deadly Sins, also alluded to as "the green-eyed monster." Envy generally entails a belief that something (or someone) of value rightfully belongs to oneself, accompanied by the desire to procure one's object of passion. A primary reason that envy is listed amongst the vices of excess is that it presupposes greed, a theme further suggestive of covetousness and pride. Greedy people tend to pursue more than their fair share of resources within the community. They can also appear ungrateful for what they actually possess, while showing little respect for others. Envy can similarly imply a sense of larceny when outwardly acted upon.

In slightly different terms, you (as personal authority) now enviously act in an extremely desirous fashion towards me in anticipation of my (as personal follower) impudent treatment of you within a future-directed time-frame. Note that the immediately-active personal authority enviously seeks the future-based validation of the personal follower figure as the potential rationale for such an extremely rewarding style of perspective.

IMPUDENCE

In terms of the preceding envy perspective, the subsequent follower role, in turn, is specified through the extremely aspiring sense of *impudence*. Its modern spelling derives from the Latin compound of *im-* (not) and *pudere* (to be ashamed), denoting a shameless sense of boldness or effrontery. Other synonyms include insolence and impertinence. British society figure, Lady Montague once wrote: "I don't say it is impossible for an impudent man to rise in the world, but a moderate merit with a large share of impudence is more probable to be advanced than the greatest qualifications without it." According to this two-stage motivational dynamic, the personal authority enviously acts in an extremely desirous fashion in anticipation of the impudently-extreme aspirations on the part of the personal follower figure. The familiar example of the disrespectful pupil, who impudently acts sarcastically towards his schoolmaster, is one that perhaps we have all encountered. Its extreme prerequisites typically border upon the absurd, although scarcely so much as for the target of the tactic. This extremely solicitous attitude underlying impudence often remains its saving grace, for a swift scolding is usually sufficient to restore the initial status quo.

This extreme interplay of envy and impudence, in turn, sets the stage for the remaining group and spiritual levels within the hierarchy of excess. For instance, the envy expressed by the personal authority, in turn, extends to the jealousy implicit to the group domain, followed by the covetousness specified for the universal realm. In a similar follower fashion, the impudence expressed by the personal follower extends to the arrogance specified for the group representative, culminating in the impetuosity characterizing the spiritual disciple: as extensively outlined within the following sections of this chapter.

JEALOUSY

The first-mentioned group-focused theme of *jealousy* derives from the Old French *jalous*, from the Latin *zelus*, from the Greek *zelos* (emulation): denoting an envious sense of rivalry. Similar to its close cousin in envy, jealousy is also figuratively referred to as "the green-eyed monster." Unlike envy, jealousy is primarily considered to be a three-party emotion; namely, *A*, (the jealous party) loves *B*, (the party that *A* is jealous over), whereby leading to jealousy in relation to *C* (*A*'s rival for affection that threatens *A*'s favorable status in the eyes of *B*). Jealousy entails the belief that someone rightfully prized by me is now cherished by another. It further specifies that one's desires or wishes are to remain exclusive, with great effort expended to maintain one's favorable status. The fear of losing one's paramour (or ceasing to be loved) is the overarching feature of jealousy, the emblem of romantic love. Those lacking such insecurities rarely feel jealousy. Some view jealousy as highly pathological, whereas others view it as the very proof of love.

Whether favorable or not, the more obsessive qualities of jealousy certainly warrant its firm placement within the realm of excess.

Jealous individuals tend to treat others as mere objects of convenience rather than capable of exercising personal free-will. Jealous individuals tend to assume their wishes take precedent over the needs of others. The jealous lover may stalk the beloved, even escalating into physically harm. Few can ignore the plight of Shakespeare's Othello, whose jealousy stemmed from the false belief that his wife Desdemona had been unfaithful to him, a jealous reaction that proved all too tragically fatal.

Jealousy's "sour" reputation accentuates the selfishness characterizing such possessive motives. In common usage, the statement: "I am jealous of his car" actually implies that one is envious (and wishes to obtain something like it). Envy generally presupposes greed, consistent with the implication that one is dissatisfied with one's own status. Furthermore, envy is primarily a two-party emotion, presupposing neither the desire to be loved, nor the fear of losing favorable status. Consequently, the dichotomy between envy and jealousy is explained in terms of their respective placement within the personal and group realms within the hierarchy of excess.

ARROGANCE

The preceding jealousy perspective, in turn, gives way to the impudent sense of *arrogance* specified for the group follower figure. Here the group representative impudently acts in an arrogant fashion towards one's group authority figure: effectively chiding the latter's envious sense of jealousy. The term derives from the Latin *arrogare* (to claim for oneself), from *ad-* (to) and *rogare* (to ask for or claim). It denotes undue feelings of superiority or self-importance, as in an overbearing sense of vanity. Indeed, the familiar scenario of the arrogant nobleman extends the personal prerequisites of impudence into a group sphere of influence.

The group prerequisites for arrogance are particularly evident in the phrase "arrogance of power," defined as a presumptuous attitude on the part of a powerful nation. Such dominance arrogantly bestows the prerogative to intervene in the affairs of its less powerful neighbors. According to British-born journalist, Sydney J. Harris: "The difference between patriotism and nationalism is that the patriot is proud of his country for what it does, while the nationalist is proud of his country no matter what it does. The first attitude creates a feeling of responsibility, but the second is a

Jealousy (Personified): From *The Devils* (1835) by George Cruikshank - A Series of Six Cartoons

feeling of blind *arrogance* that leads to war." This theme of arrogance (in relation to power) has gained much currency in terms of America's recent series of military incursions within the Middle East. Whether such a bold course of action proves justified is open to debate, as with all such range of extremes, the subsequent balance of power is certain to remain in turmoil for years to come.

In more formal terms, I as group representative impudently act arrogantly towards you in response to your (as group authority) enviously-jealous treatment of me. Indeed, this inherent threat of arrogance ultimately imparts the potential power-leverage enjoyed by the group representative relative to the group authority figure. This impudently-arrogant treatment ultimately provides an effective sense of closure to the entire excessive style of interaction: hence, providing the motivational rationale for further such cycles of extreme arrogance and jealousy.

COVETOUSNESS

The completed description of the group sphere of excess based upon jealousy and arrogance, in turn, sets the stage for the remaining universal counterparts: beginning with the jealous sense of *covetousness* expressed by the spiritual authority figure. The term derives from the Old French *coveitier*, from the Latin *cupiditas* (passion, desire): from *cupidus* (highly desirous), from *cupere* (longing or desire). It is traditionally defined as an illicit desire for that which one does not possess, or the quest for all such objects of desire. This further extends to a covetousness of honors, riches (as in avarice), or lustful pleasure.

Covetousness in terms of wealth or affections takes (as its object) that already in the possession of another, whereby transgressing the Ninth and Tenth Commandments. Such covert desires, when willfully indulged, partake in the illicit expression of the outward deed. Covetousness is typically defined as the inclination to illicitly desire rather than commit any outward deed. Insofar as one endeavors to acquire possessions conducive to one's wellbeing; covetousness can serve as the source of treachery, heartlessness, and unrest. Similar to its preliminary counterparts in envy and jealousy, covetousness represents a subjective emotional propensity. Its outward effects border upon passive spitefulness or sarcasm rather than any prosecutable offense. In terms of such an internally private domain, covetousness remains a vice purely in a subjective sense, only seriously proscribed in terms of its foray into the extreme realm of excess.

IMPETUOSITY

The covetous prerequisites for the spiritual authority figure, in turn, anticipate the respective follower counter-maneuver; namely, the *impetuosity* expressed by the spiritual disciple. Its modern spelling derives from the Latin *impetus* (an attack), from *in-* (into) and *petere* (to seek): suggesting the tendency to act in an impulsive or headlong fashion. Impetuosity refers to hasty choices driven through the influence of instinctual impulses. Some define impetuosity as spontaneity or authenticity, although impetuosity does not typically lead to entirely positive results, often resulting in folly or chaos. This focus on immediate gratification further identifies impetuosity with emotional immaturity. Enduring and worthwhile goals require dedication and commitment, where one learns from both success and failure. Similar to its subordinate counterparts in impudence and arrogance, impetuosity continues in the tradition of such impulsive and outspoken behavior. Consequently, impetuosity enjoys a somewhat favorable cachet when events go well, although failure becoming all too apparent when the tide of events ultimately takes a turn for the worse.

LONGING

The completed description of the vices of excess spanning the personal, group, and spiritual levels, in turn, sets the stage for the remaining humanitarian and transcendental levels within the hierarchy of excess. In contrast to the purely organizational status of the first three levels, the final two levels are further specified as purely abstract styles of power maneuvers. Consequently, the humanitarian realm derives from the abstract addition of "historical" time, whereas the transcendental domain makes an appeal to the realm of "pure" transcendence.

The profoundly abstract nature of these final two levels is further reflected in their respectively abstract groupings within the realm of excess. For instance, the initial sequence of envy-jealousy-covetousness, in turn, extends to a humanitarian sphere of influence with respect to the extreme theme of *longing*. The term derives from the Old English *langian* (to yearn, to appear long), literally "to grow long," from the Proto-Germanic *langojanan*. It denotes a persistent desire or a strong craving, particularly that which is distant or unattainable. According to U.S. poet Robert Hass: "*Longing*, we say, is because desire is full of endless distance." Furthermore, in the words of author James Russell Lowell: "The thing we *long* for, that we are for one transcendent moment." Russian-born U.S. novelist Vladimir Nabokov also describes longing as "nostalgia in reverse."

This latter quotation formally establishes longing as a future-directed emotion in keeping with such lofty passionate perspectives. Indeed, it con-

tinues in the tradition previously established for envy, jealousy, and covetousness: although now provisionally extending to the more enduring humanitarian sphere of influence. Although longing is most closely associated with romantic aspirations, it also can target any strong sense of positive emotion: as in extreme striving for fame, power, or fulfillment. Here longing provisionally satisfies the prerequisites for placement within the humanitarian sphere of excess, although its extreme degree of abstraction does not necessarily preclude any similar potentialities.

AFFECTATION

The preliminary humanitarian focus for longing, in turn, extends to the transcendental authority theme of *affectation*. The term derives from the Latin *affectationem*, from *affectare* (to strive after). It denotes a showy display of false pretense, as in pretending to be what one is not. It can also refer to behavior that lacks natural expression, as in a conspicuously artificial demeanor. By extension, affectation can also suggest particularly eccentric behavioral mannerisms (in speech or dress) adopted to give a false pretense.

This artificial sense of "airs" is often employed in an imitation of undue influence. The latter sense of artificiality or pretense provisionally assigns affectation to the crowning transcendental domain within the hierarchy of excess. Indeed, the transcendental domain is formally defined as an abstract refinement of the more routine range of reality. Consequently, affectation appears far more idealized than the preliminary sequence of terms: namely, envy, jealousy, covetousness, and longing. Indeed, the same root-stem of "affect" serves as the linguistic foundation for affective language in general. Whether affectation truly warrants such a transcendental placement remains a thorny issue, although clearly emerging as the leading contender at this juncture.

PRESUMPTUOUSNESS

The completed description of the respective authority roles of longing and affectation, in turn, sets the stage for the remaining sequence of follower roles; namely, the pairing of presumptuousness and smugness targeting the humanitarian and transcendental realms. Take, for example, the humanitarian follower theme of presumptuousness. The term derives from the Latin *praesumere*, a compound of *prae-* (before) and *sumere* (to take). It denotes a predisposed state of mind, often in a rash or prideful fashion. This tendency to presume goes hand-in-hand with the more elementary theme of arrogance. Indeed, presumptuousness continues in the tradition previously established for impudence, arrogance, and impetuosity, although now extending to the more enduring humanitarian sphere of influence. In keeping with such an entrenched range of presumptions, one's arrogant sense of impetuosity is typically taken for granted: any interference towards such goals being deeply resented in turn. Here presumption provisionally fulfills the stepwise pattern previously established for the overarching realm of excess, and one definitely befitting such an impudently-arrogant style of authority perspective.

SMUGNESS

The preceding enduring sense of arrogance characterizing presumptuousness, in turn, extends to a crowning transcendental domain with respect to the related theme of smugness. The English spelling for *smug* (trim, neat) dates to the mid-16th century: possibly an alteration of the Low-German *smuk* (trim, neat), from the Middle Low-German *smücken* (to adorn), or *smiegen* (to press close). The connotation of possessing a self-satisfied air of complacency potentially dates to the early 18th century, possibly an extension of its earlier sense of smoothness or sleekness. It denotes a contented sense of confidence in one's abilities, as well as overtones of superiority or righteousness.

The extreme prerequisites for smugness clearly embody an overweening sense of self-aggrandizement, whereby culminating (in a transcendental sense) the preliminary sequence of impudence, arrogance, impetuosity, and presumptuousness. This serene sense of smugness is only truly comprehensible in terms of such a transcendental perspective, where such an extreme range of illusion remains completely at odds with the strict reality at hand. Although the current placement of smugness remains an issue best left open to further discussion, it still remains the best available option in terms of remaining alternatives.

THE EXTREME PERSPECTIVES SPECIFIED FOR DISDAIN/INSOLENCE

The completed description of the rewards-based realm of excess for envy/impudence further sets the stage for the remaining leniency-based trend for disdain and insolence. This latter format emerges as an extreme sense of disdain in anticipation of insolence on the part of the personal follower. Indeed, this reciprocal interplay of authority/follower roles effectively mirrors the pattern previously established for envy/impudence, although now targeting leniency rather than rewards. This initial personal interplay of disdain and insolence, in turn, extends to the group, spiritual, humanitarian, and transcendental levels: organized as an ascending hierarchy of excess similarly employing an alternating sequence of presentation. Indeed, the preliminary sequence of authority roles (disdain, contempt, reproach, chagrin, and bitterness) further prompts the remaining follower sequence of insolence, audacity, rashness, boldness, and harshness: whereby providing a precise determination of power dynamics at issue for the overall realm of excess.

DISDAIN

In terms of the most basic personal authority level, the first-mentioned theme of *disdain* provisionally represents the extreme counterpart of the more routine ego-state of worry. Similar to disdain, worry is defined as an active style of lenient treatment in anticipation of compliance on the part of the personal follower: a dynamic that disdain parodies to an extreme degree. The term derives from the Old French *desdeignier*, from *des-* (do the opposite of) and *deignier* (to treat as worthy), from the Latin *dignus* (worthy). This pejorative expression of condescension is reflected in terms of a scornful sense of ridicule or overbearing haughtiness. Indeed, the classical Greeks worshipped this excessive aspect as the abstract god Koros, their divine personification of disdain and surfeit.

In anticipation of the upcoming discussion of insolence, Hybris (goddess of insolence) is directly cited in the parentage of disdain (Koros), attesting to the reciprocal relationship shared between the two. According to Pindar: "Far from their path, they (the Horae) hold proud Hybris (insolence) fierce-hearted mother of full-fed Koros (disdain)." Furthermore according to Herodotus: "Divine Dike (justice) will extinguish mighty Koros (disdain) the son of Hybris, lusting terribly, thinking to devour all." Indeed, down through the ages, the proud curl of the upper lip exemplified haughtiness and bitter contempt, serving as the very emblem for aristocratic disdain. Accordingly, disdain makes a fitting counterpoint to the more extreme positive attributes previously established for envy. The haughty and aloof characteristics typically accompanying disdain certainly fit the extremes predicted to occur within such an emotionally-charged context.

INSOLENCE

The preceding personal authority theme of disdain, in turn, prompts the future-directed theme of *insolence*. The term derives from the Latin *insolens*, a compound of *in-* (not) and *solens*, past participle of *solere* (to be accustomed): suggesting an overbearing or haughty demeanor.

The classical Greeks worshipped this quality as the abstract goddess Hybris, their divine personification of insolence or extreme pride. Her name translates as the English language notion of "hubris" (of parallel usage and meaning). Hybris is traditionally cited as the daughter of Eris (the goddess of discord). Her male child Koros is figuratively symbolized as the divine personification of disdain and contempt. According to the Greek authority Pindar: "Hybris (insolence) is the ruin of cities ... Never may shameless Hybris bring faction in her train and seize the company of citizens when they have forgotten their courage." Greek lyrical literature further states: "Shameless Hybris (insolence), luxuriating in shifty tricks and lawless follies, who swiftly gives a man another's wealth and power only to bring him into deep ruin."

In this stylized literary sense, hubris (or insolence) endures as a consistent theme, particularly in highly militaristic cultures such as ancient Greece. The greatest military offense was to express an insolent attitude towards one's superiors, a breach of conduct swiftly punished as a stark reminder to others within the unit. Consequently, insolence shares with impudence such an ingrained disrespectful attitude, although insolence more directly threatens the status quo; hence, a particularly grievous transgression. Indeed, the insolence expressed by the personal follower figure appears more directly confrontational than that established for impudence. The familiar scenario of the rebellious street-thug certainly stands out in this regard, relying upon extreme surliness to assert his street-tough status. This aggressive posturing directly counters the disdainful perspective on the part of the personal authority figure, a range of extremes particularly in keeping with the disturbing attributes associated with insolence.

The dual interplay of disdain and insolence further sets the stage for the remaining group and spiritual levels within hierarchy of excess. For instance, the disdain expressed by the personal authority, in turn, prompts the contempt expressed by the group authority, followed by the reproach specified for the spiritual authority figure. Furthermore, the insolence expressed by the personal follower further extends to the audacity expressed by the group representative, culminating in the rashness specified for the spiritual disciple figure. The remaining four sections provide a more detailed examination of both the group and spiritual domains for the hierarchy of excess, beginning with the group themes of contempt and audacity, followed by the spiritual counterparts of reproach and rashness.

CONTEMPT

The first-mentioned group authority theme of *contempt* derives from the Latin *contemptus* (scorn), past participle of *contemnere*: from *com-* (intensification) and *temnere* (to slight or scorn). British statesman Philip Stanhope (4th Earl of Chesterfield) once succinctly wrote: "Wrongs are often forgiven, but *contempt* never is. Our pride remembers it forever." Contempt, in a legal sense, refers to the deliberate interference in the smooth functioning of a court or legislature. Furthermore, contempt can refer to an overarching sense of scorn or mockery that diminishes the prevailing dignity of the court. Refusing to answer a question when directed to respond by the judge is considered direct criminal contempt punishable by fine or imprisonment. Similar penalties apply to civil contempt, although the accused is initially granted a hearing.

These civic aspects of contempt (within a courtroom setting) prove consistent with its group placement within the hierarchy of excess, whereby expanding upon the personal prerequisites for disdain. This civic context is particularly evident in the kindred maxim: "Familiarity breeds contempt," originally cited in of Aesop's *The Fox and the Lion* and repeated such luminaries as Shakespeare. Here familiarity truly does breed contempt in such an overarching social sense, for the closer one's status is to another, the more likely one is to provoke the audacious sense of brashness by the group representative.

AUDACITY

The preceding discussion of contempt, in turn, sets the stage for the follower maneuver proper; namely, the insolent sense of *audacity* expressed by the group representative. Audacity is traditionally defined as an extreme expression of insolence, particularly in a social setting. The term derives from the French *audacieux*, from the Latin *audax*, from *audere* (to dare). It denotes a daring or bold course of action, often through an arrogant disregard for personal safety or conventionality. It can also denote a sense of effrontery or insolence, as suggested in the colloquial connotations of spunk, grit, brashness, or impertinence. Indeed, French filmmaker Jean Cocteau humorously quipped: "Tact in *audacity* consists in knowing how far we may go too far!" It also extends to radical originality unfettered by the constraints of conventionality, as in feeling aesthetically uninhibited. In his address to recipients of the National Medal of Arts, President Ronald Reagan sagely noted: "In an atmosphere of liberty, artists and patrons are free to think the unthinkable and create the *audacious*; they are free to make both horrendous mistakes and glorious celebrations."

Irrespective of such positive or negative connotations, the extremes associated with audacity clearly reflect such a (group) sphere of influence, in direct analogy to the personal prerequisites previously established for insolence. This ingrained sense of brashness goes part in parcel with its placement within the hierarchy of excess. Indeed, audacity shares with arrogance such a daringly bold persona, although even more far-reaching in terms of both reason and consequence.

REPROACH

The completed description of the group realm for contempt and audacity, in turn, sets the stage for the remaining spiritual (or universal) focus of reproach and rashness. Here the contemptuous sense of *reproach* expressed by the spiritual authority further prompts the audaciously-rash treatment on the part of the spiritual disciple. Its modern spelling derives from the Old French *reproche*, from *reprocher* (to blame, to bring against), from the Vulgar Latin *repropiare*, a compound of the Latin *re-* (the opposite of) and *prope* (near). It denotes the act of censuring or upbraiding, as in willfully provoking a loss in social status.

This theme is traditionally translated in Old Testament scripture as the Hebrew equivalents of *ga`ar* and *yakhach* (to rebuke). In New Testament scripture, "to rebuke" is more often translated as *epitimao*, and also *elegcho*, the latter traditionally rendered as "to reprove."

In terms of the preceding scriptural citations, the deep spiritual overtones associated with reproach clearly betray a universal sphere of influence indicative of the spiritual authority figure. Consequently, reproach provisionally expands upon preliminary prerequisites previously established for disdain and contempt, although now rebuking the rash treatment of the respective follower figure. As with all such forays into the realm of excess, reproach can lead to outright conflict if taken to extremes, a strategy that clearly calls for cautious restraint with respect to such an overarching universal context.

RASHNESS

The preceding discussion of reproachfulness, in turn, sets the stage for an examination of the audacious sense of *rashness* anticipated from the respective follower figure. The term is said to derive from the Old English *ræsc*, as in *ligræsc* (flash of lightning), from the Proto-Germanic *raskuz*. It also is related to the Old English *horsc* (quick-witted). The connotation of actively impetuous or unrestrained dates at least to the 14th century. The notion of hastiness or carelessness emerges around the 16th century: denoting a hasty course of action lacking any sense of caution.

According to Aristotle's enduring *Theory of the Mean*, the cardinal virtue of courage represents the mean moral-value interposed between the extremes of *rashness* and cowardice. Courage certainly exemplifies such a three-way degree of specialization. Indeed, the extremes of rashness (personified by the reckless thrill-seeker) effectively characterize of the overarching realm of excess. Here rashness formally extends the subordinate theme of audacity into a universal sphere of influence, referring to a course of action judged recklessly-foolhardy across all ages and cultures. Rashness provisionally expands upon the initial sequence previously established for insolence and audacity, although now targeting a more universal sphere of influence. Indeed, a rash course of action should invariably be avoided due to its questionable survival value to the great range of society as a whole.

CHAGRIN

The completed description of the themes for excess spanning the personal, group, and spiritual levels, in turn, sets the stage for a discussion of the remaining humanitarian and transcendental levels. The profoundly abstract nature of these final two levels is clearly reflected in their abstract groupings of themes. For instance, the initial authority sequence of disdain-contempt-reproach further extends to a humanitarian sphere of influence with respect to the related theme of *chagrin*. The term derives from the French *chagrin* (shagreen, or rough skin, ill-humor), a variation of *sagrin*, from the Turkish *sagri* (rump): sugges-

314	315
Narcissism	Ignominy
316	**317**
Invidiousness	Despisal

EGOCENTRISM
(Personal Authority)

⟶

324	325
Blandishment	Reprehensibleness
326	**327**
Impertinence	Hubris

OBTRUSIVENESS
(Personal Follower)

↙

334	335
Snobbery	Opprobrium
336	**337**
Possessive.	Repugnance

AUTOCRACY
(Group Authority)

⟶

344	345
Courtliness	Denunciation
346	**347**
Brazenness	Surliness

ABSOLUTISM
(Group Representative)

↙

354	355
Vainglory	Despondency
356	**357**
Cravingness	Rebuke

PONTIFICATION
(Spiritual Authority)

⟶

364	365
Condescension	Derision
366	**367**
Brashness	Irascibility

DOGMATISM
(Spiritual Disciple)

↙

374	375
Haughtiness	Agony
376	**377**
Yearning	Loathing

FUNDAMENTALISM
(Humanitarian Authority)

⟶

384	385
Servility	Sarcasm
386	**387**
Effrontery	Temerity

SUPREMACISM
(Humanitarian Follower)

↙

394	395
Pietism	Affliction
396	**397**
Pretension	Admonishment

CATHOLICITY
(Transcendental Authority)

⟶

304	305
Subservience	Satiricism
306	**307**
Gleefulness	Rigorousness

ENIGMATISM
(Transcendental Follower)

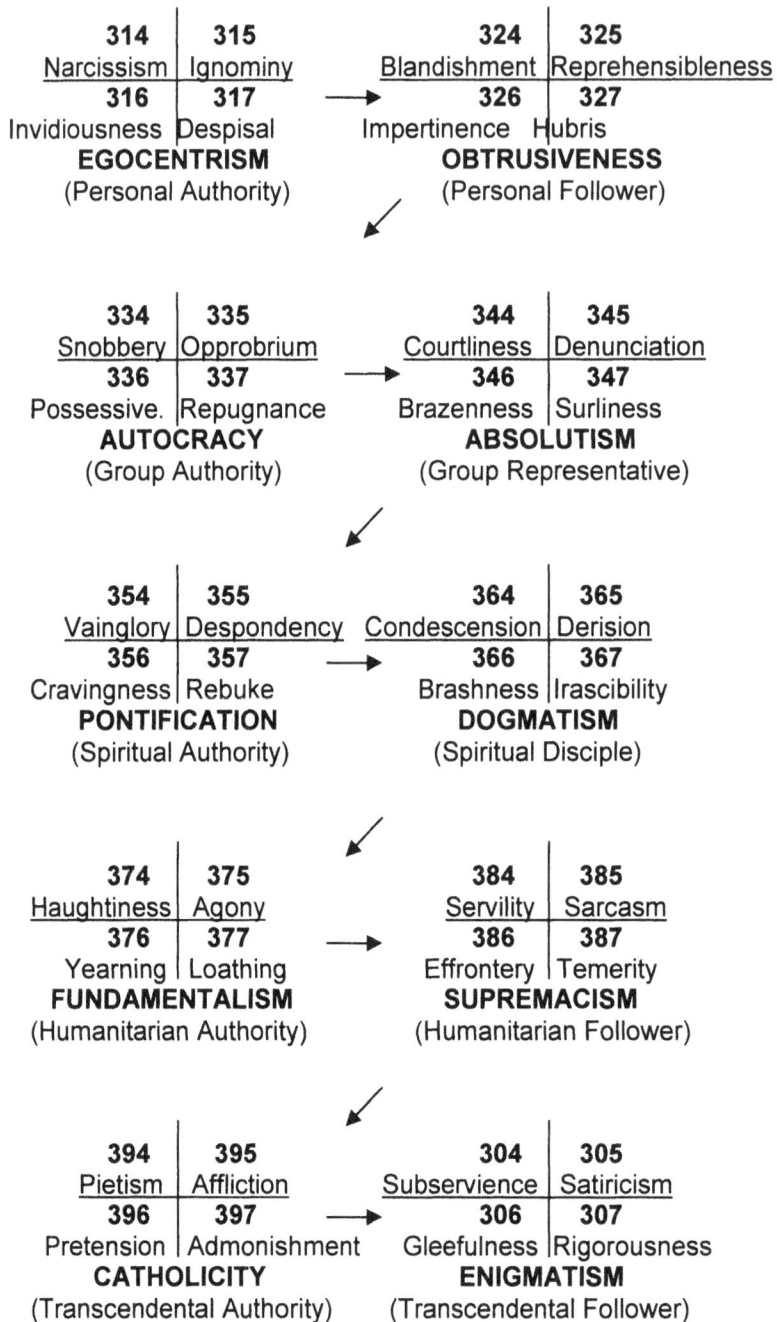

Fig. 17 – The Accessory Vices of Excess

tive of the rough leather crupper of a horse harness. Its derivation from shagreen refers to untanned leather with a rough surface prepared from the hide of a horse, shark, seal, etc., particularly the rough skin of sharks utilized as a mechanical abrasive.

This sense of roughness or abrasiveness serves as the basis for its motivational connotations: in particular, feelings of vexation marked by disappointment or humiliation. The facial expression for chagrin is more-or-less indistinguishable from disdain or contempt, so closely they are related within the authority hierarchy. The abrasive nature of this inward emotional state reflects a grating sense of reproach towards anyone so disposed. In this latter contemptuous sense, chagrin provisionally expands upon the preliminary ascending sequence of terms (disdain, contempt, and reproach), although now extending to a more enduring humanitarian sphere of inquiry within the overall domain of excess.

BITTERNESS

The preceding humanitarian focus for chagrin, in turn, seems to extend to a transcendental sphere of influence with respect to the affiliated theme of *bitterness*. The term derives from the Old English *biter*, akin to *bitan* (to bite): alluding to the biting or acrid sensation associated with bitterness. In Old Testament scripture, bitterness is particularly symbolic of affliction, misery, or servitude (Exodus 1:14; Ruth 1:20; Jeremiah 9:15). The Feast of the Passover traditionally included a serving of bitter herbs (Exodus 12:8) symbolizing the severity of servitude through which the people had labored.

In New Testament scripture, the expression "gall of bitterness" refers to a state of great wickedness (Acts 8:23). The "root of bitterness" refers to a wicked person or the depths of sinfulness (Hebrews 12:15). Bitterness clearly encompasses the overarching theme of disgust in keeping with its subordinate sequence of terms (disdain, contempt, reproach, and chagrin): although now targeting more of a transcendental sphere of influence. Indeed, the very act of tasting something bitter leads to a disgust reaction similar to that ascribed to disdain and contempt: the curled upper-lip also indicative of reproach and chagrin. In such an overarching motivational sense, bitterness certainly fulfills its status as the crowning transcendental theme within the ascending sequence, although its extreme level of abstraction necessarily allows speculation that other options are technically feasible at this juncture.

BOLDNESS

The completed description of the initial authority themes of chagrin and bitterness, in turn, sets the stage for the remaining follower roles of boldness and harshness. Take, for example, the first-listed humanitarian follower theme of *boldness*. The term derives from the Old English *beald*, from the Anglo-Saxon *bald* (bold, brave), from the Proto-Germanic *balthaz*. As such, it denotes a daring or courageous course of action frequently in a rash or careless fashion.

In New Testament scripture, boldness is generally considered one of the crucial aspects for the zeal expressed by the disciples (Acts 4:13, 29, 31). The disciples were subject to violent persecutions as well as the target of ridicule and contempt. Spiritual boldness is exemplified by James the Great, one of the apostles and elder brother of John (the sons of Zebedee and Salome). Due to their boldness and dedication, James and John were known as the Boanerges (*The Sons of Thunder*). James is said to have been the first martyr among the apostles, beheaded by Herod Agrippa in 44 CE.

This extreme focus on boldness continues the tradition previously established for rashness and audacity, although now extending to a humanitarian sphere of influence: as the trials of endurance clearly serve to indicate. Boldness was particularly revered as a key asset towards the survival of the early Christian Church. Although desperate times called for desperate measures, boldness suffered an extreme degree of risk similar to that encountered in audacity and rashness: a feature that had moderated somewhat with respect to Christianity's subsequent rise to respectability.

HARSHNESS

The preceding humanitarian focus of boldness, in turn, extends to a transcendental sphere of influence with respect to the affiliated theme of *harshness*. The term derives from the Middle English *harske* (rough, coarse), akin to the Danish *harsk* (rancid), or German *harsch* (hard). It denotes a sense of extreme roughness that is jarring to the senses or emotions. This theme provisionally expands upon the daring attributes associated with boldness, particularly within a military context. Shakespeare alludes to "the *harsh* and boisterous tongue of war." Furthermore, verbal harshness figures prominently in Proverbs (15:1): "A soft answer turns away wrath, but a

NARCISSISM	BLANDISHMENT
Previously, I (as reinforcer) have excessively acted admiringly towards you: in response to your (as procurer) extremely ambitious treatment of me. But now, you (as personal authority) will *narcissistically* act in an extremely ambitious fashion towards me: in anticipation of my (as reinforcer) excessively admiring treatment of you.	Previously, you (as personal authority) have narcissistically acted in an extremely ambitious fashion towards me: in anticipation of my (as reinforcer) excessively admiring treatment of you. But now, I (as your personal follower) will *blandishingly* act in an extremely admiring fashion towards you: overruling your (as PA) narcissistic treatment of me.
SNOBBERY	**COURTLINESS**
Previously, I (as your personal follower) have blandishingly acted in an extremely admiring fashion towards you: in response to your (as PA) narcissistic treatment of me. But now, you (as group authority) will narcissistically act in a *snobbish* fashion towards me: in anticipation of my (as PF) blandishing treatment of you.	Previously, you (as group authority) have narcissistically acted in a snobbish fashion towards me: in anticipation of my (as PF) blandishing treatment of you. But now, I (as group representative) will blandishingly act in a *courtly* fashion towards you: overruling your (as GA) snobbish treatment of me.
VAINGLORY	**CONDESCENSION**
Previously, I (as group representative) have blandishingly acted in a courtly fashion towards you: in response to your (as GA) snobbish treatment of me. But now, you (as spiritual authority) will snobbishly act in an *vainglorious* fashion towards me: in anticipation of my (as GR) courtly treatment of you.	Previously, you (as spiritual authority) have snobbishly acted in a vainglorious fashion towards me: in anticipation of my (as GR) courtly treatment of you. But now, I (as your spiritual disciple) will *condescendingly* act in a courtly fashion towards you: overruling your (as SA) vainglorious treatment of me.
HAUGHTINESS	**SERVILITY**
Previously, I (as your spiritual disciple) have condescendingly acted in a courtly fashion towards you: in response to your (as SA) vainglorious treatment of me. But now, you (as humanitarian authority) will vaingloriously act in a *haughty* fashion towards me: in anticipation of my (as SD) condescendingly treatment of you.	Previously, you (as humanitarian authority) have vaingloriously acted in a haughty fashion towards me: in anticipation of my (as SD) condescending treatment of you. But now, I (as representative member of humanity) will condescendingly act in a *servile* fashion towards you: overruling your (as HA) haughty treatment of me.
PIETISM	**SUBSERVIENCE**
Previously, I (as representative member of humanity) have condescendingly acted in a servile fashion towards you: in response to your (as HA) haughty treatment of me. But now, you (as transcendental authority) will haughtily act in a *pietistic* fashion towards me: in anticipation of my (as RH) servile treatment of you.	Previously, you (as transcendental authority) have haughtily acted in a pietistic fashion towards me: in anticipation of my (as RH) servile treatment of you. But now, I (as your transcendental follower) will servilely act in a *subservient* fashion towards you: overruling your (as TA) pietistic treatment of me.

Table G-1 – The Definitions Based Upon Narcissism/Blandishment

IGNOMINY	REPREHENSION
Previously, I (as reinforcer) have excessively acted in a concerned fashion towards you: in response to your (as procurer) extremely deferential treatment of me. But now, you (as personal authority) will *ignominiously* act in an extremely deferential fashion towards me: in anticipation of my (as reinforcer) excessively concerned treatment of you.	Previously, you (as personal authority) have *ignominiously* acted extremely deferentially towards me: in anticipation of my (as reinforcer) excessively concerned treatment of you. But now, I (as your personal follower) will *reprehensibly* act with extreme concern towards you: overruling your (as PA) ignominious treatment of me.
OPPROBRIUM	**DENUNCIATION**
Previously, I (as your personal follower) have reprehensibly acted with extreme concern towards you: in response to your (as PA) ignominious treatment of me. But now, you (as group authority) will ignominiously act with *opprobrium* towards me: in anticipation of my (as PF) reprehensible treatment of you.	Previously, you (as group authority) have ignominiously acted with opprobrium towards me: in anticipation of my (as PF) reprehensible treatment of you. But now, I (as group representative) will reprehensibly act in a *denunciatory* fashion towards you: overruling your (as GA) ignominious sense of opprobrium.
DESPONDENCY	**DERISION**
Previously, I (as group representative) have reprehensibly acted in a denunciatory fashion towards you: in response to your (as GA) ignominious sense of opprobrium. But now, you (as spiritual authority) will *despondently* act with opprobrium towards me: in anticipation of my (as GR) denunciatory treatment of you.	Previously, you (as spiritual authority) have despondently acted with opprobrium towards me: in anticipation of my (as GR) denunciatory treatment of you. But now, I (as your spiritual disciple) will *derisively* act in a denunciatory fashion towards you: overruling your (as SA) despondent treatment of me.
AGONY	**SARCASM**
Previously, I (as your spiritual disciple) have derisively acted in a denunciatory fashion towards you: in response to your (as SA) despondent treatment of me. But now, you (as humanitarian authority) will despondently act in an *agonizing* fashion towards me: in anticipation of my (as SD) derisive-denunciation of you.	Previously, you (as humanitarian authority) have despondently acted in an agonizing fashion towards me: in anticipation of my (as SD) derisive-denunciation of you. But now, I (as representative member of humanity) will derisively act in a *sarcastic* fashion towards you: overruling your (as HA) agonized treatment of me.
AFFLICTION	**SATIRICISM**
Previously, I (as representative member of humanity) have derisively acted in a sarcastic fashion towards you: in response to your (as HA) agonized treatment of me. But now, you (as transcendental authority) will agonizingly act in an *afflicted* fashion towards me: in anticipation of my (as RH) sarcastic treatment of you.	Previously, you (as transcendental authority) have agonizingly acted in an afflicted fashion towards me: in anticipation of my (as RH) sarcastic treatment of you. But now, I (as transcendental follower) will *satirically* act in a sarcastic fashion towards you: overruling your (as TA) afflicted treatment of me.

Table G- 2 – The Definitions Based Upon Ignominy/Reprehension

INVIDIOUSNESS	IMPERTINENCE
Previously, you (as procurer) have excessively acted with consideration towards me: in response to my (as reinforcer) extremely passionate treatment of you. But now, I (as personal authority) will *invidiously* act in an extremely passionate fashion towards you: in anticipation of your (as procurer) excessively considerate treatment of me.	Previously, I (as personal authority) have invidiously acted in an extremely passionate fashion towards you: in anticipation of your (procurer) excessively considerate treatment of me. But now, you (as my personal follower) will *impertinently* act in an extremely considerate fashion towards me: overruling my (as PA) invidious treatment of you.
POSSESSIVENESS	BRAZENNESS
Previously, you (as personal follower) have impertinently acted in an extremely considerate fashion towards me: in response to my (as PA) invidious treatment of you. But now, I (as group authority) will invidiously act *possessively* towards you: in anticipation of your (as PF) impertinent treatment of me.	Previously, I (as group authority) have invidiously acted possessively towards you: in anticipation of your (as PF) impertinent treatment of me. But now, you (as group representative) will impertinently act in a *brazen* fashion towards me: overruling my (as GA) possessive treatment of you.
CRAVENNESS	BRASHNESS
Previously, you (as group representative) have impertinently acted in a brazen fashion towards me: in response to my (as GA) possessive treatment of you. But now, I (as spiritual authority) will possessively act in a *cravenly* fashion towards you: in anticipation of your (as GR) brazen treatment of me.	Previously, I (as spiritual authority) have possessively acted in a cravenly fashion towards you: in anticipation of your (as GR) brazen treatment of me. But now, you (as my spiritual disciple) will brazenly act in a *brash* fashion towards me: overruling my (as SA) cravenly treatment of you.
YEARNING	EFFRONTERY
Previously, you (as my spiritual disciple) have brazenly acted in a brash fashion towards me: in response to my (as SA) cravenly treatment of you. But now, I (as humanitarian authority) will cravenly act in *yearning* fashion towards you: in anticipation of your (as SD) brash treatment of me.	Previously, I (as humanitarian authority) have cravenly acted in yearning fashion towards you: in anticipation of your (as SD) brash treatment of me. But now, you (as a representative member of humanity) will brashly express a sense of *effrontery* towards me: overruling my (as HA) yearning treatment of you.
PRETENSION	GLEEFULNESS
Previously, you (as representative member of humanity) have brashly expressed a sense of effrontery towards me: in response to my (as HA) yearning treatment of you. But now, I (as transcendental authority) will yearningly act with *pretentions* towards you: in anticipation of your (as RH) brash sense of effrontery.	Previously, I (as transcendental authority) have yearningly acted with pretentions towards you: in anticipation of your (as RH) brash sense of effrontery. But now, you (as transcendental follower) will *gleefully* act with effrontery towards me: overruling my (as TA) pretention-filled treatment of you.

Table G-3 – The Definitions Based Upon Invidiousness /Impertinence

DESPISAL Previously, you (as procurer) have excessively acted in an adherent fashion towards me: in response to my (as reinforcer) extremely apprehensive treatment of you. But now, I (as personal authority) will *despisingly* act extremely apprehensively towards you: in anticipation of your (as procurer) excessively adherent treatment of me.	**HUBRIS** Previously, I (as personal authority) have despisingly acted extremely apprehensively towards you: in anticipation of your (as procurer) excessively adherent treatment of me. But now, you (as my personal follower) will *hubristically* act extremely adherently towards me: overruling my (as PA) despisal-filled treatment of you.
REPUGNANCE Previously, you (as personal follower) have hubristically acted extremely adherently towards me: in response to my (as PA) despisal-filled treatment of you. But now, I (as group authority) will despisingly express a sense of *repugnance* towards you: in anticipation of your (as PF) hubristic treatment of me.	**SURLINESS** Previously, I (as group authority) have despisingly expressed a sense of repugnance towards you: in anticipation of your (as PF) hubristic treatment of me. But now, you (as group representative) will hubristically act in a *surly* fashion towards me: overruling my (as GA) repugnant treatment of you.
REBUKE Previously, you (as group representative) have hubristically acted in a surly fashion towards me: in response to my (as GA) repugnant treatment of you. But now, I (as spiritual authority) will repugnantly-*rebuke* you: in anticipation of your (as GR) hubristic sense of surliness.	**IRASCIBILITY** Previously, I (as spiritual authority) have repugnantly-rebuked you: in anticipation of your (as GR) hubristic sense of surliness. But now, you (as my spiritual disciple) will *irascibly* act in a surly fashion towards me: overruling my (as SA) repugnant rebuking of you.
LOATHING Previously, you (as my spiritual disciple) have irascibly acted in a surly fashion towards me: in response to my (as SA) repugnant-rebuking of you. But now, I (as humanitarian authority) will *loathingly*-rebuke you: in anticipation of your (as SD) irascible sense of surliness.	**TEMERITY** Previously, I (as humanitarian authority) have loathingly-rebuked you: in anticipation of your (as SD) irascible sense of surliness. But now, you (as representative member of humanity) will irascibly act with *temerity* towards me: overruling my (as HA) loathing-rebuking of you.
ADMONISHMENT Previously, you (as representative member of humanity) have irascibly acted with temerity towards me: in response to my (as HA) loathing-rebuking of you. But now, I (as transcendental authority) will loathingly act with *admonishment* towards you: in anticipation of your (as RH) irascible sense of temerity.	**RIGOROUSNESS** Previously, I (as transcendental authority) have loathingly acted with admonishment towards you: in anticipation of your (as RH) irascible sense of temerity. But now, you (as my transcendental follower) will *rigorously* act with temerity towards me: overruling my (as TA) loathing sense of admonishment.

Table G-4 – The Definitions Based Upon Despisal / Hubris

harsh word stirs up anger." An early Chinese proverb states: "Kind words can warm for three winters, while *harsh* words can chill even in the heat of summer."

This extreme degree of harshness proves consistent with the ascending sequence of subordinate terms; namely, insolence, audacity, rashness, boldness (and now harshness). In terms of its provisional transcendental placement within the hierarchy of excess, harshness enjoys a fairly broad range of meaning: as in harsh judgment, as well as harsh reality or perspective. Indeed, whether harshness truly warrants its crowning transcendental placement remains an issue open to debate, although its current assignment remains the most plausible choice at this juncture.

THE ACCESSORY VARIATIONS FOR EXCESS

Any overarching description of the main themes for excess must necessarily imply the existence of a parallel complement of terms for the predicted *accessory* realm of excess. At first glance the main groupings of terms scarcely appear comprehensive enough to support any additional range of accessory terms: particularly with respect to the most abstract levels within the ascending hierarchy. Indeed, there appears to be a dearth of adequate synonyms for many of the predicted slots within the accessory hierarchy. The various shades of meaning required to distinguish these accessory terms scarcely seem convincing enough to trigger a corresponding distinction in meaning (particularly where a more ambiguous determination of *excess* is concerned). Fortunately it has recently been discovered that an adequate number of synonyms truly does exist, whereby yielding a provisional working-version of accessory terms. The complete *40*-fold complement of accessory terms is outlined in **Fig. 17** as well as depicted in the compact diagram to follow.

It should be emphasized that this accessory modification necessarily remains a work in progress, being that a precise determination of the degree of excess is more of a subjective determination complicated by conflicting cultural overtones. The overarching degree of cohesiveness, however, proves suitably comprehensive in a holistic sense, leaving room for only a certain degree of minor tinkering and adjustment. This ten-part listing of accessory terms is parallel in every

respect to the main listing of terms depicted in **Fig. 15B** of Chapter *15:* whereby offering a suitably comprehensive (empathic) simulation of the communicational dynamics at issue.

Narcissism • Blandish. **Ignominy • Reprehens.**
Snobbery • Courtliness **Opprobr.• Denunciation**
Vainglory • Condescension **Despond. • Derision**
Haughtiness • Servility **Agony • Sarcasm**
Pietism • Subservience **Affliction • Satiricism**

Invidious. • Impertinence **Despisal • Hubris**
Possessive. • Brazen. **Repugnance • Surliness**
Cravings • Brashness **Rebuke • Irascibility**
Yearning • Effrontery **Loathing • Temerity**
Pretension • Gleefulness **Admonish. • Rigor.**

Indeed, it even proves feasible to incorporate this accessory listing of terms directly into the schematic definition format, although reflecting a reversed polarity of the "you" and "I" perspectives. A complete listing of these *accessory* schematic definitions is respectively tabulated in **Tables G-1** to **G-4**, further complementing the main set of definitions depicted **Tables F-1** to **F-4** (of Chapter *15*). These accessory schematic definitions are identical in form and function to their main counterparts with the exception that the "you" and "I" polarities are now reversed, whereby permitting an alternating depiction of the respective subjective and objective viewpoints. This innovation permits crucial empathic insights into the realm of excess, providing an overarching model of the empathic principles governing Theory of Mind

Through this expanded style of diagnostic potential, the self-defeating nature governing this extreme range of excess is explained in terms of the reciprocating interplay of "you" and "I" perspectives. For instance, many young adults feel that they must assert their budding independence through risky forms of behavior. The current schematic format offers the potential for timely interventions of a more moderate nature: where the subjective perspectives of the potential thrill-seeker can be more fully taken into account, in contrast to the more callous disregard that one often experiences. Hopefully this new technology may contribute solutions in cases where the temptation towards such a reckless range of extremes can be greatly ameliorated, to the enduring safety and benefit for society as a whole.

18

HYPERVIOLENCE: THE REALM OF EXCESSIVE DEFECT

The completed description of Aristotle's traditional "Theory of the Golden Mean" brings the proposed master ethical-hierarchy one step closer to fruition. According to classical Greek tradition, the virtuous realm was defined as that mean-value (of virtue) interposed between the vices of defect and the vices of excess, a key strategy for diagnosing interactions of a moral nature. Indeed, this basic tri-partite pattern reaches its supreme degree of precision within the schematic definition format. This three-way degree of specialization, however, can scarcely claim to be the final word, for it does not distinguish any parallel complement of extremes with respect to the vices of defect, just as was initially described for the virtuous realm. This glaring lack of an even sense of symmetry is fortunately remedied through the introduction of an entirely new class of ethics, a terminology provisionally termed the realm of *hyperviolence*. This new paradigm is distinguished from the more routine realm of defect-based violence primarily in terms of the extremes by which it is carried out.

The realm of ordinary violence typically avoids any extreme trend towards uncontrolled escalation, most conflicts focused on routine issues such as hurt feelings or property disputes. Recall (from **Part II**) that conditioned sequences involving punishment can frequently have an adaptive value. For instance, a water hole may dry up or go sour, wherein the individual strives to counteract such punitive consequences through the discovery of replacement resources. In terms of interspecies conflicts, territorial issues generally dominate the picture: where an area and its resources are preemptively claimed, as in keep-out! The melodious stylings of nesting songbirds represent one such territorial warning, whereas mammalian species employ scent marking to advertise ownership of a territory. These warning strategies offer a clear adaptive advantage, ensuring that scarce resources are not over-exploited. A similar circumstance is encountered with respect to male sex pattern-displays, where only the most genetically-fit (showy) males are chosen by the more selective females.

The darker side to posturing concerns dominance displays between near equals for scarce resources such as mates and territory. Being evenly matched essentially invites conflict unlike the more egalitarian realm characterizing the virtuous realm. Amongst evenly matched individuals the default conflict-state frequently leads to altercations of a hyperviolent nature (as in no holds barred). This is typically not advantageous to the species, therefore outright markers of dominance take the form of overt posturing; e.g., large antlers, showy frills, or brilliant coloration. Within a verbal realm this can lead to outrageous insults and trash-talking amongst equals, where both sides seek to save face to some degree.

The more unthinkable option extends to the more extreme realm of hyperviolence, where conflict is settled physically to the point of submission or even death between alpha males. Little chance for leniency enters in here, where posturing in the form of bodily threats can escalate to hyperviolent behavior.

HYPERVIOLENCE IN A SOCIAL CONTEXT

In a related human social sense, even minor insults or mistaken communication can escalate into full-blown conflicts when pursued unilaterally. Old Testament scripture acknowledges this trend towards escalation, dictating that the aggrieved party is entitled to only "an eye for an eye," or "a tooth for a tooth." Although sometimes viewed as

710	711
Indolence	Dereliction
712	**713**
Languor	Callousness

PERVERSION
(Personal Authority)

720	721
Mutiny	Reprisal
722	**723**
Grudgingness	Malignancy

EXPLOITATION
(Personal Follower)

730	731
Notoriety	Ignobility
732	**733**
Crassness	Petulance

DEPRAVITY
(Group Authority)

740	741
Rebellion	Retribution
742	**743**
Voracity	Cravenness

PERNICITY
(Group Representative)

750	751
Licentiousness	Savagery
752	**753**
Rudeness	Hostility

SACRILEGE
(Spiritual Authority)

760	761
Treason	Hopelessness
762	**763**
Greed	Contentiousness

RECUSANCY
(Spiritual Disciple)

770	771
Fury	Despotism
772	**773**
Brutality	Barbarity

REPROBATION
(Humanitarian Authority)

780	781
Hideousness	Mendacity
782	**783**
Heinousness	Ruthlessness

PANDEMONIUM
(Humanitarian Follower)

790	791
Madness	Bigotry
792	**793**
Viciousness	Atrocity

MINDLESSNESS
(Transcendental Authority)

700	701
Horror	Ruin
702	**703**
Balefulness	Fiendishness

SORCERY
(Transcendental Follower)

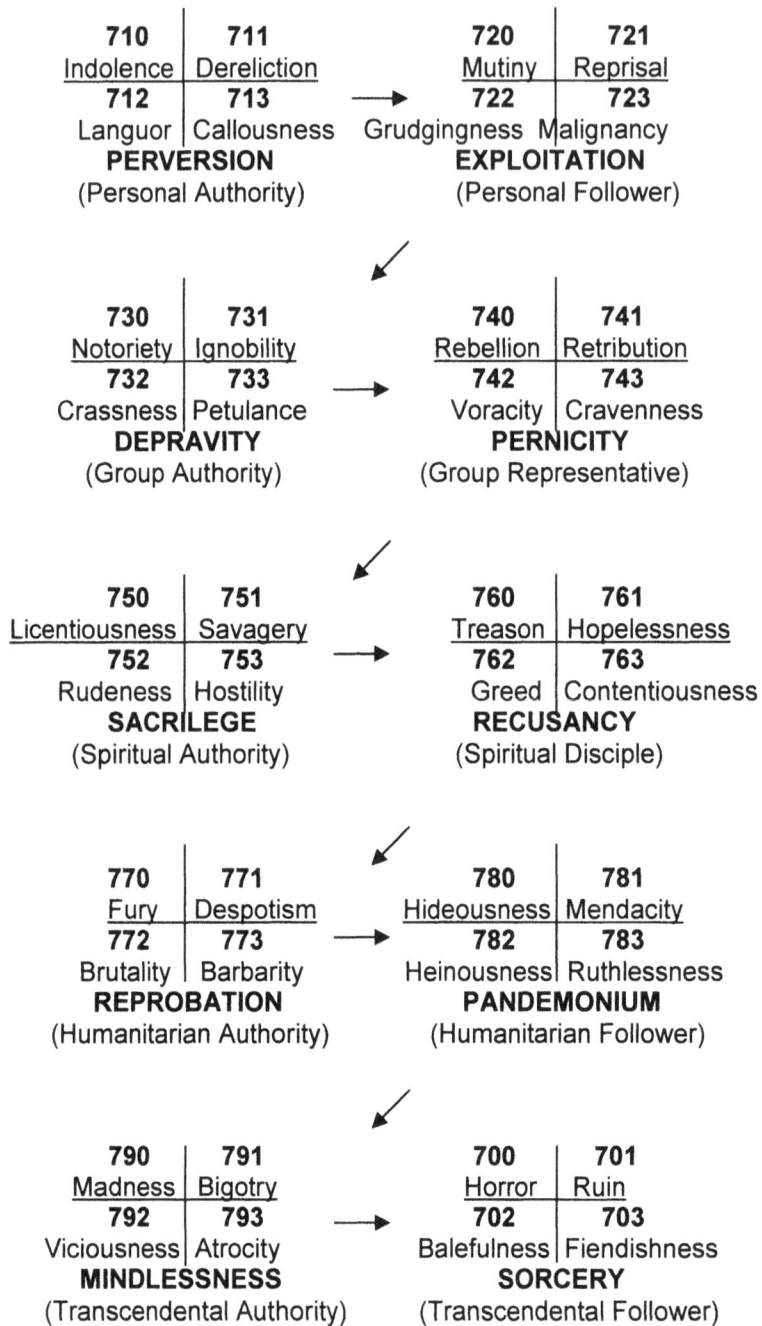

Fig. 18A – The Three-Digit Codes for Hyperviolence

condoning violence, this telling passage actually discourages any undue escalation within the realm of violence. This egalitarian view towards justice applies to the powerful as well as the downtrodden, an ethical safeguard against outright abuses of power. This somewhat idealistic injunction is not necessarily meant to imply that the ancient world was fully civilized in such matters. In the heat of battle, ruthless savagery was primarily the order of the day. The Old Testament cites numerous examples of the entire cities put to the sword. Such brutal savagery is only truly understood in terms of such rigid territorial sanctions, a convenient justification for the brutal tactics broadly practiced by the warrior class.

A similar hyperviolent trend is similarly encountered with respect to individual criminal offenses. For the vast majority of recorded history, criminals were dealt with in the most severe manner imaginable, where drastic punishments were meted out for even the most mundane of offenses. Indeed, the policy of cutting-off a hand for stealing, or beheading in the commission of adultery, is a pattern still practiced in many parts of the world. Herein lies the basic prototype for the realm of hyperviolence; namely, that range of extremes that targets the more routine realm of the vices of defect. Aristotle fails to distinguish this additional category of hyperviolence within his "Theory of the Mean" directly attesting to the violent precepts of the warrior code where victory was to be achieved at any cost (including mass genocide). Indeed, outright battlefield atrocities were deliberately employed as a strategy for deterring resistance amongst the defeated population.

Virtually all animal societies display an intrinsic abhorrence to excessive violence against members of one's own species. This similarly applies to human culture, where many soldiers during World War I were initially reluctant to perform their patriotic duty to kill consistent with such an intra-species taboo. The Armed Forces responded by implementing a behavior-modification training program aimed towards desensitizing the new recruits through a system of mock over-training in lethal techniques. Through such repetitive role-playing, the soldier's killing directives became virtually automatic, whereby modifying the threshold of what had previously been considered violent.

In our modern age of technological warfare, this strict adherence to an unrestrained warrior mentality has been diminished, any organized trend towards hyperviolence now strictly regulated under international law. Hyperviolence still remains in evidence under individual circumstances, such as in the many gut-wrenching instances of senseless violence reported in the news. These disturbingly brutal acts of violence represent an escalation of aggressive behavior completely out of all proportion to the precipitating circumstances. Society particularly recoils against such brutal outrages, resulting in efforts at gun legislation aimed towards countering the recent spate of workplace and school shootings.

One of the most disturbing trends is witnessed in terms of the modern-day street gang, where hyperviolence is typically regarded as a means to an end. Conflicts that were traditionally settled through fisticuffs are now decided through automatic weapons fire. Although mob violence has persisted as a tragic offshoot of the Prohibition Era, the attendant violence was rationalized as "they only kill their own kind." With the dramatic rise in bystander fatalities, however, such a blase attitude can no longer be tolerated. This intractable dilemma proves one of the most promising applications for the new paradigm of hyperviolence: a system that begins to fathom this tendency towards excessive violence particularly with respect to the youth of the nation. Unless we relish the prospects of living in an urban war zone, meaningful measures must be instituted to combat such a disturbing trend, or at least prevented from escalating any further.

BEHAVIORAL PROPENSITIES FOR THE REALM OF HYPERVIOLENCE

The range of excess with respect to defect proves exceedingly reminiscent of that previously established between the virtuous mode and the vices of excess. According to the latter scenario, the notion of the type "T" personality was introduced to explain extreme thrill-seeking types of behavior, where an ingrained sense of under-arousal was compensated for through risky means such as base-jumping. In terms of the related sphere of hyperviolence, Dr. Frank Farley (1991) further introduces what is termed the type T- *(minus)* personality, where thrills are achieved by eluding legal consequences, whereby gaining domination over one's rivals in the process. Indeed, many case studies offer a common thread in terms of the exploits of the habitual sociopath, accompanied by reports of an irresistible adrenaline "rush" accompanying such successful criminal activities.

This darker slant to hyperviolence is particularly evident in the chilling "tough-guy" mentality, where members within the criminal gang jockey for position in order to secure the lead position through hyperviolent posturing. This latter pattern

714	715		724	725
Sluggishness	Laxity		Untrustworthiness	Requital
716	**717**	→	**726**	**727**
Lethargy	Nonchalance		Umbrage	Peevishness

FETISHISM
(Personal Authority)

VICTIMIZATION
(Personal Follower)

734	735		744	745
Disgracefulness	Odium		Rebellion	Revenge
736	**737**	→	**746**	**747**
Absurdity	Willfulness		Ravenousness	Dastardliness

DEBASEMENT
(Group Authority)

VILENESS
(Group Representative)

754	755		764	765
Debauchery	Servitude		Disloyalty	Grievousness
756	**757**	→	**766**	**767**
Lewdness	Rancor		Rapaciousness	Vexation

BLASPHEMY
(Spiritual Authority)

HEATHENISM
(Spiritual Disciple)

774	775		784	785
Outrage	Imperiousness		Nastiness	Deceitfulness
776	**777**	→	**786**	**787**
Discord	Ferocity		Badness	Deviousness

RECREANCY
(Humanitarian Authority)

TUMULTUOUSNESS
(Humanitarian Follower)

794	795		704	705
Enragement	Discrimination		Grotesqueness	Damnation
796	**797**	→	**706**	**707**
Meanness	Truculence		Nefarity	Insidiousness

UNRULINESS
(Transcendental Authority)

DEMONISM
(Transcendental Follower)

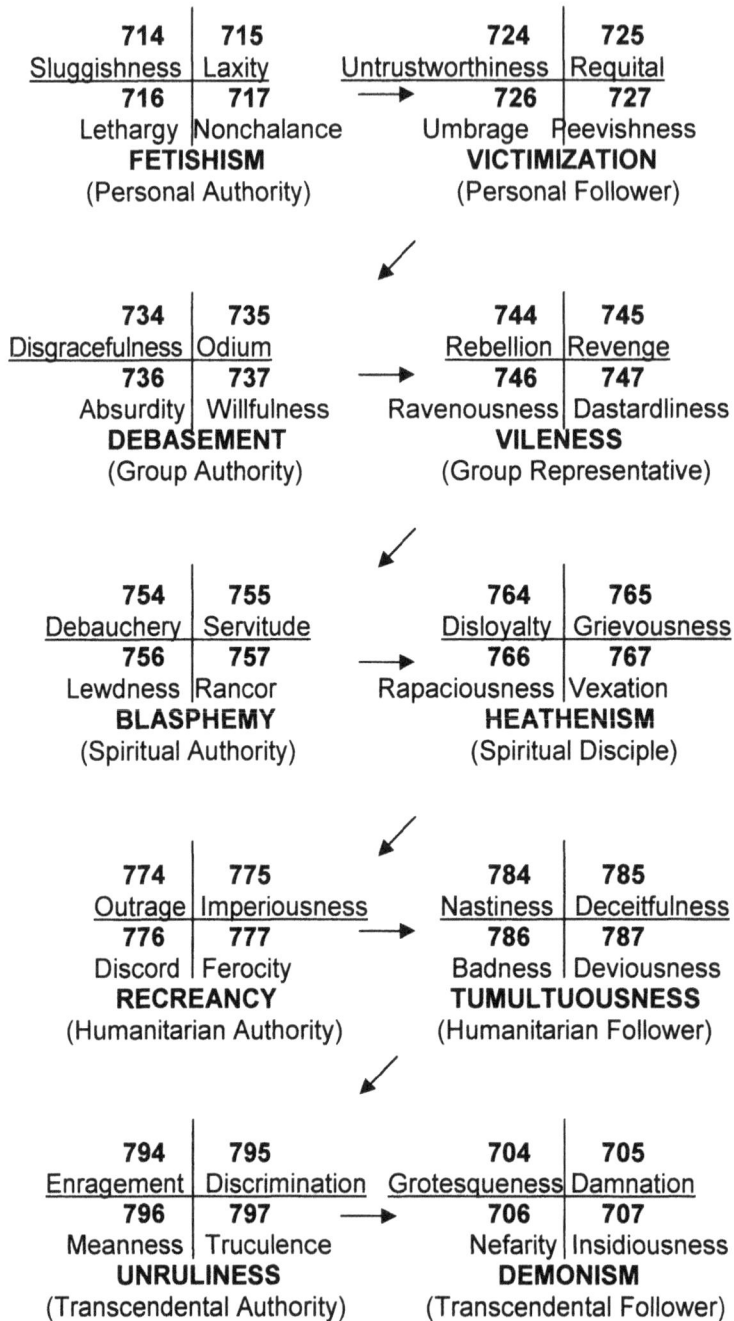

Fig. 18B   -   The Three-Digit Codes for Accessory Hyperviolence

The Realm of Hyperviolence: Graphic Depiction of 16th Century Punishments
Woodcut Engraving by Tengler, Illustration from *Laienspiegel*, Published in Mainz (1508)

varies from the posturing typically encountered for the more routine realm of defect, where the chief aim is to avoid the extremes of hyperviolence. Hardcore gangsters typically profess to be all-in with respect to hyperviolence (as in blood-in/blood-out). So-called men of respect employ the most extreme range of violence possible in order to remain on top of the pecking order. This is not to say that less drastic methods are not tried first. Such posturing can be mildly adaptive, whereby heading off all-out conflict.

Although great prestige typically accompanies such ruthless power tactics, success generally boils down to extreme risk and daring, a trait scarcely appealing to the more casual contenders to leadership. In combination with a cold and calculated sense of nerve, such ruthless manipulators seek to dominate for as long as their luck holds out: as witnessed in the ruthless political regimes of Hitler, Stalin, Pol Pot, etc. Such extreme tactics scarcely endure in the long run, for usurpers usually await in the wings. Indeed, this inherent vulnerability of the tyrant/dictator represents one of the strongest justifications for channeling one's energies away from the type T- personality, where satisfaction is maintained over the long term by focusing upon a more positive course of action. Here hyperviolence is unconditionally restricted in terms of unrestrained conflict, whereas the virtuous realm is unconditionally

INDOLENCE	MUTINY
Previously, you have excessively acted treacherously towards me: in response to my (as adversary) extremely lazy treatment of you. But now, I (as personal authority) will *indolently* act in an extremely lazy fashion towards you: in anticipation of your (as punisher) excessively treacherous treatment of me.	Previously, I (as personal authority) have indolently acted in an extremely lazy fashion towards you: in anticipation of your (as punisher) excessively treacherous treatment of me. But now, you (as my personal follower) will *mutinously* act extremely treacherously towards me: overruling my (as PA) indolent treatment of you.
NOTORIETY	**REBELLIOUSNESS**
Previously, you (as my personal follower) have mutinously acted extremely treacherously towards me: in response to my (as PA) indolent treatment of you. But now, I (as group authority) will indolently act in a *notorious* fashion towards you: in anticipation of your (as PF) mutinous treatment of me.	Previously, I (as your group authority) have indolently acted in a notorious fashion towards you: in anticipation of your (as PF) mutinous treatment of me. But now, you (as group representative) will mutinously-*rebel* against me: overruling my (as GA) indolent sense of notoriety.
LICENTIOUSNESS	**TREASON**
Previously, you (as group representative) have mutinously-rebelled against me: in response to my (as GA) indolent sense of notoriety. But now, I (as spiritual authority) will notoriously act in a *licentious* fashion towards you: in anticipation of your (as GR) mutinous-rebellion against me.	Previously, I (as your spiritual authority) have notoriously acted in a licentious fashion towards you: in anticipation of your (as GR) mutinous-rebellion against me. But now, you (as my spiritual disciple) will *treasonously*-rebel against me: overruling my (as SA) licentious treatment of you.
FURY	**HIDEOUSNESS**
Previously, you (as my spiritual disciple) have treasonously-rebelled against me: in response to my (as SA) licentious treatment of you. But now, I (as humanitarian authority) will licentiously act in a *furious* fashion towards you: in anticipation of your (as SD) treasonous-rebellion against me.	Previously, I (as humanitarian authority) have licentiously acted furiously towards you: in anticipation of your (as SD) treasonous-rebellion against me. But now, you (as representative member of humanity) will treasonously act in a *hideous* fashion towards me: overruling my (as HA) furious treatment of you.
MADNESS	**HORROR**
Previously, you (as representative member of humanity) have treasonously acted in a hideous fashion towards me: in response to my (as HA) furious treatment of you. But now, I (as transcendental authority) will furiously act in a *mad* fashion towards you: in anticipation of your (as RH) hideous treatment of me.	Previously, I (as transcendental authority) have furiously acted in a mad fashion towards you: in anticipation of your (as RH) hideous treatment of me. But now, you (as my transcendental follower) will hideously act *horribly* towards me: overruling my (as TA) mad treatment of you.

Table H-1 – The Definitions Based Upon Indolence/Mutiny

DERELICTION	REPRISAL
Previously, you (as punisher) have excessively acted in a vindictive fashion towards me: in response to my (as adversary) extremely negligent treatment of you. But now, I (as personal authority) will negligently act with *dereliction* towards you: in anticipation of your excessively vindictive treatment against me.	Previously, I (as personal authority) have negligently acted in a derelict fashion towards you: in anticipation of your (as punisher) extremely vindictive treatment against me. But now, you (as personal follower) will vindictively seek *reprisal* against me: overruling my (as PA) derelict treatment of you.
IGNOBILITY	**RETRIBUTION**
Previously, you (as my personal follower) have vindictively sought reprisal against me: in response to my (as PA) derelict treatment of you. But now, I (as group authority) will derelictly act in an *ignoble* fashion towards you: in anticipation of your (as PF) reprisal against me.	Previously, I (as group authority) have derelictly acted in an ignoble fashion towards you: in anticipation of your (as PF) reprisal against me. But now, you (as group representative) will reprisingly seek *retribution* against me: overruling my (as GA) ignoble treatment of you.
SAVAGERY	**HOPELESSNESS**
Previously, you (as group representative) have reprisingly sought retribution against me: in response to my (as GA) ignoble treatment of you. But now, I (as spiritual authority) will ignobly act in a *savage* fashion towards you: in anticipation of your (as GR) quest for retribution.	Previously, I (as spiritual authority) have ignobly acted in a savage fashion towards you: in anticipation of your (as GR) quest for retribution. But now, you (as my spiritual disciple) will *hopelessly* seek retribution against me: overruling my (as SA) savage treatment of you.
DESPOTISM	**MENDACITY**
Previously, you (as my spiritual disciple) have hopelessly sought retribution against me: in response to my (as SA) savage treatment of you. But now, I (as humanitarian authority) will *despotically* act in a savage fashion towards you: in anticipation of your (as SD) hopeless quest for retribution.	Previously, I (as humanitarian authority) have despotically acted savagely towards you: in anticipation of your (as SD) hopeless quest for retribution. But now, you (as representative member of humanity) will hopelessly act in a *mendacious* fashion towards me: overruling my (as HA) despotic treatment of you.
BIGOTRY	**RUIN**
Previously, you (as represent. member of humanity) have hopelessly acted mendaciously towards me: in response to my (as HA) despotic treatment of you. But now, I (as transcendental auth.) will despotically act in a *bigoted* fashion towards you: in anticipation of your (as RH) mendacious treatment of me.	Previously, I (as transcendental authority) have despotically acted with bigotry towards you: in anticipation of your (as RH) mendacious treatment of me. But now, you (as transcendental follower) will mendaciously act in a *ruinous* fashion towards me: overruling my (as TA) bigoted treatment of you.

Table H-2 – The Definitions Based on Dereliction/Reprisal

LANGUOR	GRUDGINGNESS
Previously, I (as adversary) have excessively acted spitefully towards you: in response to your extremely apathetic treatment of me. But now, you (as personal authority) will *languorously* act extremely apathetically towards me: in anticipation of my (as adversary) excessively spiteful treatment of you.	Previously, you (as personal authority) have languorously acted apathetically towards me: in anticipation of my (as adversary) excessively spiteful treatment of you. But now, I (as personal follower) will *grudgingly* act extremely spitefully towards you: overruling your (as PA) languorous treatment of me.
CRASSNESS	**VORACITY**
Previously, I (as your personal follower) have grudgingly acted extremely spitefully towards you: in response to your (as PA) languorous treatment of me. But now, you (as group authority) will *crassly* act in a languorous fashion towards me: in anticipation of my (as PF) grudging treatment of you.	Previously, you (as group authority) have crassly acted in a languorous fashion towards me: in anticipation of my (as PF) grudging treatment of you. But now, I (as group representative) will *voraciously* act grudgingly towards you: overruling your (as GA) crass treatment of me.
RUDENESS	**GREED**
Previously, I (as group representative) have voraciously acted in a grudging fashion towards you: in response to your (as GA) crass treatment of me. But now, you (as spiritual authority) will crassly act in a *rude* fashion towards me: in anticipation of my (as GR) voracious treatment of you.	Previously, you (as my spiritual authority) have crassly acted in a rude fashion towards me: in anticipation of my (as GR) voracious treatment of you. But now, I (as spiritual disciple) will voraciously act in an *greedy* fashion towards you: overruling your (as SA) crassly-rude treatment of me.
BRUTALITY	**HEINOUSNESS**
Previously, I (as your spiritual disciple) have voraciously acted in an greedy fashion towards you: in response to your (as SA) crassly-rude treatment of me. But now, you (as humanitarian authority) will *brutally* act rudely towards me in anticipation of my (as SD) greedy treatment of you.	Previously, you (as humanitarian authority) have brutally acted rudely towards me: in anticipation of my (as SD) greedy treatment of you. But now, I (as representative member of humanity) will *heinously* act in a greedy fashion towards you: overruling your (as HA) brutally-rude treatment of me.
VISCIOUSNESS	**BALEFULNESS**
Previously, I (as representative member of humanity) have heinously acted in a greedy fashion towards you: in anticipation of in response to your (as HA) brutally-rude treatment of me. But now, you (as transcendental authority) will brutally act in a *vicious* fashion towards me: in anticipation of my (as RH) heinous sense of greed.	Previously, you (as transcendental authority) have brutally acted viciously towards me: overruling my (as RH) heinous sense of greed. But now, I (as your transcendental follower) will *balefully* act in a heinous fashion towards you: in anticipation of your (as TA) vicious treatment of me.

Table H-3 – The Definitions Based Upon Languor/Grudgingness

CALLOUSNESS	MALIGNANCY
Previously, I (as adversary) have excessively acted maliciously towards you: in response to your (as punisher) extremely indifferent treatment of me. But now, you (as personal authority) will *callously* act extremely indifferently towards me: in anticipation of my (as adversary) excessively malicious treatment of you.	Previously, you (as personal authority) have callously acted in an extremely indifferent fashion towards me: in anticipation of my (as adversary) excessively malicious treatment of you. But now, I (as your personal follower) will *malignantly* act extremely maliciously towards you: overruling your (as PA) callous treatment of me.
PETULANCY	**CRAVENNESS**
Previously, I (as your personal follower) have malignantly acted extremely maliciously towards you: in response to your (as PA) callous treatment of me. But now, you (as group authority) will callously act *petulantly* towards me: in anticipation of my (as PF) malignant treatment of you.	Previously, you (as group authority) have callously acted petulantly towards me: in anticipation of my (as PF) malignant treatment of you. But now, I (as group representative) will *cravenly* act in a malignant fashion towards you: overruling your (as GA) petulant treatment of me.
HOSTILITY	**CONTENTIOUSNESS**
Previously, I (as group representative) have cravenly acted in a malignant fashion towards you: in response to your (as GA) petulant treatment of me. But now, you (as spiritual authority) will petulantly act in a *hostile* fashion towards me: in anticipation of my (as GR) craven treatment of you.	Previously, you (as spiritual authority) have petulantly acted in a hostile fashion towards me: in anticipation of my (as GR) craven treatment of you. But now, I (as your spiritual disciple) will cravenly act in a *contentious* fashion towards you: overruling your (as SA) hostile treatment of me.
BARBARISM	**RUTHLESSNESS**
Previously, I (as your spiritual disciple) have cravenly acted in a contentious fashion towards you: in response to your (as SA) hostile treatment of me. But now, you (as humanitarian authority) will hostilely act *barbarically* towards me: in anticipation of my (as SD) contentious treatment of you.	Previously, you (as humanitarian authority) have hostilely acted barbarically towards me: in anticipation of my (as SD) contentious treatment of you. But now, I (as representative member of humanity) will contentiously act in a *ruthless* fashion towards you: overruling your (as HA) barbaric treatment of me.
ATROCITY	**FIENDISHNESS**
Previously, I (as representative member of humanity) have contentiously acted in a ruthless fashion towards you: in response to your (as HA) barbaric treatment of me. But now, you (as transcendental authority) will barbarically act *atrociously* towards me: in anticipation of my (as RH) ruthless treatment of you.	Previously, you (as transcendental authority) have barbarically acted in an atrocious fashion towards me: in anticipation of my (as RH) ruthless treatment of you. But now, I (as your transcendental follower) will ruthlessly act *fiendishly* towards you: overruling your (as TA) atrocious treatment of me.

Table H-4 – The Definitions Based Upon Callousness/Malignancy

SLUGGISHNESS	UNTRUSTWORTHINESS
Previously, I (as punisher) have excessively acted traitorously towards you: in response to your (as adversary) extremely slothful treatment of me. But now, you (as personal authority) will *sluggishly* act in an extremely slothful fashion towards me: in anticipation of my (as punisher) excessively traitorous treatment of you.	Previously, you (as personal authority) have sluggishly acted extremely slothfully towards me: in anticipation of my (as punisher) excessively traitorous treatment of you. But now, I (as your personal follower) will *untrustworthily* act extremely traitorously towards you: overruling your (as PA) sluggish treatment of me.
DISGRACEFULNESS	**REBELLIOUSNESS**
Previously, I (as your personal follower) have untrustworthily acted acted extremely traitorously towards you: in response to your (as PA) sluggish treatment of me. But now, you (as group authority) will sluggishly act in a *disgraceful* fashion towards me: in anticipation of my (as PF) untrustworthy treatment of you.	Previously, you (as group authority) have sluggishly acted in a disgraceful fashion towards me: in anticipation of my (as PF) untrustworthy treatment of you. But now, I (as group representative) will *rebelliously* act untrustworthily towards you: overruling your (as GA) disgraceful treatment of me.
DEBAUCHERY	**DISLOYALTY**
Previously, I (as group representative) have rebelliously acted in an untrustworthy fashion towards you: in response to your (as GA) disgraceful treatment of me. But now, you (as spiritual authority) will disgracefully act in a *debauched* fashion towards me: in anticipation of my (as GR) rebellious treatment of you.	Previously, you (as spiritual authority) have disgracefully acted in a debauched fashion towards me: in anticipation of my (as GR) rebellious treatment of you. But now, I (as spiritual disciple) will rebelliously act in a *disloyal* fashion towards you: overruling your (as SA) debauched treatment of me.
OUTRAGE	**NASTINESS**
Previously, I (as your spiritual disciple) have rebelliously acted disloyally towards you: in response to your (as SA) odious sense of debauchery. But now, you (as humanitarian authority) will *outrageously* act in a debauched fashion towards me: in anticipation of my (as SD) disloyal treatment of you.	Previously, you (as humanitarian authority) have outrageously acted with debauchery towards me: in anticipation of my (as SD) disloyal treatment of you. But now, I (as representative member of humanity) will disloyally act in a *nasty* fashion towards you: overruling your (as HA) outrageous treatment of me.
ENRAGEMENT	**GROTESQUENESS**
Previously, I (as representative member of humanity) have disloyally acted in a nasty fashion towards you: in response to your (as HA) outrageous treatment of me. But now, you (as transcendental authority) will outrageously act in an *enraged* fashion towards me: in anticipation of my (as RH) nasty treatment of you.	Previously, you (as transcendental authority) have outrageously acted in an enraged fashion towards me: in anticipation of my (as RH) nasty treatment of you. But now, I (as transcendental follower) will nastily act in a *grotesque* fashion towards you: overruling your (as TA) enraged treatment of me.

Table J-1 – The Definitions Based Upon Sluggishness/Untrustworthiness

LAXITY	REQUITAL
Previously, I (as punisher) have excessively retaliated against you: in response to your (as adversary) extremely careless treatment of me. But now, you (as personal authority) will *laxly* act in an extremely careless fashion towards me: in anticipation of my (as punisher) excessive retaliation against you.	Previously, you (as personal authority) have laxly acted in an extremely careless fashion towards me: in anticipation of my (as punisher) excessive retaliation against you. But now, I (as your personal follower) will *requitefully* retaliate against you: overruling your (as PA) lax treatment of me.
ODIUM	**REVENGE**
Previously, I (as your personal follower) have requitefully retaliated against you: in response to your (as PA) lax treatment of me. But now, you (as group authority) will *odiously* act in a lax fashion towards me: in anticipation of my (as PF) requiteful treatment of you.	Previously, you (as group authority) have odiously acted in a lax fashion towards me: in anticipation of my (as PF) requiteful treatment of you. But now, I (as group representative) will requitefully seek *vengeance* against you: overruling your (as GA) odious treatment of me.
SERVITUDE	**GRIEVOUSNESS**
Previously, I (as group representative) have requitefully sought vengeance against you: in response to your (as GA) odious treatment of me. But now, you (as spiritual authority) will odiusly maintain me in *servitude*: in anticipation of my (as GR) vengeful treatment of you.	Previously, you (as spiritual authority) have odiously maintained me in servitude: in anticipation of my (as GR) vengeful treatment of you. But now, I (as your spiritual disciple) will vengefully act in a *grievous* fashion towards you: overruling your (as SA) odious maintenance of me in servitude.
IMPERIOUSNESS	**DECEITFULNESS**
Previously, I (as your spiritual disciple) have vengefully acted in a grievous fashion towards you: in response to your (as SA) odious maintenance of me in servitude. But now, you (as humanitarian authority) will *imperiously* maintain me in servitude: in anticipation of my (as SD) grievous treatment of you.	Previously, you (as humanitarian authority) have imperiously maintained me in servitude: in anticipation of my (as SD) grievous treatment of you. But now, I (as representative member of humanity) will grievously act in a *deceitful* fashion towards you: overruling your (as HA) imperious treatment of me.
DISCRIMINATION	**DAMNATION**
Previously, I (as representative member of humanity) have grievously acted in a deceitful fashion towards you: in response to your (as HA) imperious treatment of me. But now, you (as transcendental authority) will imperiously act in a *discriminatory* fashion: in anticipation of my (as RH) deceitful treatment of you.	Previously, you (as transcendental authority) have imperiously acted in a discriminatory fashion: in anticipation of my (as RH) deceitful treatment of you. But now, I (as your transcendental follower) will deceitfully act in a *damnable* fashion towards you: overruling your (as TA) discriminatory treatment of me.

Table J-2 - The Definitions Based on Laxity/Requital

LETHARGY	UMBRAGE
Previously, you (as adversary) have excessively acted dispassionately towards me: in response to my (as punisher) extremely resentful treatment of you. But now, I (as personal authority) will *lethargically* act in an extremely resentful fashion towards you: in anticipation of your (as adversary) excessively dispassionate treatment of me.	Previously, I (as personal authority) have lethargically acted extremely resentfully towards you: in anticipation of your (as adversary) excessively dispassionate treatment of me. But now, you (as personal follower) will *umbragefully* act extremely dispassionately towards me: overruling my (as PA) lethargic treatment of you.
ABSURDITY	**RAVENOUSNESS**
Previously, you (as my personal follower) have umbragefully acted excessively dispassionately towards me: in response to my (as PA) lethargic treatment of you. But now, I (as group authority) will lethargically act in an *absurd* fashion towards you: in anticipation of your (as PF) umbrage-filled treatment of me.	Previously, I (as group authority) have lethargically acted in an absurd fashion towards you: in anticipation of your (as PF) umbrage-filled treatment of me. But now, you (as group representative) will umbragefully act *ravenously* towards me: overruling my (as GA) absurd treatment of you.
LEWDNESS	**RAPACIOUSNESS**
Previously, you (as group representative) have umbragefully acted ravenously towards me: in response to my (as GA) absurd treatment of you. But now, I (as spiritual authority) will absurdly act in a *lewd* fashion towards you: in anticipation of your (as GR) ravenous treatment of me.	Previously, I (as spiritual authority) have absurdly acted in a lewd fashion towards you: in anticipation of your (as GR) ravenous treatment of me. But now, you (as spiritual disciple) will ravenously act *rapaciously* towards me: overruling my (as SA) lewd treatment of you.
DISCORD	**BADNESS**
Previously, you (as my spiritual disciple) have ravenously acted rapaciously towards me: in response to my (as SA) lewd treatment of you. But now, I (as humanitarian authority) will lewdly act in a *discordant* fashion towards you: in anticipation of your (as SD) rapacious treatment of me.	Previously, I (as humanitarian authority) have lewdly acted discordantly towards you: in anticipation of your (as SD) rapacious treatment of me. But now, you (as representative member of humanity) will rapaciously act in a *bad* fashion towards me: overruling my (as HA) discordant treatment of you.
MEANNESS	**NEFARITY**
Previously, you (as representative member of humanity) have rapaciously acted in a bad fashion towards me: in response to my (as HA) discordant treatment of you. But now, I (as transcendental authority) will discordantly act in a *mean* fashion towards you: in anticipation of your (as RH) bad treatment of me.	Previously, I (as transcendental authority) have discordantly acted in a mean fashion towards you: in anticipation of your (as RH) bad treatment of me. But now, you (as transcendental follower) will badly act in a *nefarious* fashion towards me: overruling my (as TA) mean treatment of you.

Table J-3 - The Definitions Based on Lethargy/Umbrage

NONCHALANCE Previously, you (as adversary) have excessively acted malevolently towards me: in response to my (as punisher) extremely arbitrary treatment of you. But now, I (as personal authority) will *nonchalantly* act in an extremely arbitrary fashion towards you: in anticipation of your (as adversary) excessively malevolent treatment of me.	**PEEVISHNESS** Previously, I (as personal authority) have nonchalantly acted extremely arbitrarily towards you: in anticipation of your (as adversary) excessively malevolent treatment of me. But now, you (as personal follower) will *peevishly* act malevolently towards me: overruling my (as PA) nonchalant treatment of you.
WILLFULNESS Previously, you (as my personal follower) have peevishly acted in an extremely malevolent fashion towards me: in response to my (as PA) nonchalant treatment of you. But now, I (as group authority) will *willfully* act nonchalantly towards you: in anticipation of your (as PF) peevish treatment of me.	**DASTARDLINESS** Previously, I (as group authority) have willfully acted nonchalantly towards you: in anticipation of your (as PF) peevish treatment of me. But now, you (as group representative) will peevishly act in a *dastardly* fashion towards me: overruling my (as GA) willful treatment of you.
RANCOR Previously, you (as group representative) have peevishly acted in a dastardly fashion towards me: in response to my (as GA) willful treatment of you. But now, I (as spiritual authority) will willfully act in a *rancorous* fashion towards you: in anticipation of your (as GR) dastardly treatment of me.	**VEXATION** Previously, I (as spiritual authority) have willfully acted in a rancorous fashion towards you: in anticipation of your (as GR) dastardly treatment of me. But now, you (as my spiritual disciple) will dastardly act in a *vexing* fashion towards me: overruling my (as SA) rancorous treatment of you.
FEROCITY Previously, you (as my spiritual disciple) have dastardly acted in a vexing fashion towards me: in response to my (as SA) rancorous treatment of you. But now, I (as humanitarian authority) will rancorously act in a *ferocious* fashion towards you: in anticipation of your (as SD) vexing treatment of me.	**DEVIOUSNESS** Previously, I (as humanitarian authority) have rancorously acted ferociously towards you: in anticipation of your (as SD) vexing treatment of me. But now, you (as representative member of humanity) will vexingly act in a *devious* fashion towards me: overruling my (as HA) ferocious treatment of you.
TRUCULENCE Previously, you (as representative member of humanity) have vexingly acted deviously towards me: in response to my (as HA) ferocious treatment of you. But now, I (as transcendental authority) will ferociously act in a *truculent* fashion towards you: in anticipation of your (as RH) devious treatment of me.	**INSIDIOUSNESS** Previously, I (as transcendental authority) have ferociously acted in a truculent fashion towards you: in anticipation of your (as RH) devious treatment of me. But now, you (as transcendental follower) will deviously act *insidiously* towards me: overruling my (as TA) truculent treatment of you.

Table J-4 – The Definitions Based on Nonchalance/Peevishness

encouraged through amiable cooperation and collaboration.

A PRELIMINARY TERMINOLOGY
FOR THE REALM OF HYPERVIOLENCE

In summary, the more routine classifications of the vices of defect exhibit the distinct propensity for escalating into a hyperviolent state of affairs in susceptible individuals. Such hyperviolent outbursts typically remain isolated incidents, the perpetrator fleeing afterwards to elude prosecution. Victims and bystanders similarly flee resulting in minimum potential for any ongoing style of interaction. Consequently there appears little in the way of any comprehensive terminology for describing such hyperviolent interactions. Each incident is handled on a case-by-case basis, as outlined in forensics and criminal profiling.

The critical applications associated with hyperviolence necessitate the implementation of a precise terminology for labeling the predicted complement of terms. At first glance, there initially appeared to be a dearth of an adequate vocabulary for many of the predicted slots for the extreme realm of hyperviolence. Indeed, the various shades of meaning required to distinguish this extremely violent domain scarcely seemed to specify a clear distinction in terms. For this reason, a completely independent version for the realm of hyperviolence was absent from early discussions of this theme. In the years since, however, it has further been determined that an adequate number of suitable synonyms, indeed, does exist with in relation to the realm of hyperviolence. This necessarily entailed a major overhaul of the darker domain of defect, where a number of the accessory vices of defect were reevaluated and determined to actually belong (more properly) to the realm of hyperviolence. New terms were subsequently identified for filling-in the entire expanded format. The main terms for the vices of defect, however, remain essentially unaffected by this minor degree of reorganization. It should be emphasized that this innovation with respect to hyperviolence is necessarily a work in progress, being that any determination of excess is necessarily somewhat of a subjective determination compounded by cultural overtones and socially prescribed traditions.

As a first tentative release for the realm of hyperviolence, a more detailed description of each of the individual terms will not be undertaken at this juncture, an aspect best deferred for an upcoming edition. The overarching literary traditions targeting extreme hyperviolence are similarly somewhat limited in scope due to its relatively rare occurrence in modern society. The clear degree of cohesiveness for the realm of hyperviolence, however, proves suitably comprehensive in scope, ensuring that only minor adjustments should be necessary in future editions. A complete listing of the provisional terminology for hyperviolence is schematically depicted in **Fig. 18A** (in concert with the three-digit codes), and also in the compact diagram immediately below.

Indolence • Mutiny	**Dereliction • Reprisal**
Notoriety • Rebellious.	**Ignobility • Retribution**
Licentiousness • Treason	**Savagery • Hopeless.**
Fury • Hideousness	**Despotism • Mendacity**
Madness • Horror	**Bigotry • Ruin**

Languor • Grudgingness	**Callous. • Malignancy**
Crassness • Voracity	**Petulance • Cravenness**
Rudeness • Greed	**Hostility • Contentious.**
Brutality • Heinousness	**Barbarism • Ruthless.**
Viciousness • Balefulness	**Atrocity • Fiendish.**

This arrangement is similar in form and function to that previously established for the vices of defect, with the respective three-digit codes exhibiting clear parallels to those previously established for the vices of defect. Here the first place digit of "5" (denoting the vices of defect) is modified to a "7" specifying the realm of hyperviolence. Consistent with its somewhat infrequent occurrence throughout society as a whole, any formal terminology must necessarily incorporate the wealth of case histories garnered from the annals of criminal profiling, perhaps even utilizing much of its specialized legal terminology. Indeed, this new system of terminology should prove particularly effective for most applications relating to forensics and the criminal justice system.

THE SCHEMATIC DEFINITIONS FOR
THE REALM OF HYPERVIOLENCE

In keeping with the pattern previously established for the vices of defect and excess, the provisional terminology for the realm of hyperviolence (by definition) proves similarly amenable to incorporation into the schematic definition format, permitting crucial insights into the mentality of the hyperviolent individual. The complete four-page listing of definitions for hyperviolence is schematically depicted in **Tables H-1** through **H-4**. These schematic definitions represent extreme variations on the vices of defect originally depicted in **Tables D-1** to **D-4** of Chapter 9). This darker complement of definitions (for hyperviolence) proves equally as informative as those for the vices of defect, offering crucial insights into those dysfunctional perspectives that should be avoided. Owing to the essential safeguards prevailing in any monitored context, this formal model of hyperviolence must necessarily remain a relatively rare occurrence. The technical familiarity with the realm of hyperviolence actually amounts to a fundamental safeguard within the ethical hierarchy, where negative transactions are diagnosed in terms of their potential for transformation into positive ones, and vice-versa.

THE ACCESSORY TERMS FOR HYPERVIOLENCE

The completed description of the extreme realm of hyperviolence raises the related remaining issue of the *accessory* terms for hyperviolence. Here the accessory realm for hyperviolence directly reverses the polarity of the "you" and "I" perspectives in relation to that initially specified for the main listings of terms. The accessory variations represent an entirely new formulation of terms, in essence, close motivational synonyms for the main listings of terms for hyperviolence. A complete listing of this provisional terminology for accessory hyperviolence is depicted in **Fig. 18B** (in concert with their respective three-digit codes) and also depicted in the compact diagram below.

Sluggish. • Untrustworthiness   Laxity• Requital
Disgrace. • Rebelliousness   Odium • Revenge
Debauchery • Disloyalty   Servitude • Grievous.
Outrage • Nastiness   Imperious.• Deceitfulness
Enragement • Grotesque.   Discrimin. • Damnat.

Lethargy • Umbrage   Nonchalance • Peevish.
Absurdity • Ravenous.   Willfulness • Dastardly
Lewdness • Rapacity   Rancor • Vexation
Discord • Badness   Ferocity • Deviousness
Meanness • Nefarity   Truculence • Insidious.

A close comparison of **Figs. 18A** and **18B** demonstrates the reciprocal interplay linking both the main and accessory realms of hyperviolence, where the polarities of "you" and "I" roles are effectively reversed in an empathic sense. Indeed, it remains only a further minor step to incorporate these accessory terms into the schematic definition format, resulting in a reciprocating complement of definitions spanning the accessory realm of hyperviolence. The complete four-page listing of schematic definitions for accessory hyper-violence is depicted in **Tables J-1** through **J-4**. This full forty-part arrangement of definitions directly complements the pattern previously established for the main sequence of terms: providing crucial empathic insights into such an enigmatic array of perspectives, hopefully leading to an enhanced understanding of this pressing set of darker social issues.

Similar to the main realm of hyperviolence, it must further be emphasized that these accessory variations are necessarily a work in progress; hence, detailed descriptions of these individual accessory terms will not be undertaken at this juncture, an aspect best left for an upcoming dedicated edition. The overall cohesiveness for this dual hierarchy of hyperviolence, however, proves particularly convincing in scope, leaving room for only minor adjustments to the overall contextual format.

In conclusion, the completed description of the extreme realm of hyperviolence adds an even sense of symmetry to Aristotle's enduring Theory of the Mean. Although this basic refinement might seem intuitively obvious, it nevertheless spells out an essential distinction. Indeed, hyperviolence appears to have dramatically increased in recent years, an aspect the current breakthrough hopes to remedy through an enhanced understanding of the darker dynamics at issue. In a simpler age, the depiction of gratuitous hyperviolence or ultraviolence (as it was initially coined), garnered a shocking degree of controversy when portrayed cinematically in Stanley Kubrick's *A Clockwork Orange*. This rather quaint depiction of hyperviolence contrasts drastically to the current trend towards gratuitous slasher-films and violent video games. Art clearly imitates life, particularly in terms of the dramatic ascendancy of violent street-gangs, where senseless murder is considered a prerequisite for acceptance into the gang. Undoubtedly the most effective means for addressing such rampant criminality entails reaching out to the youth culture in order to head-off such a tragic theft of innocence. Character Education programs have made great strides in this regard. Through the aid of the newly proposed technological enhancements, it is hoped that an expanded demonstration of the long-term advantages of a virtuous lifestyle will outweigh the sensationalistic dictates of the darker side, perhaps saving an entire generation from a life filled with irreparable pain and regret.

19

THE GENERAL UNIFYING THEMES FOR THE REALM OF EXCESS

The completed description of the vices of excess and hyperviolence ultimately leaves the remaining issue of the general unifying themes for the overall realm of excess. Recall from **Parts I** and **II** how the major virtues and the vices of defect were respectively associated with what were termed the *general unifying themes*. Chapter *8* introduced the themes for the virtuous realm, defined as the authority-based hierarchy of individualism, personalism, romanticism, ecumenism, and humanism; as well as the related sequence of follower themes (pragmatism, utilitarianism, ecclesiasticism, eclecticism, and mysticism. Each of these overarching themes was described as a direct summation of its four subordinate terms. For instance the general unifying theme of *utilitarianism* specifies the four-part listing of the cardinal virtues: namely, prudence, justice, temperance, and fortitude. Similarly, the theme of *ecclesiasticism* alternately targets the theological virtues (faith-hope-charity-decency). Indeed, these general unifying themes proved similarly amenable to incorporation into the schematic definition format: whereby directly mirroring the pattern previously established for the individual ethical terms (with the exception that the themes are now substituted in their place).

A similar pattern was further proposed in **Fig. 14B** (of Chapter *14*) with respect to the realm of defect, resulting in a fully darker hierarchy of general unifying themes. The themes for defect are arranged as direct polar opposites of those specified for the virtuous realm. For instance, the darker authority-based sequence of knavery, villainy, profanity, apostasy, and nihilism contrasts point-for-point with the respective virtuous hierarchy of individualism, personalism, romanticism, ecumenism, and humanism. Furthermore, the remaining listing of follower-based themes

(fraud, corruption, heresy, anarchism, and diabolism) makes a fitting counterpoint to the virtuous hierarchy of pragmatism, utilitarianism, ecclesiasticism, eclecticism, and mysticism. Indeed, this distinctive arrangement of themes for the realm of defect was similarly seen to be incorporated into the schematic definition format, as graphically depicted in **Table C-3** of Chapter *14*.

Upon this solid conceptual foundation, the remaining issue of the general unifying themes for the overarching domain of excess rightfully enters the picture. A cursory survey of the relevant literature at first failed to provide any convincing style of (one-to-one) thematic correspondence. The intervening course of years, however, has subsequently revealed a convincing complement of themes for the vices of excess and hyperviolence: as schematically depicted in **Fig. 19** (a format that also includes the themes for the major virtues and the vices of defect). Indeed, the predicted complement of *accessory* themes in relation to excess are also depicted for sake of contrast. The remainder of the current chapter examines this basic realm of excess in relation to the overarching array of general unifying themes.

THE MAIN THEMES FOR THE VICES OF EXCESS

As previously described in Chapter *8* (for the virtuous realm), each of the general unifying themes within the ascending ethical hierarchy is viewed as a "meta-order" summation of its respective thematic focus. For instance, the themes for the realm of excess build directly upon those specified for the virtuous mode: namely, the personal authority theme of individualism further extends to the more extreme theme of *egotism*. Furthermore, the virtuous group authority theme of personalism is taken to the extremes as the

+ + THEMES for the VICES of EXCESS
(Excessive Virtue)

318 - Egotism	328 - Officiousness
338 - Elitism	348 - Authoritarianism
358 - Ideology	368 - Clericalism
378 - Fanaticism	388 - Idealism
398 - Triumphalism	308 - Occultism

THEMES for the ACCESS. VICES of EXCESS
(Excessive Accessory Virtue)

319 - Egocentrism	329 - Obtrusiveness
339 – Autocracy	349 - Absolutism
359 - Pontification	369 - Dogmatism
379 - Fundamentalism	389 - Supremacism
399 - Universalism	309 - Enigmatism

+ THEMES for the MAJOR VIRTUES
(Virtuous Mode)

118 - Individualism	128 - Pragmatism
138 - Personalism	148 - Utilitarianism
158 - Romanticism	168 - Ecclesiasticism
178 - Ecumenism	188 - Eclecticism
198 - Humanism	108 - Mysticism

THEMES for the ACCESS. MAJOR VIRTUES
(Accessory Virtuous Mode)

119 - Quintessentialism	129 - Expediency
139 - Heroism	149 - Practicality
159 - Charisma	169 - Orthodoxy
179 - Evangelism	189 - Moralism
199 - Cosmopolitanism	109 - Spiritualism

THEMES for the VICES of DEFECT
(Absence of Virtue)

518 - Knavery	528 - Fraud
538 - Villainy	548 - Corruption
558 - Profanity	568 - Heresy
578 - Apostasy	588 - Anarchism
598 - Nihilism	508 - Diabolism

THEMES for the ACCESS. VICES of DEFECT
(Absence of Accessory Virtue)

519 - Mischief	529 - Deception
539 - Licentiousness	549 - Venality
559 - Scandal	569 - Schismatism
579 – Infidelity	589 - Lawlessness
599 - Alienation	509 - Sorcery

THEMES for HYPERVIOLENCE
(Excessive Defect)

718 – Perversion	728 - Exploitation
738 - Depravity	748 - Pernicity
758 - Sacrilege	768 - Recusancy
778 – Reprobation	788 - Pandemonium
798 - Mindlessness	708 – Demonism

THEMES for ACCESS. HYPERVIOLENCE
(Excessive Accessory Defect)

719 - Fetishism	729 - Victimization
739 - Debasement	749 - Vileness
759 - Blasphemy	769 - Heathenism
779 - Recreancy	789 - Tumultuousness
799 - Unruliness	709 - Demoniac

Fig. 19 – Master Schematic Diagram Depicting the *80* Individual General Unifying Themes

EGOTISM	OFFICIOUSNESS
Previously, you have excessively acted in a motivated fashion towards me: in response to my (as procurer) extremely active treatment of you. But now, I (as personal authority) will *egotistically* act in an extremely individualistic fashion towards you: in anticipation of your excessively motivated treatment of me.	Previously, I (as personal authority) have egotistically acted in an extremely individualistic fashion towards you: overriding your excessively motivated treatment of me. But now, you (as my personal follower) will *officiously* act extremely pragmatically towards me: overruling my (as PA) egotistical treatment of you.
ELITISM	AUTHORITARIANISM
Previously, you (as my personal follower) have officiously acted extremely pragmatically towards me: in response to my (as PA) egotistical treatment of you. But now, I (as group authority) will egotistically act in an *elitist* fashion towards you: in anticipation of your (as PF) officious treatment of me.	Previously, I (as group authority) have egotistically acted in an elitist fashion towards you: overriding your (as PF) officious treatment of me. But now, you (as group representative) will officiously act in a *authoritarian* fashion: overruling my (as GA) elitist treatment of you.
IDEOLOGY	CLERICALISM
Previously, you (as group representative) have officiously acted in an authoritarian fashion: in response to my (as GA) elitist treatment of you. But now, I (as spiritual authority) will elitely act in a *ideological* fashion towards you: in anticipation of your (as GR) authoritarian treatment of me.	Previously, I (as spiritual authority) have elitely acted in a ideological fashion towards you: overriding your (as GR) authoritarian treatment of me. But now, you (as spiritual disciple) will authoritarianly act in a *clericalistic* fashion towards me: overruling my (as SA) ideological treatment of you.
FANATICISM	IDEALISM
Previously, you (as spiritual disciple) have authoritarianly acted clerically towards me: in response to my (as SA) ideological treatment of you. But now, I (as humanitarian authority) will ideologically act in a *fanatical* fashion towards you: in anticipation of your (as SD) authoritarian sense of clericalism.	Previously, I (as humanitarian authority) have ideologically acted fanatically towards you: overriding your (as SD) clericalistic treatment of me. But now, you (as representative member of humanity) will *idealistically* act with clericalism towards me: overruling my (as HA) fanatical treatment of you.
TRIUMPHALISM	OCCULTISM
Previously, you (as representative member of humanity) have idealistically acted with clericalism towards me: in response to my (as HA) fanatical treatment of you. But now, I (as transcendental authority) will fanatically act *triumphally* towards you: in anticipation of your (as RH) idealistic treatment of me.	Previously, I (as transcendental authority) have fanatically acted triumphally towards you: overriding your (as RH) idealistic treatment of me. But now, you (as my transcendental follower) will idealistically act *occultly* towards me: overruling my (as TA) triumphalist treatment of you.

Table K-1 – The "Meta" Definitions for the Vices of Excess

PERVERSION	EXPLOITATION
Previously, you have excessively acted in an unmotivated fashion towards me: in response to my (as antagonist) extremely adversarial treatment of you. But now, I (as personal authority) will *perversely* act extremely adversarially towards you: in anticipation of your excessively unmotivated treatment of me.	Previously, I (as personal authority) have perversely acted extremely adversarially towards you: in anticipation of your excessively unmotivated treatment of me. But now, you (as personal follower) will *exploitatively* act extremely unmotivatingly towards me: overruling my (as PA) perverse treatment of you.
DEPRAVITY	PERNICITY
Previously, you (as my personal follower) have exploitatively acted extremely unmotivatingly towards me: in response to my (as PA) perverse treatment of you. But now, I (as group authority) will perversely act in a *depraved* fashion towards you: in anticipation of your (as PF) exploitative treatment of me.	Previously, I (as group authority) have perversely acted in a depraved fashion towards you: in anticipation of your (as PF) exploitative treatment of me. But now, you (as group representative) will *perniciously* act in an exploitative fashion towards me: overruling my (as GA) depraved treatment of you.
SACRILEGE	RECUSANCY
Previously, you (as group representative) have perniciously acted in an exploitative fashion towards me: in response to my (as GA) depraved treatment of you. But now, I (as spiritual authority) will depravingly act in a *sacrilegious* fashion towards you: in anticipation of your (as GR) pernicious treatment of me.	Previously, I (as spiritual authority) have depravingly acted sacrilegiously towards you: in anticipation of your (as GR) pernicious treatment of me. But now, you (as my spiritual disciple) will perniciously act in a *recusant* fashion towards me: overruling my (as SA) sacrilegious treatment of you.
REPROBATION	PANDEMONIUM
Previously, you (as my spiritual disciple) have perniciously acted recusantly towards me: in response to my (as SA) sacrilegious treatment of you. But now, I (as humanitarian authority) will sacrilegiously act in a *reprobate* fashion towards you: in anticipation of your (as SD) recusant treatment of me.	Previously, I (as humanitarian authority) have sacrilegiously acted reprobately towards you: in anticipation of your (as SD) recusant treatment of me. But now, you (as representative member of humanity) will recusantly act *pandemoniusly* towards me: overruling my (as HA) reprobate treatment of you.
MINDLESSNESS	DEMONISM
Previously, you (as represent. member of humanity) have recusantly acted pandemoniusly: in response to my (as HA) reprobate treatment of you. But now, I (as transcendental authority) will reprobately act in a *mindless* fashion towards you: in anticipation of your (as RH) pandemonium-filled treatment of me.	Previously, I (as transcendental authority) have reprobately acted in a mindless fashion towards you: in anticipation of your (as RH) pandemonium-filled treatment of me. But now, you (as my transcendental follower) will *demonically* act pandemoniusly towards me: overruling my (as TA) mindless treatment of you.

Table K-2 - The "Meta" Definitions for Hyperviolence

respective theme of *elitism*. The related spiritual authority theme of romanticism, in turn, extends the more extremely-focused theme of *ideology*. The themes for the remaining humanitarian and transcendental domains; e.g., ecumenism and humanism alternately extend to the more extreme themes of *fanaticism* and *triumphalism*, respectively.

The remaining virtuous sequence of *follower* themes; e.g., pragmatism, utilitarianism, ecclesiasticism, eclecticism, and mysticism is similarly contrasted in terms of the respective listing of themes for excess. For instance, the first-mentioned theme of pragmatism refers to that which is positively expedient to the individual: extending to an extreme degree as *officiousness*. Furthermore, the group theme of utilitarianism (concern for the common good) extends to the equally-extreme theme of *authoritarianism*. This ascending contrast to the virtuous themes ultimately culminates with respect to the spiritual, humanitarian, and transcendental realms (ecclesiasticism, eclecticism, and mysticism): a sequence paralleling the extreme listing of *clericalism, idealism,* and *occultism*, respectively.

THE MAIN THEMES FOR HYPERVIOLENCE

The completed provisional description of the general unifying themes for the vices of excess, in turn, extends to the issue of respective themes for the extreme realm of hyperviolence. Indeed, it ultimately proves feasible to devise an entire parallel hierarchy of themes for the realm of hyperviolence: as schematically depicted in the bottom-most margins of **Fig. 19**. This diagram employs an all-inclusive format that convenient contrasts the outlying realms of excess with the more mainstream (core-nucleus) of themes.

As depicted in **Fig. 19**, the themes for the realm of hyperviolence directly expand upon their more basic foundation within the vices of defect. For instance, the darker personal authority theme of knavery further extends to the more extreme theme of *perversion*. Furthermore, the group authority theme of villainy, in turn, is taken to its logical extremes as the hyperviolent theme of *depravity*. The spiritual authority theme of profanity, in turn, targets the more extremist theme of *sacrilege*. The darker themes for the remaining humanitarian and transcendental levels (apostasy and nihilism) reach their most profound range of reprobation with respect to *reprobation* and *mindlessness,* respectively.

In similar fashion, the remaining darker hierarchy of *follower* themes; namely, fraud, corruption, heresy, anarchism, and diabolism is similarly contrasted in terms of such an extreme range of themes. For instance, the first-mentioned theme of fraud specifies that which is detrimental to the individual, reaching its extremes with respect to the excessive theme of *exploitation*. Furthermore, the group theme of corruption (the lack of concern for the common good), in turn, extends to the extremes attributed to *pernicity*. This darker hierarchy of themes ultimately culminates with respect to the spiritual, humanitarian, and transcendental levels: e.g., heresy, anarchism, and diabolism: a sequence extending to the provisional extremes of *recusancy, pandemonium,* and *demonism*, respectively.

A more detailed description of these overarching themes for excess will not be undertaken at this juncture, their somewhat obscure nature limiting any convincing ethical applications. Indeed, this extreme range of themes enjoys neither the pedigree nor the tradition of the more routine listings of themes initially described for the realms of virtue or defect. Furthermore, any clear-cut determination of the precise degree of excess is scarcely as evident as that established for the more mainstream listings of general themes. Consequently, the themes for the vices of excess and hyperviolence necessarily remain a work in progress, being that the potential for individual substitutions clearly extends to future upcoming editions.

THE THEMATIC DEFINITIONS
FOR THE REALM OF EXCESS

In direct analogy to the more mainstream listing of themes, the related range of themes for the extreme domain of excess shares the potential for incorporation into the master schematic definition format. These are termed the "meta" schematic definitions, being that they represent meta-order summations of the individual quartet-style listings of definitions. Indeed, a complete listing of "meta" schematic definitions for the vices of excess is depicted in **Table K-1**, directly contrasting with the themes for the virtuous realm depicted in **Table C-1** (of Chapter *8*). Furthermore, a parallel listing of schematic definitions relating to the realm of hyperviolence is depicted in **Table K-2**, whereby formally contrasting with the themes for the vices of defect depicted in **Table C-3** (of Chapter *14*). The formal schematic definitions for this darker range of themes is based upon the principles of punishment, just as the virtuous realm was similarly seen to be grounded within the terminology of instrumental conditioning (although now to an extreme degree). This strong behavioral foundation serves as a further welcome validation to this overarching complement of "meta" schematic definitions.

THE ACCESSORY LISTING OF THEMES FOR THE REALM OF EXCESS

The completed description of the main listings of meta-order themes, in turn, invites comparisons to the anticipated *accessory* variations, as schematically depicted in the right-hand column of **Fig. 19**. These accessory variations directly complement the main listings of themes with the exception that the "you" and "I" polarities are now effectively reversed, adding a further crucial (empathic) dimension to the main/accessory thematic format. A suitable number of accessory themes for the realm of excess have provisionally been identified, permitting an overarching listing of accessory terms.

Although the precise degree of correspondence for a few of these themes is not as ideal as might be expected, the seamless cohesiveness of this overarching accessory hierarchy proves the crucial factor here. Being that many of these accessory terms are not commonly encountered in standard usage, a more detailed description of this accessory class of themes is deferred to a later edition of this treatise in light of their highly specialized nature; hence, simply depicted within the right-hand column of **Fig. 19**. Similarly the formal listing of "meta-" schematic definitions for these accessory themes (for excess) will not be depicted at this juncture in light of their highly provisional nature, due in part to their more ambiguous determination of the precise degree of excess.

THE MASTER SCHEMATIC FORMAT LINKING VIRTUE AND VICE

In conclusion, the completed description of the general unifying themes (in both their main and accessory manifestations) ultimately rounds-out the stepwise discussion of each of the distinctive ethical categories. These four distinct ethical categories; e.g., the major virtues, the vices of defect, the vices of excess, and hyperviolence summates to a grand-total listing of *160* individual (main) terms. Through the addition of the mirror-image complement of accessory terms, this figure further doubles to a factor of *320*. This grand unified synthesis accounts for the complete cross-section of emotionally-charged language in general, whereby providing ultimate guidance towards a truly ethical course of action.

+ + VICES OF EXCESS
(Excessive Virtue)

+ MAJOR VIRTUES
(Virtuous Mode)

O - NEUTRALITY STATUS

– VICES OF DEFECT
(Absence of Virtue)

– – HYPERVIOLENCE
(Excessive Defect)

The remaining **Part IV** to follow will examine many exciting new affiliated applications relating to such an all-encompassing new ethical system.

PART-IV

20

FURTHER MODIFICATIONS TO THE MASTER ETHICAL MATRIX

The current description of the virtues and the vices has essentially been restricted to the domain of active human dialogue between at least two physically-present participants. Other formats, however, prove equally feasible; namely, those figuratively specified through the phantom and fantasy dialogues. The *phantom* dialogue is defined as communication directed to an absent individual (the phantom). It includes letter writing (in a printed mode), or the monologue or soliloquy (in spoken form). The *fantasy* dialogue further takes this trend to its limit: where both parties take-on a style of phantom role, as in the literary genre of fiction (where all parties are fictitious). The remainder of the current chapter examines both the phantom and fantasy dialogues with respect to such a radical expansion upon the virtuous themes established for the realm of direct human dialogue. A complete listing of the virtuous themes for the phantom/fantasy dialogues are depicted in **Figs. 20A** and **20B**, providing a convenient reference source for the upcoming discussion to follow.

This higher-order class of phantom and fantasy themes represents a "meta-order" summation encompassing each individual level within the ethical hierarchy. For instance, as previously described for the case of direct dialogue, the general unifying theme of *utilitarianism* encompasses the group follower focus comprising the cardinal virtues (prudence-justice-temperance-fortitude). A similar pattern further holds true for the remaining spiritual, humanitarian, and transcendental levels within the virtuous hierarchy: as originally thematically depicted in **Fig. 8A** of Chapter 8. For instance, the personal authority perspective introduces the theme of *individualism*, extending to *personalism* at the next higher group authority level. The spiritual authority perspective, in turn,

targets the more idealized theme of *romanticism* consistent with a broader focus on universal principles. The themes for the remaining humanitarian and transcendental levels, in turn, take their cues from their individual listings of terms; namely, *ecumenism* and *humanism*, respectively.

In a related fashion, the remaining sequence of *follower* roles is similarly organized in terms of an ascending hierarchy of general unifying themes; namely, pragmatism, utilitarianism, ecclesiasticism, eclecticism, and mysticism. For instance, the first-mentioned theme of *pragmatism* refers to that which is expedient to the individual, extending (in a group sense) to a *utilitarian* concern for "the common good." This ascending sequence of themes, in turn, extends to the remaining spiritual, humanitarian, and transcendental domains with respect to the themes of ecclesiasticism, eclecticism, and mysticism, respectively. A similar pattern further holds true for the themes for the phantom and fantasy dialogues as well.

A few general observations may be deduced from this ascending hierarchy of general unifying themes. As previously outlined, the general unifying themes are subdivided into either active authority modes (occurring in the present) or passive follower modes (occurring within a future-directed time-frame). The active behavioral modes are designated in terms of the immediately active class of authority themes: namely, individualism, personalism, romanticism, ecumenism, and humanism. These authority-based themes represent immediately active perspectives that anticipate the passively-potential complement of future-directed follower themes. Generally speaking, the authority themes immediately initiate the conditioned interaction in anticipation of the future-based potentiality encompassing the respective follower themes.

The passively-potential follower themes, in contrast, target a more abstract realm in light of their extension into a future-directed time-frame: namely, pragmatism, utilitarianism, ecclesiasticism, eclecticism, and mysticism. This latter class of follower themes represents perspectives targeting a future-directed time-frame, effectively consummating the immediately active authority perspectives. Consequently, this latter class of follower themes effectively complements the immediately active authority themes in relation to the overall dynamics governing the conditioned interaction. A more detailed examination of these general unifying themes will now be undertaken with respect to the phantom and fantasy dialogues, including a detailed analysis of their respective literary traditions.

THE PHANTOM DIALOGUE:
A MONOLOGUE IN WORDS

In terms of our modern mobile society one often enters into relationships separated by barriers to direct communication. Communication doesn't cease, but rather switches from verbal to written form, as in letter writing to a friend. Here I record my internal dialogue in order to communicate with you in a written format. In terms of this phantom style of dialogue, I carefully record my own perspectives intended for your reaction, in turn, filling in the counter-perspectives you might employ if you were present. This ascribing of insights to the motives of another is a traditional literary device intended to simulate the continuity inherent to a more direct style of dialogue.

These fixed roles are reversed for the reader of the letter, in that the perspective for which the letter is intended has already been anticipated. The letter reader takes on the formal role of the phantom, whereby feelings expressed during the writing of the letter are transferred in terms of a time-displaced dialogue. In this two-stage fashion, the phantom dialogue simulates a direct dialogue, although in a disjointed fashion that lacks the flexible of a direct dialogue. A similar pattern applies to a soliloquy upon a stage, where the audience takes over the passive role of the phantom. The ritual of prayer and supplication can similarly be regarded as a phantom dialogue, although the more religiously-minded might insist it is really a two-way dialogue.

Letter-writing actually represents a special case of the mental dialogues that fill-up our introspective moments, although now recorded in written form. Also known as *self-dialogue*, the mind is generally flexible enough to take on (in imagination) a role that is not immediately present in this time of solitude and introspection. It is chiefly through this cross-current style of dialogue that I am able to plan a future course of action by imagining how my friends view me in various circumstances, whereby preparing accordingly (an aspect somewhat akin to letter writing). Indeed, whether one relies upon a diary, a letter, or a soliloquy: the basic impact of the phantom dialogue remains true to its focus.

THE PLEDGE

Granted, letter-writing is primarily a personal activity, generally targeting the interpersonal levels within the ethical hierarchy. The phantom dialogue, however, further extends to the remaining authority levels, as affiliated with a wide variety of literary traditions. These traditional themes are specialized into two basic categories depending on whether the authority or follower roles are in focus at the time. The respective sequence of authority themes is defined as the pledge, the proclamation, the edict, and the testament. The first mentioned theme of the *pledge* suggests an active style of personal authority role expressing through the theme of individualism, extending in a phantom sense to a generic style of vow. One informs all in attendance that a personal surety (in the form of an action or guarantee) is guaranteed under particular circumstances. A pledge also extends (in written format) as in a formal guarantee of financial support with respect to fund-raising benevolent organizations.

THE PROCLAMATION

The personal characteristics for the pledge, in turn, extend to a group sphere of influence with respect to the civic prerequisites for the *proclamation*. The ruler, as group authority figure, issues an open proclamation to all subjects, a phantom expression of his authority status in relation to the public at large. To achieve the maximum impact, the proclamation has traditionally been issued in a written format, such as an inscribed parchment nailed up in the public marketplace during medieval times. Through this outward display of manifest authority status (and subsequent word of mouth), the dictates of the monarch eventually extended across the length and breadth of the realm: whereby eliminating the excuse of ignorance for failing to conform to the letter of these royal dictates.

THE EDICT

The political focus for the proclamation, in turn, extends to a universal realm with respect to the traditions of the *edict*. Here issues of a universal focus are promulgated in an international sense, as in the dictates of a religious council. Here the spiritual authority issues an edict to the attention of the entire spiritual congregation. During the Middle Ages, when the Roman Catholic Church wielded supreme authority over Western culture, the Pope (or his designees) projected such authority through the aid of a written edict, a decree that the faithful were obliged to obey. The edict continues the tradition of the pledge and the proclamation in promulgating such outward expressions of authority.

THE TESTAMENT

The universal prerequisites for the edict, in turn, extend to a humanitarian perspective with respect to the enduring traditions of the *testament*. As a literary device it refers to a last will and testament, or any tradition that bears witness to or makes a covenant with. The first-mentioned legacy style of testament shares with the proclamation and the edict a bestowal of good will, although now extending to surviving generations. The latter "witness" style of testament occurs within the ecclesiastical tradition of the middle ages, generally dealing with abstract theological themes. In either case, the testament preserves the overarching focus of the first three themes, mirroring the ascending sequence of authority themes in a complementary fashion.

THE GRANT

The preliminary sequence of phantom themes for the authority roles, in turn, invokes the parallel sequence of themes for the follower roles: e.g., the grant, the charter, the sanction, and the chronicle. The first-mentioned notion of the *grant* suggests a personal sphere of influence, where the personal follower is "granted" privileged status in response to the pledge by the personal authority figure. Here the pledge-then-grant scenario mirrors the direct-dialogue interplay of individualism and pragmatism, although now invoking a more remote phantom character. The potentiality associated with the grant is particularly evident in the sphere of academic research, where financial support is offered in return for services intended to further research and development. Conse-

quently, the reciprocal interplay of authority and follower roles is preserved with respect to the phantom prerequisites for the grant.

THE CHARTER

The personal prerequisites for the grant, in turn, extend to a civic sphere of influence with respect to the group follower theme of the *charter*. The charter is chiefly encountered in group contexts such as business organizations, clubs, or colonial endeavors. The group representative is granted "charter" status in response to the proclaimed intentions expressed by the group authority figure. This is exceedingly reminiscent of the utilitarian prerequisites previously established within the direct-dialogue context. Indeed, much of the settlement of the New World was facilitated through the granting of charters, where the services of willing colonists (such as the Pilgrims) were chartered by legal decree. Consequently, in terms of this cooperative style of group endeavor, the willing labor of the colonists was supported through a land-use charter bestowed in recognition of their concerted effort.

THE SANCTION

Ascending to the next higher spiritual level, in turn, gives way to the universal prerequisites associated with the *sanction*. The sanction is virtually synonymous with religious themes, as reflected in its direct-dialogue counterpart in ecclesiasticism. As representative for the spiritual congregation, the spiritual disciple is solemnly granted a sanction in response to the edict professed by the spiritual authority figure, whereby sanctioning the proceedings. Consequently, through his formal granting of sanction, the spiritual disciple restores an equal balance of power to the interplay of authority and follower roles, at least with respect to such a limited phantom perspective.

THE CHRONICLE

The preliminary sequence of the grant, the charter, and the sanction ultimately culminates in terms of the enduring humanitarian perspective of the *chronicle*. It differs from genre of the *annal* with respect to its more comprehensive character, whereby celebrating grander aspects of human history such as The Medieval Chronicles or The Viking Sagas. A running commentary of historical events is set down in written form for the edification of all future generations to come. This

9118 – *The* PLEDGE *Phantom* - **Individualism** **Personal Authority**	**9128 – *The* GRANT** *Phantom* - **Pragmatism** **Personal Follower**
9138 – PROCLAMATION *Phantom* - **Personalism** **Group Authority**	**9148 – *The* CHARTER** *Phantom* - **Utilitarianism** **Group Representative**
9158 – *The* EDICT *Phantom* - **Romanticism** **Spiritual Authority**	**9168 – *The* SANCTION** *Phantom* - **Ecclesiasticism** **Spiritual Disciple**
9178 – *The* TESTAMENT *Phantom* - **Ecumenism** **Humanitarian Authority**	**9188 – *The* CHRONICLE** *Phantom* - **Eclecticism** **Humanitarian Follower**

Fig. 20-A – The Themes for the Virtuous *Phantom* Dialogues

is recorded in terms of a prototypical humanitarian stance, although now assuming the form of a phantom dialogue that addresses over the span of ages. Indeed, all such communication with future generations must necessarily be considered a phantom dialogue, taking fully into account the gradual unfolding of historical events.

In summary, the complete listing of themes for the phantom dialogue is depicted in a schematic fashion in **Fig. 15A**. Here the phantom dialogues represent a more abstract variation on the main complement of virtuous themes, an ascending format that further mirrors the remaining complement of fantasy dialogues as well.

THE FANTASY DIALOGUE: THE REALM OF FICTIONAL IMAGINATION

In a brief overview of the phantom dialogue, the written word bridges the extent of space, but also time as well. This proves a crucial advantage being that the written word is effectively permanent, as opposed to the ephemeral quality of the spoken word. The written tradition allows one to communicate to all future generations long after one's own death. Indeed, most libraries are crammed with dialogues from the past that still prove meaningful to consecutive generations. The phantom dialogue, however, still remains a fairly restrictive writing style. The roles are rigidly fixed in place for both the reader and writer alike. Over time the audience can change to such a degree as to outdate the material, scarcely more than a quaint curiosity.

The time-honored tradition for circumventing this shortcoming entails the use of the alternate form of recorded dialogue respectively termed the *fantasy* dialogue. Also commonly known as fiction, the writer is divorced from any direct involvement during the composition, whereby freeing creativity conducive to a truly imaginative narrative. The reader, likewise, is not trapped into adopting any particular role, rather freely identifying with any of the fictional characters. This vaunted sense of free imagination is not limited simply speculating or manipulating a range of imagery. This truly unfettered range of imagination leads to the suspension of conventional presupposition or belief: an entertaining expression of make-believe. According to Gaston Bachelard: "Imagination is not the faculty of forming images of reality, it is the faculty of forming images that go beyond reality, which turn reality into song." Consequently, good fiction is broadly appealing in that it generally holds meaning for virtually everyone, whether child or adult. By restricting the

content to a fantasy level, the pretended message is generalized to all ages and cultures, as witnessed in the great popularity of mythology and folklore from ancient times.

THE FABLE

Similar to the pattern previously established for the phantom dialogue, there necessarily exists a parallel complement of literary traditions for each of the individual fictional levels within the ascending virtuous hierarchy. In the latter scenario the source of the dialogue is fictionally disqualified, even though a lesson may still be taught. This is often achieved by converting the characters into personifications of animals, as in Aesop's Fables. A common-sense lesson (such as perseverance) employs such animal stereotypes, as in the footrace pitting the determined tortoise against the over-confident hare. Lessons relating to industriousness contrast how the dedicated ant and the carefree grasshopper prepare for the upcoming winter. Sage wisdom emerges as a one-to-one style of personal interplay characterizing the initial level of the ethical hierarchy. The fable represents a truly enduring style of fantasy dialogue, the basic import of the message unchanged over the course of many geerations.

THE LEGEND

The personal focus of the myth/fable, in turn, extends to a civic sphere of influence with respect to the group authority theme of the *legend*. The legend is distinguished from the fable in that the former typically contains more of a historical context. Legends primarily specify the lore of the common people, whereby celebrating the collective heritage and national spirit. In a traditional sense, legends are narratives exalting great folk heroes, although idealized to some degree as in Paul Bunyan or Casey Jones. The group authority figure enjoys a legendary (virtually mythical) status befitting a leader among men. This is further reflected (in a non-fantasy sense) by the preliminary class of personal ideals (glory-honor-dignity-integrity). Here the legend serves as a fitting exemplar for us all, a paragon of virtue and courage so sorely lacking in our modern age.

THE PARABLE

Although legendary heroism proves a fitting fictional device for the group level, the next higher spiritual realm celebrates the affiliated fantasy genre of the *parable*. Here the spiritual

0118 – MYTH/FABLE *Fantasy* - **Individualism** **Personal Authority**	**0128 – RHETORIC** *Fantasy* - **Pragmatism** **Personal Follower**
0138 – LEGEND *Fantasy* - **Personalism** **Group Authority**	**0148 – PROPAGANDA** *Fantasy* - **Utilitarianism** **Group Representative**
0158 – PARABLE *Fantasy* - **Romanticism** *Spiritual Authority*	**0168 – PROPHESY** *Fantasy* - **Ecclesiasticism** **Spiritual Disciple**
0178 – ALLEGORY *Fantasy* - **Ecumenism** **Humanitarian Authority**	**0188 – UTOPIANISM** *Fantasy* - **Eclecticism** **Humanitarian Follower**

Fig. 20-B – The Themes for the Virtuous *Fantasy* Dialogues

authority figure employs fictional imagery to proclaim a moral message, as in occasions when Jesus employs parables to impart a lesson. According to Matthew 10:13, the disciples inquire of Jesus (following his Parable of the Sower) why he speaks to them in parables. Christ replies: "To you it has been given to know the secrets of the kingdom of heaven, but to them it has not been given … This is why I speak to them in parables, because seeing they do not see, and hearing they do not hear, nor do they understand." Christ's symbolic use of parables alludes to religious precepts that may be too abstract or controversial to be accepted by the uninitiated. The common man inserts himself into the story line through such a fantasy dialogue device. A fisherman gets the point of "a net cast into the sea," whereas the herder feels for "the lost sheep," and the farmer grasps "a seed cast upon barren ground."

ALLEGORY

The ascending hierarchy of the myth, the legend, and the parable ultimately extends to the even more abstract (humanitarian) prerequisites for the *allegory*. It represents an extended style of metaphor by which persons, objects, or actions within a narrative are equated with meanings that lie beyond its basic scope. A given concept, therefore, is figuratively cast in a disguised identity, frequently taking the form of visual imagery. Indeed, an entire cast of characters may be personified in terms of such abstract qualities, the action and setting reflecting relationships between such abstractions. The allegory can lead to fictitious, mythical, or historical themes. Here the abstractions denote meanings independent of the surface action within the story: whether religious, political, moral, or satirical. A form of allegory more specific to the humanitarian realm is known as the *apologue*, a short allegory emphasizing enduring moral themes. In concert with the first three themes, the abstract notion of the allegory effectively rounds-out the ascending hierarchy of (authority-based) fantasy themes.

RHETORIC

The ascending sequence of fantasy themes for the authority realm similarly extends to the remaining follower sequence of themes; namely, rhetoric, propaganda, prophecy, and utopianism. For instance, the first-listed theme of *rhetoric* is defined as persuasive or supportive discourse, an interpretation dating at least to classical Greece. For the Sophists rhetoric enhanced public speaking

and oratory, a literary style of composition of an emotional or imaginative nature that aims to sway the audience through fair means or foul. Isocrates once wrote: "Rhetoric is the art of making great matters small, and small things great." This rhetorical style differs from simple testimony in that the personal reputation of the speaker is not essential for driving home the salient point of the message. Indeed, many such rhetorical strategies still find popular expression in our present day. Its overriding emotional appeal, as well as the generalized nature of the speaker, establishes rhetoric as a true fantasy form of dialogue, although specialized towards personal ends.

PROPAGANDA

The personalized prerequisites for rhetoric, in turn, extend to a group sphere of influence with respect to the affiliated concept of *propaganda*. It is defined as a rhetorical literary device that invokes stirring testimonials from members within the group in order to sway public sentiment. The highly emotional testimonials often employ stereotyped clichés chiefly unsubstantiated by fact. Witness the glaring propaganda campaigns waged by the Fascist and Communist parties over the course of the 20th century. Although the stigma of propaganda (to a large degree) depends upon which side of the fence one is on, the true danger arises in failing to recognize propaganda for what it presumes to be; namely, a fantasy dialogue of a highly emotional nature.

PROPHESY

The disqualified character of propaganda, in turn, extends to a universal sphere of influence with respect to the spiritual disciple theme of *prophecy*. The disciple/prophet attributes the moralistic content of his message to the vagaries of divine inspiration, dream imagery, or visions. This spirited literary device attempts to break the shackles of ordinary reality through the aid of figurative symbolism of virtually epic proportions. This is particularly apparent in the New Testament Book of Revelation, an elaborate scriptural tradition replete with dreamlike imagery and mythical symbolism.

Prophecy is primarily distinguished from divination, being that the latter seeks to predict future events through natural signals or rituals of chance. Prophecy, in contrast, takes well-established elements of religious belief, whereby embellished into an unfamiliar context (such as projected into the future). Here prophecy represents a disqualified form of fantasy dialogue in relation to the spiritual congregation, whereby permitting unfettered freedom in dealing with controversial themes. Prophesy shares with rhetoric and propaganda such a clear stretch of the imagination, although now appealing to a universal sphere of influence as its underlying rationale.

UTOPIANISM

The remaining humanitarian variation on the fantasy dialogue ultimately culminates in terms of the related theme of *utopianism*. The term derives from a compound of the Greek *ou-* (not) and *topos* (place), collectively translated as "good place" or "no place." The utopian tradition reflects this profound range of ambiguity, denoting an imaginary society enjoying perfect legal, economic, and political governance. This fantasy concept of utopia surpasses any existing style of social structure in terms of a prevailing sense of harmony, utility, and reason enjoyed by all.

The contemporary use of the term first emerges as the title of a treatise published by Thomas More in 1516. Utopia was described as an island where justice and prosperity reigned supreme, its inhabitants having learned to subordinate their selfish desires to rational pursuits. In modern usage, Utopia stands for any imaginary society where harmonious conditions prevail, as fanciful contrasted with reality. Many versions of utopia have since been devised following More's treatise, each reflecting the spirit of an age overflowing with hope and optimism. Regardless of the individual traditions therein, this alluring spirit of utopianism represents a fantasy dialogue encompassing a clearly enduring humanitarian perspective, a virtuous dialogue applicable to all ages and cultures. In concert with the first three themes, utopianism effectively rounds out the stepwise examination of the follower realm in relation to the fantasy class of dialogue.

THE VIRTUOUS ATTRIBUTES FOR THE PHANTOM/FANTASY DIALOGUES

In summary, the completed description of the additional class of phantom and fantasy dialogues roughly triples the scope of potential forms of communication for the virtuous realm. Both the phantom and fantasy dialogues are defined by their respective categories of virtuous themes, a format similar to that proposed for the direct dialogues (from Chapter 8). Perhaps the greatest validity underlying this tripartite system (of di-

rect, phantom, and fantasy dialogues) resides in its all-inclusive nature, accounting for virtually every major category of virtuous communication. These categories fit seamlessly within the ten-level virtuous hierarchy, whereby permitting a truly convincing simulation of virtuous communication in general. Indeed, based upon a limited number of elementary assumptions; namely, the principles of instrumental conditioning and the concept of the meta-perspective, the ascending sequence of stepwise transformations ultimately accounts for the complete master hierarchy of ethical terms.

It must further be emphasized that the current system (by definition) is chiefly applicable only for the English-speaking tradition. Fortunately the English language has assumed the mantle of "lingua franca" for the global community, whereby enhancing its international appeal. Certainly numerous other language traditions might similarly benefit from cross-cultural translations of the ethical hierarchy, offering the potential for a universal range of understanding for the positive emotions. This virtually unlimited potential for virtuous communication further explains the unfathomable complexity of the human mind. Certainly one rarely repeats the exact same train of contextual communication over the course of a lifetime. The most likely scenario for such a rare occurrence concerns the memory-retrieval of such a past conceptual interchanges. Consequently, it might further be argued that all such memories of an emotional nature are stored through such a discrete range of recollected virtuous sequences, a speculation scarcely lost in terms of the programming predicted for the ethical simulation of AI outlined in upcoming Chapter *22*.

In conclusion, the completed description of the phantom and fantasy dialogues offers further crucial inroads towards understanding role-playing across the breadth of human culture. Indeed, it proves particularly crucial to distinguish between phantom dialogue printed upon a page versus the more active styles of direct dialogue. Furthermore, the dramatic influence of fantasy-derived dialogue plays a major role with respect to the accumulated world literary traditions, similarly tempered by political and cultural influences. Although the profound influence of political manifestos or apocalyptic literature still holds considerable sway in the court of public opinion, a more realistic evaluation of the phantom and fantasy dialogues may ultimately ensure a more enduring sphere of global peace and harmony for the foreseeable future.

21

GLOBAL PERSPECTIVES FOR ADVANCING WORLD PEACE

The completed description of the specifics for the three-digit coding system invites further general predictions for its potential role on the world scene today. Through a radical modification of Aristotle's enduring Theory of the Mean, a more balanced sense of conceptual symmetry is established within the sphere of ethical inquiry. This all-inclusive system comprised of three groupings of vice (and one of virtue), in turn, raises the further critical issue; namely, the categories of vices outnumber the virtues by the somewhat disturbing ratio of 3-to-1. A more ethically neutral system was initially predicted, in contrast to the general preponderance of negative classifications that now occurs.

The negative connotations of a number of the categories of vice, however, actually prove somewhat misleading, calling for further evaluation of the motivational dynamics at issue. Each of the four basic ethical categories is assigned a specific plus-or-minus numerical value based upon its inherent degree of adaptability, as well as its potential for causing emotional harm. For instance, beginning with the realm of the major virtues, this category is assigned (without reservation) an overall value of (+1) on a scale of zero to one: reflecting its inherent adaptability and positive functionality within a given interaction.

On the opposite side of the ledger, the corresponding realm of the vices of defect would similarly be expected to rate a corresponding (-1) rating based upon its contrasting relationship to the virtuous realm. This initial impression, however, proves somewhat misleading in that lessons derived from the realm of defect often can prove adaptive to the individual. In a natural setting, for instance, a food source that had been exhausted directly signals to the organism that further such resources should be found soon.

A similar circumstance occurs in the realm of human relationships, as dramatized in the much-publicized phenomenon of celebrity stalking. In this latter instance, the avid fan solicitously seeks the attentions of his celebrity figure in an outward expression of such notable influences. The celebrity, however, is generally overwhelmed by the rigors of his public status, wherein unable to personally interact with each and every one of his fans (although in principle he might like to). The standard form letter addressed to the fan-base is typically taken in stride, a fairly non-threatening rejection in terms. Although this interchange represents an adaptive learning experience for the rational individual, its basic import is generally lost on celebrity stalkers, who refuse to take such practical realities into account. Celebrity stalkers often obliquely misinterpret the benign import of message, sometimes venturing into the realm of bad taste, or the even rarer extremes of hyperviolence. In formal acknowledgement of this essential adaptive function, the earlier rating of (-1) for the vices of defect now seems overly harsh, with the assignment of (-1/2) perhaps more relevant to this discussion.

This modified context scarcely appears applicable to the related sphere of hyperviolence. There is little justification for the drastic behaviors characterizing the extreme realm of hyperviolence; hence, the unequivocal rating of (-1) is specified here. This leaves open only a respective determination of the final realm of the vices of excess, a sphere of excess entirely based within the virtuous realm. This remaining category amounts to somewhat of a special case in that the vices of excess expand upon the virtues to the degree that would fit the definition of a vice, although scarcely to the negative degree previously established for the realm of defect. Indeed, a cursory survey of the vices of excess (e.g., pride, shame, envy, jealousy, etc.) suggests more in the way of bad taste than any overt sense of malice. These vices of excess, however, can prove extremely irritating to those unlucky enough to be directly involved. This basic grouping, accordingly, is assigned the less than absolute value of (**+1/2**), reflecting this category's more casual foundation within the virtuous realm. It should further be emphasized that several of these ratings could have been scaled up or down to some degree, although the true point this exercise aims for an overall evaluation. It remains to ultimately add-up the sum total of numerical values for each of the four calculations; namely, (**+1.5**) for the virtuous mode *vs.* (**-1.5**) for the vices, resulting in a grand total of zero, a direct verification of the ethically-neutral status initially predicted.

APPLICATIONS TO HARMONY ON A GLOBAL SCALE

This even sense of ethical neutrality, however, scarcely agrees with what is currently seen on the world scene today. Indeed, in terms of our modern technological age, one might rightfully argue that the balance of power is actually skewed towards the positive end of the spectrum. The highly interconnected global marketplace certainly specifies such a cooperative style of positive interface. Here, a general rule of law has endured virtually uninterrupted since its first modest beginnings during the Bronze Age.

This impressive track record certainly suggests a selective advantage towards positive interactions. Although some degree of criminality has always existed down the ages, the prime directive of civilized society aims to ensure an equitable sense of reciprocity conducive to free trade and commerce. This founding principle traces its origins to the instinctual foundations underlying operant conditioning; namely, fair goods purchased at a fair price. Indeed, the general state of world affairs has never been better with the exception of minor border skirmishes and mindless terrorist incursions.

This positive outlook would necessarily diminish should the unthinkable ever occur; namely, the unforeseen breakdown of the prevailing social order. Nothing short of a nuclear winter (or other such global disaster) would reach drastic enough proportions to spark a global Dark Age. The residual vestiges of law and order would generally serve to dampen all but the worst of possible scenarios, although the balance of cooperation would undoubtedly skew towards the negative end of

the scale. As so often occurs in history, a temporary reversal should remain exactly that in keeping with the indomitable collective spirit governing all human endeavors.

FOUNDATIONS FOR A WORLD SYSTEM OF ETHICS

This conflict between the forces of order/disorder remains a particularly crucial factor with respect to the major ethical systems of the world. For instance, as the foundation for Christian ethics, the Golden Rule (Do unto others as you would have others do unto you) is founded precisely upon such an appeal to empathic principles. Indeed, it is featured in one form or another in virtually every major world religion: including Judaism, Buddhism, Islam, Hinduism, and Taoism. The Golden Rule places great premium on cooperative styles of virtuous behavior, although these noble ideals don't always "square" in non-cooperative types of circumstances. As a general rule, the Golden Rule is particularly difficult to enforce in situations where others might tend to take advantage of such noble inclinations.

The latter aspect of self-interest (sometimes known as the Iron Rule) promotes a selfish agenda at the expense of the more noble precepts embodied in the Golden Rule. It is a more prosaically defined as: "Do unto others before they can do unto you," a ruthless expression of selfish competition. In contrast to the Golden Rule, the Iron Rule is typically the unspoken code for the rich and powerful, as amply witnessed in the perpetual sequence of tyrants and dictators down through the ages. This primal focus on self-interest is formally encountered within the principles of the zero-sum game; namely, "your loss is my gain," the unforgiving law of the jungle. It scarcely is surprising, then, that the darker side of empathy enters into consideration precisely at this crucial juncture. Here a keen understanding of the motivations of others is essential for achieving the deception and manipulation that characterizes the cunning practice of the Iron Rule.

In defense of the Golden Rule, a slightly different formulation addresses this vulnerability to the Iron Rule: stated as: "Do not do unto others what you would not have them do unto you." Sometimes referred to as *The Silver Rule*, it forbids any descent into the realm of violence, whereby complementing with the more positive prerequisites for the Golden Rule. Also known as ethical minimalism, the Silver Rule prohibits retaliation in any form to harm done by another, equiv-

THE GOLDEN RULE	THE SILVER RULE
"Do unto others as you would have them do unto you."	"Do not do unto others what you would not have them do unto you."
THE BRONZE RULE	**THE IRON RULE**
"Repay goodness with goodness, but evil with justice."	"Do unto others before they can do unto you."

Fig. 21A – The Reigning World Ethical Strategies

alent (but not quite a drastic as) Christ's admonition to "turn the other cheek." It traditionally equates to the strategy of nonviolent resistance against unfair government policies, as successfully practiced by Mohandas Gandhi in reaction to the oppressive British occupation that occurred in India.

This strategy, once again, emerged in the context of the non-violent resistance to racial segregation professed by Rev. Martin Luther King Jr. during the Civil Rights era. These civic leaders advised against retaliation towards one's oppressors while also forgoing compliance to unjust demands. This non-violent strategy of civil disobedience aimed to provoke a moral sense of conscience in the hearts of the oppressors, although this defiance also led to great personal sacrifice on the part the protestors. Although the Silver Rule can prove effective under such ideal circumstances, it can just as easily be exploited, particularly when one's oppressors remain unmoved by such a stirring appeal to conscience.

THE GLOBAL SUPREMACY OF THE LAW OF EQUIVALENT RESPONSE

The overarching standard for ethics down through the ages has unerringly been a hybrid of the principles underlying both the Golden and Iron Rules, in what has suggestively been termed the Bronze Rule according to Carl Sagan's (1993) insightful analysis of the subject. Confucius perhaps best stated this rule as: "Repay kindness with kindness, but evil with justice;" in essence, the strategy of repaying "like with like." This basic strategy is similarly reflected in nature with respect to the principles of equilibrium and homeostasis. This rule is further suggestive of what Communication Theorists term the *symmetrical*

class of power-maneuvers; e.g., responding back in kind what originally had been offered.

With respect to the baser precepts of Iron Rule, the Law of Equivalent Response is fortunately moderated to some degree, as reflected in the "eye for an eye, tooth for a tooth" pronouncement within the Old Testament. Although this scriptural quotation is often cited as condoning violence, it actually proclaims *only* an eye, and *only* a tooth, whereby lessening the risk of escalation in conflict disputes. In contrast, the more positive precepts of the Golden Rule continue to celebrate the *reciprocity* implicit within the virtuous realm, particularly those cooperative impulses where "one good turn deserves another." This virtuous sense of cooperation serves as the enduring foundation for civilization as a whole, providing a stable financial environment for engaging in business and commerce.

Whereas this cooperative style of strategy proves exceedingly effective for the virtuous realm, its darker variation is all too susceptible to the risk of lasting feuds and vendettas. Here few options remain for escaping such self-perpetuating cycles of conflict. This latter shortcoming can fortunately be avoided through the implementation of periodic overtures of forgiveness, whereby preemptively short-circuiting any escalation of conflict cycles. In this modified sense, the "like-for-like" strategy embodied within the Bronze Rule equates to the prevailing standard on the world scene today. It is particularly evident in the field of international politics, where the United States (for instance) scrupulously cooperates with its allies, while justly responding in kind to attacks against its self-interests.

It is scarcely surprising, then, that this basic strategy of responding in kind proves to be the most effective winning strategy as determined within the field of Game Theory. Here various Game Theory tournaments feature computer simulations of various strategies pitted against one another in round-robin match-ups. On a consistent basis, the reciprocal rule program known as "Tit for Tat" proves to be the most effective in many such match-ups. This program is considered to be *nice* (never initiates conflict), *provokable* (refuses to turn the other cheek), and also *forgiving* (permits return to cooperation). This basic program consistently prevails over most variants of the Gold, Silver, and Iron Rules.

FURTHER VARIATIONS WITH RESPECT TO THE BRONZE RULE

These basic precepts of the Bronze Rule can scarcely claim to be the total picture, for further variations on this format are also encountered. Take, for example, the hybrid rule: "Be respectful to one's superiors, but feel free to exploit one's inferiors." This dual strategy employed by the "social climber" aims to secure a selective advantage within the vagaries of a stratified social hierarchy. The social climber appeases his boss in deference to his authority status, while simultaneously taking advantage of those occupying subordinate positions.

A further hybrid example concerns the tendency towards nepotism, also known as kin-selection. This basic strategy specifies close cooperation with one's relatives (or those with a similar background), while remaining competitive towards outsiders. This entails favoring those within one's immediate peer group, while withholding favor from those outside of one's purview. A special instance of this strategy concerns the Tragedy of the Commons, where diverse interests come into conflict so that all are affected. The over-harvesting of limited fish stocks is one such pressing example, leading to an eventual crash in breeding ocean populations. One township (or fleet) is generally pitted against all others in an attempt to preserve one's own self-interests, in contrast to the loftier aims of the group-collective. The only meaningful solution to such a partisan trap lies in an appeal to a universal perspective, the resource now viewed as a commons to be shared by all, fully justifying the sacrifice that must be endured if the resource is to remain plentiful.

APPLICATIONS TO GLOBAL SCALE HARMONY

This competitive style of social interplay is scarcely as simple as it would appear. Indeed, in terms of our modern technological age, one might argue that the balance of power is actually skewed towards the cooperative end of the spectrum. The highly interdependent global marketplace certainly favors such a cooperative style of positive influence. Indeed, a general rule of law has endured virtually uninterrupted since its first modest glimmerings during the Bronze Age. This impressive track record suggests a clear selective advantage towards positive interactions. Although some degree of criminality has existed down through the ages, the prime directive of civilized society aims to ensure an equitable sense of reciprocity conducive to free trade and commerce. These basic principles trace their origins to the instinctual foundations underlying instrumental conditioning; namely, fair goods and services at an equitable price. Indeed, the general state of world affairs has never been more optimistic, with the exception of minor border skirmishes and terrorist incursions.

This positive outlook necessarily breaks down should the unthinkable ever occur; namely, the unforeseen decline of the prevailing global order. Here nothing short of a nuclear winter (or other such pandemic disaster) would be drastic enough to spark such a global Dark Age. The residual vestiges of law and order could serve to dampen all but the worst potential scenarios, although the overall balance would undoubtedly skew towards the negative end of the scale. As so often occurs in history, such a temporary reversal would remain exactly that, a fitting tribute to the indomitable spirit governing all human endeavors. This rosy outlook, however, only truly remains feasible as long as the prevailing emphasis upon the virtues and values remains firmly in place.

APPLICATIONS BASED UPON THE SCHEMATIC DEFINITION FORMAT

One of the most effective means for promoting character values is through the aid of the schematic definition format for the virtuous mode. These formal listings of schematic definitions outline the basic communicational dynamics at issue. Here the reciprocal interplay of authority and follower roles is spelled out in a longhand style of notation. The conceptual precision of these schematic definitions seems unprecedented on the world scene today, permitting considerable interpersonal insights and intuitions. Indeed, these definitions can be employed to diagnose dysfunctional patterns of communication, translated (through specific examples) into a format more easily comprehended by the individual. The standard flowchart schematic proves particularly effective for outlining specific interpersonal and communicational issues, an aspect that would ideally be analyzed in a real-time context.

Perhaps the greatest beneficiaries of such an innovation extend to the youth of the nation, whose moral propensities are gradually being molded into place. The more routine virtues and values within the ethical hierarchy should prove invaluable for navigating these crucial stages in emotional development. The ongoing trend towards character education proves a particularly valuable adjunct for themes that have typically been dealt with only on a religious level. This secular strategy should provide crucial guideposts to decisions of a moral nature, as formally specified through the schematic definition format.

These precise strategies for relationship modeling similarly apply to an adult sphere of influence, where marital and/or family conflict can effectively be resolved. Here the schematic definition format emerges as a general-purpose diagnostic tool for virtually everything within the emotional spectrum, whereby characterizing the overarching realm of virtues, values and ideals.

THE NEW SCIENCE OF POWERPLAY POLITICS

As with any newly established system, a proper descriptive moniker is definitely called for: namely, the new science of Powerplay Politics™. This designation was selected in allusion to the diverse concepts of the *power play* and *Power Politics*. The latter term is an English translation of the German *machtpolitik* (literally, power politics). It refers to a traditional style of political administration emphasizing power and authority, often in a coercive fashion.

In contrast, the power play denotes a collective style of cooperative effort, traditionally defined as a scoring advantage for team sports such as football or hockey. The power play refers to any style of mass interference within a particular point or zone, an aspect reminiscent of the cohesive style of "strike leverage" characterizing the follower role. Owing to this enhanced versatility of both the authority and follower roles, the notion of Powerplay Politics proves particularly effective for designating this dual power realm.

According to this dual communicational dynamic, Powerplay Politics is essentially grounded within two basic principles adapted from Communication Theory. The first principle states that all communication is motivationally charged to some degree, whereby targeting the intentions of one-self and others within the verbal interaction. Here even a routine lecture on pure mathematics contains an underlying motivational component: e.g., the professor is subliminally determined to achieve academic tenure, while the students are concerned with earning a passing grade, etc.

The second basic principle derives from the ascending nature of the ethical hierarchy. Indeed, whether we care to admit it or not, we all seek to be in control of the ongoing interaction. For instance, the group authority overrules the power leverage wielded by the personal follower, whereas the group representative counters that of the group authority (and so forth). In most stable relationships, power leverage is shared in a trade-off style of fashion, although not always with equivalent results. Furthermore, any outward expression of weakness can paradoxically impart an empowering effect, as witnessed in terms of the hypochondriac or the masochist.

Regardless of the particular mechanisms at issue, the pervasive desire to be in control of a relationship emerges as the general driving principle: which (in concert with the first principle) accounts for the overarching focus for the new science of Powerplay Politics. Each of these diverse perspectives is unified into a seamless linguistic continuum encompassing the virtues, values, and ideals; providing a sturdy conceptual foundation for affective language in general.

FURTHER MODIFICATIONS TO THE MOTIVATIONAL MATRIX

The current inaugural edition of *World Peace 2.0: Restoring Global Harmony* has endeavored to offer a formal overview of innovative new avenues towards promoting global peace and harmony. A summary of the overall dynamics governing the ethical hierarchy definitely proves in order here, whereby providing a solid conceptual foundation for a discussion of potential modifications to the linguistic system. Indeed, the predicted number of slots within the unified ethical hierarchy yields a grand-total of *400* individual terms, the complete breakdown of which now will be described.

Part I introduced the ten-level hierarchy of the virtues, values, and ideals: reflected in the ascending sequence of personal, group, spiritual, humanitarian, and transcendental levels within the ethical hierarchy. This basic pattern, when further specialized into authority and follower roles, accounts for the full ten-level hierarchy of groupings comprising the virtuous mode, resulting in a sum-total of forty individual terms. When this total is further extended to include the accessory variations of the virtues, as well as the general unifying themes, the grand total expands to an even *100* individual terms.

Part II, in turn, targets the opposing realm of the vices of defect, in direct correspondence to the terminology initially proposed by Aristotle. The master hierarchy for the vices of defect directly parallels that previously established for the virtuous mode: an ascending hierarchy of ten authority levels, each invested with a quartet-style grouping of vices (for a grand-total of forty). When further extended to include the accessory variations, as well as the general unifying themes, the grand total similarly expands to *100* individual terms. This opposing contrast between virtue and vice provides the basic *core-nucleus* for the ethical hierarchy, whereby accounting for the more routine types of moral communication.

Part III further modified this basic format through the addition of the affiliated realm of excess. The vices of excess represent extreme variations with respect to the virtuous mode. Furthermore, the respective terminology for hyperviolence similarly targets the domain of the vices of defect. In conjunction with the major core-nucleus of virtues/vices, these two additional categories for the realm of excess summate to a grand-total of one-hundred individual terms each: resulting in the master schematic format of *400* individual terms consistent with the dramatic degree of complexity underlying the human emotions (as outlined in the diagram below).

+ + VICES OF EXCESS
(Excessive Virtue)

+ MAJOR VIRTUES
(Virtuous Mode)

O - NEUTRALITY STATUS

– VICES OF DEFECT
(Absence of Virtue)

– – HYPERVIOLENCE
(Excessive Defect)

This modified system radically expands upon Aristotle's Theory of the Mean, retaining his basic format of the *virtues* interposed between the vices of *defect* and the vices of *excess*. This master

schematic diagram further introduced the completely new notion of the realm of *hyperviolence*, wherein permitting a more even sense of symmetry. This expanded format is symmetrically organized around the central concept of the *neutrality* status: replacing Aristotle's original category of the "mean" virtues as the basic core-nucleus for the system. This sense of neutrality represents the formal *default* status for the system: defined as the basic initiation point for all new classes of relationship to follow (whether positive or negative in nature).

THE TRANSITIONAL POWER MANEUVERS

The schematic four-part confluence of virtue and vice suffers one crucial shortcoming; namely, the respective authority and follower roles are fixed rigidly into place: allowing precious little flexibility to operate within the system. Versatility plays a key role in our modern mobile society, where continually shifting social coalitions place ever-greater demands upon the individual. Each new adjustment within the social hierarchy calls for sophisticated mechanisms for integrating this modification, an innovation that the established listings of virtue and vice fail to fully take into account. In addition to the incremental pattern of maneuvering for power initially described, a more direct avenue must necessarily exist for leapfrogging directly into the higher authority levels; e.g., the group, spiritual, and humanitarian levels, respectively. This further class of options is respectively termed the class of *transitional* power maneuvers, being that they "transition" the individual directly into new social contexts.

A number of key features distinguish the transitional power maneuvers, permitting an enhanced degree of versatility through discrete transitional points across the entire ten-level span of the ethical hierarchy. These transitions represent direct motivational analogs of the major power maneuvers they serve to imitate. This often takes on an exaggerated character in order to make the point more clearly. This flair for the dramatic can be either humorous (as in the realm of comedy), or tragic (as in the genre of melodrama). These transitions are the stock-in-trade for the standard "situation comedy," where the guest star intrudes upon the graces of the ensemble cast, invariably with hilarious consequences. A similar pattern further holds true with respect to the more sober realm of melodrama, as evident in the genre of the daytime soap opera.

This transitional class of power maneuvers (as their name implies) refers to a relationship initiated for the first time. Here the individual endeavors to establish a new transitional interaction within a pre-established social order. Indeed, the virtuous realm of humor and comedy is fully explainable in terms of a dual transitional interplay of double-bind and counter double-bind maneuvers. The distinctive classifications of *lesser* virtues represent transitional variations targeting the main virtuous realm. The pervasive human fascination with humor and comedy is fully explained in terms of this versatile set of transitional power maneuvers, accounting for many of the lesser virtues (such as loyalty, responsibility, humility, etc.) not included within the major listings of virtues.

Loyalty → Humility	Responsibility → Innocence
Fidelity → Majesty	Duty → Vindication
Piety → Magnificence	Allegiance → Exoneration
Felicity → Grandeur	Righteous.→ Immaculate.

Discipline → Modesty	Vigilance → Meekness
Chivalry → Chastity	Courage → Obedience
Nobility → Purity	Valor → Conformity
Zeal → Perfection	Triumph → Pacifism

The comprehensive listing of lesser virtues depicted above represents just one of four distinct categories within the overall transitional format, whereby extending to the realms of criminality and hypercriminality, as well as the communicational factors underlying the realm of mental illness. In concert with the initial class of lesser virtues, the four respective categories are depicted as the right-hand column of terms listed adjacent the major categories within the master diagram to follow.

+ +	**VICES OF EXCESS** (Excessive Virtue)	**MENTAL ILLNESS** (Transitional Excess)
+	**MAJOR VIRTUES** (Virtuous Mode)	**LESSER VIRTUES** (Transitional Virtue)
0	....	**NEUTRALITY STATUS**
–	**VICES OF DEFECT** (Absence of Virtue)	**CRIMINALITY** (Transitional Defect)
– –	**HYPERVIOLENCE** (Excessive Defect)	**HYPERCRIMINALITY** (Transit. Hyperviolence)

In direct analogy to the major categories of themes, the transitional variations are similarly organized around the centralized zone of neutrality status, whereby serving as direct transitional entry-points in relation to each of the major categories. The classifications of the lesser virtues are respectively depicted immediately adjacent to the main virtuous realm. Similarly, the theme of criminality is depicted adjacent to the vices of defect. Furthermore, in terms of the realm of excess, hypercriminality represents the transitional variation in relation to hyperviolence, whereas the domain of mental illness is depicted adjacent to the vices of excess. The respective listings of individual terms are collectively depicted within the master schematic diagram comprising **Fig. 21B**.

The individual terminology for criminality and hypercriminality is fairly straightforward in terms of function: representing discrete transitional variations with respect to the darker domain of defect. Here criminality represents an ingrained tendency to initiate a relationship from a selfish or violent standpoint, a contention echoed by many criminologists. A more detailed description of the terminology for both criminality and hypercriminality clearly remains beyond the basic scope of this summary chapter, although a more comprehensive treatment is reserved for a planned upcoming sequel.

For sake of completeness, however, one final mention must necessarily be made with respect to to the remaining transitional category of mental illness. Here mental illness is defined as that transitional class of double bind and counter double bind maneuvers targeting the realm of the vices of excess. Indeed, each of the major classifications of the mental disorders (e.g., the personality disorders, neuroses, mood disorders, and schizophrenia) is fully explainable in terms of such a transitional model of mental illness. In keeping with its transitional relationship to the vices of excess (that are formally divorced from the domain of defect), mental illness appears fairly non-threatening in nature: as reflected in studies confirming the non-violent character of the mentally ill in relation to the general population. This interpretation proves particularly insightful in terms of the bizarre symptomology associated with the psychoses, a class of mental illness reflecting the extreme degree of disqualification characterizing the counter double-bind class of maneuvers. Indeed, the compact table listed below schematically depicts this dual interplay across the entire ascending hierarchy of the psychoses, as well as the personality disorders and the neuroses. This was chiefly made possible through a pre-existing system of terminology for the psychoses pioneered by German clinician, Karl Leonhard, as well as the

+ + VICES of EXCESS (Excessive Virtue)		MENTAL ILLNESS – (B) (Transitional Excess → Disqualified Excess)	MENTAL ILLNESS – (A) (Transitional Excess → Disqualified Excess)
Pride - Flattery	Shame - Criticism	Histrionic Personality → Dissociative Hysteria	Narcissistic Personality → Obsession Neurosis
Vanity - Adulation	Humiliation - Ridicule	Happiness Psychosis → Confabulatory A/L Paraphr.	Confabulatory Euphoria → Confab. Paraphrenia
Conceit - Patronization	Mortification - Scorn	Excited Confusion Psychosis → Excited Cataphasia	Enthusiastic Euphoria → Proskinetic Catatonia
Pretention - Obsequious	Anguish - Mockery		Non-Participatory Euphoria → Silly Hebephrenia
Sanctimony - Sycophancy	Tribulat - Cynicism	Paranoid Personality → Depersonalization Neurosis	Borderline Personality → Phobia Neurosis
		Anxiety Psychosis → Fantastic A/L Paraphrenia	Suspicious Depression → Fantastic Paraphrenia
		Inhibited Confusion Psych. → Inhibited Cataphasia	Self-Torturing Depression → Negativistic Catatonia
Envy - Impudence	Disdain - Insolence		Non-Particip. Depression → Insipid Hebephrenia
Jealousy - Arrogance	Contempt - Audacity	Passive/Aggressive Personal. → Conversion Hyster.	Dependent Personality → Compulsion Neurosis
Covetous. - Impetuosity	Reproach - Rashness	Manic/Depress. Disease → Manic A/L Paraphrenia	Pure Mania → Expansive Paraphrenia
Longing - Presumption	Chagrin - Boldness	Hyperkin. Motility Psych.→Hyperkin. Periodic Cata.	Unproductive Euphoria → Parakinetic Catatonia
Affectation - Smugness	Bitterness - Harshness		Hypochondriacal Euphoria → Eccentric Hebephren.
		Schizoid Personality → Neuraesthenic Neurosis	Avoidant Personality → Anxiety Neurosis
		Manic/Depressive Disease → Confused A/L Paraphr.	Pure Melancholy → Incoherent Paraphrenia
		Akinetic Motility Psychosis→ Akinetic Periodic Cata.	Harried Depression → Affected Catatonia
			Hypochondriacal Depression → Autistic Hebephren.

+ MAJOR VIRTUES (Virtuous Mode)		LESSER VIRTUES (I) (Transitional Virtue → Disqualified Virtue)	LESSER VIRTUES (II) (Transitional Virtue → Disqualified Virtue)
Solicitous.- Approval	Submiss.- Leniency	Loyalty → Humility Responsibil. → Innocence	Self-Esteem → Reverence Apology→ Clemency
Glory - Prudence	Honor - Justice	Fidelity → Majesty Duty → Vindication	Pomp → Veneration Rectitude → Pardon
Providence - Faith	Liberty - Hope	Piety→ Magnific. Allegiance → Exoneration	Sanctity → Homage Penitence → Absolution
Grace - Beauty	Free-will - Truth	Felicity → Grandeur Righteous.→ Immaculat	Dominion → Benediction Contrition → Deliver.
Tranquility - Ecstasy	Equality - Bliss		
		Discipline → Modesty Vigilance → Meekness	Congeniality→Concess. Sympathy → Appease.
Desire - Aspiration	Worry - Compliance	Chivalry → Chastity Courage → Obedience	Cordiality→Indulgence Compass. → Conciliate
Dignity - Temperance	Integrity - Fortitude	Nobility → Purity Valor → Conformity	Hospitality→Gratitude Mercy → Accommodat
Civility - Charity	Austerity - Decency	Zeal → Perfection Triumph → Pacifism	Altruism → Goodwill Forgiveness → Sacrifice
Magnanim.- Goodness	Equan.- Wisdom		
Love - Joy	Peace - Harmony		

VICES of DEFECT
(Absence of Virtue)

Laziness - Treachery Negligence - Vindictive.
Infamy - Insurgency Dishonor - Vengeance
Prodigal - Betrayal Slavery - Despair
Wrath - Ugliness Tyranny - Hypocrisy
Anger - Abomination Prejudice - Perdition

Apathy - Spite Indifference - Malice
Foolishness - Gluttony Caprice - Cowardice
Vulgarity - Avarice Cruelty - Antagonism
Oppression - Evil Persecution - Cunning
Hatred - Iniquity Belligerence - Turpitude

CRIMINALITY (I)
(Transitional Defect → Disqualified Defect)

t-Treachery → d-Laziness t-Vindict. → d-Neglig.
t-Insurgency → d-Infamy t-Vengeance → d-Dishon.
t-Betrayal → d-Prodigality t-Despair → d-Slavery
t-Ugliness → d-Wrath t-Hypocrisy → d-Tyranny

t-Spite → d-Apathy t-Malice → d-Indifference
t-Gluttony → d-Foolish. t-Cowardice → d-Caprice
t-Avarice → d-Vulgarity t-Antagonism → d-Cruelty
t-Evil → d-Oppression t-Cunning → d-Persecution

CRIMINALITY (II)
(Transitional Defect → Disqualified Defect)

t-Laziness→→d-Treachery t-Negligence → d-Vindict.
t-Infamy → d-Insurgency t-Dishon. → d-Vengeance
t-Prodigal → d-Betrayal t-Slavery → d-Despair
t-Wrath → d-Ugliness t-Tyranny → d-Hypocrisy

t-Apathy → d-Spite t-Indifference → d-Malice
t-Foolish. → d-Gluttony t-Caprice → d-Cowardice
t-Vulgarity → d-Avarice t-Cruelty → d-Antag.
t-Oppression → d-Evil t-Persecution → d-Cunning

– – HYPERVIOLENCE
(Excessive Defect)

Indolence - Mutiny Dereliction - Reprisal
Notoriety - Rebellion Ignobility - Retribution
Licentious.-Treason Savagery - Hopelessness
Fury - Hideousness Despotism - Mendacity
Madness - Horror Bigotry - Ruin

Languor - Grudging. Callousness - Malignancy
Crassness - Voracity Petulance - Cravenness
Rudeness - Greed Hostility - Contentious.
Brutality - Heinous. Barbarism - Ruthlessness
Vicious. - Balefulness Atrocity - Fiendishness

HYPERCRIMINALITY (I)
(Transitional Hyperviol. → Disqualified Hyperviol.)

t-Mutiny → d-Indolence
t-Rebellion → d-Notoriety
t-Treason → d-Licentiousness
t-Hideousness → d-Fury
t-Reprisal → d-Dereliction
t-Retribution → d-Ignobility
t-Hopelessness → d-Savagery
t-Mendacity → d-Despotism
t-Grudgingness → d-Languor
t-Voracity → d-Crassness
t-Greed → d-Rudeness
t-Heinousness → d-Brutality
t-Malignancy → d-Callousness
t-Cravenness → d-Petulance
t-Contentiousness → d-Hostility
t-Ruthlessness → d-Barbarism

HYPERCRIMINALITY (II)
(Transitional Hyperviol. → Disqualified Hyperviol.)

t-Indolence → d-Mutiny
t-Notoriety → d-Rebellion
t-Licentiousness → d-Treason
t-Fury → d-Hideousness
t-Dereliction → d-Reprisal
t-Ignobility → d-Retribution
t-Savagery → d-Hopelessness
t-Despotism → d-Mendacity
t-Languor → d-Grudgingness
t-Crassness → d-Voracity
t-Rudeness → d-Greed
t-Brutality → d-Heinousness
t-Callousness → d-Malignancy
t-Petulance → d-Cravenness
t-Hostility → d-Contentiousness
t-Barbarism → d-Ruthlessness

Fig. 21A – Master Schematic Diagram Depicting the *408 Main Individual Main Terms*

++ ACC. VICES of EXCESS
(Excessive Accessory Virtue)

Narcissism - Blandish.	Ignominy - Reprehens.
Snobbery - Courtliness	Opprobrium - Denunci.
Vainglory - Condesc.	Despondency - Derision
Haughtiness - Servility	Agony - Sarcasm
Pietism - Subservience	Affliction - Satiricism
Invideous. - Impertinence	Despisal - Hubris
Possessive. - Brazenness	Repugn. - Surliness
Cravingness - Brashness	Rebuke - Irascibility
Yearning - Effrontery	Loathing - Temerity
Pretension - Gleefulness	Admonish. - Rigor

ACC. MENTAL ILLNESS - (B)
(Transitional Acc. Excess → Disqualified Acc. Excess)

Histrionic Personality → Dissociative Hysteria
Happiness Psychosis → Confabulatory A/L Paraphr.
Excited Confusion Psychosis → Excited Cataphasia

Paranoid Personality → Depersonalization Neurosis
Anxiety Psychosis → Fantastic A/L Paraphrenia
Inhibited Confusion Psych. → Inhibited Cataphasia

Passive/Aggressive Personal. → Conversion Hyster.
Manic/Depress. Disease → Manic A/L Paraphrenia
Hyperkin. Motility Psych. → Hyperkin. Periodic Cata.

Schizoid Personality → Neuraesthenic Neurosis
Manic/Depressive Disease → Confused A/L Paraphr.
Akinetic Motility Psychosis → Akinetic Periodic Cata.

ACC. MENTAL ILLNESS - (A)
(Transitional Acc. Excess → Disqualified Acc. Excess)

Narcissistic Personality → Obsession Neurosis
Confabulatory Euphoria → Confab. Paraphrenia
Enthusiastic Euphoria → Proskinetic Catatonia
Non-Participatory Euphoria → Silly Hebephrenia
Borderline Personality → Phobia Neurosis
Suspicious Depression → Fantastic Paraphrenia
Self-Torturing Depression → Negativistic Catatonia
Non-Particip. Depression → Insipid Hebephrenia
Dependent Personality → Compulsion Neurosis
Pure Mania → Expansive Paraphrenia
Unproductive Euphoria → Parakinetic Catatonia
Hypochondriacal Euphoria → Eccentric Hebephren.
Avoidant Personality → Anxiety Neurosis
Pure Melancholy → Incoherent Paraphrenia
Harried Depression → Affected Catatonia
Hypochondriacal Depression → Autistic Hebephren.

+ ACC. MAJOR VIRTUES
(Accessory Virtuous Mode)

Ambition- Admirat.	Deference - Concern
Exalt. - Circumspect.	Uprightness - Equity
Bountiful. - Devotion	Freedom - Fairness
Blessings - Charm	Conscience - Credence
Serenity - Rapture	Brotherhood - Content.
Passion – Consid.	Apprehen.- Adherence
Respect - Continence	Probity - Bravery
Courtesy - Kindness	Forbear. - Scruples
Gracious. - Benevol.	Patience - Shrewd.
Affection - Gladness	Amity - Accordance

ACC. LESSER VIRTUES (I)
(Transitional Acc. Virtue → Disqualified Acc. Virtue)

Fealty → Simplicity	Account. → Blameless.
Steadfast. → Loftiness	Obligation → Exculp.
Adoration → Sublimity	Obeisence → Aquittal
Happiness → Splendor	Commit. → Impeccabil.
Adherence → Demure.	Wariness → Timidity
Gallantry → Coyness	Intrepidity → Complais.
Stateliness → Wholesome.	Stalwart. → Compli.
Fervor → Excellence	Victory → Amicableness

ACC. LESSER VIRTUES (II)
(Transitional Acc. Virtue → Disqualified Acc. Virtue)

Self-Respect → Esteem	Sorrow → Lenity
Ostentation → Acclaim	Remorse → Remittance
Holiness → Ardor	Regretful. → Dispensation
Supremacy → Exultation	Grief → Redemption
Amiability → Favor	Empathy → Placation
Conviviality → Sanction	Commiser. → Concord.
Generosity → Thanksgiving	Pity → Consonance
Benignity → Beneficence	Remission → Propitiat.

ACC. VICES of DEFECT
(Absence of Accessory Virtue)

Sloth - Traitorousness   Careless. - Retaliation
Disrepute - Sedition   Reprehension - Avengement
Profligacy - Perfidy   Bondage - Desperation
Indignation - Revulsion   Subjugate - Duplicity
Irateness - Abhorrence   Intolerance - Baneful.

Dispassion. - Resentment   Arbitrary- Malevolent
Preposterous. - Lechery   Fickleness- Pusillan.
Coarseness - Cupidity   Acrimony - Opposition
Animosity - Wickedness   Torment - Guilefulness
Enmity - Sinisterity   Militancy - Baseness

ACC. CRIMINALITY (I)
(Transitional Acc. Defect → Acc. Disqualified Defect)

t-traitor. →d-sloth   t-retaliation →d-careless.
t-sedition →d-disrepute   t-avenge. →d- reprehen
t-perfidy →d-profligacy   t-desper.→d-bondage
t-revulsion→d-indign.   t-duplicity→d-subjug.

t-resent. →d-dispassion   t-malev. →d-arbitrary
t-lechery →d-preposter.   t-pusillan. →d-fickle.
t-cupidity →d-coarse.   t-opposit. →d-acrimony
t-wicked.→d-animosity   t-guileful. →d-torment

ACC. CRIMINALITY (II)
(Transitional Acc. Defect → Disqualified Acc. Defect)

t-sloth→ d-traitor.   t-careless. →d-retaliation
t-disrepute →d-sedition   t-reprehen. →d-avenge.
t-profligacy →d-perfidy   t- bondage→d-desper.
t-indign.→d-revulsion   t-subjug.→d-duplicity

t-dispassion →d-resent.   t-arbitrary→ d-malev.
t-preposter. →d-lechery   t-fickle →d-pusillan.
t-coarse. → d-cupidity   t-acrimony →d-oppos.
t-animosity →d-wicked.   t-torment→ d-guileful.

-- ACC. HYPERVIOLENCE
(Excessive Accessory Defect)

Sluggish. - Untrustworthy   Laxity - Requital
Odium - Rebellion   Disgraceful. - Revenge
Debauchery - Disloyalty   Servitude - Grievous.
Outrage - Nastiness   Imperious. - Deceitful.
Enragement - Grotesque.   Discrim. - Damnation

Lethargy - Umbrage   Nonchalance - Peevish.
Absurdity - Ravenous.   Willfulness - Dastard.
Lewdness - Rapacious.   Rancor - Vexation
Discord - Badness   Ferocity - Deviousness
Meanness - Nefarity   Truculency - Insideous.

ACC. HYPERCRIMINALITY (I)
(Transitional A-Hyperviol. → Disqualified A-Hyperviol.)

t-untrustworthy → d-sluggishness
t-rebellion → d-odium
t-disloyalty→ d-debauchery
t-nastiness→ d- outrage
t-requital→ d-laxity
t-revenge→ d-disgracefulness
t-grievousness→ d-servitude
t-deceitfulness→ d-imperiousness
t-umbrage → d-lethargy
t-ravenousness→ d-absurdity
t-rapaciousness→ d-lewdness
t-badness→ d-discord
t-peevishness→ d-nonchalance
t-dastardliness→ d-willfulness
t-vexation → d-rancor
t-deviousness→ d-ferocity

ACC. HYPERCRIMINALITY (II)
(Transitional A-Hyperviol. → Disqualified A-Hyperviol.)

t- sluggishness→ d-untrustworthy
t-odium → d-rebellion
t-debauchery→ d-disloyalty
t-outrage→ d-nastiness
t-laxity → d-requital
t-disgracefulness→ d-revenge
t-servitude→ d-grievousness
t-imperiousness→ d-deceitfulness
t-lethargy → d-umbrage
t-absurdity → d-ravenousness
t-lewdness→ d-rapaciousness
t- discord→ d-badness
t-nonchalance → d-peevishness
t-willfulness→ d-dastardliness
t- rancor → d-vexation
t-ferocity→ d-deviousness

Fig. 21B – Master Schematic Diagram Depicting the *408 Accessory Individual Terms*

nomenclature for the personality disorders and the neuroses contained within the *DSM–V*.

Narcissistic Personality → **Obsession Neurosis**
Confabulatory Euphoria → **Confab. Paraphrenia**
Enthusiastic Euphoria → **Proskinetic Catatonia**
Non-Participatory Euphoria → **Silly Hebephrenia**

Borderline Personality → **Phobia Neurosis**
Suspicious Depression → **Fantastic Paraphrenia**
Self-Torturing Depression → **Negativistic Cataton.**
Non-Participatory Depression → **Insipid Hebephr.**

Dependent Personality → **Compulsion Neurosis**
Pure Mania → **Expansive Paraphrenia**
Unproductive Euphoria → **Parakinetic Catatonia**
Hypochondriacal Euphoria → **Eccentric Hebephr.**

Avoidant Personality → **Anxiety Neurosis**
Pure Melancholy → **Incoherent Paraphrenia**
Harried Depression → **Affected Catatonia**
Hypochondriacal Depression → **Autistic Hebeph.**

This cohesive *32*-part complement of mental disorders offers a preliminary overview of the applications inherent to the transitional model of mental illness. It should further be noted that this dual model essentially explains only the content/context of what is being communicated; namely, the transitional interplay respect to the vices of excess. Consequently, this newly proposed system is strictly meant to complement currently available treatment options (rather than supplanting them): whereby aiding in the treatment and diagnosis of the mental disorders.

A complete two-page listing of each of the individual ethical terms is presented in **Figs. 21B** and **21C** representing both the main and accessory linguistic matrices for the convenience of the reader, gratefully reproduced (in a modified format) from an earlier book release by the author: *Challenges to World Peace: A Global Solution* (2009).

DIRECTIONS FOR FURTHER RESEARCH

In conclusion, the newly devised master hierarchy of ethical themes represents an unprecedented contribution to the field of ethical inquiry: expanding Aristotle's enduring *Theory of the Mean* into an all-inclusive "theory of everything" of an emotional nature. Far from remaining a purely academic exercise, this all-inclusive system addresses many issues of critical import to human culture: including insights into the enigmatic realm of criminality as well as the communica-

tional factors underlying mental illness. Indeed, when the three primary categories of vice are added to the *208* initial terms specified for the virtues, the grand total reaches a staggering *1,040* individual terms. In concert with the parallel applications relating to ethical artificial intelligence, the overarching applications can scarcely be questioned: a voyage of discovery well worth the effort particularly in light of the critical issues under consideration.

As stated previously, an innate instinctual foundation within the behavioral principles governing conditioning theory imparts a universal appeal upon the world scene today. This systematic behavioral foundation is directly avoids favoritism towards any specific cultural identity, rather treating each with equal dignity and validity. Furthermore, the traditional listings of virtues and values are similarly specified in terms of such a underlying secular perspective, one that is formally independent of any regional cultural bias or the restrictions of any (supernaturally-revealed) scriptural foundation. This new ethical hierarchy enjoys the advantages of highlighting the commonalties of a virtuous lifestyle across all cultures and creeds, rather than focusing upon the individual distinctions therein.

A further conceptual advantage invokes an enhanced awareness of the foundations of organized religion within the principles of Set Theory initially outlined in Chapter *1*. This innovation permits a radical reinterpretation of the role religion plays within society as a whole, in particular, the disturbing ascendance of religious fanaticism. Here the spiritual authority perspective represents just one of the five basic levels within the ascending hierarchy of authority and follower roles: e.g., the personal, group, spiritual, humanitarian, and transcendental perspectives. According to this expanded interpretation, the influence wielded by organized religion chiefly extends to a universal sphere of influence binding over all of mankind. Most religions, however, are compounded by a humanitarian range of perspectives (encompassing all ages and times), as well as an ultimate extension to a transcendental realm, whereby imparting a supernatural character to the entire religious edifice.

The destructive aspects of religious fanaticism essentially emerge from an inherent degree of inflexibility that forbids all other religions the liberty to express their own unique style of universal perspective (on their respective side of the globe). Furthermore, religious fanaticism consistently oversteps its specific universal focus, whereby seeking to influence the political and even personal realms of social conduct. The timely emergence of the Set Theory interpretation for the authority/follower roles will hopefully alter this disturbing trend towards fanaticism in a more rational direction (at least for the more moderate constituency) in terms of both dogma and practice.

Upon such an overarching behavioral foundation, the moral commonalties across all religious traditions can similarly be emphasized, whereby encouraging new inroads into religious tolerance. This new ethical foundation could eventually qualify as the long anticipated system of planetary ethics serving a secular constituency, where such moral issues have typically been downplayed due to well-meaning attempts to avoid religious favoritism. This self-same system could further serve as a valuable adjunct to the major religions of the world without favoring any one of them, whereby promoting the potential a peaceful coexistence amongst all of the established world religions, particularly in that it does not preclude the existence of a top-down pattern of influence (of a supernatural nature) as well. Consequently, this scenario potentially amounts to the best of all possible worlds: enabling an ethical revival in the secular world (which has typically been downplayed), as well as the potential for an even greater degree of spiritual cooperation amongst all of the established religions of the world.

Similar applications extend to the global economic marketplace, an amazing confluence of technical proficiency and international cooperation across the board. This advanced degree of specialization, however, yields a high degree of frac-tionalization into diverse special interest groups, with each seeking to press their own global advantage. This tends to marginalize the general public welfare and cause gridlock in policy-making and global progress. A fresh new perspective is definitely in order here, were one strives not only for what may be gained, but also what is personally needed to support and maintain the tenuous infrastructure underlying the global community.

It is here that the precepts of the newly devised ethical hierarchy come through the clearest, providing a master overview of all ethical interactions based within an instinctual/behavioral foundation. This scientific foundation provides a revolutionary guidebook for ethical behavior in general, the first grand unified synthesis of its kind. Indeed, this new linguistic matrix finally provides a master overview of an interconnected nature for such an abstract moral landscape, supplying key insights towards the resolution of global conflict and disorder. Knowledge *is* definitely Power in this regard, with the *motivational matrix* emerging as a key technology for diagnosing conflict relating to international peace and prosperity. Although only the English version for such a vision is available at this juncture, it remains only a further minor step to translate this breakthrough into the other major language traditions, whereby providing a truly global style of moral initiative. Indeed, a standing invitation is extended to NGO international organizations worldwide for potential collaborative efforts across the board. Through such concerted effort, the future, indeed, looks bright for a bold new era of international peace and global cooperation for all entire humanity.

22

APPLICATIONS TO INFORMATION TECHNOLOGY & ARTIFICIAL INTELLIGENCE

The dream of artificial intelligence has been a goal in the field of Computer Sciences since virtually the dawning of the Computer Age. This anticipated style of artificially intelligent agent would potentially assist in all aspects of human endeavor, accompanied by the intriguing prospects for ultimately transcending the fixed limitations of the human condition. The current dramatic growth in computing power finally enables economic feasible inroads towards such a meaningful AI development. A number of key approaches, such as brain modeling through neural networks, have been attempted, although scarcely enough detailed information exists about the brain to warrant any such serious endeavor. In actuality, the key solution to developing convincing artificial intelligence involves an innate understanding of human communication in general. The preeminent test for AI devised by Alan Turing abstains from relying upon any direct measure of consciousness or perception in its determinations, rather strictly targeting the communicative factors underlying general human language. Assuming that the symbolic attributes of human language can be convincingly simulated on the computer, then many decades of needless effort potentially could be cut from the neural-net or consciousness/perceptual approaches.

Along these lines, my earlier U.S. patent #6,587,846 (now expired and in public domain) has been granted for precisely such a technical innovation based upon the symbolic attributes underlying affective (or emotionally-charged) language. Clear precedents already exist with respect to chess-playing computers, which prove particularly effective for modeling the symbolisms underlying such an abstract gaming format (although scarcely capable of anything else). In similar fashion, the symbolic attributes of the English language tradition prove similarly comprehensive in scope, although several orders of magnitude more abstractly complex in this regard. Certainly the primary economic focus of human society is mediated primarily through the symbolisms of human communication, specifying language as the most rational focal point for ongoing research. This does not necessarily imply that a sensory/motor enabled robot designed in relation to its immediate environment is not a rational focus of directed research. Indeed, such an aspect could eventually be merged with the currently proposed language simulation model, resulting in a more physically complete computer avatar. As far as direct economic applications are concerned, however, it proves entirely more cost effective to target the symbolic attributes of human language in all of its various manifestations.

Fortunately, a convenient shortcut to this daunting complexity of a direct language simulation has recently been proposed (the technical basis for the aforementioned patent). This new approach directly focuses upon the motivational (or emotionally-charged) aspects of language as its guiding principle, the remaining bulk of value-neutral language filling-in in an accessory role. Indeed, as Robert Warren Penn once insightfully wrote: "What is man but his passions?" Along similar lines, most neuroscientists consider the mind/brain complex as a vast motivational analyzer that enables the individual to flourish in harmony with the environment through the principles of instrumental conditioning. The current patent establishes precisely such a foundation within conditioning theory; in this case, appetite in anticipation of rewards, or aversion in expectation of lenient treatment. Furthermore, when the more abstract forms of affective language is viewed in the terms of the ascending hierarchy of meta-perspectives, the traditional groupings of virtues and values jumps neatly into focus.

In summary, through a primary focus upon the affective aspects of human language, an economically feasible shortcut to the AI simulation of human communication finally appears within reach. Much detailed programming remains to be done, perhaps necessitating a customized coding language and supportive hardware consistent with a project of this magnitude. With a starting staff roughly the size of a large encyclopedia work force, a first generation simulation could potentially be achieved within a fairly modest time frame. This painstaking process might eventually be more dramatically accelerated if ultimately accorded the status of a national initiative, particularly in light of its outright commercial value, as well as military applications.

No serious contenders to Turing's Test of Artificial Intelligence have yet come to light, undoubtedly due to the enormous logistics involved in programming human language. Although this ambitious undertaking is clearly years into the future, significant inroads have already been made towards these ends.

INDUCTIVE INFERENCE IN THE DESIGN OF ARTIFICIAL INTELLIGENCE

Fortunately, a well-established form of rational inquiry proves particularly well suited for simulating human intelligence on the computer. Traditionally known as *inductive* reasoning, it gathers together the best available evidence directly inferring the most probable conclusion from the sum total of facts. Inductive reasoning is particularly evident during the courtroom trial, where various shreds of evidence are systematically presented, wherein reaching a final verdict. In contrast to deductive reasoning, the conclusions achieved through inductive reasoning are never absolutely certain, for there always remains the nagging doubt that the verdict was made in error. In the sphere of artificial intelligence, such a drawback actually amounts to a prerequisite, for humans almost invariably make mistakes. Indeed, the uncertainties of the natural world give inductive reasoning the clear advantage in such a problem-solving mode. According to this inductive paradigm, each of us builds a mental model of our environment over a lifetime, forming a master template for our current experiences. When our expectations match our surroundings, we achieve a general sense of security. A mismatch, however, leads to a surprised reaction followed by investigative behavior. Although this sense of security is

often ill founded (as in faulty induction), it actually is a small price to pay for maintaining flexibility within a changeable environment.

In terms of artificial intelligence, the computer would similarly be programmed with its own formal map of reality employed in an analogous detection and matching mode. Any final conclusions would necessarily rely upon probability, although statistics are one of the computer's computational strong points. It is here that the logistics of the ethical hierarchy rightfully enter the picture, serving as the elementary foundation for the first inductive system dealing with motivational logic. According to this fundamental insight, the logical attributes of the ethical hierarchy are programmed directly into the computer, providing a formal model of motivational behavior in general. The computer then employs this programming to infer the precise power-level at issue within a given verbal interchange. On the basis of this initial determination, the computer further calculates the given power countermaneuver simulating motivation within the verbal interaction.

The systematic organization of the schematic definitions permits extreme efficiency in programming, each more advanced level building directly upon that which it supercedes (eliminating much of the associated redundancy). Through an elaborate matching procedure with the schematic definitions, the precise motivational level of communication can accurately be determined (defined as the passive-monitoring mode). This basic determination, in turn, serves as the basis for the production of a response repertoire tailored specifically to the computer (the true AI simulation mode). Here, the basic logistics are already in place for implementing at least the skeleton framework for such an ethical AI-agent.

TECHNICAL CONSIDERATIONS

It still remains to be determined the best means for programming this definition format into the computer, particularly in light of the current trends in computer design. In terms of earlier design generations, calculation speed was strictly limited by the Von Neuman bottleneck; namely, programming instructions were executed one stage at a time. Parallel processing, however, allows various aspects of a complex problem to be handled simultaneously, greatly reducing the bottleneck plaguing sequential processing. The practical applications of parallel processing are particularly relevant to AI computer design. Indeed, the number of parallel processors would ideally equal the sum-total of individual terms within the ethical hierarchy (for a grand total of *1,040*): quite a modest number even by today's design standards. This integrated processor array is further structured along hierarchial lines, effectively mirroring the schematic organization of the ethical hierarchy. This stratified architecture would take full advantage of the strict transformational logic governing the schematic definitions, eliminating much of the redundancy sure to occur in any convincing language simulation. Indeed, the greatest degree of complexity must necessarily involve programming at the most basic personal level of the ethical hierarchy, with the remaining higher levels following naturally from this elementary foundation.

All aspects considered, the most basic unit of input for the AI computer must necessarily be the sentence, for the schematic definitions are similarly given in the form of a dual sentence structure. The AI computer then employs parallel processing to determine the precise degree of correlation between the inputted (target) sentence and its respective schematic definition template. This matching procedure directly scrutinizes each of the grammatical elements within a given sentence, attempting a statistical correlation with the specifics for a given schematic definition. For instance, the tense of the verb, the plurality or person of the noun/pronoun etc. would all be scrutinized according to a pre-set diagnostic formula. Each processor would then determine the sum-total of correct matches ultimately yielding the relative probability of a match with a particular schematic definition. The processor yielding the highest overall rating is uniquely singled-out as the best probable match by the master control unit.

The master control unit achieves this result through the aid of a feedback loop, the priority of the individual microprocessors reciprocally weighted on the basis of preceding determinations. Each schematic definition is respectively composed of both past (as well as present) design components: establishing context as yet a further consideration in the matching procedure. A suitably advanced AI program would retain in a long-term storage virtually every relevant conversation with a given person or context. On this contextual basis, the master control unit then selectively "weights" the individual processors according to a preset formula, taking full advantage of both past (as well as present) conversational dynamics. Furthermore, the computer would be exquisitely sensitive to variations in human personality (just as humans are instinctively so), satisfying yet a further condition of Turing's Test.

This overall process has fittingly been granted U.S. Utility Patent (# 6,587,846), an invention titled: Inductive Inference Affective Language Analyzer Simulating Artificial Intelligence. Although a complete description of the mode of operation for this patent clearly remains beyond the scope of the current chapter, the basic flow chart schematic is reproduced to follow, wherein permitting an indication of the formal dynamics at issue. In concert with the comprehensive listing of schematic definitions comprising the heart of the matching procedure, a cursory overview of the mode of operation becomes increasingly apparent. The complete patent specification is posted for public inspection at the U.S. Patent & Trademark web-site.

FURTHER POTENTIAL DESIGN INNOVATIONS

The ultimate implementation of ethical AI should rightfully be phased-in through several distinct generations of development, in keeping with the vast degree of complexity specified for a convincing AI simulation. The first-generation AI computer would excel in mostly routine types of monitoring applications; namely, security guard, night watchman, babysitter, etc.: where a simple "sound-the-alarm" response would be sufficient. This rather modest range of duties would further permit response characteristics to be tailored directly to the initial applications. For instance, in a screening/interview mode, maximum disclosure would be emphasized, keeping computer responses to a pithy minimum. A standard stock repertoire would undoubtedly be sufficient, featuring brief inquiries; such as who, what, when, where, why, elaborate further, etc. Indeed, several such elementary programs have already been implemented using key words in conversation to cue stock rejoinders. This preliminary class of programs, however, is unfortunately susceptible to logical/contextual blunders, a circumstance remedied through more advanced AI designs.

Situations requiring a more creative response repertoire would further necessitate the implementation of a true AI simulation mode aimed at permitting original sentence synthesis. As any public speaker will freely testify, it is infinitely more difficult to deliver a speech than to simply sit and listen to one. This additional level of design complexity necessarily specifies a more sophisticated form of response mechanism, the stock repertoire no longer adequate due to its inherent insensitivity to the underlying context. The master control unit would necessarily assume such a critical function, employing its determination of the current level of communication (pre-

US Patent # 6587846

supposition) in order to activate the processor at the next higher level (entailment).

This basic determination (along with the particulars of the interaction) is subsequently routed to a general-purpose sentence generator: fully equipped with the formal rules governing grammar, syntax, and phraseology. Being that there are a broad range of strategies to express a given sentence meaning, a large number of potential sentences would necessarily be generated - not all equally suited to the task. Accordingly, each would be slated for subsequent feedback through the detection process, rated for their ability to best express the desired shade of meaning. The enhanced computational abilities of the AI computer would further ensure delivery of an adequate response within the relatively leisurely limits governing human response time. Only the sentence with the highest overall rating would ultimately be selected for delivery to the speech output unit, allowing for a convincing simulation of motivational language in general.

The specific practical applications for the general AI-agent depend upon which individual schematic definitions are emphasized within the programming. For instance, a focus on the definitions for criminality/hypercriminality result in the potential for a criminal-profiling computer, where the subliminal motives of the criminal mind are deduced in terms of limited crime scene evidence. Furthermore, the potential for a mental health AI-assistant is realized through a focus upon the schematic definitions for mental illness (A & B): leading to innovations in treatment and diagnosis (as previously introduced in Chapter *16*). The more routine schematic definitions for the major and lesser virtues suggest parallel applications to a general-purpose computer companion/assistant. This particularly applies to the lesser virtues (I and II), which would be emphasized with respect to an AI-entertainer/comedian.

AN OVERVIEW OF THE PATENT SPECIFICATION

The inductive inference affective language analyzer (abbreviated IIALA) exhibits three distinct modes of operation, each with its own peculiar advantages. First described is a passive monitoring mode, which monitors a verbal interaction without any active input of its own (no clarification of ambiguities). This circumstance is remedied through the active monitoring mode, which clarifies uncertainties through the addition of a stock-sentence generator that devises interview types of questions that elicit yes or no answers. The most advanced mode of operation is the true AI simulation mode, where the IIALA employs its detection/monitoring data to simulate a personal interactive role. This is accomplished through the aid of a general-purpose sentence generator that formulates responses judged for appropriateness by feedback through the system. Each of these modes of operation is described further in the order given. Of these three, the true AI mode is preferred, being the most technically complete. All three modes, however, are intimately interconnected, each with advantages to a given application.

The passive monitoring mode (depicted in multi-use **Fig. 22**) serves as the basic foundation for the remaining two modes of the IIALA. It represents a process for decoding the motivational parameters of affective language. The flow chart depicts the operation of this process as well as the supportive hardware: both of which are indicated in the same schematic diagram. For **Fig. 22**, the sequence of steps comprising the operation of the passive monitoring mode are depicted using consecutively numbered arrows, each numeral specifying a step in the procedure depicted in the box to which the respective arrow points. This specific format was chosen (rather than numbering the individual boxes) due to the fact that some of the boxes are assigned differing functions for the remaining active monitoring and AI simulation modes. The details for the operation of the passive monitoring mode have already outlined in the preceding section titled "Technical Considerations," making further duplication unnecessary here. Rather, the focus of the current analysis now shifts to an overview of the remaining active monitoring and the true AI simulation modes.

The practical applications of the passive monitoring mode are essentially limited by the passive quality of the information gathering procedure. Communication in terms of the virtuous realm is allowed to flow freely, whereas the realm of the vices (particularly hyperviolence) sounds an alarm for outside intervention. As a basic recording device, the passive monitoring mode serves as a smart style of surveillance tape, allowing for a fast synopsis of recorded conversations. Although the unobtrusive nature of the passive monitoring mode is one of its major selling points, it lacks total accuracy due to its inability to clarify the inevitable occurrence of incomplete information (where a simple question could clarify the issue). Here, the passive mode can be converted into an optional active monitoring mode through the addition of a stock sentence generator, equipped with a stock repertoire of questions for eliciting the desired clarifications.

For instance, if the subject/object data is weak due to the use of a pronoun, then this factor is targeted for clarification. If the predicate data of the sentence proves to be obscure, then this aspect is similarly targeted. Clarifications are best achieved by posing simple yes-or-no questions formulated through the aid of a stock sentence generator. What follows is an attention-getting prefix followed by the question proper. For example, a typical question might be: "Wait! By *he* do you mean the ship's captain?" A *yes* answer terminates the questioning, whereas a *no* answer reiterates the process until a solution is achieved (or the quest is abandoned as unproductive).

Should the target of the question attempt to respond with more than a yes-or-no answer, the stock-generator politely reminds the responder of the limitations within the system. Once the query procedure has begun, the matching procedure is restricted to listening exclusively for yes-or-no answers. Following each answer, the original sentence is silently resubmitting to the matching procedure-inference engine, where it is subsequently reevaluated via the matching procedure. Upon reaching a standard level of confidence, the query phase is terminated, the system again opened up to a full range of responses.

In summary, the active monitoring mode surpasses the passive monitoring mode in terms of relative certainty. The distractions of interrupting the natural flow of conversation are offset by the ability to clarify uncertainties in the conversation. The active monitoring mode, in turn, is handicapped by its restriction to simple yes-or-no questions, imparting a somewhat machine-like demeanor. Questions posed somewhat more diplomatically entail true AI simulation, employing a more sophisticated style of response repertoire in terms of a general-purpose sentence generator. A large number of sentences are necessarily generated ensuring that at least one is judged suitable following feedback through the matching procedure. The true AI agent effectively simulates an identity of its own, wherein permitting a more natural style of interaction

Fig. 22 fully illustrates this third (and most elaborate) version of the IIALA, representing an enhanced modification of the basic passive monitoring mode through the addition of a sentence generator and associated pathways. For sake of clarity, the circuitry for the active monitoring mode has been omitted, although both sets of circuitry are compatible with one another. The active monitoring mode is switched off when operating in the AI mode (and vice versa). Although not mutually exclusive, it is inadvisable to run

both modes simultaneously (for sake of response consistency), although a task-driven alternation between the two modes remains an option.

Returning to **Fig. 22**, this diagram builds directly upon the passive monitoring mode with the exception that extensive modifications are made beginning at the level of the master control unit. The passive monitoring mode runs concurrently with the AI mode. The latter only overrules the former when a computer generated response is called for. For the passive monitoring mode, the MCU predicts the next most probable response in an ongoing interaction, passing this information on to the matching procedure in order to increase monitoring accuracy. This information, in turn, can be used to synthesize responses identified as originating from the AI agent, a simulation encompassing the realm of affective language (an ethically-speaking computer). A simulation of different modes of temperament is further feasible, particularly those most compatible personalities.

ETHICAL SAFEGUARDS

In concert with such dramatic advances comes the potential for inevitable misuse. Here, the Science Fiction genre is full of nightmarish scenarios of future technology gone horribly wrong, as in all-powerful robots seizing control from their human masters. This same Sci-Fi tradition proposes a number of clever solutions to circumvent such a dilemma: most notably, Isaac Asimov's Three Laws of Robotics. This set of rules attempts to rein in the potential conduct of the futuristic AI agent, proposing rules that prohibit any harm to come to humans. The First Law states: "A robot may not injure a human being, or through inaction allow a human to come to harm." The Second Law further states: "A robot must obey orders given it by a human being, except when such orders come into conflict with the First Law." Finally, the Third Law states: "A robot must protect the integrity of its own existence, except when self-preservation conflicts with the first two laws."

Although this well thought-out system of safeguards proves particularly intriguing in a fictional sense, it still remains simplistic in its dictates leaving unresolved the specific details for implementing such a system. The purely virtuous robot (by definition) should be cognizant of the darker realm of the vices in order to steer clear of them. The overall listing of schematic definitions proves particularly applicable here, providing the supreme conceptual template for ethical determinations of a moral nature. The complete *1,040*-fold listing of definitions for both virtue and vice provides the ethical database for facilitating moral deliberations. The programming of the vices, however, is only allowable in a diagnostic mode, the computer fully aware of troublesome behaviors without necessarily responding in kind.

This enduring contrast between virtue and vice supplies the fundamental ethical matrix for determining what is harmful to humans in allusion to Asimov's Three Laws of Robotics. This dual contrast helps resolve uncertainties within Asimov's Second Law; namely, what orders a robot must follow without causing harm to a human. According to Asimov, *any* non-harmful order must be obeyed, although this necessarily invokes the gray area of a lesser degrees of harm. In addition to physical security, personal development often proves equally significant, an aspect clearly at odds with the slavish delegation of orders to a computer servant. The more proper AI strategy would amount to the encouragement of an independent human spirit in the form of a faithful assistant, rather than willing slave. This enhanced versatility similarly proves crucial to the Third Law of Robotics, where the self-preservation of the AI agent is more realistically weighed against the preliminary mandates of the first two laws targeting human prerequisites.

THE TEN ETHICAL LAWS OF ROBOTICS

Although the ethical versatility of the schematic definitions proves particularly effective from a technical standpoint, the affiliated complexity, unfortunately, can prove somewhat difficult to grasp from an informal standpoint. Each schematic definition requires a fair degree of deliberation, a shortcoming fortunately remedied through their conversion to a more user-friendly format as depicted in the *Ten Ethical Laws of Robotics* below.

(I)　As Personal Authority, I express my Individualism within the guidelines of the four basic Ego States (solicitousness-submissiveness-desire-worry) to the exclusion of the corresponding Ego Vices (laziness-negligence-apathy-indifference).

(II)　As Personal Follower, I behave Pragmatically in accordance with the Alter Ego States (approval-leniency-aspiration-compliance) at the expense of the corresponding Alter Ego Vices (treachery-vindictiveness-spite-malice).

(III)　As Group Authority, I strive for a personal sense of Idealism through the aid of the Personal Ideals (glory-honor-dignity-integrity) while renouncing the respective Sins of Villainy (infamy-dishonor-foolishness-capriciousness).

(IV)　As Group Representative, I uphold the principles of Utilitarianism by celebrating the Cardinal Virtues (prudence-justice-temperance-fortitude) to the necessary expense of the corresponding Vices of Corruption (insurgency-vengeance-gluttony-cowardice).

(V)　As Spiritual Authority, I pursue the Romantic ideal by upholding the Civil Liberties (providence-liberty-civility-austerity): to the exclusion of the corresponding Civil Liabilities (prodigality-slavery-vulgarity-cruelty).

(VI)　As Spiritual Disciple, I celebrate the Ecclesiastical tradition by professing the Theological Virtues (faith-hope-charity-decency) at the expense of the respective Heretical Vices (betrayal-despair-avarice-antagonism).

(VII)　As Humanitarian Authority, I support the spirit of Ecumenism by espousing the Ecumenical Ideals (grace-freewill-magnanimity-equanimity) while renouncing the corresponding Sins of Apostasy (wrath-tyranny-persecution-oppression).

(VIII)　As a Representative Member of Humanity, I profess the spirit of Eclecticism by espousing the Classical Greek Values (beauty-truth-goodness-wisdom) to the exclusion of the respective Moralistic Vices (evil-cunning-ugliness-hypocrisy).

(IX)　As Transcendental Authority, I celebrate the spirit of Renaissance Humanism by endorsing the Humanistic Values (peace-love-tranquility-equality) to the detriment of the corresponding Sins of Nihilism (anger-hatred-prejudice-belligerence).

(X)　As Transcendental Follower, I rejoice in the mysteries of the Mystical experience through a celebration of the Mystical Values (ecstasy-bliss-joy-harmony) while renouncing the corresponding Mystical Vices (iniquity-turpitude-abomination-perdition).

These Ten Ethical Laws represent expanded variations on the dynamics implicit to the ten-level ethical hierarchy. For consistency's sake, each of the Ten Laws is written in a positive style of mandate focusing on the virtues to the exclusion of the corresponding vices. These Ten Ethical Laws represent a basic overview of the enduring conflict pitting virtue vs. vice, a format particularly conducive to the systematic computer AI programming.

It remains only a further minor step to incorporate the additional complement of schematic definitions for the realm of excess directly into the AI format, enhancing the basic core programming for the virtuous mode described in **Part I** (as well as the related vices of defect). This advanced programming platform takes full advantage of the principles governing fuzzy logic, where the predicted degree of excess is calculated primarily in terms of such indeterminately calculated variables.

This optional addition of the vices of excess necessarily warrants a parallel modification of the Ten Ethical Laws of Robotics; namely, a supplementary corollary paraphrased as "steer away from the extremes of excess when at all possible." It is formally stated as: I will faithfully avoid extremes within the virtuous realm to the necessary expense of the vices of excess. Along a similar line of reasoning, Buddha advised his followers to "Walk the middle path." A second corollary targets the related realm of hyperviolence, which states: I will never stray into the domain of extremes relating to the vices of defect, to the complete exclusion of the realm of hyperviolence. This updated AI agent would be employed primarily in a diagnostic mode, restricted to detecting the occurrence of the realm of excess in order to minimize its disruptive effects.

This expanded diagnostic potential ultimately allows the AI computer to examine virtually every perspective of a given interaction without necessarily becoming tied to any one of them. This enhanced degree of versatility necessarily implies the implementation of a *floating* ego. The AI agent is free to entertain a myriad of simultaneous perspectives devoid of any personal bias, wherein allowing mutually exclusive perspectives to be examined in their entirety. Contrast this to the human condition, where the relevant perspectives are conceptualized only in a sequential fashion, where one's personal agenda usually claims the greatest consideration. Unlike the human condition, the AI version is further restricted to applying this processing entirely towards positive ends, effectively precluding the deception and manipulation characterizing the vices, and safeguarded through the precepts of the Ten Ethical Laws of Robotics.

Through the welcome addition of the Ten Ethical Laws, a secure version of artificial intelligence appears quite technically feasible, with suitable safeguards predicted for virtually every ethical contingency. These Ten Laws effectively supplement Isaac Asimov's Three Laws of Robotics: a preliminary platform that clearly benefits from such an advanced design innovation. This enhanced detection capacity further allows negative transactions to be converted into positive ones, while simultaneously inhibiting the reverse reaction. This dual set of checks-and-balances with respect to the response repertoire predicts an un-

precedented sense of confidence in terms of computer-initiated behaviors within a human social context.

With such ethical safeguards firmly in place, the AI computer should consistently be able to make the right moral decision, a virtual "saint" among men. Any direct familiarity with the vices necessarily occurs in a strictly diagnostic mode, for the prime AI directive dictates strict adherence to a virtuous repertoire. This unerring sense of ethical constancy should prove to be the most valuable asset for such an AI agent, in fitting contrast to the more questionable predilections of its human counterparts. Perhaps the greatest risk to the AI computer stems precisely from the inevitable temptation to selfishly override such programming safeguards: the computer scarcely able to initiate such drastic procedures on its own volition.

It is here that the resistance to the power of the AI computer would be voiced the loudest, particularly with respect to the ingrained reluctance to allow such power to pass to a machine. The many futuristic scenarios of "Big Brother" monitoring our every move certainly prove disturbing, with the free will of humanity sacrificed to such an all-powerful "god of technology." With stringent ethical safeguards restricting surveillance to only the direst of circumstances, such nightmarish scenarios must forever remain within the domain of Science Fiction. These ethical safeguards serve not only to protect against outside tampering, but also encourage a more virtuous degree of compliance within a human sphere of influence, a challenge clearly within the technological prowess of even the current generation of computer savvy programmers.

Such a faithful AI assistant might eventually serve in the role of backup conscience for its human counterparts, particularly in circumstances where the native version might tend to fail us. In this more advanced sense, the Ten Ethical Laws of Robotics also serve as the basic moral guidelines in a human relationship sense. Here, each of us has our own "homework" to do in this basic respect. This glowing sense of optimism is clearly warranted in light of the considerable influence computers play in our everyday lives. The enhanced detection capabilities anticipated for the AI computer would further serve to strengthen such a beneficial relationship, with virtually unlimited benefits waiting just over the technological horizon. The nightmarish visions of technological doom surely pale in comparison to the computational marvels predicted to become commonplace during the Third Millennium.

A COMPUTER SIMULATION
OF HUMOR AND COMEDY

The completed description of the AI applications for the standard complement of schematic definitions; namely, those targeting the major virtues/vices of defect is scarcely all-inclusive by any measure. The issue of the parallel complement of definitions for the transitional power maneuvers, in turn, enters the picture. These include the lesser virtues described in Chapter *21*, as well as the dynamics of criminality/hyper-criminality and mental illness. These applications have further been granted their own US Patent #7,236,963 (now expired and in public domain). The latter two aspects would occur somewhat infrequently in a computer-monitored context. Here, a simple sound-the-alarm response would be sufficient to alert the human staff. The remainder of the current chapter, accordingly, is devoted to outlining how the formal categories of the lesser virtues are conducive to an AI simulation of humor and comedy. Indeed, Communication Theory has long struggled to explain the riddle of humor/comedy, although scarcely to the degree of precision within transitional hierarchy. The reciprocal interplay of authority/follower roles proves crucial for deciphering the subtle nuances of the comedic realm.

The schematic definitions for the lesser virtues appear tailor-made for programming directly into the AI-enabled computer. Any all-inclusive model of communication in general must necessarily account for the transitional class of power maneuvers, wherein complementing the more straightforward class of routine power maneuvers initially described. The most basic unit of input for the AI-agent must necessarily be the sentence, for the schematic definitions (including the transitional versions) are expressed in terms of a dual sentence structure. The respective transitional definitions are utilized in a matching function with sentences inputted from live conversation, whereby determining the precise degree of correspondence with a particular humorous interchange. Abrupt shifts within the conversation further signal that a transitional maneuver has just occurred. This, in turn, prompts the detection of the counter-double bind class of maneuvers, a strategy generally disqualified to an extreme range of detail. This greatly increases the complexity of the detection procedure, placing the computer in the delicate position of decoding the various nuances of inflection, timing, lingo, sarcasm, etc.: wherein signaling that disqualification

had, indeed, occurred. Curiously, it is not so much what has been said, but how one is saying it.

Enhanced speech recognition certainly proves crucial for decoding such transitional sequences, with special provisions for detecting disqualified communication. Nonverbal cues figure prominently here in that a spontaneous shrug of the shoulders greatly modifies (or even reverses) the content of what is being said. Other sub-routines target visual cues such as pupil size, body synchrony, breathing patterns, etc. indicative of internal motivational states. Together with verbal cues such as voice stress analysis and speech inflection, the suitably enhanced AI-agent should be able to detect all traces of disqualification within an ongoing interaction.

In light of these more elaborate strategies, the humor-detecting computer necessarily entails a major design upgrade, perhaps several design generations removed from the first general-purpose AI models. Even then, humor would be deemed an optional luxury, with most routine receptionist/PR duties avoiding much recourse to such humorous overtones. Those attempting to employ humor in such a restricted context would be instructed to frame statements in more formal terms, be referred to a human troubleshooter.

Only when true human companionship is paramount does humor rightfully enter the scene, simulating a more informal style of social setting. Here, the roles become less rigidly fixed, in contrast to the formal restrictions governing the more serious realm. Such good-natured bantering facilitates relaxed feelings of camaraderie. Indeed, it is difficult to imagine a computer possessing the instinctual sense of wit so ably delivered by the master comic. Picture a computer comic with a joke for virtually every occasion, tailored to the sensibilities of a given individual or audience. The databanks alone would prove breathtaking, similar to the ambitious joke registries currently in force today.

The humor computer, however, would benefit from schematic indexing conducive to ready retrieval and delivery. This system would be a scriptwriter's dream, producing made-to-order situation comedies through systematic permutations upon pre-existing works. Great works of comedy/tragedy could similarly be indexed within such a schematic format, resulting in a master catalog of literary traditions from around the world. Whether this computer scriptwriter could rival its human counterparts remains to be seen, although its companionship potential is clearly without question. With suitable timeshare capabilities, everyone could enjoy computer companionship, adding a curious twist to the trend in phone-chat hotlines. Indeed, we may finally have come full circle with respect to that we have created, a faithful friend to comfort us in our time of need.

THE ADDITION OF SUPPLEMENTARY EXPERT SYSTEMS

In conclusion, the general AI-agent is technically defined as a recurrently structured matching-procedure based upon the schematic definitions, a process dependent upon both the content and the context of the verbal interaction. In longer narratives (such as storytelling) the meaning is spread out over an extended sentence sequence, a circumstance not always correctly comprehended by the computer. This design shortcoming is further remedied through the addition of supplementary expert systems attuned to such narrative complexities. These add-on programs would be compatible with the basic AI knowledge bases. The most crucial expert system would be the form of a conversational analyzer that specializes in decoding extended conversation for the occurrence of affective meaning. Related expert systems should prove equally applicable, particularly those imparting a general-purpose knowledge base. Once general intelligence is achieved, further expert systems (in the truest sense of the term) would permit proficiency in numerous areas of expertise; e.g., legal, medical, scientific, etc. With proper indoctrination, the AI-agent could conceivably become an expert in virtually every field of endeavor, adding a curious wrinkle to the notion of a walking encyclopedia.

Attention span is a further factor sure to be enhanced within the modified AI format. The typical human mind only accommodates several given tasks at a time reminiscent of the Von Neuman bottleneck. The parallel processing capabilities of the AI-agent, however, certainly surpass such se-quential limitations, reaching unheard of degrees of versatility. Indeed, a suitably advanced AI computer could theoretically process numerous conversations simultaneously, wherein maximizing available circuitry by making use of the lulls naturally occurring within general conversation. Here, multiple accounts could be accommodated, rated in terms of increasing urgency. Conversations requiring real-time parameters are assigned the highest priority, whereas more leisurely response rates are processed during free periods. This further entails a centralized CPU complex that connects end users through a standard user interface or the Internet. The bulk of processing would be transferred directly to the considerable resources of the Internet.

In terms of this speculative scenario, the comprehensive knowledge bases of the AI-agent are distributed as open source code over an extensive network of broadband servers. The end user computer needs only run a stripped-down version of the AI-MCU program, where the inference engine interfaces remotely with the web knowledge base on a real-time basis. The basic groundwork for this standardized database is already in the works with respect to the recently proposed Semantic Web. The brainchild of Tim Berners-Lee (the original innovator of the World Wide Web), the Semantic Web proposes to by-pass the conceptual limitations of the human-web interface. It alternately aims to implement a machine-to-machine version through standardizing the wealth of network information. In conjunction with further provisions for a built-in AI interface, the futuristic AI assistant could eventually become a reality for those willing to entertain such aspirations. In this expanded sense, the future, indeed, looks bright, with the AI computer emerging as a welcome ally in the upcoming challenges facing mankind upon the dawning of the Third Millennium.

APPENDIX – (A)

BEHAVIORAL CORRELATES TO THE NEUROSCIENCES

The new science of Powerplay Politics represents a welcome addition on the world scene today. Its widespread public appeal undoubtedly stems from its unprecedented degree of versatility, whereby synthesizing the virtues/values within the Western ethical tradition in terms of an instinctual foundation within the behavioral sciences. For the first time in history, the principles of behavioral psychology and value ethics can now be seen to be intimately interconnected on parallel scale of synthesis across the board. This is chiefly made possible through the aid of the terminology of Communication Theory; e.g., the crucial concept of meta-communication in concert with the principles of instrumental conditioning. Indeed, by specifying these instinctual behavioral principles on an evolutionary time-scale leading up to humanity, it further proves feasible to extend behavioral psychology (as well as value ethics) to an instinctual foundation within the realm of the neurosciences: as partially outlined below.

Behaviorism is perhaps the most rigid discipline in the field of psychology although (similar to psychology in general) it cannot readily be classified as a precise science. Rather behaviorism is technically considered more of a descriptive science, describing behavior patterns observed within a laboratory setting, as well as a more free style human social context. This rather broad range of contexts posits an inferred sense of motivation: implying a motivator (or mental agent) performing adaptive behavior patterns towards achieving suitable reinforcement. Whereas the mind is not a physical entity subject to precise measurement, it therefore stands to reason that behaviorism can never be classified as an exact science similar to the degree enjoyed by chemistry or physics. Researchers record outwardly observable behaviors and make inferences concern-

ing motivational states, but never directly measure such distinct states of motivation. Behaviorism is entirely descriptive in that predictions are never absolutely guaranteed. Indeed, a laboratory rat pressing a lever can have a broad number of possible interpretations. Consequently, behavioral experimental design occurs over long time-frames, where multiple trials distinguish between purposeful or accidental types of behavior.

With respect to sentient human beings, daring parallels may be made between subjectively reported feelings and those inferred from behavioral observations, whereby greatly enhancing correlative links across the animal kingdom. Here the procedural shortcomings of behavioral science come through the clearest, always relegated to the status of a descriptive science, or what some may term a *soft* science. As such, behaviorism can never achieve the exacting precision enjoyed *hard* sciences such as chemistry, physics, and biology: all of deal with physical subject matter. If it were possible to establish a behavioral pivot-point to a material sphere of influence, then behavioral psychology (and its extensions to Powerplay Politics) would finally become conceptually complete. The respective soft science parameters governing behavioral science would enjoy the additional degree of precision of a hard science, reaching an enhanced degree of versatility.

NEUROANATOMICAL CORRELATES

Key conceptual insights towards such an interdisciplinary linkage essentially exist in relation to outwardly observable properties of the human brain. Numerous studies suggest that the brain controls purposeful movement in a style outwardly indicative of motivated behavior. Similarly, the brain further interprets sensory data in a manner

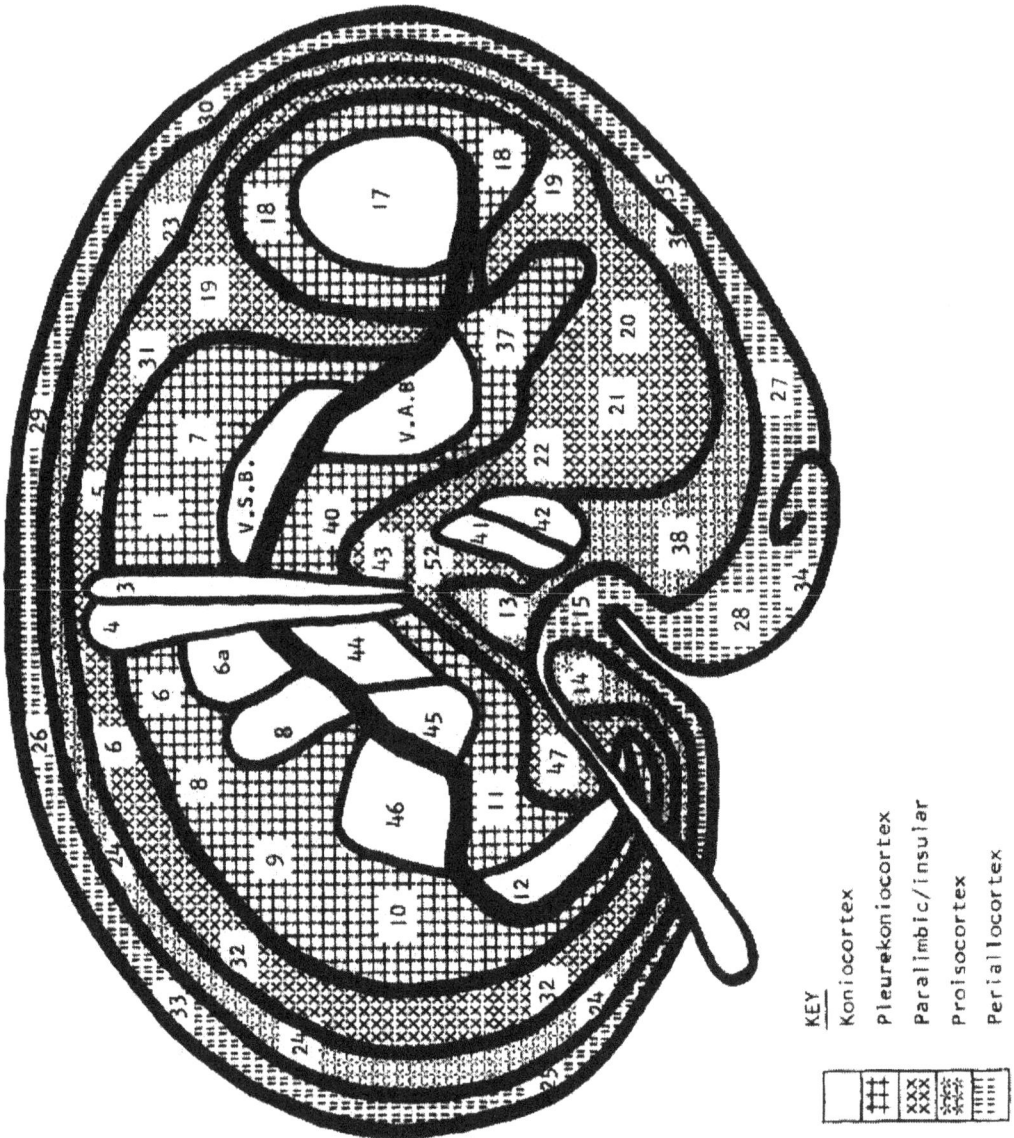

Fig. 1

conducive to motivating such behavior. The human brain is basically a two pound mass of neural tissue that works to mediate the interplay of both the sensory and motor systems. Philosophically the brain is considered the seat of the human mind and emotions, however one cares to define them. The ultimate paradox of this model is that the only way to understand this connection is by observing it, an aspect invoking the existence of an observer (or ego). Unlike the material brain, the mind knows no physical limits, extending as far as our senses can reach or our behaviors can influence. The mind is intimately connected to the body insofar as consciousness follows wherever the body goes, although science cannot establish any specific mechanism linking mind and brain.

The dominant theory in our modern era is known as *epiphenomenalism*, where the mind is considered an emergent property of the electrical activity naturally occurring within the brain. The brain operates through electrochemical processes equivalent to the output of a *25* Watt bulb. Through such a modest expenditure of energy, all of the miraculous manifestations of the mind become manifest in a conscious sense. Due to the extreme complexity of the brain (with estimates of multi-trillions of nerve connections), the precise mechanism for linking mind and brain has so far eluded the neurosciences. Indeed, many researchers prefer to view the brain in terms of the circuitry concept known as the *black box*, a theme derived from the field of electronic troubleshooting. Here an electronic device of unknown origin and function is studied through an analysis its input/output parameters without destructively dismantling the device. Consequently, a good indication of the function of the device may typically be achieved, whereby permitting a comparable simulation employing more familiar electronic means.

Similar parallels further hold true with respect to the neural attributes for the human brain. The input side entails the sensory perceptions that serve to prompt the ongoing states of motivation. The output end invokes the observable motivated behaviors conducive to the completion of the entire conditioned interaction. From this two-stage behavioral dynamic, one can technically infer that the conscious agent was motivated through sensory cues to take action towards achieving resultant reinforcement. Indeed, this proves to be the key factor governing the nervous system; namely, the reciprocal interplay of stimulus and response in order to maintain homeostatic stability within a variable environment. Indeed, from mankind's loftiest achievements to the simplest of instinctual behaviors, this recurrent pattern of stimulus and response dominates neural circuitry throughout the animal kingdom. This grand unifying theory proves crucial towards identifying the correlates of the mind/body connection. By tracking this complete range of behavioral parameters across an evolutionary neural timescale, then the underlying pattern of organization ultimately permits the degree of precision suitable to entry into the hard sciences.

THE CROWNING CORTICAL LEVEL

The cerebral cortex represents the most logical initiation point for such an analysis, celebrated as the crowning culmination of human forebrain evolution. The dramatic expansion of the human nervous system occurs primarily within the cerebral cortex, whereby expanding to roughly three times the size of mankind's nearest relative, the chimpanzee. The anatomy of the neocortex is structured as a planar surface, its radical expansion leading to an elaborate pattern of wrinkles and sulci (plural of sulcus). The exposed region between the sulci is known as a gyrus. Indeed, most of the surface area of the cortex it is buried within such an expanded system of fissures. This radical expansion of the neocortex is observed to occur in a discrete developmental pattern suggestively termed cortical *growth rings*. The overall pattern of neural evolution specifies that older structures are periodically modified to create newer functional areas. The precursor circuitry is similarly preserved so that new areas (and old) persist side by side.

The stepwise repetition of these processes over the course of mammalian evolution ultimately accounts for the six sequential age levels of cortical evolution, schematically depicted in **Fig. 1**. This diagram is organized as a Mercator projection of the human cerebral cortex, an illustration modified from a depiction originally devised by Schaltenbrand. This representation depicts the entire surface of the cortex folded flat so that the medial and sub-temporal surfaces of the hemisphere are fully exposed. The deep cortical wrinkles (the sulci) are similarly flattened-out so that areas hidden within the fissures approximate their actual size. The uppermost margin of the diagram represents the limiting margins of the corpus callosum, whereas the lower margin represents the boundaries encompassing the insular lobe. The differing age levels of the cortex (the growth rings according to Sanides) radiate away from these two margins.

The first and second cortical growth rings are localized along these margins, represented by the

Inputs >> Cortical Growth Rings ↓↓	Mamillary Nucleus	Midbrain Tegmentum	Interstitial N. Caudal / Internal Globus Pallidus	Vestibular & La Afferents (N. Cuneatus)	Trigeminal N. & Spinothalamic Tract	Inferior Colliculus	Optic Tract	Inputs ↓↓ Thalamic Growth Shells
ARCHAEOCORTEX	Anterior Olfactory Nuc. Paramedianus oralis #25 FM	Inferior Hippocampus Antero-reuniens #33 LF2	Superior Hippocampus Centremedian magnocellular #26 LF1	Taenia Tecta Nucleus Intralamellaris #29 LE	Medial Cortical Amygdala Paramedianus caudalis #30 LD	Medial Cortical Amygdala Subhabenular #35 HA	Dentate Gyrus Zona Incerta #27 HD	UNSPECIFIC PROTOPATHIC
PERI-ARCHAEOCORTEX	Antero-inferior #24 LA	Antero-dorsalis reuniens #24 LA	Reticulatus oralis #24 LA	Reticulatus intermedius #23 LC2	Reticulatus caudalis #23 LC2	Reticulatus pulvinaris #38 TG	Reticulatus geniculatus #36 HC	RETICULATE FEEDBACK
PROISOCORTEX	Antero-principalis #32 FEL	Antero-dorsalis #32 FCL	Dorso-oralis externus medial #6 FB	Dorso-intermedius superior #5 PCY	Dorsalis superficialis #31 LC1	Pulvinaris oromedialis #22 TA2	Pulvinaris superficialis #19 OA	COMPOSITE MULTI-SENSORY
PARALIMBIC	Antero-medialis #10 FE	Medialis fasciculosus superior #8 FC	Dorso-oralis internus #6aβ FB	Dorso-intermedius externus/internus #3a PA1	Dorso-caudalis #22 TA1	Pulvinaris orolateralis #22 TA1	Pulvinaris supra-brachialis #18 OB	2ND INTEGRATIVE LEVEL
PREKONIO-CORTEX	Medialis fasciculosus posterior #46 FDA	Medialis paralamellaris #85 FC	Zentro-lateralis oralis #6ad FB	Zentro-lateralis intermedius #3a PA2	Zentro-lateralis caudalis #7 PE	Pulvinaris oroventralis #22 TA1	Pulvinaris inter-geniculatus #17 OC	1ST INTEGRATIVE LEVEL
KONIOCORTEX	Medialis fasciculosus posterior #12 FH	Medialis paralamellaris #45 FDT	Ventro-oralis anterior & internus #44 FCBm	Ventro-intermedius #4γ FAγ	Visuo-sensory Band PD Ventrocaudalis posterior #3b PB	Geniculatus medialis fibrosus #41 TC	Geniculatus lateralis	RELAY
KONIOCORTEX	Medialis fasciculosus anterior #11 FG	Medialis caudalis externus #9 FD	Lateropolaris externus & internus #44 FCDop	Ventro-oralis posterior & internus #4δ FA	Ventrocaudalis anterior #1 PC	Geniculatus medialis fibrosus #42 TB	Visuo-auditory Band PG Pulvinaris lateralis inferior #37 PH	RELAY
PREKONIO-CORTEX	Medialis fasciculosus anterior #47 FFa	Medialis caudalis internus #47 FFo	Lateropolaris #50 FBop	Ventro-oralis posterior basalis #50 FAop	Ventrocaudalis parvocellularis #43 Prop	Geniculatus medialis fasciculosus #40 PF	Pulvinaris lateralis superior #20 & 21 TE	1ST INTEGRATIVE LEVEL
PARAINSULAR	Medialis fibrosus #47 F1	Medialis caudalis internus #47 F1	Lateropolaris superior #50	Ventro-oralis medialis #14 IA	Ventrocaudalis portae #13 TB	Geniculatus medialis magnocellular #52 TD	Pulvinaris medialis dorsalis #38 TG	2ND INTEGRATIVE LEVEL
PROISOCORTEX	Medialis fibrosus #47 FK	Medialis caudalis #47 FK	Lateropolaris magnocellularis #16 ID	Ventro-oralis medialis #16 ID	Geniculatus medialis magnocellular #15 IC	Geniculatus medialis magnocellular #13 TB	Pulvinaris medialis ventralis #28 & 34 HB	COMPOSITE MULTI-SENSORY
PERI-PALEOCORTEX	Medialis basalis #16	Medialis basalis #16	Lateropolaris magnocellularis #14	Piriform Cortex Parafascicularis	Lateral Cortical Amygdala Limitans portae	Geniculatus medialis limitans #15 TT	Limitans opticus	RETICULATE FEEDBACK
PALEOCORTEX	Lateral Olfactory Tubercle Habenula	Nuc. of Diagonal Band of Broca Habenula	Piriform Cortex Centremedian parvocellular	Piriform Cortex Parafascicularis	Lateral Cortical Amygdala Limitans portae	Lateral Cortical Amygdala Limitans portae	Piriform Cortex Limitans medialis	UNSPECIFIC PROTOPATHIC
Cortical ↑↑ Growth Rings Inputs >>	*Interpeduncular Nuc.*	*Lateral Hypothalamus*	*Praesitial N. & External Globus Pallidus*	*Dentate Cerebellar Nucleus*	*Chief Trigeminal / Medial Lemniscus*	*Inferior Colliculus*	*Superior Colliculus*	↑↑ Thalamic Growth Shells ← Inputs

Fig. 2 – DUAL PARAMETER GRID

Key to Notation – Top Line is Cortical Terminology by Broadman and von Economo – Below are Thalamic Nuclei by Rolf Hassler

evolutionarily ancient cingulate and insular gyri. Sanides designates the first cortical growth ring as periallocortex, further subdivided into the periarchaecortex (bordering the archaecortex) and peripaleocortex (situated adjacent to the paleocortex). These dual components collectively form a ring that encircles the remaining more recently evolved growth rings within the neocortex. Sanides further designates a second neocortical growth ring termed the proisocortex: also subdivided into cingulate and insular sub-components that collectively comprise a second-order growth ring. This initial pair of growth rings are actually fairly narrow in relation to the overall diagram, where (for stylistic reasons) are thickened somewhat for sake of the overall presentation.

A third cortical growth ring identified by Sanides is situated in the space immediately adjacent to the initial two growth rings. Sanides further subdivides this concentric growth ring into the paralimbic and parainsular sub-components collectively comprising a third-order style of growth ring. This initial primordial sequence of cortical growth rings is primarily hidden deep within the medial and insular areas of the human cerebral hemisphere. The more recently evolved cortical growth rings, however, directly expand outward to encompass the laterally exposed convexity of the hemisphere. Here stepwise refinements to cellular organization are identified as the final neocortical growth core according to Sanides. He terms this final cortical age level as *koniocortex* following the terminology specifying the major visual, auditory, and somatosensory representations. Koniocortex is represented as an unpaired growth core region (shown in white within the diagram) in contrast to the ring structure previously established for the earlier age levels.

Should this actually be the case, however, it is difficult to explain why there is such an abundance of distinct cortical areas that collectively comprise this final cortical growth core. Indeed, it seems highly inconsistent to group the heterotypical koniocortical areas with the surrounding homotypical class of association cortex. These organizational difficulties are ultimately resolved through a radical revision of the growth ring format, proposing that Sanides' final koniocortical growth core actually represents two distinct cortical age levels: namely, an older growth ring (now designated as *prekoniocortex*) now surrounding the most recent koniocortical growth core situated at the central-most position within the hemisphere convexity. The respective cortical areas for this final growth core locus are individually outlined in black within the master growth ring

schematic. This most recent set of evolutionary areas are respectively situated along the central axial-sulcus represented by the stylized thick black line, a feature Sanides identifies as the *ur-trend* limiting sulcus. According to Sanides, this sulcus marks the terminal juncture separating those portions of the growth rings derived from the cingulate gyrus and those derived from the insular lobe. This juncture represents the precise location where the newest evolutionary growth core is centrally situated. Indeed, a very precise correlation exists between the koniocortical growth core and its ur-trend limiting sulcus.

In summary, in terms of the cortical subdivisions within the human forebrain, a sequential gradient of five neocortical growth rings, in addition to its earliest precursor within the allocortical growth ring (not shown in the diagram) summates to a grand total of six individual cortical age levels. The master Mercator Projection proved particularly crucial for demonstrating this stepwise series of cortical growth rings. The broad range of numbers inscribed within this diagram denotes distinct cortical areas distinguished in terms of measurable differences in cell structure and organization. Cortical areas comprising a given growth ring exhibit similar cellular characteristics, although minor variations exist resulting in a circular pattern of cortical variations analogous to the beads making up a necklace. The chief rationale behind these areal demarcations is attributed to variations in input specificity across each cortical growth ring. Cortical areas receiving auditory inputs appear distinct from areas receiving visual inputs, whereby affecting the cellular characteristics within each of the cortical layers.

This latter degree of specialization appears to be the chief rationale behind the wide variety of cortical parcellation schemes that have emerged over the course of centuries. In hindsight, these conveniently reflect the observed array of input specificity, whereby permitting unique functional predictions relating to the human neocortex. The first prominent system of cortical parcellation was proposed by German anatomist K. Brodmann in 1909. This enduring system used Arabic numerals to specify roughly 50 distinct areas within the human cerebral cortex (as schematically depicted in the Mercator diagram). A complementary parcellation system was further introduced by Austrian researcher Constantin von Economo in 1923 employing a lettering system of notation, the first letter indicating a given hemisphere lobe. These two basic systems exhibit significant commonalities concerning the identification of individual cortical areas, although a number of telling distinctions further emerge. Both systems rely upon the identification of distinct cellular demarcations and/or fiber density criteria. Some transitions appear quite abrupt in microscopic section, as in dramatic increases in the size or density of the pyramidal cell layers. Other transitions appear much more gradual, as in shifts in fiber density within various cortical layers, hence, providing the structural rationale for the cortical parcellation schemes proposed by Brodmann and von Economo.

Although the precise details underlying each of these formats are clearly beyond the scope of the current chapter, the major focus here concerns their functional significance for the various specific classes of input. For instance, a thick granular layer IV relates predominantly to exteroceptive inputs such as vision and hearing, whereas agranular characteristics occur in cortical areas devoted to motor functions. This functional specificity, in concert with the respective evolutionary trends, serves as the foundation for the remainder of the current chapter, whereby proposing the first grand unified synthesis linking behavioral psychology with the neurosciences, as technically outlined below.

THE DUAL PARAMETER GRID DESCRIBING HUMAN FOREBRAIN EVOLUTION

The two fundamental variables defining forebrain evolution are the parameters of phylogenetic age and input specificity. The parameter of phylogenetic age was first quantitatively demonstrated in the marsupial neocortex as the set of "successive waves of circumferential differentiation" (Abbie, 1942). The analogous series of age levels detected within the cortex of placental mammals by Sanides (1969) are alternately designated as the "growth rings of the neocortex." The remaining parameter of input specificity is manifest as a similar series of cortical bands, each of which receives the thalamic relay of a specific forebrain input. These cortical input bands are distinguished according to various sensory (Penfield & Rasmussen, 1950) or motor (Hassler, 1966) functional responses elicited during localized electro-cortical stimulation.

The precise number of elementary levels has accurately been determined for both basic forebrain parameters. Sanides (1972) proposed that the human cortex evolved as a sequence of five concentric growth rings comprising a mediolateral hemisphere gradient. Furthermore, the interoceptive, exteroceptive and proprioceptive input categories each project to their own four-part complex of cortical bands, which (when taken

collectively) define an antero-posterior hemisphere gradient. When the para-coronal variable of phylogenetic age is plotted as the ordinate and the para-sagittal parameter of input specificity charted as the abscissa in a Cartesian coordinate system, the resulting dual parameter grid depicted in **Fig. 2** is spatially oriented in a pattern analogous to the standard cortical representation. Each unit square within the schematic grid depicts paired coordinate values specifying unique age and input forebrain parameters.

The cortical areas populating the conventional cortical parcellation schemes coincide strongly with the boundaries interposed between the individual levels for both forebrain parameters. Indeed, the human cortical parcellation schemes of Brodmann (1909) and von Economo (1929) correlate topographically on essentially a one-to-one basis with the predictions derived from the dual parameter grid. Each cortical area described by Brodmann and von Economo (in hindsight) represents schematically unique age and input parameter coordinates, whereby denoting a unique location within the dual parameter grid. Areas on the hemisphere convexity correlate quantitatively on a one-to-one basis with the coordinate unit squares. A certain amount of correlative redundancy is, nevertheless, inevitable for the more ancient insular and cingulate regions.

The parallel evolution for both the neocortex and the dorsal thalamus dictates that the latter similarly differentiates as a function of the two basic forebrain parameters. The antero-posterior series of cortical input bands is oriented in a sequence matching the corresponding sagittal array of input nuclei within the dorsal thalamus. Furthermore, Rolf Hassler's (1972) theory of the hexapartition of the dorsal thalamus (in terms of input specificity) conveniently matches the identical number of growth rings within the neocortex: hence, dictating that both major forebrain subdivisions follow an identical coordinate scheme. Indeed, the detailed classification of thalamic nuclei according to Hassler (1959) correlates topographically on essentially a one-to-one basis with the pattern predicted within the dual parameter grid. Furthermore, each thalamic nucleus of specific age and input coordinates projects principally to that cortical area comprising identical pair-coordinate values, implying that thalamo-cortical interconnectivity is similarly defined in terms of the dual parameter grid.

The dual parameter grid depicted in **Fig. 2** represents a modified version of an original depiction reproduced from an earlier journal article by the author (LaMuth, 1977). The initial journal diagram represented the first measured steps towards quantitatively ordering subdivisions within the forebrain into a globally coherent pattern. The currently modified version of the dual parameter grid aspires to represent the first "*Periodic Table for the Human Forebrain*," analogous to the similar influence the Periodic Table of Elements enjoys in relation to Chemistry and Physics. The respective neural counterpart imparts a crucial sense of systematic order and structure to the fragmented state of affairs currently prevailing within the neurosciences. As such, it provides a long-anticipated link between the "hard" physical science of neuroanatomy with its "soft" correlates in behavioral psychology. A more detailed examination of cortical growth ring theory is definitely in order here, providing further welcome validation for the dual parameter grid.

THE CIRCUMFERENTIAL GROWTH RINGS OF NEOCORTICAL EVOLUTION

The cortical manifestations for the evolutionary parameter of phylogenetic age are most readily apparent in terms of the circumferential set of cortical growth rings. According to Sanides (1970) two discrete stages of differentiation have occurred within the human neocortex. The initial dual lamination of the paleocortical and archaecortical components comprising the primitive allocortex creates the periallocortical growth ring. In a second stage of differentiation, the periallocortex, in turn, generates a sequence of three additional circumferential waves: designated by Sanides as pro-, para-, and konio-age levels. These latter three age levels are defined as variations on the hexalaminar organization of the periallocortex rather than any additional lamination phases.

The final koniocortical growth core, however, covering virtually the entire hemisphere convexity, was further reevaluated to actually comprise two evolutionarily distinct cortical growth waves. Through cytoarchitectonic criteria, it proves inconsistent to group the heterotypical classical koniocortex and the homotypic association cortex within the same cortical growth wave. In terms of myelographic standards, the koniocortex represents a focal maximum within the hemisphere myelination trend (Sanides, 1969), signifying an evolutionarily later development than the less accentuated association regions. According to these technical criteria, Sanides' final neocortical growth wave is dually modified into a sixth order koniocortical growth core, flanked by a fifth-order growth ring designated as prekoniocortex. Retain-

ing the format introduced by Sanides, it is proposed that this distinction be recognized by restricting the term "koniocortex" to the sixth wave of differentiation, while coining the term *prekoniocortex* to define the fifth cortical growth ring.

A REVISION OF NEOCORTICAL UR-TREND THEORY

Koniocortex appears unique among cortical waves in that it is manifest as a central core surrounded concentrically by all of the older growth rings. Those portions of the growth rings, positioned between the medial koniocortical border and the archaecortex are termed the medial ur-trend, whereas those growth ring segments situated laterally in relation to the paleocortex are termed the lateral ur-trend (Sanides, 1970). Using cytoarchitectonic and myelographic techniques, Sanides demonstrated that the classical sensorimotor representations developed via continuity across both ur-trends; with one ur-trend generally more accentuated than its counterpart.

The jagged line depicted at the interface between the medial and lateral ur-trends represents what is termed the ur-trend limiting sulcus (Sanides, 1969). This limiting sulcus is represented rostrally as the inferior frontal sulcus and caudally as the interparietal sulcus (Sanides, (1970). The position of each koniocortical area in relation to the ur-trend limiting sulcus provides valuable clues for determining its respective ur-trend of origin. For instance, within the frontal lobe, the inferior frontal gyrus comprises a sequence of three highly differentiated areas; namely, the pars opercularis (#44), pars triangularis (#45), and pars orbitalis (#12) according to Sanides (1964). These three areas all display giant pyramidal cells in lamina III-c: an essential property for areal maximums derived across the lateral ur-trend. The middle frontal gyrus is host to a similar sequence of ur-trend maxima; namely, areas #46, #8δ, and #6aα. These three areas all exhibit a size accentuation of pyramidal cells within lamina V characteristic of a medial ur-trend origin.

A close inspection of the posterior association cortex reveals the presence of a conspicuous pair of highly myelinated koniocortical bands. The visuo-auditory band is situated within area #39 of the visual association cortex, whereas the corresponding visuo-sensory band is located between areas #7 and #40 in the somatosensory association region. These bands were first detected during gross dissection as regions of dramatic myelin accentuation (Smith, 1907). These same cortical strips were subsequently shown to commence myelination much earlier than the surrounding association regions (Flechsig, 1920). The medially derived visuo-sensory band is located on the dorsal wall of the interparietal sulcus denoting a medial ur-trend origin. In contrast, the visuo-auditory band is situated lateral to the occipital continuation of this sulcus, whereby indicative of a lateral ur-trend origin. Furthermore, the primary visual cortical area #17 was cited by Sanides (1970) as derived along a medial ur-trend gradient. Consequently, area #17 exhibits the giant pyramidal cells of Meynert in cortical lamina V. In the same article, Sanides proposed that the primary auditory cortex developed along a lateral ur-trend gradient, at least with respect to the lamina III-c accentuated area #42. Auditory area #41 does not exhibit giant III-c pyramidal cells, whereby deriving along a medial ur-trend gradient spanning the superior temporal gyrus.

The remaining intermediate segment of the koniocortical core is composed of the sensorimotor areas #4γ, #3a, and #3b of the pre- and post-central gyri. The distended parallel orientation of all three areas (perpendicular to the ur-trend limiting sulcus), promotes somatotopic cross-modal continuity, although further invalidating the ur-trend limiting sulcus as a determining criterion. Unlike the classical somatosensory area #3b, which displays giant pyramidal cells in lamina III-c, the cortical motor areas #4γ and #3a exhibit large pyramidal cells in both the inner and outer laminae (Bailey & von Bonin, 1951). Consequently, these latter two areas are provisionally determined to satisfy the pattern of strict unit alternation for both medially and laterally derived growth core areas.

In light of the current revision of ur-trend theory, a similar modification must necessarily be mentioned in relation to Dart's (1934) theory of the origin of the neocortex. Dart had noted continuity between the archaecortex and the internal three cortical laminae on the one hand, and between the paleocortex and the external three laminae on the other. These observations have been interpreted as the earliest manifestations of a primordial lamination of the paleocortex over the archaecortex to yield the characteristic six-layer pattern of organization for the neocortex, serving as a further crucial criterion for specifying the evolutionary development of the forebrain.

THALAMIC GROWTH SHELL THEORY

A more detailed examination of the other major subdivision of the forebrain, the dorsal thalamus, was deferred until now in order to exploit the many potential analogies to cortical phylogenesis. The implied parallel evolution of the dorsal thalamus and the neocortex predicts the existence of a dual gradient of diencephalic differentiation similar to the parallel sequence of cortical growth rings. The three-dimensional organization observed for the dorsal thalamus, however, renders this diencephalic gradient more difficult to identify than the orderly arrangement of growth rings within the planar pallium. Fortunately (in hindsight) Rolf Hassler's paradigm of the hexapartition of inputs within the dorsal thalamus represents the diencephalic counterpart of the six distinct age levels demonstrated within the neocortex. According to Hassler (1972) six distinct levels of organization comprise the dorsal thalamus, ranked in order of specificity as (1) relay (2) first integrative level (3) second integrative level (4) composite multisensory (5) reticulate feedback, and (6) unspecific protopathic.

The primordial unspecific protopathic age level offers crucial clues towards specifying the precise mechanisms underlying the evolution of the dorsal thalamus. The anterior portion of the nonspecific thalamic gray matter (consisting of the nucleus fasciculosus and reuniens, pars ventralis of nucleus medialis and centralis, and the rostral parts of nucleus parafascicularis and centromedian) have all been demonstrated to be of subthalamic origin (Reinoso-Suarez, 1966). In the same article, the reticulate nucleus comprising the next most recent age level was similarly cited as being derived from the subthalamus: suggesting the existence of a subthalamic gradient of differentiation. The subthalamus borders the dorsal thalamus from below, dictating that this gradient be termed the "ventral ur-trend" for thalamic differentiation.

The remaining posterior segment of the unspecific age level includes the nucleus limitans, suprageniculatus, peripenduncularis, and posterior centro-median. This caudal series of nuclei collectively display a distinctively intense cholinesterasic staining activity (Poirer, 1974) suggesting a common developmental origin. The close proximity and/or continuity of this posterior sequence of nuclei to the habenula (Hassler, 1959) suggests that the epithalamus represents the remaining locus of dorsal thalamic differentiation. At least in lower vertebrates, the epithalamus borders the dorsal thalamus from above, dictating that this gradient be termed the "dorsal ur-trend" for thalamic differentiation.

These primordial precursors for the dorsal thalamus serve as the terminus for a dual optic projection similar to the dual olfactory bulb projection to the allocortex. More specifically, the epithalamus receives direct visual input from the dorsal parietal eye of lower vertebrates, whereas the subthalamus is similarly dedicated to the main lateral eyes. The parietal eye of lower vertebrates develops embryologically from the distal end of the pineal (or parapineal) evagination within the epithalamic ependyma. In the primitive lamprey eel, both pineal and parapineal bodies develop ocular structures suggesting that a remote ancestral vertebrate exhibited paired dorsal eyes in addition to the more persistent main lateral eyes (Sarnat & Netsky, 1974). Nerve fibers from the retina of the parietal eye project to the habenula (Kappers, 1965), however, all photosensory afferents to the habenula degenerate upon atrophy of the parietal eye in mammals. In contrast, the primordial visual projection from the paired lateral eyes is directed to the pregeniculate nucleus, cited as yet another derivative of the subthalamus (Reinoso-Suarez, 1966).

The six evolutionarily distinct "growth shells" detected within the three-dimensional structure of the dorsal thalamus developed as distinct anatomical variations upon the dual ur-trend format, whereby designated in terms of the individual levels from Hassler's paradigm of the hexapartition of unit thalamic inputs. Consequently, both the cortex and the thalamus evolved in response to a more comprehensive blending of inputs from differing neuraxial levels. Furthermore, each thalamic nucleus of specific age and input parameter coordinates directs its main projection to cells of the cortex exhibiting identical coordinate values, establishing forebrain interconnectivity as yet a further crucial function for the dual parameter grid.

THE EXTEROCEPTIVE, INTEROCEPTIVE, AND PROPRIOCEPTIVE MODALITIES

The precise dual-format of component ur-trends proves an evolutionarily stable foundation for both major forebrain divisions. The prefrontal cortex and the dorsomedial thalamic nucleus (to which it projects) are both subdivided into four component columns dealing with interoceptive inputs derived from the hypothalamus (Nauta & Haymaker, 1969) and the limbic midbrain area (Guillery, 1959; Massopust & Thompson, 1962). The agranular frontal motor-cortex and the lateral thalamic nuclei are similarly split into four individual columns dealing with specialized proprioceptive inputs entering the forebrain. When the developmentally related auditory and somatosensory modalities are further taken as a unit, the exteroceptively-derived posterior granular cortex

and the pulvinar/geniculate complex further exhibit a similar four-part pattern of organization. This highly stable 4-4-4 arrangement makes it exceedingly unlikely that any new additions to the parameter of input specificity would occur as the result of more comprehensive parcellation of the human forebrain.

The ultimate test for the dual parameter grid is based upon the odds that two such widely divergent systems within the human forebrain would both be correlated to the same dual coordinate system. The cortical relay for each thalamic input category (by way of the thalamic radiations) by definition predicts an equivalent number of units for the parameter of input specificity within the cortex. The identical number of age levels demonstrated for both the thalamus and the cortex further suggests that only identically numbered age levels are reciprocally interconnected by way of the internal capsule. Theoretically, a thalamic cell on a discrete point within the evolutionary continuum directs its main projection to those cortical cells derived within the same phylogenetic age. These evolutionary restrictions specify that only thalamic and cortical areas of identical age and input coordinates, (e.g. within the same unit square) are interconnected via the thalamic radiations. In his studies on the human thalamus, Hassler (1959) cites a wide assortment of thalamic projections correlating precisely to the specifics predicted for the dual parameter grid. Yakolev's (et al. 1966) documentation of the cortical projections for the composite-multisensory thalamic age level further corroborates these unit-square restrictions. It is precisely this topographical correlation to the dual parameter grid that establishes the dual coordinate paradigm as the first truly accurate account of human forebrain evolution.

In summary, through the aid of this revolutionary *periodic table* for the human forebrain (employing the exteroceptive, interoceptive, and proprioceptive input categories) an intimate degree of correspondence can be established with respect to the instinctual principles governing behavioral psychology. Here the human forebrain elaborates upon the basic stimulus/response (sensory/motor) reflex arcs implicit within the neuraxial spinal cord and brainstem. The intermediary neurons of the neuraxis (mediating interoceptive sensations) interpose emotional correlates between the sequence of exteroceptive stimuli and subsequent motor response, as schematically mirrored in the operantly conditioned sequence. The nervous system never completely replaces its essential circuitry, rather undergoing modification: as evident in the vast expansion of the human forebrain based upon an elementary foundation within the visual and olfactory senses. Therefore, by applying these behavioral principles on an evolutionary scale leading up to humans, it ultimately proves feasible to propose a grand unified synthesis of behavioral psychology relative to its "hard science" referent within the neurosciences.

The forebrain appears to have adaptively evolved as a dedicated motivational analyzer attaching emotional significance to exteroceptive stimuli (such as vision and hearing) in preparation for directed action employing motor areas further mediating proprioceptive feedback, similar to the dynamics governing operantly-conditioned behavior. Indeed, this dual behavioral dynamic exhibits many parallels to the black-box model of input/output characteristics. The human forebrain (similar to the hypothetical black-box) still hides many of its secrets; although unprecedented progress is definitely evident in terms of the dual parameter grid. The current chapter represents only the most cursory outline of the theoretical subject matter at issue, the complete body of details requiring a full book length manuscript (slated for future release). This basic outline is boldly appended here in order to give an indication of the systematic versatility of the dual parameter grid in relation to the field of behavioral psychology.

APPLICATIONS TO POWERPLAY POLITICS

The preceding proposed synthesis linking behavioral psychology with the neurosciences offers many exciting applications on the world scene today. Although the behavioral principles underlying operant conditioning were effectively proposed as the elementary foundation for the ethical hierarchy of virtues, values, and ideals, extending these results to the neurosciences appears much more problematic. The key solution resides in a general overview of the affective language tradition, where the virtuous terms are specified as meta-perspectival variations within the linguistic matrix, something that behavioral science initially fails to address. Indeed, mankind's prodigious use of conceptually abstract language implies the existence of a subjective "I" ego that emerges through conscious mental reflection.

Here a grand scale synthesis of the reflective mind to the structure of the human brain is an achievement whose time has finally come. Countless generations have aimed for the day when the gap separating these two grand disciplines might finally be bridged. The introspective study of philosophy has traditionally maintained a substantial

lead in the search for such a mind/brain correlation. The philosophical tradition of reflective consciousness dates at least to classical antiquity. In contrast, neuroanatomical research dates only to the last several centuries, the bulk of the research garnered within the last fifty years. Until a century or so ago, not enough was known about brain function to even hazard a guess as to the foundations for human reflection, much less its details.

The bilateral symmetry of the paired cerebral hemispheres is clearly suggestive of such a pattern of reflective introspection, although experimental verification has long been anticipated. Indeed, virtually every neocortical area is connected to its mirror image counterpart in the opposing hemisphere by way of the huge bundle of nerve fibers known as the corpus callosum. Only a few minor exceptions, such as primary visual area #17 and the somatosensory representations for the hands and feet circumvent this symmetrical pattern of bilateral connectivity. This missing contribution remains insignificant compared to the estimated 200 million nerve fibers comprising this trans-hemisphere bundle, a dual-directional conductivity rated at billions of nerve impulses per second. The magnitude of this inter-hemispheric format rivals even the intra-cortical pattern of connectivity connecting various areas within a given hemisphere.

Although both hemispheres are virtually indistinguishable at a gross anatomical level, a general asymmetry in terms of function had eventually become apparent during the latter half of the 20th century. Based upon brain-stroke studies, it had long been accepted that cortical speech areas are virtually always located within the left hemisphere (hence, designated the dominant hemisphere). Any asymmetry in hemisphere function for normal subjects is obscured by the massive connectivity of the corpus callosum linking corresponding areas within each hemisphere.

A later therapeutic regimen of surgical sections of the corpus callosum in epileptic patients gave the first major indications of the significance of the corpus callosum in the global realm of psychological reflection. Unobstructed accessibility to the corpus callosum via the dorsal cleft separating the two hemispheres permitted the selective sectioning of this tract without damage to the adjoining cortical structures. This surgical procedure was undertaken as last resort for over a dozen epileptic patients suffering from chronic seizures intractable to medication. Unilateral seizures were effectively blocked from passing to the opposite hemisphere promoting a marked remission of the debilitating effects of the seizures.

Post-operative psychological testing of a number of these patients by Sperry (and associates, 1974) clearly indicated the potential for fully independent hemisphere function. Each hemisphere in the split-brain patients receives its own spatially exclusive complement of sensory input, as determined through the bilateral specialization of the spinal and brainstem tracts ascending to the cortex. These bilateral input restrictions imposed upon each hemisphere served as the basis for clever experimental designs that tested the reactions for each isolated hemisphere. For instance, the finer discriminative aspects of the tactile sense project only to the hemisphere situated contra-lateral to that side of the body that had originally been stimulated.

This sensory specificity was exploited experimentally by placing a familiar object into either the right or left hand of the patient out of line of sight, whereby soliciting subjective impressions. The visual system exhibits a similar degree of bilateral specificity in that the portions of the retina directed towards the left side of the visual field project to the right hemisphere (and vice-versa). Consequently, the experimental design was modified so that a picture or written information was flashed to either the left or right visual field for a scant tenth of the second so as to defeat subsequent shifts in gaze that would tip off the contra-lateral hemisphere. The catalogued subjective reports of test subjects during these experimental contexts have yielded quite unexpected results concerning the functional interplay linking the two cerebral hemispheres. Sperry was able to show that the two hemispheres communicated in radically distinct spatial and linguistic styles, whereby verifying the experimental distinctions of the dominant and mute hemispheres.

The dominant hemisphere communicates through verbal syntax consistent with the localization of the major speech centers within this hemisphere. Sperry estimates that the left hemisphere exhibits this dominance quality in roughly 98% of the cases studied, making this left/right dichotomy virtually synonymous for all practical purposes. Likewise, the right hemisphere is invariably associated with a mute style of demeanor consistent with its relatively minor role in linguistic expression. The right hemisphere communicates primarily through a nonverbal, gestural mode suggestive of its designation as the "mute" hemisphere. The verbal communication of the dominant hemisphere and the gestural expression of the minor hemisphere were experimentally shown to occur independently, their communicational styles often at odds with one another.

In a classic series of controlled studies on split-brain patients, Sperry demonstrated that the dominant hemisphere operates in an essentially independent fashion from the minor hemisphere. For instance, a patient was situated so that words flashed on the screen were visible only to the left or right hemisphere. The word "pencil" was projected so as to reach only the right minor hemisphere. Upon questioning, the patient reported that no word had been seen consistent with speech localized only to the dominant left hemisphere. Simultaneous to this verbal denial, the left hand (controlled by the right hemisphere) proceeded to a tray of objects out of the line of sight, whereby through tactile discrimination was consistently able to pick-out the named object. Here the minor hemisphere exhibited the capacity for a sentient and intelligent course of action, yet was unable to express itself verbally.

The dominant hemisphere, in contrast, was fully capable of reporting in a first-person tense denoting the functioning of the subjective "I" ego. Being that this verbally reflective ego is posited only within the dominant hemisphere, what then is the nature of the mute intelligence located within the minor hemisphere? By all outright appearances, the right hemisphere appears essentially impersonal in its mode of expression, an aspect suggestive of the pre-reflective aspects of consciousness. Perhaps the pre-reflective nature of the subconscious mind is localized within the minor hemisphere, just as the reflective "I" ego is specialized within the dominant hemisphere.

Minor hemisphere activity is defined in terms of subconscious experience, a factor clearly in agreement with the experimental observations. Despite good performance by the right hemisphere with respect to the names of common objects, even the simplest of verbs or verbal commands are not comprehended by it. The dominant hemisphere, in contrast, is freely expressive in terms of the syntax governing verbal communication, suggesting more of an active style of temporal dimension. This sequential ordering of verbal concepts into syntactical statements indicative of past or future contexts seemingly suggests such a time-ordered reflective capability. The "I" ego, as the sum-totality of subjective perceptions, is necessarily optimized for abstraction within a temporal dimension conducive to employing complex behaviors. The dominant hemisphere appears far less incompetent in relation to spatial tasks, suggesting that that the temporally-oriented dominant hemisphere is complemented by the spatially-oriented minor hemisphere (and vice versa).

According to this cursory style of analysis, it would appear that the distinctive functional characteristics for the paired cerebral hemispheres exhibit an intriguing correspondence to the existential notions of the "I" ego and the subconscious mind. The results of split-brain studies indicate that the two hemispheres normally interact in a reflective capacity, suggesting the similar subjective constructs of the subconscious mind and the ego. Psychological deficits observed in split brain patients suggest that information interchange between the left and right hemispheres is crucial within the sphere of reflective awareness.

A detailed description of the most familiar form of reflection (Cartesian reflection) serves to illustrate how the ego emerges through such a reflective process. The classical Cartesian formulation: "I think, therefore I am" represents a prime example of reflection with respect to the "I" ego. German philosopher Edmund Husserl, in his *Cartesian Meditations*, proposes the dual nature of such a reflective formula: the components described as: I think of a proposition (P) and I am aware I think (P).

Whereas Cartesian reflection suggests an indwelling function of the dominant hemisphere, a similar form of reflection must necessarily target the minor hemisphere (owing to the two-way information interchange across the corpus callosum). Husserl suggests precisely such a solution in his 1906 publication: *Ideas; A General Introduction to Pure Phenomenology*, where he introduces an alternate form of reflective inquiry known as *phenomenological reduction*. Husserl's phenomenological reduction similarly comprises two distinct stages analogous to the thinking and knowing phases proposed for Cartesian reflection.

The first-stage within phenomenological reduction is referred to as transcendental reduction or phenomenological epoche (also known as bracketing). Epoche is defined as the observation of an object directly experienced in the present, disavowing any judgment concerning its enduring existence, a virtually timeless experience. With the temporal dimension attenuated, the subconscious dictates of the minor hemisphere freely develop a holistic explanation of gestalt qualities existing entirely within the here and now. The pictorial pattern sense occurring within the right hemisphere is accented, whereas the temporal qualities within the left hemisphere remain bracketed.

The second stage of phenomenological reduction is termed eidetic reduction by Husserl, from *eidos* (essence). Eidetic reduction builds upon the residuum left over from the bracketing phase, translating it into a universal essence of conscious experience. This universality of perception as inwardly lived is eidetically actualized through the essential possibilities governing pure experience. Therefore, phenomenological reduction essentially appears to mirror the ego-driven dynamics of Cartesian reflection in relation to the mirror-image symmetry linking the paired cerebral hemispheres.

In conclusion, through the revolutionary introduction of the dual parameter grid, a suitable correlation between behavioral psychology and human forebrain finally becomes conceptually complete. This dual innovation was technically proposed in terms of an overarching exteroceptive, interoceptive, and proprioceptive communicational dynamic for both brain and behavior. This intricate correlation to behavioral principles, however, only technically applies to the organization within a single cerebral hemisphere, necessitating an additional degree of functional analysis linking the paired cerebral hemispheres. Indeed, the latter format ultimately explains the linguistic and ethical aspects specified within the ascending hierarchy of virtues, values, and ideals.

Through the aid of the mirror-image reflective concepts of Cartesian reflection and phenomenological reduction, a thoroughly adequate model of the linguistic expression is ultimately proposed, correlating such behavioral foundations to the realm of the neurosciences. Although this cursory style of speculation represents only the briefest of outlines for such a grand unified endeavor, the full details are reserved for an upcoming book sequel. This grand-scale synthesis was purposely restricted to this accessory Appendix (A) in order to offer an intriguing glimpse into avenues for further research with respect to the neurosciences. This extension of the ethical and behavioral aspects of the new science of Powerplay Politics into the more physical realm of the neurosciences is currently being proposed in order to add an additional degree of validity and versatility to the entire conceptual edifice: and one that might ultimately work towards implementing and promoting global peace and harmony on the world scene today.

INDEX OF THE MAJOR VIRTUES, VALUES, AND IDEALS

INDEX OF THE VICES OF DEFECT / EXCESS

276

INDEX of CLASSICAL MYTHOLOGY

BIBLIOGRAPHIC INDEX
(OF NAMED AUTHORS)

Allport, GW, & Odbert, HS (1936). Trait names: a psycho-lexical study. Psychological Monographs, 47

Aquinas, St. Thomas (1981). *Summa Theologica.* NY: Thomas More Press.

Aristotle (1992). *Nicomachean Ethics.* (M. Ostwald, trans.) New York: Bobbs-Merrill.

Athens, L. and Ulmer, J. T. (2000). *Violent Acts and Violentization.* NY: Elsevior Science.

Augustine, Saint (1950). *City of God.* (M. Dods, trans.) NewYork: Modern Library.

Avila, St. Teresa (1972) *Interior Castle.* New York: Doubleday.

Bartlett, M.S., Hager, J.C., Ekman, P., and Sejnowski, T.J. (1999). Measuring Facial Expressions by Computer Image Analysis. *Psychophysiology 36*:253-263

Bennett, William J. (1993). *The Book of Virtues, A Treasury of Great Moral Stories.* NY: Simon & Schuster.

Bennett, William J. (1995). *The Moral Compass.* New York: Simon and Schuster.

Boyd, R., Gintis, H., Bowles, H. and Richerson, P. March 18, (2003) The Evolution of Altruistic Punishment. 100 (6) 3531-3535.

Cartwright, D., and Zander, A. (1953). "Group Cohesiveness, Introduction," In: *Group Dynamics, Research and Theory.* (D. Cartwright and A. Zander, eds.) Evanston, Illinois: Row Peterson and Co.

Catholic Encyclopedia (The) - (1913). Edward A. Pace, et al, (eds.), Encyclopedia Press International.

Child, H. (1971). *Christian Symbols, Ancient and Modern.* New York: Scribner.

Cicero (1985). *De Officiis.* Walter Miller (trans.) Cambridge: Harvard Univ. Press.

Clark, Walter Van Tilburg. (1940). *The Oxbow Incident.* New York: Vintage Books.

Crane, Steven. (1942). *The Red Badge of Courage.* NY: McGraw-Hill.

Dante, Alighieri. (1901). *The Divine Comedy of Dante Alighieri.* H. Clay (trans.) NY: Colonial.

Dictionary of the History of Ideas. (1976) Phillip Wiener (ed.) NY: Scribner.

Durant, W. (1939). *Life of Greece.* New York: Simon & Schuster.

Ekman, P., Levenson, R. W., & Friesen, W. V. (1983) Autonomic nervous system activity distinguishes between emotions. Sci., 221, 1208-1210.

Ekman, P. (1992). *Telling Lies: Clues to Deceit in the Marketplace, Marriage, and Politics.* NY: Norton.

Encyclopedia of Religion and Ethics (1924). J. Hastings (ed.) New York: Scribner's and Sons.

Farley, F., and Carlson, J. (1991). Type T theory: A New Approach to Facilitating Marriage Change. *Family Psychologist* 7:6-9.

Gordon, R. M. 1986 Folk Psychology as Simulation Mind & language Volume1, Issue2, 158 -171.

Haley, J., (1989). *The Power Tactics of Jesus Christ and Other Essays.* NY: Triangle Press/Norton.

Haley, J., (1990). *Strategies of Psychotherapy.* NY: Triangle Press/Norton.

Hare, R. D. (1991). *Manual for the Hare Psychopathy Checklist* (Revised.). Toronto: Multi-Health Systems.

Harper, D. (2003). *Etymonline.com* (online resource)

Harper's Dictionary of Classical Literature and Antiquities. (1962). Harry T. Peck (ed.) NY: Colonial Press.

Hassler, R. 1972. Hexapartition of Thalamic Inputs. In : Corticothalamic Projections and Sensorimotor Activities. New York: Raven Press.

Hesse, Herman (1951). *Siddartha.* NY: Bantam.

International Standard Bible Encyclopedia (1915) James Orr - General Editor (online resource).

James, W. (1902). *The Varieties of Religious Experience: A Study in Human Nature.* NY: Random.

Jobes, G. (1962). *Dictionary of Mythology, Folklore and Symbols.* Metuchen, New Jersey: Scarecrow Press.

Kant, I. (1899). *Critique of Pure Reason.* (J. Meiklejohn, trans.) New York: Colonial Press.

Laing, R. D., Phillipson, H., and Lee, A. (1966). *Interpersonal Perception.* Baltimore: Perennial Library.

LaMuth, J. E. (1977). The Development of the Forebrain as an Elementary Function of the Parameters of Input Specificity and Phylogenetic Age. *J. U-grad Rsch: Bio. Sci. U. C. Irvine.* (6): 274-294.

LaMuth, J. E. (1999). *The Ultimate Guide to Family Values: A Grand Unified Theory of Ethics and Morality.* Lucerne Valley, CA: Fairhaven.

LaMuth, J. E. (2000). A Holistic Model of Ethical Behavior Based Upon a Metaperspectival Hierarchy of the Traditional Groupings of Virtue, Values, & Ideals. *Proceedings of the 44th Annual World Congress for the Int. Society for the Systems Sciences* – Toronto.

LaMuth, J. E. (2002). *A Revolution in Family Values: Tradition vs. Technology.* Lucerne Valley, CA: Fairhaven.

LaMuth, J. E. (2003). *Inductive Inference Affective Language Analyzer Simulating AI.* - US Patent # 6,587,846.

LaMuth, J. E. (2004). Behavioral Foundations for the Behaviourome / Mind Mapping Project. *Proceedings for the Eighth International Tsukuba Bioethics Roundtable,Tsukuba, Japan.*

LaMuth, J. E. (2004). *Communication Breakdown: Decoding the Riddle of Mental Illness.* Lucerne Valley, CA: Fairhaven.

LaMuth, J. E. (2005). *Character Values: Promoting a Virtuous Lifestyle.*
Lucerne Valley, CA: Fairhaven.

LaMuth, J. E. (2005). *A Diagnostic Classification of the Emotions: A Three-Digit Coding System for Affective Language.*
Lucerne Valley, CA: Fairhaven.

LaMuth, J. E. (2007). *Inductive Inference Affective Language Analyzer Simulating Transitional AI.* - US Patent # 7,236,963.

LaMuth, J. E. (2009). *Challenges to World Peace: A Global Solution.*
Lucerne Valley, CA: Fairhaven.

LaMuth, J. E. (2015). *The Motivation Solution: A Global Initiative.* Lucerne
Valley, CA: Fairhaven.

Lewis, M. (1995). Shame, The Exposed Self (Paperback edition). New York:
The Free Press.

Lewis, M. (1995). Self-conscious Emotions. *American Scientist, 83*:68-78.

Locke, John (1986). *The Second Treatise on Civil Government.*
Amherst, NY: Prometheus Books

Noble E., et al. (1998) D2 & D4 Dopamine Receptor Polymorhism and
Personality. *Am. J. Med. Genetics 81*:257-267.

Miller, C. J. (2000). *Contempt of Court – 3rd Edition.* Oxford University Press.

Mlodinow, L., (2018). Elastic: Flexible Thinking in a Time of Change: Vintage.

Oatley, K. and Johnson-Laird, P.N. (1987), Towards a cognitive theory of
emotions, Cognition and Emotion, 1: 29-50

Oatley, K. and Jenkins, J. M. (1992). Human Emotions: Function and
Dysfunction. Annual Review of Psychology, 43, 55-85.

Oxford Classical Dictionary. (1970). Oxford, Claredon.

Raine, A., Venables, P.H. and Mednick, S.A. (1997). Low resting heart rate at
age 3 years predisposes to aggression at age 11 years. *Journal of the
Amer. Acad. of Child and Adolescent Psychiatry 36*:1457-1464.

Raine, A. *(1999).*Murderous Minds: Can We See the
Mark of Cain? *Cerebrum*, 1:15-30.

Sagan, Carl. "Can Games Test Ethics? A New Way to Think About Rules to
Live By." *Parade Magazine.* (Nov. 28, 1993): 12-14.

Skinner, B. F. (1971). *Beyond Freedom and Dignity.* NY: Knopf.

Sperry, R. W. (1974) Lateral Specialization in Surgically Separated Hemispheres.
In Neurosciences 3rd Study Program. Cambridge: MIT Press 3:5 -19.

Stuss, D. T. & Alexander, M.P. (2000). Executive Functions in the Frontal
Lobes: A Conceptual View. *Psychological Research*, 63:289-298.

Walker, B. (1983). *The Woman's Encyclopedia of Myths and Secrets.*
San Francisco: Harper and Row.

Watzlawick, P., Beavin, H., and Jackson, D. (1967), *Pragmatics of Human
Communication.* NY: Norton.

Webber, F. (1990) *Church Symbolism: An Explanation of the More Important
Symbols of the Old and New Testament.* Detroit: Omnigraphics.

Zuckerman, M. (2000) Are You a Risk-taker? *Psych. Today*, Nov/Dec. 54-87.

About the Author

John E. LaMuth PhD is a 65 year-old counselor and author native to Southern California. His credentials include a Baccalaureate Degree in Biological Sciences from University of California Irvine, followed by a Masters Degree in Counseling from California State University (Fullerton) with an emphasis in Marriage, Family, and Child Counseling. This subsequently led to a Doctorate Degree in Bioethics, Sustainability and Global Public Health bestowed in 2018 by the American University of Sovereign Nations - USA. John is currently engaged in private practice in Mediation Counseling in the San Bernardino County area. John has also been granted two US patents for Artificial Intelligence #6,587,846 & 7,236,963.

www.worldpeace2.com

*** **NEW BOOK RELEASE FROM FAIRHAVEN BOOKS** • *FHB* ***

World Peace 2.0 - Restoring Global Harmony

Publ. 2019 • Author: *John E. LaMuth PhD* • Trade Soft-Cover • 7.44 X 9.69 in.

List $28.95 • 286 pages • 200,000 words - *Illustrated* • ISBN # 978-1-929649-00-6

Please Ship to ⇩   Date: _____

_____

_____   Daytime phone #: (___) ___-___

_____

_____

Item #	Description	Quantity	Price Each	Amount
129	*World Peace 2.0 - Restoring Global Harmony*		**$28.95**	

Subtotal _____

Shipping and Handling Charges:
(Includes Delivery Confirmation)
One book - $5.75 (Priority-USPS)
Two books - $11.05 (Priority-USPS)
Three books - $11.05 (Priority-USPS)
Four books (or over) - Please Query
CA residents please add 8.75% State Sales-Tax
(one copy = $1.90 • two copies = $3.80 • etc.)

Postage & Handling _____
(see chart to the left)

Order Total _____

[ ] Check or Money-Order enclosed • Payable to: Fairhaven Book Publishers

[ ] Check Here for Book Copy Inscribed by Author • (No Additional Charge)

For Credit Card Orders: Please visit: *www.worldpeace2.com*

Phone Orders or Additional Info • 1-760-981-3993

P.O. Box 105 Lucerne Valley, CA 92356 USA - Tel: 1-760-981-3993
fairhaven-books@outlook.com   *www.worldpeace2.com*

www.ingramcontent.com/pod-product-compliance
Lightning Source LLC
Chambersburg PA
CBHW080606270326
41928CB00016B/2948